FROM BABEL
TO DRAGOMANS

Also by Bernard Lewis

FROM BABEL
TO DRAGOMANS

INTERPRETING THE MIDDLE EAST

BERNARD LEWIS

Weidenfeld & Nicolson

LONDON

First published in Great Britain in 2004
by Weidenfeld & Nicolson

A CIP catalogue record for this book is available from the British Library.

ISBN 0 297 84884 4

Printed in Great Britain by
Butler & Tanner Ltd, Frome and London

Weidenfeld & Nicolson

The Orion Publishing Group Ltd
Orion House
5 Upper Saint Martin's Lane
London, WC2H 9EA

ACKNOWLEDGMENTS

My thanks are due to the editors and publishers of the various journals and volumes in which many of these articles were originally published.

I would also like to express my thanks to my editor, Ms. Susan Ferber, at Oxford University Press, for many constructive suggestions, and to Ms. Helen Mules for her production assistance; to my friend Ms. Buntzie Churchill for her keen judgment and wise counsel; to Mr. Eli Alshech and Mr. Jesse Ferris for help of various kinds, and, once again, to my assistant Ms. Annamarie Cerminaro, for the care and skill with which she tended this volume from the first drafts to the final published version.

B.L.

CONTENTS

PART TWO: CURRENT HISTORY

PART THREE: ABOUT HISTORY

CREDITS

❦❦❦❦

PART ONE: PAST HISTORY

1. An Islamic Mosque.   This essay first appeared as one of a series published in *The Times Educational Supplement* in London, and republished in book form under the title *Temples and Faith*, edited by Walter James, Skeffington, London, 1958. The ten articles in the series dealt with a variety of temples, both ancient and Eastern, and churches, as well as synagogues and a mosque. The aim was to try and explain religions not, in the usual way, through their texts and liturgies, but through their places of worship. I was asked to contribute a paper on Islam and to choose a mosque. My choice was one of the many great mosques of Istanbul.

2. From Babel to Dragomans.   This was presented to the British Academy on 19 May 1998, as the Elie Kedourie Memorial Lecture, and published in the proceedings of the British Academy, vol. 101 (1998) *Lectures and Memoirs*, pp. 37–54. © The British Academy 1999. Reproduced by permission from Proceedings of the British Academy, vol. 101 (1998).

3. Middle East Feasts.   This article attempts to review the available evidence on the production, commerce, and preparation of food in their economic, social, and political context. It was first published as "In the Finger Zone" in *The New York Review of Books*, vol. XLIX, no. 9, May 23, 2002, pp. 61–63.

4. Iran in History.   An attempt to explain and assess the importance of Iran, its people and its culture, in the history of the Middle East and the world, from the earliest recorded antiquity until modern times. It was originally given as a guest lecture in the University of Tel Aviv, and published by them on their website on September 28, 2001. It has not hitherto appeared in print.

5. Palimpsests of Jewish History: Christian, Muslim and Secular Diaspora. Originally presented as a paper to the Tenth World Congress of Jewish Studies, and published in their series *Jewish Studies*, vol. 30 (1990), pp. 7–13.

6. Some Notes on Land, Money and Power in Medieval Islam.   Published in a Festschrift in honor of Robert Anhegger, *Türkische Miszellen*, Istanbul 1987, pp. 237–42.

7. An Interpretation of Fatimid History.   This paper was presented to an international colloquium held in Cairo in 1969, to celebrate the thousandth anniversary of the foundation of the city. It was published in the proceedings of the conference *Colloque International sur l'Histoire du Caire*, Cairo, 1972, pp. 287–95.

8. Propaganda in the Pre-Modern Middle East: A Preliminary Classification.   Published by the Hebrew University of Jerusalem, The Faculty of Humanities in their series, *Jerusalem Studies in Arabic and Islam*, vol. 25 (2001), pp. 1–14.

9. Monarchy in the Middle East.   A paper presented to a conference and published in *Middle East Monarchies: The Challenge of Modernity*, edited by Joseph Kostiner, pp. 15–22. Copyright © 2000 by Lynne Rienner Publishers, Inc. Reprinted with permission. Its theme is Middle Eastern attitudes to the institution of monarchy, from biblical to modern times.

10. Religion and Murder in the Middle East.   An earlier version of this paper was presented to the Rabin conference in Tel Aviv and published in Hebrew translation in the conference proceedings. *Political Assassination: The Murder of Rabin and Political Assassinations in the Middle East*, ed. Charles S. Liebman, published by the Yitzhak Rabin Center for Israel Studies and Am Oved, Tel Aviv, 1998, pp. 109–17. The original English text has been slightly revised.

11. The Mughals and the Ottomans.   *Pakistan Quarterly*, Summer, 1958, pp. 4–9.

12. Europe and the Turks: The Civilization of the Ottoman Empire.   *History Today*, London, October, 1953, pp. 673–80. Reflections on the quincentennial of the Turkish conquest of Constantinople in May 1453.

13. Europe and Islam: Muslim Perceptions and Experience.   Presented to a conference held in the Hofburg, Vienna, November 29–December 2, 1994, under the auspices of the Institut für die Wissenschaften vom Menschen, and published in German translation in *Das Europa der Religionen: Ein Kontinent zwischen Säkularisierung und Fundamentalismus*, ed. Otto Kallscheuer (Frankfurt-am-Main: Fischer Verlag, 1996), 67–95. The original English text has been slightly revised.

14. **Cold War and Détente in the Sixteenth Century.** Originally published in *Survey*, no. 3/4, 1976, pp. 95–96. This was written in response to an editor's request to compare the struggle between the West and the Soviets at that time with the 16th-century struggle between Christendom and the Ottomans.

15. **From Pilgrims to Tourists: A Survey of Middle Eastern Travel.** A previously unpublished paper.

16. **The British Mandate for Palestine in Historical Perspective.** This was delivered as a talk at a conference on "Jerusalem and the British Mandate: Interaction and Legacy" held in Jerusalem in the spring of 2001. The text was published in Hebrew translation in a volume edited by Yehoshu Ben-Arieh in Jerusalem in 2003.

17. **Pan-Arabism.** This article was commissioned by the *Enciclopedia del Novecento*, and published by them in Italian translation in Volume V, Rome, 1981, pp. 67–78. The English original, hitherto unpublished, was completed in 1978.

18. **The Emergence of Modern Israel.** *Middle Eastern Studies*, vol. VIII, October 1972, pp. 421–27.

19. **Orientalist Notes on the Soviet–United Arab Republic Treaty of 27 May 1971.** Published in *The Princeton Papers in Near Eastern Studies*, no. 2, 1993, pp. 57–65. A comparative textual analysis of four texts of the Treaty—the official Arabic and Russian versions, and the somewhat divergent English translations published in Moscow and Cairo. A shorter earlier discussion of the treaty was published in *The Times* newspaper of London, October 8, 1971, under the title: "Small Print of the Soviet-Egyptian Treaty."

20. **A Taxonomy of Group Hatred.** Published in German in the Viennese review *Transit*, vol. 16, Winter 1998–1999, pp. 3–13, under the title *Der widerspenstige Andere zu einer Typologie des Gruppenhasses*.

21. **Islam and the West.** Published in *National and International Policies in the Middle East: Essays in honour of Elie Kedourie*, edited by Edward Ingram (London: Frank Cass, 1986), pp. 16–30.

PART TWO: CURRENT HISTORY

22. **The Middle East, Westernized Despite Itself.** *Middle East Quarterly*, Philadelphia, March 1996, pp. 53–61.

23. The Middle East in World Affairs. This paper was presented to a conference on "Tensions in the Middle East" held at the School of Advanced International Studies of the Johns Hopkins University, in Washington, in the last week of August 1957. It was published in the proceedings of the conference, edited by Philip W. Thayer (Baltimore: Johns Hopkins Press, 1958), pp. 50–60.

24. Friends and Enemies: Reflections After a War. Reflections on the situation after the Arab-Israel War of June 1967. *Encounter*, London, February 1968, pp. 3–7.

25. Return to Cairo. Impressions of a visit to Egypt in 1969. It was published in *Encounter*, August 1969, pp. 76–86, under the pseudonym Ibn al-'Assal, so as not to endanger Egyptian friends.

26. Middle East at Prayer. *The Spectator,* 2 August 1969, pp. 142–43.

27. At the United Nations. A review of Senator Daniel Patrick Moynihan's book *A Dangerous Place*, New York, 1979. The review was published in *Commentary*, vol. 67, no. 3, March 1979, pp. 82–84.

28. The Anti-Zionist Resolution. Reprinted by permission of *Foreign Affairs*, October, 1976, pp. 54–64. © 1976 by the Council on Foreign Relations, Inc.

29. Right and Left in Lebanon. Published in *The New Republic*, September 10, 1977, pp. 20–23.

30. The Shi'a. *New York Review of Books*, August 15, 1985, pp. 7–9. This and the two following articles are comments on the course of the Islamic Revolution in Iran.

31. Islamic Revolution. *New York Review of Books*, January 21, 1988, pp. 46–51.

32. The Enemies of God. *New York Review of Books*, March 25, 1993, pp. 30–32.

33. The Roots of Muslim Rage. Under the title "Western Civilization: A View from the East," this was delivered as the Jefferson Lecture for 1990, under the auspices of the National Endowment for the Humanities. A slightly shortened version was published in *The Atlantic Monthly*, September 1990, pp. 47–60. This version is reprinted here.

34. The Other Middle East Problems. A lecture at Tel Aviv University, published in their series *Middle East Lectures*, no. 1, Tel Aviv, 1995, pp. 45–58. This attempts to draw attention to some other Middle East problems beyond the Arab-Israel conflict and the Revolution in Iran.

35. Did You Say "American Imperialism"?: Power, Weakness, and Choices in the Middle East. *National Review*, Washington, December 17, 2001, pp. 26–30. © 2001 by National Review, Inc., 215 Lexington Avenue, New York, NY 10016. Reprinted by permission.

36. The Law of Islam. *The Washington Post*, Washington, D.C., Friday, February 24, 1989. A contemporary comment on the condemnation of Salman Rushdi's book *The Satanic Verses* and the death sentence passed on its author by the Ayatollah Khomeini.

37. Not Everybody Hates Saddam. *The Wall Street Journal*, August 13, 1990. Written after Saddam Hussein's conquest and annexation of Kuwait, but before the American response.

38. Mideast States: Pawns No Longer in Imperial Games. *The Wall Street Journal*, April 11, 1991. Reviews the new situation after the Gulf War and the liberation of Kuwait.

39. What Saddam Wrought. *The Wall Street Journal*, August 2, 1991. Reviews policy choices for both Middle Eastern and outside powers.

40. The "Sick Man" of Today Coughs Closer to Home. *The Wall Street Journal*, December 26, 1991. Some lessons from the Ottoman past for present-day governments.

41. Revisiting the Paradox of Modern Turkey. *The Wall Street Journal*, November 12, 1996, p. A18. Published soon after the fifty-eighth anniversary of the death of Kemal Ataürk.

42. We Must Be Clear. *The Washington Post*, September 16, 2001. Written immediately after the events of September 11, 2001.

43. Deconstructing Osama and His Evil Appeal. *The Wall Street Journal*, August 23, 2002. An attempt to explain the continuing popularity of Osama bin Ladin among many Muslims.

44. Targeted by a History of Hatred. *The Washington Post*, September 10, 2002, p. A15. A discussion of the sources and varieties of anti-Americanism in the Muslim world.

45. A Time for Toppling. *The Wall Street Journal*, September 28, 2002.

PART THREE: ABOUT HISTORY

46. In Defense of History. A lecture given to the American Philosophical Society on November 15, 1997, and published in the *Proceedings of the American Philosophical Society*, vol. 143, no. 4, December, 1999, pp. 573–87.

47. First-Person Narrative in the Middle East. Published in *Middle Eastern Lives: The Practice of Biography and Self-Narrative*, edited by Martin Kramer, Syracuse University Press, 1991, pp. 20–34.

48. Reflections on Islamic Historiography. A lecture given at Tel Aviv University and published in their series, *Middle Eastern Lectures*, no. 2, 1997, pp. 69–80.

49. The Ottoman Archives: A Source for European History. Presented to a meeting of the American Oriental Society in Baltimore on April 10, 1956, and printed in the *Report on Current Research*, Spring, 1956, of the Middle East Institute in Washington, D.C. A slightly modified version was published in *Archives: The Journal of the British Records Association*, vol. IV, no. 24, 1960, pp. 226–30.

50. History Writing and National Revival in Turkey. *Middle Eastern Affairs*, New York, vol. IV, 1953, pp. 218–27.

51. On Occidentalism and Orientalism. Previously unpublished.

FROM BABEL TO DRAGOMANS

Introduction

꒰ꕤ꒱

Most of the articles, studies and lectures assembled in this volume date from the period of my professional life which began in the autumn of 1949, when I was appointed to the newly-created chair of the History of the Near and Middle East at the School of Oriental and African Studies in the University of London.

I first set foot in the school as an undergraduate student in 1933. Already then I was not entirely a newcomer to Middle Eastern studies. My initiation had begun at an early age, when I was confronted with the need to study a difficult, ancient Middle Eastern text—to be precise, part of Chapter 26 of the Book of Leviticus. At the age of eleven or twelve, along with most Jewish children, I was instructed in the rudiments of Hebrew to prepare me for my Bar Mitzvah, the synagogue ceremony by which Jewish boys—and in modern times also girls—are formally recognized as full, adult members of the community. At that time and in that place, this normally implied only learning the alphabet, memorizing the tunes, and acquiring a sufficient command of the Hebrew script to read and chant the text without understanding it. In the normal course of events, no more than that was expected of pupils; no more was provided by teachers. But for me, another language, and more especially another script, offered new excitement, and led to the joyous discovery that Hebrew was not merely a kind of encipherment of prayers and rituals, to be memorized and recited parrot-fashion. It was a language with a grammar, which one could actually learn like the Latin or French that I was learning at school—or rather, like both of them at the same time, since Hebrew was at once a classical and a modern language. By good fortune, I had a teacher who could respond to my childish enthusiasm, and it was he who helped me find my way on one of the two paths that led to my subsequent career—the fascination with exotic languages.

It was therefore natural that I should continue my Hebrew studies, under his direction, after the completion of the Bar Mitzvah ceremony, and by the time I was ready to go to university, I had read widely and deeply in Hebrew. All this whetted my appetite for more of the same. The more serious study of Hebrew led inevitably to Aramaic, and later, in a more adventurous shift, to Arabic. Though I never made much progress with Aramaic, I became much more interested in Arabic, and was able to indulge that interest more effectively when I went to university. At one stage I was engaged simultaneously in the study of Latin, Greek, Biblical Hebrew and Classical Arabic—a rather heavy program of dead languages for a mere undergraduate. As a graduate student, I expanded my study of Arabic, and added Persian and Turkish.

My main subject of interest, however, was history. I had always been greatly attracted to this subject, and even as a child I had a curious desire to know the history of the other side. In England, when I was at primary school, history basically meant English history, and for a long time this, as taught at that level, consisted largely of wars with the French. From this, I developed a curiosity about French history and asked my father to get me a history of France—in English, of course. He did so, and I was able to consider the history of the Anglo-French wars from both sides. I found it both a rewarding and a stimulating experience.

A little later, chapters in my history textbooks on such topics as the Crusades and the Eastern Question raised similar questions. Here too my Bar Mitzvah marked a turning point. Like most other Bar Mitzvah boys, I received a number of presents, one of which was an outline of Jewish history, a subject about which I previously knew very little. My eager and immediate reading of this book brought me to such fascinating and exotic places as Moorish Cordova, Baghdad under the Caliphs, and Ottoman Istanbul. These were no doubt the first steps on the path which led to my career as an historian of the Middle East.

The degree structure at the University of London at that time made it possible for me to take an honours (that is to say, specialized) degree in history with special reference to the Middle East. This enabled me to continue my linguistic adventures, and at the same time to find my true vocation as a historian. As far as I know, there was no comparable undergraduate program available at any other university at the time. I therefore chose that university and that syllabus— choices and opportunities for which I remain profoundly grateful.

After some years of study in Middle Eastern history and languages at the School of Oriental (later also "and African") Studies in the University of London, my professor, the late Sir Hamilton Gibb, summoned me and said: "You have now been studying the Middle East for four years. Don't you think it's time you saw the place?" A traveling fellowship from the Royal Asiatic Society, given to me on Professor Gibb's recommendation, enabled me to follow his advice, and in the academic year 1937–1938 I set out on my first trip to the Middle East.

My first port of call was Egypt. Arriving (by sea, of course) at Port Said, I remembered the English Arabist Edward Lane's description of his first arrival in the region whose language and culture had so fascinated him. As he put it, I felt like a Muslim bridegroom meeting the bride with whom he is to spend the rest of his life, and seeing her for the first time after the wedding.

At first, communication was not easy. Though the syllabus and the courses I attended included modern history, my main interest was in the period that in European history is called medieval, a term not very appropriate to the great age of Arab and Islamic civilization. My language studies followed the same line. When I arrived in Egypt the only Arabic I knew was classical Arabic, which was about as useful for conversation as Ciceronian Latin would be in present-day Naples. But I managed to acquire some colloquial Arabic, and enrolled as an "auditor" in Cairo University. I did what students usually do—attended lectures and meetings, read books and newspapers, talked, and—more especially—listened, and on one occasion even attended a student demonstration, I can no longer recall for what cause. From Egypt, I traveled extensively in Palestine, Syria, Lebanon and Turkey, and in the early summer of 1938 returned to London, where I settled down to serious work. My main task during that period was study rather than research, though I did manage to make some progress in the collection of materials for my dissertation, which I completed after my return to England.

In 1938 the University of London offered me a position as an assistant lecturer in Islamic History. The first class I taught in 1938 consisted of four students, three Arabs and an Iranian. I remember my father asking me in wonderment at the time why the University of London would pay me a salary to teach Arab history to Arabs. Many others have asked more or less the same question, in a variety of forms. Some also asked why Arab students would come to England to study their own history, and were given—by both the students and their teachers—a variety of answers. For whatever reasons, they continued to come, and for the rest of my teaching career in England a varying number of my undergraduate students and a steady majority of my graduate students were Arabs from Arab countries.

A year after my appointment, war broke out, and in due course I, along with everyone else, went into the armed forces. I was initially assigned to the Royal Armoured Corps, but soon, either because of my aptitude for languages or my ineptitude with tanks, I was transferred to Intelligence. From there, in 1941–1945, I was attached to a department of the Foreign Office dealing with Middle Eastern matters. I was in Cairo when the war ended, and, thanks to an accelerated release, was back at the University on 1 September 1945.

It was not easy to resume an academic career after an interval of almost six years doing very different work. I had acquired a close, intense but highly specialized knowledge of some aspects of the modern situation in the Middle East in the course of my wartime duties, but I had to relearn my profession, both as a teacher and as a researcher. In 1949 I was appointed to the new chair in Near and Middle Eastern History at the age of 33, one of a generation that was still young in years but prematurely aged in experience and, one hoped, in wisdom. The immediate post-war period was a good time for young scholars just starting or re-starting their careers—a time of rapid and extensive development in the universities, which faced a double challenge: a five-year backlog of students who had gone straight from high school to the armed forces and wished to resume their academic education, and a skeletal academic apparatus, in urgent need of expansion and development to meet the demands of a new age. One of the answers to this demand was the creation of new teaching positions in previously neglected subjects, notably in the field of Oriental and African studies.

The university, wisely, decided that I should begin my tenure by going on what was called "study leave," to update and broaden my acquaintance with the region whose history I was to reach and research. When I set out on my third tour of the Middle East, beginning in the autumn of 1949, the situation in the region had been transformed beyond recognition. In the aftermath of the Arab-Israel War of 1948, severe restrictions were imposed by Arab governments on access and even entry by Jews, and this considerably reduced the number of places to which I could go, and in which I could work. Since then, there has been some easing of this rule in some but not all Arab countries, and it became possible for me to renew and extend my acquaintances with the Arab east. But in 1949, for Jewish scholars interested in the Middle East, only three countries in the region were open—Turkey, Iran and Israel. It was in these three countries therefore that I arranged to spend the academic year 1949–1950, most of the time in Turkey and in Iran. Iran was a new experience—the first of many visits over the years. My previous direct experience of Turkey was limited to a very short visit, as a student, in the spring of 1938.

I began in Istanbul, which because of the unique richness of its libraries and archives, offered special attractions to the historian of the Middle East. My primary interest remained classical Islamic civilization, an interest which I now extended to the great age of the Ottoman Empire. I counted on being able to use the collections of Arabic and other Islamic manuscripts in Turkish libraries. I also applied, with little expectation of success, for permission to use the Imperial Ottoman Archives. These archives had been described by various Turkish scholars, and a number of documents had been published, mostly in Turkish scholarly journals, in the course of the years—enough to whet, but not to satisfy a historian's appetite. No Westerner had however been admitted to these archives, apart from a very small number of expert archivists brought in as consultants. These were the central archives of the Ottoman Empire, extending over many centuries. It was known that they contained tens of thousands of bound registers and letter-books, and millions of documents. It was obvious that these archives would be a precious, indeed an indispensable, source for the history of all the lands that had ever formed part of the Ottoman Empire, and of value even for others, like Iran, that had been involved with the Ottomans in one way or another. But so far access had only been allowed to Turkish scholars.

It was my good fortune, rather than any particular merit on my part, that I submitted my application precisely at the moment when the custodians of the archives decided to pursue a more liberal policy, and I was both astonished and delighted to receive the coveted permit. Feeling rather like a child turned loose in a toy shop, or like an intruder in Ali Baba's cave, I hardly knew where to turn first.

Publications are of course an essential part of any academic career, both as a means of self-expression, and as a ladder for advancement. My earliest publications followed the usual pattern in our profession. First came some articles, developed from seminar papers, and placed in learned journals by the good offices of my professors. Second—and the first in book form—was my doctoral dissertation. I had finished this just before the outbreak of war, and when the University of London offered me the opportunity, through a subvention, to transform a dissertation into a real, published book, I responded eagerly. The future looked very problematic at the time, and I wanted to leave something behind me. In retrospect, I do not think it was such a good idea, as the thesis was not ready for publication. It was completed in great haste because of the war that was looming, and was published in five hundred copies in 1940, under the title *The Origins of Ismailism*, dealing with the historical and religious background of the Fatimid Caliphs, a dynasty that came to power in North Africa in 909, and conquered Egypt in 969 C.E. It took at least ten years to sell the whole edition. I was however very gratified when an Arabic translation was published in Baghdad in 1947. This was the first of many Arabic (and later also Persian and Turkish) translations of my books. For this one the publishers actually asked my permission, which I gave with alacrity, and sent me some complimentary copies, which I received with delight.

My next publication, apart from minor odds and ends, was a little book called *The Arabs in History*. A London publishing house was preparing a series of short books under the editorship of a very distinguished medieval historian, Sir Maurice Powicke. He gave me the title and asked me to write not a short history of the Arabs, but an interpretative essay on the role of Arabs in history. I was much attracted by this idea and was enormously flattered that a famous historian had actually written to me asking me for this book. The publishers even offered me money, in the form a small advance—a new experience at the time. This was my first serious attempt to deal with a broader subject over a longer period, and to do so in a form addressed not solely to a few academic colleagues and/or rivals but to a previously unknown species—the general reader.

As a student of the Middle East, my interests and training were primarily historical rather than—as with most of my predecessors, teachers and contemporaries—philological and literary. I did however serve a brief apprenticeship in these disciplines and am profoundly grateful for having done so. The first and most rudimentary test of an historian's competence is that he should be able to read his sources, and this is not always easy, as for example when the language is classical Arabic or the writing is a crabbed Ottoman bureaucratic script.

And that is not all. The historian of a region, of a period, of a group of people, or even of a topic, must know something of its cultural context, and for this literature is an indispensable guide. Fortunately, this was one part of my studies and of my subsequent researches which I particularly enjoyed. As a child and for a while as a young man, I cherished delusions of a literary career, seeing myself first as a poet, and then as an essayist. In time, with more or less regret, I abandoned these delusions, and devoted whatever literary skills I could muster to the presentation of my work as a historian, supplemented and in a sense illustrated by translations.

The surest test of one's understanding of a text in another language is translating it into one's own. One may believe that one has really grasped the meaning of a text, only to find, in the process of translation, that one's understanding has serious gaps and even flaws. As a schoolboy and then as a student, I was of course required to translate texts from—and in accordance with English educational usage at that time, into—the languages I was studying. My translations into these languages were usually a disaster, though no doubt they served some educational purpose. But the task of translating from these languages into English was stimulating, challenging, even exciting, and I continued to do it long after it ceased to be a pedagogic requirement. A not inconsiderable part of my published work consists of translations of texts, generally pre-modern, in various Middle Eastern languages. In most of them my purpose was to offer the student or other reader some insight into how Middle Eastern history looks as seen through Middle Eastern eyes. Occasionally, I attempted to give the reader of English some experience, however diminished, of the pleasures of Middle Eastern literature.

A new phase in my professional and personal life began with my move from London to Princeton in 1974. This gave me several very substantial advantages. The first was more free time. Since my appointment was a joint one between Princeton University and the Institute for Advanced Study, I taught only one semester a year; the rest of my time was free of teaching responsibilities—except of course for the supervision of graduate students preparing dissertations. For a teacher with a sense of responsibility towards his students—that means most of us—this is a task that goes on all through the year and often continues for years after the student has completed his formal studies and requirements. I count such relationships with former students, many of them now professors, among the most rewarding that the academic profession has to offer.

A second advantage was that being a newcomer from another country and a part-timer in both institutions, I was free from the kind of administrative and bureaucratic entanglements that had built up, over decades, in England. This was a most welcome relief. I must confess that I never had much taste for administrative responsibilities. Had that been my desire, I would have either gone into business, in pursuit of real money, or into government, in pursuit of real power. I would not have stayed in the university, where neither the money nor the power is real. The satisfactions of the scholarly life are of quite a different character.

Finally, at Princeton I was provided with the kind of infrastructure which English universities simply could not afford, such as hiring student assistants to find and fetch me books from the library, to check references and help with other tedious and time-consuming but essential tasks. Here, too, the time-saving was enormous.

There was another important change; I was growing older, at least physically, and I decided that it was time to start closing the files. During the course of my work as a researcher and as a teacher, perhaps most of all simply as a reader, I had built up a series of files on topics which aroused my special interest. Whenever I came across anything relevant, I made a note of it and put it in the appropriate file. What I have been doing since coming to Princeton is taking these accumulations of material built up over the course of the years, organizing and where necessary, expanding them by further research, and preparing them for publication. This is the explanation of what might otherwise seem a large output in a relatively short time, as contrasted with a rather small output in a much longer time previously.

Some of these resulted in books preceded and followed by a scatter of articles—the political language of Islam, the Judaeo-Islamic tradition, race and slavery in the Middle East, the emergence of modern Turkey, the Muslim discovery of Europe. These last formed part of a larger topic, of deeper concern. I have always been interested in the relations between the Islamic Middle East and the Christian and post-Christian West—the Islamic advance into Europe from the South West and then the South East, and the Christian reconquest and counterattack; the impact of both Western action and Western civilization on the Islamic peoples and societies of the Middle East; the successive phases of Middle Eastern response; the perception and the study, or lack of study, of each by the other.

During the last half century, in the domains of religion, nationhood, and society, far-reaching and significant changes took place, including both successes and failures, both in the return to old traditions and in the pursuit of new ideas. My work involved a study of these changes, the new perceptions of freedom, both national and personal, and the attempts being made to achieve it; the changing content and significance of national and patriotic loyalties; and the resurgence of religious and communal identities and commitments. In looking at these processes, I tried to situate them in both a global and a regional context—in the shifting interplay of regional and global powers on the one hand,

and in the far-reaching changes in Middle Eastern economies and societies on the other. Many of these topics, inevitably, are highly controversial, and evoke passionate debate among scholars and others, both in the region and abroad.

A few years ago, in the course of an interview, I was asked: "Why do you always deal with sensitive subjects?" To which I responded: "The answer to your question is contained in the metaphor you have used. The sensitive place in the body, physical or social, is where something is wrong. Sensitivity is a signal the body sends us, that something needs attention, which is what I try to give. I don't agree with the implicit meaning of your question that there are taboo subjects."

There are, of course, in other societies, many taboo subjects. Some people in our own society and more particularly in the academic community wish to impose similar constraints, notably in the discussion of non-Western civilizations and religions, and even of contemporary non-Western leaders and movements. This approach, now widespread especially in the universities and the media, is defended—sometimes indeed enforced—in the name of sensitivity and is challenged or derided—usually by those whose careers are not at stake—as censorship or "political correctness." Some critics of Western scholarship, including some Westerners, even question the very right of outsiders to research, write, or teach Middle Eastern or Islamic history. Others go still further, accusing such outsiders of pursuing a hidden agenda and of devising or using special methods to serve it.

I have sometimes been asked about the "special methods" that I and my colleagues use. I don't think that there is a special method for studying Islamic or Middle Eastern history, different from the methods we would use for studying any other kind of history. History is history—our motivations may be different; our purposes may be different, and certainly the subject matter will be different, but the method is basically the same. To use one method for studying our own history and another method for studying someone else's history would be dishonest. The serious study of history, one's own or anyone else's, must be based on primary sources, and these must be examined in the original, not through the filter of translation, adaptation, or summary. All of these may easily be slanted to serve some political, ideological or other purpose. They will inevitably reflect the filtrator's perceptions. Learning a language for such study is not necessarily a predatory intrusion. It is more likely to be inspired by respect and above all by intellectual curiosity.

What is the historian trying to do? First, on the most rudimentary level, to find out what happened. Then, at a rather more sophisticated level, to find out how it happened. And, for the intellectually ambitious, why it happened. This is surely the really interesting part of understanding the past.

The study of recent and contemporary history presents special problems to the historian. There is the obvious difficulty arising from the fragmentary and usually secondary quality of documentation. In compensation there is the immediacy of his own experience of the events of his own time. This in turn brings another danger—that of the historian's personal involvement and commitments. We are all, including historians, the children of our time and place, with loyalties, or at least predispositions, determined by country, race, gender, religion, ideology, and economic, social, and cultural background. Some have argued that, since complete impartiality is impossible, the historian should abandon the attempt as false and hypocritical, and present himself frankly as a partisan of his cause. If his cause is just, according to this view, his story will to that degree be authentic. If his cause is unjust, his story will be flawed and should be dismissed accordingly.

I adhere to a different view: that the historian owes it to himself and to his readers to try, to the best of his ability, to be objective or at least to be fair—to be conscious of his own commitments and concerns and make due allowance and, where necessary, correction for them; and to try and present the different aspects of a problem and the different sides to a dispute in such a way as to allow the reader to form his own independent judgment. Above all, the historian should not prejudge issues and predetermine results by the arbitrary definition of topic and selection of evidence, and the use of emotionally charged or biased language. As a famous economist once remarked, "Complete asepsis is impossible, but one does not for that reason perform surgery in a sewer."

My readers will judge for themselves how far I have succeeded over the years in my antiseptic precautions to avoid infection. I derive some reassurance from the reception of the first edition of one of my books on recent and contemporary history. It was translated and published both in Hebrew, by the publishing house of the Israeli Ministry of Defense, and in Arabic, by the Muslim Brothers. The translator of the Arabic version, in his introductory remarks, observed that the author of this book was one of two things: a candid friend or an honorable enemy, and in either case, one who does not distort or evade the truth. I am content to abide by that judgment.

The study of past history is illuminated by what we see happening around us, just as our understanding of what we see happening around us now is enriched by knowledge of past experiences. But this does not mean that one has to slant past history so as to serve some present purpose, or let the grievances of today distort our understanding of yesterday.

In a free society, different historians put forward different points of views, with changes of theme and emphasis even when discussing the same events and evidence. At one time, when religion was generally agreed to be the crucial element in human affairs, scholars and others who wrote about the history of the Middle East and its relations with the West saw their topic almost entirely in terms of the religious encounters between Islam and Christianity, with Judaism somewhere in the middle. In the nineteenth century, with the rise of nationalism and ethnic awareness, historians once again looked back into the past from their own time and perceived not just Muslims and Christians, but Arabs,

Persians, and Turks. More recently, economic and social historians have looked with a new awareness and acuteness at the structures of Middle Eastern economies and societies, in remote as well as recent times. Like the historians of religion, historians of ethnicity and of society were at times guilty of some over-emphasis, but by bringing these perceptions from the modern West to the study of the medieval Middle East, they were able to enrich and deepen our understanding of religious, ethnic and socio-economic relationships, in the past as well as the present.

In my early studies I was mainly interested in the period when the Islamic Middle East was most different from the West, least affected by the West, and in most respects far in advance of the West. I never lost my interest in early Islamic history, but it ceased to be my primary concern. The opportunity to enter the hitherto sealed Ottoman archives in 1949 was too good to miss; it provided me with a chance to pursue a topic in which I was already deeply interested—the history of the Ottoman Empire. Most of my published work since then has spanned the medieval, Ottoman, and modern periods, or some combination of the three.

But no specialist on the Middle East—not even an Assyriologist or an Egyptologist—can wholly ignore the contemporary scene. My war service gave me an intimate knowledge of some aspects of modern Middle Eastern life and politics. My travels in Middle Eastern countries, my occasional meetings with Middle Eastern monarchs and other rulers, more extensively with academic colleagues, and, perhaps most of all, my encounters with Middle Eastern students, kept me in touch with what was happening on the ground. From time to time I ceded to the temptation to make some public pronouncement on Middle Eastern events, usually in the form of an interview or article in some review or magazine or, occasionally, newspaper. Since coming to America I have written at greater length on recent and contemporary topics.

Anyone who studies the evolution of a civilization must, in the course of time, devote some thought to the broader and more general aspects of his topic, as distinct from the more specific objects of his immediate research. Any writer or teacher of history must from time to time explore, at least in his mind, the larger implications of the historic process. And, on a more mundane level, any professional scholar must, at times, pause and consider the state and needs of the field of scholarship in which he works, more especially when, as now, this field, and indeed scholarship itself, are under attack. Some of my thoughts on these matters are included in this volume.

The following pieces were written over a period of half a century, and cover a wide variety of topics. Most of them appeared in periodicals of one sort or another, ranging from learned quarterlies to daily newspapers, and their topics correspondingly range from problems of early medieval history to yesterday's headlines and tomorrow's challenges. Some were lectures. Others were contributions to colloquia and symposia held in various places, and originally published in the proceedings of these gatherings. Several of these were held in foreign countries and published in foreign languages. My English originals of such papers are published here for the first time. Some of the papers have not previously been published in any form.

With a few minor changes, I have kept all these essays in the form in which they were originally published. In a few places, I have made cuts, usually to avoid overlaps and repetitions, occasionally to remove matter no longer of any current interest. Such cuts are indicated in the usual way. In a very few places, I have inserted a brief explanatory note, in brackets.

In general, I have excluded specialist, technical studies, based directly on primary sources and heavily footnoted. These are accessible to specialists in the learned journals where they originally appeared; they would offer little of interest to the general reader.

All the articles in this volume deal with history in one form or another. I have divided them into three main groups—past history, present history, and about history. Clearly, the first and second at least overlap. What I have tried to do is to limit the second category, current history, to discussions of events or at least of processes while they were actually occurring. The third—about history—considers the tasks and duties of the historian, and in particular the problems of writing the history of the Middle East, both from inside and outside the region.

PART ONE
PAST HISTORY

1

An Islamic Mosque

❧❦❧❦

The Suleymaniye Mosque in Istanbul was begun in 1550 and completed in 1556. It is one of the supreme masterpieces of Mimar Sinan (*c.* 1489–1588), by common consent the greatest of Ottoman architects. It bears the name of Sultan Suleyman, known to Europe as the Magnificent. His reign (1520–66) is generally regarded as the apogee of Ottoman Imperial greatness.

The structure and decoration of this mosque, begun almost a century after the Turkish conquest of Constantinople, illustrate both the enrichment of Islam by earlier streams of tradition and the essential originality of its own religious and aesthetic creations. Though the mosque shows clear signs of both Persian and Byzantine influence, there is something distinctively and characteristically Ottoman in the harmonious contrast of minarets and dome, in the lightness of touch in the use of the dome itself, and in the spacious and elegant interior.

Islam is an Arabic word meaning surrender, and denotes the act of submission of the believer—the Muslim—who surrenders himself to the will of God as revealed through the Prophet Muhammad. It is the name of the monotheist religion founded by Muhammad in Western Arabia in the early part of the seventh century; it is also used of the whole complex civilization, with its own distinctive political and legal, social and cultural patterns, that grew up under the aegis of that religion. In Western terms, it would thus correspond roughly to both the words Christianity and Christendom.

Within the Islamic religion and society of the classical period many elements of diverse origin can be traced: Christian, Jewish, and old oriental ideas of prophecy and revelation, Persian and Byzantine notions of government and statecraft, Hellenistic science, philosophy, and architecture. But despite the persistence and pervasiveness of these influences from earlier times, Islamic civilization is neither a revival nor an imitation of previous cultures, but a new creation, in which all these elements are fused into something fresh and distinctive, recognizable and characteristic in every facet of its achievement.

It is perhaps in art and architecture that we can see most clearly how Islam modifies and reshapes the many divergent local traditions, imposing on them the unmistakable stamp of the Islamic way of life and the Islamic pattern of culture.

The most striking feature of the Suleymaniye mosque, the great central cupola, clearly owes much to the example of Santa Sophia, which in turn reflects the merging of Hellenism, Christianity, and older Asian traditions. But the Ottoman architect made several significant changes. Centuries earlier the Arab Muslim conquerors, when they carried their new faith out of Arabia into the Near East, North Africa, and Spain, had been faced with the need to adapt the Christian churches, which were their principal models, to the different needs of Muslim worship, and had responded with the great mosques of Damascus, Kayrawan, and Cordova, masterpieces of a new, Islamic style of religious architecture. The Ottoman Turks, encountering the same problem again, found a new solution to it, in harmony both with their own traditions and with those of the lands and peoples among which they held sway.

In the Suleymaniye mosque we still find the central cupola buttressed by two half-domes, but these are no longer supported by great semicircular niches as in Santa Sophia. By finding a different solution to the problem of giving strength and balance to the central dome, Sinan was able to clear the central space under it of pillars and other encumbrances, and thus to obtain the wide extension needed for Muslim worship.

In the public prayer, held every Friday, the worshippers stand side by side, in long rows, facing the *qibla* wall which shows the direction of Mecca. They are led by the Imam, whom they must follow exactly, and there is special merit in being in the front row, preferably to the right of the Imam. Unlike the church, the mosque is therefore usually planned in breadth, with naves parallel to the *qibla* wall.

In the earlier Arab and other Mediterranean mosques there was usually a wide chamber opening on a great open court. In the colder climate of Turkey, however, an enclosed and sheltered space was needed. The Ottoman architects evolved, among others, the solution of a large cupola supported on walls on a hexagonal plan. The disposition in breadth and the removal of the central supports gave room for the wide rows of worshippers, with a clear and unbroken view of the Imam and the *qibla*.

The interior of the mosque is simple and austere. There is no altar and no sanctuary, for Islam has no sacraments and no ordained priesthood. The Imam has no priestly function, but is only a leader in prayer. Any Muslim who knows the prayers and ritual may perform the task, though in practice the Imamate usually becomes a permanent professional office. Communal prayer takes place at midday on Friday, and consists of certain prescribed prostrations and formulas, chiefly taken from the Qur'an, the book which Muslims believe to contain the word of God as revealed to Muhammad. Besides the Friday prayer, the Muslim is required to pray five times daily—at sunrise, midday, afternoon, sunset, and evening.

Inside the mosque the two chief foci are the *minbar* and the *mihrab*. The first of these is a kind of raised pulpit, used in the larger mosques during the Friday prayer. In earlier times, when the mosque was still the social and political as well as the religious centre of the community, it was from the *minbar* that the ruler or his representative made important announcements. It is still used for the sermon, which forms a part of the Friday service.

The *mihrab* is a niche in the *qibla* wall, showing the direction of Mecca, the birthplace of the Prophet, towards which all Muslims turn in prayer. It is usually placed in the centre of the wall, and determines the axis of symmetry of the building.

Muslim public prayer is a disciplined, communal act of submission to the Creator, to the One, remote and immaterial God. It admits of no drama and no mystery, and has no place for liturgical music or poetry, nor for representational painting or sculpture, which Muslim tradition rejects as blasphemy verging on idolatry. In their place, Muslim artists used abstract and geometrical design, and based their decorative schemes on the extensive and systematic use of inscriptions. The names of God, the Prophet, and the earlier Caliphs, the Muslim creed that 'there is no God but God and Muhammad is the Prophet of God', and verses or even whole chapters of the Koran—these are used to decorate the walls and ceilings of the mosque. The text is divine, and to write or read it is in itself an act of worship. Many different styles of writing are used, and in the hands of the great masters the art of calligraphy achieved an intricate and recondite beauty, the mainsprings of which are not easy of access for one brought up in the western tradition. These decorative texts are the hymns and fugues and icons of Muslim devotion; they are a key to the understanding both of Muslim piety and of Muslim aesthetics.

The most familiar and characteristic outward feature of the mosque is the minaret, usually a separate structure, from the top of which the muezzin summons the faithful to prayer. It typifies both the unity and variety of the Muslim world. Everywhere it serves the same religious and social purpose, soaring above the crowded alleys and markets, a signal and a warning to the believers. But at the same time each of the great regions of Islam has its own style of minaret, often preserving the remembered outline of some earlier structure, not always a religious one—the step-towers of Babylon, the church steeples of Syria, the lighthouses of Egypt. In the slender beauty of the Turkish minaret there is an ethereal quality in which all memory of a non-Islamic or non-religious past seems to have been effaced; the grouped fingers of stone around the Suleymaniye point heavenward in a gesture of devotion and submission.

2

From Babel to Dragomans

And the Lord said, Behold, the people is one, and they have all one
language . . . and now nothing will be restrained from them, which
they have imagined to do. Go to, let us go down, and there confound
their language, that they may not understand one another's speech.

Genesis 11: 6–7

This famous passage from the Book of Genesis expresses the recognition
of a distinctive feature of the Middle Eastern region as contrasted with
the two other regions of ancient civilisation in the old world. China had
substantially one classical language, one script, one civilisation; ancient India
likewise, with relatively minor variations. The Middle East had many different
unrelated civilisations and many languages which, from the earliest times, created
problems of communication. The problem was apparently still unresolved by the
time of the New Testament, and there again we have a reference to the situation
created by the Tower of Babel, which was, when necessary, solved by what in
Christian parlance is called 'the miracle of tongues'. Let me quote another passage: 'And how hear we every man in our own tongue, wherein we were born?
Parthians, and Medes, and Elamites, and the dwellers in Mesopotamia, and in
Judea, and Cappadocra, in Pontus etc . . . we do hear them speak in our tongues
the wonderful works of God' (Acts 2: 8–11). And again 'In my name shall they
cast out devils; they shall speak with new tongues' (Mark 16:17). And again 'If
any man speak in an unknown tongue, let it be by two, or at the most by three,
and that by course; and let one interpret' (1 Corinthians 14:27).

By this time, clearly, the office and function of the interpreter were well
understood.

The interpreter—the one who translates from one language to another, who makes communication possible between different peoples speaking different languages, appears very early. Again I go back to the book of Genesis, where we learn that Joseph, as a high Egyptian official, spoke to his brothers newly arrived from Canaan, and they did not know that he understood them when they spoke among themselves—'For he spake unto them by an interpreter'. (Genesis 42: 23). The word used in the Hebrew is *melitz* (מליץ). Melitz has a number of meanings; more often it means something like intercessor or advocate or even ambassador. But in this case, interestingly, the Authorized Version translates it as interpreter (obviously interpreting between Egyptian and Hebrew), and if we look at one of the earliest translations from the Hebrew text into Aramaic, we find that the word *melitz* is rendered as *meturgeman* (מתורגמן). Here we have an early form of what later, in English, came to be called 'dragoman'. A *meturgeman* is a translator; the word is very old, and goes back to Assyrian, where *ragamu* means to speak, *rigmu* is a word and the *taf'el* form indicates one who facilitates communication.

This word *meturgeman*, also *turgeman*, passed from Aramaic to Hebrew, to Arabic, to Turkish, to Italian, to French, to English, and many other languages. It occurs in Italian in the form *turcimanno*, no longer used in modern Italian. In French it becomes *truchement*, in English, dragoman and drogman. The Hebrew word *Targum* is from the same root.

The earliest discussions of translation are in the context of the translation of scriptures such as the *Targum*, the translation of the Hebrew Bible into Aramaic. There is an interesting difference between the attitudes of the scriptural religions to this question. Jews decided at an early stage that it is permissible to translate scripture, and translations of the Hebrew Bible were made into Aramaic, later into Greek and into other languages, especially Judaeo-Arabic, Judaeo-Persian, and of course Judaeo-German, better known as Yiddish.

For Christians, translation is not only permitted, it is required, and some translations acquire the status of scriptures themselves. Such is the Latin translation, the Vulgate; the Syriac translation, the Ethiopic translation and, one might add, the Luther German Bible and the King James English Bible. Indeed it has been suggested, with some plausibility, that parts of the Greek New Testament are themselves translations from an earlier original in some other language, presumably Aramaic.

The Muslim position on the other hand is quite different; translation of the Qur'an is not only not encouraged, it is expressly forbidden. The text is divine, inimitable, uncreated and eternal, and to translate it would be an act of presumption and impiety. Of course they do translate it. Most Muslims nowadays do not understand Arabic, and the contents have somehow to be conveyed to them, but this is presented as interpretation, not as translation. Certainly there is no translation of the Qur'an which has the status of the Vulgate or the Septuagint or the Targum. It is interesting that the Qur'an itself refers in a number of places to the fact that it is in Arabic: the Hebrew Bible does not refer to the fact that it is in Hebrew. On the contrary, the word Hebrew, meaning a language as distinct from its use as an ethnic designation, does not occur in the Hebrew Bible, which usually refers to the language used by the ancient Israelites as *'yehudit'* (Jewish) (2 Kings 18: 26 cf. Isaiah 36: 11; Nehemiah 13: 24; 2 Chronicles 32: 18) or *Sefat Kena'an* (language of Canaan) (Isaiah 19: 18).

My concern today is not with translations of scriptural texts, but rather with translations for more practical purposes, for purposes of government, diplomacy, trade, war, and the like. Here again we have some very early examples. A passage in the Book of Esther tells us that in the Persian empire an order was sent 'to the lieutenants, and the deputies and rulers of the provinces which are from India unto Ethiopia, an hundred and twenty-seven provinces, unto every province according to the writing thereof, and unto every people after their language' (Esther 8: 9). A considerable task, to translate an imperial order into presumably 127 languages so that the ruler's orders would be understood in all the provinces of his empire, from India even unto Ethiopia.

Who did the translations? How did it happen? We have literally hard evidence, in the form of inscriptions on stone, of the concern of the rulers of multinational empires that their edicts and orders should be understood; we have bi-lingual and tri-lingual inscriptions, the most famous of course being the inscription at Behistoun in Iran and the Rosetta stone from Egypt, now in the British Museum. In these the same text is given in different languages, so that it may be understood by different elements of the population.

Translation requires a translator. Somebody has to know both languages, so as to understand a text in the source language and be able to express it in the target language. The Roman author Pliny (*Natural History*, vi. 5) tells us that the peoples of the Caucasus spoke many different languages, so much so that the Romans needed 130 different interpreters [*interpres*] to deal with the Caucasian kings and princes—even exceeding the Persian empire.

Another classical author, Plutarch, tells us that among the many qualities of Cleopatra, she was an accomplished linguist: 'And her tongue, like an instrument of many strings, she could readily turn to whatever language she pleased, so that in her interviews with barbarians she very seldom had need of an interpreter [ἑρμηνεύς], but made her replies to most of them herself and unassisted, whether they were Ethiopians, Troglodytes, Hebrews, Arabians, Syrians, Medes or Parthians.'[1]

One of our earliest accounts of a diplomatic communication in the Middle Ages comes from an Arabic chronicler called Awhadi. He tells us that a European queen, Bertha the daughter of Lothar, queen of Franja [Frankland] and its dependencies, sent a gift and a letter to the Abbasid Caliph al-Muktafi in the year 293 of the Hijra (906 CE). With them was a further message, not included in the letter, but addressed directly to the Caliph. The letter, says the Arab historian, was written on white silk 'in a writing resembling the Greek writing but straighter' (presumably this was Latin writing: the queen from Italy would obviously have used the Latin script). The message, he says, was a request to the Caliph for marriage and friendship—a rather odd listing; one cannot help but wonder whether there was some mistranslation here.[2]

How did they read this message in Latin? Who could there have been in tenth-century Baghdad that could read a letter in Latin? Awhadi tells us: they searched for someone to translate the letter, and in the clothing store they found a Frankish slave who was able 'to read the writing of that people'. He was brought into the Caliph's presence, where he translated the letter from Latin writing into Greek writing. They then brought the famous scientific translator Ishaq ibn Hunain and he translated it from Greek into Arabic.

Not surprisingly, nothing seems to have resulted from this embassy, neither by way of marriage nor of friendship. But it does give us an interesting early example of a method which we hear of much more, and that is the two-tier translation: translation through an intermediate language. It became very common in the later Middle Ages and the early modern period, when increasingly, we find a language which is, so to speak, accepted as a diplomatic and commercial lingua franca. In the later Middle Ages, Italian served this purpose in the Mediterranean; it continued until the beginning of the nineteenth century to be the most widely used European language in the region. Communications, for example, between the English and the Turks passed through Italian. An Englishman who had something to say to a Turkish official said it to someone who translated it into Italian and then someone else translated it from Italian into Turkish. The answer came back by the same route.

My main concern in this paper is with communications, through interpreters and dragomans, between the two major Mediterranean civilisations—the civilisations of Christendom and of Islam. It might be useful first to point to one or two relevant differences between these two cultures. On the Christian side, there was a well-established need to learn languages. Christians of whatever native language had two classical languages to learn if they wished to be considered educated: Latin and Greek, and two more if they wanted to read their scriptures in the original: Hebrew and Aramaic. In addition to that, they had a multiplicity of spoken languages: Rashid al-Din, the fourteenth-century Persian historian, notes with astonishment that 'the Franks have twenty-five different languages which they use among themselves, and nobody understands the language of anybody else'.[3]

In 1492, a year well known also for some other events, a Spanish humanist called Antonio de Nebrija published a grammar of the Castilian language. This, as far as I am aware, is the first time that anyone had treated a colloquial language seriously. He tried to establish rules, and launched the process by which the Castilian dialect became the Spanish language. Very soon after that, Italian, French, English, German, and all the other vernaculars of Europe became recognized written languages with rules and eventually grammars and even dictionaries.

The situation on the Islamic side was entirely different. The many languages of antiquity either disappeared or dwindled into insignificance, surviving as written languages, if at all, in scriptures and rituals. After the spread of Islam, there was only one language that mattered—Arabic. It was the language of scripture, of the classics, of commerce, of government, of science. And although, like Latin in the west, it developed a number of vernaculars, they did not, like French and Spanish and Italian and Portuguese, develop into autonomous languages. Colloquially of course they did, but that development was never formally recognised or recorded. Just one language met all needs, and there was therefore no need to learn any other. Why would an Arabic speaker bother to learn the barbarous idioms of infidels and savages beyond the imperial frontier? Arabic provided all his needs, and if anyone wanted to talk to him, they would learn Arabic. One finds a similar attitude in parts of the English-speaking world at the present time.

A little later, first one, then another language was added: first Persian, then Turkish. In the Islamic Middle East and North Africa there were no more. Others were at most local dialects. A medieval (probably tenth-century) Arabic writer explains: 'The perfect language is the language of the Arabs and the perfection of eloquence is the speech of the Arabs, all others being deficient. The Arabic language among languages is like the human form among beasts. Just as humanity emerged as the final form among the animals, so is the Arabic language the final perfection of human language and of the art of writing, after which there is no more'[4]—a remarkable anticipation of the later concept of evolution.

Nevertheless, there was need for communication—in commerce, in war, and in some other matters. From an early date, and especially during the Crusades and after, there are numerous references to interpreters, mostly professional interpreters who came to be known in Arabic as *tarjumān*. The same word found its way, as I mentioned before, into a variety of western languages.

Who were these interpreters? Why does anyone set out to learn a foreign language, to learn the language of another people and learn it well enough to understand and interpret what are often very complex statements? The commonest and most widespread reason for learning a language is that it is the language of your masters, and it is wise, expedient, useful, or necessary to know the language of your masters. I am using the word 'master' in three different senses: a slave learns the language of his master, that is his owner, needing it in order to do his job, to receive his orders, to survive. The owner does not learn the language of the slave. The same is true of the master in the sense of ruler: the subject needs to learn the language of his ruler. In British India, Indians learned English; very few Englishmen learned the languages of India and when they did, for the most part they didn't learn them very well. One finds much the same thing in French North Africa and in the various other empires that have flourished. Many Central Asians know Russian, very few Russians, even in Central Asia, knew the languages of Central Asia.

In a third sense of master, meaning teacher, the learner sees some earlier civilisation, some other culture as having classical status. The Greeks and the Romans provide us with examples of both. The Romans learned Greek because Greek was their classical language, the language of science and philosophy and the highest literature known to them. The Greeks eventually learned Latin because the Romans conquered and ruled Greece.

Another group who find it expedient and convenient to learn a language are refugees: those who flee from one world to another. There were considerable numbers of refugees who fled from Christian Europe to the lands of Islam in the Middle Ages and the early modern period; there were very few who went in the opposite direction. Among these refugees from Europe were many Jews, notably those who came after the expulsion from Spain in 1492. Some of them learned Turkish and were able to make themselves useful to the Turkish empire in a variety of ways.

A distinctive group among the newcomers consisted of those who changed their religion, and made a new career—those whom the Christians call renegade and whom the Muslims call *Muhtadi*, one who had found the true path of God. Considerable numbers of Christian—shall we say adventurers?—went from various parts of Europe into the Muslim lands, bringing useful skills—military, commercial, technical, and also linguistic—for which they were able to find a ready market.

All these groups—slaves, refugees, renegades—came in from the outside. There were also those who went out from the inside; there were prisoners-of-war, not too many, but we do know of some people from the Muslim lands who were captured by one or other Christian state and spent some years in a Christian country before they were ransomed or escaped, and went home. These are remarkably disappointing. Very few of them wrote anything about their experiences and even fewer appear to have played any sort of role on their return. There were also merchants who travelled abroad and returned home; they normally seem to have been non-Muslims—Christian and Jewish subjects of the Muslim states, and they have left little record.

There were also sailors. When Prince Jem, brother of Sultan Mehmed II, fled to Europe and spent a little while as the guest of various European rulers, the Ottoman government was not unnaturally concerned about what he was doing and what he might be plotting with the enemies of the empire. So they sent a spy to Italy and to France to keep an eye on the exiled prince and report on his activities. But whom could they send, whom would they have that could move around in Italy and France? They sent a sea-captain, who had been to Europe and apparently had sufficient language skill, not to pass as a native, but to sail, so to speak, around under his own flag, as a sailor, and communicate and report.[5] The Venetian Father Toderini, who visited the Turkish naval school in the late eighteenth century, found that almost all the teachers were foreigners, Europeans who had learned Turkish, but he did find one Muslim, a native Algerian seaman, who had learned Italian and was able to help him.[6] They were not a large group, but they were not insignificant. They have left their record in the European loanwords in Ottoman Turkish. Until the beginning of the nineteenth century, and the massive intrusion of new ideas and objects and words to designate them, European loanwords in Turkish were very few, and most of them were Italian and maritime.

By far the most important of those who went out and came back were Christians. From the seventeenth century, wealthy Christian families began to send their sons (not daughters of course) to Europe, principally to Italy, to study in the universities. They returned with a serious knowledge of at least one European language and usually some other useful skills as well. These came to play an increasingly important part.

In doing so they replaced the Jews. Jews had come from Europe in the fourteenth, more especially in the fifteenth and early sixteenth centuries. They came with a knowledge of languages and countries and for a while were very useful. But they lost their usefulness; no new ones were coming, and the second generation born in Turkey no longer possessed the skills and knowledge that their parents had brought from Europe. They were replaced by Greeks, and to a much lesser extent Armenians, who went out and came back, and took over many of the roles which Jews had formerly played in the Ottoman lands.

What were these roles? Who employed interpreters? We have rather scattered information, showing that they were employed at various levels, including the lower levels. They were needed locally. An imperial government has to have people who know the local language, for practical purposes like collecting taxes and maintaining order. For this, local people were usually used.

Jews served especially in the customs administration, where their knowledge of European languages and conditions was useful. Those who came from Europe could speak Spanish and often Italian too. We find for example great numbers of customs receipts in the Venetian archives, in Hebrew letters. A customs receipt is given so that the recipient can show it to another customs officer, and if the other customs officer was also likely to be Jewish, it made good sense to write the customs receipt in Hebrew letters. In the Venetian archives there are boxes of customs receipts given by Sephardic Jews in the Ottoman service to Venetian merchants.

There were more important interpreters, at government level, who served in negotiations between the Ottoman government and the various European embassies. This is the period when something new was developing, that is to say, resident embassies conducting continuous diplomacy. One after another the European states—the Venetians, the Genoese, the French, the English, and the rest—established embassies in Istanbul to negotiate with the Ottoman government on matters of concern, primarily of course on commerce.

How did they talk to each other? Ottoman officials did not know any English or French or Italian or any other Christian European language, nor did these westerners know any Turkish. Communication was carried on through first one and then two groups of intermediaries—those employed by the Sublime Porte, and those employed by the embassies, each side hiring and paying its own interpreters.

The earliest dragomans of the Sublime Porte about whom we have information seem to have been renegades, or from a Muslim point of view *Muhtadi*, and they seem to have come in the main from the periphery of the empire, including Hungarians, Poles, Germans, and Italians. These were gradually replaced by Greeks, who were of course Ottoman subjects. There were a few Jews, but not in major positions. In most of the jobs they had held, Jews were replaced by western-educated members of the Greek patrician class of Istanbul. They came to be known as the Phanariots, from the district in Istanbul where many of them lived and where the office of the Greek Patriarch was situated. These, generation after generation, continued to send their sons to Italy, where they graduated from Italian universities, came back with a thorough knowledge of Italian and of European conditions and were able to serve the Sublime Porte consistently, effectively and remarkably loyally for many generations. The earliest to bear the title of Grand Dragoman was a certain Panayotis Nicosias, a Greek who was appointed by his patron, Köprülü Ahmed Pasha, in 1661. He was followed by a medical doctor called Alexander Mavrokordato, founder of one of the great dragoman dynasties.

On whom did the embassies rely? They drew on a rather different group of people, whom it has become customary to call Levantines. The word levantine comes from Italian—Levante is the sunrise; people who come from the east are politely called 'people from the sunrise' *levantini*. Those who came from the west were sometimes called *ponentini*, people from the sunset. Levantine came to be something of a term of abuse; it came to mean people who are European but not really European; who have a veneer and a smattering of European ways and education but are really local; and yet who don't possess the real local culture. The Turks called the Levantines *tatlısu frengi*, sweet-water Franks, as opposed to the genuine article, who are salt-water Franks.

The Levantines flourished for several centuries. They were overwhelmingly Catholic by religion; mostly they spoke Italian. Many of them seem to have been of Italian origin, though they intermarried freely with Greeks, especially with Catholic Greeks, and they formed a more or less self-contained, autonomous society, not only in the capital but also in many provincial cities, since dragomans were needed not only at the embassies but also at consulates, vice-consulates and trading posts and the like. Both embassies and consultes relied very largely on Levantines to do these jobs.

Almost from the start, we find continual complaints about the Levantines in the diplomatic documents of the European powers. Sometimes the interpreters are accused of incompetence; they pretend to know Turkish well but they don't. That appears on the whole to be an unjustified complaint. There may have been some who were not able to do their job properly, but on the whole, they seem to have been pretty competent.

A more serious complaint is disloyalty: they are accused of serving their own interests, of selling their services to the highest bidder, of forming a sort of self-contained, coherent Levantine dragoman group which owed no real loyalty to anybody. Certainly there are quite awful stories told by many ambassadors about dragomans selling secrets to another embassy, or exchanging secrets with colleagues. They were mostly related to each other, so that a dragoman of the British embassy might be the first cousin of a dragoman of the French embassy. At a time of acute Anglo-French rivalry, this would give rise to interesting possibilities for both of them.

Another accusation, made very frequently and certainly justified by the evidence, is that they were frightened—too frightened to do their job properly. They were after all not Englishmen or Frenchmen or Austrians; they were local people who lived in Turkey. They were not citizens in the modern sense (the word has no relevance to that time) but they and their families were subjects of the Ottoman Sultan, and entirely at his mercy. They did not enjoy any kind of diplomatic status (not that the Ottomans in the high period of Ottoman rule cared all that much for diplomatic status, though they generally respected it). But the Levantine dragomans, until a very late stage, were not diplomats, and the embassies almost all agreed that they were far too scared of the Turkish authorities to deliver any unpalatable message honestly. Thus for example when the British or the French or the Austrian ambassador wanted to deliver a severe message, the severity disappeared entirely. The severe message as transmitted by the dragoman to the *reis efendi* or whatever other Ottoman official he dealt with became a humble supplication.

As an example of a dragoman's style I may quote one example. A man called George Aide or Aida, who was the dragoman of the British consulate in Aleppo, working for the Levant Company and the consulate—by his name one would assume a Syrian Christian—got into trouble for reasons which are not quite clear, and was imprisoned in the Citadel. He asked the British ambassador to help him. The ambassador responded and eventually managed to get Aida released. But as precaution, the dragoman also sent a petition from the citadel, when he was imprisoned, to the Aga of the janissaries, the highest military officer in Turkey. One passage will suffice to give the flavour of such documents.

> This is the petition of the dragoman to the Aga of the janissaries: Having bowed my head in submission, and rubbed my slavish brow in utter humility and complete abjection and supplication to the beneficent dust beneath the feet of my mighty, gracious, condescending, compassionate, merciful benefactor, my most generous and open-handed master, I pray that the peerless and almighty provider of remedies may bless your lofty person, the extremity of benefit, protect my benefactor from the vicissi-

tudes and afflictions of time, prolong the days of his life, his might and his splendour and perpetuate the shadow of his pity and mercy upon this slave.[7]

It goes on like this at some length. If this was how a dragoman addressed a high Ottoman functionary, one can understand a certain concern on the part of European diplomats about the form in which their words—written or spoken—were transmitted to their Ottoman addressees.

Sir James Porter, an ambassador writing in the mid-eighteenth century, notes with regret that ambassadors

> are under a necessity of trusting other men to transmit their thoughts and sentiments to these unknown ministers; or, which is still worse, are obliged to have recourse to writing, and if the Turkish ministry happen to not like the subject, it will never produce an answer. Hence arises a great perplexity to zealous ministers, for if they entrust their secret to interpreters, who with large families live upon a small salary, and are used to Oriental luxury, the temptation of money from others is with difficulty withstood by them [Sir James is very considerate in putting it that way] and even exclusive of any considerations of gain, they are often excited by mere vanity to discover [meaning to reveal] the secret they are entrusted with in order to show their own importance.[8]

This became a serious source of concern, and various ways were found of dealing with it. In time the system broke down on both sides—the use of the Levantines by the embassies, the use of the Phanariot Greeks by the Porte; they broke down in different ways and for different reasons.

Most of the European powers decided, sooner or later, that they could no longer rely on these people, and that the only real answer was to train people of their own. And so young Englishmen, young Frenchmen, young Austrians, young Russians—these being the four Powers mainly concerned—were assigned to learn the language. There is a long and interesting story about how attempts were made and finally succeeded—to some extent. The French began with what they called '*les jeunes de langue*', a *jeune de langue* being a kind of language cadet. They were sent from France, where they had some preliminary training in a Middle Eastern language, and then attached as what we would nowadays call, I suppose, interns, to the French embassy. The Austrians at one stage even insisted that their ambassador must speak Turkish. The Russians, according to the testimony of Adolphus Slade, one of the best British observers, had a much simpler method: when they wanted something, they would say 'Do so or I will declare war' and this, apparently, was normally effective.[9]

By the nineteenth century, the older system was dying, though it persisted quite far into the century, and for a while young Englishmen and Levantine dragomans served side by side, naturally with not very happy relations between them. On the Ottoman side, the end came with the Greek war of independence. The last of the Greek grand dragomans, Stavraki Aristarchi, was hanged in 1821 on suspicion of complicity with the rebels. I have no idea whether the suspicion was well grounded or not; I am inclined to think not. The Phanariot bureaucratic families showed very little sympathy with the rebels; they had a long record of attachment to the Ottoman state which continued even after these events. Indeed, as late as 1840, the first Ottoman envoy to independent Athens was a Phanariot Greek, Kostaki Musurus, later Ottoman ambassador in London.

But it was no longer considered safe to entrust what had become a crucial post, in the newly important field of foreign policy, to non-Muslims. The basic change was in the relationship between the Ottoman empire and the western world. In the new balance of power, the Ottomans could no longer afford the attitude of easy disdain, of contemptuous unconcern for the barbarous peoples of Europe and their absurd dialects. It became necessary to learn languages. After the hanging of the chief dragoman, Aristarchi, we are told by the contemporary Turkish historians that there was total confusion in the office of the grand dragoman; papers were piling up and there was no one that could read them. So they brought the chief professor of the naval school, a Jew converted to Islam who knew several European languages, and he held this office for a while.

With the increasing importance of relations with European countries the chief translator became more than a chief translator; he became in effect a minister of foreign affairs, conducting the policies and drafting the letters, not just translating them. Later the Ottomans established a translation office, and that soon became the main avenue to power in Turkish bureaucratic politics in the late nineteenth and early twentieth centuries. In other words, on both sides—the Ottoman government on the one hand and the foreign embassies on the other— they were tending more and more to use their own people.

An important question is that of mistranslation, not just mistranslation by simple error or ignorance, but systematic, intentional mistranslation, of which there are interesting examples. I had occasion some time ago to look at the correspondence between London and Istanbul in the late sixteenth century, after the establishment of the first English embassy to the Ottoman government: letters from the Ottoman Sultans to the Queen of England and replies from the Queen to the Sultans; also correspondence with the Grand Vizier and other functionaries. The Sultan's missives were of course in Turkish; a contemporary translation was provided in Italian which the English could understand; the reply was drafted in English, sent in Italian and presumably translated into Turkish. We do not have the letters from the Queen of England which reached the Sultan in their Turkish form; we have originals in English and translations in Italian but not the final form. We do have the successive versions the other way round, and they show systematic mistranslation right through.

From the Ottoman point of view, the Ottoman Sultan was the ruler of the world; outside there were enemies or vassals, and Ottoman protocol was not willing to use the full titles which these outside rulers claimed for themselves. Thus, in letters addressed to Queen Elizabeth—polite, friendly letters—she is addressed as 'Queen of the vilayet of England'. The Holy Roman Emperor himself, in Vienna, is called 'the king of Vienna'. The words used for 'king' and 'queen'—*kural* and *kiraliçe*—are European, not Turkish or Islamic. The Ottomans in Europe, like the British in India, used native titles for native princes.

The letters themselves reveal the same sort of approach, so that when the Sultan writes a friendly letter to the Queen of England, the purport of what he says is that he is happy to add her to the vassals of his imperial throne, and hopes, in the formal phrase, that she will 'continue to be firm-footed on the path of devotion and fidelity'. None of this appears in the translation, which was made for the English ambassador in Italian and communicated by him to London in English. In these the language is one of equal negotiation between sovereigns. Thus, for example, in the berat (diploma) granted by Murad III to Queen Elizabeth authorising English merchants to trade in the Ottoman lands, the Sultan speaks of the Queen as having 'demonstrated her subservience and devotion and declared her servitude and attachment' (*izhar-i ubudiyet ve ihlas ve ish'ar-i rıkkiyet ve ıhtısas*). The contemporary Italian translation renders this 'sincera amicizia'.[10]

It was, it seems, the general practice for the dragomans discreetly to modify the language, making it less imperious and more polite. One may safely assume that they were doing the same thing the other way round, and that when, for example, the Queen wrote to the Sultan expressing good will and friendship, in the Turkish version which reached the Sultan this became loyalty and humble submission.

In the early stages, the Embassies were not aware of these discrepancies and there was no way they could have been aware of them. Later there was a growing realisation that the interpreters employed by the embassies were systematically misrepresenting their texts. That became more and more of a problem, and the subject of frequently expressed concern. An ambassador negotiating with a foreign minister needs to know exactly what is being said. A certain amount of sprucing up and tidying up is permissible, but when it comes to misrepresentation, falsifying the atmosphere that exists between two governments—that is not acceptable. At a fairly early stage, certainly by the eighteenth century (and there are some suggestions even earlier than that), diplomats were becoming very dissatisfied with their interpreters. We don't find this on the Ottoman side, with reason. The Ottomans knew with whom they were dealing; their interpreters were their own subjects, working for them, their livelihoods and even their lives being entirely dependent on them.

That is one kind of mistranslation—the mistranslation of diplomatic documents, and I suspect that this continued into modern times, indeed may still be going on. A second type of mistranslation—perhaps more dangerous—occurs in treaties. A treaty is drawn up between at least two parties; it is usually elaborately negotiated and an agreed text is produced which both parties sign. What exactly is this agreed text?

Two examples may suffice. The first, the treaty of Küchük Kaynarja between Russia and Turkey, was signed in 1774 after a Russian victory in a war. The treaty was drawn up in Italian, still at that time the main diplomatic language. The last article of the Treaty (Article XXVIII) says that the Treaty will be signed and sealed in two versions—one in Italian and Russian, the other in Italian and Turkish, so that each of the two signatory nations would have a version in their own language. The Italian version, which is the same for both, was obviously the binding one. Yet the Russians used the Russian version and the Turks used the Turkish version, and quite considerable discrepancies appear between the two, both nominally based on the same Italian text.

A second example is the treaty of friendship signed in 1971 between the Soviet Union and the United Arab Republic. According to the text of the treaty, it was drawn up in two languages—Russian and Arabic, of equal validity. Unlike many other treaties, this has no agreed common version. Both Moscow and Cairo published English translations, but they are markedly different. We do not know in what language the treaty was negotiated and agreed. It may have been Russian or Arabic, with extensive use of interpreters all the way. It cannot have been English, since the Moscow English text is clearly translated from the Russian and the Cairo English text is clearly translated from the Arabic. There are a number of significant differences between them.

Today, the dragoman has given way to the highly trained professional translator, a member of an immense and still rapidly growing profession. Despite the widespread use and understanding of a few major languages, translators are now more in demand than ever before. Bodies like the United Nations and the European Union require that speeches and documents be translated into all the official languages. Sometimes even purely domestic speeches and documents must be translated, in countries with more than one official language.

For the official translator, elegance is of no significance. What matters is accuracy. But even today, startling discrepancies may sometimes arise. Thus, for example, Article (i) of Security Council Resolution 242 of 22 November 1967 requires the 'withdrawal of Israeli armed forces from territories occupied in the recent conflict'. The omission of the definite article before 'territories' has usually been taken to mean that the required withdrawal relates to some but not necessarily all of the territories in question. This fine but crucial distinction is lost in both the French and Russian versions. The French text includes the definite article, since French grammar requires it. The Russian texts omits the definite article, since in Russian none exists. The Arabic translation, for both stylistic and political reasons, includes the article, but at that time Arabic was not an official UN language.

In translating and interpreting official documents, the purpose is not to evoke aesthetic appreciation but accurately—and in some but not all situations unequivocally—to convey the meaning of the original. In such translations the issues are not literary or linguistic, but political and even military.

Speed of movement and ease of communication have greatly increased both the range and scope of the translator's work, and the need for his services. The impact of these new methods and opportunities can be seen in literary as well as bureaucratic translation. In this century the craft of the literary translator has flourished as never before, and more texts of more kinds are being translated from more languages into more languages than at any time in history. The Bible, still easily the most translated book, is constantly reaching ever new readers in ever new languages, in some of which a Bible translation is the first text ever committed to writing. With the growth of literacy and the improvement in communication, works of literature rapidly become known far outside their place of origin, and books are being translated into an ever-widening range of languages. In countries using lesser-known languages, a majority of the books offered for sale in bookshops are translations from other languages. Even in countries using a major world language, a significant proportion of new publications are translated from other languages, including some previously little-known languages. The first to benefit from this were the Scandinavians. Nineteenth-century writers like the Norwegian Henrik Ibsen, the Swede August Strindberg, the Danes Hans Andersen and Søren Kierkegaard, were able, through translation, to achieve world fame. Others, geographically, linguistically, and culturally less accessible than the Scandinavians, took a little longer—but only a little. The twentieth century brought such previously hidden talents as the Czech Karel Čapek and, most recently, the Albanian Ismail Kadare before a world audience.

The literary consensus on the quality of translation is on the whole pessimistic. As far back as the seventeenth century, the English writer James Howell remarked that some held translations to be 'not unlike . . . the wrong side of a Turkish tapestry'. In the nineteenth century George Borrow sadly remarked that 'translation is at best an echo'. A similar sentiment inspired the Turkish poet Ahmet Hashim who, when asked what was the essence of poetry, replied: 'That which is lost in translation.' A French wit is quoted as likening translations to wives—'some are beautiful, some are faithful, few are both'. A classical Italian phrase sums it up: 'Traduttore traditore'—translator, traitor.[11]

Notes

1. Plutarch, *Lives*, IX, *Anthony*, 27: 4, edited and translated by Bernadette Perrin, Loeb Classical Library (1920) p. 197.

2. Ed. M. Hamidullah in "Embassy of Queen Bertha to Caliph al-Muktafi billah in Baghdad 293/906." *Journal of the Pakistan Historical Society*, 1 (1953), 272–300.

3. *Histoire des Franks*, ed. and trans. K. Jahn (Leiden, 1951), p. 11 of Persian text, p. 24 of translation. A Persian writer added: "All they have in common is letters and numbers."

4. *Rasā'il Ikhwān al-Safā*, III (Cairo, 1928), p. 152.

5. V. L. Ménage, "The Mission of an Ottoman Secret Agent in France in 1486," in *Journal of the Royal Asiatic Society* (1965), 112–32.

6. G. Toderini, *Letteratura turchesca* (Venice, 1787), vol. I, pp. 177.

7. Document in the Public Record Office, S.P. 102/62.

8. *Observations on the Religion, Law, Government and Manners of the Turks* (1771), p. 211.

9. Adolphus Slade, *Records of Travels in Turkey, Greece, etc.* (1833), vol. II, p. 192.

10. Documents in the Public Record Office, S.P. 102/61 ff. For a study of some of these documents, see S. A. Skilliter, *William Harborne and the Trade with Turkey 1578–1582: a documentary study of the first Anglo-Ottoman relations* (1977).

11. An abridged version of this lecture was published in *The Times Literary Supplement* of 23 April 1999.

3

Middle East Feasts

ॐ

1.

The Promised Land is defined by its frontiers and then by its abundant if basic food supply—"a land flowing with milk and honey." The Lord's Prayer deals with eternal truths, and with one practical request—for "our daily bread." The pagan ancient Greeks, imagining the life of the immortals on Mount Olympus, provided for their sustenance—ambrosia and nectar, the food and drink of the gods.

The systematic study of the history of food is comparatively recent, but historians have already made impressive progress. This kind of history, like any other, requires evidence, and in the Middle East, the home of the most ancient civilization known to history, such evidence is fortunately plentiful.* A major source of historical information consists of the actual words and names that we use to designate the foodstuffs that we eat and drink. In this, as in everything else, language is a primary and often very illuminating, though sometimes rather tricky, source of information. A few examples may suffice to illustrate the value and the pitfalls of verbal evidence. One is that familiar fruit, the orange: in English "orange," from French *orange*, from Spanish *naranja*, from Arabic *naranj*, from Persian *narang*, which is of course related to the Hebrew *etrog*, from the

---

*Useful surveys of various aspects of the subject, with bibliographical details, will be found in two major works of reference, the *Encyclopedia Iranica* and the *Encyclopedia of Islam*. In the first, reference may be made to the articles on "Cooking," "Fisheries and fishing," "Fruit," etc. The *Encyclopedia of Islam* is published in English and French, but the articles are, for the most part, listed under their Arabic names. Of particular value are the articles on food (*Ghidhā'*), drinks (*Mashrūbāt*), and cooking (*Matbakh*). There are also valuable articles on more limited and specific themes, such as coffee (*Ḳahwa*), wine (*Khamr*), and tea (*Shay*).

Persian *turung*. An interesting term of Middle Eastern origin, traceable in various forms, designating citrus fruit.

But then we find something very puzzling. Most of the languages of Europe use a word of Persian origin to designate this fruit, but in the languages of the Middle East, in Turkish, in Persian, and in Arabic they call it *Portugal*. So why is the fruit which we in the West call by a Middle Eastern name called in the Middle East by the name of a West European country? This question, fortunately, is not difficult to answer. The *narang* is the small bitter orange, used for conserves, for flavoring, sometimes also for perfume and medicinal purposes. The sweet orange came from China and was unknown in the Middle East until it was brought by Portuguese merchants, who had picked it up in the Far East, brought it around the Cape, and then reexported it from Western Europe to the Middle East. The Germans got it right when they called it *Apfelsin*, the apple of China.

As for the peach, the English name comes from the French *pêche*, from Italian *pesca*, from Greek *persica*—referring to the "Persian fruit." The Greek term also found its way into Hebrew in the form *afarsek*. This again is an instructive verbal route which one can retrace without too much difficulty.

Sometimes names can lead us astray. In the autumn of 1949 I was in Turkey, working in the Turkish state archives. This was just at the time when a new relationship was developing between the United States and Turkey, which culminated a couple of years later in the inclusion of Turkey in NATO. On Thanksgiving in 1949, President Truman, no doubt on the advice of his specialist advisers, thought it would be a gracious and pleasant gesture to present a turkey to the president of Turkey. In Istanbul, I could observe the general bewilderment. Nowadays of course they would understand immediately. But at that time people in Turkey didn't know very much about the United States, and there was much mystification. They appreciated what was clearly meant as a friendly gesture, but they were very puzzled when a large dead bird arrived at Çankaya, the Turkish presidential residence, delivered by a special diplomatic courier.

The reason for the mystery is that the bird which in English is called "turkey," in Turkish is called *hindi*, Indian. It was an American bird, unknown in the Eastern Hemisphere before the discoveries of the American continents. Wanting to give it an exotic name, something odd, something different, Europeans made do with the most exotic they could think of. So people called it the the Indian bird, *dinde* (*d'Inde*) in French, and equivalents in other languages. In time the bird reached the Middle East, where, in Arabic, it is called *dik habashi* or *dik rumi*, the Ethiopian bird or the Greek bird. In fact, the bird is neither Ethiopian nor Greek, neither Turkish nor Indian. All these words simply mean something strange and exotic from a far and unknown place.

The same thing happens with maize, that distinctively American cereal, also unknown in the Eastern Hemisphere before the discoveries. The first English settlers in North America called it "Indian corn." "Corn" of course in English meant wheat, and still does in England. But in America it was "Indian corn." Eventually there was no need to repeat the word "Indian" all the time, so "corn" came to be maize. In Europe it has various names. In Italian it's called *gran turco*, Turkish grain; in Turkey it's called *mısır*, Egypt; in Egypt it's called *dura shamiyya*, Syrian sorghum. All these names serve the same purpose; to indicate that this is something foreign and exotic.

There are other ways in which etymology can be either misleading or instructive. In Hebrew *leḥem* means bread, whereas the Arabic *laḥm* means meat. Both obviously derive from the same word, and designate a major foodstuff. Similarly, *samn* in Arabic means clarified butter; the cognate Hebrew word *shemen* means oil. A moment's thought is enough to explain the difference. For the pastoral Arabs, these basic words designated meat and butter; for the agricultural Hebrews, bread and oil.

A second major group of sources is literary works, literary in the broad sense. Some deal explicitly with food and drink. One is surprised at how much there is, going back to remote antiquity. We have for example cookbooks with recipes in ancient Assyrian cuneiform inscriptions, and there is a fairly extensive culinary literature in classical Arabic, as well as in later writings. An important topic is spices. The same commodities often turn up as spices, perfumes, and medicines, and in all three capacities they evoked a considerable scientific literature, including, by the way, a book by Maimonides.

Travel literature is of particular interest. Pilgrimage is one of the basic obligations of the Muslim faith, and every Muslim is required to go on pilgrimage to the holy cities of Mecca and Medina at least once in a lifetime. This brought pilgrims every year, traveling great distances from all the lands of Islam, in what must surely be the most important example of voluntary, personal mobility in pre-modern times. Many of the pilgrims wrote accounts of their travels, including descriptions of the places that they visited, the people that they met, and— more relevantly—the foodstuffs that they encountered and consumed in the course of their peregrinations.

An important contribution of the medieval historians is the lists of taxes and tributes which they sometimes provide. Many of these were levied in kind, and the enumeration of places, products, quantities, and prices can also be extremely informative.

There is also much to be learned from literature in the stricter and narrower sense: stories, poetry, even anecdotes. A characteristic example, related by a fourteenth-century Persian writer, deals with the eggplant, known in Persian as *Badinjan*, from which "aubergine" and other European names are derived:

One day when Sultan Mahmud [reigned 998–1010] was hungry, they brought him a dish of eggplant. He liked it very much and said,

"Eggplant is an excellent food." A courtier began to praise the eggplant with great eloquence. When the sultan grew tired of the dish he said, "Eggplant is a very harmful thing," whereupon the courtier began to speak in hyperbole of the harmful qualities of the eggplant. "Man alive," said the sultan, "have you not just now uttered the praises of the eggplant?" "Yes," said the courtier, "but I am your courtier and not the eggplant's courtier."

One Persian poet deserves special mention. His name is Abu Ishaq, usually shortened to Boshaq, and he is known as Boshaq-i at'ima, Boshaq of the foodstuffs, because he devoted almost his entire literary output to writing poems about food. He was obviously fascinated by the subject. He flourished in the late fourteenth and early fifteenth centuries in Shiraz. His major work is called *Kanz al-Ishtihā*, or *Treasure of Appetite*. He also wrote an epic called *Dastan-i Muza'far o Bughrā, The Epic of Saffron-Flavored Rice and Meat Pie*; a story in prose and verse called *Mājerā-i Berenj o Bughrā, The Adventures of Rice and Pie*; and even a dictionary of culinary terms, the *Farhang-i Dīvan-i at'imā*, or *The Science of Foodstuffs*, mainly rather humorous definitions of food terms.

Another category of particular importance in this region, though perhaps less so in others, is religious and juristic writings, which deal, often quite extensively, with what may or may not be eaten or drunk, and lay down rules and restrictions concerning food and drink. These are primarily Jewish and Muslim. Christians may eat or drink anything.

This literature begins with ancient religious texts; it continues right through to the modern period. There are many legal and administrative texts dealing with the lawfulness or otherwise of foodstuffs, their pricing and distribution, and other related matters.

A recurring problem was that of wine, forbidden to Muslims but not to non-Muslims. Difficulties inevitably arose when two groups of people, Jews and Christians, were free to make, sell, and drink wine, and the Muslim majority was not. There are numerous decrees and regulations dealing with such questions—how one prevents the Jews and Christians from selling wine to the Muslims, and even the problem of Muslim guests at Jewish or Christian weddings, at which wine is served.

A third category of evidence consists of documents, meaning not literary works, but actual documentary texts. Here again the Ottoman archives, both central and provincial, offer millions of documents. They cover the whole food process from production, reflected in detailed lists of taxes in kind, to preparation and consumption, illustrated by kitchen accounts from the palace, the military, and a chain of hospices providing free meals to the needy.

We also have some much more ancient documents. Sometime between 884 and 859 BC, the Assyrian king Ashur Nasirpal II thought it worthwhile, in a major inscription near the doorway to his throne, to include a description of a banquet which he gave. The usual purpose of these royal inscriptions was to say: Look how great I am, look how strong I am, look what I accomplished. The normal pattern is: I conquered so many territories, I enslaved so many peoples.

But Ashur Nasirpal II was a man of kindlier disposition, and he describes in great detail a banquet which lasted ten days, with food and drink for 69,574 invited guests, both men and—remarkably—women. The food served is specified and enumerated in this inscription, in very great detail; so many head of cattle, cows, sheep, lambs, stags, gazelles, ducks, geese, pigeons and other birds, fish, eggs, bread, vegetables, fruits, nuts, condiments, and spices, and also 10,000 kegs of beer and 10,000 skins of wine. There are several references in the Bible to royal feasts, given by Pharaoh (Genesis 40:20), Solomon (1 Kings 3:15), and Ahasuerus (Esther 1:3–5; 2:18; 8:17; 9:17–22), but Ashur Nasirpal's would appear to be the oldest described in detail.

Another category of evidence is archaeology, and particularly what is nowadays called "archaeo-chemistry." Forty-four years ago an expedition from the University of Pennsylvania excavated some ruins at Gordion, an ancient Phrygian site in central Turkey, where they found the remains of a funeral feast for a king, perhaps the famous Midas himself. The king had died, and in accordance with the custom of the time and the place, there was a great farewell dinner for him. Whether through drunkenness, carelessness, or obedience to custom, they did no washing up. The king was buried with the entire remains of the feast: the dirty plates and dishes, the unwashed glasses, the leftovers.

We are told that when the archaeologists went and opened the ruins, their nostrils were assailed by the stink of rancid meat. They couldn't do much about it at the time, but since then new techniques have been evolved for the chemical analysis of organic remains. These have now produced extremely interesting data about what they ate and what they drank 2,700 years ago in Turkey.

2.

What were the ingredients of ancient cuisine? We start of course with milk and honey. Milk is a very basic foodstuff, taken sweet, curdled, clarified, and various other ways. One can, in a sense, divide the civilizations of this planet into three zones: the sweet-milk zone, the sour-milk zone, and the no-milk zone. The sweet-milk zone is Europe and the Americas; the sour-milk zone the Islamic lands and India; the no-milk zone China and Japan, where they neither drink it nor use it in their traditional cuisine—no milk, no cheese, no butter.

Honey was also important. It wasn't until comparatively recently that sugar became known, and before that honey was the main sweetener. It was also used to make alcoholic drinks. Cereals are attested to from an early date: wheat, barley, sorghum. Rice seems to have been introduced from India. There is some evidence that it was cultivated immediately before the advent of Islam in Iraq and Iran, but probably not long before. It wasn't known to the Greco-Roman world.

We have a rather interesting description from an early Arab source of their first encounter with rice, at the time of the Arab conquest in the seventh century. Some Persian scouts whom an Arab armed force surprised in the marshes took flight, leaving behind them two baskets: one containing dates, and the other what they afterward learned to be unhusked rice. The Arab leader told his men: eat the dates, but leave this other thing, for it might be poison which the enemy has prepared for you. They therefore ate the dates, and avoided the other basket. But while they were eating, one of their horses broke loose and started to eat the rice. They were about to slaughter the horse, so that they could eat it before its flesh was also poisoned, but the horse's owner told them to wait, and said that he would see to it in due course.

The following morning, finding the horse was still in excellent condition, they lit a fire under the rice and burned off the husks. "And their commander said: pronounce the name of Allah over it and eat. And they ate of it and they found it a most tasty food."

Bread of course is attested to from a very early time, and even acquired a kind of sanctity. Here is a passage from no less an author than al-Ghazali, the great Muslim theologian who died in 1111. In a treatise on table manners, on the correct way to behave while eating, he says: One should eat from the round-ness of the loaf, except where there is only a little bread. A person should break bread and not cut it with a knife. That is disrespectful to the bread. The Prophet is quoted as saying: Tear it with your teeth. No bowl or other vessel should be placed on the bread, but only foodstuffs. Honor bread, which Almighty God sent down as a blessing from heaven. Don't wipe your hand with bread. If anyone lets a mouthful of bread drop, he should pick it up, remove any dirt on it, and not leave it for the devil. A kind of respect for bread still survives in many parts of this region to the present day.

Meat was for most of antiquity something rare and precious, not something for ordinary everyday people. But we have indications of the various birds and beasts that were consumed, and those that were forbidden. Some historians have even argued that the ban on pork set the limits of Islamic expansion. The Islamic religion came out of Arabia in the seventh century, spread very rapidly eastward and westward and northward and southward, and then came to a stop in Spain, the Balkans, and China, three regions depending very heavily on pig husbandry.

Another theory sets the limits of the Islamic expansion in terms of the olive, the cultivation of olives and the production of olive oil, a staple of virtually all cuisine in the Middle Eastern region. That idea seems even more far-fetched than the pork theory, since Islam has after all spread very extensively in lands where the olive is not cultivated or known.

We find plenty of references to fruits and vegetables, including figs, dates, grapes, peaches; eggplant is a great staple. The apple seems to be so basic that it even serves as a sort of generic term for fruits and vegetables, so that something unfamiliar is called a kind of apple. An Italian pilgrim, describing his first encounter with a banana in Egypt in 1384, calls it a "paradise apple." When the potato, an American innovation, first appeared, the French called it *pomme de terre*. When modern Israel needed names for oranges and potatoes, lacking in biblical and rabbinic Hebrew, they both became apples of a kind: "golden apples" and "earth apples." And when the tomato was introduced to Italy, it was the "golden apple," the *pomodoro*, which eventually passed into Arabic in the forms *banadura* and *bandura*.

A word or two about side dishes, condiments, flavorings—things which are not part of a main dish, but are used in various ways to give it flavor. There are the obvious ones, onions, leeks and garlic, all attested to in remote antiquity. Sugar is an interesting additional item, which came from India via Iran, and was either unknown or very little known in Greco-Roman antiquity. We find occasional references to what might be sugar, but they certainly didn't use it normally for cuisine, and when it first appeared it was used for medicinal purposes. After the Islamic conquests sugar spread very rapidly—first its use, then its cultivation: from Persia to Egypt, to North Africa, to Spain, and from Spain to the Atlantic islands and to the New World. From the New World it came back to the Middle East. European powers were able to grow sugar more cheaply and more efficiently on their plantations than in the home countries. The same happened a little later with coffee.

Spices were of course very important. Mas'udi, a major Arabic writer of the Middle Ages, lists twenty-five different spices. Oddly enough, he does not include pepper, the most widely used of all of them, of which another author tells us there were seven hundred varieties. Spices are important also in another respect, and that is through commerce, both with Europe and Southeast Asia.

Mention has already been made of milk as a basic drink. The other most frequently mentioned in antiquity is alcoholic drink of various kinds, principally by fermentation, i.e., wine, or by brewing, i.e., beer. Distilling, making spirits, came later. We have a good deal of literary, archaeological, and even linguistic evidence on the history of wine.

Despite the explicit prohibition of all alcoholic drinks, they were widely indulged in, and there is a whole literature of wine poetry in Arabic, Persian, Turkish, and other Islamic languages. Pious attempts to explain wine as a metaphor for mystical ecstasy are not always persuasive.

Where did they go for a drink? There were of course no taverns in Islamic lands, and no vintners. Christians were allowed to make wine, and Christian monasteries, then as now, there as elsewhere, often specialized in the production of fine wine. So in classical and medieval poetry, both Arabic and Persian, the convent, the *der*, appears almost in the sense of the tavern.

Hot drinks come surprisingly late. Fruit juices or infusions may have been heated, though even that is questionable. But the familiar hot drinks, tea, coffee, cocoa, were totally unknown in the Mediterranean and adjoining regions in antiquity and in the Middle Ages. We do find occasional reference in Arab travel books to the infusion of tea leaves in China. But they describe it with puzzlement and distaste, and don't seem to have been tempted to import this. There is some evidence that when the Mongols conquered Iran in the thirteenth century they brought tea drinking with them, but it didn't take. It wasn't until much later that tea was reintroduced to the Middle East by Europeans. Sometimes it came over land from North China, sometimes by sea from South China. The North Chinese word for tea is *chai*, the South Chinese *tey*, two dialectal pronunciations of the same word, designated by the same Chinese character.

Coffee is better documented. It originated in Ethiopia, probably taking its name from the province of Kaffa, where coffee grows wild. One can only marvel at the ingenuity of the people who discovered how to make coffee from the coffee bean. Most of the basic foodstuffs and drinks are fairly simple; for coffee, they had to go through a long and elaborate process in order to get drinkable coffee from the beans that grow wild in Kaffa. But it happened, fortunately for all of us.

Coffee was imported from Ethiopia to Yemen, from Yemen through Arabia in the sixteenth century to Egypt and Syria, then to Turkey, and from Turkey to Europe. Tea came to the Middle East from Europe, ultimately from China. Coffee was at first a subject of astonishment among Europeans; some even spoke of it with a certain disgust.

A famous English book, Robert Burton's *Anatomy of Melancholy*, written in 1621, offers this comment:

> The Turks have a drink called coffa (for they use no wine), so named of a berry as black as soot and as bitter . . . which they sip still of, and sup as warm as they can suffer. They spend much time in those coffa houses, which are somewhat like our ale houses or taverns, and there they sit chatting and drinking to drive away the time, and to be merry together, because they find by experience, that kind of drink so used helpeth digestion and procureth alacrity.

Like sugar, coffee was also taken by Europeans to their colonies in the West Indies and in Southeast Asia. By the eighteenth century both coffee and sugar figure among the imports to the Middle East from Europe.

Two other herbs are "drunk" in Arabic, though not in English: hashish and tobacco. Hashish is of course indigenous to the Middle East and goes back a long time; tobacco is another American import. Here we have precise documentation. It was brought at the beginning of the seventeenth century, by English merchants, who presumably brought it from the American colonies, and it caught on very rapidly. About both coffee and tobacco, there was a long argument whether they were permitted or forbidden according to Shari'a. For a while smoking was not only forbidden, but was treated as a capital offense. It is still forbidden by the Wahhabis and their disciples.

3.

We know from antiquity of two places for preparing food. One is the oven, called *tannur*, a word that goes back to Assyro-Babylonian antiquity. It was used for baking bread and also for baking pies. The other is the hearth, in Arabic *mustawqad*, where a fire was made in one way or another for boiling, stewing, grilling, and sometimes frying, though that seems to have been comparatively rare, no doubt because of the high cost of oil. We have a fair amount of information on utensils, and even a quantity of utensils preserved.

Foodstuffs were of course an important item of trade. Obviously a large part of what people ate was perishable, bulky, and inexpensive, and therefore unsuitable for long-distance commerce and of no interest to business. But there was nevertheless quite a lot to interest the traders. Spices were very important; also sugar, olive oil, alcoholic drinks. We also find nuts, dried fruits, honey, tea, coffee, and pulses (beans and lentils) listed among commodities.

The generality of Western travelers seem to agree that very few people, other than the great and the wealthy, cooked food in their own homes. They bought cooked food in marketplaces, in cook-shops, from a widely ramified range of professional cooks. An account of the city of Istanbul prepared by order of the Sultan Murad IV in 1638, cited by Evliya Çelebi, a Turkish writer of the time, lists the "guilds and professions" of the city. Among those concerned with food, the first group consists of the cultivators, the people who grow food. The second group, led by the chief of the bakers, includes bakers, salt-makers, cracker-bakers, and pastry cooks, followed by millers, flour merchants, purifiers of corn, sieve-makers, bag-makers, starch-makers, and biscuit-makers. Then come what he calls "the Egyptian merchants." These are importers of rice, coffee, and sugar. Then the purveyors of rice and lentils, of sugar and sweets, of sherbets and of coffee: three hundred men and shops, all Greek and all rich, he says.

The next group consists of the butchers—the slaughterers, the beef butchers, the Jewish butchers, the sheep butchers; and a number of others concerned with the care, slaughter, and sale of animals. Then come the dairymen, divided into purveyors of buffalo milk and sheep's milk, cheese-mongers, cream merchants, butter merchants, and yogurt sellers. Then come the cooks, and those who prepare food for sale in the public places. He enumerates the different kinds of food they sell: dried meats and salt meats, and also liver, tripe, pickled fruits and vegetables, garlic and onions. There are various groups who cook for the poor and a separate guild of carvers. In every cook-shop there is at least one carver who, after having set the dish before the guest, says *bismillah* (in the name of God), eats two morsels, and then bids the guest to eat. This is presumably to show that it is not poisoned. Then there are roasters and stewers and preparers of pilaf, of *dolma*, of eggplant, vine-leaves, onions, mustard, syrups, sherbets, and many kinds of fish.

The Middle East doesn't seem to have had restaurants. At the beginning of the nineteenth century an Egyptian sheikh from al-Azhar, Rifaʻa Rafiʻal-Tahtawi, visited Paris, and wrote a fascinating account of his experiences and observations in the mysterious Occident. One of the oddities of Paris that he noticed was a place called a restaurant. He spells out the word "restaurant" in Arabic script and explains what it is.

We take tables and chairs for granted in places where we eat—we sit on chairs and have the food served on tables. But that is by no means a law of nature. Tables and chairs seem to have existed in the ancient Middle East; they disappeared in the medieval and early modern periods. In a society where wood was rare and precious, and wool and leather cheap and plentiful, they had different arrangements for seating and serving.

With what did they eat the food? Here again we may divide the world into three zones—the cutlery zone in the West, the chopstick zone in the East, and the finger zone in the middle. Chopsticks seem to be a very ancient invention in the Far East. Cutlery is much more recent in the West. A knife was of course necessary, but was not a utensil for eating. The fork was the main one, and seems to have been a Byzantine innovation, introduced to England in the early seventeenth century. English travelers found it in Italy, and they were most impressed by it. The English word "fork" comes from the Italian *forchetta*. The Italians, it was noted, are rather fastidious and don't like getting their fingers or their napkins dirty. We find a couple of references to this new device, a fork, in the plays of Ben Jonson (d. 1637). It hadn't yet arrived in Shakespeare's time.

We have a number of descriptions of Eastern banquets by Western travelers, and of Western banquets by Eastern travelers. They noticed different things; they were struck by different things. One thing that struck Eastern travelers to the West was that men and women actually dined together. This happened in antiquity, but it was not customary in Islamic times, and it astonished—or even shocked—Middle Eastern visitors to Europe. One such visitor, a certain Vahid Efendi, Ottoman ambassador to France, wrote in 1806 or 1807: "At European banquets many women are present. The women sit at table, while the men sit behind them, watching like hungry animals as the women eat. If the women take pity on them, they give them something to eat, and if not, the men go hungry."

I don't know which banquets he attended, but let me just say this: his account of a Western banquet is not more fantastic than some of the Western travelers' accounts of Middle Eastern life. But these comments take us into a different area, from alimentary and culinary to social and cultural history—in a word, from eating to dining. And that is another story.

4

Iran in History

❧❦❧

In attempting to attain some perspective on Iran in history, I begin, as I think one must, with the Arab-Islamic conquests in the seventh century—that series of epoch-making events following the advent of Islam, the mission of the Prophet Muhammad and the carrying of his message to vast areas east and west from Arabia, and the incorporation of many lands, from the Atlantic and the Pyrenees to the borders of India and China and beyond, into the new Arab-Islamic empire. These events have been variously seen in Iran: by some as a blessing, the advent of the true faith, the end of the age of ignorance and heathenism; by others as a humiliating national defeat, the conquest and subjugation of the country by foreign invaders. Both perceptions are of course valid, depending on one's angle of vision.

What I would like first to bring to your attention is a significant and indeed remarkable difference between what happened in Iran and what happened in all the other countries of the Middle East and North Africa that were conquered by the Arabs and incorporated in the Islamic caliphate in the seventh and eighth centuries.

These other countries of ancient civilization, Iraq, Syria, Egypt, North Africa, were Islamized and Arabized in a remarkably short time. Their old religions were either abandoned entirely or dwindled into small minorities; their old languages almost disappeared. Some survived in scriptures and liturgies, some were still spoken in a few remote villages, but in most places, among most people, the previous languages were forgotten, the identities expressed in those languages were replaced, and the ancient civilizations of Iraq, Syria, and Egypt gave way to what we nowadays call the Arab world.

Iran was indeed Islamized, but it was not Arabized. Persians remained Persians. And after an interval of silence, Iran reemerged as a separate, different and distinctive element within Islam, eventually adding a new element even to Islam itself. Culturally, politically, and most remarkable of all even religiously, the Iranian contribution to this new Islamic civilization is of immense importance. The work of Iranians can be seen in every field of cultural endeavor, including Arabic poetry, to which poets of Iranian origin composing their poems in Arabic made a very significant contribution. In a sense, Iranian Islam is a second advent of Islam itself, a new Islam sometimes referred to as *Islam-i Ajam*. It was this Persian Islam, rather than the original Arab Islam, that was brought to new areas and new peoples: to the Turks, first in Central Asia and then in the Middle East in the country which came to be called Turkey, and of course to India. The Ottoman Turks brought a form of Iranian civilization to the walls of Vienna. A seventeenth-century Turkish visitor who went to Vienna as part of an Ottoman embassy, notes with curiosity that the language which they speak in Vienna is a corrupt form of Persian. He had of course observed the basic Indo-European kinship between Persian and German, and the fact that the Germans say *ist* and the Persians say *ast*, almost the same thing, for the verb "to be," present indicative third-person singular.

By the time of the great Mongol invasions of the thirteenth century, Iranian Islam had become not only an important component; it had become a dominant element in Islam itself, and for several centuries the main centers of Islamic power and civilization were in countries that were, if not Iranian, at least marked by Iranian civilization. For a while this supremacy was challenged by the last center of power in the Arab world, the Mamluk Sultanate based in Egypt. But even that last stronghold disappeared, after the contest between the Persians and the Ottomans to decide which should conquer Egypt and the Ottoman success in what might be called the preliminary elimination bout. Arabian Islam under Arab sovereignty survived only in Arabia and in remote outposts like Morocco. The center of the Islamic world was under Turkish and Persian states, both shaped by Iranian culture. The major centers of Islam in the late medieval and early modern periods, the centers of both political and cultural power, such as India, Central Asia, Iran, Turkey, were all part of this Iranian civilization. Although much of it spoke various forms of Turkish, as well as other local languages, their classical and cultural language was Persian. Arabic was of course the language of scripture and law, but Persian was the language of poetry and literature.

The Iranian Exception

Why this difference? Why is it that while the ancient civilizations of Iraq, Syria, and Egypt were submerged and forgotten, that of Iran survived, and reemerged in a different form?

Various answers have been offered to this question. One suggestion is that the difference is language. The peoples of Iraq, Syria, Palestine, spoke various forms of Aramaic. Aramaic is a Semitic language related to Arabic, and the transition from Aramaic to Arabic was much easier than would have been the transition from Persian, an Indo-European language, to Arabic. There is some force in that argument. But then Coptic, the language of Egypt, was not a Semitic language either, yet this did not impede the Arabization of Egypt. Coptic survived for a while among the Christians, but eventually died even among them, except as a liturgical language used in the rituals of the Coptic Church.

Some have seen this difference as due to the possession by the Persians of a superior culture. A higher culture absorbs a lower culture. They quote as a parallel the famous Latin dictum: "conquered Greece conquers its fierce conquerors"—in other words the Romans adopt Greek culture. It is a tempting but not convincing parallel. The Romans conquered and ruled Greece, as the Arabs conquered and ruled Iran, but the Romans learned Greek, they admired Greek civilization, they read, translated, imitated Greek books. The Arabs did not learn Persian, the Persians learned Arabic. And the direct Persian literary influence on Arabic is minimal and came only through Persian converts.

Perhaps a closer parallel would be what happened in England after 1066, the conquest of the Anglo-Saxons by the Normans, and the transformation of the Anglo-Saxon language under the impact of Norman French into what we now call English. There are interesting parallels between the Norman conquest of England and the Arab conquest of Iran—a new language, created by the breakdown and simplification of the old language and the importation of an enormous vocabulary of words from the language of the conquerors; the creation of a new and compound identity, embracing both the conquerors and the conquered. I remember as a small boy at school in England learning about the Norman conquest, and being taught somehow to identify with both sides with a new legitimacy created by conquest, which in the case of Iran, though not of course of England, was also buttressed by a new religion based on a new revelation.

Most of the other conquered peoples in Iraq, in Syria, in Egypt, also had higher civilizations than that brought by the nomadic invaders from the Arabian desert. Yet they were absorbed, as the Persians were not. So we may have slightly modified or restated the question; we haven't answered it. Another perhaps more plausible explanation is the political difference, the elements of power and memory. These other states conquered by the Arabs—Iraq, Syria, Palestine, Egypt and the rest—were long-subjugated provinces of empires located elsewhere. They had been conquered again and again; they had undergone military, then political, then cultural, and then religious transformations, long before the Arabs arrived there. In these places, the Arab-Islamic conquest meant yet one more change of masters, yet one more change of teachers. This was not the case in Iran. Iran too had been conquered by Alexander, and formed part of the great Hellenistic Empire—but only briefly. Iran was never conquered by Rome, and therefore the cultural impact of Hellenistic civilization in Iran was much less than in the countries of the Levant, Egypt and North Africa, where it was buttressed, sustained and in a sense imposed through the agency of Roman imperial power. The Hellenistic impact on Iran in the time of Alexander and his immediate successors was no doubt considerable, but it was less deep and less enduring than in the Mediterranean lands, and it was ended by a resurgence, at once national, political and religious, and the rebirth of an Iranian polity under the Parthians and then the Sasanids. A new empire arose in Iran which was the peer and the rival of the empires of Rome and later of Byzantium.

This meant that at the time of the Arab conquest and immediately after, the Persians, unlike their neighbors in the West, were sustained by recent memories, one might even say current memories, of power and glory. This sense of ancient glory, of pride in identity, comes out very clearly in Persian writings of the Islamic period, written that is to say in Islamic Persian in the Arabic script, with a large vocabulary of Arabic words. We see the difference in a number of ways: in the emergence of a kind of national epic poetry, which has no parallel in Iraq or Syria or Egypt or any of these other places; and in the choice of personal names. In the Fertile Crescent and westwards, the names that parents gave their children were mostly names from the Qur'an or from pagan Arabia— 'Ali, Muhammad, Ahmad, and the like. These names were also used in Iran among Muslim Persians. But in addition, they used distinctively Persian names: Khusraw, Shapur, Mehyar and other names derived from a Persian past—a recent Persian past, that of the Sasanids, but nevertheless Persian. We do not find Iraqis calling their sons Nebuchadnezzar or Sennacherib, nor Egyptians calling their sons Tutankhamen or Amenhotep. These civilizations were indeed dead and forgotten. The Persian sense of pride did not rest on a history retained and remembered, because their history too, except for the most recent chapters, was lost and forgotten, no less than the ancient glories of Egypt and Babylon. All that they had was myth and saga; a sketchy memory of only the most recent chapters of the pre-Islamic history of Iran, none at all of the earlier periods.

The Islamic view of history may serve as an explanation of this—why does one bother to study history, what is the importance of history? History is the record of the working out of God's purpose for humanity, and from a Muslim, particularly a Sunni Muslim point of view, it has a special importance as establishing the precedents of the Prophet, the Companions and the early "rightly-guided" rulers of Islam, who set the pattern of correct law and behavior. That means of course that the only history that matters is Muslim history, and the history of picturesque barbarians in remote places, even of picturesque barbarians who may happen to be one's ancestors, has no moral or religious value, and is therefore not worth retaining. By the time the Persians recovered their voice, after the Islamic conquest, they had lost their memory—though not, as we shall see, permanently.

The history of ancient Iran prior to the Sasanids, the immediate predecessors of Islam, was obliterated by successive changes. The ancient language was replaced by Muslim Persian, the ancient scripts were forgotten and replaced by the Arabic script modified to suit Persian phonetic needs. The old language and script survived among the dwindling minority who remained faithful to the Zoroastrian religion, but that was of little importance. Even the personal names to which I alluded a moment ago were forgotten, except for the most recent. Thus, for example, the name of Cyrus, in modern times acclaimed as the greatest of the ancient Persian kings, was forgotten. The Persians remembered the name of Alexander in the form Iskandar, but they did not remember the name of Cyrus. Alexander was remembered better among the Persians than were the Persian kings against whom he fought.

Iran, Greeks and Jews

What little information survived about ancient Iran was that which was recorded by two peoples, the Jews and the Greeks, the only peoples active in the ancient Middle East who preserved their memories, their voices and their languages. Both the Greeks and the Jews remembered Cyrus; the Persians did not. The Greeks and the Jews alone provided such information as existed about ancient Iran until comparatively modern times, when the store of information was vastly increased by Orientalists, that is to say western archeologists and philologists who found a way to recover the ancient texts and decipher the ancient scripts.

Let me pause for a moment to look at the image of Iran as preserved in the Bible and the Greek classics, that is to say, as preserved by the Jews and the Greeks. The Greek view, as one would expect, is dominated by the long struggles, beginning with the Persian invasion of Greece and culminating in the great Greek counter-attack by Alexander. This is a major theme in ancient Greek historiography; the contrast between Greek democracy and Persian autocracy also forms an important theme of Greek political writings. But despite the fact that the history was mainly one of conflict, the tone of ancient Greek writing about Persia is mostly respectful, and sometimes even compassionate, notably for example in the play *The Persians* by Aeschylus, himself a veteran of the Persian wars, who shows real compassion for the defeated Persian enemy.

The Bible gives us a uniquely positive picture of ancient Iran, in a literature which does not normally deal indulgently with strangers, nor even with its own people. The earliest occurrences of the name Persia, *Paras*, are in the Book of Ezekiel, where *Paras* is listed along with other exotic and outlandish names to indicate the outer limits of the known world. *Paras* has something like the significance of *ultima thule* in western usage. The name makes a more dramatic appearance in the story of the writing on the wall at Belshazzar's feast, where the inscription *Mene mene, tekel upharsin* informed the hapless Babylonian monarch that he was weighed in the balances and found wanting, and that his realms would be shared by the Medes and Persians.

And then of course comes Cyrus, mentioned more particularly in the later chapters of Isaiah, what the Bible critics call Deutero-Isaiah, that part of the

Book of Isaiah dating from after the Babylonian captivity. The language used of Cyrus is little short of astonishing. He is spoken of in the Hebrew text as God's anointed, messiah, and he is accorded greater respect, not only than any other non-Jewish ruler, but almost any Jewish ruler.

Inevitably the question arises—why? Why does the Bible speak in such glowing terms of this heathen potentate? There is of course one obvious answer, that Cyrus was, so to speak, the Balfour of his day. He issued a declaration authorizing the Jews to return to their land and restore their political existence. But that doesn't really answer the question; it merely restates the question. Why did he do that? A series of conquests had brought a multitude of ethnic groups, as we say nowadays, under Persian rule. Why should Cyrus take such a step on behalf of one of them? We only know the Jewish side of this, we don't know the Persian side, and one can only venture a guess as to the reason. My suggestion is that there was, shall we say, a perceived affinity, between those who professed two spiritual, ethical religions, surrounded on all sides by ignorant polytheists and idolaters. One can see this sense of affinity in the latest books of the Old Testament, and also in subsequent Jewish writings. One notes for example a number of Persian words, some already in the Bible, many more in the post-Biblical Jewish literature.

This encounter between Iranian religion and Jewish religion was of far-reaching significance in world history. We can discern unmistakable traces of Persian influence, both intellectual and material, on the development of post-exilic Jewry, and therefore also of Christendom, and corresponding influence in the late Greco-Roman and Byzantine world, and therefore ultimately in Europe.

Let me just take a few examples, first on the practical side. The early Arabic sources tell us that the Persians invented a new device for riding, a device called the stirrup, previously unknown. We can easily see why this device, which revolutionized transport, communications and also warfare, created so great an impression. A mounted soldier in armor, on an armored horse, with a lance, could launch a much more devastating charge with stirrups than without them, when he was in imminent danger of being dismounted. We hear vivid stories, specially from the Byzantine writers, of the advent of this new and devastating instrument of warfare, the mounted, armored horseman, the cataphract.

The stirrup also helped the Persians to develop the postal system. Their system, described with admiration by the Greeks, consisted of a network of couriers and relay stations all over the realm. It was known in Arabic as *barid*, which comes of course from the Persian verb *burdan*, meaning to carry. The post-horse was the *paraveredos*, from which comes the German *Pferd*. Another innovation credited to Iran, though the evidence here is conflicting, is the mill, the use of wind and water to generate power. This was the first and for millennia the only source of energy other than human and animal muscle.

In another area the Persians are accredited with the invention of board games, particularly chess, which still uses a Persian terminology—the Shah—and also the game which is variously known as trik-trak, shish-besh, backgammon and other names.

We are on stronger ground in ascribing to Persians—and here we come back to the theme of cultural history—the book, that is the book in the form of a codex. The Greco-Roman world used scrolls, and so did much of the ancient Middle East. The codex, stitched and bound in the form which we now know as a book, seems to have originated in Iran. The cultural impact of such an innovation was obviously immense.

But let me turn to what is ultimately the more important theme, and that is the influence of ideas. From Iran, from Iranian religion, comes the concept of a cosmic struggle between almost equal forces of good and evil. The Devil, as you know, was Iranian by birth, although he is now given a local habitation and a name in the Western Hemisphere. The idea of a power of evil, opposite and almost equal, is characteristic of ancient Persian religion: Ahriman is the predecessor of Satan, Mephistopheles, or whatever else we may choose to call him. Linked with that was the idea of judgment and retribution, of heaven and hell; and here I would remind you that paradise is also a Persian word. The *para* is the same as the Greek *peri; perideśos* in ancient Persian means walled enclosure.

Messianism too seems to have Persian antecedents, in the doctrine that at the end of time a figure will arise from the sacred seed of Zoroaster, who will establish all that is good on earth. It is not without significance that the Messianic idea does not appear in the Hebrew Bible until after the return from Babylon, that is to say after the time when the Jews came under Persian influence. The importance of messianism in the Judaeo-Christian tradition is obvious. Linked with this is the idea and the practice of a religious establishment—a hierarchy of priests with ranks, under the supreme authority of the chief priest, the *Mobedhan Mobedh*, the Priest of Priests. And by the way, that form of title, the Priest of Priests, the King of Kings, and the like, is characteristically Iranian. It is used in many Iranian titles in antiquity; it was adopted into Arabic: *Amīr al-Umarā'*— the Amir of Amirs, *Qāḍī al-Quḍāt*—the Qadi of Qadis. Perhaps even the title of the Pope in Rome: the Servant of the Servants of God—*Servus Servorum Dei*— may be ascribed to indirect Iranian influence. The whole idea of a church, not in the sense of a building, a place of worship, but a hierarchy under a supreme head, may well owe a good deal to Zoroastrian example.

The ancient religion of Iran survives. Zoroastrianism is still the faith of small, dwindling, but not unimportant minorities, in India, in Pakistan, and to some extent in Iran. They preserved the ancient writings, in the ancient script, and a knowledge of the ancient language, and it was these which enabled the first European Orientalists to learn Middle Iranian and to use it to rediscover the still more ancient languages of Iran.

Iran and Shi'ism

For at least a millennium, Iran has been associated with Islam, and in the more recent centuries with Shi'ite Islam, which some have seen as an expression, a reappearance of the Persian national genius in an Islamic disguise. Some have gone even further—nineteenth-century European writers like Gobineau claimed to see the triumph of Shi'ism as the resurgence of the Aryanism of Iran against the Semitism of Islam. Such ideas are rather discredited nowadays, though they were popular at one time, and still have their adherents.

The difficulty about such theories is that Shi'ism, like Islam itself, was brought to Iran by Arabs. The first Shi'ites in Iran—and for a long time this remained so—were Arabs. The city of Qomm, the stronghold and center of Iranian Shi'ism, was an Arab foundation, and the first settlers in Qomm were Arabs. (I remember being taken round Qomm by a Persian friend who pointed to the deserts that surround it, and remarked: "Who but an Arab would build a town in a place like this?") Shi'ism was reintroduced and imposed by the Safavids many centuries later, and they, I would remind you, were Turks. Until then Iran was a largely Sunni country. But no doubt that with the establishment of the Shi'ite Safavid state a new era began, one of a distinctively Iranian Shi'ite character.

The accession of the Safavids marks a new era in Persian history and the establishment, for the first time in many centuries, of a unified dynastic state. The Safavids brought certain important new features. One I have already alluded to—unity. Under the first Arab conquerors the whole of Iran was under one rule, that of the Caliphs situated in Medina, then in Damascus, then in Baghdad. But with the break-up of the Caliphate, Iran broke up into its various regions, under local rulers of one kind or another. The Safavids for the first time created a united realm of Iran, more or less within its present frontiers—not just diverse regions, Pars and Khurasan and the rest of them, but a single realm with a single ruler. It has remained so ever since, in spite of the immense ethnic diversity which characterizes that country to the present day. If you look, for example, round the periphery, starting in the north-west, you have the Turkish-speaking Azarbaijanis. To the south of them are Kurds, to the south of them are more Turks, the Qashqais, to the south of them, in Khuzistan are Arabs, in the south-east the Baluchis and then the Turkmen. These form a periphery, all around the center, of peoples speaking different non-Persian languages. Nevertheless, the culture of the Persian language and the distinctive Shi'ite version of Islam helped to maintain the unity that was imposed by the Safavids and maintained by their successors.

Shi'ism brought a second important feature, and that is differentiation from all the neighbors: from the Ottomans in the west, from the central Asian states in the north-east, from the Indian-Muslim states in the south-east. Practically all of these were Sunni states. True, Persian was used as a classical language, a literary language and even at times a diplomatic language by all three neighbors, the Ottomans, the Central Asians, and the Indians. But the crucial difference between the Sunni and Shi'ite realms remained.

Another interesting development of the period, particularly under the late Safavids and their successors, is the emergence of the notion of Iran. I have been using the terms Persia and Persians, to speak of the land and the people, as was customary in Western languages until recently. The name Iran is ancient, but its current use is modern. We first find the word in ancient Persian inscriptions. In the inscription of Darius for example, in the ancient Persian language, he describes himself as King of the Aryans. Iran is the same word as Aryan; it means "noble" in the ancient languages of Iran and of India. The King was the King *Aryanum*, which is a genitive plural, King of the Aryans. It survives in the myths and sagas of the early medieval period, in the *Shāhnāma* and related stories of the great struggle between Iran and Turan; it reappears in the nineteenth century as the name of the country in common rather than official usage. It did not become official usage until much later, probably under the influence of the Third Reich. The German government of the time, which needed various facilities and help from Iran, went to some pains to assure the people of that country that they were Iranians, which is the same as Aryans, that they were therefore different from and superior to all their neighbors, and that the Nuremberg Laws did not apply to them. It was at that time that the name of the country, in foreign languages as well as in Persian, was officially changed to Iran.

Let us look at another turning-point in history, the Islamic Revolution, and its creation the Islamic Republic. This was indeed a revolution. The word revolution has been much used in the Middle East in modern times, to designate a whole series of coups d'état, palace revolts, assassinations, civil wars and the like. What happened in Iran, for better or for worse, was a real revolution, in the sense that the French Revolution and the Russian Revolution were real revolutions. And like them, the Iranian revolution had a tremendous impact in all those countries with which it shares a common universe of discourse, in other words in the Islamic world.

As with these earlier revolutions, there are contrasting views of the Islamic revolution in Iran. In one of them, we see actions and statements which have made the name of Iran, even the name of Islam, stand for a regime of bloodthirsty bigots, maintained by tyranny at home and by terror both at home and abroad. In the other, that which they themselves prefer to present, we see an alternative diagnosis and an alternative prescription for the ills and sufferings of the region, an alternative, that is, to the alien and infidel ways that have long prevailed, and a return to authenticity.

At the present time, with the ending of direct outside rule and the rapid diminution even of outside influence, a familiar pattern is beginning to reemerge in the Middle East. Today there are again two major powers in the region, this time the Turkish Republic and the Islamic Republic of Iran. In the sixteenth century, in the same countries, two rival powers, the Ottoman Sultan and the Safavid Shah, representing the Sunni and the Shi'ite versions of Islam, fought for the headship of the Islamic world.

A thousand years earlier, in the sixth century, in the same countries, two rivals, the Byzantine emperors and the Sasanids of Iran, embodied rival civilizations and rival visions of the world. Both Sasanids and Byzantines were conquered and overwhelmed by Islam. Both the Ottoman Sultans and the Safavid Shahs were swept aside by new forces from outside and also from inside their realms.

Today the rivals are two regimes, both established by revolution, both embodying certain basic ideologies, secular democracy in Turkey, Islamic theocracy in Iran. As in earlier times, neither is impervious to the temptations of the other. In Turkey we have seen religious parties win large shares of the votes in free elections and play an important and growing role in national politics. We do not know how many Iranians would prefer secular democracy, since in an Islamic theocracy they are not permitted to express that preference. But from various indications one may say that their number is not inconsiderable.

The struggle continues, within these two countries and elsewhere, between two different versions of what was originally a common civilization. The outcome remains far from certain.

5

Palimpsests of Jewish History
Christian, Muslim and Secular Diaspora

❧❧❧

The purpose of my talk is to offer some general observations on the nature of Jewish history, the documentation of Jewish history and, finally, the writing and teaching of Jewish history in that long period that intervened between ancient and modern times, that is to say between the two periods when Jewish history, like that of most other peoples, was somehow focused on a place and a state. Between those two eras, between the ending of the ancient Jewish commonwealth and the foundation of the modern Jewish commonwealth, Jews, Judaism, Jewish life and Jewish culture seemed to have flourished only under Christian or Muslim rule. There were other possibilities in the world. There were vast areas of Asia—India, China, which were neither Muslim nor Christian, but in which Judaism never took root. Jews settled in these places, but in spite of the absence of certain disadvantages which affected Jewish life under both Christian and Muslim rule, Judaism did not flourish. It barely survived, but rather stagnated in these places. It was only under the aegis of what in this company I may call the two daughter religions that Judaism seems to have been able to grow, to expand, to live, to flourish, to continue an original religious and cultural life.

The reason for this is not too difficult to find. These two religions are both in a sense offshoots of the Jewish religious tradition and have considerable affinities both with one another and with Judaism. When throughout the Middle Ages and into early modern times Christendom and Islam were engaged in what Gibbon called "the Great Debate" and denounced each other as infidels, by the mere fact of so doing they were revealing their essential kinship. The Jews, like the rabbi in the story, agreed tactfully with both. There is a considerable shared heritage, much of it, though not all of it, Judaic, and even the non-Judaic parts of the shared heritage of Christendom and Islam, that of the

Hellenistic culture and the remnants of the ancient Middle East, are also shared by Judaism.

In a sense Christian and Muslim civilization were pupils of Judaism, not only in an historical and metaphorical sense, but even in the most literal and personal sense. Christian and Muslim men of learning and even theologians turned to Jewish sages for guidance on many issues. Sometimes they were denounced for this, but they nevertheless persisted. When Jerome was preparing his Latin translation of the Hebrew Bible, he naturally, and wisely, sought the help of Jewish scholars—and was denounced for his pains as a Judaiser. This resort to Jewish help continued through the Middle Ages, the Renaissance, the Reformation, and to the beginnings of modern Hebrew scholarship in the universities of the Christian world.

In the Islamic world the connection was much less direct. The Muslims, unlike the Christians, did not retain the Hebrew Bible as part of the canon, regarding it as superseded. Whereas for Christians the Old Testament was supplemented by their dispensation, for Muslims it was replaced—an altogether different situation. Muslims were therefore not interested in the Hebrew language or in the Hebrew text, but even so there was a considerable interest in the supplementary information which Jewish scholars were able to provide concerning certain personalities and certain episodes mentioned in the Qur'an. There was sometimes an element of suspicion towards this Jewish material; the word *Isrā'īlıyyāt*, meaning material derived from Jewish sources, sometimes acquired the meaning of superstitious nonsense. But in spite of this, there is a great deal of Jewish material in Muslim writings, particularly though not exclusively in relation to Old Testament figures in their Qur'anic guise.

There is of course a fundamental difference in the attitude of the two religions, Christianity and Islam, towards Jews, alike in the extent, the form and in the manner of toleration. Both claimed a world mission, whence the continuous conflict, the clash of jihad and crusade, between them. For both of them, Judaism as a predecessor was entitled, by the logic of their own beliefs, to a certain, albeit limited, measure of tolerance. In the relations between the three religions, the sequence is crucial. Universal religions can tolerate a predecessor, but not a successor. Both Christians and Muslims were firmly convinced that they possessed God's complete and final word to mankind. For Christians, the Jews had last year's model—not as good as their own, but passable. For Muslims, Christians and Jews were in the same position. For Christians of course, Islam, being post-Christian, was not acceptable, just as for Muslims post-Islamic religions like Baha'ism are not acceptable.

But the difference is not only in sequence, in respect of which there is no basic difference between the Christian and Muslim positions regarding Judaism. There is a vast difference—I mean no disrespect by using this expression—between the foundation myths of the two major religions. The founders of both came into conflict with Jews, but in those conflicts one lost, the other won. That made a profound difference to the perception of Jews in their sacred history, in the memories enshrined in the sacred writings which formed the core of the self-awareness of both religious communities. Muhammad won his battle with the Jews and his successors were therefore able, shall we say, to adopt a more relaxed attitude.

There is also a difference in their claims. The Christian dispensation claims to be the fulfillment of promises made to the Jews, the accomplishment of Jewish prophecies. In a view officially held until quite recently, and sometimes reasserted even more recently, the convenant with the Jews was taken over and Israel was, so to speak, replaced by the true Israel, *verus Israel*, which is the Church. Jewish survival and still more Jewish refusal were thus seen as somehow impugning the authenticity of the Christian dispensation. Muhammad and his successors made no such claim, and the conversion of the Jews was therefore a matter of little concern to them. This difference can be seen very clearly in the polemical literature. There is in medieval and even in modern Christendom a vast polemical literature by Christian theologians the purpose of which is to persuade Jews of the truth of the Christian dispensation. Islam shows nothing remotely comparable. A few Muslims wrote polemics against Judaism; most of them were Jewish converts. Otherwise there is little interest in Judaism, and no equivalent to the continuing Christian concern with the Jewish obduracy and the need to overcome it.

Besides the doctrinal difference, there was also a quite significant practical difference in the two situations. In Christendom, which until the dawn of the modern era substantially meant Europe, Jews were the only religious minority in an otherwise religiously and to large extent even racially homogeneous society. The Islamic world on the contrary was international, one might say intercontinental, embracing peoples in Asia, Africa and Europe; they formed a pluralistic and varied society in which Jews were one among a number of minorities and for the most part not the most important and certainly not, in Muslim eyes, the most dangerous.

This raises what has become the delicate and difficult question of influences. Jewish influence on Christianity and Islam is well-known and much discussed, particularly in innumerable nineteenth century doctoral dissertations. But influence flows both ways. In the early 1970s there was a Festival of Islam in London, a great cultural event, organized with the cooperation of many Muslim governments which provided funds and lent objects. Among the ground rules for the Festival of Islam—the lectures, publications, exhibitions and the like—was a guideline laid down by the sponsors: Islam influences, Islam is not influenced. The discussion of possible influences on Islam was avoided. I have the uneasy feeling that a rather similar point of view is beginning to gain ground, I won't say to prevail, in some circles in Israel. It is wrong and dangerous. For almost two millennia, Jews were a minority in a large, developing and relatively advanced civilization and society, and it requires no great effort of scholarship to detect influences going both ways. It is not my purpose to go into any detail on this, but merely to draw your attention to one or two examples. Even in a matter as intimate and personal as marriage, we see the Jews of the Islamic world adopting procedures regarding marriage roughly in accord with those of the Islamic world. There are differences, notably in the prohibition of concubinage, but the rule of polygamy was maintained. On the other hand, in the Christian world there was the famous *takana* outlawing polygamy and imposing the Christian-inspired rule of monogamy.

If Jewish religious law can be determined in a matter as central as marriage by the dominant culture, on the very sound principle of *dina de-malkhuta dina*, the law of the state is (religious) law, then we shall not be surprised to find other resemblances. The rabbis, who in the Christian world, particularly in western Christendom, tend to become clergymen, in the Islamic world tend to become *ulema*. Sometimes in the Western world they also become *ulema*, but that is another question. We can see the same acculturation in architecture, and strikingly even in theology. There is a story told of an Anglican scholar who was a specialist on Judaism and published a book entitled *The Systematic Theology of the Synagogue*. It was reviewed by a rabbi who began his review by saying, "first of all there is no such thing as 'the Synagogue,' and if there were, it wouldn't have a theology and if it did, it wouldn't be systematic." Nevertheless, there is a Jewish theology, which developed at a relatively late date; it is on the whole rather systematic, and the external influences on the development of this systematic theology are plainly visible.

I have spoken of two of the diasporas, the Christian and the Muslim, and tried to compare and contrast them. There is also a third, the secular. Here it is important to note a distinction between secularism and pluralism. Secular societies are usually pluralist. Pluralist societies are not necessarily secular. There are many examples of pluralist societies in which one group, one religion, usually one ethnic–religious group is dominant, but permits others to survive or even to flourish, subject to the acceptance of certain limitations. On the whole, Jews have done rather better in pluralist societies of this kind, such as the medieval Islamic caliphates, or the empires of the Ottomans and the Hapsburgs in the Middle East and in Central Europe. In these, Jews had the status, in the better periods, of a tolerated minority subject to certain restrictions, the scale and effectiveness of which varied considerably, in different times and places, from minor inconvenience to major disability. In the secular state, which officially has no religion at all, and in which there is no involvement of the state in religion and no involvement of religion in the state, Judaism theoretically has the same status of any other religion. There are not many secular states of that type in the world. Most of the countries of Western Europe have a state church, though at the present time this is not very meaningful. The communist states in Eastern Europe were in principle secular, but in reality their secularism had little effect. They were atheists, but not godless. They had no theology, but they did have a creed. They had no religion, but they certainly had a church, complete with scriptures and dogmas, prelates and hierarchs, orthodoxy, heresies and, above all, an inquisition. This church too, coincidentally, was founded by one of Jewish origin and background. One might even argue that he too was to some extent inspired by Jewish prophetic vision and Jewish messianism. Fortunately, unlike his predecessors, he did not come into collision with his Jewish co-religionists, and the Jews are therefore not cast, in Marxist sacred history, in an adversarial role as they are in Christian and to a lesser extent in Muslim history. It is perhaps fortunate that the modern secular religion has not claimed Spinoza as its founder.

In this secular religion, there is little room for tolerance—less than in either Christendom or Islam; there is little prospect for long term survival. It is a more demanding religion, or was until very recently, than either Christianity or Islam, and less tolerant of dissent, deviation, or unbelief.

Real secularism, that is to say the separation of church and state, the abandonment of any kind of formal religious commitment by the state, begins in fairly modern times, theoretically from the seventeenth century, constitutionally with the American and French Revolutions. In principle, this separation provided the first opportunity for Jewish equality, not just legal equality but genuine equality with full membership and participation. Just three hundred years ago the English philosopher John Locke published his *Letter concerning Toleration* in which he observed that "neither pagan, nor Mohammedan, nor Jew ought to be excluded from the civil rights of the commonwealth because of his religion." George Washington, in a letter to a Jewish community leader in Newport, Rhode Island, dismissed the idea of toleration as essentially intolerant, as if "it was by the indulgence of one class of people that another enjoyed the exercise of their inherent natural rights." These are noble sentiments. In our own time they express a growing reality.

These modern secular societies offer a real possibility of separate Jewish survival as part of the larger society; of assimilation without betrayal or at least without a sense of betrayal. Even here, of course, there are the dangers which Ahad Ha'am, speaking of another more assimilated but less tolerant society, described as "slavery in freedom," and which some anonymous Cartesian in America summarized as the philosophy of *incognito ergo sum*.

I come now to my final topic, the documentation and writing of Jewish history. The mere fact of the variety of languages needed for this study is a sufficient demonstration of the essential interconnection between Jewish history and what in Israel I have learnt to call general history, a term previously unknown to me. There are other languages besides Hebrew which are important to Jewish history and which, though not Jewish in origin, became in a sense Jewish languages—Aramaic, used in the two Talmuds and many other writings; Greek, no longer a Jewish language, but the medium of Josephus and perhaps more importantly Philo; Arabic, the vehicle of a rich Judaeo-Arabic culture which has for all practical purposes ceased to exist, but which has left us the heritage of

Maimonides and Yehuda Halevi and Saadya and so many others. Perhaps German for a while was approaching such a status, perhaps English now may be approaching such a status—I don't know, but it is not impossible.

What does all this mean in relation to the writing, study and teaching of Jewish history? The history of the Jews can rightly be described as a long and glorious history, but it would be difficult to justify the use of either adjective for Jewish historiography. Short and inglorious might perhaps be a more appropriate description. It had a very promising beginning. The historical books of the Hebrew Bible set a magnificent example of historiography at its best—frank, honest, self-critical, showing even the greatest national and religious heroes with all their faults and all their sins and no attempt at concealment. In this, the historical books of the Hebrew Bible served as a model for much of early Christian historiography and to a lesser extent for Muslim historiography—but not, oddly enough, for Jewish historiography, which, within the community, virtually came to an end some time after the return from Babylon and did not resume until comparatively modern times.

The lack of Jewish historiography for this long period must be seen not as a failure but as a rejection. It is not that they failed to produce historians; it is that they did not want historians and they did not want history. The books of Maccabees were rejected from the canon and survive only in translation. Josephus, one of the greatest historians of antiquity, was a renegade Jew writing in a foreign language for a foreign audience. Maimonides even went so far as to denounce the study of history as of no moral or intellectual value and a waste of time.

During this long period from antiquity to the beginning of modern intellectual curiosity, the leaders and spokesmen of the Jews, those who enjoyed prestige and exercised power among them, relied on transmitted authority. Those who rely on transmitted authority are usually reluctant to subject the process of transmission to critical scrutiny. There is an important distinction between what one might call official historiography, the purpose of which is to legitimize and strengthen authority, and critical historiography, which sometimes intentionally, sometimes unintentionally, may have the effect of undermining authority. Official historiography needs some sponsoring agency—a throne, a church, a city. These were the sponsors of the historical writings of Islam and Christendom, which provided a function and a livelihood for historians. There were no such sponsoring agencies among the Jews, but on the contrary, as I tried to suggest, a certain suspicion of historians and of what they might do.

For the centuries during which we have no real Jewish historical literature, there is nevertheless an immense variety of historical data. But even this is found only in certain periods. In other periods the material is limited and scattered, sometimes very rich for intellectual history, but very poor in any kind of archival documentation. The treasure of the Geniza, which is not an archive but a wastepaper basket on a grand scale, demonstrates how much we have lost by not having the archives from which the Geniza represents some scattered fragments.

Historiography is thin and very sparse. Jewish historical writing begins again with the Renaissance in Europe, and is essentially a European phenomenon. The same intellectual curiosity, the same new philological approach, inspired the first Jewish historical writing of European type, albeit written in Hebrew. It is no accident that the first Jewish histories of the Ottoman Empire were written not in the Ottoman Empire, but in Western Europe or in Crete, at the time a Venetian possession.

Since then, Jewish historical studies have developed in several different directions. A notable feature, from the nineteenth century, is the growing professionalization of Jewish historical studies, the stages of which can be indicated by mentioning three names: Graetz, Dubnov and Baron. And after Baron came the collective histories written by numerous specialists, bringing Jewish history into accord with general scholarly practice.

The establishment of the State of Israel created a new situation, because for the first time Jewish history is compulsorily taught in schools to a young generation under the authority of the State or of some agency within the State. This creates a new challenge, new problems and also, I would venture to suggest, new dangers. What does one aim at in teaching history to children in schools? We have many examples of this if we look around the region. In one country it will be taught in order to strengthen religious belief and to reaffirm the control of the state by the senior members of the religious hierarchy. I am referring of course to Iran. In another country, according to a circular by the Ministry of Education, the purpose of teaching history in the schools is to strengthen national pride and to reinforce patriotic loyalty. The country in question is Syria. Is that where you would like to look for examples, for guidance to follow as to the nature of historical teaching? I would rather think that the purpose of teaching history should be critical and accurate self-knowledge, self-awareness, consciousness of one's place in history, personal and communal, without which we are all blundering amnesiacs. It is quite impossible to understand Jewish history without at the same time understanding the societies of which Jews in every aspect of their lives, including their religious life, were a part. What is needed in this is binocular not monocular vision. Because, make no mistake about it, if we are not prepared to confront the past, we shall be unable to understand the present and unfit to face the future.

6

Some Notes on Land, Money and Power in Medieval Islam

ᘓ᠕᠖᠕᠗᠘

Betewen the advent of Islam in the 7th century and the coming of the Mongols in the 13th—that is to say, in the period of Middle Eastern history delimited by two major invasions, conquests and dominations—a political, social and economic order emerged in these lands which it is customary to designate as Islamic. A feature of this order was a series of legal, fiscal and administrative arrangements, based on certain linkages between land-tenure, taxes and rents, service and recompense, authority and allegiance. In recent years it has become common practice among historians to describe these arrangements as "feudal."

The term feudalism, strictly speaking, relates to the west European context from which it emerged. Any use of the word feudalism and other terms associated with it (fief and enfeoffment, vassal, etc.) of other times and places is at best an analogy and can be seriously misleading. However, the term has become common not only among western historians, who first applied it to the Middle East, but also in the Arab world where, in the loan-translation *iqṭāʿiyya*, it is used—in a kind of two-layered analogy—as an ideological designation for an old and disapproved order. It may therefore be useful to clarify a few points concerning the working of this order in medieval Islamic states, and concerning the changing meanings of the verb *aqṭaʿa* (from *qaṭaʿa*, to cut, lop or slice), from which the present-day Arabic equivalent of feudalism is derived.

The distinctively Islamic social and economic order began, as in most other societies, with a conquest and an ascendancy. During the lifetime of the Prophet, conquest was in the main limited to the Arabian peninsula, and the conquered, apart from some Jews and Christians, were seen as heathens and idolaters, and were given the choice of conversion or death. Those who accepted Islam retained their lands, and by their acceptance became members of the Islamic ascendancy.

There were, however, exceptions who, though perhaps insignificant numerically, were of great importance as a pattern for future development. The Jewish inhabitants of the oases of Khaybar and Wadi'l-Qurâ, north of Medina, were conquered by Muhammad himself. Being followers of a revealed religion and possessors of what Islam recognized as a holy book, they were allowed to practice their faith and to till the soil which they had formerly owned, in return for the payment of half their crop to Muhammad. The Christians of Najran, in southern Arabia, made voluntary submission through an embassy. They were given a treaty in which the Prophet agreed to their retaining both their religion and their lands, in return for a stipulated tribute. These agreements, though later abrogated by the Muslim decision to expel all non-Muslims from Arabia other than the south, nevertheless constituted precedents, backed by the authority of the Prophet himself, for dealings between the Muslim state on the one hand and conquered or surrendered peoples on the other.

Immediately after the death of the Prophet, when the Islamic order extended beyond Arabia to embrace the ancient civilizations of the Middle East and North Africa, the existing non-Muslim inhabitants of these countries were left to cultivate their lands but were required to pay a tax which the Muslims called *kharāj*, a term already in use in Byzantine times. This word was at first used in the general sense of tax or tribute paid by the non-Muslim subject peoples to the Muslim state; it was later specialized, in the technical vocabulary of Muslim law, to denote the land tax of up to 50% paid by non-Muslims, in accordance with the canonical precedent of Khaybar. The percentage might be varied according to the quality and situation of the land. If the ownership of the land passed, through either transfer or conversion, into Muslim hands, the Muslim owner was liable to pay only the tithe (*'ushr*). Former state lands and church lands inherited by the Muslim state, as well as lands abandoned through the death or flight of their former owners, were classified as *fay'*, a term meaning booty, more particularly that which was taken without fighting from the unbelievers. This category also included "dead lands" i.e., uncultivated lands and large estates from which the previous (Byzantine or Persian) owners had fled but on which the peasants remained.

These *fay'* lands were seen as the property of the Muslim community of which the Caliph was, so to speak, the trustee. In principle the Caliph could not alienate these lands, whether by gift or sale, since they were community property. In fact, the practice grew up whereby many of them were assigned by a form of grant to members of the Prophet's family and to other prominent figures among the new aristocracy created by the Arab conquests. These grants were called *qatī'a* (plural *qatâ'i'*) from an Arabic noun meaning a section or slice, because they were, so to speak, sliced away from the communal domain. The recipient of a *qatī'a* was called a *muqta'*.

According to some traditions *qatâ'i'* were granted during the lifetime of the Prophet. This may be questionable, but such grants became common under the early Caliphs and perhaps owed something to the example of the Byzantine *emphyteusis* and analogous Iranian arrangements.

The early *qaṭīʿa* is not the same as the later arrangement called *iqṭāʿ*, from the same Arabic root but with a very different practical meaning. The recipient of a *qaṭīʿa* was obliged to cultivate the land within a stipulated period, and to pay taxes to the government. While the non-Muslim tenants and landowners paid the full rates of taxation inherited from the previous regimes and later replaced by the Islamic *kharāj*, the Arab Muslim *muqtaʿ* was, in the first century of the *hijra*, liable only for the tithe. As a result of the acquisition of land outside Arabia by Arab Muslims on the one hand, and of the conversion of non-Arab landowners to Islam on the other hand, the treasury suffered a serious loss of revenue, and the transformation of *kharāj*-land into tithe-land was therefore stopped. Thereafter by a legal fiction the tax was deemed to be due from the land and not from the landowner, and all *kharāj*-land paid *kharāj*, irrespective of any changes in the religion of the owner or cultivator. The only remaining fiscal privilege of the Muslim was that he was exempt from the *jizya*, the poll-tax paid by all non-Muslims.

The *qaṭīʿa* was in essence a grant of lands from the state domain. It was in practice alienable and heritable, and thus in effect though not in law became freehold property. The *muqtaʿ*, while thus having the rights of a freehold land-owner, had no others. Unlike the European fiefholder, he enjoyed no fiscal or judicial immunities, and exercised no jurisdiction over his tenants. He did not normally reside on his *qaṭīʿa* but in the imperial or provincial capital, and cultivated his land with native tenant or semiservile labor. Another major difference was that the *muqtaʿ* did not allot parts of his grant in smaller grants, on the same or similar terms, to his own henchmen. All grants were held directly from the ruler, and thus did not resemble the Western practice of sub-infeudation.

Besides the large estates, which were comparatively few in number, the *qaṭāʾiʿ* were usually small; the normal size seems to have been a holding sufficient to sustain one family at the level appropriate to a conqueror aristocracy. The increase in number of *qaṭāʾiʿ* thus led to the formation of something like a middle class of tithe-paying Muslim freeholders. Though in theory tithe-land and *kharāj*-land existed side by side, this made little difference to the cultivators, since the tithe-paying *muqtaʿ*, usually non-resident, collected *kharāj* or its equivalent from his tenants. After the freezing of the *kharāj*-lands, this led to the emergence, in the 8th and 9th centuries, of a new type of grant.

In this, the *muqtaʿ* is given a grant of *kharāj*-land, from which he himself collects the *kharāj*, but on which he pays the government only a tithe. The difference between the tithe and the *kharāj* thus constitutes his profit, and the *muqtaʿ* becomes an intermediary between the state and the cultivator.

At some stage another intermediary appears between the tax-payer and the state: the tax-farmer who buys the right to collect the taxes of one or more districts. Frequently the holders of *qaṭā'iʿ* became tax-farmers not only for their own but also for neighboring lands and, by blurring the distinction between *muqtaʿ* and tax-farmer, were able in practice greatly to extend their holdings. This tendency toward the formation of larger estates was also helped by a process not unlike the west European recommendation, whereby in times of insecurity and fiscal oppression small landowners took refuge (*talji'a*) with great ones. Sometimes the right of "protection" (*himāya*), with police powers, was actually conferred on a great landowner by the public authority, by this time normally military. This conferred no judical authority in Islamic terms—i.e. the right to appoint qadis to administer Shariʿa law. This right was retained by the ruler or governor, with jurisdiction over marriage and divorce, inheritance, and other matters where Shariʿa law prevailed. It did however confer police powers, which in the common practice of medieval Islamic states, included criminal jurisdiction.

By the 10th century a new kind of grant, differing in several important respects from the earlier forms, made its appearance. Despite the general commercial prosperity of the age, the government was in a state of chronic financial crisis. A spendthrift court, an inflated and corrupt bureaucracy, and a mercenary army made exorbitant demands on resources that were already diminishing through the loss of provincial lands to local dynasts and, later the exhaustion or loss to invaders of gold and silver mines.

The farming out (*damān*) of state revenues had become a common practice, and soon the government found a precarious remedy for its shortage of ready cash by leasing out state revenues to officers and high officials in lieu of pay. Unlike the earlier *qaṭā'iʿ*, these grants were not of property rights in state lands; they were grants of the right to collect taxes from *kharāj*-paying lands outside the state domains, and thus constituted a further development of the second type of *qaṭā'iʿ* described above. Unlike both the earlier *muqtaʿ* and the tax-farmer; the recipient of this kind of grant owed no money payment to the state. He was not a landowner, and did not reside on his *iqṭāʿ*, from which he merely drew his revenues through a steward. The tax-farmers continued to function, but now farmed from the great grant-holders. State revenues were alienated to the grantees, and the small peasant freeholders were crushed out of existence. There was as yet no sub-infeudation, all grants being held directly from the state.

Before long, provincial governors were given the tax-farms of the provinces they governed, with the obligation only of remitting an agreed sum to the central treasury after having met the cost of the provincial forces and administration. These farmer-governors thus became what might be called vassals or tenants-in-chief of the central power; soon they became the real rulers of the empire, the more so when *iqṭāʿs* and governorships became the prerogative of the military class, who alone had the strength and authority needed for the task. The collapse of civilian and bureaucratic government, and its replacement by a kind of ruling caste of alien praetorians was reflected in the emergence of a new pattern of authority in which all power, financial as well as military and police, was concentrated in the hands of the provincial governors. In earlier times there had been a strict separation between administrative and financial powers in the provinces. From the 9th century onwards provincial governors usually controlled the revenues as well as the armed forces in their province, and indeed the same word, *iqṭāʿ*, is often used to denote an assignment of revenues and an appointment to a governorship. The governorships became in effect sovereign states and the governors themselves assigned grants to their military and civilian officials. At this point Islamic usage approaches the European practice of sub-infeudation, though it is still limited to two levels. The granting of such assignments, which by this time we may not unreasonably call fiefs, becomes the normal form of remuneration given by rulers to those who carry out military and civilian tasks for them.

Many of the innovations that at one time were attributed by historians to the early Seljuqs seem in fact to have originated in the Buyid period. The Seljuqs systematized and extended the practice of their predecessors. In time they also introduced a number of innovations, notably the large *iqṭāʿ* of a city, district or province, granted as a form of governorship or as an appanage to a member of the reigning family. A new kind of *iqṭāʿ* seems to have first appeared in border or steppe areas where it was imposed by the conditions of insecurity. Its use became generalized as this insecurity spread across the Seljuq dominions, largely as the result of the migrations of the Turkish tribes. In this order, the *muqtaʿ* was given firmer tenure and greater discretion. In theory the *iqṭāʿ* carried a right to the collection of taxes; it was a remuneration, granted for a limited time, and could be revoked. This was in fact the case under the first Seljuq sultans. Later, however, the *iqṭāʿ* tended to become permanent and even hereditary. The state was interested in military service rather than in revenue, and this new form of *iqṭāʿ* was no longer defined by its fiscal value but by the military service rendered, i.e., the number of soldiers maintained. By the late Seljuq period, the *iqṭāʿ* is no longer a lease of taxes but a hereditary landed fief over which the *muqtaʿ* exercises seigniorial powers and in return for which he renders military service and maintains a specified number of soldiers. These soldiers really become *his* men, answerable and loyal to him, and paid by him either with money or with smaller *iqṭāʿs* from within his own *iqṭāʿ*. It is at this point that Islamic feudalism approximates most closely the west European pattern. While the tendency to form a hereditary feudal class with stable functions thus existed, until Ottoman times no regime was immune from invasion and overthrow for a sufficiently long period to permit the completion of this process.

This kind of "feudalism" was carried by the Seljuqs into Anatolia, where it eventually evolved along independent lines into the distinctively Ottoman system. It was also carried by the Seljuqs and Zangids into Syria and by the Ayyubids into Egypt, where local conditions and special circumstances started it on another line of development which reached its maturity in the Mamluk system.

But by this time the Mongol conquests had brought profound changes, and led among other things to the emergence of new patterns of organization not only in the lands which were for a while under the Mongol rule but even in others like Egypt never conquered by the Mongols but deeply influenced by their example.

7

An Interpretation of Fatimid History

❧❦❧

The story is told that when the Fatimid Caliph al-Muʿizz came to Egypt, and was questioned by the representatives of the *ashraf* concerning his pedigree and his proofs, he half-drew his sword from his scabbard and said: "This is my pedigree," and then scattered gold among them and added: "And these are my proofs."[1]

The story is dramatic and amusing, but is self-evidently false. Its purpose is to depict al-Muʿizz as an adventurer—an unscrupulous upstart who had gained power by force and maintained it by corruption. But this is precisely what al-Muʿizz was not, and nothing is less likely than that he would, in this brazen way, have declared himself an impostor.

A much more accurate idea of the image of al-Muʿizz, as seen by his followers and projected to his new subjects, may be found in the poems of Ibn Hāniʾ, his Andalusian panegyrist.[2] The poet, in medieval Islamic courts, often had an important public function. As panegyrist, he praised his patron; as satirist, he abused his enemies. In a society that was sophisticated and literate, but without mass media, poetry could to some extent take their place; the poet devised, for publication and dissemination, versions of events or sketches of personalities which were vivid, memorable—and slanted. He was the propagandist, or, as we might now say, the public relations officer and image-maker of the ruler, and his compositions can tell us a great deal about the policies and intentions of rulers and sometimes even about the responses of the ruled.

The image of the Fatimid Caliph, as portrayed by his aulic poets, is not just that of a successful soldier or politician, but of a great world leader, at once spiritual and imperial. As a victorious dynastic ruler, he represents the emergence of a new power, which is young, fresh and vigorous, in contrast with his effete and degenerate opponents. But that is not all. The Fatimid state is not just another principality, carved out of the 'Abbasid Empire by an ambitious governor or a mutinous soldier. Such adventures had become commonplace; the rise of the Fatimids was something new, and their advent marks an era in the history of Egypt and indeed of all Islam.

During the first four centuries of Islam, Egypt went through three major phases, each of which has left its mark in the capital city. During the first phase, for more than two centuries after the Arab conquest, Egypt was a province of an Empire with its capital elsewhere. The administrative centre was Fustat, a provincial garrison city set up by the conquerors, conveniently near both the desert that was their line of communication with home, and the bureaucratic cadres bequeathed by the previous empire. The rulers of Egypt were governors, appointed by and answerable to the Caliph in the East; her corn fed Arabia; her revenues enriched the imperial treasury.

The second phase began in 254/868, with the arrival in Egypt of Ahmad ibn Tulun. At first a subordinate with strictly limited powers, subject to the authority of his superiors in Baghdad, he succeeded within a few years in creating a virtually independent state—the first in Muslim Egypt. By reducing the drain of revenue to the East and encouraging agriculture and commerce, he accumulated great wealth; with it he built a new capital, the combined fortress, palace and city of al-Qata'i', hard by the site of Fustat.

The establishment of the Tulunid state, and its revival and continuance by subsequent rulers, mark a significant change in the history of medieval Egypt. Ibn Tulun, the Ikhshid and Kafur were all foreigners in Egypt; their aims were personal or at most dynastic, and were limited in both territorial extent and political content. As Sunni Muslims, they had no desire to withdraw from the Islamic oecumene headed by the Caliph, still less to challenge the 'Abbasids for the Caliphate itself. Their aim was to rule Egypt, together with such adjoining countries as could conveniently be added to it, and to do so, if at all possible, with the approval of the Caliph and under his suzerainty. Though they were patrons of the arts and of letters, their rule did not foster any national or cultural renaissance, such as accompanied the emergence of similar principalities in Iran.

Yet, despite these and other limitations, the Tulunids and Ikhshidids inaugurated the separate history of Islamic Egypt, pursued recognizably Egyptian policies, and earned strong Egyptian loyalty and support. Under their rule the Nile Valley again became, for the first time since the Ptolemies, the seat of an independent political, military and economic power, with growing influence and importance in the affairs of the whole region.

With the coming of the Fatimids in 358/969, the role of Egypt in the Islamic world was vastly increased and totally transformed. The new masters of Egypt were moved by more than personal or dynastic ambition. They were the heads of a great religious movement, which aimed at nothing less than the transformation and renewal of all Islam. As Isma'ili Shi'ites, they refused to offer even token submission to the 'Abbasid Caliphs, whom they denounced as wrongdoers and usurpers; they and they alone were the true Imams, by descent and by God's choice the sole rightful heads of the whole Islamic community. The Caliphate was therefore theirs by right, and they would take it from the ʿAbbasids as the ʿAbbasids had taken it from the Umayyads.

In preparing the accomplishment of this plan, the Fatimid followed very closely on the pattern set by the ʿAbbasids. Like the ʿAbbasids in their early days, they appealed to all those who felt that the community of Islam had taken a wrong path, and they argued that only an Imām of the house of the Prophet could restore it to the true one. Like the ʿAbbasids again, they created a secret mission, to preach their cause and to organize those who adhered to it. The ʿAbbasids had begun by establishing themselves in the remote province of Khurasan, on the eastern borders of the Empire; the Fatimids, using the same tactics, concentrated their missionary and political effort first in the Yemen, and then in North Africa. The ʿAbbasids had harnessed the warlike Khurasanis to their purposes; the Fatimids mobilized the Berbers. The ʿAbbasids, sweeping westwards from Khurasan, chose a new central province, Iraq, and built themselves a new capital in Baghdad. The Fatimids, advancing eastwards from Tunisia, moved the centre to Egypt, and, near the camps and cantonments of Fusṭāṭ and al-Qataʾiʿ, founded a great new imperial metropolis, the city of Cairo. The poet Ibn Haniʾ, in celebrating the victories of al-Muʿizz in Egypt, looks forward in poetic vision to the next and final stages—the invasion of Iraq, the capture of Baghdad, the advance on the ancient highway to the East.[3]

At this point, however, the resemblance ceases, for the vision was not fulfilled. The ʿAbbasid triumph was complete, that of the Fatimids only partial. Except for the distant and isolated province of Spain, all Islam submitted to the ʿAbbasids, and even in Spain the Umayyad survivors did not seriously challenge their Caliphate. The Fatimids won great victories, and at the time it must have seemed that they were about to engulf the whole world of Islam. But they did not. The ʿAbbasids, defeated and weakened, themselves under the domination of a Shiʿite though not Ismaʿili dynasty of mayors of the palace, nevertheless managed to hold on in their old capital, and served as a rallying point for all the forces of Sunni Islam. In the following century, those forces were immensely strengthened by the advent of the Seljuq Turks and the creation of a new and powerful military empire in the East, the great Sultanate. The reinforcement was religious as well as political. The Seljuq Sultans were devout Sunnis. True, they dominated the Caliphate, but unlike the Shiʿite Buyids whom they replaced, they treated the Caliphs with honour and respect as the supreme religious authority in Sunni Islam, and their advent greatly increased the prestige and influence of the ʿAbbasid house. The containment of the Fatimid danger was not achieved by military and political means alone, though these were essential and in large measure successful. In the *madrasa*, Sunni Islam created a new and crucial weapon in the struggle for religious unity. In these great colleges, spreading all over the East, the scholars and theologians of the Sunna devised and taught the orthodox answer to the Isma'ili intellectual challenge.

Both the 'Abbasids and the Fāṭimids, in their hour of victory, confronted the dilemma which sooner or later faces all successful rebels—the conflict between the responsibilities of power and the expectations of those who brought them to it. The 'Abbasids, after a brief attempt to persuade the Muslims that their accession had really brought the promised millennium, chose the path of stability and orthodoxy. The radical doctrines were forgotten, the radical leaders murdered. The messianic epithets became regnal titles, the black banners of revolt became a dynastic livery—even the very word *dawla*, which originally connoted revolution and change, came to mean the dynasty and then the state.[4]

The same problem arose for the victorious Fatimids, but in a more complex form, since their victory was slower and incomplete. Sixty years and three unsuccessful attempts intervened between the establishment of the Fatimid Caliphate in Tunisia and its extension to Egypt. The further conquest of the Islamic East was never accomplished. The Fatimid Caliphs, like the first 'Abbasids, found that the views and wishes of the missionaries did not always accord with the needs of the state, and from time to time, both in the Tunisian and in the Egyptian phases, there are indications of disagreement and repression within the Isma'ili fold—even of secession. But the Fatimids, unlike the 'Abbasids, could not afford to break completely with the mission, since there was still important work for the mission to do. The aim of the Fatimids, at least until al-Mustanṣir, was to overthrow and supersede the 'Abbasid Caliphate—to establish their own Imamate and their Isma'ili faith in the whole world of Islam. For more than a century the activities of the Fatimid government in Cairo and of its agents at home and abroad were directed towards this objective.

These activities were not always pursued with equal vigour. There were times when the Fatimids were distracted by other problems—unrest in the provinces, trouble on the Mediterranean or Byzantine frontiers—and found it expedient to reach a *modus vivendi* with their rivals in the East. But their ultimate objective, necessarily, was still the establishment of the universal Isma'ili Imamate.

The Fatimid Caliphate thus represents a phenomenon which was new though not unique in history—a regime at once imperial and revolutionary. Within his own domains, the Fatimid Caliph was a sovereign—the supreme ruler of a vast empire which he sought to extend by conventional military and political means. Its centre was Egypt; its provinces at its peak included North Africa, Sicily, Palestine, Syria, the Red Sea coast of Africa, the Yemen, and, of special importance, the Hijaz, possession of which conferred great prestige on a Muslim ruler and enabled him to use the potent weapon of the pilgrimage to his advantage.

His capital city, Cairo, was the thriving centre of this vast realm. The tribute of empire now flowed into Egypt, not out of it. The material prosperity of the country was sustained by a flourishing agriculture and an extensive commerce;

the opportunities of Cairo attracted men of talent and ambition from all over the Fatimid domains and beyond. Policy and circumstance combined to encourage a great flowering of intellectual and artistic life.

But the Caliph was not only an imperial sovereign. He was also the Isma'ili Imam, the spiritual head of the faithful wherever they were, the embodiment of God's purpose and guidance on earth. As such, he was the dedicated enemy of the existing order in the East, the hope and refuge of those who sought to overthrow it. All over the 'Abbasid realms, he commanded a great army of missionaries, agents and followers, elaborately and secretly organized under the supreme direction of the Chief Missionary *(Dā'ī 'l-du'āt)* in Cairo. It is significant that the Chief Missionary himself was almost invariably an Easterner, with personal experience of service in the Mission. One of the greatest of them, al-Mu'ayyad fi'l-Dīn al-Shinazi, has left a fascinating autobiographical work describing his adventures as a Fatimid missionary in Persia, as a political emissary in Iraq, and as Chief Missionary in Cairo.[5]

In traditional Islamic states, the business of government was carried on by two main groups, known as the men of the sword *(arbāb al-suyūf)* and the men of the pen *(arbāb al-aqlām)*. The former were the armed forces, the latter the civilian bureaucrats. Their relative importance and influence varied according to the type of regime, but the two together were commonly agreed to be the twin pillars of the state. The Fatimids, for the first time in Islamic history, added a third—the Mission. In the Sunni Caliphate, the professional men of religion had stood aside from the state, neither serving it nor accepting its direction. The Fatimids organized them into a third branch of government, with its own functions, structure, and hierarchy, under the direction of the Chief Missionary and the ultimate authority of the Caliph in his capacity as Imam. The Fatimids thus created something previously unknown to Islam—an institutional church. Their example was followed by some later rulers, who found in this new relationship between religion and the state a powerful reinforcement of their authority.

The work of the Mission had many different facets. It was known as the *da'wa*, and in classical Arabic usage is perhaps sufficiently described by that richly associative word. In modern categories and terminology, some elaboration of the different functions of the *da'wa* might be useful.

One of these was what we nowadays call ideology—the organized and exclusive system of ideas adopted and propagated by a movement or a regime. Generally speaking, Islamic regimes had no ideology other than Islam itself—and that in the broadest and most tolerant definition. Muslim governments took care not to impose, or even espouse, any intellectual orthodoxy, but to allow, within reasonable limits, the co-existence of diverse opinions. The oft-cited saying *Ikhtilāfu ummatī raḥma*, difference of opinion within my community is part of God's mercy, accurately reflects traditional Islamic attitudes and practice. The 'Abbasids used a radical religious ideology to gain power, but swiftly abandoned it when they had done so. Their one attempt to impose an official creed on the

Islamic community was a total failure, and it is significant that the Muʿtazili doctrine which they sponsored is one of the few major religious trends in Islam to have completely disappeared.

The Fatimids did not abandon their distinctive doctrines, but on the contrary gave them a central importance in their whole political system. Ismaʿili theology provided the basis on which the Fatimids rested their claim to the Caliphate and denied that of the ʿAbbasids. As long as the ʿAbbasids survived, the Fatimids were engaged in a religious—i.e., an ideological conflict, in which doctrine was one of their most powerful weapons. In a sense, they were caught in a vicious circle. Because of their initial failure to win over all Islam, they were obliged to maintain their ideological challenge; yet, by so doing, they isolated themselves from the central consensus of Islam, and thus ensured their own ultimate defeat and disappearance.

It was, however, some time before that defeat became apparent. While the struggle continued, the Fatimids accorded prime importance to the formulation and elaboration of their creed. First in North Africa and then in Egypt, a series of distinguished theologians wrote what became the classical works of Ismaʿili literature. Most of the authors had served in the Mission; some like Ḥamid al-Dīn al-Kirmānī and al-Muʾayyad fiʾl-Dīn al-Shinazi, had been its chiefs.[6]

The process was not without difficulty. Already at the beginning of the Fatimid Caliphate, in North Africa, the Imam as ruler proved different from the Imam as claimant. The needs of government required some changes of approach, and the adoption, in the words of a modern Ismaʾili scholar, of "a graver and more conservative attitude towards the then existing institutions of Islam."[7] Within the Mission itself, there were disputes between radicals and conservatives, between the revealers and the preservers of the esoteric mysteries. Sometimes their disputes were no more than arguments between colleagues; sometimes they led to defections, schism, and even conflict.

Until the death of al-Mustansir, these defections were of minor importance, and the main body of Ismaʿili remained faithful to the reigning Fatimid Caliph and to the officially sponsored Ismaʿili creed.

It was not enough merely to formulate ideology; there was also the more practical business of disseminating it. In this respect, the Mission performed many tasks which a modern observer, depending on his point of observation, might classify as education or propaganda. In Cairo, the Fatimids founded great libraries and colleges among whose purposes was the training of missionaries to go out into the field, and the further instruction of those converts whom they sent home for this purpose. Many eager aspirants came to Cairo from Sunni lands in the East, to imbibe wisdom at the fountainhead, and then return to their own countries as exponents of the Ismaʿili message and workers for the Fatimid cause. One such was the Persian poet and philosopher Nasir-i Khusraw. A convert to Ismaʿilism, he went to Egypt in 439/1047, and returned to preach the faith in Iran and Central Asia, where he won a considerable following. Another was the redoubtable Hasan-i Sabbah, the founder of the order of the Assassins. Converted by a Fatimid agent in Iran, he went to Egypt in 471/1078, and stayed there for about three years.

The Isma'ili message had considerable appeal, to many different elements in the population. It was a time of great upheavals in the Islamic world—of economic change, political disruption and intellectual malaise. As in late Umayyad times, there were many who felt that the Islamic community had gone astray and that a new leader, with a new message, was needed to restore it to the true path. There was a withdrawal of consent from the existing order, a loss of confidence in hitherto accepted answers. The 'Abbasid Caliphate, and with it the Sunni order, seemed to be breaking up; some new principle of unity and authority was required to save Islam and the Muslims from destruction.

To many it seemed that the Isma'ilis could offer such a principle—a design for a new and just world order, under the Imam. To the devout, the doubtful and the discontented alike, the Isma'ili missionaries brought a message of comfort and hope, appropriate to the needs of each; for the pious, a deep, spiritual faith, sustained by the example of the suffering of the Imams and the self-sacrifice of their followers; for the intellectual, a comprehensive explanation of the universe, synthesizing the data of revelation and philosophy, science and mysticism; for the rebellious, a well-organized and widespread movement, supported by a rich and powerful ruler far away, and offering a seductive prospect of radical change. One of the important functions of the missionaries, where conditions were favorable, was what one might now call subversion.

In the nature of things, secret activities such as subversion, especially when successful, leave few traces for the historian to examine. There are, however, some scraps of information, from here and there, which throw light on the work of the Fatimid emissaries. Pieced together, and compared with other evidence, they suggest that the operations of the Mission were centrally directed and were part of a grand strategy, the ultimate aim of which was to destroy the Sunni Caliphate and establish the Fatimid Imamate in its place.

This grand strategy can be discerned over a vast area, in which the imperial purposes of the Fatimid state and the universal aims of the Isma'ili faith met and merged. Fatimid statesmen and soldiers harried the rulers and realms of the Sunnī world; Isma'ili authors and missionaries attacked the loyalty of their subjects. And at the same time, Cairo waged a form of what modern strategists call economic warfare, in which the Egyptian or Tunisian merchant, the Isma'ili missionary, and the Fatimid diplomat all had their different but associated parts.

The pattern of rivalry between the powers that dominated the eastern and the western or Mediterranean halves of the Middle East is an ancient one, which long antedated and survived the Fatimid-'Abbasid confrontation. The western power might be called Egyptian, Hittite, Greek, Roman, Byzantine, Fatimid, Mamlūk or Ottoman; the Eastern, Assyrian, Babylonian, Persian, 'Abbasid, Seljuq, Mongol or Safavid. The names, forms, characters, even locations of these rival powers varied greatly; so too did the circumstances and results of their rivalries. Yet through the variety, certain geographical constants may be discerned.

One of these is the competition between the two trade routes leading to the further east—the one from Egypt through the Red Sea, the other from Iraq and Iran through the Persian Gulf. To some extent these have been complementary, each serving a different area. But in times of great power conflict, they have often represented alternative opportunities, and inspired opposing ambitions. Rival powers in the Middle East have an obvious interest in controlling at least one and preferably both of these routes, and in blocking what they cannot control.

The Fatimid rulers of Cairo appear to have been well aware of the importance of these matters, and to have devised policies for dealing with them. As far as is known, there is no direct or explicit evidence on Fatimid eastern strategy. The evidence we have is indirect and inferential, but persuasive. One aspect is Fatimid activity in the Red Sea, the domination of which was vital to their larger plans. Their aim, clearly, was to control both the African and the Arabian shores and the southern exit; in this they were, for a while, largely successful. On the African side, they developed the great seaport of 'Aydhab, as a centre for the eastern trade and a rival to Basra and Ubulla. On the Arabian side, the Yemen was the country where the Fatimid cause had gained its first major success, and the area remained one of prime concern to them—the scene of considerable religious and political effort. Even today, the Yemen contains one of the only two surviving Isma'ili communities in the Arab world; the other is in Syria. The Fatimid interest in the Yemen, without ideological complications, was maintained by their Sunni successors in Egypt, the Ayyubids and the Mamluks, no doubt for some of the same reasons.[8]

In the letters sent by the Caliph al-Mustansir to the Isma'ili ruler of the Yemen, the Caliph expresses his satisfaction with the work of the Mission in southern Arabia, and suggests its extension eastwards. 'Uman was a suitable area for attention—and in al-Aḥsa representatives of the cause were already at work.[9] The interest in this area was not new. It was here that the Carmathians had set up their famous republic, described by the pro-Fatimid travellers Ibn Hawqal and Nasir-i Khusraw.[10] In another passage, Ibn Hawqal tells how the Baluchi brigands of southern Iran, who terrorised the roads of "all Kermān, the steppes of Sijistān, and the borders of Fārs," had belonged to the Fatimid mission, as part of the mission-district jazira of Khurasan.[11] The Carmathians in Eastern Arabia harassed the land communications of Iraq with Arabia and Syria; the brigands and pirates of Kerman and the Baluchi coasts harassed both the land and sea routes from Iraq to India. It is difficult to resist the conclusion that, while protecting their own communications through the Red Sea, the Fatimids were trying to disrupt those of their rivals in the East.

Fatimid interest was not limited to the routes to India; it extended to India itself. Ismaʿili missionaries, from an early date, were active at the two main points of entry into India, by land and sea, from the Middle East—by the North West frontier, and in the ports of the western seaboard. On the coast of Sind, and in the inland city of Multan, the Ismaʿilis made great efforts and were even able to gain power at certain times. The traveller al-Muqaddasi, who visited Multan in 375/985–6, records that the bidding-prayer was recited in the name of the Fatimid Caliph, that they followed his orders in matters of faith and law, and that messengers and gifts went regularly to Egypt.[12] Small communities of Ismaʿilis are still to be found in North Western Pakistan, in Afghanistan, in the Pamir, in eastern Iran—strung out along the trans-Asian highways. On the Gujerati coast, Fatimid commercial activities were accompanied by a vigorous religious propaganda, and the planting of what in time became the great Ismaʿili community of India. It is perhaps significant that these Ismaʿilis are still known as Bohra, a Gujerati word meaning merchant. Again, the inference is strong that the Fatimids were concerned both to strengthen their own position and to weaken and dominate that of their rivals.[13]

This does not of course mean that the Fatimid state engaged directly in commerce, or that the *daʿwa* itself was a trading organization[14]—the connection between mission and trade, between ideological and economic penetration, is rarely quite so obvious. It is not unlikely, however, that the Fatimids were aware of that connection, and tried in various ways to make use of it. Two facts may be mentioned here—the prominence of North Africans among the eastern traders, and the role of qadi's as officially recognized representatives of the merchants.[15]

The high water mark of Fatimid expansion came in the years 448–451/1057–9, when a Turkish general in Iraq called Arslan al-Basasiri went over to the Fatimid side and proclaimed the Fatimid Caliph first in Mosul and then, for a year, in Baghdad itself. Despite the efforts of the Chief Missionary, however, the Fatimid government was unable to provide effective support, and the strongly Sunni Seljuqs drove al-Basasiri out of Baghdad. The Ghaznavid ruler in the East had already opted for Sunnism, to which he brought powerful reinforcement. The Ismaʿilis of Multan were crushed—those of Persia and Iraq subjected to both repression and counter-propaganda.

The Fatimids failed to complete the ʿAbbasid pattern of advance—from the periphery to the centre, from revolt to empire. They followed, however, at an accelerated pace, on the ʿAbbasid road to ruin. The ʿAbbasid Caliphate, with all its troubles, lasted for half a millennium; the Fatimid Caliphate was terminated by Saladin after barely half that time.

What went wrong? In the present state of knowledge, it is not possible to offer more than the most tentative of answers. The fall of empires, the failure of ideologies, are subjects of the greatest complexity, and the historian at his peril attempts to unravel the tangled web of interacting causes, symptoms and effects. Some phenomena—they should not be more closely defined than that—can however be enumerated, as having some bearing on the failure of the Fatimid bid for leadership and power.

One such phenomenon was the espousal and retention, by the Fatimid regime, of a religious system that was basically alien and ultimately unacceptable to Sunni Muslims. The Isma'ili creed, as elaborated by the Fatimid theologians, represents a very high level of intellectual and spiritual achievement; it was however remote from what had become the main stream of Islamic belief and thought, and, with the Sunni revival of the 11th and 12th centuries, its final rejection became certain. That rejection also involved the regime that was inextricably associated with it.

In their foreign adventures, the Fatimids scored many successes. In one crucial area, however, they suffered repeated and disastrous setbacks—in Syria. Here, on their doorstep, they encountered their greatest difficulties—difficulties which contributed in no small measure to their final failure. Despite the pro-Shi'ite and even pro-Isma'ili sympathies of sections of the population, the Fatimids were never able to establish themselves really firmly in Syria. Their troubles began with their arrival, when their forces advancing from Egypt to Syria had to cope with Bedouin assailants in Palestine, dissident Carmathian raiders from Arabia, the adventurer Alptekin in Damascus and the volatile Hamdanids in the North. In the pacification of Syria, their successes were temporary, their troubles recurring. Already fully stretched in dealing with local opponents, they had to face major threats from outside—the Byzantines, the Turks, and finally the Crusaders. It was in Syria that the great Fatimid drive to the East was delayed and halted; in Syria, too, that a new force emerged which finally destroyed them.

The Fatimids were unfortunate in that their rule in Egypt coincided with great changes in other parts of the world—on the one side the revival of Christian power, which manifested itself in the Byzantine offensives, the reconquest of much of Spain and Sicily, and the coming of the Crusaders to the East; on the other the migration of the steppe peoples, which brought the Turks to Iraq and then to Syria, and created a new power and a new order in South West Asia. In the looming contest between Islam and Christendom, there was no room for a schismatic division on the Muslim side. The Fatimids were in decline, their faith was on the wane. The Turks and their associates were the new great power in Islam, the Sunni revival the new moral force. Between them, they gave to the Muslim peoples the strength to hold and repel the Crusaders from the West, and the endurance to survive the far more terrible invasion, still to come, of the Mongols from the East.

These misadventures abroad no doubt contributed to the growing troubles at home in Egypt. While factional strife led the government of the country into a vicious circle of disorder and tyranny, economic upheavals culminated in a series of disastrous famines, which, according to the chroniclers, reduced the people to eating cats and dogs. Finally, in 466/1073, an able soldier, Badr al-Jamali, established an authoritarian regime which restored order and some measure of prosperity. He assumed the title of *Amir al-Juyūsh*, the Commander of armies.

The regime of Badr al-Jamālī and his successors in the same office saved the Fatimid state from collapse, and postponed the end of the dynasty for nearly a century. At first, the new order retained and indeed revived the universal claims and aims of the Fatimid Caliphate. In the inscriptions of Badr al-Jamālī, in addition to his military and political titles, he is styled guardian of the *qadis* of the Muslims (*Kāfil quḍāt al-Muslimīn*) and guide of the *dā'īs* of the Believers (*Hādī du'ʿāt al-Mu'minīn*), symbolising his control of the religious as well as the military and bureaucratic establishments. He is even credited with the authorship of an Ismaʿili book.[16] Responding to the challenge of the Seljuq power in the East, he pursued an active policy in Syria, Arabia and elsewhere, using both religious and worldly weapons. The published *Sijills* of al-Mustansir, most of which belong to this period, show how this policy was applied in the Yemen, which became a centre for Fatimid activities in Arabia and even in India.[17]

But the cause was lost. In Syria the Fatimid armies suffered repeated defeats; in Arabia, Fatimid influence was finally brought to an end. Badr's son and successor, al-Afdal, in effect renounced the claims of the Fatimid Caliphate to the universal leadership of Islam. On the death of al-Mustansir in 487/1094, the *Amir al-Juyūsh* made a choice of successor which was rejected by the Ismaʿilis of the East, now infused with a new revolutionary fervour under the leadership of Hasan-i Sabbah. After the death of al-Amir in 525/1130, even those Ismaʿilis, chiefly in the Yemen, who had remained faithful to the Cairo Caliphate refused to recognize his successor. The divergence between the state and revolution, which had begun to appear from early Fāṭimid times, was now complete. The ruler of Egypt, perhaps intentionally, had alienated the militant Ismaʿilis in the lands under Sunni rule, and dissociated the interests and policies of the Egyptian state from their radical doctrines and terrorist actions. The Fatimids still had some time to reign, and much to accomplish; but the great adventure, with its opportunities, its excitements and its heavy price, was over.

Notes

1. Ibn Khallikan, *Kitāb Wafayāt al-aʿyān*, Būlāq 1275, ii, 326–27; cf. ibid., ii, 135; Abu'l-Maḥāsin ibn Taghribirdī, *Al-Nujūm al-zāhira*, iv, Cairo 1352/1933, 77. Ibn Khallikān, who cites the story from the *K. al-Duwal al-munqaṭiʿa*, rejects it as false on the ground that ʿAbdallah ibn Ṭabāṭabā, the ʿAlid who is supposed to have questioned al-Muʿizz, was already dead at the time when al-Muʿizz arrived in Egypt. For a discussion of the legend see P. H. Mamour, *Polemics on the origin of the Fatimi Caliphs*, London, 1934, 180–83.

2. For an evaluation, see M. Canard, "L'Impérialisme *des Fātimides* et leur propagande," in *Annales de l'Institut d'Études Orientales* (Algiers), vi (1942–1947), 156–93. See further *EI²* (*Encyclopaedia of Islam*, 2nd edition), s. v. "Ibn Hāni'" (by F. Dachraoui).

3. Ibn Hani', *Dīwān*, ed. Zāhid ʿAlī, Cairo 1356, 408; cf. Canard, 185.

4. See *EI²*, s. v. "Dawla" (by F. Rosenthal); B. Lewis, "The regnal titles of the first

'Abbāsid Caliphs," in *Dr. Zakir Husain Presentation Volume*, New Delhi, 1968, 13–22; idem, "Islamic Concepts of Revolution" in P. J. Vatikiotis (ed), *Revolution in the Middle East*. Totowa NJ, 1972, 30–40.

5. *Sīrat al-Mu'ayyad fī'l-Dīn* . . . , ed. Muḥammad Kāmil Ḥusayn, Cairo, 1949. On the Fatimid *daʿwa* see further M. Canard, op. cit.; W. Ivanow, "The organization of the Fatimid propaganda," in *Journal of the Bombay Branch of the Royal Asiatic Society*, xv (1939), 1–35; A. E. Bertels, *Nasir-i Khosrov i Ismailizm*, Moscow, 1959 (Persian translation, Tehran, 1968); B. Lewis, *The Assassins*, London, 1967; Ḥasan al-Bāshā, *Al-Funūn al-Islāmiyya* . . . , ii, Cairo, 1966, 507–11; *EI²*, s. vv. "Dāʿī" (by M. G. S. Hodgson) and "Daʿwa" (by M. Canard), where further references are given.

6. On this literature, see W. Ivanow, *Ismaili literature, a bibliographical survey*, second edition, Tehran, 1963. The major Isma'ili bibliography, known as *Fihrist al-Majdūʿ*, was edited by Alinaqi Monzavi, Tehran 1966.

7. H. Hamdani, "Some unknown Ismāʿīlī authors and their works," in *Journal of the Royal Asiatic Society* (1933), 365. On the conflicts within Isma'ilism, see further S. M. Stern, "Heterodox Ismailism at the time of al-Muʿizz," in *Bulletin of the School of Oriental and African Studies*, xvii (1955), 10–33; W. Madelung, "Das Imamat in der frühen ismailitischen Lehre," in *Der Islam*, xxvii (1961), 43–135.

8. On Fatimid activities in the Yemen, see Ḥusayn al-Hamdani, in association with Ḥasan Sulaymān Maḥmūd al-Juhanī, *Al-Ṣulayḥiyyūn wa'l-ḥaraka al-Fāṭimiyya fī'l-Yaman (268–625)*, Cairo n. d. (preface dated 1955).

9. *Al-Sijillāt al-Mustanṣiriyya*, ed. ʿAbd al-Munʿim Mājid, Cairo, 1954, 168, 176–79, 205. For evaluations of these documents see H. F. al-Hamdānī, "The letters of Al-Mustanṣir bi'llāh," in *Bulletin of the School of Oriental Studies*, vii (1934), 307–24; idem, *Al-Ṣulayḥiyyūn*; ʿAbd al-Munʿim Mājid, *Al-Imām al-Mustanṣir bi'llah al-Fāṭimī*, Cairo, 1961, especially 101 ff.

10. Ibn Ḥawqal, *Al-Masālik wa'l-mamālik*, ed. M. J. de Goeje, Leiden, 1873, 21–22; new edition, *Ṣūrat al-arḍ*, ed. J. H. Kramers, Leiden, 1938, 25–27; French translation by J. H. Kramers and G. Wiet, *Configuration de la terre*, i, Paris, 1964, 24–26. Nāṣir-i Khusraw, *Sefer Nameh (Safar-Nāma)*, edited with French translation by Ch. Schéfer, Paris, 1881, text 82–85; translation 225–33; Kaviani edition, Berlin, 1841, 123–27. On Carmathian and Ismāʿīlī activities in this area see further M. J. de Goeje, *Mémoire sur les Carmathes du Bahrain et les Fatimides*, 2nd edition, Leiden, 1886; B. Lewis, *The origins of Ismāʿīlism*, Cambridge, 1940; W. Madelung, "Fatimiden und Baḥrainqarmaṭen," in *Der Islam*, xxxiv (1958), 34–88; Ḥusayn al-Hamdānī, *Al-Ṣulayḥiyyūn* . . . , 221 ff.

11. *Masālik*, 221; *Ṣūrat al-arḍ*, ii, 310; French translation, ii, 304. There is a slight difference between the two versions. On Ismāʿīlī use of the term *jazīra* see Lewis, *Assassins*, 48–49.

12. *Aḥsan al-taqāsīm*, 2nd ed. by M. J. de Goeje, Leiden 1906, 485. On Fatimid activities in India see Abbas H. al-Hamdani, *The beginnings of the Ismāʿīlī daʿwa in northern India*, Cairo, 1956, where further sources and studies are cited.

13. On Fatimid policies in East and West see B. Lewis, "The Fatimids and the route to India," in *Revue de la Faculté des Sciences Economiques de l'Université d'Istanbul*, xi (1949–50), 50–54; Abbas Hamdani, "Some considerations on the Fāṭimid Caliphate as a Mediterranean power," in *Atti del III Congresso di Studi Arabi e Islamici (Ravello 1966)*, Naples 1967, 385–96. When the above was written I did not have access to the following works: Muḥammad Djamāl al-Dīn Surūr, *Siyāsat al-Fāṭimiyyīn al-khārijiyya*, Cairo, 1967; ʿAbd al-Munʿim Mājid, *Ẓuhūr khilāfat al-Fāṭimiyyīn wa-suqūṭuhā fī Miṣr*, Cairo, 1968.

14. It may however be noted that in a *Sijill* of al-Mustanṣir, dated Dhu'l-Qaʿda 481/Feb. 1089, a *dāʿī* in ʿUmān is accused of neglecting his duties and travelling in pursuit of business. *al-takhallī fī'l-Khidma wa'l-zikāḍ fī ṭalab al-tijāra (Al-Sidjillāt al-Mustanṣiriyya*, 168). This

would appear to mean that a reasonable but not excessive concern with commerce is permissible to a *dā'ī*.

15. For Geniza evidence on the trade with India see S. D. Goitein "From the Mediterranean to India; documents on the trade to India, South Arabia and East Africa from the eleventh and twelfth centuries," in *Speculum*, xxix (1954), 181–97; idem, "Letters and documents on the India trade in medieval times," in *Islamic Culture*, xxvii (1963), 188–205; idem, *A Mediterranean Society: the Jewish communities of the Arab world as portrayed in the documents of the Cairo Geniza*, i, *Economic foundations*, Berkeley and Los Angeles 1967. On the predominance of North African merchants in the India trade, and the role of the qāḍis see "Letters . . .," 199–200 and 202.

16. W. Ivanow, *Ismaili Literature* . . . , 49; Inscriptions in *Répertoire chronologique d'épigraphie arabe*, vii, Cairo 1936, 210, 238, 248, 259 etc.; cf. Max van Berchem, *Matériaux pour un Corpus Inscriptionum arabicarum*, i, Egypte, fasc. i, *Le Caire*, Paris, 1894, 54ff. On the significance of these titles see Ḥasan al-Bāshā, *Al-Funūn al-Islamiyya*, ii, 940–42.

17. See above, notes 9–10.

8

Propaganda in the
Pre-Modern Middle East

A Preliminary Classification

❧❧❧❧

The word propaganda has gone through many changes of meaning. It apparently dates from 1622, when a committee of cardinals was appointed by the Roman Catholic Church, with responsibility for the care and oversight of foreign missions engaged in the propagation of the faith; by the nineteenth century it had acquired the more general meaning of efforts made to promote a particular doctrine or practice, religious or other.

The emergence of a certain type of modern state, at once ideological and dictatorial, together with the vast extension of the technology of communication, has given the whole business of propaganda a new scope and intensity. Two states in particular, Nazi Germany and Soviet Russia, created an immense apparatus for the propagation of both their general world view and their specific state policies.

The Reich Propaganda Ministry and Soviet Agitprop between them brought the term "propaganda" into disrepute, and it is now mostly used in a negative, even a dismissive, sense. In most countries and circles nowadays, "propaganda" and its equivalents in other languages denote what our opponents put out; what we provide is "information," "guidance" and the like. A relatively new term, public relations, spans the border area between propaganda and advertising, and covers the arts and techniques of persuasion and marketing—of an idea or programme, a person or party, a commodity or service. Today, even the term public relations, often abbreviated to P.R., has begun to acquire negative associations, while to describe a statement as propaganda is tantamount to condemning it as falsehood.

A parallel development may be observed in Arabic. The modern Arabic term is *di'āya*, which carries the same negative connotation as "propaganda." It too has a religious origin, and derives from the verb *da'ā* which includes, among its meanings, to pray, to call, to summon, to appeal, and, in a religious sense, to try and convert another to one's faith. In the Qur'ān, the Prophet is described as *dā'ī Allāh*, the summoner to God (46: 31–32); in another passage the true *da'wa, da'wat al-ḥaqq* (13: 14) is the call or prayer addressed to the one true God. In the early Islamic jihad, the term *da'wa* commonly denoted the challenge of the Muslim fighters to the unbelievers to embrace Islam, pay the poll-tax, or fight. In later usage, particularly but not exclusively in radical Shi'ite circles, the *dā'ī* was the equivalent of the missionary, the *da'wa* of the mission. These terms have been and in some circles still are used with a positive connotation. There are however also negative terms derived from the same root, notably *da'ī*, a braggart or imposter, and the verb *idda'ā*, to allege or to put forward a (usually false) claim. *Di'āya* is a modern coinage, and is now used only in a negative sense. It is thus the equivalent of the present-day Western use of the term "propaganda." Positive terms for the same activity are the relatively neutral *akhbār*, information, and the more purposeful *irshād*, guidance.

The most usual form of propaganda in the past was religious, as one would expect in a region inhabited by Muslims, Christians and Jews, with obvious divergences between and also within these faiths. The ostensible purpose of the propagandist is to promote the religious beliefs of the side that he represents, to discredit differing, still more opposing, religious sects, beliefs and causes, and to win over their adherents. Very often, this simply means using religious arguments to promote or oppose a holder or seeker of power. In the past Islam, unlike Christendom, had no organized churches or ecclesiastical institutions, and religiously formulated propagandist activities among Muslims tended on the whole to be sporadic and due to personal or sectarian initiatives. This is no longer true. In several Muslim countries, religious hierarchies have emerged, with the functional, though not the doctrinal, equivalents of a church and an episcopate.

Propaganda in its original Christian religious sense did however have a partial Islamic equivalent in the medieval Middle East. The Isma'ili Fatimid caliphs in Cairo attached great importance to the propagation of their doctrines. This task was entrusted to an organization known as the *da'wa*, which maintained a network of emissaries called *dā'ī*, in Fatimid dominions to preach to their own subjects, and beyond their frontiers to win over the subjects of the Sunnī 'Abbasid caliphate. Like the 'Abbasids before them, the Fatimids owed their success, in no small measure, to the work of a subversive opposition (*da'wa*); unlike the 'Abbasids, the Fatimid retained and institutionalized the *da'wa* after they came to power. The Cairo caliphs, it should be remembered, were not merely rebellious rulers achieving some kind of local autonomy or independence, as happened in many places during the decline of 'Abbasid power. They were challenging not just the suzerainty but the very legitimacy of the 'Abbasid caliphs. For them, the 'Abbasids were usurpers, and their Islam was corrupted. According to Isma'ili teaching, the Fatimids represented the authentic line of heirs of the Prophet, and their Isma'ili doctrine was the true Islam. The tenth and eleventh centuries thus saw a major struggle for the control of the Middle Eastern Islamic world between two competing caliphates, representing two rival versions of the Islamic religion. Occasionally this conflict took military form. More often, it was carried on by means of economic and more especially propaganda warfare.

The propaganda of the Fatimids was very elaborate and well organized.[1] It amounted to a third branch of government, alongside the military and the financial establishments which were customary in Middle Eastern states; a kind of ministry of propaganda and almost, one might say, a kind of church. The Fāṭimid *da'wa* also had an elaborate system of training, hierarchy and financing. Its head, the *dā'ī al-du'āt* or chief *dā'ī*, was one of the highest and most influential officers of the Fātimid state. In Isma'ili documents, he is often given the title of Gate (*bāb*), or Gate of Gates (*bāb al-abwāb*). The autobiography of al-Mu'ayyad, one of the leaders of Fatimid propaganda in Iran, describes his adventures there, his journey to the headquarters in Cairo, and his subsequent activities as head of the *da'wa*. When he arrived in Cairo in about 1045, he found that the mission which he had served, and in which he had placed such high hopes, was in a bad way, and "the product was sluggish and unsaleable," a remarkable prefigurement of modern public relations imagery.[2]

The 'Abbasid caliph and the Sunni *'ulamā'*, confronted with this double challenge, both political and doctrinal, had no choice but to respond, and they did. It was in this period that the Islamic institution of higher education, the *madrasa*, was rapidly developed and expanded, and assumed the central position that it has retained ever since. In its origin, its immediate task was counter-propaganda—to devise and disseminate an answer to the challenge of Isma'ili doctrines and of Fatimid power. As the historical record shows, it was successful in both.

The propaganda struggle within the Islamic world did not begin with the rise of the Fatimids, nor did it end with their disappearance. Propaganda of various kinds was conducted by the parties to the early civil wars in the Islamic community, and notably by pro-'Abbasid emissaries in Khurasan and elsewhere, impugning the legitimacy of the Umayyads. This propaganda contributed significantly to their fall and their replacement by the 'Abbasids.[3] The launching of a jihad, and the accompanying mobilization of volunteer fighters, also involved extensive propaganda addressed to prospective recruits. Examples of jihad propaganda may be found in *ḥadīth*; in the heroic narratives of war on the frontiers, especially with the Byzantines; in the call to the counter-Crusade and in the Ottoman *ghāzī* literature.[4]

The use of propaganda and many of its characteristic themes and methods can be traced back to antiquity—Christian and Jewish, Roman and Greek, and beyond them to the earliest use of writing and imagery in the region. There were always conflicts or at least rivalries between states, tribes and families, towns, neighborhoods and provinces, religions and sects, rulers and claimants, and factions and causes of many kinds. Religious propaganda against non-Muslim religions is rare, and when it occurs it is due to specific, usually political and economic, circumstances. Religious propaganda between Muslim groups is much more common. This could be inter-governmental, e.g. between ʿAbbasids and Fatimids, or later, between Sunnī Ottomans and Shiʿite Safavids. More frequently, it arises from a radical challenge to the existing order. Obvious examples are the Kharijites, the Ismaʿilis, the Almohades, and the Wahhabis.

Propaganda was also sometimes directed against specific tribal, ethnic or regional groups to which the propagandist or his employer was opposed. During the second century of the caliphate, the rivalry between Arabs on the one hand and non-Arabs, more particularly Persians, on the other, gave rise to propaganda literature, both poetry and prose, in which the propagandists extolled the merits and expressed the grievances of their own side and insulted or ridiculed their opponents. Other ethnic, racial, and regional conflicts in different parts of the Islamic world gave rise to similar literary propaganda.

A preliminary classification of the vehicles, methods and themes of propaganda may be useful. Propaganda may be verbal or non-verbal, i.e. visual. The pre-modern use of music as propaganda still awaits study. Verbal propaganda may be written or spoken, or some combination of the two. The recorded history of propaganda begins with the invention of writing and, indeed, a large proportion of surviving ancient texts may be classified under that heading, consisting as they do of statements by rulers proclaiming their greatness, or by religious teachers promulgating their doctrines. A major step was the invention of the alphabet, and the replacement of the cumbrous writing systems—cuneiform, hieroglyphs and the like—of the most ancient civilizations. With the advent of the alphabet, writing was no longer a specialized craft or mystery, knowledge of which was confined to a small class of priests and scribes. In contrast to the earlier systems of writing, it could easily be taught and mastered, and could bring the message of a written text to a much wider circle. This was still far short of universal literacy, but it was a great improvement on what went before, and significantly eased the task of propagandists of every kind.

Written propaganda is attested by hard evidence in the most literal sense— writings on stone and metal, detailing the name, authority, achievements and claims of the ruler. From early times, these titles and claims were asserted on coins, which passed through many hands; on inscriptions, clear and visible in public places, as well as in letters and other documents.

We are fortunate in having vast numbers of coins that have come down to us from many times and places in the Islamic world. The right to strike coins (*sikka*) was one of the two major prerogatives of sovereignty, the other being the *khuṭba*, of which more later. The inscription on the coinage became a standard method of asserting or recognizing sovereignty, as well as of accepting or renouncing the suzerainty of some superior ruler elsewhere. When a local or provincial ruler or governor struck coins in his own name, omitting the name of the caliph or sultan who previously held sway over that province, this was, like omission from the *khuṭba*, a public declaration of independence. The quality and weight of the metal might also convey a message. When the Umayyad Caliph ʿAbd al-Malik introduced a new gold coinage—hitherto a Roman and Byzantine prerogative—with inscriptions in Arabic, using the Islamic creed to replace the diadem and cross of the Byzantine emperors, his purpose was clear. It was well understood by the emperor in Constantinople, who saw it as a casus *belli* and responded accordingly. Coins and their inscriptions were also a way by which rebels would announce their rebellion and even make statements. The brothers ʿAbdullah and Musʿab b. al-Zubayr, asserting their claim to the Caliphate against the Umayyads, struck coins in their names. There are other coins struck by rebel groups such as the Carmathians, the Zanj, and the Assassins.[5]

Coins and inscriptions are the only hard evidence that we have for most of the medieval period; that is to say, the only genuine contemporary records from a period from which practically no archives have remained intact and only scattered individual documents have survived. The papyri and the Geniza, though not archives, comprise significant numbers of such documents, but they are limited in time, in place (both are from Egypt) and in content. The inscriptions tend to be rather monotonous and repetitive, particularly on coins. They do however provide important information, especially inscriptions in mosques, on gates, in markets, at fountains and other public services, to advertise (I use the word advisedly) the name of the benefactor and to gain good will and support. Inscriptions may be used to claim credit for good works, to indicate the extension of one's authority and—a favorite—to remit taxes. A recurring problem for medieval Islamic governments was the imposition of the so-called *mukūs*, illegal taxes; illegal, that is to say, in the sense that they are not approved by the Holy Law. The Holy Law is very detailed and very explicit on the subject of taxation. But the taxes approved by the Holy Law rarely sufficed for the needs of government. A whole series of taxes was therefore imposed by administrative action, by customary law, by a ruler's decree and other methods, which were strongly disapproved by the doctors of the Holy Law. One of the commonplaces in describing the piety of a pious ruler is that he abolishes the illegal taxes. To judge from the inscriptions, the same illegal taxes were abolished again and again, without any documentary evidence that they were ever reimposed.

Inscriptions were sometimes used to proclaim victories, for the edification of residents and visitors. A notable example is Saladin's simple and modest inscription on the *minbar* of the Aqsa mosque in Jerusalem, celebrating his reconquest of the city from the Crusaders.

More commonly, such announcements were made by the so-called victory letter, which a ruler sent to his colleagues and others, announcing a victory. This might be the defeat of an enemy in battle, the conquest or recovery of territory, or other military successes. Such letters were promulgated by the caliphs, both ʿAbbasid and Fatimid, and by most other Muslim dynasties. Qalqashandı, in his encyclopedia of bureaucratic usage, devotes a whole chapter to documents of this kind.[6] Some scholars have seen in them a continuation of the Roman *Litterae Laureatae*; others connect them with the old Arabian *maghāzī*, heroic narratives of the exploits of the Arabian tribes and, later, of the Prophet, his companions, and his successors. In time the victory letter became an art form, almost a kind of heroic narrative.

According to ancient tradition, the two arts which the Arabs most admired and in which they most excelled were poetry and eloquence—the first partly, the second wholly concerned with persuasion. Classical Arabic literature in general and historiography in particular quote many examples of contests and of victories in which poets and orators exercised their skills in what a modern observer can readily recognize as propaganda.[7]

In pre-modern times, poetry was in many ways the most interesting and the most elusive of the means of propaganda. In the days before journalists and public relations officers, poets fulfilled these functions for tribes, chiefs and rulers. They had been engaged in these tasks for a long time. The Roman Emperor Augustus, for example, had his court poets in Rome doing public relations work for the empire in general and the emperor in particular. One might even argue that Virgil's great epic, the *Aeneid*, is a public relations job for the Roman imperial idea.

The propagandist function of poetry in ancient Arabia is familiar to all students of Arabic literature. The traditional classification of the different types of poetry includes at least three that have an important element of propaganda: the *fakhr* or boast in which the poet makes propaganda on behalf of himself and his tribe; the *madīḥ* or panegyric, in which he promotes his ruler or patron, and the *hijāʾ*[8] or satire, consisting of negative propaganda against hostile or rival groups or persons. In its earliest and simplest form, as described by the Arab literary historians, the *fakhr* is a technique of battlefield propaganda, designed to strengthen the morale of one's own fighters while undermining that of the enemy. A more peaceful form of propaganda was the *mufākhara*, a kind of friendly contest in which poets and orators from different tribes competed against each other, boasting of their own merits and achievements and belittling their rivals. Poets seem at times to have played an active and even important part in some of the wars and conflicts of early Islamic history, as propagandists on behalf of one or another individual or faction. There are episodes in the biography of the Prophet in which different poets appear among both his supporters and his opponents. From the narrative it is clear that their propaganda efforts, on both sides, were considered important, even dangerous.[9]

The Umayyad Caliphs, and thereafter virtually all Muslim rulers, had court poets. There were also lesser figures who employed poets for advertising and public relations. In this way poetry became, for some, a kind of business, and we have quite detailed information about such matters as the rates of remuneration. These obviously depended on the standing of the patron and the skill of the poet. As in other fields of propaganda, the same material could be re-used. A poem in praise of one ruler could, with slight necessary adjustments, be resold to another. There are many stories in the literary histories of poets moving from the service of one prince to that of another, and sometimes recycling the same poems. The tenth-century Syrian prince Sayf al-Dawla had a staff of poets who, in a sense, are still working for him at the present day, and have misled some insufficiently wary historians into accepting the propaganda line. The Isma'ili Fatimid caliphs, as one would expect, had ideological poets. Ibn Hani', the court poet of the conqueror of Egypt, al-Mu'izz, ably presents the Fatimid case against the 'Abbasids.

Just as coins and inscriptions could be seen by everyone, so poems could be memorized, recited and sung, thus reaching a very wide audience.

Some of the chroniclers of the period give us lists of the official poets. Qa-lqashandī tells us that the Fatimids kept a staff of poets attached to the chancery, divided into two groups—Sunni poets who wrote more respectable Sunni praise, and Isma'ili poets who went in for the much more extreme Isma'ili adulation of the ruler as Imam.[10]

Rulers were not the only ones who employed poets for public relations. They were also used by rebels and sectarian leaders, to disseminate seditious propaganda, and sometimes even for purely personal ends. Poetry was also used for what we would nowadays call the social column, as a way of announcing births, deaths, marriages, and other events of this kind.

Poetry was of course spoken as well as written—indeed, recitation was the primary form of publication, and the written text was in origin merely auxiliary to this purpose.

The advent of Islam introduced a new and immensely important instrument of communication and persuasion—the *khuṭba*, the Friday sermon in the Mosque.[11] Being named in the *khuṭba* is one of the major symbols of authority, going back to very early Islamic times; it is one of the two standard, most widely and generally accepted tokens of sovereignty. Mention in the *khuṭba* is the recognized way of accepting and submitting to the sovereignty or suzerainty of a ruler. Omitting the name from the *khuṭba* is the recognized way of declaring one's independence from a suzerain.

Already in medieval times the *khuṭba* was a major vehicle of communication from the rulers to the ruled. It was an accepted method of proclaiming the deposition or accession of a ruler, the nomination of an heir, and more generally, the presentation of both the achievements and the intentions of rulers. It was also a way of making known, in suitable terms, such major events as the beginning or an end of war, and more particularly, the winning of a victory.

Another form of oratory is that denoted by the Arabic terms *wa'ẓ* or *maw-'iẓa*, a word related to the Hebrew *yo'eṣ*, advisor, and *'ēṣa*, advice or council. The Arabic *wa'ẓ*, with a connotation of guidance or admonition, occurs frequently in the Qur'ān, particularly in reference to revelation and prophecy. Sometimes, as for example in Sūra 24:17, dealing with the calumniators of ʿAʾisha, it has the meaning rather of rebuke. The term *waʿẓ* may denote the admonitions and warnings that poets, scholars and others, like the Old Testament prophets, sometimes addressed publicly to their rulers of the world.

More directly concerned with the arts of persuasion was the *qāṣṣ*, the narrator or reciter. Though often used in the general sense of preacher or orator, the term refers specifically to the practice of telling stories of the great deeds of the past in order to urge an audience to emulate them. The *qāṣṣ* might speak in the mosque or in the street; he might also address the troops before a battle to strengthen morale. The *waʿiẓ* and the *qāṣṣ* had a social and moral role in Islamic society, going far beyond mere propaganda. But the propagandist impact, especially in the early period, was not insignificant.

A very important form of propaganda in all periods is the use of slogans or war cries shouted in unison. In earlier as in modern times, these can be a very effective way of mobilizing support and arousing passion.

Historiography provides useful information about propaganda, and is at times itself an instrument of propaganda. Sunni historical writing is on the whole very sober. In the Sunni view, what happens is important because it represents the working out of God's purpose for mankind, and history is therefore a source of guidance on theology and law, a tangible expression and realization of the Sunna. The Shiʿa by contrast took the view that after the murder of ʿAli and the resignation of his son, history had, so to speak, taken a wrong turn; all non-ʿAlid regimes were illegitimate and all existing societies were, in a sense, living in sin. The defense of the existing order is therefore an important theme of Sunni historiography. Early writing was much affected by this; it was also much affected by the struggles of the time, between family and family, tribe and tribe, faction and faction, region and region. All of these are reflected in the different, sometimes contrasting, narratives that have been meticulously preserved for us by the classical Arab historians.

The historians of medieval Islam, unlike some of their modern colleagues, seem to have been remarkably free from pressure, and expressed themselves with astonishing frankness. But sometimes they were willing, like historians in other times and places, to interpret events in such ways as to support certain ideas, their own or the predominant ideas of the society. Even Tabari, the most meticulous collector of variant narratives, admits to suppressing some stories because they are repugnant or shameful.[12] Sometimes, more specifically, historians slant what they tell to serve a ruler or patron, or more loosely, a faction, a sect, or a tribe. There were many such groups, each with its own propagandist historiography.

Historiography directly sponsored by the ruler to serve the ruler's purpose is much less common in the Islamic world than in Christendom. It appears, however, in the time of the Fatimids, and then more frequently under the Iranian and Turkish dynasties.[13] In the Ottoman Empire it was formalized in the office of the *vakanüvis*, the imperial historiographer.

It is, in the nature of things, more difficult to assemble evidence of the use and effectiveness of visual, as distinct from verbal, propaganda. Islam, like Judaism and unlike Christianity, bans the use of images and makes only limited use of symbols. Because of this tradition, the Middle East has been much less responsive than the countries of Christendom to visual imagery and evocation. Nevertheless, visual propaganda, sometimes relying on living beings as well as on images and symbols, has often been used to arouse sympathy, to gain support, or to project power.

The use of display, of pageantry, of processions, and of ceremony to convey religious and political messages, was familiar in the region since antiquity. A classical example was the black flags of the ʿAbbāsids. Like the red flag in Europe a millennium later, it first appeared as a call to revolution, and was transformed into an emblem of the ruling regime. Display of various kinds was widely used in the ʿAbbasid period and still more in the time of the Fatimids.[14] Some emblems and symbols are primarily religious; others are more specifically related to power, and their use, display and flourishing is intended to strike fear, to overawe or, at the very least, to impress. The short spear or sword is used in a variety of contexts, for example by the *khaṭīb* when he goes up to read the *khuṭba*. Pictures of birds and beasts of prey, a panther or tiger seizing a deer, a hawk pouncing on a bird, such as we can see in the mosaics and frescoes of the Umayyad Palace in Jericho, project an image of power, authority and ferocity. The subliminal message is very clear: this is what will happen to you if you don't behave yourself, if you are disloyal to the ruler. Even architecture may serve a propagandist purpose, as has been demonstrated for both ʿAbbāsid and present-day Baghdad.[15]

An interesting case of visual propaganda occurred after the battle of Varna in 1444, when a Crusader army sent to fight the Ottomans was defeated and the Ottoman sultan Murad II captured a group of Frankish knights, gorgeously attired and caparisoned. He sent them all the way across the Middle East, to Afghanistan and back. The propaganda purpose is obvious: the Ottoman sultan, still in an early stage of Ottoman greatness, was saying to all his neighbors, colleagues and of course rivals: "Look at what I did!" "Look at what I got!" These Frankish knights in full war-kit must have been quite impressive, though they were probably rather tattered by the time they got to Afghanistan.

The methods and techniques of the medieval propagandist are surprisingly similar to those of his modern successors. His main purposes are to promote the cause of his client, and to denigrate possible rivals or opponents. Propagandists for opposing causes may handle the same themes and facts in very different ways, resorting to such familiar devices as selection, suppression, shading, and, when feasible, downright invention.

A favorite trick of propagandists of all times and places is to discredit an

opponent by attributing to him bad or ridiculous characteristics and, more relevantly, bad intentions. Many of these arise from, or give rise to, stereotypes.
These are particularly useful in attacking religious, ethnic or regional opponents.
Propaganda of this kind made extensive use of standardized abusive epithets and
curses, often in the form of rhymes and jingles.

Falsehood is probably as old as speech and certainly much older than writing.
A significant proportion of ancient texts consists of lies, written with the intent
to deceive as part of some propaganda effort. Accusations of falsehood in antiquity
are not unusual. Even the great Greek historian, Herodotus, acclaimed by some
as the "Father of History," was already in antiquity denounced by others as the
"Father of Lies." Ancient religion as well as ancient morality show awareness of
the danger. The ninth of the Ten Commandments forbids the bearing of "false
witness"—the original Hebrew text simply reads "lies." The inscription of Darius
at Persepolis prays to Ahuramazda to protect the land from the three great
enemies—foe, famine, and falsehood.[16]

In the simpler kind of falsehood, the writer simply tells lies in his own name.
In a more complex and insidious kind of falsehood, he fabricates written statements and attributes them to others in order to give them greater credibility
and impact. The same technique may be used without written texts, simply by
starting a rumor. *Flusterpropaganda*, that is, whisper propaganda, was extensively
used by the Third Reich during World War II and then by others. In the Soviet
Union, the manufacture and dissemination of false news was entrusted to a department of the KGB and was given a new name—disinformation.

Modern usage has adopted the terms "black propaganda" and "gray propaganda" to designate propaganda put out under false auspices, the first purporting
to come from the enemy, the second from uninvolved and therefore presumably
impartial outsiders. Though these terms were of course not used, both black and
gray propaganda have a long history.

Even inscriptions could be falsified. A famous example is the construction
text inscribed in the Dome of the Rock in Jerusalem. As is well known, this
great monument was erected by the Umayyad Caliph ʿAbd al-Malik in the year
A.H. 72, corresponding to 691–692 C.E. An inscription in the mosque records
the construction, the date, and the name of the ruler who built it. There is
something odd about the inscription. The name of the ruler is given as ʿAbd
Allāh al-Maʾmūn, and the writing is cramped to fit into a space too narrow to
hold it. What happened can easily be guessed. At a later date, those responsible
for ʿAbbāsid propaganda were uncomfortable with the idea of such excellent
publicity for the dynasty that had been overthrown and superseded by them.
The forger therefore set to work to change the inscription and attribute the
construction, not to the Umayyad Caliph, ʿAbd al-Malik, but to the ʿAbbasid
Caliph ʿAbd Allāh al-Maʾmūn. The forger did not do a very good job. From
the difference in the writing, the name has obviously been changed; to make
matters worse, the forger either forgot or did not think it necessary to change

the date, so that the original date of construction remains. Most forgers, working in materials rather more malleable than stone, do a better job.

Fabrications are usually of two kinds. In the first, the forger—as in the Dome of the Rock—takes an authentic existing text and changes it to suit his purpose. In the second, he fabricates the text in its entirety, and attributes it to a real or imaginary author of his own choosing or invention.

In the early Islamic centuries there could be no better way of promoting a cause, an opinion, or a faction, than to cite an appropriate action or utterance of the Prophet—in a word, a *ḥadīth*. The many conflicts of early Islamic history inevitably gave rise to a good deal of propagandist distortion and invention. At a very early date, Muslim scholars became aware of the dangers of spurious or dubious *ḥadīth*, created or adapted to serve some ulterior purpose. They responded to this danger by devising and applying an elaborate science of *ḥadīth* criticism, designed to distinguish the true from the false. Remarkably, the creation of new *ḥadīths* designed to serve some political purpose has continued even to our own time. A tradition published in the Jerusalem daily newspaper *al-Nahār* on 15 December 1990, and described as "currently in wide circulation," quotes the Prophet as predicting that "the Greeks and Franks will join with Egypt in the desert against a man named Ṣādim, and not one of them will return." The allusion is clearly to the build-up of coalition forces leading up to the Gulf War. It has not been possible to find any reference to this tradition earlier than 1990, and it is not difficult to guess when, where and for what purpose this *ḥadīth* was invented.[17]

This obviously spurious *ḥadīth* is a typical example of a favorite technique of the forger. He begins with a "prediction" which is remarkably accurate, because it was in fact written *after* the events which it predicts, and having thus gained the confidence of the listener, he continues with a prediction of events yet to occur. The second, genuine prediction, as in this case, is usually wrong.

Predictions of this kind were central to another form of propaganda, the apocalyptic and eschatological tracts known as *malāḥim* (sg. *malḥama*). Writings of this kind circulated among Jews and Christians, both before and after the advent of Islam. Examples may be found in both the Old and New Testaments. Muslim predictions often have a specific political agenda. They purport to describe the struggles at the end of time between good and evil and the final triumph of a messianic figure who, in the common phrase, "will fill the world with justice and equity as it is now filled with injustice and oppression." These predictions were used to convey a message of religious dissent and protest against the existing order, and to support the claim of a rebel pretender to the headship of the Islamic community. Such pretenders made a great effort to conform to prophecies that were current at the time and thus to cast themselves in the role of the expected savior. The implication was clear; the existing regime was evil, and the rebel leader would establish a truly just society. Such claims and promises were characteristic of the propaganda of the ʿAbbasids, the Fatimids, the

Almohades and some other regimes that grew out of revolutionary movements. The first caliphs of both the ʿAbbāsid and Fāṭimid dynasties adopted regnal titles with messianic implications, no doubt to persuade their subjects that these rulers were indeed engaged in the messianic mission of establishing the kingdom of heaven on earth.[18] After the first few caliphs of both dynasties, the claim began to wear rather thin, and the titles adopted by later caliphs had somewhat less ambitious formulations.

The themes of propaganda may be grouped under four main headings: political, principally personal and dynastic; ethnic, reflecting inter-Arab rivalries and then rivalries between Arabs and other groups; local—exchanges of abuse and sometimes merely of good-humored banter between rival provinces, cities, or neighbourhoods. A different expression of this is the so-called *faḍāʾil* literature,[19] lauding the merits of particular places—a blend of local pride and tourist propaganda. Related to these are the books on *ziyārāt*, visits to the graves of saints and other holy places, designed for the pilgrim trade.[20] Another type of *faḍāʾil* book appears at the time of the Crusades and deals with some lost territories in the Syro-Palestinian area. Here again the propaganda theme is obvious. And, finally, in many ways the most important is religious propaganda, arising from the unending debate about doctrines and practices, leadership and power.

The introduction of modern technologies of communication—the printing press and the newspaper, telegraph and telephone, radio and television, fax and internet—have enormously increased and accelerated the production and distribution of propaganda. They have, however, added remarkably little to its basic themes and purposes.

Notes

1. The classical studies on this subject are W. Ivanow, "The Organization of the Fatimid Propaganda," in *Journal of the Bombay Branch of the Royal Asiatic Society*, 15 (1939): 1–35, and Marius Canard, "L'impérialisme des Fatimides et leur propagande," in *Annales de l'Institut de'Études Orientales de la Faculté des Lettres d'Alger* 5 (1939–1941): 151–93. For a more recent study, see Farhad Daftary, *The Ismāʿīlīs: Their History and Doctrines*, Cambridge, 1990.

2. The Arabic phrase he uses is *"Al-biḍāʿa bāʿira kāsida."* Al-Muʾayyad fiʾl-Dīn, *Sīra*, ed. Muḥammad Kāmil Ḥusayn, Cairo, 1949, p. 79.

3. On ʿAbbāsid propaganda, see especially Moshe Sharon, *Black Banners from the East*, Jerusalem–Leiden, 1983; Jacob Lassner, *Islamic Revolution and Historical Memory: an Inquiry into the Art of ʿAbbāsid Apologetics,* New Haven, Connecticut, 1986.

4. Emmanuel Sivan, *L'Islam et la Croisade: idéologie et propagande dans les réactions musulmanes aux Croisades*, Paris, 1968; Cemal Kafadar, *Between Two Worlds: the Construction of the Ottoman State*, Berkeley–Los Angeles, 1995, especially pp. 62 ff.

5. See for example, John Walker, "A Rare Coin of the Zanj," in *JRAS* (1933):651–55; Paul Casanova, "Monnaie des Assassins de Perse," in *Révue Numismatique* 11 (1893), 3e *série* XI, pp. 343–52; idem, "Monnaie du chef des Zendj (264/877–8)," in *RN* 11 (1893), 3e série XI, pp. 510–16; Antonio Prieto y Vives, "Numismatica Qarmata" in *al-Andalus*, (1933), pp. 301–5. Carmathian coins appear in several collections; see for example L. A. Mayer, *Bibliography of Muslim Numismatics* 2, London, 1954, items 986, 1276, 1277, 1373, 1383.

6. Qalqashandī, *Ṣubḥ al-aʿshā*, Cairo 1334/1915, vol. 8, pp. 274–290 (cf. vol. 7, p. 366).

7. The report of a colloquium, *Prédication et propagande au Moyen Age: Islam, Byzance, Occident*, Paris 1983, includes essays on poetry and more especially on preaching. On the role of various types of preachers, see Johannes Pedersen, "The Islamic Preacher: wāʿiẓ, mudhakkir, qāṣṣ" in *Ignáce Goldziher Memorial Volume*, Budapest, 1948, pp. 226–51 and idem, "Den Arabiske og Muhammedanske Taler," in *Religionshistoriska Studier tillägnade Edvard Lehmann, den 19 Aug. 1927*, pp. 152–64.

8. There is also a magical element in poetry. It is surely significant that the Arabic word for satire *hijāʾ* is akin to the Hebrew root h - g - h/y, meaning witchcraft, or casting a spell (cf. Isaiah 8:19). Satire does not just mean being nasty; it is being nasty to practical effect.

9. See for example the accounts of the events after the battle of Badr and after the capture of Mecca, in Ibn Hishām, *Sīrat Rasūl Allāh*, ed. F. Wüstenfeld, Göttingen, 1858–60, pp. 819–20, 994–96. For contrasting discussions by modern scholars see W. Montgomery Watt, *Muhammad at Medina*, Oxford, 1956, pp. 15, 68, and Maxime Rodinson, *Mohammed* (English translation), London, 1961, pp. 157–58, 171–72, 261–62. At the time of the Salman Rushdie affair, the killings of poets and singers described in these pages were cited by some in Iran as a prophetic endorsement of execution by assassination.

10. Qalqashandī, *Ṣubḥ al-aʿshā*, vol. 3, p. 497.

11. See El², s.vv. "Khaṭīb," (J. Pedersen) and "Khuṭba," (A.J. Wensinck) also Albrecht Noth, *Quellenkritische Studien zu Themen, Formen und Tendenzen frühislamischer Geschichtsüberlieferung*, Bonn, 1973, pp. 81–90.

12. See e.g., Ṭabarī, *Taʾrīkh*, i, pp. 2862, 2965, 2980.

13. Historians directly in the service of a royal or quasi-royal patron include ʿUtbī (for Maḥmūd of Ghaznā), Rāwandī (for the Seljuqs), ʿImād al-Dīn and Bahā al-Dīn (for Saladin), Juvaynī (for the Mongols), Tursun (for Mehmed II), Niẓām al-Dīn Shāmī (for Timur Lang), etc.

14. See Paula Sanders, *Ritual, Politics and the City in Fatimid Cairo*, New York, 1994, especially chapters 4 and 6.

15. For the first, see Jacob Lassner, *The Shaping of ʿAbbāsid Rule*, Princeton, 1980, pp. 163ff; for the latter, Samir al-Khalil, *The Monument: Art, Vulgarity and Responsibility in Iraq*, Berkeley–Los Angeles, 1991.

16. Mary Boyce, *Textual Sources for the Study of Zoroastrianism*, Chicago, 1984, p. 105.

17. Cited in Michael Cook, "Eschatology and the Dating of Traditions," in *Princeton Papers in Near Eastern Studies* 1 (1992): 25–6.

18. B. Lewis, "The Regnal Titles of the First ʿAbbāsid Caliphs," in *Dr. Zakir Husain Presentation Volume*, New Delhi, 1968, pp. 13–22.

19. See El², s.v. "Faḍīla." (R. Sellheim).

20. The first modern scholar to draw attention to this literature was Ignaz Goldziher, in his *Muhammedanische Studien*, Halle, 1890, vol. 2, p. 318. For a more recent survey see, Janine Sourdel-Thomine, *Guide des lieux de pèlerinage* (translation of al-Harawī), Damascus, 1957, pp. xxx–xxxv.

9

Monarchy in the Middle East

֍

The word *monarchy* has been, and at times still is, used in two different senses. One of them is indicated by its etymology, from two Greek words, the first meaning "single" or "alone," the second meaning "rule." In this sense monarchy means one-man personal rule—the rule of an individual—as contrasted in ancient and medieval times with aristocracy and oligarchy, or in modern times with democracy. Often the term also carries a connotation of arbitrary rule. The Arabic term used to render monarchy in this sense, *istibdād*, usually has this connotation and is contrasted with *shūrā* or *mashwara* (consultation). *Istibdād* conveys the idea of a ruler who governs in accordance with his personal desires and caprice without consulting those whom it would be appropriate to consult.[1] Traditional Islamic literature lays great emphasis on the importance of consultation, with both statesmen and men of religion.

The other connotation of the term "monarchy" relates not to the exercise but to the acquisition of supreme sovereign authority. In this sense monarchy means hereditary, that is, dynastic rule, in which the headship of the state is transmitted from one member to another of the same family. It is membership of this family that confers legitimacy, that is, the primary basis of entitlement of whoever accedes to the supreme sovereign office after the death or removal of his predecessor. In this sense, the converse of a monarchy is a republic.

The two connotations of monarchy are not the same, though they may overlap. At some times and in some places, especially in recent years, they may even appear to be contradictory. In Europe, for example, the surviving monarchies are without exception constitutional democracies. Most of them have been so for a long time and show every sign of continuing along the same path. Most of the democratic republics, in contrast, have a brief and checkered history. The surviving tyrannies in the modern world are with few exceptions republics, not monarchies.

The Arabic term *malik* has been used to convey both meanings of "monarch." If you consult an English-Arabic or Arabic-English dictionary, you will be told with the laconic and sometimes specious certitude of lexicographers that *malik* equals "king" and "king" equals *malik*. This is, of course, misleading. There are times and places when that equation may be correct. But mostly, the connotations of these terms, and for that matter of other equivalent terms in various languages, differ considerably.

In talking about the use of royal titles among the Arabs, we are not obliged to rely only on literary evidence, itself often based on fallible human memory. We have hard evidence—coins and inscriptions, many of them dated—where we can follow the development and ramification of royal titulature.

The earliest uses of the title are on the whole positive. There were the kings of Kinda and of Hira, known from the literary tradition. The oldest surviving inscription in the Arabic language, an epitaph of 328 C.E. found at Namara, commemorates a "king (*malik*) of all the Arabs, who wore the diadem. . . . No king until this time had attained what he had attained."[2] The last Byzantine emperor to rule over Egypt and the Syrian lands before the advent of Islam, Heraklius, adopted the king-title *basileus*, in addition to the usual Byzantine title *autokrator*, to celebrate the Christian victory over the infidel Persians, in particular the recovery of the Holy Land and the Holy City of Jerusalem. The term *basileus* brought with it an echo of the ancient kings of Israel celebrated in the Bible and of Christ the king.

But among the ancient Arabs kingship often had a negative connotation. The Bedouin, like other nomads, dislike any kind of central authority. An Arabic word, *liqāh*, is explained as meaning "those who had never submitted to a king," and there is a poem attributed to the pre-Islamic Arabic poet Abid ibn al-Abras in which he says in praise of his own tribe: "They refused to be servants of kings, and were never ruled by any. But when they were called on for help in war, they responded gladly."[3]

The earliest specifically Islamic references to kings and kingship are mostly negative and very much resemble the picture that emerges from the Hebrew Bible, particularly from the Book of Samuel, of the events that led to the troubled beginnings of the Israelite monarchy. In both Qur'an and *hadith* the word *malik* is sometimes used as a divine epithet, in which case of course it has a positive meaning. As applied to mortals, it often carries a connotation of presumption and even of paganism.[4] Both David and Solomon appear in the Qur'an and both are positively portrayed. But both are prophets and, though depicted in royal splendor, are not designated by the word *malik*. The only one of the ancient Israelite kings expressly designated as such in the Qur'an is Saul, in the Qur'anic version called Talut, and he has the same rather equivocal image in the Qur'an as in the Book of Samuel.[5]

In the early Islamic centuries the words *king* and *kingship* often retain this rather negative connotation, especially when contrasted with *caliph* and *caliphate*. An early narrative preserved by Tabari records a conversation between the caliph 'Umar and the Persian convert Salman: "Salman said that 'Umar said to him: 'Am I a king or a caliph?' And Salman answered: 'If you have taxed the lands of the Muslim one dirham, or more, or less, and applied to unlawful purposes, then you are a king not a caliph.' And 'Umar wept."[6] The contrast between *kingship* and *caliphate* is clearly indicated in this anecdote. The essential difference is not between elective and dynastic succession, since the latter very rapidly became the norm in the caliphate, too, but between arbitrary rule and government in accordance with the divine law.

The term *malik* was thus used in the early Islamic centuries to denote rulers whose authority was primarily military and political—or, as we might say, "secular"—rather than religious and whose manner of ruling was arbitrary and personal rather than lawful and religious. But the dynastic principle was not seriously challenged and was argued in an extreme form by the Shi'a for whom the only legitimate dynasty is that of the descendants of the Prophet. The title *king* (*malik*) was not replaced but rather overtopped by more exalted titles with an imperial rather than a royal connotation. These may be Arab, like *sulṭān*, or Persian, like *shāh* and *pādishāh*, or Turkish and Mongol, like *khaqan* and *khan*.

As the use of these titles became more general among Muslim dynasties, the title *king* acquired another and different negative connotation—that of subordination. With the rise of independent principalities within the caliphate, more or less the title was used by many of the new princes. Their titulature makes it clear that it was no longer a title of sovereignty. The king, the *malik*, was less than the caliph and the sultan, and while asserting his own authority he nevertheless recognized the higher authority of a suzerain. Another distinctive feature is that the king in this period does not claim kingship of any place or people. His title is simply *al-malik*, usually followed by some adjective, such as "the Excellent," "the Perfect," and the like.

The title *king*, followed by an enumeration of the peoples and lands over which kingship is claimed or exercised, was at first used principally of foreign and infidel rulers. These include the Byzantine emperor, the king of Nubia, and various Christian European kings collectively known as *mulūk al-kuffār* (the kings of the unbelievers) or even as *mulūk al-kufr* (the kings of unbelief). Tabari tells a revealing story about an exchange of diplomatic messages between the Byzantine emperor Nikephorus and the caliph Harun al-Rashid. Nikephorus addressed the caliph as "Harun, king of the Arabs." From the point of view of the emperor this was no doubt a correct title, since he himself used the title *king* (*basileus*) and was king of the Romans. He was doing Harun the honor of giving him the same kind of title as he used himself. But for the caliph—"the commander of the faithful"—to be called "king of the Arabs" was a double insult. It implied that he was only a king—and only of the Arabs! He expressed his anger in his reply to the emperor, headed "From Harun, Commander of the Faithful, to Nikephorus, Dog of the Romans" (Min Hārūn, amīr al-mu'minīn ilā Niqfūr, Kalb al-Rūm).[7]

In later medieval centuries, both territorial and ethnic titles begin to appear in Muslim royal titulature. Some of these are rather vague: for example, *Malik al-Barrayn wa'l-Bahrayn* (King of the Two Lands and the Two Seas), used by the Mamluks and later adopted by the Ottomans. For the Mamluks the two seas were the Mediterranean and the Red Sea; for the Ottomans, the Mediterranean and the Black Sea. An even earlier title used by the Seljuks was *Malik al-Mashriq wa'l-Maghrib* (King of the East and the West), which looks rather like a claim to universal sovereignty. Another interesting title is *Malik al-Mulūk* (King of Kings), clearly a translation of the Persian *Shāhanshāh*. The Buyid dynasty also used such titles as *Malik al-Umam* (King of the Nations) and even *Malik al-Dawla* (King of the State). Some titles appear to be ethnic. Thus, Mamluk sultans called themselves, as part of a string of titles, *Malik al-'Arab wa'l-'Ajam* (King of the Arabs and Persians); perhaps a fair translation would be "King of the Arabs and everyone else."[8] In Ottoman times this becomes *al 'Arab wa'l-'Ajam wa'l-Rūm* (King of the Arabs and non-Arabs and the Rum), *Rum* at that time meaning the Ottomans and the Ottoman lands. These are not claims to ethnic leadership but rather denote the assertion of universal supreme sovereignty.

Titles defining a territorial or national kingdom, commonplace in Europe, were until the twentieth century almost unknown in the Islamic world. A few Turkish rulers in pre-Ottoman Anatolia, no doubt influenced by the usage of the peoples whom they had just conquered, sometimes struck coins or wrote inscriptions with territorial titles. But these are rare and atypical and were of brief duration. In the later medieval and subsequent centuries the petty sovereignties and autonomous principalities typical of the Islamic Middle Ages had for the most part disappeared. Most of the Islamic Middle East was divided among a small number of major states, the rulers of which used imperial rather than royal titles. The term *malik* survived principally in two contexts: as a component, of no special significance, in the string of titles and honorifics used by the Ottoman and other emperors; and as a designation for European and other infidel rulers. It was in the latter but not in the former context that the term denoted sovereignty and related to a particular place and people. In Turkish these monarchs were usually given the title *kiral*, a loan-word from Slavic or Hungarian. In Arabic they were called "*malik*" sometimes replaced by the explicitly condemnatory term "*ṭāghiya*" or "*taghūt*", with a connotation of insolence and usurpation.

In the twentieth century the *malik* title enjoyed both a revival of popularity and an improvement in status. This change is a reflection of Western, more particularly British, usage and derived its popularity and prestige from the sovereign institution of what was then the greatest empire in the world. The first modern Muslim ruler to use the title appears to have been Sharif Hussein, who declared himself king of the Hijaz in 1916. He was followed by his son Faysal, who proclaimed an Arab kingdom in Syria in 1920 and, after the failure of that adventure, became king of Iraq in 1921. In 1922 he was followed by the ruler of Egypt, where the ruling dynasty had changed its titles several times. The line of Muhammad Ali came to power in Egypt as Ottoman pashas. They changed their titles successively to *khedive*, to declare their autonomy under the Ottoman sultan, and then to *sultan*—using the Ottoman suzerain's own title—to declare their independence. In the same way the title *king*—that used by the ruler of Britain himself—served to proclaim independence from Britain.

Others followed. The most important was Ibn Saud, who in 1926 proclaimed himself king of the Hijaz and sultan of Najd. In 1932 the two were merged in a kingdom with a new name—Saudi Arabia. Later in Morocco, Jordan, and Libya the adoption of the royal title served the same purpose as it had in Egypt at an earlier date, namely, that of declaring independence against a European suzerain power.

Through all these changes, the dynastic principle and the practice of hereditary succession remained powerful, deep-rooted, and virtually universal in the Islamic Middle East. Even in the nomadic tribes, the *shaikh* is normally chosen from among the members of one family, who have a recognized hereditary claim to the headship of the tribe and very often to the custody of some sacred place or object—the palladium or ark of the covenant, so to speak. Similar practices may be observed also among Iranian and Turkic nomads. The principle of primogeniture—of succession from father to eldest son in the direct—is a European idea. It was not accepted among the ancient Arabs, and it never took root in the great Muslim dynastic empires. Descent in the male line from the founding and the ruling families was the sole requirement. The most usual practice was for the ruler to designate his successor, choosing whichever of his uncles, brothers, nephews, or sons might be the most suitable. Sometimes the ruler might designate more than one in line, though this was neither usual nor required.

The advent of Islam changed this only briefly. The death of the Prophet posed an immediate question of succession. As Prophet, he could have no successor. But the Prophet had not only created a religious community; he had also founded a state, which was rapidly becoming an empire, and that state urgently needed a sovereign. At a very early date the famous split occurred between the Sunni and the Shi'ite views, the Shi'a doctrine being frankly dynastic. According to them, only the lineal descendants of the Prophet are entitled to rule as his successors. Since the Prophet had no descendants in the male line, a unique exception is made in favor of the descendants of his daughter, Fatima. The Sunni view, in contrast, as formerly set forth, was that the caliphate should be elective. This should not be understood in modern terms of universal suffrage. The juristic concept of election means that on the death of the caliph the most suitable successor is chosen by a small college of qualified electors.

The first four caliphs after the death of the Prophet were indeed elected in the sense that none of them had a hereditary claim to the succession. If one asks the pragmatic question—did the elective system work?—the answer must surely be that it did not. Of the four elective caliphs three were murdered—the last two by fellow Muslims—and the whole system collapsed in a bloody civil war. The emergence of the dynastic caliphates and sultanates was the result.

Republican, that is, nonhereditary, sovereignties were not unknown in the Islamic world. We have descriptions from Arabic and Turkish writers of the Italian republics in the Middle Ages and of the Dutch and English republics in the seventeenth century. But they showed no great interest in this form of government. The first European republic to obtrude itself forcibly on Muslim attention was the French republic. Early reactions to it were almost uniformly negative. The Ottoman historian Asim at the beginning of the nineteenth century likens the politics of the French republic to "the rumblings and crepitations of a queasy stomach."[9] But republicanism, often confused with democracy, began to exercise an increasing fascination, and during the twentieth century republicanism—and with it republican forms of government—developed rapidly. The earliest republics were those established in the Muslim territories of the fallen Russian Empire, when the temporary relaxation of pressure from the capital after the revolutions of 1917 allowed a brief interval of local independence and experimentation. In May 1918, after the dissolution of the short-lived Trans-Caucasian Federation, the Azerbaijani members of the Trans-Caucasian Parliament declared Azerbaijan an independent republic—the first Muslim republic in modern times. It was of brief duration and in April 1920 was conquered by the Red Army and reconstituted as a Soviet republic. The same pattern was followed by other Turkic and Muslim peoples of the Russian Empire, whose short-lived national republics were all in due course taken over and reconstituted as Soviet republics or regions within the USSR. The first Muslim republic to be established outside the Russian Empire seems to have been the Tripolitanian Republic, proclaimed in November 1918. It was later incorporated in the Italian colony of Libya. The first independent republic that remained both independent and a republic was that of Turkey, established on 29 October 1923. Republican institutions were created by the French in the mandated territories of Syria and Lebanon.

In the aftermath of World War II, the decline of the once dominant British Empire and the rise to power and prominence of the United States and the Soviet Union contributed to the devaluation of royalty and the new popularity of republics. In one country after another monarchs were overthrown, by coup or revolution, and replaced by presidents and leaders presiding over republics of various complexions: Egypt in 1953, Sudan in 1956, Iraq in 1958, Tunisia in 1959, Yemen in 1962, Afghanistan in 1973, Iran in 1979. In many of these states the term *republic* denotes neither the Islamic converse of arbitrary rule nor the Western converse of dynasticism.

The institution of kingship or, more specifically, the use of royal titles, was under attack from various sides: by liberals and leftists who saw a republican form of government as more in accord with their ideologies and aspirations; by Muslim fundamentalists who had revived the tradition of Islamic condemnation of royal pomp and titulature; and more generally by those who felt that monarchy was old-fashioned and republics were modern and progressive.

Monarchies are now clearly a minority in the Middle East, yet the dynastic principle has remained extremely powerful even to the present day. The last and most enduring of the great Islamic empires, that of the Ottomans, took its name and identity from the founding and ruling dynasty—the House of Osman ('Uthmān). In the same way, Saudi Arabia, probably the most Arab and most Islamic of the states in the region, takes its name and identity from the founding and ruling dynasty. More remarkably, even in the modern, avowedly secular regimes of Syria and Iraq, it is striking that both Saddam Hussein and Hafiz al-Asad seemed determined to found dynasties or at least to ensure the succession of their sons. Both royalty and democracy are under siege in the Middle East, but dynasticism, it would seem, is alive and well.

Bibliographical Note

The numismatic and epigraphic evidence in the use of *malik* in medieval Islamic states was reviewed and analyzed by Hasan al-Basha, *Al-Alqāb al-Islāmiyya f'il-ta'rīkh wa'l-watha'iq wa'l-āthār* (Cairo: Maktabat al-Nahda al-Misriyya, 1957), pp. 496–506, and al-Basha, *Al-Funūn al-Islāmiyya wasl-wazaif ala al-Arabiyya*, 3 (Cairo: Maktabat al-Nahda al-Misriyya, 1966), pp. 1139–42. The literary evidence relating to pre-Islamic Arabia was examined by Emile Tyan, *Institutions du droit public musulman*, 1, *Le Califat* (Paris, 1954), pp. 75–84, and Francesco Gabrieli, *Tribu e Stato nell'antica poesia araba*, in his *L'Islam nella storia* (Bari, 1966), pp. 9–26. The reappearance of monarchical titles and their use by Muslim rulers have been studied by Wilferd Madelung, "The Assumption of the Title Shahanshah by the Buyids" and the "Reign of the Daylam Dawlat al-Daylam," *Journal of Near Eastern Studies*, 28 (1969), pp. 84–108 and 168–83, and by C. E. Bosworth, "The Titulature of the Early Ghaznavids," *Oriens*, 15 (1962), pp. 210–33. The revival and use of the term in the nineteenth and twentieth centuries was studied by Ami Ayalon, "Malik in Modern Middle Eastern Titulature," in *Die Welt des Islam*, 23–24 (1984), pp. 306–19. On royal titles in general, see Bernard Lewis, *The Political Language of Islam* (Chicago: University of Chicago Press, 1988), pp. 96ff.

Notes

An earlier version of some parts of this chapter was published in my article, "Malik," in *Cahiers de Tunisie*, Tunis, 35, no. 139–40 (1987), pp. 101–9.

1. B. Lewis, "Usurpers and Tyrants; Notes on Some Islamic Political Terms," in Roger M. Savory and Dionisius A. Agius (eds.), *Logos Islamikos: Studia Islamica in honorem Georgiii Michaelis Wickens*, Papers in Mediaeval Studies 6 (Toronto: Pontifical Institute of Mediaeval Studies, 1984), pp. 259–267.

2. *RCEA (Repertoire Chronologique d'Epigraphie arabe)*, 1 (Cairo, 1931), n. 1.

3. The *diwans* of Abid b. al-Abras and Amir b. at-Tufayl, ed. and tr. Sir Charles Lyall (Leiden, 1913), p. 64; text, p. 81 (London, printed for the trustees of the "E.J.W. Gibb Memorial" by Luzac).

4. See, for example, Qur'an 12, where *malik* is commonly used for pharaoh; cf. 27, 34, where the queen of Sheba remarks to Solomon: "When kings enter a city, they pillage it and make its nobles destitute. Thus do kings."

5. Qur'an 2, 247 ff.

6. Tabari, *Ta'rīkh al-Rusul wa'l-Mulūk*, 1, p. 2754.

7. Ibid., 3, pp. 695–96.

8. Al-Basha, *Al-Alqāb al-Islāmiyya fi'l-ta'rīkh wa'l-wathā'iq wa'l-āthār* (Cairo, 1957), pp. 497, 502–5; RCEA, 6, p. 2177, 7, pp. 2377, 2378, 2707, 2734, 2760; 9, p. 3509; 10, p. 3739; 11, pp. 3273, 4308;12, p. 4554.

9. Ahmed Asim, *Tarikh* (Istanbul, n.d.), 1, p. 78.

10

Religion and Murder
in the Middle East

❧❧❧❧

The theme of this meeting is "The Modern State and Political Assassination." My purpose is to add some dimensions, both of time and space, to the topic—extending it outward to the Middle East as a region and backward at least until Biblical times, and to emphasize one aspect which has received passing attention but not, I suspect, sufficient for our purposes. That is the religious aspect—the citing of religion as a motive and as a justification for murder.

Let me start with the year 656 C.E. and the assassination of 'Uthman, the third caliph, that is to say, the third in the succession to the Prophet in the headship of the Muslim community. Of the first four caliphs, three were murdered, but the third was crucial. The second, 'Umar, was murdered by a disgruntled slave, who was neither a Muslim nor an Arab; his act therefore had no religious or political significance. 'Uthman was murdered by Muslim Arab mutineers, and his murder was the signal for a devastating civil war.

The issue in this civil war may be simply stated. Was the killing of 'Uthman, as some claimed, an act of rebellion, a crime the perpetrators of which should be punished? Or was it, as others claimed, an act of justice; not a murder but an execution, the killing of a ruler who was a tyrant and more important, a usurper, whose removal therefore was the duty of every good Muslim? This was the issue in the first civil war in Islam—a war which in a sense continues to the present day. Those who adopted the first point of view, that this was a crime, came to be known as the Sunni Muslims, while those who adopted the opposing point of view, that this was the punishment of a crime, came to be known as the Shi'a. A little later, 'Uthman's successor, 'Ali, was also murdered, this time by a dissident within his own camp, exemplifying the second major theme of religious-political murder in the Middle East.

For religious cults to be based on victims is not unusual. It is less common, but by no means unknown, for religious cults to center not on the victims but on the perpetrators. The idea of tyrannicide was not new. The Middle East had for centuries been part of the Greco-Roman world, and tyrannicide—murdering the tyrant and ridding society of oppression—was a familiar theme. Among the more famous victims were Philip II of Macedon, Tiberius Gracchus and, most famous of all, Julius Caesar, whose murder provided Shakespeare with the theme of what is certainly the best dramatic presentation of political assassination.

There was also a Jewish background in antiquity. One could argue that the first recorded murder in history, the murder of Abel by Cain, was a religiously motivated assassination, since its cause was that while both were competing for God's attention, one felt that the other was getting an unfair advantage. There are other stories of assassinations in the Old Testament and Apocrypha, with such notable assassins as Ehud and Judith. But these are different in that they were murdering foreigners, oppressors of Israel. Much more relevant is the case of Jehu, who received, so he believed, a message from God transmitted to him through a great religious leader, instructing him to kill the king and take his place. We have in our modern language an Oedipus Complex, which we draw from ancient Greek drama. We might adopt another psychological term—a Jehu Complex—drawn from the Hebrew Testament. Such a complex surely affected that notorious group of organized assassins known as the Zealots or Sicarii, who were active in the final stages of ancient Jewish statehood, and perhaps contributed to its ending.

In the early centuries of the Islamic era, from about the 8th century onwards, religious murder becomes a recurring theme, and we find the curious phenomenon of religious sects which practise murder as a religious obligation. There are several distinctive features about these, for example, the specialization on a single way of committing murder. This has a ritual, an almost sacramental significance. One group of murderers only strangled their victims—an obvious resemblance, perhaps a connection, with the Indian Thugs. Another group clubbed them to death, believing that only on the Day of Judgment would they be allowed to use steel. The most famous of the assassins, those from whom the name is derived, only used daggers. It is striking that they avoided poison, missile weapons and other relatively safe methods of dispatching an opponent. The close personal contact between killer and victim was important, as was the element of self-sacrifice.

Two excerpts from medieval sources typify two different perceptions of the role of the assassin.

The first is from a Persian poet of the early 13th century, himself a supporter, probably a member, of the Assassin order: "Brothers," he says, "when the time of triumph comes . . . then by one single warrior on foot a king may be stricken with terror, though he own more than a hundred thousand horsemen."[1] That expresses, vividly and simply, the self-perception of the political assassin, or, as we might say nowadays, of the terrorist.

The second comes from a European source. When the Assassins, that is to say the group in Syria to which the name was first applied, terrorized both the Crusaders and the Muslim princes, they nevertheless spared and even paid tribute to the two Christian knightly orders, the Knights Templar and the Knights Hospitaler. The medieval French historian Joinville explains why. Speaking of the head of the Assassin order he says: "He paid tribute to the Templars and to the Hospitalers because they feared nothing from his Assassins, since the leader of the Assassins could gain nothing if he caused the Master of the Temple or the Master of the Hospital to be killed; for he knew very well that if he had one killed another just as good would replace him, and for this reason he did not wish to lose assassins where he could gain nothing by it."[2]

One might argue that democracies have a similar advantage. Assassination is effective in autocratic regimes and, indeed, it emerged from a society where autocracy was the norm. Then as now, much could be accomplished by the removal of a dictator, but assassin chiefs might well hesitate to waste assassins on a readily replaceable politician. Modern terrorism, mostly directed against democracies, may perhaps be the assassins' answer to this dilemma.

Medieval accounts of the Assassins focus mainly on the victims—known and public figures, publicly dispatched. They also provide some, mostly hearsay reports about the mysterious chief who trained and sent the assassin to perform his deadly task. They say very little about the killer himself, who appears from nowhere, to kill and die in silence.

But a few points emerge. One, fairly obvious, is that the assassin is a dedicated volunteer; this is no work for conscripts or mercenaries. Another is that he does not expect—or perhaps even desire—to survive his mission. According to some accounts it was considered disgraceful for him to survive. He had to get up close to his victim and made no attempt to escape—not that there would have been much chance anyway. The story is told of one who survived and escaped; his mother went into mourning in shame for her son. The medieval Persian author Hamdullah Mustawfi tells us that among these people, to commit no murder was regarded as a great sin.[3] The suicide bomber, so to speak, has a long history.

Another recurring theme is that of the delights of paradise, promised to the assassin as an immediate and eternal reward.[4] These aroused the curiosity of European visitors as early as the Middle Ages, and are said to be a major motivation of present-day suicide bombers. There are however important differences between then and now. The medieval assassin did not die by his own hand, but awaited—indeed welcomed—death at the hands of his enemies. Another difference is that the medieval Assassin, at the risk—or rather cost—of his own life, killed only his designated and carefully chosen victim. The random slaughter of uninvolved bystanders, such as market shoppers, bus passengers, café patrons, and school parties, is a modern innovation.

The tactics of the medieval Assassins are probably the earliest example of what one can legitimately call state terrorism. They did not merely operate as an illegal opposition. They seized territory, held castles, and established small principalities of their own. Where this was not feasible, they sometimes managed to secure the complicity of a local ruler—the prince of a city, the governor of a district or the like. For this complicity they paid in money and of course promises of protection, and also by carrying out an occasional assassination which was not part of their own agenda but which might be of service to their accomplice. In this way and probably for the first time in history, the terrorists had at their disposal a kind of state, and consequently were able to attain the level of organization, preparation, training, which this could provide.

A recurring theme is that of elaborate planning and preparation. There are many stories which indicate that an assassination was something prepared over a long period of time, requiring special training, concealment, disguise and infiltration. This, clearly, in its method and more particularly in its purposes, went beyond individual murder.

There is a rather striking geographical resemblance between the medieval Assassins and some modern terrorist movements. They began in Iran and spread to Syria, and these remained their principal bases throughout the medieval period. For most if not all of that time, the Syrian mission was subject to the direction of the Assassin headquarters in Iran.

What was their objective? What was the purpose of all this? The first reports reached the West from the Crusaders, who brought back all sorts of strange and wonderful stories about these people, including the term assassin itself, from the Arabic *ḥashīshiyya*.[5] The Crusaders were convinced that they themselves were the main target, that the Assassins were there in order to fight and destroy them. This impression, which has persisted into modern times, is quite false. There were very few Crusader victims among the scores who fell to the daggers of the Assassins between the 11th and 13th centuries. Most of their victims were Muslims—caliphs, sultans, amirs, generals, judges and high ministers of state. In the few cases where they did murder a Crusader, there is good evidence that they did so as a service to a Muslim ally rather than for any reasons of their own. They were not terribly interested in the Crusaders who were, so to speak, outside their world. Their aim was to overthrow the existing order in the Islamic lands and to take over. They rejected Sunni Islam, they condemned the political, military and religious leaders who maintained it; they represented—they would not of course have used this term but in the early 21st century we may—a revolutionary opposition and, as they saw it, an alternative, a true Islam and a true caliphate.

This also suggests a parallel to the modern situation. Are we as mistaken as the Crusaders were in thinking that the main objective of Islamic terrorism is Israel? It is a legitimate question, and the answer may well be the same as in the Middle Ages. The literature of the fundamentalists shows that they are much more preoccupied with their Islamic enemies, with the Muslim governments that they denounce as not truly Islamic, as tyrants and usurpers. The usurpation is more important than the tyranny. Tyranny is difficult to define in an area where authoritarian government is the norm; usurpation is explicit and unambiguous.

Take for example the murder of President Sadat of Egypt in 1981. In Israel and in most of the Western world, it was assumed that Sadat was murdered because he made peace with Israel and opened good relations with the United States. That is not the impression that one gets from reading, for example, the transcript of the interrogation of his murderers. From this, and from some of the statements of the accused in court, one sees that they did not approve the peace with Israel and the opening to the United States; on the contrary, they objected to them very strongly. But for them, these were symptoms, not causes—the kind of thing that they would expect from what they saw as a neo-pagan government, headed by a ruler who had renounced Islam, disestablished the Islamic holy law, and introduced pagan, foreign, i.e. western notions and practices. The charges against the Shah in Iran, against Sadat in Egypt, against the military rulers of Algeria and others elsewhere are primarily internal. They come from movements directed against their own rulers, seeking to take power and, as they see it, regenerate, that is to say, re-Islamize, society. Except of course for those most immediately affected by their presence, the Israelis, like the Crusaders in the same place some centuries ago, are so to speak, incidental; their arrival is seen as a consequence, rather than the true cause, of a deeper, more pervasive evil.

A crucial feature of the medieval Assassins is their total and final failure. They did not overthrow a single regime; they did not seize power in any Muslim country of any importance. They continued to carry out an occasional assassination but, eventually, they became less like zealots and more like hired hitmen, until they were finally extinguished in the 13th century, in Iran by the Mongols, in Syria by the Mamluks. Obviously, one should not draw too close a parallel between the medieval Assassins and their modern successors, but the ignominious end of the Assassin endeavor may carry a lesson.

The tactics, perhaps the strategy of the Assassin, have reappeared in modern times. So too has their self-bestowed name. "Assassin" was not used by them; it was applied to them by their enemies. The term they used for themselves is *fidā'ī*, one who is prepared to sacrifice his life for the cause which he serves. This medieval term was revived and used in the 19th century and, more extensively, in the 20th, with approximately the same connotation—those who are prepared to sacrifice their lives in an act of terror and violence in order to promote what they believe to be the true cause of authentic Islam. To the best of my knowledge, the term, in its modern form, first appears in 1859 when it was adopted by a small group of Ottoman conspirators. It reappears later in Iran, in the movement of the *Fidā'iyān-i Islam*, the devotees of Islam, a religious terrorist group active in Iran between 1943 and 1955, and of course the Palestine Liberation Organization from 1964 to the present day.

In the modern Middle East there have been many murders—kings, prime ministers, other ministers, intellectuals, writers, most of them by religiously motivated murderers. Apart from Sadat, the two most celebrated victims were the Persian Prime Minister 'Alī Razmārā, killed by the *Fidā'iyān-i Islam* in 1951, and the Egyptian Prime Minister Mahmud Fahmi Noqrashī killed by the Muslim Brethren in 1948. The list is long and may still grow longer.

In conclusion, we may look at one particular assassination that did not take place—the projected killing of Salman Rushdie. The facts are well known. Mr. Rushdie published a novel. The Ayatollah Khomeini, who knew no English and had apparently never read the novel, condemned it and issued a *fatwā* concerning its author. Issuing a *fatwā* is not, as is sometimes thought, the Muslim equivalent of the American term "putting out a contract." A *fatwā* is a juristic ruling—the equivalent of the Roman Responsa or Rabbinical Teshuvot, providing an answer to a question on a point of law. In this *fatwā* Khomeini ruled that it would be appropriate to kill Salman Rushdie, and indicated why and—to some extent—how.

A few points may be noted. Rushdie was accused of two offenses. One is insulting the Prophet. For Muslims, of course, this is an extremely serious matter, the equivalent of blasphemy. Shari'a law prescribes various penalties for insulting the Prophet, depending on the circumstances, the seriousness, the form of the insult, and other factors. One of these penalties is execution, but it is not the only one. However, the sin or rather the crime of insulting the Prophet is normally discussed in the context of a non-Muslim subject of the Muslim state. When a Muslim insults the Prophet it is much more serious, because insulting the Prophet is considered to be tantamount to apostasy, and apostasy—that is to say, abandoning Islam—is a capital crime under any interpretation. The offense, therefore, for which Salman Rushdie was sentenced to death was apostasy, being a renegade from Islam.

Crime, judgment, punishment—all these raise obvious questions concerning the procedure of adjudication. The chief Mufti of Egypt at the time was asked about his views. He agreed that insulting the Prophet was a major sin, and renouncing Islam a capital crime. But, as with any accusation in Shari'a as in any system of law, there had to be an arraignment, a trial, confrontation between the accused and his accuser, judicial consideration, verdict and, if appropriate, sentence. No such procedure preceded the death sentence pronounced on Salman Rushdie. There is a *hadith*, that is, a saying attributed to the Prophet, accepted by Shi'ites and by a small minority of Sunnis in Central Asia, according to which the Prophet said: "If anyone insults me, then any Muslim who hears him must kill him immediately, without any need to refer to the imam or the sultan," in other words, without needing to refer to the judicial or police authorities. Even in this rather extreme form, the tradition speaks of a spontaneous response by one who actually hears someone insult the Prophet. It says nothing about an arranged killing for a reported insult in an unread book in a far place, and Khomeini clearly was making law rather than following it.

The accusation, verdict and sentence thus summarily attained still left an important question—how was it to be carried out? Rushdie was living in England, and no British court was going to extradite him to Iran to stand trial on a capital charge of apostasy. The Iranian authorities therefore decided to procure Rushdie's execution by assassination, and offered a reward, or bounty, to anyone who accomplished it—or rather two rewards. Khomeini's own statement urged any self-respecting Muslim to go to England and kill this man in order to avenge the honor of Islam, and by way of reward he promised the delights of paradise for eternity if the assassin was himself killed. For fear lest this be insufficient inducement, a pious Islamic charitable foundation offered a reward of 20 million tumans for an Iranian (at the official rate at that time, $3 million; at the unofficial rate, $170,000). For a non-Iranian the reward was stated as $1 million, United States currency. Since 1989, when the *fatwā* was issued, the reward has been increased several times. It has not yet been claimed.

Perhaps the most extraordinary aspect of this episode is the argumentation adduced in Iran to defend, in Islamic terms, what to outsiders might look like hiring a hitman to commit murder for a fee. The traditional Muslim way of defending any idea or action is by showing that it was the practice of the Prophet. So in the Islamic Republic of Iran, from 1989 onwards, articles from time to time appeared in the press, (e.g. *Tehran Times, International Weekly*, February 23, 1989, p. 12) saying that on this or that occasion, according to reliable biographical traditions, the Prophet condoned or approved or instigated the murder of one or other of his opponents. A poet, for example, who composed poetry lampooning the Prophet, a singing girl whose offence was singing some of these poems, were murdered, according to these traditions, with the approval, or even at the behest, of the Prophet.

For any outsider, and surely for most Muslims, this would be regarded as defaming the Prophet in the worst possible way; in Iran this was done for the exact opposite purpose. Claiming that the Prophet instigated murder had as its purpose not to defame the Prophet but to justify murder by showing that the Prophet himself had encouraged it. It is an argument with far-reaching implications and devastating consequences.

Notes

1. W. Ivanow, "An Ismaili poem in praise of Fidawis," in *JBBRAS*, xiv (1938), 71; cf. Bernard Lewis, *The Assassins: A Radical Sect in Islam*, London, 1967, new edition New York, 1987, p. 130.

2. Joinville, *Histoire de Saint Louis*, ed. A. Pauphilet in *Historiens et Chroniqueurs du moyen âge*, Paris, 1952, Chapter lxxxix, p. 307.

3. Hamdullah Mustawfi, *Tārīkh-i Guzīda*, ed. E. G. Browne, London–Leiden, 1910, pp. 455–6; French trans by Charles Defrémery, in *JA*, 4ᵉ sér., xii (1848), p. 275.

4. On some medieval Western accounts of the promise of Paradise, see Lewis, *The Assassins: A Radical Sect in Islam*, London, 1967, pp. 6 ff. For studies of the Muslim sources, see *Encyclopædia of Islam*, 2, *svv.* "Djanna" and "Hūr." For a recent Muslim discussion see Muhammad ʿAlī Abuʾl-ʿAbbās. *Nisāʾahl al-janna: aṣnāfuhunna, ḥusnuhunna, awṣāfuhunna, jamāluhunna*, Cairo, n.d.

5. On this term and its significance, see *Encyclopædia of Islam*, 2, *s.v.*

11

The Mughals and the Ottomans

❧❦❧

The first recorded exchange of diplomatic missions between the Ottoman Sultans and the Muslim rulers of the subcontinent dates from the years 1481–82, when embassies, letters, and gifts were exchanged between the Bahmanid kings Muhammad Shah (1463–82) and Mahmud Shah (1482–1518) and the Ottoman Sultans Mehmet II (1451–81) and Bayezid II (1481–1512).

In the early years of the 16th century, the great victories of Selim I (1512–20) against Iran and Egypt aroused interest in India as well as in other countries. Among the many letters received by the victorious Sultan was one from Muzaffar Shah II (1511–22), the king of Gujerat, congratulating the Sultan on his victories in Iran and telling of his own success in capturing Mandu from the Rajputs. Another letter, from the Indian general Malik Ayas, the governor of Surat, congratulated the Sultan on his victory over the Mamluks and his conquest of Egypt.

The establishment of Ottoman rule in Egypt in 1516–17, followed by the extension of their power down both shores of the Red Sea, involved the Ottomans more intimately in Asian affairs, and brought them for the first time into direct contact with the Indian sub-continent and her problems. Their arrival on the Indian Ocean coincided with the coming of the Portuguese, and they soon found themselves committed to a decisive struggle for power in eastern waters. It was naturally to the Ottoman Sultan, as the major Muslim sovereign of the day, that the Muslim rulers of Asia turned for help. The Ottomans made several attempts to give it, the most important of which was the naval expedition of 1537–38, commanded by Khadim Suleyman Pasha. (A number of Suleyman Pasha's letters, sent from Egypt, Jedda, and Aden, were published in Turkey in 1940).

Despite the inconclusive outcome of this expedition, the Ottomans did not give up hope of accomplishing something in the East. The journey of the Ottoman admiral Sidi Ali Reis to India in 1553–56 is well-known. Less well-known was the attempt of the Ottomans to send help to Acheh in Sumatra. In 1563, the Muslim king of Acheh sent an embassy to Istanbul to ask for help against the Portuguese. If the Ottomans would only come and save them, he said, the infidel rulers of Calicut and Ceylon would embrace Islam. A large-scale Ottoman expedition was prepared, but at the last minute had to be diverted to Aden to deal with an insurrection in Yemen. Instead, two ships with supplies and military technicians, chiefly gunners and gun-founders, were sent.

The Ottomans were well aware of the issues at stake. In a book written in about 1580, describing the European voyages of discovery and the New World, an Ottoman geographical writer warns the Sultan of the dangers to the Islamic lands and the disturbance to Islamic trade resulting from the discoveries, and suggests: "Let a channel be cut from the Mediterranean to Suez, and let a great fleet be prepared in the port of Suez; then, with the capture of the ports of India and Sind, it will be easy to chase away the infidels and bring the precious wares of those places to our capital. . . ." The same or similar ideas may also be found in other Ottoman writers of the late 16th and early 17th centuries.

The idea of a canal through the isthmus of Suez received serious consideration, and in 1568 the project is mentioned in a *ferman* from the Sultan to the governor of Egypt. But such a canal was beyond the technical resources of the time, and finally the Ottomans abandoned the unequal struggle against the superior naval power of the Europeans in the East. From the end of the 16th century Ottoman relations with India were purely commercial and diplomatic. It is with the diplomatic relations between the Ottomans and the Mughals, who had meanwhile established themselves as the dominant power on the sub-continent, that we are now concerned—more specifically, with the information given about these relations in Ottoman chronicles and documents.

The first reference to the Mughals in Ottoman sources dates from the year 1536 when, according to the chronicler Ferdi, the Lodi prince Burhan Bey, the son of Sikandar Shah, arrived in Istanbul. Fleeing before the invasion of the Chaghatayan armies, he sought refuge at the Ottoman court. "He was granted the privilege of kissing the Imperial hand and allowed a daily pension of 300 aspers." At about the same time, an embassy from King Bahadur Shah of Gujerat arrived in Istanbul, to ask for help against the encroachments both of Humayun and of the Portuguese.

Possibly because of their alliance with the kings of Gujerat, the Ottomans seem at first to have regarded the rise of the Mughals with some suspicion. This was reinforced in 1588, when reports were received from Ottoman spies in India that Akbar was conspiring with the Portuguese, and was planning a naval expedition to strike at the ports of Yemen. This fantastic story was taken seriously by the Ottomans, who ordered reinforcements and supplies not only to Yemen but also to Basra and Suez.

The next report dates from the year 1632. In this year, the Ottoman historian Naima tells us, the Mughal prince Baysunkur Mirza, the grandson of Akbar, came to Istanbul "to rub his brow on the Imperial Gate." He set up house in the suburb of Üsküdar. Naima relates at some length how the Mughal family had been massacred by Shah Jehan, and how Baysunkur escaped to Iran. Finding a cold reception there, he continued his journey to Istanbul, and sought hospitality and help from the Ottoman Sultan Mura IV (1623–40).

The Mughal prince seems to have made a bad impression at the Turkish court. Naima describes him as boastful, arrogant, and discourteous. Full of pride at his own royal descent he failed to comply with the ceremonial of the Ottoman court and was even so tactless as to brag of his ancestor Timur—not very wise on the part of a Timurid guest of an Ottoman Sultan. When he was given a sum of money for his expenses he distributed it, as soon as he came out of the audience, among the porters and guards. As a result of these acts of discourtesy the Sultan ceased to rise from his seat when the prince called on him, and eventually stopped receiving him altogether. Baysunkur, however, went on demanding an army from the Sultan, to win him the throne of India. The Sultan was not interested. His relations with Shah Jehan, he said, were good, and the Mughal Emperor had already sent him two embassies, with gifts and protestations of friendship. In any case such an expedition, to so remote a country, would be enormously difficult, and even if one could be sent, it would be wasted effort. Baysunkur's incapacity was well known even if an Ottoman army placed him on his throne, he would soon lose it through his own folly. Eventually Baysunkur gave up hope of winning Turkish support and left the country. "What became of him is not known for certain," says Naima, "but some say he became a dervish."

In 1638, Naima reports the arrival of an ambassador, Mir Zarif, sent by Shah Jehan to Murad IV. He travelled *via* the Red Sea, landed at Jedda and eventually reached the Sultan at Mosul. The ambassador brought sumptuous gifts, including a girdle worth 15,000 piastres, and a shield of elephant's ear and rhinoceros' hide. The letter he brought was less gratifying. Shah Jehan urged on Murad the need for a close alliance between the two Sunni emperors against the Shi'a heretics in Iran but in such terms as to reproach the Ottoman Sultan for dilatoriness and lack of zeal. Murad's reply is not extant, but its tone may be inferred from the next Indian letter, which complains of a lack of courtesy on the Ottoman side. This Ottoman reply was taken to India by an ambassador called Arslan Agha. In 1642 he returned to Istanbul, bringing unmistakable indications of Shah Jehan's displeasure. No presents were sent by the Emperor, and only a few of slight value by his vizier. No letter was sent by Shah Jehan to Sultan Ibrahim (1640–48), who had meanwhile succeeded Murad IV on the Ottoman throne. Instead, there was a letter from the Indian to the Ottoman Grand Vizier, complaining at the insufficiently respectful forms of address used in the Ottoman letter, and describing the power and extent of the Mughal Empire. A dignified and restrained reply from the Ottoman Grand Vizier failed to appease Shah Jehan's anger, and a period of silence followed, during which even the customary

Turkish letter announcing the accession of Sultan Mehmet IV in 1649 appears to have remained for a while unanswered.

It was not until 1652 that a new Mughal ambassador, called Sayyid Ahmad, arrived in Istanbul. He came with the Ottoman Muhyi'd-Din, who had carried Mehmet IV's letter to India. Muhyi'd-Din's mission had not been purely formal. Besides announcing the accession of the new Sultan, he had been instructed to win Mughal support for the Khan of the Uzbegs, and to ask the Mughal to use his good offices in settling a dispute which had arisen between the Khan and his son. The Mughal reply stated that the matter of the Uzbegs had been attended to even before the arrival of the Ottoman embassy, but that the Khan had been attacked by rebels and had died soon after. It seems likely that one of the factors that induced the Mughal to resume relations with the Ottoman Sultan was the despatch, some years earlier, of a private embassy from Dara Shikoh to Istanbul. The letter of Dara Shikoh and the reply of the Ottoman Grand Vizier, which are preserved in a Turkish collection of letters, give no hint of the real purpose of the embassy, but refer to the verbal message carried by Dara's envoy, the Molla Shaki. We can only guess at its content.

The embassy of Sayyid Ahmad was a personal triumph. Naima describes him as a man of learning, charm, and wit, and remarks that no ambassador had ever been received with such attention and honour. His welcome was no doubt made warmer by the gifts he brought. These, which were valued at 300,000 piastres, included a turban ornament with a diamond bigger than that worn by the Sultan. The Ambassador was feted and entertained, and given rich presents to take home with him.

The question now arose of appointing a Turkish ambassador to go on a return mission. On this subject Naima is both caustic and entertaining. The ancient custom he says, was to send a man of affairs from among the Ulama or the scribes, or a man of eloquence from among the men of learning and refinement. In fact these necessary conditions were disregarded. Dhu'l-Fikar Agha, the brother of Salih Pasha (the late Grand Vizier), asked for this embassy, and said: "I want no expense money; I shall pay the expenses out of my own pocket." This argument, Naima tells us, proved irresistible, and, he remarks acidly, "on the principle that a cheap hire makes a good companion, this ignorant Bosniak was appointed ambassador." The Sultan, Naima says, was deeply impressed by the wit and learning of the Mughal envoy, and was anxious to send someone of comparable quality to represent him in India, since "ambassadors are the honour of kings." The Mufti, the vizier, and other advisors, however, persuaded the Sultan of the superior merits of an ambassador who would pay his own expenses, and he therefore nominated the ignorant but wealthy Dhu'l-Fikar.

It now became Dhu'l-Fikar's duty to call on his Indian colleague, and then invite him to an entertainment in his own house. Naima's description of these proceedings is richly comic. "Go to the ambassador's house," Dhu'l-Fikar was instructed "and pay your respects, and then give him a party at your house . . .

but stand silent and don't say a word." In spite of this good advice Dhu'l-Fikar managed to disgrace himself by his stupid and boorish behaviour. Naima describes the dinner party, the wit and grace of the Mughal ambassador, the stupidity of Dhu'l-Fikar. When they parted, Dhu'l-Fikar observed to his cronies: "He talked to me in fancy language, but I answered him back in plain Turkish." The Indian, says Naima, was heard to say to his companions, as he left Dhu'l-Fikar's house: "Glory be to God, who created an ox in the form of a man."

The whole episode, says Naima, caused deep distress in Istanbul. As one of the Turkish guests at the ill-fated dinner-party remarked: "If we look at it impartially, at a time when there are so many men of learning, culture, and refinement available, is it proper to send such vulgarians on embassies merely for the sake of their money?" This, says Naima, reflected the general opinion, and many wondered how the Chief Mufti Baha'i Efendi could have given his consent to it.

Dhu'l-Fikar proceeded on his embassy to India, for part of the journey in the reluctant company of the Mughal ambassador. Three years later, in 1656, he returned to Turkey, accompanied by a new Indian envoy called Ka'im Bey. This new ambassador from Shah Jahan was well received, and this time a man of real ability was appointed to return with him to India. Manzade Huseyn was one of the chief Chamberlains of the Ottoman Court, and, so it would seem, a man of some distinction. He was, incidentally, the son of Fakhr ad-Din Ma'n, the famous Druze leader in Lebanon, who was executed for rebellion in 1635.

Manzade Husein returned to Turkey in 1659, and was thus present in India during part of the struggle for power at the end of the reign of Shah Jahan. Unfortunately his report on India is not available, though some allusions to it appear in Naima's History. He was received in India by Murad Bakhsh, who accepted his letters and gifts, and replied to them as sovereign. It was shortly after this that Murad Bakhsh was overpowered by his brother Aurangzeb. The Ottoman ambassador had thus backed the wrong horse, and it may be for this reason that we hear of only one mission to India during the reign of Aurangzeb— and that one not very successful. In 1690 the Ottoman Sultan Suleyman II (1687–91), hard pressed by his enemies, sent a letter to the Mughal asking for support. According to Indian sources a reply was sent, but none has so far come to light in Ottoman chronicles or records.

The Ottoman chronicles of the 18th century contain a few allusions to diplomatic exchanges between the Courts of Delhi and Istanbul. Thus, among the events of the year 1717, the Imperial historiographer Rashid records the departure of an Indian embassy, after a long stay in Istanbul. Apart from the usual details about the exchange of gifts, no information is given.

We hear a little more about an exchange of missions in 1744. The Imperial historiographer Izzi tells us that the Mughal Emperor and the Ottoman Sultan had long been friends. In this year an ambassador called Seyyid Ataullah, by origin a Bukharan, landed in Basra, and travelled overland to Üsküdar and thence to Istanbul. The texts of the letters exchanged are given by Izzi, and these, together with other documents, make the purpose of the mission clear. The Mughal ambassador had come to warn the Ottomans, then at war with Nadir Shah, not to be misled by his overtures for peace. Though he might for the moment seek Turkish friendship, his intentions against Turkey were no less hostile than against Mughal India, and he would certainly betray any trust that was reposed in him. The two prospective victims of Nadir Shah's aggression would be wise to make common cause against him. In a report presented by the ambassador himself to the Ottoman authorities, he gives specific evidence of Nadir Shah's hostility and of Indian good will. Thus, for example, Nadir Shah had sent a mission to India to buy ships, but when it was learnt that they were for use against Turkey, their sale was prohibited. Now Nadir Shah was trying to make peace with the Ottomans. If they agreed to this, he would turn against India, and then, greatly enriched in arms, men, ships, supplies, and money, would return to the final conquest of the Ottoman realm. The Ottomans should not therefore be taken in by Nadir Shah's deceitful peace-proposals, but should continue the war.

The Sultan's return embassy was led by a certain Salim Efendi, an official of the finance department. The Ottoman reply, "written in gold letters," expresses general agreement, and promises to take all possible precautions. In fact the war continued until 1747, when Nadir Shah, who had won a decisive victory, was able to secure a peace. He was assassinated shortly after.

In 1750 Izzi reports another embassy from India. Its purpose, he says, was to renew the friendship between the two empires. There was the usual exchange of gifts, which are described in some detail.

These were certainly not the only embassies exchanged between Delhi and Istanbul. The Ottoman sources contain a number of passing allusions to other missions which are not described in the Imperial chronicles. Thus, for example, in the biography of Mehmet Emin Pasha, who became Grand Vizier in 1769, we are told that he was the son of Hajji Yusuf Agha, who had gone on an embassy to India, and that he himself had accompanied his father on this mission. A more detailed investigation of the Ottoman sources and especially of the vast Ottoman archives, would no doubt reveal more information about these exchanges and the varying purposes that inspired them.

On the whole, Ottoman relations with India after the 16th century seem to have been infrequent and of relatively minor importance. There was a time, during the reign of Suleyman the Magnificent, when the Ottomans were for a while actively concerned with the affairs of south Asia. Towards the end of the 16th century, however, they withdrew from active participation, and thereafter their links with India were chiefly commercial—and even these began to weaken, as the Western powers established themselves more firmly in the East and diverted a good deal of the trade from the Middle Eastern transit routes to the open ocean.

There seems to have been some cultural contact between the two countries, mainly through individual travellers. Thus the Ottoman architect Mimar Yusuf, a disciple of the great Mimar Sinan (1490–1578), by common consent the greatest of Ottoman architects, went to India and entered the service of Akbar. He is reputed to have had some hand in the buildings of Agra and Delhi.

From the 16th to the 18th century the Ottoman Sultan and the Mughal Emperor were the two greatest Sunni Muslim rulers. They were, however, too remote to interest one another very much, either as allies or as rivals. The Ottomans had their eyes fixed on Europe first—as an area of expansion, then as an area of danger, against which it was the principal concern of the Ottoman Sultans to protect themselves. The Mughals on their side were preoccupied with Indian affairs—with the many problems of their vast Empire. Only one thing brought them together—the common threat, offered to both of them, by the Shi'ite Empire of Iran. When the Turks were fighting near Baghdad, or the Mughals near Kandahar, their thoughts began to turn to a second front on the far side of their enemy's territory—and it was on these occasions that embassies began to travel by sea between the Ottoman and the Indian ports.

In the 19th century, the pattern of relationship between Turkey and the Muslims of the sub-continent began to change. The formal exchanges of diplomatic missions between the Ottoman Sultans and Mughal Emperors ceased, but a new intimacy arose between their subjects who, already linked by many ties of religion, culture, and history, now found themselves confronting the common challenge of the modern world.

12

Europe and the Turks

The Civilization of the Ottoman Empire

ᶜᴶᶜᶜᵔᶜ

This year [1953] the Turks have been celebrating the 500th anniversary of their conquest of Constantinople. Turkish rule in Europe began nearly a century earlier, and was firmly established by the time that the occupation of the Imperial city rounded off the Turkish dominions and made Constantinople once again the capital of a great empire. But the anniversary may serve as the occasion for some reflections on the place of the Ottoman Empire in the history of Europe and of the world.

For most Europeans, the loss of Constantinople is a great historical disaster, a defeat of Christendom which has never been repaired. In spite of the present friendly relations between Turkey and the West, there is still a reserve of mistrust, and even at times of hostility, with roots deep in the European Christian past. For most literate West Europeans, the words "Turk" and "Turkey" have complex emotional associations, coloured by centuries of strife; and for East Europeans the traditional picture of the Turkish oppressor has become part of the national folk-lore.

This Western image of the Turk has several sources. The first of these is fear, imprinted on the Western mind during the long period when the Turks were thrusting into the heart of Europe and seemed to threaten the very existence of Christendom. Richard Knolles, the Elizabethan chronicler of the Turks, expressed the feelings of Europe when he spoke of the Turk as "the present terror of the world." . . .

This sense of fear was augmented by the religious hostility between Christendom and Islam, dating back to the first Arab-Muslim conquests, which had wrested the Christian provinces of Syria, Egypt, North Africa and Spain from the West and incorporated them in the Islamic world. The clash was renewed by the Christian counter-attack in the Western Mediterranean and in the

Crusades, and again by the new Muslim offensive launched into Europe by the Ottoman Turks. Even the secularization of Europe from Renaissance times onwards did not seriously diminish this hostility to Islam. Religious ill-will usually outlives religious belief. Western travellers in Turkey, who were the major source of information to the Western world, with few exceptions reinforced these prejudices. Most of them lacked the perceptiveness and imagination to realize that though the familiar good qualities that they appreciated at home were missing in Turkey, there were others present of a different kind. They did not understand that this was another civilization, with its own ethics and its own standards and values. In more recent times, Western hostility to the Turk was perpetuated by the enthusiasm of the philhellenes who, in their just admiration for Greece, did less than justice to the Turk, seeing in him only the brutal destroyer of the liberties of Hellas, and forgetting the famous words of the Byzantine dignitary Lucas Notaras, "It is better to see in the city the power of the Turkish turban than that of the Latin tiara."

In our own time, yet another source of misinformation has been added. Since the spread of nationalism to the Balkans and the Near East, more than a dozen states have risen from the ruins of the Ottoman Empire, each with its own national legends of liberation and its own brand of national historiography. Like most liberated peoples, the Balkan, and later the Arab, states tended to blame all the defects and shortcomings of their societies upon the misrule of the fallen imperial masters. More articulate in Western terms than the Turks, they have succeeded in persuading most Western observers of the truth of their version of history.

It might have been expected that the revival of learning in Europe and the growth of scientific history would have brought about a more impartial view and a less prejudiced approach. In fact, they did not. Prejudice, as so often, has been swollen by ignorance. Though it is generally accepted that one does not write French history without some reference to French sources, Western Europeans continued to write Turkish history—renamed the Eastern Question—without any reference to what the Turks themselves had to say about it. But Turkish sources do exist in vast numbers—histories, chronicles, archive documents by the million, many of which have been published. There is no longer any need to view the Turks only through the eyes of their rivals and enemies.

This negative attitude to the Turks, while predominant, is not the only one. There is also what one might call a positive legend of the Turk in Europe—and here I am not speaking of the political and military considerations which from time to time led European powers to sup with the Turk, though with a long spoon. The West also had a romantic or heroic legend of the Turk, which again has diverse origins. Sometimes it was the Western doctrine of the "noble savage"—with the Turk unflatteringly cast in that role. Sometimes the Turk, like other exotic peoples, was used as a vehicle for social comment in the West; sometimes, too, as a means of anti-Christian—or more specifically anti-Catholic controversy, as when sixteenth-century Protestant polemists contrasted Turkish tolerance with Catholic repression. Occasionally, one or other national or social group in the West experienced or imagined a feeling of affinity with the Turks. Such, for example, was the pan-turanian myth advanced by some Hungarian intellectuals, who sought a Magyar-Turkish alliance against the common threat of pan-slavism. Such, too, was the attitude of some elements amongst the English ruling classes, who saw in the Ottoman Muslim a gentleman of the established church, and in the Ottoman Christian a factious nonconformist. Broadly, there are two prototypes of the Turk in Western legend, the one expressed in the adjective "unspeakable," the other in the noun "gentleman." Both have little to do with the real Turkey. In what follows, I propose to examine some of the specific charges brought against the Turks, or rather, some of their alleged defects, the existence of which is tacitly assumed as axiomatic, and to see how far they are justified by an impartial examination of the evidence.

A common assumption is that the Turk was a brutal barbarian without culture. But the Ottoman Turks have a rich literature, going back to the thirteenth century in Turkey, and still earlier among the Eastern Turkish peoples of Central Asia. If not of the level of the earlier Muslim literatures in Arabic and Persian, there is still much that is of more than local value, especially in the great tradition of historical writing. Ottoman historiography consists not merely of annals, but of real history, sometimes achieving even an epic quality. This literature is little known in the West—but that is hardly the fault of the Turks. More accessible to foreign visitors are the glories of Ottoman art and architecture—the magnificent mosques that still grace Turkey and the successor states: miniatures, metal-work, and the products of the industrial and decorative arts. Not least of these is the characteristic art of calligraphy, often underestimated or misunderstood by Western observers, but capable of reaching a high level of artistic self-expression. Turkish culture is, as one would expect, mainly Islamic, and the educated Ottoman was as familiar with the Arabic and Persian classics as his Western contemporaries with those of Greece and Rome. Even an interest in Western civilization, though very limited, was not entirely lacking. Mehmet the Conqueror had a knowledge of Greek, and a library of Greek books. His entourage included the Italian humanist, Ciriaco Pizzocolli of Ancona, and the Greek humanist, Critoboulos. The latter—who was Mehmet's biographer—mentions his interest in Greek antiquities and remains, and, when describing Mehmet's wonderment at the Parthenon, even confers upon him the title of "Philhellene." After the capture of Constantinople, Mehmet had to keep his promise to his victorious troops to give them free rein for three days in the conquered city, but both Greek and Western writers attest that on the fourth day he took measures to safeguard manuscripts, buildings and relics. Some scholars say that the Turkish conquest of Constantinople was less destructive than that of the Western Crusaders in 1204.

A word often used to describe the Ottoman Empire is ramshackle, and there is a general impression that Ottoman Government was always incompetent, venal and inept. Yet the countless documents in the Istanbul archives show that up to the sixteenth century the Empire was governed by an elaborate bureaucratic organization, extremely conscientious in its task of administering a vast Empire. One series of registers alone contains a record, in over 1,000 volumes, of towns, villages, population and revenue for the whole Empire from Budapest to Baghdad. The 50,000 and more bound registers, and the millions of papers, still preserved in the Turkish record office show that whatever may have been the faults of Ottoman administration, it was, in the early and middle periods, anything but ramshackle.

Against the charge of destructiveness that is often brought against Turkish rule, the same evidence may be cited. The registers show an increase in population and prosperity in most areas after the conquest, which the travellers—by no means friendly witnesses—confirm. In the Arab lands, Ottoman rule brought peace and security after the heady nightmare of late Mameluke rule. In the Balkans, too, Ottoman Government brought unity and security in the place of previous conflict and disorder. In the wars of conquest, a large part of the old landowning aristocracy was destroyed and their ownerless estates were incorporated into the Ottoman feudal system and granted as fiefs to Ottoman soldiers. Under the Ottoman order, the fief-holder was concerned only with revenue and had no seigneurial rights. Thus, the peasants enjoyed far greater freedom on their farms than previously, while the operation of Ottoman law prevented both the fragmentation and the concentration of land-ownership. This security and prosperity, given to peasant agriculture by a Government which had inherited the ancient loyalty owned by the Balkan peoples to the Imperial Byzantine throne, did much to reconcile them to the other imperfections of Ottoman rule, and account in large measure for the long tranquillity that reigned in the Balkans until the explosive eruption of nationalist ideas from the West. Even to Constantinople, the Ottoman conquest brought a new prosperity, as the city was transformed from a fossil into the flourishing capital of a great Empire.

Another charge is that of tyranny. Certainly the Sultan was no democrat; but after all, democracy, as we know and practise it, has flourished in only a few places, and in most of them is recent and precarious. The Sultan was not a true despot, but the supreme custodian of the God-given Holy Law of Islam, to which he himself was subject. It is true that the Holy Law granted him almost despotic power, and that it did not provide for its own enforcement against him. But ultimately the Holy Law remained the basis of the social and political structure of the Empire, and was observed by the Sultans, whose sovereignty was accepted and respected by the people, both Muslims and Christian, as right and inevitable.

Two other qualities which have been attributed to the Turks are fanaticism and intolerance. The Ottoman Turks were indeed fanatical Muslims, dedicated to the maintenance and expansion of the Islamic state. But toleration is a relative matter. According to the principles professed by modern democracies, toleration means the absence of discrimination. In that sense, the Ottomans were not tolerant, since non-Muslims were not the civic and social equals of the followers of the dominant faith, but were subject to a number of legal disabilities. But this kind of toleration is new and insecure, even in Europe, and it is not reasonable to look for it in the old Ottoman Empire. If we define toleration as the absence, not of discrimination, but of persecution, then the Ottoman record until the late nineteenth century is excellent. The well-known preference of the fifteenth-century Greeks for Muslim rather than Frankish rule was not without its reasons. The confrontation of Christendom and Islam has sometimes been compared with the Cold War. The comparison is valid at many points, but we must remember in making it that the main movement of refugees in the fifteenth and sixteenth centuries was from Europe to Turkey and not the other way. When Ottoman rule in the Balkans ended, the Balkan peoples resumed their national existence, with their own religions and languages and national cultures intact. After the Christian conquest, no Muslims remained in Spain or Sicily, and no speakers of Arabic.

A good example of the way in which European travellers and diplomats misunderstood and misinterpreted Ottoman institutions is provided by the word "rayah." According to most of the Western travellers, followed by most Western historians, the word rayah means cattle, and was applied to the Christian subjects of the Porte, whose predatory attitude to them is expressed in the term. In fact, Ottoman usage until the middle of the eighteenth century applied the term to the peasant population of the Empire, irrespective of religion. Thus Muslim peasants were rayahs and Christian towns people were not. The word itself comes from an Arabic root, meaning to graze, and would be better translated as flocks, expressing the well-known pastoral ideal of Government, which is common to Christendom and Islam. It is a curious comment on the pattern of Western influence on Turkey, that from the middle of the eighteenth century the Western misinterpretation of the term passed to the Turks themselves, who began to use it—and sometimes apply it—in the once mistaken Western sense.

With the decline of the Ottoman Empire, some of the traditional charges against the Turks become in part justified. Ottoman culture declined into mere repetition and imitation of earlier models. Ottoman administration ran down until the Empire really was ramshackle. Increasing weakness in the face of foreign invasion and internal rebellion often led to oppression and brutality and tyranny. Suspicion, hatred, fear—and sometimes, we may add, the example of Western intolerance—transformed the Turkish attitude to the subject peoples.

But when all is said and done, it will be argued, the Turks are an alien and hostile element in Europe. Until very recently this description was undeniably merited. But the point should not be exaggerated. It was not barbarians from the Central Asian Steppes who conquered south-eastern Europe, but a civilized Muslim people, and Islam, despite its long conflict with Christendom, has much in common with it. Both share the Hebrew heritage of prophecy, revelation, ethical monotheism and divine law. Both shared—or rather, divided—the Hellenistic heritage, of which Islam preserved the philosophy and science, while the West kept the literature and art. Islam is far more akin to Europe in its cultural traditions than to the true Orient, in India and China. But the Turks were familiar in a nearer and more material sense. They had been in Anatolia since the 11th century, absorbing the ancient races of the peninsula; in Europe since the fourteenth century. By the time that they conquered Constantinople, they were well acclimatized in the Balkans, mingled with Greek, Slavonic and Albanian blood. Men of Christian birth were prominent at the court and in the army—the corps of janissaries consisted exclusively of such. Mehmet the Conqueror was at home both in Greek and in Greece. In many senses, the Turks were less alien to Constantinople than were the Western Christians.

The loss of Constantinople was certainly a defeat of Christendom and of Europe—though perhaps not so total as was once feared. It is not without significance that the Turks today are celebrating the 500th anniversary of their great victory by the Gregorian and not by the Muslim calendar. Nor was it a victory of barbarism, but rather of another and not undistinguished civilization. The four slender minarets that the Turks added to the Church of Santa Sophia may be, for the Christian, a desecration. They are not a defacement.

13

Europe and Islam

Muslim Perceptions and Experience

❧❦❧❦

urope is a European idea, conceived in Greece, nurtured in Rome, and now, after a long and troubled childhood and adolescence in Christendom, approaching maturity in a secular, supranational community.

Asia and Africa are also European ideas, European ways of describing the Other. All human groups have terms, often derogatory, to designate those who are outside the group. Some of these terms have acquired an almost universal significance. Barbarians were originally non-Greeks, gentiles are non-Jews, Asian and Africans are non-Europeans and were sub-divided geographically into the east and the south. Barbarians did not of course regard themselves as barbarians, nor did gentiles regard themselves as gentiles, until both were taught, by the processes of Hellenization and Christianization, to see themselves in this alien light. The Hellenization of the barbarians took place in antiquity; the Christianization of the gentiles in the Middle Ages. The awareness among Asians and Africans of this European-imposed identity dates in the main from modern times, when they were taught this classification by European rulers, teachers and preachers. By the present day, the Greek invention of the three continents of the Old World has been universally accepted. The enterprise and ingenuity of mostly European explorers and geographers have added several more.

Medieval Muslims were keenly interested in geography, and produced a rich geographical literature in Arabic, Persian and later Turkish. But in this literature, and in the administrative geography which it reflects, the name of Asia is unknown, and Africa, in the form *Ifrīqiya*, is, as in Roman usage, simply the name of a province on the Mediterranean coast roughly corresponding to present-day Tunisia. The name Europe, in the form *Urūfa*, makes a brief appearance in early medieval geographical works, translated or adapted from Greek originals, and then disappears.

Early Muslim geographical literature used two systems of classification to subdivide the world, one of them physical, the other at once religious and political. The physical division was into "climates" (*iqlīm*), a word and a system derived from the Greeks. It is purely geographical and has no reference to religion, ethnicity, culture or political sovereignty. It figures only in geographical writings and is not usually mentioned elsewhere.

Far more important was the religio-political classification, which dominated, and in some circles still dominates, Muslim discussions of the world in which they live and of their relations with others. The basic division of the world, in the traditional Muslim perception, is between the "House of Islam" (*Dār al-Islām*) and the "House of War" (*Dār al-Ḥarb*); that is to say, between the regions where a Muslim government rules and Muslim law prevails, and the rest. Not everyone in the House of Islam is Muslim. Indeed, large and important communities of non-Muslims remain and are allowed to practice their religions and, within limits, run their affairs. But an essential condition of this tolerance is their acceptance of the supremacy of Islam and the primacy of the Muslims.

Beyond the frontiers of Muslim power lies the House of War, lands not only inhabited but also—more important—ruled by non-Muslims. It is the moral and religious duty of Muslims to share their good fortune with the rest of the world, not selfishly to keep God's final revelation for themselves, but to strive unceasingly to bring it to all humankind, if possible in peace, if necessary by war. This is one of the basic obligations of the Muslim faith. It is called *jihād*, a word which literally means "striving," and is usually translated "holy war."

Not all unbelievers were the same, nor were they all seen in the same light. South and east of the Islamic lands, in what Europeans but not Muslims called Asia and Africa, there were polytheists and idolaters, with many gods and no divine scripture recognized as such by Islam. Some were primitive, others were civilized, and might even have useful lessons to teach the Muslims in the arts and sciences. But there was no world religion to compete with Islam, and no world empire to rival the Caliphate. China, which might have seemed an exception, was remote and little-known, and in any case the Chinese made no great effort to impose their beliefs, their culture, or their power beyond their immediate neighbors. For the Muslim world, the east and the south were inhabited by teachable barbarians who could in time be converted to Islam and recruited into the service of the Muslim state and faith. This was indeed the historical experience of Islam in Asia and Africa.

The situation on the northwest frontier of the Islamic lands, in the regions known to some of their inhabitants though not to the Muslims as Europe, was very different. Immediately to the north were people whom modern scholarship has called Byzantines, but who called themselves and were recognized by their Muslim neighbors as Romans. In this ancient empire, ruled by a line of Caesars and professing the Christian religion, Muslims recognized a state, a faith, and a mission of their own kind—a rival dispensation, maintained by a rival power, disputing with them the possession of God's final truth and the universal mission of bringing it to all the world.

In a sense, early Islam defined itself against Christian faith and power. The earliest Muslim religious monuments, the Dome of the Rock in Jerusalem and the great Umayyad mosque in Damascus, were consciously built to vie with the Church of the Resurrection in Jerusalem and the great Christian churches of Syria. The inscriptions inside the Dome and on the gold coins, struck by the Caliphs in deliberate defiance of what had until then been a Roman prerogative, announce the rejection of Christian errors and the supersession of Roman power by the bearers of the new Islamic order. In medieval Muslim writings, the Byzantine Empire is the "House of War" par excellence, against which the final and greatest *jihād* must be waged. These were no simple heathens to be instructed and absorbed, but the supreme rivals, and they are treated with the suspicion—and respect—appropriate to that status.

Medieval Muslim writings show little suspicion and no respect for the remaining peoples of Europe. Information about these was sparse, and there was no great desire or incentive to add to it. There were a few intrepid travellers who ventured into darkest Europe, and the strange stories they brought home provided most of the limited stock of information. It was known that to the west of the Romans there were people called Franks, and that at a certain moment they had erected a kind of empire of their own, to which, however, little importance was attached. The name, which probably reached the Muslims from Byzantium, was originally used of the empire of Charlemagne, and later applied to Europeans in general, more particularly to the Catholic and later also Protestant countries of Europe. Orthodox Christians, including those within the realms of the Caliphate, were known as "Romans" (*Rūm*), though some of them were believed have connections with, the *Saqāliba*—Slavs—living further north. In the still remoter north, there were pagan peoples known in Arabic writings as *Majūs* or "Magians," a term originally used of the Zoroastrians of pre-Islamic Persia, but later also applied to the Vikings and other Norsemen, in the belief that they practiced a similar form of paganism. What little was known of the geography of Europe came from an Arabic adaptation of Ptolemy's *Geographikē Hyphēgēsis*, supplemented by scraps of information brought by merchants, diplomats, and an occasional returning prisoner of war.

For the medieval Muslims, Europe thus presented a double challenge. On the one hand, there was the Christian imperial rival to confront and overcome; on the other, there was the mission, felt by other empire-builders before them and after them, to conquer, convert and civilize the barbarous peoples beyond the imperial frontiers.

Western history and myth have portrayed the victory of Charles Martel over the Saracens at the battle of Tours et Poitiers in 732 as the turning-point in the struggle between Christendom and Islam, the decisive battle which halted and repelled the Muslim advance and ensured the survival of Christian Europe. This battle receives at most only minor notice in Muslim writings. This was not because they were concealing a defeat—classical Muslim historians are often remarkably honest in recording defeats as well as victories—but because of a different, and, in the longer and broader perspective of history, more accurate perception.

For the Western Christians, this was the decisive battle between Christendom and Islam. For the Muslims, it was a minor skirmish involving a group of raiders in the wild country far beyond the imperial frontier. A Western parallel might be a reverse suffered by some scouting party from nineteenth-century British India, caught by tribesmen in the wilds of Afghanistan. Early medieval Muslims were very conscious of the great struggle in which they were engaged against Christendom—of the issues and the stakes involved. They were also well aware of their defeat in the attempt to conquer and convert Europe. But in their perception, the real turning point in the attack on Europe was the repeated failure of the armies and fleets of the Caliphate to capture Constantinople in the late seventh and early eighth centuries. The Byzantine capital was rightly seen as the citadel of Christendom, the successful defense of which saved Europe from Islamization. And when the attempt was abandoned, the capture of Constantinople was postponed to an eschatological future, and became the subject of a whole series of traditions and legends. All this enormously increased the religious significance of the eventual fall of the city, in 1453, to a Turkish sultan bearing the name of the Prophet of Islam.

The Muslim attempt to conquer Europe falls into three main phases—those of the Arabs, the Tatars, and the Turks. When the Muslim armies burst out of Arabia in the seventh century, the Levant, Egypt, and North Africa were still Christian and, in fact or in principle, part of a Christian empire. Indeed, the Persian geographer Ibn Khurradādhbih (died 846), one of the few who mentions the name of Europe, includes North Africa in it.[1] The wave of conquest that engulfed these lands continued, and for a while Sicily and the other Mediterranean islands, almost the whole of the Iberian peninsula, and even, briefly, parts of southern France, were incorporated in the Islamic Empire. The Crusades, the great attempt to recover by holy war some of the Christian lands of the East that had been lost by holy war, ended in failure. But the longer struggle to recover Sicily, Spain and Portugal was successful, and was completed in 1492 with the reconquest of Granada, the last Muslim foothold on West European soil.

The second wave, that of the so-called Tatars, for a while brought much of Eastern Europe under Muslim rule. The Kipchak Turks, who conquered a large part of southern Russia, were not originally Muslims, but in time they were converted to Islam, as were also the vastly more powerful Mongols who conquered Russia in the thirteenth century. With the conversion of the Mongol Khan of the Golden Horde to Islam, a major Muslim military power ruled much of Eastern Europe, and many of the local Christian princes, including the rulers of Moscow, were subject to his sway. In eastern as in southwestern Europe, a series of wars of reconquest finally ended what Russians called "the Tatar Yoke," and recovered these lands for Christendom. Thus, at both its eastern and southwestern extremities, the limits and in a sense even the identity of Europe were established through first the advance, and then the retreat, of Islam.

The latest, and in many ways the greatest, of the Muslim attacks on Europe was that of the Turks, led first by the Seljuq and then by the Ottoman dynasties. Already in the eleventh century, the Seljuq Turks wrested Anatolia from the Byzantines, and transformed it from a Greek Christian to a Turkish Muslim land. In the thirteenth century, an Ottoman expeditionary force crossed the straits into Europe and began what developed into a vast expansion of Ottoman power. At its height, the Ottoman Empire, with the Crimean khanate under Ottoman suzerainty, included all the shores of the Black Sea, the whole of the Balkan peninsula and half of Hungary. In 1480 an Ottoman naval expedition from Albania seized Otranto in Italy, while Ottoman advance units raided within sight of Venice. Most important of all, they were twice able to lay siege to Vienna. The second siege, in 1683, was the first unequivocal defeat, and it was followed by the first peace treaty—Carlowitz, 1699—in which the Ottoman sultan had to submit to the will of victorious Christian enemies.

Until then, Islam, in its own perception at least, was triumphant; the absorption of the obdurate European barbarians could be delayed, but not prevented. True, there were some losses in remote and little-known regions, like Spain and Russia, and even an occasional setback like the naval defeat at Lepanto in 1571, a battle that caused great but brief elation in Europe but had little effect on the immediate balance of power. As long as the Muslim forces remained dominant in the central lands, they continued—again, like other empire-builders before them and after—securely believing in the supremacy of their arms and the immutable superiority of their beliefs and their way of life.

Ottoman awareness of Christian Europe was somewhat greater than that of their medieval Saracen predecessors, but was still very limited. Ottoman officials were of course well-informed about the Christian European peoples under their rule, and the documents preserved in the imperial Ottoman archives in Istanbul reflect in some detail the day-by-day dealings of the Ottoman authorities with these communities at all levels. But there is little reflection of this in Ottoman literature or even historiography.

There was still less interest in the Christian European peoples beyond the Ottoman frontiers. Thus for example, even such major events as the Thirty Years' War, involving regions very close to the Ottoman-held lands, and raising issues directly relevant to Ottoman concerns, received very little mention in contemporary Ottoman writings, and even that little is sometimes inaccurate. Of the intellectual life of Europe, virtually nothing was known. Some of the Sultans had their portraits painted by European artists; a very few scientific works, mainly medical and geographical, were translated. Ottoman officials show some awareness of the struggle between Protestants and Catholics, and tried on occasion in a rather desultory way to turn them to advantage. But neither the Renaissance nor the Reformation aroused interest or evoked concern. An account of Christianity by an Ottoman scholar of the seventeenth century is based on medieval Arabic accounts. It devotes great attention to the Christological controversies of the early church councils, but says nothing about the schism of Photios or the heresy of Luther, which, one might have thought, would be of greater interest to Ottoman readers.

Nor were the Turks unduly concerned by the reconquest of Spain. Events on the periphery of Islam were of relatively little importance. What mattered was the position at the center, and at the center the forces of Islam were doing very well.

For more than a thousand years, Europe, that is to say Christendom, was under constant threat of Islamic attack and conquest. If the Muslims were repelled in one region, they appeared in greater strength in another. As far away as Iceland, Christians still prayed in their churches for God to save them from the "terror of the Turk." These fears were not unfounded, since in 1627 Muslim corsairs from North Africa raided their coasts and carried off four hundred captives, for sale in the slave market of Algiers.

The events of the late seventeenth century—the failure to take Vienna in 1683, the loss of Buda, for a century and a half the seat of a Turkish pasha, in 1686, the retreat of the Turks through the Balkans, and the sealing of their defeat in the Treaty of Carlowitz of 1699, were of more than local or even regional significance. They marked a major turning point in the relationship between European Christendom and Ottoman Islam.

The Turks themselves had no illusions about the magnitude of the change. In the negotiations which led to the signing of the Treaty of Carlowitz in 1699, they sought and obtained the help of the British and Dutch ambassadors, whose governments were concerned at what they saw as an undue increase in Austrian power. After the peace, the Ottoman government embarked on the first of a long series of attempts to reform and modernize their armies, to enable them to confront their European enemies.

Thus, at the beginning of the eighteenth century, the rulers of the leading Islamic state in confrontation with Europe initiated a new strategy, both diplomatic and military. In both respects, they were following European methods. In both, their purpose was to use these methods against Europe. The adoption of European-style diplomacy, and of European drill and weaponry, did not suffice to restore the waning power of Islam, but they enabled the Ottoman state to fight a long drawn-out rearguard battle before its final extinction.

For two and a half centuries, from the Turkish retreat from central Europe until the retreat of the great West European empires from Asia and Africa in the mid-twentieth century, it was Europe—which the Muslims saw as Christendom—that took the offensive, and Islam that knew the danger, and, over most of its territories and for most of its people, the reality, of foreign, that is, Christian, domination.

The two phases, the first of Muslim advance and Christian retreat, the second of Christian advance and Muslim retreat, were not consecutive, but rather overlapping. In some regions, the reversal of roles began centuries before the siege of Vienna. Already in medieval times, Christians were trying to repel and expel the Muslim invaders of Christendom, and to recover their lost lands. As far back as the ninth century, when a Saracen fleet captured Ostia, sailed up the Tiber, and sacked Rome, the Pope of the time called on the kings and princes of Christendom to send armies to defend the faith. Some of the language used by him and by his immediate successors, trying to rally Christian strength against the invaders, both echo the Muslim language of *jihād* and prefigure the later Christian language of crusade.

There was of course an important difference between the two. The *jihād* was a sacred mission enjoined by scripture and incorporated in the holy law, to continue until all the world was open to the light of Islam. The crusade was a human enterprise, not enjoined—some might rather say forbidden—by Christian scripture, and undertaken for a limited purpose, to defend, or, where lost, to recover, Christian territories. The medieval crusades were successful in recovering from Islamic rule the lost lands of Italy, Iberia and Russia. They failed in the Levant. Their successes in the one, and their failures in the other, defined what came to be the accepted boundaries of Europe.

At the time these boundaries were by no means established. Neither the Spaniards and Portuguese in the southwest, nor the Russians in the east, saw any reason to stop their victorious pursuit of their defeated former masters when they had reached the limits of what subsequently came to constitute their national territories. In the east, the Russians pursued the Tatars into Asia; in the southwest, the Portuguese and the Spaniards followed the Moors into Africa and round Africa into southern Asia. Already in the early sixteenth century, some Ottoman statesmen were aware of the looming danger of European naval power. When Sultan Selim I (1512–20), who had already added Egypt and Syria to the Ottoman realms, remarked to his chief adviser that he intended to conquer the land of the Franks, the adviser replied: "My Sultan, you live in a city whose benefactor is the sea. When the sea is unsafe, no ship comes; when no ship comes, Istanbul's prosperity is lost." A few years later, Lutfi Pasha, the Grand Vizier of Suleyman the Magnificent, raised the matter again with his sovereign, and told him: "Of the previous Sultans, there were many who ruled the land, but few who ruled the sea. In the conduct of war at sea, the infidels are superior to us. We must overcome them."[2]

But the Turks did not overcome the maritime powers at sea, and later in the sixteenth century other voices were raised, warning of the new dangers posed to the Ottomans and to Islam by the extension of European naval and commercial activity to Asia, and at the same time, by the overland advance of the Russians southward and eastward. The Ottomans made some attempt to counter European expansion. In 1569, the Sultan's government considered a plan to dig a canal from the Don to the Volga river, through which Ottoman fleets could sail from the Black Sea into the Caspian. It proved unworkable. Naval expeditions were sent from Ottoman ports on the Red Sea and the Persian Gulf to help their distressed co-religionists in India and Sumatra, but were no match for the ocean-going vessels of the maritime powers, built to face the Atlantic, and therefore able to carry a heavier complement of arms and men. The Ottomans, primarily concerned with Europe, abandoned the attempt in both directions, and concentrated on what seemed at the time the wiser course—to strike straight at the heart of the enemy.

But the blow to the heart of the enemy was held and averted, and in the course of the eighteenth century, the European counter-attack against the Islamic lands gained strength at the center and advanced rapidly at the extremities. By the end of the eighteenth century, much of Muslim India and Southeast Asia were under European imperial domination. The two major Middle Eastern rulers, the Sultan of Turkey and the Shah of Persia, were well aware of these dangers, but could do nothing to help, since they themselves were now facing the direct threat of European advance in their own home territories.

The Russian annexation of the Crimea in 1786 marked another turning point. Until then, the Ottomans had been forced to relinquish many rich provinces in southeastern Europe, but they had all been conquered lands with predominantly Christian populations. The withdrawal affected chiefly Ottoman soldiers and administrators, leaving only relatively small Muslim minorities behind them. But the Crimea had been Muslim and Turkish land since the Middle Ages, and its loss was a bitter blow. This was followed by the rapid expansion of Russian power east and west of the Crimea, along the northern shores of what had once been a Muslim-dominated sea. The Russian seaport of Odessa, it may be recalled, was founded in 1796 on the ruins of a Tatar village. In a series of wars at the end of the eighteenth and the beginning of the nineteenth century, Russian power was extended far into former Persian and Ottoman territory.

So far, these events had affected only the Turkish and Persian-speaking peoples, whose historic awareness of the danger from the north remained vivid until modern times. In the course of the nineteenth century, the advance of the European empires first touched and finally engulfed much of the previously unaffected Arab world. This too began at the extremities, with the French in Algeria in 1830 and the British in Aden in 1839, and in less than a century, involved, in varying degrees, almost the whole Islamic world.

With European dominance came European perceptions and classifications. Sheikh Rifāʿa Rāfiʿ al-Ṭahṭāwi, an Egyptian from Al-Azhar University, who stayed in Paris from 1826–31 as religious preceptor to the Egyptian Student Mission, wrote the first influential Arabic account of a European country: "You should know," he tells his readers, "that the geographers of the Franks have divided the world, from north to south and from east to west, into five parts, which are the lands of Europe, Asia, Africa, America, and the islands of the surrounding Ocean."[3] He then goes on to describe the physical and political geography of Europe, as a preliminary to his discussion and explanation of the governments and laws, the manners and customs, of the French. This was the beginning of what became an extensive literature, both original and translated, in Arabic, Persian, Turkish and other languages, informing Muslim readers and students about the new, challenging, and menacing power of Europe.

By 1920, it seemed that the triumph of Europe over Islam was complete. In Afghanistan and inner Arabia and a few other places difficult of access and offering no attraction, independent Muslim rulers maintained the old ways. Otherwise, new rulers and new ways, introduced or imitated from Europe, prevailed everywhere. Even in the former Russian empire, riven by revolution and civil war, Moscow was reasserting its control over the former, briefly liberated, Muslim dominions of the tsars.

The once great Ottoman Empire was defeated and occupied, its Muslim provinces parcelled out among the victorious powers. Persia, though technically neutral, had been overrun by British and Russian forces, sometimes as allies, sometimes as rivals, sometimes as both. The rest of the Muslim world was incorporated in one or other of the great European empires. It seemed that the long struggle between Islam and Christendom, between the Islamic empires and Europe, had ended in a decisive victory for the West.

But the victory was illusory and of brief duration. The West European empires, by the very nature of the culture, the institutions, even the languages which they brought with them and imposed on their colonial subjects, demonstrated the ultimate incompatibility of democracy and empire, and sealed the doom of their own domination. They taught their subjects English, French and Dutch because they needed clerks in their offices and counting houses. But once these subjects had mastered a Western European language, as did increasing numbers of Muslims in Western-dominated Asia and Africa, they found a new world open to them, full of new and dangerous ideas such as political freedom and national sovereignty and representative government by the consent of the governed.

These ideas powerfully affected both the subjects and masters of the Western empires, making the one unwilling to accept, the other, to impose, an old-style autocratic domination. In the nineteenth century, these ideas had encouraged the Christian subject peoples of the Ottoman Empire to rebel and demand their independence. In the twentieth century, the same ideas had the same effect on the Muslim subject peoples of the European empires, and this time the imperial masters were forced to recognize their own principles and ideals being used against them.

Some of the movements of revolt against Western rule were inspired by religion and fought in the name of Islam. But the most effective at the time—

those that actually won political independence—were led by Westernized intellectuals who fought the West with its own intellectual weapons. Sometimes
indeed they fought the West with Western help and encouragement; Western
sympathizers played a significant and sometimes forgotten role in the development of Turkish, Arab, Indian, and other nationalisms.

From the mid-twentieth century onwards, it became increasingly clear that
the era of European preeminence, in the Islamic lands as elsewhere, had ended.
Most of the Muslim world was now ruled by independent governments, and the
external forces and influences that still affected them came not from Europe, but
from the two new superpowers, the Soviet Union and the United States of America. Though the cultures of both of these derived from European roots, they had
grown into something different and distinctive, and after some initial misunderstandings, this fact was well-recognized in most of the Islamic world. Alien
power and alien penetration were still very much an issue in these lands, but
since they were no longer seen as European, Muslims, even the most passionate,
were able to see Europe in a more friendly, or at least a more neutral, light.

In one sense, the new relationship between Europe and the Islamic world was
a reversion to an earlier phase. Even at times of major clashes between Christendom and Islam—the crusaders in the East, the Ottomans in Austria—there was
a lively commerce between the two worlds, mainly due to European enterprise
and activity. In 1174 Saladin, the hero of the counter-crusade, wrote to the Caliph
in Baghdad to explain his decision to allow the European Christian merchants
to remain in the Levant ports even after they had been reconquered. These merchants, he said, rendered a valuable service, bringing the choicest of Western
products, and in particular, weapons and other war materials.[4] Christian authorities, not surprisingly, took a less benign view of this trade, and the Holy See
in particular tried to stop it by decrees of prohibition and threats of excom-
munication. But all these efforts were of no avail. This profitable traffic continued, and even as the Ottoman armies were advancing into the heart of Europe,
there were Christian merchants eager to supply their needs, and Christian bankers
willing to finance their purchases. The modern purveyors of advanced weaponry
to Saddam Hussein and his peers are the products of a long history.

One of the main reasons for the extent and persistence of this trade was the
relative poverty of Europe and the relative wealth of the Islamic lands. In medieval, even in early Ottoman times, this disparity was very clear. It was primarily the bullion and resources of the New World and of other European
colonial dependencies that fuelled the series of changes by which Europe was
enriched and the world of Islam impoverished. The exhaustion of Europe after
1945 on the one hand, and the immense wealth accruing from oil on the other,
for a while restored the earlier relationship, and placed new and powerful economic weapons in Muslim hands. So far, however, they have not done very well
in the use of these weapons. Oil wealth is unevenly distributed between Muslim
countries and even within the oil-rich countries themselves.

In one respect however, oil wealth has significantly affected Islamic attitudes and activities, in that it has enabled some Muslim governments and an increasing number of wealthy individuals to finance Islamic activities of various kinds in the Muslim world, and, notably, among the new Muslim communities in Europe. European Muslims have received special attention from radical and fundamentalist groups in Muslim countries, profiting from a freedom of propaganda and ease of communication which for the most part they do not enjoy in their homelands. The Iranian revolution in 1979, it will be recalled, was planned and directed from Neauphle-le-Chateau near Paris. There are other movements at the present time, the leaders of which find it easier to operate in a European or American city, combining the liberties and amenities of the West with the potential support of large, resident Muslim communities.

The emergence of these communities has transformed the relationship between Europe and Islam, and added a new element to the Muslim experience of Europe. The Christian reconquest in Italy and Iberia was followed by the total extirpation of Islam in these countries. The ebbing tide of the Tatars in Russia and the Turks in the Balkans left small minorities behind them, among predominantly Christian populations. But these minorities were old-established, often of indigenous origins, and fairly well acculturated. This acculturation did not by any means render them immune from conflicts with their neighbors, as the expulsion of Turks from communist Bulgaria and the recent and current tragedy in Bosnia amply demonstrate. But despite these troubles, it remains clear that the Bosnians are essentially Europeans, having far more in common with their non-Muslim neighbors than with their non-European co-religionists.

The reverse is true of the new Muslim minorities formed by immigration in most of the countries of Western Europe. The very existence of such minorities marks an astonishing change in Muslim attitudes and perceptions. Muslim law and tradition date from the early centuries of Islam, when the Islamic state and faith were in a process of almost continual expansion. Muslim jurists and theologians therefore deal extensively with the situation of non-Muslims living in a Muslim state, and with the proper way to treat them. They devote some but not much attention to the problems of a Muslim living in a non-Muslim state.

The section on this topic, which in law books usually comes in the chapter on *jihād*, deals with the plight of such a Muslim under three different headings. The first is the involuntary traveller—the Muslim who has the misfortune to be taken prisoner of war, or otherwise captured or enslaved and taken to a Christian country, where he remains under duress. The second case is that of "the infidel in the land of the infidels" who sees the light and embraces Islam, and thus finds himself isolated among unbelievers and alienated from his own kin. The third case, mostly discussed during the reconquest of Spain and Sicily and the brief rule of the Crusaders in the Levant, is that of the Muslim whose homeland is conquered by Christians, and who thus finds himself under Christian rule. The consensus of the jurists for all three classes of involuntary sojourners in "the lands of unbelief" is that they must leave and go to a country where a Muslim government rules and where Muslim law prevails. When, in God's good time, the light of Islam is extended or restored to their homelands, they or their descendants may return.

There are however differences of opinion in the application of this rule. For some, the more rigorous, the obligation to depart is immediate and unconditional. According to this view, to stay under non-Muslim rule is, for a Muslim, an act of impiety and a breach of a basic obligation of the holy law. Other, more lenient jurists, while recognizing the basic obligation to depart, attach a number of qualifications which in effect amount to a license to remain under an infidel government provided that that infidel government allows them the free exercise of their religion. This of course raises the further question of what constitutes for a Muslim "the free exercise of his religion," and in particular how far this involves the observance and enforcement of Muslim holy law.

A similar disagreement between the rigorist and lenient schools of juristic interpretation arises in discussions of the voluntary Muslim visitor to non-Muslim lands. The movement of Muslim merchants, and even the establishment of Muslim communities among the idolaters and polytheists in Asia and Africa, seem to have aroused little or no concern. But the voluntary movement of Muslims to Christendom, to the lands of the arch-rival of Islam, was another matter. For the most rigorous, there is only one legitimate reason for a Muslim to travel to Christendom, and that is to negotiate the ransoming or exchange of captives. This could be extended into a general license for ambassadors, though it should be noted that the Muslim states, in contrast to the Christian states, established no resident embassies abroad until the end of the eighteenth century, and very few until the nineteenth. The usual practice was to send an ambassador when there was something to say, and to recall him when he had said it. Most of the early Moroccan embassy reports from Europe are headed "Report on a Mission for the Ransoming of Captives" or words to that effect—presumably to avoid possible legal troubles for the ambassador or for the ruler who sent him.

Some jurists also permitted travel for purposes of trade, but limited this to the purchase of provisions in times of dearth. This too was extended by the more lenient into a general license for Muslim merchants to travel to Europe. Very few however availed themselves of this right, and most of the trade was carried on through Christian—and to a much lesser extent Jewish—visitors and residents in the lands of Islam.

The question of travel for study did not arise, since clearly there was nothing to be learnt from the benighted infidels of the outer wilderness. It was not until the early nineteenth century that the Pasha of Egypt, followed by the Sultan of Turkey and the Shah of Persia, sent the first student missions to Europe. Their main purpose in sending these missions was the modernization of their armed forces, and their action could therefore be justified by the ruling of earlier jurists that it is permissible to learn from the enemy in order more effectively to fight him.

The one contingency that never seems to have occurred to any of those engaged in these discussions was that Muslims, singly or in groups, might chose of their own free will to leave the lands of Islam and to go and settle in a non-Muslim country.

Great numbers did, however, go and settle in Europe in the post-imperial years. Many of them went from former dependencies to the homelands of their former rulers—North Africans to France, south Asians to Britain, Indonesians to Holland, Trans-Caucasians and Central Asians to Russia. But these were not all. There were also many immigrants from countries that had never known imperial rule, notably economic migrants from Turkey and political and religious refugees from Iran. By now there are many millions of Muslim residents in most of the countries of Western Europe, an increasing proportion born and brought up in these countries, with all the expectations to which their birth entitles them and which their education prepares them to demand.

Europe has a long history of dealing with religious minorities—Protestants in Catholic countries, Catholics in Protestant countries, Jews in both. It is a chequered history, marked by dissent and repression, persecution and expulsion, and at times religious wars. In our own time, after an appalling finale under Nazi rule and influence, most people in most European countries have agreed to accept diversity and coexistence, and there are few if any who can justly complain of religious persecution.

But the Muslim presence in Europe raises new questions. In part this is because most of the Muslim immigrants are racially different from Europeans, and racial prejudice is alive and well in much of Europe. But even in the purely religious sphere, there is an important new element in the situation. Islam is not only a different religion; it also embodies a different conception of what religion means—of what it defines, delimits and requires. For most modern Europeans, religion is primarily concerned with belief and worship; religious freedom means the right to hold, express and teach these beliefs, and to organize and conduct the appropriate worship, all this without suffering discrimination in other walks of life. For traditional Muslims Islam has meant all that and much more. In particular, it has meant the right to live by the holy law of Islam, which is concerned not only with belief and worship, but also with a whole range of civil, criminal and especially personal matters.

For Muslims, as for all other people, their expectations are shaped by their own history and traditions. In the great Muslim empires, when Islam was dominant and the various Christian denominations were tolerated minorities, these minorities enjoyed a large measure of communal autonomy, including the running of their own educational systems, and even the enforcement of their own laws, insofar as these did not conflict with the basic laws of the state. Their communal authorities exercised real power, with the right to levy taxes, to adjudicate disputes, and even to impose punishments on offenders. It is understandable that Muslims, finding themselves a minority in Christian countries, should expect the same level, and more explicitly, the same kind of tolerance, from a Christian government as Christian minorities had been given by Muslim governments. This expectation was not weakened but confirmed by their recent experience in their home countries under European imperial rulers, who were generally rather cautious and conservative in matters of education, personal status and law.

Asian and African Muslims, living as minorities in modern European democracies, thus find themselves in possession of both more and less freedom than they want, expect and can use. The basic rights of the citizen and even of the permanent resident are naturally welcome, and often constitute some improvement on their previous condition. But the Western perception of the status of women has for many Muslims been deeply troubling. The kind of communal and cultural, even social and legal autonomy that was customary in the Muslim empires is impossible in modern Europe, and the attempts on the one side to acquire this autonomy, on the other to refuse it, have led to misunderstanding and friction.

There are several possible futures for the Muslim minorities in Western Europe. There are some who argue that the next generation, European by birth and education, will follow the path blazed by the Jews, who in an earlier age emerged from the ghettos to become part of the mainstream of civilized Europe. There are others who point to the powerful European forces that sometimes blocked or even reversed that process, noting that Muslims are present in far greater numbers than the Jews, and moreover, unlike the Jews, are sustained and reinforced by a vast Muslim world outside Europe. There are some who see their future rather as distinctive cultural and even social enclaves within a larger, more tolerant, more open European community, and others again who even see Europe itself as destined, finally, to become part of the House of Islam.

Whatever their future, two things are already clear. First, there is now a large, significant, and irremovable Muslim presence in Western Europe, which will henceforth play an increasing part in European life. And second, these communities, through the thousand links that they will inevitably retain with their ancestral homelands, will play an increasingly important part in the future development of the Muslim world as a whole.

Notes

1. Ibn Khurradādhbeh, *Kitāb al-masālik wa'l-mamālik*, ed. M. J. de Goeje (Leiden, 1889), p. 155.

2. *Das Asafname des Lutfi Pascha*, ed. and trans. R. Tschudi (Berlin, 1910), p. 34.

3. *Takhlīṣ al-Ibrīz fītalkhīṣ Bārīz*, ed. Mahdī 'Allam, Aḥmad Aḥmad Badawī and Anwar Lūqa (Cairo, 1958), p. 69.

4. Abū Shāma, *Al-Rawḍatayn fīakhbār al-dawlatayn*, eds. M. Ḥilmī, M. Aḥmad and M. Muṣṭafa Ziyāda (Cairo, 1962), I/ii, 621–23.

14

Cold War and Détente
in the 16th Century

❧❧❧❧

The drawing of historical parallels has fallen into disrepute of late, partly no doubt as a result of some strikingly inept and widely disseminated recent examples. The working historian is accustomed to evidence which is fragmentary, unreliable, inconsistent and often contradictory, thus accurately reflecting the human condition. It is for this reason that history is one of the most valuable of educational and intellectual disciplines; for this reason too that historical statements are much more tentative, much more hypothetical than is normally expected in the comparativist social sciences. The historian knows that his materials are friable and unsafe, and he can only watch with wonderment and alarm as the model-building social scientists raise great structures of the bricks which he reluctantly supplies to them.

A common form of comparison involves the use of modern Western statements about non-modern or non-Western societies, thus, in effect, arguing in a circle. If, for example, we compare the Crusades with current events in the Middle East, and do so on the basis of a modern Western historian of the Crusades, then we are in fact not making a comparison between two sequences of events at different times, but between two modern views, one of the medieval, the other of the present-day Middle East, the first inevitably contaminated by the second. Such a comparison is of little value, since the similarities lie not in the events or situations, but in the eye of the observer.

Sometimes, however, it happens that an authentic contemporary document depicts a situation which suggests striking parallels with our own day. The comparison is often made between the confrontation of the free world and the Soviet Union at the present time, and the confrontation of Christendom and Islam, the Hapsburgs and the Ottomans, in the sixteenth century. Then as now, two different worlds, two different ideologies, two different ways of life stood face to face and contended for the mastery of the known world. There were times when it seemed that the centralized, disciplined power of the Turk was over-whelming and that Christian Europe, weak, divided and irresolute, was doomed. To complete the parallel, the Turk was hampered by the presence of another, rival Islamic power on his Eastern flank—the Shi'ite Empire of Persia, which prevented him from concentrating all his forces in the West and thus gave Europe a respite from destruction. All these points are graphically made in a letter dated 1 June 1560 and written in Istanbul by Ogier Ghiselin de Busbecq, the Hapsburg Ambassador to the Ottoman Court. Busbecq describes the patience, sobriety and strict discipline of the Turks and goes on to say:

> How different are our soldiers, who on campaign despise ordinary food and expect dainty dishes . . . and elaborate meals. If these are not supplied, they mutiny and cause their own ruin; and even if they are supplied, they ruin themselves just the same. For each man is his own worst enemy and has no more deadly foe than his own intemperance which kills him if the enemy is slow to do so. I tremble when I think of what the future must bring when I compare the Turkish system with our own; one army must prevail and the other be destroyed, for certainly both cannot remain un-scathed. On their side are the resources of a mighty empire, strength unimpaired, experience and practice in fighting, a veteran soldiery, ha-bituation to victory, endurance of toil, unity, order, discipline, frugality, and watchfulness. On our side is public poverty, private luxury, impaired strength, broken spirit, lack of endurance and training; the soldiers are insubordinate, the officers avaricious; there is contempt for discipline; li-cence, recklessness, drunkenness, and debauchery are rife; and, worst of all, the enemy is accustomed to victory, and we to defeat. Can we doubt what the result will be? Persia alone interposes in our favour; for the enemy, as he hastens to attack, must keep an eye on this menace in his rear. But Persia is only delaying our fate; it cannot save us. When the Turks have settled with Persia, they will fly at our throats supported by the might of the whole East; how unprepared we are I dare not say![1]

To Busbecq and his contemporaries it may well have seemed that Europe was doomed. Yet how wrong they were. Though the Ottoman power was still to survive for some time, it had already passed its peak. The Turks did not in fact settle with Persia but continued to fight wars against them until the eighteenth century, after which both Turkey and Persia ceased to pose a serious threat. The great age of the Eastern empires was past; the great age of Christian Europe was just beginning.

Note

1. Edward Seymour Forster (trans.), *The Turkish Letters of Ogier Ghiselin de Busbecq* (Oxford, Clarendon Press, 1927), pp. 111–12.

15

From Pilgrims to Tourists
A *Survey of Middle Eastern Travel*

❧❦❧

Let me begin with a word or two of definition. By travel, I mean what one might call personal journeys, undertaken by an individual, either by his own decision or by the decision of some other individual who chose and sent him for a particular reason. I am including neither the migrations of nomads nor the invasions of armies. These are obviously of far greater historical importance, but they are not my present subject, which is limited to individual travel, and of course, necessarily and inevitably, to journeys that left some kind of record.

I start with pilgrims, not because they are the earliest chronologically (they are not); but because the pilgrimage—more specifically the Muslim pilgrimage to Mecca and Medina—is the first really major factor of personal travel over vast distances in human history, and for long it remained the most important single factor.

There were of course pilgrimages before the advent of Islam; pilgrimage was practiced by both Jews and Christians as well as in some of the eastern religions. But it is usually, almost invariably, what one might call in modern parlance an optional extra.

It is not optional in Islam. A Muslim is required, as one of the five pillars of his faith, on par with belief, prayer, fasting and charity, to go at least once in a lifetime to the sacred places in Mecca and Medina where the Prophet was born and carried out his mission, and to do so at a specified time in the year, in the sacred month of communal pilgrimage. Christians and Jews could go on pilgrimage to Jerusalem at any time, whenever convenient. Muslims could also go on a pilgrimage to Mecca and Medina at any time, but this was the lesser pilgrimage—the *'Umra*. The major pilgrimage, the *Ḥajj* properly so-called, takes place every year on prescribed days in the Muslim calendar, in the month accordingly known as Dhu'l-Ḥijja. Since the Muslim religious calendar is purely lunar, the month of pilgrimage is not identified with any season, and rotates through the solar year three times a century.

Almost from the beginning the Hajj brought travellers from the entire world of Islam (already in medieval times reaching from Spain and Morocco at one end to Southeast Asia and Central Asia at the other), to join together at one time, in one place, and engage in certain common rituals and other activities. This, clearly, has been a factor of enormous importance in the cultural and social history of the Islamic world. Every year, great numbers of Muslims, from many countries and from different races and social strata, leave their homes and travel, often over vast distances, to take part in a common act of worship. These journeys, unlike the mindless collective migrations familiar in ancient and medieval times, are voluntary and individual. Each is a personal act, following a personal decision, and resulting in a wide range of significant personal experience.

This degree of physical mobility, without parallel in pre-modern societies, involves important social, intellectual and economic consequences. The pilgrim, if wealthy, may be accompanied by slaves, some of whom he sells on the way to pay the expenses of his journey. If he is a merchant, he may combine his pilgrimage with a business trip, buying and selling commodities in the places through which he travels, and thus learning to know the products, markets, merchants, customs and practices of many lands. If he is a scholar, he may take the opportunity to attend lectures, meet colleagues, and acquire books, thus participating in the diffusion and exchange of knowledge and ideas. The needs of the pilgrimage—the demands of the faith reinforcing the requirements of government and commerce—help to maintain a network of communications between the far-flung Muslim lands; the experience of the pilgrimage gives rise to a rich literature of travel, bringing information about distant places, and a heightened awareness of belonging to a larger whole. This awareness is reinforced by participation in the common rituals and ceremonies of the pilgrimage in Mecca and Medina, and the communion with fellow-Muslims of other lands and peoples. The physical mobility of important groups of people entails a measure of social and cultural mobility, and a corresponding evolution of institutions.

Islamic history offers many examples of the impact of the pilgrimage; the biographies of learned and holy men are full of accounts of formative meetings and studies in the Holy Cities, on the way there, and on the way back. The wandering scholar is a familiar feature of medieval societies: the pilgrimage ensured that the wanderers met, at a determined time and place. It provided the Islamic world as a whole with a centre and a forum, which already in medieval times contributed greatly to the formation and maintenance of an Islamic consensus—almost, one might say, an Islamic public opinion.

The effect of the pilgrimage on communications and commerce, on ideas and institutions, has not been adequately explored; it may never be, since much of it will, in the nature of things, have gone unrecorded. There can, however, be no doubt that this institution—the most important agency of voluntary, personal mobility before the age of the great European discoveries—must have had profound effects on all the communities from which the pilgrims came, through which they traveled, and to which they returned. This vast movement of great numbers of people every year required a system of communication, contact, relay stations, covering the whole of the Islamic world.

There are other, lesser pilgrimages. One, already mentioned, is the *'Umra,* the pilgrimage to Mecca and Medina at some time other than the Hajj; there are also other pilgrimages to holy places, which the Muslims call *Ziyāra*—literally a visit: visits to the tombs of holy men and the like. There are of course parallels to this in both Judaism and Christianity.

A very important difference between the Christian and Muslim experience, of great relevance to the cultural history of both civilizations, is that whereas the major Christian holy places were under Muslim rule, Muslims had no holy places under Christian rule. Christians were not required, but felt it to be a moral and religious obligation to visit the places where Christ was born and lived and died. And so, through the centuries, a stream of Christian pilgrims from different parts of the Christian world traveled to the Holy Land to visit these places. The same is true of Jews, who came to the Holy Land to visit their holy places; and like the Christians they too came not only from within but also from outside the Muslim world. The Muslims, and for that matter the Jews living in the Muslim world, had no comparable need to visit the lands of Christendom. There were of course Christians living under Muslim rule, but they were mostly not of the Roman communion and for long had no incentive to visit Rome.

Beside pilgrims, there were other kinds of religiously-inspired travelers. An obvious example is the missionary. Organized missionary activity is distinctively Christian, and from early times Christian missions were active on and beyond the frontiers of Christendom. For centuries this activity did not include the lands of Islam, for a very good reason: apostasy in Muslim law is a capital offence, involving the execution both of the apostate and of his seducer. This did rather put a damper on Christian missionary activities among Muslims.

But the wars of religion following the Reformation in Europe created a new need and, since Muslim authorities had no objection to Christians proselytizing each other, a new opportunity. This gave rise to a great effort by European Christian missionaries to recruit the Eastern churches to either the Protestant or the Catholic cause. Here was, so to speak, a large reserve of uncommitted Christians in the East: Christians who were neither Protestants nor Catholics, and who might provide a useful addition to one or other of the warring parties in the Western Christian world. So we find intensive activity, especially from Rome. . . . Their efforts achieved a fair measure of success in creating Uniate churches, i.e. groups that broke away from the Coptic, Armenian, Greek and other eastern churches and entered into communion with Rome.

This process established a new and important line of communication between

Christian Europe and the Middle East. Many Europeans—scholars, missionaries, clergymen of various sorts, traveled to the eastern lands to establish links with the local Christian communities, and before very long, Christians from those parts began to travel to Europe. Arabic-speaking Christians, notably Maronites from Lebanon, but also others from eastern churches in communion with Rome, traveled to Italy, to France, to Germany, to Spain, a few even to England—and, among other things, played a role of some importance in the beginning and development of Arabic and Syriac studies in European universities. In the eighteenth century members of the Maronite al-Sam'ānī family, for example, whose name was Italianized into Assemani, cataloged and described Eastern manuscripts in the Vatican Library and in other collections in Florence and Venice. Another Maronite scholar, Michael Casiri (Ghazīrī), published a magnificent catalog of the Arabic collection in the Escurial Library in Madrid (two volumes, 1776–1790). A Chaldean Uniate priest from Mosul in Iraq visited the Spanish colonies in America between 1668 and 1683 and gave us what is certainly the first Arabic description of the New World, including South and Central America as far north as Mexico. His account, in Arabic, was published by the Jesuit fathers in Beirut, almost a hundred years ago.[1]

Muslims did not engage in organized missionary activity. But of course there were the wandering Sufis who carried the faith, particularly eastwards into Central Asia, India and other places. We have much less record of that, though there is some. We have accounts also by disciples, both of holy men and of learned teachers, who traveled great distances to sit at the feet of the great masters of the faith. Some of them even compiled books containing short biographies of the teachers whose courses they had attended.

This created a fairly considerable movement and left a not uninteresting literature. There were also men of religion of one sort or another, sent to take up an appointment; sent for example from Rome to supervise the Catholic missions and Uniate communitites, or sent from various other European countries, sometimes by churches, sometimes by missionary societies, sometimes by commercial companies and—increasingly—by governments. A notable example was Edward Pococke (1604–1691) who spent some years in Aleppo as chaplain to the English merchants of the Levant Company. While there he studied Arabic first under a Jewish and then under an Arab teacher. On his return to England in 1636 he was appointed to the newly-created Chair of Arabic at Oxford University. These religious travelers also have Muslim equivalents—men sent out to take up an appointment as a Mufti or a Qadi. They did not usually leave much written record, but there are some, and because of their rarity they are of greater interest. One may add archaeologists, whose writings are not limited to archaeology, nor were their activities always so limited. They too have left us some very interesting travel records.

I have spoken almost entirely of western travelers to the East. What about eastern travelers to the West? As noted, there were no places of pilgrimage, no teachers or scholars or centers of learning to which they thought it worth going, that is to say, not until the early nineteenth century. In the Middle Ages, there were European scholars and students who went to what were then the great Arab Muslim universities in Spain and in Sicily. But that came to an end, and those who had been students became teachers. Those who had been teachers should have become students, but it took them some time to realize that fact.

Finally they did, and from the beginning of the nineteenth century, increasing numbers of students traveled from the Middle East to the West. Usually they went in student missions, groups of students sent by their governments to study in western countries. The Pasha of Egypt, the Sultan of Turkey, the Shah of Iran, all sent such missions; and, as one can readily imagine, this created considerable problems. These were people to whom it had been virtually inconceivable that one would go by one's own choice to an infidel country. In the past it was universally agreed among the juristic authorities of Islam that it was a bad thing for Muslims to go to a country ruled by non-Muslims. The usual view was that such a thing was categorically prohibited; that Muslims must not go to a non-Muslim country voluntarily. Some allowed it in certain narrowly-defined circumstances—to redeem captives, to go on a mission to negotiate the redemption of captives and perhaps to buy supplies in times of dearth or of critical shortage.

Naturally this changed in the course of time, particularly with the spread of Christian rule to vast areas of the Muslim world where a mass exodus was hardly feasible.

At the beginning of the nineteenth century, student missions were sent to Paris, then to London and to various other European cities. At first they were mostly military, but they included also some others. We have a fascinating account by an Egyptian Sheikh, Rifā'a Rāfi'al-Tahtāwī, from an unreformed Al-Azhar, who was sent to Paris in 1826, not as a member of the student mission but as a sort of chaplain, to attend to the students' spiritual welfare. He wrote a fascinating book about what he saw and experienced.[2] Some of the other missions have left some record, though on the whole regrettably little.

A second major category is travel related to war: I did at the beginning exclude invasions, expulsions and other military movements, but there is still a certain amount of individual travel related to war and its preparation. In principle, there was of course a permanent state of war between Islam and Christendom as laid down by Shari'a; the one is the Dar al-Islam (House of Islam); the other is the Dar al-Harb (the house of war). Theoretically there could be truces but no permanent peace. In point of fact reasonably peaceful relations were at times maintained between some Christian and some Muslim governments.

An interesting category of travelers is captives. During the ongoing state of war between Islam and Christendom from the early Middle Ages until the nineteenth century, great numbers were captured on both sides; by armies or raiding parties on land, by corsairs at sea or on the coasts. From the Muslim side, Tatars raided eastern and south-eastern Europe; corsairs from North Africa raided the shores and shipping of western Europe, reaching as far as the British Isles and on occasion even as far as Madeira and Iceland. Similarly, there were the Christian orders who conducted holy war against Muslim shipping in the Mediterranean and also collected a fair amount of booty, including captives. The departure into captivity is entirely involuntary and is therefore not part of our present topic. However, a fair proportion of these captives either escaped or were redeemed and some of them have left written records of their adventures—whom they met, what they did, what was done to them and what they saw.

Some of these, though brief and simple, are quite informative. The Corsairs carried off great numbers of European Christians, some of whom were later freed and wrote accounts of their handling by the corsairs. One of the most fascinating of these accounts was written by an Icelandic priest called Olufr Eigilsson, who with several hundred other captives was taken from Iceland. He was eventually redeemed, returned home and wrote about his experiences—a very interesting comment from the far end of the world about the corsairs and their behavior.[3]

A striking difference is that while we have many accounts written by Christians who escaped or were redeemed from Muslim captivity, we have hardly any accounts written by Muslims returning from Christian captivity. There were many who either escaped or were redeemed or were exchanged, but I am aware of only two who wrote about it. One was a Turkish Qadi who in April 1597 was on his way to take up an appointment in Cyprus, and was captured by the Knights of St. John and taken to Malta. Two years later he was released, and wrote a short account of his misadventures.[4] The other was an Ottoman interpreter, Osman Aga, who was captured by the Habsburg forces and held prisoner for some time; he could speak German and therefore was able to communicate with his captors. He was taken around to various places and eventually released. Exceptionally, in 1724–5 he wrote two accounts of his adventures among the infidels. Clearly, they did not evoke much interest. Each survives in a single manuscript. Both are in European collections, and seem to be totally unknown in the east.[5] The same is true of the Qadi's account of his travels and misadventures. Obviously there was a great curiosity on the one side; there seems to have been no corresponding curiosity on the other. The captives would surely have told their story if there had been anyone interested, but it seems that there was none.

Another category of travelers related to war and its preparation is spies. In the nature of things, the surviving documentation regarding espionage is scanty and ambiguous. It has been well said that a secret service that isn't secret doesn't serve. There are indications, even pieces of evidence, and they give us some kind of a picture, but it is fragmentary and tantalizing. Obviously there was espionage between the Christian and Muslim worlds. We have sufficient references to indicate that this was carried on a fairly extensive scale, but our information about it is very limited.

Already in medieval times there were Byzantine spies among the Christian populations in Syria and Iraq who reported, generally through ecclesiastical channels, but not exclusively so. A famous Byzantine work on how to run the empire: *De Administrando Imperio*,[6] gives material obviously obtained by intelligence services about the Islamic lands. Apart from that, there are odd references: for example the migration of Spanish Jews from Spain to the Ottoman Empire in the 15th and 16th centuries created perhaps opportunity, certainly suspicion both ways. . . .

Espionage becomes more of a source for the historian in modern times. In the nineteenth and twentieth centuries, the scale of operation is vastly increased and, through the opening of archives, information is more readily though not immediately accessible.

Another category of travelers somehow related to war might be lumped together under the heading of "experts". From quite an early date, Muslim armies realized the value of European weapons, and there were always Christian European merchants willing to bring and sell them. In Ottoman times the English Levant company maintained a gunshop in Istanbul selling choice weapons of war to the Turks to help them in their invasion of Christian Europe. All the Christian countries participated in this trade. From the seventeenth century onwards, they offered not just weapons, but also expertise. Sometimes the experts went as adventurers; sometimes they became what the Christians called renegades and what the Muslims called Muhtadi, one who has found the true path—the same thing of course, from a different perspective. A number of European officers went and served in various Middle Eastern armies in the seventeenth and eighteenth centuries; some were converted to Islam, some not.

From the late eighteenth century, they began to come with the approval and even often by the appointment of their governments. The Baron de Tott, a French officer of Hungarian origin who went to Turkey in 1755 to learn Turkish, noted what was wrong with the Turkish forces and then, from 1773 to 1755, went on a French-sponsored mission to help the Turks modernize their army. He was the first of many, and he wrote a fascinating book describing his adventures.[7]

Another example, a little later, was the Prussian Helmut von Moltke, a famous name in Prussian military history, who in 1835, as a young officer, went to Turkey on a private visit and was hired by the Sultan to help reorganize the Ottoman armies. He too wrote a remarkable account of what he saw and heard.[8]

A more recent example—again German—is Liman von Sanders, a German cavalry general who commanded the German forces and also for a while part of the Ottoman forces during the First World War. His book[9] is a major contribution to the history of the First World War in the Levant. There were many experts of various kinds from France, from England, from Prussia, from Italy and from other places, and there is a fairly extensive literature resulting from their activities.

One might perhaps add another military category and that is conquerors:

those who come, conquer, rule and then appear there as part of the "new administration". But these hardly qualify as individual travel.

Another major motive for travel is trade. That is probably the oldest of all, going back to remote antiquity, and here by the way Middle Eastern travelers visited the West long before westerners ever visited the Middle East. We know for example that the Phoenicians went as far as Cornwall, where they were interested in the tin mines, and of course to Spain, Marseilles and other places. Trade, unlike some other forms of economic activity, was strongly approved by the Islamic tradition. It is praised in the Qur'an, and the honorable merchant is an almost idealized figure in Muslim tradition, particularly in the Hadith, the sayings attributed to the Prophet.

Merchant travel has left us an enormous body of material. In the early centuries, Europe had very little to offer; its people produced very little by way of goods, and they had no money with which to buy, and so the commerce between the Middle East and Europe was extremely limited. The only bulk commodities they could offer to Muslim buyers were weapons (European weapons were, as noted, appreciated from an early date) and slaves.

European slaves were, again, highly appreciated for different purposes. Sometimes they were taken by capture, sometimes sold by enterprising European merchants who had no compunction in selling not their own countrymen but their 'neighbors', so to speak, into slavery. Here we may recall that the English word "slave" comes from the word Slav, because most of the early slaves in Europe were from Eastern Europe and were sold into slavery by their neighbors on either side, by Western and Central Europeans or by Turks and Tatars.

After the discovery of America, and the exploitation of its resources, particularly in the first instance the gold and silver mines of the New World, Europeans suddenly found themselves with money to spend and with something to sell. They now began to buy all sorts of interesting things from the East. Trade developed very rapidly and very extensively and has left us not only travel narratives but also, and more importantly, archival records. The European trading companies set up what they called factories, not in the modern sense of places where things are manufactured but centers of trade, in a number of Middle Eastern cities, and these have left extensive records which are a very valuable source of information on economic history. Here again, Middle Eastern travel in the West is very limited until modern times.

Another related category of travel literature, for a long time also primarily concerned with trade, is provided by embassies and those who reside or work in them. Diplomats are travelers of a sort, and occasionally have interesting things to say on matters other than diplomacy, particularly in the earlier period. The sending or the exchange of ambassadors, goes back to a very remote antiquity. The Book of Proverbs tells us "A wicked messenger falleth into mischief but a faithful ambassador is health" (xiii, 17). In the earliest books of the Hebrew Bible, there are a number of references to ambassadors being sent from one ruler to another. It is interesting that the word used for ambassador in the Hebrew Bible is *mal'akh*, messenger, which of course later is specialized to mean one special sort of messenger—one sent by God, an angel. The Greek word *angelos*, from which angel comes, also means a messenger or envoy and was later similarily specialized. The semantic evolution of the Hebrew *mal'akh* and the Greek *angelos* and its many derivatives in the languages of Christendom is parallel.

The sending of envoys was already well-established by the time of the early books of the Hebrew Bible and continued through classical antiquity into medieval and modern times. The usual practice was that when a ruler had something to say to a neighboring ruler, he sent an ambassador to say it. The ambassador said it and then went home. This eminently sensibly and thrifty procedure was maintained for many centuries, until towards the end of the Middle Ages, the beginning of the modern period, when a new practice was developed by Europeans and at first by no one else; that of maintaining continuous diplomatic contact through resident missions.

This new and unprecedented practice began with the Italian merchant communities in the Byzantine empire. There were sizeable colonies of Venetian, Genoese and later other Italian merchants who, for purposes of trade, stayed for long periods and formed resident communities. The Byzantines allowed these communities certain privileges, one of which was having a chief of their own who represented them in dealings with the government. They looked for a title to give to this chief and they took the old Roman title of a senior city official: they called him the consul. That is how the term consul began to acquire its later and present-day meaning. The Consul of the Venetians in Constantinople was recognized by the Byzantine government as the head of the Venetian community, but inevitably he also represented the government of the Venetian Republic in its dealings with Byzantium.

That was the beginning; from this there developed fairly rapidly the practice of resident embassies in the capital and resident consulates in other cities, chiefly in sea ports and trading centers. For a long time these were primarily concerned with trade, and were even, to a considerable extent, maintained and manned by merchants. Their reports deal therefore with conditions inside the country, and often contain detailed and perceptive descriptions. From the end of the eighteenth century onwards, principally as a result of the Revolutionary and Napoleonic Wars, the embassies become more professional and their reports more strictly concerned with diplomatic and political matters.

It was not until some centuries after the first European missions in Muslim lands that Muslim governments finally decided to establish resident embassies in Europe. They began rather fitfully towards the end of the eighteenth century, and they didn't really get firmly established until well into the nineteenth century.

We have a fair number of embassy reports from the Muslim side. Returning Ottoman envoys generally wrote an account of their travels, called *Sefaret-name*, embassy book.[10] From the end of the eighteenth century onwards, these became more standardized along European lines. European reports were of course far more extensive and bulky. For example—in the Public Record Office in London, Foreign Office series 7, the collections of volumes containing communications between the Foreign Office in London and the British embassy in Istanbul, for the period 1780 to 1905, consists of 5,490 volumes. Foreign Office series 60, dealing with relations with Persia for a much shorter period, 1807–1905, comprises 734 volumes. These are just the embassy files. In addition of course there are communications with the consulates and also separate files on special topics. During the nineteenth century, successive British governments were very much concerned with the suppression of the slave trade, particularly though not exclusively in the Middle East. From 1816 when they started, to 1892, there are 2,276 volumes of documents dealing with suppression of the slave trade. So whereas on other topics and other kinds of travel, we complain about lack of documentation, for this period and this kind of material, any complaint would be in the opposite direction.

After the trader and the diplomat, the third in chronological sequence among major travellers from the West to the East is the journalist. In a sense, journalism first appeared as a concomitant rather than a successor of commerce and government. In the 1790s the French Embassy in Istanbul published a newsletter, which in time became a newspaper, to bring the message of revolution to any who could read French. General Bonaparte set up a kind of newspaper in Egypt, and in the years that followed, missionaries, merchants and governments established newspapers of various kinds, first in foreign, then in Middle Eastern languages. Foreign journalists did not come to the Middle East in significant numbers or report in significant detail until the Crimean War, in which Britain and France fought on the side of the Ottoman Empire against Russia. Both Western countries already had an important daily press, and a wide range of readers who wanted daily reports from the battlefronts. This brought two important and related innovations to the Middle East. The first was the telegraph, extended from Western Europe to Istanbul, and the second, inevitably following, was the war correspondent. The first message, sent in September 1855 from Istanbul to Europe, read: "Allied Forces have entered Sebastopol."

From then until now, great numbers of correspondents from all over the world have gone to the Middle East and reported their findings for newspapers, radio, television, and eventually in books. Some of these journalists actually took the trouble to learn the languages and study the cultures of the region, and produced writings of lasting value.

By the twentieth century journalistic travellers no longer consisted exclusively of outsiders visiting the Middle East. The people of the Middle East were developing their own modern media and the journalist, alongside the officer and the politician, was coming to play an increasingly important public role. But their activities were severely hampered by the authoritarian regimes still prevailing in most of the countries of the region, and the number of publications able to send and maintain foreign correspondents is still limited. They are not for that reason unimportant.

Our final category is tourists, a term used here to denote those who do not have any discernible practical purpose in travelling other than seeking entertainment, amusement, instruction, something to talk about with their friends and the like. It is not easy to say when and where precisely the tourist makes his first appearance in the Middle East; this is largely a question of definition, but it would not be unreasonable to say that it begins with the extension eastwards of what in England was known as the Grand Tour; it may even be the origin of the term.

The Grand Tour was the practice of young gentlemen, and after a while even young ladies, of good family wandering off to France and then to the Western Mediterranean countries to see something of the world, to learn something about art and music, to enjoy the cultural amenities. After a while, they even wandered further east into the Ottoman lands—and even beyond the Ottoman lands—but that came later.

Such travel became quite popular with literary figures, and several famous writers at some stage in their careers went on an eastern tour. These were times when travel in the Middle East was often difficult, sometimes dangerous, but they went, in increasing numbers, from Europe and then also America. Among the writers who left accounts of their tours were Melville, Chateaubriand, Thackeray, Mark Twain, Gustave Flaubert, E.M. Forster and more recently George Duhamel, to name writers of English and French only. There are many others. We sometimes find aspiring politicians; a certain Benjamin Disraeli for example traveled in 1830–31 and even thought of joining the Turkish army as a volunteer in the Albanian War.[11] Byron of course chose the Greek side, but that hardly qualifies as tourism.

Some travelers were doctors, and we hear of physicians who went touring in the Middle East, perhaps because they had been told that as physicians they had opportunities which no other westerner could hope to have. A fascinating Irish physician called R. R. Madden wrote a two-volume account of his travels in Turkey, Egypt, Nubia and Palestine between 1824 and 1827. These involved frequent visits to harems, which he was able to enter as a doctor, whereas other males were of course totally forbidden: he was entirely virtuous, he hastens to assure us. He felt the ladies' pulses through a curtain, but was able to give some of the most interesting accounts of the harem.

Another category of tourists had even better access to the harem and that was of course ladies. The most notable of these is Lady Mary Wortley Montagu, whom one might call a tourist. She was the wife of the British ambassador; she therefore had no formal duties, no official function and was able to conduct herself as a tourist with the freedom and leisure which that gave her. Her letters are among the very best. There are other ladies who are certainly worth reading.

Until fairly recently, they were all Western ladies. Before the beginnings of modernization, women from the Middle East did occasionally travel to Europe, as part of the household of a diplomatic, commercial, or other traveler, but for the most part they had neither the opportunity to receive impresssions nor the education to express and record them. This began to change at the turn of the twentieth century, when for the first time literate Muslim ladies from the Middle East were able to travel to Europe, establish communication, and write about their experiences and impressions. But they remain relatively few.

There were a number of practical problems faced by both Western tourists in the Middle East and Eastern travelers to the West. One obviously was language. Nobody in the West knew any Turkish, very few knew any Arabic, and nobody in the Middle East knew English or even French, until the beginning of the nineteenth century. The only European language that was known at all was Italian, the dominant Mediterranean language, which was widely used in the Ottoman lands. Most of the interpreters who served as a medium of communication between foreign diplomats and foreign merchants and local authorities did so in Italian, usually through two-stage translation. From the early nineteenth century onwards, the problem of language becomes much easier. Turks and then others, realized that they had to learn Western languages in order to communicate with the modern world, and a knowledge first of Italian, then of French and later of English, became very widespread in all these lands.

Another difficulty was the quarantine, arising from the fear of the plague, which was often endemic in the Middle Eastern lands. The danger of contagion was well understood in the Middle Ages. We have medieval Arabic texts which talk about the danger of communicating plagues by garments, by contact, by travelers from one town to another. They were aware of the nature and danger of contagion, but they did not devise any method of dealing with it.

Europe devised the famous "quarantine," the system of isolating people who came from the Muslim lands for a period of time, in principle forty days, in what was known from the Italian as a "lazaretto," until they were deemed safe and allowed out. We have descriptions from the Middle Eastern side of the humiliation which they suffered in going to Europe, where even ambassadors were confined to a lazaretto for quarantine, before they were permitted to continue their journey. The forty day rule was not always strictly observed, the period of detention being sometimes longer, sometimes shorter. The quarantine was a major obstacle to travel, one frequently discussed by travelers both ways.

In modern times, the word travel immediately evokes the word "passport." This in its present form is a fairly recent invention. But passports and security checks were already there in the Middle Ages, and we have a number of reports, especially by Christian pilgrims, who as Christians and pilgrims were doubly suspect, about the security checks which they had to undergo while they were traveling first to Egypt, then to Jerusalem and other holy places.

A final question: How does one travel? The simplest, primary method is of course to walk. There were indeed some who felt that that was the way to do it, especially if they were going on a pilgrimage. The Hebrew for pilgrimage is indeed "going on foot." But for a pilgrimage from, shall we say, Morocco to Mecca, or from Sumatra to Mecca, walking is not very practical, and in the course of time they developed other methods of travel.

After walking, the next step is to ride. What does one ride? The first that comes to mind is the horse, and here one may mention, in passing, such major technological developments in horse-riding, as the bridle and the stirrup. The stirrup made it possible to ride fast and far, without falling off. This revolutionized calvalry warfare. It also helped the Persians, who apparently introduced the stirrup in the Middle East, to build up their remarkable network of courier routes and relay stations, which is described with admiration by Greek and other visitors.

The donkey, of course, was popular, universal, less expensive and more manageable than the horse, and better able to cope with difficult terrain, but not so good for very long distances.

The camel is the supreme technological innovation of the Middle East, remarkably efficient and cost-effective. This animal can travel great distances, carry great loads, and requires very little by way of food and water. But the camel also, in a sense, set the limits for the Muslim advance on Europe, both by the Moors in Spain and the Turks in the Balkans. The camel was superb for the Middle East and North Africa. In the more humid climate of Europe, it did not flourish.

One would expect at some stage that there would be vehicles, and their absence is very remarkable. We do hear from time to time of two-wheeled carts. But when Ibn Baṭṭūta, a great Moroccan traveler in the early fourteenth century, reached the Turkish steppes, he remarks with astonishment on a device which he found there: a four-wheeled cart. This was new and strange to him, and he was very much impressed by it.[12]

It remained unusual in the Middle East. The camel for a long time continued to be much more cost-effective than any kind of vehicle. Carts need roads, roads need upkeep; carts need to be drawn, and are dangerously open to seizure or requisition. Wheeled vehicles didn't really come into general use until the early nineteenth century, when the British were interested in establishing overland links through Egypt, between the Mediterranean and the Asian waters, as a short route to their imperial possessions in India. That is when the Middle East began to acquire roads and wheeled vehicles on those roads.

Travellers through the Middle East also made extensive use of waterways—rivers, coastal waters, and in time canals. The coming of West European ships built for the Atlantic brought a devastating impact. A ship built to withstand the Atlantic gales had to be bigger and stronger than those built for the Mediterranean or the Indian Ocean, so they could mount more guns, carry larger cargoes, travel greater distances. That was why a small country like Portugal was able to establish an empire in Asia in defiance of such mighty military powers as the sultans of Turkey, the shahs of Persia, the moguls of India. By the eighteenth century we find even Muslim pilgrims from India and Indonesia who book their passage to Arabia on west European ships, Portuguese or Dutch, because it was cheaper, quicker and safer.

Later of course, everything was changed with the coming, first of steam, and then of the petrol engine, then of aircraft, and now, the almost unlimited opportunities for travel in the mind offered by electronic devices.

Let me conclude with a warning from Lady Mary Wortley Montagu, from a letter written in 1717. She is replying to a letter from a friend, and she says: "Your whole letter is full of mistakes, from one end to the other. I see you have taken your ideas of Turkey from that worthy author, Dumont, who has writ with equal ignorance and confidence. 'Tis a particular pleasure to me here [in Istanbul, where she was writing] to read the voyages to the Levant, which are generally so far removed from truth, and so full of absurdities I am very well diverted with them. They never fail giving you an account of the women which 'tis certain they never saw, and talking very wisely of the genius of the men into whose company they were never admitted, and often describe Mosques which they dare not peep into."[13]

Notes

1. *Riḥlat Awwal Sā'iḥ Sharqī ilā Amerika (1688–1683)*, ed. Father Anṭun Rabbat, S.J., in *Al-Mashriq* (Beirut), Vol. 8, 1905, pp. 821–34, 875–81, 931–42, 974–83, 1022–33, 1080–88, 1118–29.

2. *Takhlīṣ al-Ibrīz fī talkhīṣ Bārīz*, ed. Mahdi 'Allām, Aḥmad Aḥmad Badawī, Anwar Luqā, Cairo, 1958 (and other editions).

3. A Danish version of his narrative was published after his return; the Icelandic original was edited from the manuscript in the mid-19th century. See Oluf Eigilssen, *En Kort Beretning om de Tyrkiske Sørøveres onde Medfart og Omgang* . . . (Copenhagen, 1641); Olafur Egilsson, *Lítil Saga um herhlaup Tyrkjans arid 1627* (Reykjavik, 1852). The difference between the Danish and Icelandic forms of the author's name will be noted. An English translation is in preparation.

4. The Qadi's memoirs were published by I. Parmaksızoğlu, "Bir Türk kadısının esaret hatıraları" *Tarih Dergisi* 5 (1953): 77–84.

5. Both volumes of Osman Ağa's memoirs were first published in German translation: see R. F. Kreutel and O. Spies, *Leben and Abenteuer des Dolmetschers 'Osman Ağa* (Bonn, 1954), and R. F. Kreutel, *Zwischen Paschas und Generalen* (Graz, 1966). The Turkish text of one volume has been edited by R. F. Kreutel, *Die Authbiographie des Dolmetschers 'Osman Ağa aus Temeschwar* (Cambridge, 1980).

6. Constantine Porphyrogenitus, *De Administrando Imperio, Commentary*, ed. R.H.H. Jenkins et al, London, 1962.

7. *Mémoires du Baron de Tott sur les Turcs et les Tartares,* 4 volumes, Maestricht, 1785.

8. Moltke, Helmut von, *Briefe über Zustände und Begebenheiten in der Türkei aus den Jahren 1835 bis 1839*, 5th ed., Berlin, 1891.

9. Liman von Sanders, *Fünf Jahre Türkei*, Berlin, 1920 (English translation *Five Years in Turkey,* Annapolis, 1927).

10. See Faik Reşit Unat, *Osmanli Sefirleri ve Sefâretnameleri*, Ankara, 1968.

11. See W. F. Monypenny and G. E. Buckle, *The Life of Benjamin Disraeli, Earl of Beaconsfield*, London, 1929, vol. 1, p. 162.

12. Ibn Battūta, *Riḥla*, ed. C. Defremery and B. R. Sanguinetti, vol. ii, Paris 1853–59, p. 361. English translation by H.A.R. Gibb, *The Travels of Ibn Battuta*, vol. ii, Cambridge, 1962, pp. 472–73.

13. *The Complete Letters of Lady Mary Wortley Montagu*, ed. Robert Halsband, vol. I, Oxford, 1965, p. 368.

16

The British Mandate for Palestine in Historical Perspective

Address to a Meeting in Jerusalem

෴

A ll scientific method and therefore all scholarly method is comparative. When you go to see the doctor with a pain in your right arm he also examines your left arm. The same principle is useful in examining a period in history.

At first sight, the period of British rule in this country [Israel] looks like a brief passing episode between the 400 years of Ottoman rule that preceded it and the lengthening decades of Jewish and Arab rule that have followed it. Nevertheless it is, I think, an extremely important period, and the study of that period is very rewarding for the understanding of the history not only of this country, but of the region. As I said, all scholarly method is comparative, and it may be useful to compare the record of the British Mandate here not only with what went before and with what came after, but also with what was happening in the neighborhood—with other empires, with previous and subsequent governments, and with other former British territories.

Britain seems to have come rather unwillingly to this country. At the outbreak of war in 1914, the Prime Minister Mr. Asquith, in a speech at the Guildhall, informed his audience with deep and obvious regret that the Ottoman Empire had chosen to enter the war on the other side. Until then it had been a cardinal principal of British policy in the region to preserve "the independence and integrity" of the Ottoman Empire as the best way of protecting the Middle East from other incursions. Mr. Asquith remarked on that occasion, with prophetic insight, that the Ottoman Empire in making this decision was in effect committing suicide and sealing its own doom. And he said this with obvious regret. As late as 1916 an inter-departmental committee appointed by the Prime Minister to advise the government on Middle East policy recommended that although the Ottoman Empire was now a hostile power, fighting on the other side, nevertheless British interests would be best served after the war by preserving the Ottoman Empire and maintaining its rule and jurisdiction in the Middle Eastern region. This, they said, was better than any of the probable alternatives. One wonders whether they were perhaps right after all. However, that policy was abandoned. A quite different view was adopted and different arrangements made.

As with most imperial governments, British rule in Palestine was in many respects cautiously conservative, preserving much of the old order, particularly in social and cultural matters, most important of all in religion, in the very wide Middle Eastern interpretation of that word. And here I note in passing that although more than half a century has passed since the ending of British rule, successive governments of Israel have maintained the same policy of cautious conservatism in dealing with religious institutions, with the result that today I would say that the Ottoman heritage is more perfectly preserved in Israel, certainly than in the Turkish Republic, and more, I would say, than in any of the other countries of the region. It is symbolically represented even in the costume of religious dignitaries, which mirror those of mid-level Ottoman bureaucrats of the mid-nineteenth century.

Perhaps one other point I should mention: I spoke of looking at the situation before and after the British Mandate, and I suppose that as a conscientious historian I should explain my qualifications to do this. As a professional student of Ottoman history I feel that I have something to say about what went before. As a frequent visitor and keen observer of Israel in the last half century or so, I think I may have something to say about what is going on now. Regarding the British Mandate, unfortunately, my qualifications are much less. I visited Mandatory Palestine twice, the first time in 1938 as a student with a traveling fellowship from the Royal Asiatic Society, the second time very briefly during World War Two on His Majesty's service. This may, I hope, give me some sort of a feeling for what was going on.

Much has been said about different aspects of the British legacy in this country, and I am particularly struck by some of the points made in the film we have just seen, notably such visible legacies as the use of Jerusalem stone and the like. But what I want to bring to your attention is three particular changes which seem to me to be of crucial importance.

One of them is the notion of Palestine. Obviously there have been states in this region before the Mandate, but they were not called Palestine; there were places called Palestine in this region before that, but they were not states. To remind you briefly, the name Palestine occurs in Greco-Roman antiquity. The authorized version of the Old Testament names Palestine three times. All three were removed in the revised version because they were mis-translations of the word Philistia—Hebrew *Peleshet*—the Land of the Philistines; not Palestine but Philistia. The word does not occur at all in the New Testament. It appears in late Roman times as the name of a province, then of two provinces, then of three provinces in the late Roman Empire. The name survived briefly in the early Arab Empire, and then disappeared. The Crusaders called the country the Holy Land and their state the Kingdom of Jerusalem. After the end of the ancient Jewish states, the capital of the administrative districts called Palestine were not in Jerusalem but elsewhere, in Caesarea, in Ramleh, in Lydda, in various other places. The only time between the ancient and modern Jewish states when Jerusalem was the capital was the Crusader Kingdom, the Latin Kingdom of Jerusalem as it was called. And that was a comparatively brief interlude.

Even the adjective Palestinian is comparatively new. This, I need hardly remind you, is a region of ancient civilization and of deep-rooted and often complex identities. But Palestine was not one of them. People might identify themselves for various purposes, by religion, by descent, or by allegiance to a particular state or ruler, or sometimes locality. But when they did it locally it was generally either the city and immediate district or the larger province, so they would have been Jerusalemites or Jaffaites or the like, or Syrians, identifying with the larger province of Syria, in classical Arabic usage, Sham.

The constitution or the formation of a political entity called Palestine which eventually gave rise to a nationality called Palestinian and the reconstitution of Jerusalem as the capital were, it seems to me, very important, and as it turns out, lasting innovations of the British Mandate. Even in the Ottoman period Jerusalem was the capital of the district of Jerusalem, but there were separate districts ruled from other cities such as Safed and Nabulus and Gaza. All of them sub-divisions of larger provinces governed at various times from Damascus, Sidon, or Beirut.

The second major innovation wrought by the British Mandate was the creation, with its base in Jerusalem, of a civil service. Now there is something distinctively British about this term—civil service, civil servant. It embodies a concept of authority and a concept of how one should exercise authority that is peculiarly British and I'm almost tempted to say peculiarly English. The civil servant is a servant and he is civil in several different senses of that adjective. He is something very different from the *fonctionnaire* or the *Beamte* or the *Chinovnik* even in Europe, and certainly very different from anything that had been seen previously in this region. And that I think has remained. It was also introduced in many other parts of the British Empire and it is interesting to compare the vicissitudes of civil servants and the organized civil service in those various post-imperial countries, districts, neighborhoods. In Israel I have the impression that despite some erosion here and there the notion of the civil servant and his duties, his functions, has I think, on the whole, remained as it was established in the days of the Mandate.

Parenthetically, I may cite a very interesting Ottoman document. I refer to the report of an ambassador who was sent to Prussia in 1795. He came back and wrote a report on the Kingdom of Prussia which he had visited, and ended with some recommendations concerning things which he had seen in Prussia which the Imperial Ottoman government might consider imitating. One of them was Prussian officialdom, on which he noted something quite remarkable—that officials were appointed not by patronage and clientage, as was normal, but for their competence in the area or topic in which they were dealing; in addition, they were promoted or dismissed according to their competence or incompetence. This was a revolutionary notion, and I sometimes see distressing signs of a recurrence of the older pattern, also in the modern state.

My third point is the emergence, under the aegis of the Mandatory government, and more particularly under its civil service, of what we have nowadays got into the habit of calling "the civil society." This is a term of considerable antiquity, going back to the Middle Ages, but in its modern sense it has acquired the fairly specific meaning of the network of interacting voluntary organizations. In the traditional society there are two kinds of association: the one the involuntary but strong allegiance that one owed by birth, to the tribe, the sect, the neighborhood; the other the compulsory allegiance that one owed to the ruler. There was very little between the two. The civil society is a network of groups of people bound together by choice, by a shared interest, a shared program, even a shared hobby. The sports-club is an important part of the civil society. There are beginnings of the civil society in the late Ottoman period, but this too, it seems to me, is one of the major innovations which can be credited to the British Mandate.

There's a good deal of confusion in much of the world, and particularly in the Middle East, between two different words and two different concepts: freedom and independence. In many parts of the region the two words are used as if they were synonyms. They are not synonyms. They mean very different things. And much of the world has now learned painfully not only that it is possible to have one without the other, but in many situations the two appear to be mutually exclusive. Some of the empires gave far greater freedom in the sense of individual rights to their subjects than were ever accorded by the independent states that arose on the ruins of empires. Nowadays some rather bitterly define independence as the right to be kicked in the teeth by a compatriot instead of being hit on the head by a foreigner.

In that sense, free institutions have, alas, become something of a rarity. The first really free press that we find in the Middle East, where issues could be argued freely and openly and the government could be criticized, was in British-occupied Egypt from the 1880s onwards. That country, under Imperialist domination, nevertheless became a haven of refuge for people from all over the region who had something to say and wanted to be free to say it. That again, it seems to me, is a very important part of the heritage of the British Mandate. This tradition of freedom of expression, freedom of exchange of views, freedom of organization which were well established during the mandatory period and have survived pretty well since then. Freedom, independence, civil society, freedom of association and—ensuring the freedom of them all—the civil service, it seems to me that these are not a bad record.

17

Pan-Arabism

❧❦❧

Introduction

Pan-Arabism as a political doctrine and a political movement is an application to the Arabic-speaking peoples of the 19th century European conception of the nation, namely that the nation is the basic entity into which the human race is divided, that it is defined by certain varying but ascertainable characteristics and is endowed with certain corporate political attributes, purposes and rights and, finally, that the nation thus defined is the only rightful basis of statehood. Any nation, according to this doctrine, which has not expressed its nationhood in statehood is deprived of its rights; any state in turn not based on a nation is wrongful and illegitimate.

At the beginning of the 20th century the Arabic-speaking peoples, like the rest of mankind apart from a very small segment mostly in western Europe, were not so organized. The largest and by far the most important part of the Arabic-speaking peoples was incorporated, with a greater or lesser degree of effective subordination, in the Ottoman Empire. A few in the remoter regions of Arabia still maintained substantial though not nominal independence of the powers. The remainder had passed under the rule or influence of the European empires—in southern and eastern Arabia of the British, in North Africa of the French and, in Libya from 1911–1912, the Italians.

Apart from small Christian and smaller Jewish minorities, the former chiefly in the east, the overwhelming majority of the Arabic-speaking peoples were Muslim, and it was by their allegiance to Islam that they defined themselves both socially and politically. An awareness of Arab identity of course existed and in earlier times had had a certain importance—more social and cultural than directly political. It had, however, given way to the overriding Islamic loyalty—

and in the Islamic lands for a thousand years past the Turks not the Arabs had been the dominant people. Arabs, however proud of their descent and of their culture, accepted Turkish dominance in the universal Islamic community in the same way as Dante had accepted German sovereignty in the Holy Roman Empire. Arab cultural self-awareness continued under Ottoman rule, but was combined with full identification with the Ottoman social and political order and with loyalty to the Ottoman Sultan as legitimate head of the Islamic state.

Political identity and loyalty were still basically determined by three considerations. The first was religious or rather communal, that is to say membership of the universal family of Islam. This was by far the most important and effective. At the second level came allegiance to a specific state or dynasty—the two meaning very much the same thing. For the Arabs of the Fertile Crescent this meant the Ottoman house; for those of Egypt it meant the khedivial ruling house, under Ottoman suzerainty; for those of the Arabian peninsula, a variety of local rulers. At the third and lowest level, identity was ethnic or local, but this was of the most rudimentary kind, that of the family, the clan, at best the tribe. As a basis of political allegiance to a ruler it persisted chiefly in the Arabian peninsula and its borderlands. It is interesting that the modern Arabic term for nationalism, *qawmiyya*, first appears in Turkish (*Kavmiyet*) not in Arabic, and is a term of abuse not praise, with a connotation of divisive tribalism or factionalism.

The idea of ethnic nationality as the basis of political identity was strictly European and was a product of the late 18th and early 19th centuries, associated with the French Revolution, the Napoleonic wars and the romantic movement. Its first expressions in the Islamic world were and for some time remained of foreign inspiration. For a long time the only response in Islamic countries was among the non-Muslim minorities, chiefly Christian.

The Precursors

The first phase in the rise and development of pan-Arabism begins in about 1875 and ends in 1914 with the outbreak of the First World War. During this period the movement was overwhelmingly Syrian; indeed one historian has gone so far as to say that the word Arab means Syrian in the documents and even the studies of that time. It found expression chiefly in secret societies and led to the holding of the first Arab congress in Paris in 1913.

Several factors were at work in this early development of pan-Arabism. The first of these was external, that is to say European, influence. This took several forms. One was the impact of European ideas, particularly the ideas of liberal patriotism and nationalism as developed during the 19th century. These came principally from France, Italy and Britain, and became known through translation, adaptation and oral percolation into Arabic. Rather more important than the influence of European ideas was the influence of European example, the most

relevant here being the models offered by the Germans and Italians in the creation of a single powerful nation state where there had previously been a mosaic
of small states, most of them of minor significance. The examples of Germany
and Italy were and have remained a powerful stimulus to movements of this
kind among the Muslim and Arab peoples, and there has been no lack of candidates among the states of the area for the role of Prussia or Piedmont in the
creation of a greater unity. At first the only possible candidate was the Ottoman
Empire, and the larger unity proposed was an Islamic rather than a national
one—that is to say, a pan-Islamic rather than a pan-Arab or pan-Turkish program. Later Egypt and later still other states aspired to such a role.

Another factor of importance was European interest. Several of the European
powers found some advantage in encouraging nationalist ideas among the Arabs,
and at various times France, Britain, Germany, Italy and Russia played a role in
influencing, sponsoring, and even organizing movements of this kind.

Finally a word should be said about the influence of Western romanticism,
which rediscovered the Arabs and revived an interest in their remote and glorious
past. The immediate impact of such writers as Disraeli, Washington Irving and
Lamartine in the Arab countries was minimal or perhaps nil, but their writings
initiated a chain of influences, and in time such romantic ideas began to penetrate
to the Turks and to the Arabs themselves. Among Turkish liberal patriots there
was at times a kind of romantic pro-Arabism rather akin to the obsession among
European radicals and revolutionaries first with antiquity and then with the
Middle Ages. This at times found political expression, as in the doctrine, of
which faint echoes are heard in the late 19th century, that the Ottoman Sultan-
Caliphs were usurpers and should be replaced by an Arab Caliphate. But of this
more hereafter.

As well as international influences, there were also important local, or rather
regional factors at work. Within the same Ottoman world to which the Arabs
belonged, other peoples, the Greeks, the Serbs, the Bulgarians and the Ruma-
nians had successively won their independence and set up modern national states
which seemed to be thriving, or which at least showed marked progress and
prosperity as compared with their own previous status and the continuing status
of the provinces which remained under Ottoman rule. Even the Turks themselves, the masters of the Empire, had succumbed to the nationalist virus, and
were beginning to speak in terms of a Turkish rather than an Ottoman-Islamic
loyalty. This trend was encouraged by the exiles and émigrés who came to Turkey
from among the Turkish-speaking subject peoples of the vast Russian Empire.
These, who had encountered pan-Slavism in Russia, had reacted to it with a pan-
Turkism of their own and had brought it to Turkey in the hope of inducing the
Turks to adopt the role of political leadership which this doctrine assigned to
them. In the Arabic-speaking provinces of the Ottoman Empire the new Turkish
ideologies aroused some disapproval among religious-minded Arabs, but little
serious resistance.

At first the opposition movements within the Ottoman lands were separatist rather than nationalist, though often expressed in a nationalist phraseology borrowed from Europe. The most important of these by far was that sponsored by the Khedives of Egypt. Until 1914 Egypt remained nominally part of the Ottoman Empire and under Ottoman suzerainty. In fact however it was ruled by a virtually independent dynasty which remained in office and active even after the British occupation of the country in 1882. Khedivial political aspirations led to the encouragement of Egyptian patriotism rather than Arab nationalism—an idea at that time almost equally alien but rather more suited to their purposes. However, they found it useful also to appeal for support in the territory still remaining under Ottoman rule and in this they were greatly helped by the increasing numbers of immigrants who came from Ottoman Syria and Lebanon to the relative freedom and opportunity offered by khedivial and still more by British-occupied Egypt.

A parallel movement, albeit on a much smaller scale, began in Ottoman Syria. Its main base seems to have been among the Arabic-speaking Christians of the area which is now comprised in the republic of Lebanon. These, naturally far more open than their Muslim compatriots to the influence of European ideas, seem to have thought in terms of a separate Syrian or Lebanese state within the Ottoman Empire. As in Egypt, the administrative structure and separate sense of identity which this required already existed. Their ideas were however purely local; they aroused little support within the Christian community and none at all outside it.

Both of these movements were strictly regional, that is, confined to one country. While reflecting the influence of the imported European idea of nationality, they were expressed in the form not of nationalism but rather of the kindred but distinct idea of patriotism—that is to say identity in terms of country, rather than nation, and loyalty to the state governing that country, rather than to an abstract entity.

Nevertheless, they both contributed in different ways to the emergence and development of the Arab idea. This first finds expression in the rather vague notion of an Arab Caliphate which seems to have been current among some Turkish radical circles. It appears in the form of a proposal to overthrow the Ottoman Caliphate and replace it by a new Caliphate, to be held by the Sherif of Mecca who, it was romantically believed, would restore the pristine greatness and glory of Islam in its early Arabian phase. A variant of this was the idea that the Empire might be turned into a republic in which the Sherif would exercise a kind of spiritual but no real political authority. These ideas appear chiefly in Turkish circles, though no doubt some Arabs were affected.

The first explicit statement of the idea that the Caliphate should be transferred from the Turks to the Arabs and with it the first theoretical statement of pan-Arabism is the work of a certain 'Abd al-Raḥmān al-Kawākibī (?1849–1902), nowadays generally regarded as the ideological pioneer of pan-Arabism.

Kawākibī was born in Aleppo of a distinguished family of sherifs and worked for a while both as government official and as a journalist. He seems to have fallen foul of authority and served a term of imprisonment. In 1898, like so many Syrians, he moved to Egypt, which offered wider scope for his activities. At some point he appears to have entered the service of the Khedive, and an extensive journey round Africa and into Asia seems to have been undertaken on the Khedive's behalf. He is principally remembered for two books, both of which were attacks on the Ottoman Sultanate in general and on the reigning Sultan, Abdulhamid II, in particular. It has been credibly suggested that both of these were part of a well-organized campaign sponsored by the Khedive against his suzerain. The first of these two books, *The Characteristics of Tyranny*, was published in 1900 and is very largely based on *Della Tirannide*, the famous treatise by Vittorio Alfieri, first published in 1800. A Turkish translation was printed in Geneva in 1898. The second, entitled *Umm al-Qurā* (The Mother of Cities, i.e. Mecca) was first made public in the form of a series of articles in the magazine *al-Manār*, between April 1902 and February 1903. It was published in book form after Kawākibī's death. Recently, a copy of an edition in book form has come to light, dated 1316 A.H.—i.e. 1898–1899, with Port Said named as place of publication. This was presumably a limited edition intended for clandestine distribution in the Ottoman Empire. This work is hardly more original than the other, being to a large extent a reflection of the views expressed by the English romantic Wilfred Scawen Blunt in his book *The Future of Islam*, published in 1881, and setting forth the idea of an Arab Caliphate. Kawākibī in this book was the first Arabic writer to declare openly for the Arabs as a political entity in opposition to the Turks.

The theme of the book, like that of many others of the time, is the weakness and backwardness of Islam and the problem of how to remedy this. His analysis is along the lines familiar among the Muslim, mainly Turkish, reformers of the 19th century. The Islamic community had become moribund, having lost its corporate being and loyalty. This backwardness was the result of tyranny, of the decline of Muslim civilization and the lack of genuine racial and linguistic bonds binding Muslims together. The Ottomans, in particular, had been guilty of corrupting Islam by introducing, under the influence of Byzantine cesaropapism, a system of religious hierarchy, headed by the Sultan himself, and totally alien to the true spirit of Islam. For these reasons, among others, the Ottoman Sultanate was incapable of fulfilling its duty to defend and preserve Islam. The Ottoman Empire, made up of different countries, religions and sects and with a polyglot ministerial leadership, could not accomplish the necessary regeneration. This could be done only by the Arabs, the founders and creators of Islamic civilization. An Arab Caliph residing in Mecca would provide the spiritual leadership of the greater Islamic union. His authority, Kawākibī stresses, would be religious not political, and he would serve as a symbol of Islamic unity. Kawākibī lists the reasons for the superiority of the Arabs and their entitlement to the Caliphate.

Kawākibī's motives can be and have been questioned. His departure from his birthplace after obscure quarrels in Aleppo, his service of the Khedives, have shed doubts on his integrity. His originality has also been impugned and his debt to Alfieri and Blunt demonstrated. All this however does not diminish his importance, nor even the originality and novelty of the ideas which he expressed—in the circle in which he expressed them. The new and significant elements in Kawākibī's writings are 1) his clear and explicit rejection of the Ottoman Caliphate; 2) his insistence on the Arabic-speaking peoples as a corporate entity with political rights of its own and 3), most radical of all, his idea of a spiritual Caliphate which would presumably leave politics and government to a secular authority separate from religious authority and law, and entirely within the scope of human decision and action. This marks the first significant step in the direction of secular nationalism. That the theory of a spiritual Arab Sherif in Mecca may have been designed to leave the way open for a temporal Egyptian ruler does not diminish its importance.

The second intellectual precursor of pan-Arabism was another Syrian, this time a Christian, Negib (Najīb) Azoury (birthdate unknown—died 1916). Azoury was a Maronite or Uniate Catholic Christian who studied in Istanbul and Paris and later became a provincial official in Jerusalem. He left his post in unknown circumstances and seems to have been condemned to death in absentia in 1904, when he fled to Paris. In the following year he published a book, *Le réveil de la nation arabe*. He spent most of the remaining years of his life in Paris, where he formed an organization—probably a one-man-show—called the *Ligue de la patrie arabe*, and published a monthly journal of which eighteen issues appeared, called *L'Independence arabe*. The name, it has been remarked, is reminiscent of the anti-Dreyfusard *Ligue de la patrie française*, which flourished in the late eighteen nineties. His writings reflect the anti-semitic obsessions with world-wide Jewish power which were current in anti-Dreyfusard circles, though curiously he gives comparatively little attention to the beginnings of Zionist colonization in Palestine. He had some French contributors to his journal, and made repeated attempts to obtain money from the French government, but without success.

Azoury's ideas were even more radical than those of Kawākibī. While Kawākibī had sought a transfer of the Caliphate from Turks to Arabs but presumably without any disruption of the Ottoman Islamic Empire, the Christian Azoury spoke openly in terms of secession. His plan was not merely for an Arab Caliphate but an Arab kingdom consisting of the Arabian peninsula and the Fertile Crescent. Egypt was specifically excluded in that the Egyptians were not Arabs by race, though, oddly, he proposed that the sovereign of this Arab kingdom should be a khedivial prince. Its limits would be the Tigris and Euphrates valleys, the Mediterranean, the Indian Ocean and the Suez Canal. He adopts Kawākibī's idea of the spiritual caliphate and a separation of lay and religious authority. As a member of the Christian minority he was naturally interested in religious freedom and civic equality, which he hoped to achieve in such a state.

A very different figure, and in his own day far more influential than either of these, was a third Syrian emigrant, Rashīd Riḍā (1865–1935). Born near Tripoli (now in Lebanon), Rashīd Riḍā went to Egypt in 1897 and spent the rest of his days there. He was a pupil of the famous Egyptian theologian Muḥammad 'Abduh and was the editor of the magazine he founded, *al-Manār*, which was widely read in the Islamic world.

Rashīd Riḍā was basically a theologian, not a politician, and his fundamental loyalty was Islamic not Arab. As early as 1900, however, he wrote a series of articles in *al-Manār* in which he discussed the Turks and the Arabs, comparing the characters and achievements of the two, much to the advantage of the Arabs. While conceding great qualities to the Turks and allowing their important function in Islam, he insists on the superiority of the Arabs and on the greater significance of their role in the rise and spread of Islam among mankind. It is however because of their service to Islam that Rashīd Riḍā praises the Arabs— not like later nationalist theorists, including even some Christians, who praise Islam as a manifestation of the Arab genius. There is no hint of support for separatism in his writings, which express the attitude of a loyal Muslim to the Muslim state, at that time still the Ottoman Empire. Rashīd Riḍā at first supported the Young Turk Revolution of 1908, and indeed incurred some obloquy by praising the new regime in the strongly pro-Hamidian city of Damascus. Later, however, he was alienated by what he saw as their irreligious and anti-Islamic policies, and decisively turned against them after the military coup in Istanbul, led by Enver Pasha, on 23 January 1913. He subsequently played an active role in Arab nationalist politics.

In general, the revolution of 1908 brought considerable changes to the Arab position. Until that time support for Arab movements and committees was insignificant. The committees which were formed in Syria and elsewhere aroused minimal response. On the contrary the overwhelming majority of Ottoman Arabs remained loyal subjects of the Ottoman Sultan and indeed, during the reign of Abdulhamid, seem to have enjoyed a privileged position. The Sultan himself had a small group of Arab favorites and intimates, including religious leaders and others, through whom he was able to maintain close and direct links with the Arab provinces. The concern of the Ottoman government with the Arab heartlands was manifested and strengthened by the building of the Hijaz railway from Damascus to Medina which was—ironically—completed in 1908. The Young Turk movement enjoyed Arab as well as Turkish support and several figures from the Arab provinces were prominent among its leaders, notably the Baghdadi Maḥmūd Shevket Pasha, a general who played a major role in crushing the counter-revolutionary mutiny of 1909 and later became Grand Vizier. Arabs in Istanbul founded a society for Ottoman-Arab brotherhood devoted to the ideals of the Young Turks in general, and incidentally to the welfare of the Arab provinces of the Empire.

Relations however between Turks and Arabs soon deteriorated. The very loyalty of the Arabs to Abdulhamid and the prominence of Arabs among his most intimate supporters helped to bring this about. On the one hand, the Arabs felt deprived of the positions of power and influence which they had previously held; on the other many Turks felt an animosity to the associates of the deposed sultan. Arabs, like members of other provinces of the Ottoman Empire, began to feel increasingly the pressure of Turkism, the growth of a separate sense of Turkish identity among the ruling group of the Ottoman Empire, which inevitably aroused a reaction among those who were not themselves Turks. As long as the Ottoman Empire had been conceived and presented as an Islamic monarchy, it might and did encounter difficulties from its Christian subjects; but it enjoyed the undivided loyalty of its Muslim subjects, whether their language was Turkish, Arabic, Kurdish, Albanian, Serb, or any other. But with the movement from an Ottoman towards a Turkish state and the increasing stress on Turkishness in the pronouncements and even in the actions of the Young Turk rulers, Albanian and then other non-Turkish Muslims began to feel separated. This reaction was strongest among the Balkan Muslims, closest to the centers of power and most open to the influence of European ideas through their own Christian compatriots and neighbors.

Such reactions were slower and later in the Arab lands—remoter from the capital and its affairs, and still overwhelmingly Muslim and conservative in outlook. Arab feeling did however develop in the new atmosphere, and found expression in the formation of a whole series of Arab societies, clubs and organizations—some cultural, some literary, some open, some secret, and most of them more or less political. Even at this stage there seems to have been little desire for actual separation from the Ottoman state, and these groups often seem more concerned with the politics of the capital than with the affairs of their provinces. Arab members of the Istanbul parliament formed a substantial group, and in the struggle for power between rival Young Turk parties and factions they were at times able to play a role of some importance. As regards specifically Arab aims, they seem in general to have thought in terms of decentralization, of some form of local self-government within the Arab provinces whereby they could achieve their limited political and cultural objectives. Some went a little further and spoke of a kind of Turco-Arab dual monarchy on the Austro-Hungarian model. In general their aims were to resist the policies of centralization and Turkification pursued by some of the Young Turks, and this often led them into alliance with the so-called *Entente libérale*—the party known in Turkish as *Hürriyet ve Itilâf* (Freedom and Association), in deliberate contrast with the name and doctrine of Union and Progress, adopted by the ruling group. The *Entente libérale*, founded on 21 November 1911, won many Arab supporters, one of the most notable of whom was Sayyid Ṭālib, a scion of a family of notables in Basra, who represented that city in the Ottoman parliament from 1908 to 1914, and was an acknowledged leader of the Arab group of deputies. A dominant figure in his native Basra, he was involved in 1912–1913 in what was virtually an attempt to create an autonomous emirate in southern Iraq.

The participants in Arab political movements were still overwhelmingly Syrian, though towards the end a number of Iraqis became involved. These were of particular importance in that many officers of Iraqi origin served in the Ottoman army.

The most important public activity of the Arab nationalists before the outbreak of war was the holding of an Arab congress in Paris in June 1913. It was attended by twenty-five persons, all of them, apart from two Iraqi students who happended to be in Paris at the time, from Syria-Lebanon, and including a number of prominent notables. The demands which they formulated were for administrative autonomy for the Arab provinces, a higher degree of Arab participation in central government, and the recognition of Arabic along with Turkish as an official language of the Empire. At the congress there were clear divergencies between the different groups which participated. The most important was between the French-inspired Christian Beirutis with local and basically separatist aims (for some, annexation to France) and those who thought in terms of a larger Arab entity. Such different purposes as reform, autonomy and separatism all appear in the discussions.

The congress produced no tangible results. The Ottoman government, which had sent someone to keep an eye on the congress and maintain contact with the participants, made only minor concessions, and in the meantime serious disagreements developed among the Arabs themselves. At this point there was the beginning of a shift—from semi-Westernized intellectuals in Syria to military officers in Iraq, from more moderate to more extreme attitudes, from protest to conspiracy. Egypt was still regarded as outside the scope of Arab nationalism, and only one of the early pioneers of Arab nationalist politics was an Egyptian. He was ʿAziz ʿAli al-Masrı, who left Egypt to serve in the Ottoman army. In 1914 he organized a new society, this time secret and consisting largely of army officers. He was detected, arrested, tried and sentenced to death. Fortunately for him, his brother-in-law, who was the governor of Cairo, was able to persuade the British government to intervene on his behalf, as a British-protected Egyptian subject, and secure his release and return to Egypt.

1916–1948

The first major steps towards the achievement of Arab independence and unity came during the First World War. Curiously, their inspiration was foreign, not Arab, and their first ideological expression was religious, not nationalist.

The immediate impetus to the rise of the Arab movement during the First World War came from British policy. In 1915 the British government entered into negotiations with Ḥusayn, the Sherif of Mecca, with a view to persuading him to lead a revolt against his Ottoman suzerain. Britain had a double purpose in this enterprise. One was to weaken the Ottoman Empire and in particular to relieve pressure on Egypt by deflecting attention to an Arab revolt. The second purpose was to counter the danger which was apprehended from the Ottoman jihad. After the outbreak of war the Ottoman government had proclaimed a jihad, a holy war, against the allied and associated powers. It was feared that this appeal would have dangerous effects among Muslims under British rule, especially in India and Egypt, as well as on the Muslim subjects of the French and Russian Empires. In fact this danger turned out to be largely illusory, but the idea of meeting the appeal of the Ottoman sultan with a counter-appeal from the Sherif of Mecca offered obvious attractions. Another purpose, present in the minds of at least some British officials, was to extend British influence into Palestine and Syria, and thus oust the French and consolidate the British position in Egypt. The Sherif was interested in the proposals which were put to him, for an Arab Caliphate, and for an Arab realm to be carved out of certain Ottoman provinces and placed under his rule.

Basically, however, this program was dynastic and separatist rather than nationalist. Dealings between the Sherif of Mecca and Arab nationalist societies did not go smoothly. It is significant that when he rose in revolt against the Ottomans his manifesto was expressed in traditional religious terms rather than in Arab national terms. In it he denounces the Young Turks as impious innovators who were endangering Islam and depicts his own action as being taken in defense of the faith. The idea that the Ottoman Caliphate had become corrupt and impious and that a true, regenerated Islam would arise in the Arabian peninsula, in the land of the Prophet and of his Companions, was not new. Such ideas had been propagated as far back as the 18th century by the Indian mystic Shāh Walīullāh, who lived in the Hijaz for a while, and more actively by the Wahhābīs, a powerful religious reformist movement which for a while succeeded in dominating large parts of central and northern Arabia. Similar ideas had of course figured prominently, in a more overtly political form, in the writings of Blunt, Kawākibī, and Azoury.

Several versions have been published of the texts of Ḥusayn's manifestos issued during his revolt and there is some dispute as to what he actually said. It is however noteworthy that in the earliest and most reliable texts which are extant there is little or no mention of Arabism or of Arab nationalism, the main stress being laid on Islam.

Some of the letters seem to have been drafted by Rashīd Riḍā who proffered his advice to the British authorities in Egypt in their dealings with Ḥusayn. These drafts reflect his own point of view—strongly Islamic and at times even anti-Western and anti-Christian. It was this element, particularly noticeable after Rashīd Riḍā went on a pilgrimage to the Hijaz, that no doubt led the British to dispense with his advice.

The whole problem of the Arab revolt—its military usefulness and its political significance—has been heavily overlaid with myth and propaganda, and it is only now that, thanks to the opening of the archives and a more critical study of the data, these are being perceived in their proper proportions. It is now seen that the military contribution of the Sherifian forces to the Allied victory in Syria was comparatively small, while the political support which Ḥusayn enjoyed among the Arab subjects of the Ottoman Sultans has been greatly exaggerated.

Nevertheless, the whole episode was of very considerable significance as a sort of foundation myth both of British policy and of Arab nationalism in this area.

A new phase began with the armistice in 1918 and continued until the rise of Nazi Germany in 1933. During this period the former Arab provinces of the Ottoman Empire in southwest Asia were constituted into separate states and placed under mandatory rule, British or French. These were endowed with more or less liberal institutions, each of the mandatory powers setting up regimes in its own image—republics in the French territories, constitutional monarchies in those under British mandate.

Political opinion and activity among the population of these countries went through several phases. To begin with, there was a certain revival of sympathy and kinship with the Turks, as Muslim brothers and representatives of the Muslim Sultanate and Caliphate. This affected even the leaders of the Arab revolt. In the second half of August 1918 Jemal Pasha, Commander of the Turkish Fourth Army, informed the German General Liman von Sanders that he had received a secret message from the Sherif Faysal offering to take the Jordan front over from the Turkish Fourth Army if he were given certain guarantees from the Turkish government for the formation of an Arab state. The Sherif Faysal was quoted as saying—truthfully—that a major British attack was in preparation in the coastal zone and the troops of the Fourth Army could thus be used to strengthen the front between the sea and the Jordan. Liman von Sanders tried unsuccessfully to secure the desired guarantees from the Turks, who seem to have mistrusted the offer and regarded it—mistakenly—as a British *ruse de guerre* (Liman von Sanders, *Fünf Jahre Türkei*, Berlin 1920, pp. 330–31; English translation, *Five Years in Turkey*, Annapolis, 1928, p. 212). Similar suspicions led to the rejection by the Turkish General Ali Fuat Cebesoy in October 1918 of an offer by Nuri al-Sa'id, then serving as an officer with the Sherifian forces, to join the Turks against the British (Ali Fuat Cebesoy, *Millî Mücadele hâtiralari*, Istanbul 1953, pp. 28–29).

The Kemalist movement in Turkey led to a revival of Arab sympathy and interest, and Arab delegates seem to have played some part in the congresses held by the Turkish nationalists in Anatolia. Later, however, with the firm insistance by the Kemalists on their desire for a Turkish national state and their renunciation of larger Ottoman or Islamic claims or memories, the Arabs withdrew their sympathy and support—though the Kemalist republic remained for many of them a model of successful nationalism. Sati' al-Husri, who was later to play a major role as a theoretician of Arab nationalism, was in Turkey at this time, and his writings reflect the influence both of Turkish experience and of Turkish ideology.

Another influence, powerful in the immediate post-war period was that of left-wing revolutionary movements, mostly sponsored by the Soviet Union, but often with a strong Islamic tinge. These movements enjoyed rather more support among Turks than among Arabs and died out by the early '20s leaving very little result.

During the period of the British and French Mandates, the main force of nationalist activity tended to concentrate on the political entities as constituted by the mandatory powers—that is, on Syria, Lebanon, Iraq, Palestine and Transjordan as individual countries. The principal demand was for independence rather than for freedom. Under the mandatory regimes, personal political freedom—freedom of expression—though somewhat imperfect, often limited, and occasionally suspended, was nevertheless greater than at any time before or after. Since freedom was more or less conceded and independence withheld, it was natural that the political movement should concentrate on independence and perhaps somewhat neglect freedom. Independence, in the circumstances of the time, necessarily involved the political units as they then existed, and meant, as the first objective of struggle, independence for Syria, independence for Lebanon, independence for Iraq, and the rest. The idea of a larger political grouping in which all these would be parts existed, but was of comparatively minor importance at that stage. Where the people of these countries thought of themselves as part of something larger than their immediate states, they did so in Islamic rather than Arab terms—of a pan-Islamic rather than a pan-Arab vision of unity.

A new period began in 1933, with Hitler's rise to power in Germany, followed by the Italian invasion of Ethiopia, the Spanish Civil War, and the formation of the Axis. All these events had considerable consequences in Arab lands. Three in particular were relevant to the growth of pan-Arabism.

The first of these was the persecution of the Jews in Germany and later in other countries under German rule or influence. Zionist colonization in Palestine and the British promise to the Jews contained in the Balfour Declaration had already given a special acuteness to the Arab struggle against the British Mandate and its policies in Palestine. This however remained essentially a local problem, and the cause of the Palestinian Arabs had aroused some sympathy and interest but no real concern or support in neighboring countries, which were far too absorbed with their own affairs. The rise and spread of militant anti-Semitism in Europe both intensified and dramatized this aspect of the problem. In the pre-Nazi period, Jewish immigration to Palestine had dwindled to a mere trickle and at one point was even exceeded by Jewish emigration. The Nazi persecutions led at once to an immediate and considerable rise in the rate of Jewish immigration, and gave a new point and a new urgency to the Zionist analysis of the Jewish predicament and the Zionist formula for its solution. From this time onwards the struggle for Palestine grew in scope and intensity. While the Jews of Palestine enjoyed the support of their fellow Jews and also of other sympathizers elsewhere in the world, the Arabs too attempted with increasing success to mobilize their own international community, whether conceived in Islamic or in Arab terms. Ironically it was the British government which played the major role in bringing this about.

The Nazis profited from this situation in two ways. On the one hand, by their persecutions they themselves created the problem; on the other hand they were able, by preaching hatred of Jews to willing listeners, to exploit it to their own advantage. Nazi Germany, preceded in this by Fascist Italy, directed an immense propaganda effort to the Arab countries, the purposes of which were to disseminate their own form of nationalist ideology, to undermine the position of the Western powers and thereby to extend their own influence and ultimate domination. Their seeds fell on fertile ground, and impressive results were achieved for sometimes quite small efforts. Arab nationalism was deeply influenced in this period by Nazi and Fascist ideology. Arab and indeed Muslim intellectuals were already keenly aware of the German and Italian examples, which seemed to provide a model for their own unification. Now for the first time these two countries were conducting active propaganda. Italy was the first in the field with Arabic broadcasts from Bari—the first outside the Arab world—from 1935. Italian cultural organizations and even some religious orders played a part in this propaganda campaign, on which a great deal of money was spent. One permanent memorial of Mussolini's Arab policy is the marble columns which he donated to the Aqṣā mosque in Jerusalem.

The Germans entered the field a little later—German broadcasting in Arabic did not begin until 1938—but when they did so it was with overwhelming effect. This is the first great age of pan-Arab ideology when numerous writers, most of them Syrian or Iraqi, set forth the basic tenets of the pan-Arab program. In their formulation, in their spirit, in their conception, these are obviously deeply influenced by German and Italian nationalism, especially in their chauvinistic and illiberal phase.

For such a process of unification, ideology in itself is of course insufficient. A state is also needed—a Prussia or a Piedmont—to initiate and complete the necessary political and perhaps military action. Among the Arab states there were several competing candidates for this role. The first to seek the role was Iraq, which obtained formal independence in 1932, and with it some measure of freedom of action. In the same year King Faysal projected an Arab conference in Baghdad; a leading Iraqi politician, Yāsīn al-Hāshimī, attempted without much success to set up a pan-Arab organization and meetings.

Only one of the Arab states, however, could seriously aspire to the leadership of the Arab world—and that was Egypt. By her central position, her cultural, economic, demographic and technological preponderance, Egypt was the natural leader of any larger grouping of Arabic-speaking countries. After Iraq, and apart from the desert kingdoms of Arabia, too remote and too undeveloped to play any such role, Egypt was moreover the first of the Arab states to acquire sufficient freedom of action to be able to pursue an independent foreign policy. The threat posed to both British and Egyptian interests by the Italian occupation of Ethiopia led to a change of policy in both countries, and to the conclusion of the Anglo-Egyptian treaty of 1936. After this Egypt was able to follow a more active and independent line, and began to interest herself in Arab affairs. To begin with this was merely an aspect of Egyptian foreign policy; in time it grew into something more than that, into a commitment to Arabism.

Until 1936 the parties to the Palestine conflict consisted of the United Kingdom as mandatory power, the Palestinian Arab leadership, and the Jewish Agency. From this year onwards however it was gradually extended to include other Arab countries. In that year the sovereigns of Transjordan, Iraq, Saudi Arabia and the Yemen made a joint approach to Britain in favor of the Palestine cause; it is noteworthy that the king of Egypt did not join in this demarche by the Arab monarchs. It was after this that Egypt played a part and finally assumed leadership in this movement.

At first, inter-Arab action on Palestine was at non-governmental levels—private persons, opposition parties and other non-official bodies. Pro-Palestinian committees were formed in a number of Arab countries, and in September 1937 the Damascus committee organized a conference of these groups which was held at Blūdān in Syria and was attended by more than 300 delegates from different Arab countries. The conference passed resolutions rejecting "the partition of Palestine and the establishment of a Jewish state therein."

The first inter-Arab conference at government level took place in Cairo, in October 1938. This was the "Inter-parliamentary world congress of Arab and Muslim countries," in defense of the cause of the Palestine Arabs. It was inaugurated by King Fārūq, and the participants were official representatives. The combination "Arab and Muslim" indicates that at this stage King Fārūq was still keeping both his options—Caliphate and pan-Arab leadership—open.

This meeting was preparatory to the conference convened by the British government to discuss the Palestine question, and held at St. James's Palace, London, in February 1939. The delegations of the Arab governments, following the policy previously adopted by the Arab Higher Committee of Palestine, refused officially to meet the Jewish delegates in direct negotiation. The conference therefore consisted of two sets of parallel talks, one between British and Jewish representatives, the other between British and Arab representatives. The British Colonial Office punctiliously designated the meetings "Palestine Conferences"— in the plural.

Not surprisingly, no agreement was reached. In the months that followed, the international situation deteriorated rapidly. The German annexation of Bohemia and Moravia in March and the Italian invasion of Albania in April were followed by the formation of the Berlin-Rome Axis on May 7. Axis propaganda in Arab countries was now intensified; the outbreak of war later that year hampered but by no means stopped its development.

These activities soon showed results. Some Arab groups maintained relations with the Axis governments from the start. The dramatic events of the summer of 1940 brought these contacts to government level. In June 1940 a "committee for cooperation between the Arab countries" was formed under the leadership of the Grand Mufti of Jerusalem, Ḥāj Amīn al-Ḥusaynī, and including leading politicians from Iraq, Syria and Saudi Arabia, with some contacts with Egyptian nationalists. The representatives included such well-known figures as Rashīd ʿAlī, Nājī Shawqat and Nājī al-Suwaydī from Iraq, Shukrī al-Quwwatlī and ʿĀdil Arslān from Syria, while Saudi Arabia was represented by Yūsuf Yāsīn, the (Syrian) private secretary of King Ibn Saʿūd, and by the royal counsellor, Khālid al-Hūd.

This committee decided to make contact with the Axis powers. After some preliminaries an envoy left Baghdad in July 1940 and, travelling via Istanbul, reached Berlin on 26 August. A further mission was sent in February 1941. On both occasions the Arab leaders offered to recognize German and Italian aspirations provided that the Axis powers issued a statement recognizing and confirming Arab rights and claims.

Although the Germans never publicly committed themselves to an acceptance of pan-Arab claims, which they viewed with some reluctance, they nevertheless won wide support. In Iraq under Rashīd ʿAlī and in Syria under Vichy occupation Arab leaders identified themselves openly with the Axis cause. This is the more remarkable in that the Arab leaders were well aware that Germany had conceded primacy to Italian interests in this region, and that the Italians were determined not to fetter themselves with any promises or commitments. In other Arab countries still under Allied occupation such activity was necessarily clandestine but was important and involved some leading figures of the post-war era. Even Nūrī al-Saʿīd, regarded as the faithful friend and ally of Britain, offered his services to the Germans, but once again, as when he had offered them to the Turks in 1918, his offer was refused in the wholly mistaken belief that it was inspired by a British ruse.

Rashīd ʿAlī and his associates were defeated and overthrown and fled to Germany, together with the Mufti of Jerusalem and other Arabs associated with them. The British government however judged it advisable to promote its own brand of pan-Arabism, fearing a collision with Arab nationalism during the war. This had led the British government on the one hand to adopt policies restricting the growth of the Jewish settlement in Palestine, even at the cost of refusing to admit refugees from Hitler-occupied Europe, on the other to a conflict with French interests in Syria and Lebanon.

The most significant step in this direction, however, was the formation of a league of Arab states as the result of a meeting held in Alexandria in October 1944. This body was formed under British sponsorship and guidance, and was probably intended to serve as a sort of political counterpart to the Middle East Supply Centre, which coordinated Allied problems of supply. The League, however, rapidly developed a character of its own. In time it became more or less an instrument of Egyptian policy.

Egyptian involvement in pan-Arabism was at first a slow and gradual process. In the early stages of Arab nationalism Egypt was not felt to be part of the Arab world, either by the Egyptians themselves or by their Arab neighbors in southwest Asia. Pan-Arabism in its early form was confined—in aspiration as well as in influence—to the Fertile Crescent and the Arabian peninsula, the inhabitants of which were believed to be the "real Arabs." This definition excluded Egypt and the remainder of the Arabic-speaking countries in the African continent. True, the Egyptians spoke and wrote Arabic, but this, it was argued, did not make them Arabs any more than Americans were Englishmen or Mexicans were Spaniards. The Egyptian nationalist movement in the 19th and in the early 20th centuries was concentrated wholly on Egyptian national and patriotic aspirations, conceived in terms of Egypt as a territorial nation. Insofar as Egypt was seen as part of a larger entity, this was Islamic, and indeed Ottoman, in that loyal Egyptian Muslims under British occupation felt that their rightful suzerain was the Ottoman Sultan. During the 'Aqaba crisis in 1906, when Britain, as occupying power, clashed with the Ottomans over the delimitation of the Sinai frontier, many of the Egyptian nationalists supported the Turks, though this was to the territorial disadvantage of Egypt. During the 1914–1918 war many Egyptian boys were named after the Young Turk Pashas—Enver (Anwar), Tal'at, and Jemal (Gamal). The Arab revolt against the Turks, led by the Sherif Ḥusayn, was received with great hostility in Egypt, at both the official and popular levels.

Egyptian loyalties were, at various levels, Egyptian, Ottoman, or Islamic, but not Arab. Arabs were regarded as something different and even—as on occasion when their activities as immigrants in Egypt provoked reaction—sometimes regarded with a certain hostility. Broadly speaking, however, Egyptian attitudes towards the Arabs of southwest Asia were sympathetic and friendly, wishing them well as fellow-Muslims and as sharers in a common inheritance, but not regarding them as part of the same nation. Even while Khedivial policy encouraged and subsidized pan-Arab activities, it did so for specifically Egyptian and dynastic aims, rather than as participants in a pan-Arab movement. This remained true of Egyptian activities in the period beginning 1936, which seemed to be directed towards objectives of Egyptian dynastic policy rather than of pan-Arab nationalism.

The growth of interest in Arabism was gradual. In 1936 pro-Palestine committees were formed in Egypt as in other Arabic-speaking countries, and non-official Egyptian delegates participated in the first pan-Arab pro-Palestine conference at Blūdān in 1937. In the following year, 1938, no less than three such pan-Arab conferences were held in Egypt—of students, of women, and of members of parliament, and Egypt also participated in the St. James's Palace Conference of 1939. The main centers of pan-Arabism however were still in Syria, Palestine and Iraq, and this was to remain true until after the war. Egyptian identification with pan-Arabism did not come until much later though signs of it can be discerned at a relatively early date. The Egyptian conspirator 'Azīz 'Alī al-Maṣrī remained an isolated figure with little or no influence in Egypt. During the '20s and '30s politically conscious Egyptians thought of themselves in Pharaonic and Mediterranean terms, finding their identity in the glorious memories of ancient and even of Hellenistic Egypt, rather than in the Arab past. The first pan-Arab magazines and clubs in Egypt date from the early '30s; they were still of very limited influence, and were mostly run by Syrian emigrés. In the 1940s, first under German and then British encouragement, pan-Arabism became rather stronger in Egypt, where an officially patronized "Arab union" was founded on 25 May 1942 for the purpose of promoting it. The creation of the Arab League in Egypt and the inevitably important role played by Egyptians in its functioning greatly increased the interest of this idea for Egyptians, many of whom saw in it an important role for Egypt—and Egyptians—to play.

A factor of some importance in the growth of these ideas was the writings of Sāṭi' al-Ḥuṣrī, a Syrian from Aleppo and a former Ottoman official, who wrote extensively during the 1940s propounding a pan-Arab ideology. Sāṭi' al-Ḥuṣrī, who was associated with Rashīd 'Alī in Iraq and was banished from that country after the collapse of the Rashīd 'Alī regime, was principally concerned to argue three points; first, that the individual can achieve freedom only in the nation and not outside it; second, that Egypt is an integral part of the greater Arab nation; and third, that pan-Arabism is compatible with Islam and not contrary to it. While the practical leaders, even including Nūrī al-Sa'īd (whose scheme for Arab unity submitted to the British government in 1942 excluded Egypt) still thought in terms of a purely Asian pan-Arabism, Sāṭi' al-Ḥuṣrī argued vigorously that Egypt was a part of the Arab nation, and devoted great effort to convincing the Egyptians of this fact.

Egyptian resistance to this idea had at first been strong. Many Egyptians, indeed, notably the nationalist leader, Muṣṭafā Kāmil, had regarded the scheme for a pan-Arab Caliphate as a British plot directed against the Ottomans; he had criticized the Syrian emigrants in Egypt for their attacks on the Ottoman Empire, by which, as he saw it, they were playing the British game. The distinguished Egyptian writer Luṭfī al-Sayyid, in 1938, went so far as to describe the pan-Arab idea as "pure fantasy." Similar views were expressed by the shaykh of al-Azhar and other notables. Such views were encouraged by King Fārūq whose aims at that time seem to have been directed towards an Islamic Caliphate, an objective which might well have seemed incompatible with an Arab nationalist program and leadership.

The outbreak of war and the events that followed seem to have brought a change of policy. The restoration of the Caliphate was clearly a non-starter, while the Arab nationalist idea, encouraged by both the Axis and the British, seemed to offer far better prospects. Fārūq now seems to have thought for the first time in terms of Arab leadership, a role which was adopted after him by subsequent Egyptian leaders. The Arab Society formed in 1942 had official encouragement and well-known official personalities were involved in it. It followed significantly after the declaration by Anthony Eden, the British Foreign Secretary, in May 1941 in favor of Arab unity. A memorandum presented by the Society to the Chief of the Royal Cabinet in March 1942 explaining the aims of the Society referred to this declaration and set forth the limits of the proposed Arab Union. It would include Egypt and the Sudan, the Arabian peninsula, Iraq, Syria, Lebanon, Palestine, Transjordan, and also North Africa and all other Arabic-speaking countries. It would, the memorandum went on, exclude non-Arabic speaking Muslims and therefore also the idea of a Caliphate "of which no Arab country can today bear the heavy burdens, discharge the momentous responsibilities, or pay the exorbitant price." These ideas were approved by the King and led directly to the preliminary talks, as a result of which the Arab League was established.

Anthony Eden's statement delivered at the Mansion House on 29th May 1941 is worth quoting at length. "The Arab world has made great strides since the settlement reached at the end of the last War, and many Arab thinkers desire for the Arab peoples a greater degree of unity than they now enjoy. In reaching out towards this unity they hope for our support. No such appeal from our friends should go unanswered. It seems to me both natural and right that the cultural and economic ties between the Arab countries, and the political ties too, should be strengthened. His Majesty's Government for their part will give their full support to any scheme that commands general approval." (*The Times*, 30 May 1941) Other expressions of support followed, notably, a statement by Eden in the House of Commons on 26th February 1943.

In spite of such encouragement, the Arab states were rather at a disadvantage in the years 1945–1948, when they were called upon to face the first crucial test of the effectiveness of pan-Arab unity and cooperation. As regards the Palestine problem the situation had changed in two respects to their disadvantage. The appalling discoveries in the Nazi camps had aroused universal sympathy for the efforts by the Jewish community in Palestine to provide a home and a refuge for the shattered survivors. The fall of the Axis had deprived the Arabs of their main support and indeed left many of the Arab leaders with an uneasy feeling that their complicity with the Nazis might be discovered to their disadvantage.

Before long, however, the situation changed again. The new British government showed that it would not give way to sympathy or pressure in favor of Jewish emigration to Palestine and that, though the threat of German competition had for the time being disappeared, it intended to continue its policy of supporting pan-Arabism as the best security for British interests in the Middle

East. This was confirmed in the autumn of 1945, when the British government supported the nationalists in Syria against the French, as the war-time government had done in Lebanon in 1943. As the showdown on the Palestine issue approached in the form of a direct collision between British and Jews, the Palestine Arab leadership had the Arab governments behind them, and were led to expect at least some measure of British support.

To begin with their action was diplomatic, expressed in approaches and demarches to the British and other interested governments and notably through a second London conference in 1946 which proved as useless as the preceding one. Diplomatic failure was followed by even more disastrous military failure. The first Palestine war began with local conflicts between Jewish and Arab irregular forces inside mandatory Palestine. This was followed by an invasion of the country by the regular armies of the neighboring Arab states with the declared objective of conquering the area assigned to the Jews by the United Nations partition resolution and establishing Arab authority in the whole of Palestine. Precisely what Arab authority was not clear, and one of the major factors in the Arab defeat was the disunity between the Arab states and in particular the rival ambitions of King ʿAbdullah of Transjordan and King Faruq of Egypt, each of whom envisaged an aggrandizement of his own realm.

Ideological Triumph and Political Failure

The Arab military defeat in 1948 and the humiliation resulting from it ushered in a new phase which continued until the third Arab-Israeli War in 1967.

The main feature of this period was the growth and development of a whole series of independent Arab states. To the original group in the Middle East many others were added, as the former British and French dependencies and possessions in Asia and Africa, one after another, gained political sovereignty.

During the years 1948–1967 pan-Arab ideologies enjoyed great and unchallenged popularity; but pan-Arab policies suffered some of their greatest defeats.

In the vast literature on pan-Arab ideology produced in these years, several trends can be detected, which may be divided, roughly and broadly, into conservative and radical. The former, overwhelmingly Muslim, lays great stress on Islam—as a universal religion but also as a manifestation of the Arab genius, and virtually identifies Arabism with Islam. Writers of this school sometimes call upon Christian Arabs (Jewish Arabs, whose theoretical existence is often asserted in anti-Zionist polemic, are rarely if ever mentioned in this context) to join, as Arabs, in the veneration of Muḥammad as a great Arab hero whose career and achievement gave the Arabs their rightful place in world history. At one time, there were Christian Arab writers willing to accept and indeed elaborate this idea, though this has become much rarer in recent years. One of the most cogent and intelligent exponents of this type of rather conservative, Islamic pan-

Arabism, the Iraqi statesman ʿAbd al-Rahman al-Bazzaz, likened the position of the Arabs in Islam to that of the Russians in world communism.

On the whole, the radicals were for long far more influential than the conservatives, at any rate in the area of ideological expression. While some—including some of the most extreme—have been Muslims, many have been Christians of various denominations. It may be worth noting in passing that among the Palestinian organizations, the broad-based and relatively moderate *al-Fath* is predominantly Muslim, while the extremist groups are overwhelmingly Christian in leadership. It is of course a common phenomenon for members of discontented minorities to gravitate to revolutionary and millenarian movements, in the hope of attaining thereby the equality and opportunities that have eluded them in the traditional order.

Certainly the most influential of these Christian-born radical ideologists is Michel Aflaq, born in Damascus in 1912, the co-founder, with the Muslim Ṣalāḥ al-Dīn Bīṭār, of the *Baʿth* (Renaissance) party. This party appears to have been founded in 1940, and began public activity in 1943. In 1953 it united with the Arab Socialist Party, led by a Syrian Muslim, Akram Hawrānī, and has since been known as the Arab Socialist Baʿth Party. It won considerable successes, becoming the only organized pan-Arab party with branches and followers in most of the Arab lands. On several occasions it was able to gain or share power in Syria and Iraq, but was weakened by a recurring tendency to internecine conflict. It was largely the Baʿthist leadership in Syria that procured the union with Egypt in 1958. But recriminations followed, and it was the Baʿthists again who did much to undermine the union and cause its disruption. Their subsequent political actions in Syria and Iraq won them power, but have not brought them nearer to unity.

Baʿthists describe their ideology as left-wing, revolutionary, and socialist, but it was by no means easy to disentangle what is meant by this from their extensive programmatic literature. Such parochial European terms as left-wing and right-wing have very different meanings when applied to Arab politics, and even the word socialist—as Europe herself demonstrates—may bear a variety of meanings, ranging from the Scandinavian or British Social-Democrats to the so-called "Socialist Bloc" of Soviet-dominated Eastern Europe and the National Socialist German Workers Party (NSDAP) of Adolf Hitler. Various Baʿthist pronouncements are at times suggestive of all of these; even the last named is recalled in the extreme, often chauvinistic nationalism which they express.

The long debates between Baʿthists, Nasserists and others on Arab nationalism and Arab socialism are however less important than the major developments in Arab political life.

These must be seen in the continuing struggle for Palestine, and the series of military defeats suffered by the Arabs. Defeat in war has often provoked radical change. Sometimes, as in Germany and Russia after the First World War, it can lead to far-reaching political and economic adventures. Sometimes, on the other hand, it may lead to a mood of sullen withdrawal and resentment, as happened to the South after the American Civil War and to Spain after the defeat in Cuba in 1898. The shock of defeat in 1948 was especially humiliating in that the victors were not the mighty imperial powers but the Jews, familiar as a tolerated minority. Defeat at their hands was especially galling, and led to the overthrow by violence of most of the regimes held guilty of allowing it to happen.

This in turn led to the second major development of the period: the fall of existing regimes in most of the countries of the Middle East and their replacement by self-styled revolutionaries, mostly military in origin, who established autocratic regimes by coup d'état. These new rulers proclaimed programs of revolutionary change, later designated socialism, and of Arab nationalism.

Internationally, the new radical leaders were strongly anti-Western, and like their predecessors in the '30s—in some cases indeed the self-same persons—they sought allies against the West. The Nazis had gone but there were others to take their place. The Soviet Union was now able to present itself to the Arabs as their champion—and against the same enemies, the West, the Jews, and liberal or capitalist democracy. There were remarkable resemblances in the appeal, in the hopes and fears to which it was addressed, and in the nature and identity of the response and of the respondents.

At first sight all seemed to favor the development of pan-Arabism. The Arab states had now cast off their Western bonds. There were no treaties with the Western powers, no bases, no troops or experts based on their soil and advising and thus limiting their governments and their armed forces. No Western imperialist power could now influence the Arab governments or prevent them from making a free choice for unity if they so desired. Pan-Arab propaganda was now unrestrained. Pan-Arab literature, ideological and polemic, appeared in vast quantities in all the Arabic-speaking countries. Pan Arabism became virtually official doctrine in most of these countries and Arab rulers and ministers without exception paid lip service to pan-Arab ideas and objectives, agreeing with the current fashion of denouncing regional, sectional and factional loyalties, by which were meant the specific interests and allegiances of the various Arab states.

Circumstances also seemed to favor the pan-Arab cause. One of these was language. The unity of language of the Arab countries had to a large extent been theoretical rather than real. Although they shared a common written language, the spoken languages of these various countries differed greatly from one another—rather as if France, Italy, Spain and Portugal all spoke their various languages but had continued to read and write Latin, with a medieval level of literacy. In recent years however the growth of education and the rise in Arab literacy has increased the effect of the common written language as a medium of unity. This has been further accentuated by the rapid growth of the mass media—cinema, radio, television, newspapers, to which may be added books. Publications emanating from the two main cultural centers, Cairo and Beirut, circulate all over the Arab world and the Egyptian film has brought a knowledge of Egyptian Arabic to virtually all Arab countries. The cause has been further helped by legal and public encouragement and by the adoption of pan-Arabism as the official program of at least one major party, the Baʿth, and its encouragement by others. The public and formal acceptance of pan-Arabism has indeed gone so far that it is even enshrined, or rather embalmed, in the constitutions of many Arab countries. As far back as 1956 the revised Egyptian constitution promulgated in that year proclaimed Egypt as an Arab country. This was followed by equivalent clauses in the constitutions of Iraq, Syria, Jordan, Sudan, Algeria, Kuwait, and other Arab states, and in the Charter of the P.L.O.

The inclusion of pan-Arabism in the constitutions of Arab states, alongside the guarantees of personal liberty, freedom of expression, etc., is perhaps a sign of its decline, for in this constitutional tradition, the enactment of political principles is a substitute for their enforcement, not a means of ensuring it. In fact, all attempts to create larger units by joining together existing Arab states failed. The most ambitious of these was the union of Syria and Egypt in the United Arab Republic. This was brought about in 1958 amid great rejoicing in the pan-Arab camp. It proved a difficult association, and ended in 1961 with the separation of the two and the resumption of a separate existence by Syria. Other attempts to create greater units by joining Jordan and Iraq, North and South Yemen, or Egypt and Libya have either failed or are encountering great difficulties. While paying lip service to pan-Arab ideals, the heads of Arab governments continue to pursue their various sectional interests and these preclude subordination of their own states to larger centralized units located elsewhere.

There are several reasons by which this process can be explained. One is the Arab-Israel conflict itself. The failure of the Arab League and of the Arab states to prevent the formation of Israel or to secure its dissolution is a failure of pan-Arabism—a failure either to concert effective action against Israel or to provide effective help for the Palestinian Arabs, whether by reconquest or by resettlement. Arab spokesmen were also becoming aware of a theoretical weakness in the pan-Arab position affecting their stand against Israel. If the Arabs were indeed one nation and the Arab lands one country, then they had suffered the loss only of a province and a very small one at that, compared with the enormous area of the greater Arab fatherland. The loss of territory and movement of people were far smaller and less significant than those endured by the Poles, Germans, Indians and Pakistanis between 1945 and 1947—that is, in the brutal aftermath of the Second World War and in the years immediately preceding the first Arab-Israel conflict. If, on the other hand, the Palestinians were a nation and not merely a small part of one, then their position vis-à-vis Israel was substantially different. Until 1967 Arab governments generally adopted the pan-Arab position, which entitled them to make the Palestinian Arab cause their own and also, in the case of Jordan, Egypt and Syria, to remain in possession of those parts of mandatory Palestine not included in Israel. In Jordan, Palestinian Arabs were treated as citizens and accorded equal rights. In other Arab countries, however, they remained stateless aliens and were usually treated as such.

The main factor in this period was the growing solidity and reality of the individual states. To begin with, most of these were artificial enough—carved out of former provinces of the Ottoman or Western empires, with frontiers that were lines drawn on maps by European statesmen. With the exception of Egypt and to a lesser extent of Lebanon, they had no tradition of separate existence or even of regional autonomy. Even their names reveal their artificiality—Jordan is a river, Lebanon a mountain, Iraq the name of a medieval province, not coinciding with the boundaries of the present state of that name; Syria and Libya are Greek names borrowed and used for the first time in modern Arabic. Even Palestine was a name unused since the early Middle Ages among the Muslim inhabitants of that country, until it was adopted to designate the southern parts of the Ottoman provinces of Damascus and Beirut, together with the separate district of Jerusalem, assigned to British Mandate.

Yet these states, artificial and alien as they may have been, nevertheless acquired reality. Around each one of them there grew up a ganglion of interests, careers and loyalties and, most important of all, a ruling and administering élite which made the state an effective unit—unwilling to surrender or share power or control and increasingly conscious of a separate identity and purpose. This was already clear in the disunity of the Arab states invading Palestine in 1948, even at the moment of danger. It has become much clearer in the years that have passed since then, in particular after the political and social transformations of some of these countries, which intensified the conflicts of interest between them.

The role of Egypt has been of particular importance in this process. Egypt was a late comer to pan-Arabism and for some time showed interest in it only as a possible adjunct to her own foreign policy. That policy had done Egypt little good. It involved her in a disastrous war in the Yemen, in an ill-starred union with Syria which ended amid hostility and recrimination, and above all in defeat at the hands of the Israelis. As a result Egyptian pan-Arabism has been attacked from both sides. On the one hand, there have been many Arabs who have seen Egyptian policy as an attempt to exploit pan-Arab sentiments and aspirations for Egyptian imperial purposes; on the other, there have been many Egyptians who have seen in that policy a subordination of Egyptian national interests to pan-Arab fantasies, and the squandering of Egyptian blood and treasure in a cause not their own.

Pan-Arabism was also adversely affected by the growth and spread of Soviet influence in the Arab countries. This happened in two different ways. The Soviets themselves dislike supranational ideologies not controlled by them, and discouraged pan-Arabism among their own followers, preferring to deal separately with the individual Arab states. At the same time those who were opposed to Soviet influence and who saw the Russian presence, with its treaties and its troops and its experts and its advisers, as a new imperialism, were also turning away from pan-Arabism, partly because it was pan-Arab leaders who brought the Russians into the Middle East and also, more importantly, because in a struggle against foreign penetration it is inevitably the liberation of the homeland which is the first consideration.

Finally, mention should be made of the steady growth of religious and more specifically communal sentiments, marking a partial reversion to more traditional loyalties. This trend was intensified by the Lebanese civil war of 1975–76, and by the growing weight of Saudi leadership in the Arab world.

The third Arab military defeat in 1967 intensified these processes. Egypt, Jordan and Syria lost the Palestinian territories which they had previously occupied or annexed and therefore no longer had any vested interest in denying the existence of a Palestine entity. On the contrary, the formation of militant Palestinian organizations made it possible for them to shift the main responsibility for the struggle against Israel to the Palestinians themselves and thereby in some measure to diminish their own involvement.

These processes continued after the war of October 1973 which, whatever its military outcome, was a clear political victory for the Arab states. The resulting gains were confirmed and extended by the power of oil and of the money which oil brought. But the uneven distribution of this new wealth among the Arab states, and their uneven participation in the conflict with Israel, placed new strains on inter-Arab relations. Increasingly, the governments of the individual states pursued their separate interests and purposes, sometimes to the point of open and even of armed conflict between them.

Most significant in this respect is the changing attitude of the Palestinians themselves. In the past they had been, for obvious reasons, the most enthusiastic supporters of the pan-Arab cause and the most prominent exponents of pan-Arab ideology. But they had encountered bitter disappointments. At the lowest level they found themselves treated as foreigners in virtually all Arab countries, apart from Jordan; even in the Gaza stip occupied by Egypt, apart from a brief period in 1956–57, from 1948 to 1967, they were not accorded Egyptian citizenship and not allowed freedom of travel or employment in Egyptian territory. The Arab states had either refused or proved unable to help them in their struggle against Israel, or to accept them as fellow Arabs in their own countries.

Worst of all, in these countries there was developing a strong sense of separate nationality with a growing and maturing political élite. The Palestinian élite saw their own contemporaries enjoying the fruits of power which were denied to them because they lacked a state of their own and were not admitted to full citizenship in the countries where they had found refuge. In these circumstances Palestinians began to think less of pan-Arabism and more of constituting an entity of their own in which they would be masters, and could enjoy the same political opportunities as their contemporaries in Syria, Iraq and elsewhere.

For a while Arab leaders continued to pay lip service to pan-Arabism while pursuing sectional-national objectives. In recent years even this has ceased, and some Arab leaders have begun to speak openly of their real purposes. The new frankness has not however as yet penetrated to the ideological literature, in which pan-Arabism remains the sole orthodoxy.

The present development in the Arab world suggests a parallel with South America after the ending of Spanish rule. There too there was a series of countries akin in language, culture, religion and way of life, which might have come together as did the English-speaking colonies of North America, to form one or two major states. They did not in fact do so and the opportunity, once lost, did not recur. The Arab states, too, seemed to be moving in the same direction—a community of language, culture, religion and, to some extent, of institutions and way of life, with a common Arabism which may be equivalent to the *hispanismo* of the Spanish-speaking world—but no more. This would not preclude the formation of regional groupings, of a pattern increasingly common in the world today, based on practical rather than ideological considerations. At one time it seemed that the working arrangement between Morocco, Algeria and Tunisia could be an example of this; and that relations between Egypt, Libya and perhaps also the Sudan might move in the same direction, but many difficulties have arisen, which have obstructed this development.

It may well be that at some future time, with the growth of cultural links, communications and the trend towards the formation of larger entities, the Arab countries may come together in larger political formations. But for the time being the trend is in the opposite direction.

18

The Emergence of Modern Israel

❧❦❧❦

I n the second half of the nineteenth century, when political Zionism was born, the entity known as "the Jews" consisted of several distinct and disparate groups. Two of them were, by the criteria of the societies in which they lived, nations; the rest were religious minorities, with a varying degree of acceptance and assimilation within the nations to which they belonged.

The first and larger of the two nations consisted of the Jews of Eastern Europe. Most of these were to be found in the great belt of territory stretching from the Baltic to the Black Sea, and comprising the so-called Pale of Settlement—the area within which alone, by a statute promulgated in 1804, Jews were permitted to live in the Russian Empire. The Jewish communities in these provinces came into being under the aegis of the Polish-Lithuanian State, which had accorded them tolerance and a measure of autonomy. Through the successive partitions of Poland the great majority of them had passed under the rule of the Czars of Russia, who thus acquired by conquest the Jewish subjects whom they had refused to accept by any other means. These new subjects suffered greatly by the change.

In addition to the Jews of the Russian Pale of Settlement, there were similar groups beyond the Russian western border, in other former Polish territories annexed to Prussia and Austria-Hungary, as well as in Roumania. By about 1880 the Jews in this area numbered between five and six million, that is to say some three-quarters of the entire Jewish population of the world.

This Jewish community had most, if not all, of the characteristics of a national minority in Eastern Europe—a common culture and way of life, a common religion, a putative common descent, and a common language (Yiddish) exclusive to them. They had their own literature, provided their own schools, and created a form of higher education, in the rabbinical seminaries. In a sense they even had a common territory in the Pale, based on the former Polish-Lithuanian State, and a common history extending back over many centuries within that political framework. True, they were not a majority in that area—though in a few parts of it they attained even that—but this was less of an anomaly than might at first appear in regions of very mixed population. The Yiddish nation of Eastern Europe had no political existence—but the same was true of all but a few of their neighbours. The Jews formed an ethnic but not a legal nationality, in this resembling the Poles, the Baltic peoples, the Ukrainians and many others.

The second Jewish nation was of quite a different type. This was the Jewish *Millet* in Islam, more particularly in the Ottoman Empire. Here again the Jewish entity conformed to the prevailing pattern—that of a religio-political subject community like the Armenians or the Greeks. In the early nineteenth century the word Greek in the Ottoman Empire denoted religion, not ethnic or linguistic nationality, and the term covered Orthodox Christians speaking Roumanian, Albanian, Bulgarian, Serbian and Arabic as well as Greek. The Jewish *Millet* too was multi-lingual, including speakers of Arabic, Spanish, Greek, Kurdish, Aramaic and other languages. The largest Jewish community under Muslim rule was that of the Ottoman Empire. Other, smaller, groups existed in Iran and Central Asia, in the Yemen, Morocco, and in various territories formerly under Islamic rule now incorporated in the European colonial empires, especially those of France and Russia. No reliable statistics are available for these countries, but the number of Jews under Muslim rule at the time is put at roughly one million.

The remainder of the Jewish people consisted of more or less assimilated religious minorities. The most important of these were in the lands of German culture in middle Europe—in Germany and in the western parts of the Austro-Hungarian Empire. Other, smaller, groups were to be found in Western Europe, and there were new but growing communities in the United States and other countries of European settlement overseas. These Jewish minorities were barely distinguishable in language, culture and a way of life from their compatriots of other religions. The differences were diminishing with the twin processes of emancipation and secularization, and, to the innocent optimists of the early decades of this [the 20th] century, it seemed that there would be no halt or hindrance to the continuation and completion of this process. They were to learn otherwise.

Nationalism was in the air in the nineteenth century, and Jews were variously affected. In the West, they became fervent patriots of the countries of which they were more or less equal citizens. In the East—both European and Islamic—the situation was more complex and more difficult. Theoretically, the change from religious to national identities and loyalties should have improved their position, by transforming them from a tolerated minority to an integral part of the nation. In fact, their position went from bad to worse. The old intolerance was modernized and magnified; the old restraints weakened or removed. In a time of rapid social change and heightened ethnic awareness, the Jews remained unbelievers and became aliens, exposed to a hostility which ranged, in different countries, from petty but wounding snobbery to violent persecution. For the traditional, believing Jew, suffering for his religion was a voluntary trial which he could endure with dignity, fortitude, and confidence. For the aspiring citizen it was a degradation and an affront, against which he had no inner defence of self-respect.

The new nationalism confronted the Jews with new problems; to some it also suggested a new solution. If the nation—an entity defined by descent, culture and aspiration—was the only natural and rightful basis of statehood, why then the Jews were also a nation, and must have their own State. The first precursor of modern Zionism was a Bosnian Rabbi called Yehuda Alkalai, who in 1843 produced a scheme for a man-made Jewish restoration in Palestine—without waiting for the Messiah. The problem was posed for him, in an acute form, by the anti-Jewish trouble in Damascus in 1840; the model for a solution was provided by the Serbian and Greek national revivals. In 1862 a Rabbi in Posen, in Prussian Poland, exhorted his co-religionists to "take to heart the examples of the Italians, Poles, and Hungarians." In the same year Moses Hess, an emancipated, radical German Jew, published his *Rome and Jerusalem*, the first of a long series of socialist Zionist Utopias.

In the course of the nineteenth century, the idea of a Jewish national restoration in Palestine became widely known. It aroused the interest of Jews in many lands; it even attracted the attention of Christian observers as diverse as Napoleon, Palmerston, Shaftesbury, and George Eliot.

The name Zionist and the political movement called by it were both born in Austria-Hungary—also the home of modern anti-semitism. Within the sprawling and variegated Habsburg monarchy assimilated modern Jews and un-assimilated traditional Jews lived side by side, encountering both modern and traditional antagonisms. The founder of the Zionist organization was Theodor Herzl, a Hungarian-born Viennese Jew, and the history of the movement is conventionally dated from the publication of his booklet, *The Jewish State*, in 1896.

But Herzl had many predecessors, in both theory and action. The most important of them, as also of his disciples and successors, were not Central but East Europeans.

In a very real sense, Jewish nationalism, with the State of Israel which is its ultimate result, was a creation of the Yiddish nation in Eastern Europe. Its romanticism, its socialism, its populism, its linkage of religion and nationality are familiar features of East European political thought and life.

Zionism has many sources. Some of these are traditionally and authentically Jewish. One such is the Jewish religion itself with its recurring stress on Zion, Jerusalem, and the Holy Land, and on the interwoven themes of bondage and liberation, of exile and return. These occupy a central position in the Jewish religious tradition, and a worshipper is reminded of them daily and throughout the year by the Jewish liturgy.

Another is Hassidism—the movement of religious revival which arose among Polish Jews in the late seventeenth century and affected large parts of East European Jewry. This movement, which gave new warmth and vitality to the rabbinic Judaism of that time, was an important, perhaps a necessary, prerequisite to the growth and spread of the Zionist movement. It is certainly remarkable how large a proportion of the pioneers of Zionism, and still more of the Hebrew revival, were men of Hassidic background.

Linked with this was the Jewish tradition of Messianism—the belief in a Redeemer who would rescue the Jews from captivity and restore them to their promised homeland. There were many aspirants to this role, some better known than others. The last to announce his advent and mission in purely religious terms was a seventeenth-century Turkish Jew called Shabbetai Sevi, a grotesque and tragic figure who was able for a while to win delirious support among Jews in both east and west. His failure and apostasy brought them disillusionment and despair. After this time, the Jews—now exposed to new, external influences—began to look elsewhere for the realization of their messianic hopes, and to turn from religious to secular redeemers.

There was no lack of problems requiring the attentions of a Redeemer. Throughout the Pale of Settlement, Jews were the victims of poverty, repression, permanent discrimination, and occasional persecution. The ideas, ideals and ideologies of the East European peoples among whom the Jews were living seemed to offer solutions which the gradual growth of secular knowledge among Jews made accessible and attractive to them. East European socialism, anarchism and populism all made their various contributions to the growth of one more nationalism among the others. Some believed that the Jews should seek freedom and renewal by fighting shoulder to shoulder with the peoples among whom they lived. Others—the Zionists—saw in the universal minority status of the Jews the basic cause of all their troubles, and believed that only in a Jewish country, ruled eventually by a Jewish State, would they be able to achieve true emancipation.

Many Jews found a personal solution to their problem by emigrating, above all to the United States. Between 1870 and 1900 more than half a million East European Jews migrated to the West. Between 1900 and 1914 the figure exceeded a million and a half. All in all, about one-third of the Jews of Eastern Europe are estimated to have left their homes in search of a new life in the West. Of the remainder, the overwhelming majority stayed where they were, most of them engaged exclusively in the personal struggle for survival, some—few but not unimportant—seeking a political end to their troubles, through participation in Russian revolutionary movements. Another group, insignificant in numbers but far-reaching in effect, found another way. In 1882 some young Jews, most of them students, met in Kharkov and formed an organization called Lovers of Zion. Their aim was emigration—not to the broad lands of the West, but to a remote and largely derelict Ottoman province known in Christendom but not to its inhabitants as Palestine. The settlements which they and their successors founded, in the teeth of immense difficulties and obstacles, formed the nucleus of what was eventually to be the State of Israel.

Like the white Anglo-Saxon Protestants in the United States, the East European pioneers and their descendants in Israel have ceased to form the majority of the population. Again, like their American counterparts, however, the founding fathers of Israel and their descendants have retained their primacy in two important respects. One, the more practical, is through their continued predominance in the interlocking system of personal, family and institutional loyalties which constitutes the Israeli establishment. The other, more permanent, is through the stamp which they have imposed on the very nature of the Israeli State and society. Modern Israel is in a very real sense the creation of the East European pioneers, and later immigrants, from Central Europe and from the countries of Asia and Africa, have been constrained with greater or lesser willingness to assimilate to the pattern established by these pioneers. Even the language of the East European founding fathers, like that of the English settlers in North America, has somehow imposed itself on Israel as a whole. Hebrew is of course quite a different language from Yiddish, and belongs to a different family. But the transformation of Hebrew from a learned and liturgical language into a living, modern language, while yet retaining a distinctively Jewish character, was the achievement of people who came with a distinctively Jewish language of their own—Yiddish. In a very real sense modern Hebrew is a reincarnation of Yiddish—the same soul in a new lexical body. . . .

These and related features may help to provide an answer to a question which has often puzzled observers of the Israeli scene—that democracy survives and indeed flourishes in a setting which is in every way unfavourable to it; a population the overwhelming majority of whom come from countries without any tradition of democratic government, a region in which democratic ways and processes are almost universally discredited, and a continuing struggle, since the very foundation of the State, which inevitably assigns a major role to the armed forces and lays great stress on the patriotic and martial virtues. There seemed every reason why Israel should follow her neighbours into military dictatorship— yet Israel has not done so, and shows little sign of doing so in the foreseeable future.

Perhaps the most important factor preventing the emergence and acceptance of an autocratic régime in Israel is the deep-rooted tradition of voluntarism which exists among the population. In both the Polish kingdom and the Ottoman Empire, the two States from which the overwhelming majority of Israelis originated, the Jews had enjoyed a very large measure of autonomy in the conduct of their own affairs—social, cultural and even fiscal as well as purely religious. The old Polish system of Jewish autonomy in the so-called Council of the Four Lands, like the Ottoman *Millet* system, had allowed the Jews substantial independence in running their lives. Both of these traditions of autonomy had been

eroded in the course of the nineteenth century—that of Poland by the subjection
of the greater part of Polish Jewry to the harsher rule of Czarist Russia, that of
the Ottoman Empire through the abrogation of the *Millet* system under the
influence of the centralizing reforms of the Tanzimat and after. Thanks largely
to Czarist and reformist inefficiency, however, this process of erosion had not
gone very far, and the principle of voluntary organization from within had remained very strong among communities for whom the State was remote, alien,
and marginal to most of their interests and activities. For the more important
East European community it was also an irremediably hostile entity in which
they had no share and which they could not hope to influence. The resulting
traditions—of mistrust for authority on the one hand and of voluntary self-
administration on the other—still survive very vigorously in Israel, and provide
the main basis for the flourishing network of separate autonomous organizations
through which Israel functions. . . .

The East Europeans were the first but not the only immigrants. During the
1930s they were followed by large-scale immigration from middle Europe—
from Germany, Austria, Czechoslovakia and Hungary—of Jews of a rather different kind. These were assimilated Europeans, basically members of religious
minorities in their countries of origin, and very different in culture and outlook
from the Yiddish nation. Relations between middle and East Europeans formed
an important theme in Jewish Palestine in the 1930s and early '40s, and gave
rise to many conflicts and antagonisms.

These conflicts are now for the most part settled and forgotten—largely because, after the absorption of the shattered survivors in the Displaced Persons
camps, there was not and could not be any further large-scale immigration from
these countries. Subsequent immigration from the Western world, from North
and South America, from South Africa and from Western Europe has presented
fewer problems—partly because it was much smaller in scale, partly because it
consisted very largely of Jews with—at one or two generations removed—the
same East European background as the original settlers.

Far more important, however, has been the migration, since the foundation
of the State, of great numbers of Jews from the Middle East and North Africa.
These at one time constituted a fairly small minority within the Jewish community in Palestine; they and their descendants now form more than half of the
Jewish population of Israel. For a variety of reasons they have failed to attain
anything like the share of positions of power and influence corresponding to
their numbers, and this has given rise to much complaint and bitterness. There
are many reasons for this disparity, some arising from the different standards and
qualifications brought by the immigrants, some from the inability of new groups
to penetrate the closely interlocked and well-ensconced Israeli establishment.

There is indeed a profound difference between the two communities. Some
see this difference in traditional terms, as a rivalry between Ashkenazic and
Sefardic Jews; others present it in more fashionable dress, as a conflict between

Europeans and Afro-Asians, with the latter of course cast in the role of victims. Neither interpretation quite corresponds to the realities; neither reveals the basic issues. Essentially, this is a confrontation between the Jews of Christendom and the Jews of Islam. European and American Jews are not Christians, as Middle Eastern and North African Jews are not Muslims, yet both are deeply marked by the cultures, standards, values and outlooks of their countries of origin, and even in Israel continue to maintain many of their characteristic attitudes. The encounter of two civilizations, of two worlds, within a single small State constitutes what is perhaps the major internal problem of Israel at the present day.

It is now in the process of being further complicated by the massive arrival of a third group—the Jews from Soviet Russia. These come from a background which is neither Christian nor Muslim but Communist; it remains to be seen how much they will bring with them from their country of origin, and how this will be brought into accord with what they find in Israel.

19

Orientalist Notes on the Soviet–United Arab Republic Treaty of 27 May 1971

❧❦❧❦

On 27 May 1971, a treaty of "Friendship and Cooperation" between Russia, at that time known as the Soviet Union, and Egypt, at that time known as the United Arab Republic, was signed in Cairo by Presidents Nikolai Podgorny and Anwar Sadat.[1] The treaty was drafted, signed, and ratified in two languages, Arabic and Russian, both texts being valid. The two signatory governments both published official but nonbinding English translations. Both English versions use British spelling, but otherwise differ on a number of points, some of which may be significant.[2]

The practice of drawing up international agreements in more than one language is common, though, in order to forestall misunderstandings and difficulties, it is often agreed that one text, sometimes in a language other than those of the contracting parties, will be binding. The classical case in diplomatic relations between Russia and Middle Eastern states is the Treaty of Küçük Kaynarca of 16/21 July 1774, in which the twenty-seventh and concluding article requires that the treaty be ratified by the commanders-in-chief of the Russian and Ottoman armies, who, on behalf of their sovereigns, will sign and seal the document, the one in the Turkish and Italian languages, the other in the Russian and Italian languages.[3] It would appear that the treaty was originally drafted in Russian. The situation at the time—the imposition of the treaty by a victorious Russia on a defeated Turkey—makes this probable; the actual Italian text, in Article XIII of which the Turkish title *padişah* is transcribed as *"padischag,"* following Russian orthography, makes this certain.

By the late eighteenth century, there were experts in Russia who knew Ottoman and other forms of Turkish. But a binding text in the language of the vanquished would hardly have suited the victors, and there can have been few if any in Turkey who knew Russian. A mutually acceptable and intelligible language was necessary even for an imposed treaty, and Italian, at that time the only European language in common and to some extent even in official use in Ottoman lands, was a natural choice.

In the present [twentieth] century, when knowledge of languages is much more widely diffused, a mutually acceptable third language is no longer necessary, though it is still common. A mutually agreed binding text might still serve a useful purpose where differing interpretations could arise. The possibility of this happening is the greater where the languages concerned are as far apart as modern Russian and Arabic, which differ not only lexically—a relatively minor point—but also, far more importantly, in the cultural, social, and political connotations of the terms that they use. Some inkling of these differences may immediately be gathered from the two different English translations published by the high contracting parties, the one in Moscow, the other in Cairo. A comparative textual study of the two English versions, and of the Russian and Arabic texts that underlie them, may therefore be instructive.[4]

The provenance of the text is immediately obvious. It is clearly of Russian origin, as may be seen from a comparison with other bilateral treaties concluded by the Soviet Union, notably the treaties of "Friendship, Cooperation, and Mutual Assistance" with Hungary, signed in Budapest on 7 September 1967, and with Czechoslovakia, signed in Prague on 6 May 1970.[5] Other similarly entitled treaties were signed with Finland in Moscow (6 April 1948) and with China, also in Moscow (14 February 1950). Also of relevance, though it was signed with a Western country, was the "Protocol on Cooperation" with France, signed in Moscow on 13 October 1970.[6]

From these documents, it would appear that a draft treaty was brought from Moscow and subsequently modified in whatever negotiations took place between the arrival of the Soviet delegation in Cairo on 25 May and the signature of the treaty on 27 May. In this there is a striking difference with the Soviet-Finnish treaty of 1948. The first suggestion for that treaty came in a letter from Stalin to the Finnish president, dated 23 February. Four days later, the president sent a brief acknowledgment, pointing out that foreign treaties required parliamentary approval. On 5 March, the Finnish president received the written views of parliamentary groups. Negotiations between the two governments began on 25 March, and the treaty was signed on 6 April. A Finnish diplomat, contrasting this with the speedy conclusion of the treaties between the Soviet Union and its East European neighbors, pointed to the timetable of negotiation as "an eloquent assertion of Finnish independence, and a demonstration of the democratic process."[7] The Soviet-UAR treaty was initiated, negotiated, and concluded in three days.

Several clauses of the treaty bear on internal as well as regional and international matters. Article 2 in the Soviet English version, for example, lays down that the Soviet Union "as a socialist state" and the United Arab Republic, "which has set itself the aim of reconstructing society along socialist lines," will cooperate in all fields to ensure conditions "for preserving and further developing the social and economic gains of their peoples." The Cairo English version has a slightly more cautious translation of the last phrase, omitting the words "in all fields," and "further," and stating simply that the two governments "will cooperate closely to create the necessary conditions for safeguarding and maintaining the development of their two peoples' social and economic gains." It is obvious that the Egyptian understanding of "socialism," in the context of their own ideology of Arab socialism, differed radically from the Soviet interpretation of the same term. Both meanings were advanced in the internal debate in Egypt, the one being called "Arab socialism," the other, "scientific" socialism. At the present time, both countries would probably agree that socialism is neither Arab nor scientific.

This paragraph was apparently inspired by Article 5 of the Soviet-Czechoslovak treaty, which reads, "the high contracting parties, expressing their unswerving resolve to proceed along the path of the construction of socialism and communism, will undertake the necessary measures for the defense of socialist gains of the peoples and for the security and independence of both countries, and will strive to develop all-around relations between the states of the socialist commonwealth, and to act in the spirit of consolidating their unity, friendship, and fraternity." This article, and similar articles in other Soviet treaties with countries in the Soviet bloc, embody the principle that came to be known in the West as the Brezhnev Doctrine. In the Soviet reading of Article 2 of the Soviet-UAR treaty, the UAR government committed itself to "maintain and extend socialism"—presumably meaning, in this context, something that the Soviet government would recognize as socialism. When at a later date the government of Egypt decided to abandon socialist policies, this article could no doubt have been cited by the Soviet Union to justify an intervention "in defense of socialism," had such an intervention been in other respects feasible.

Article 7 is clearly, though not explicitly, concerned with the Middle East. In the Soviet version, "In the event of situations developing which, in the opinion of both sides, create a danger to peace or a violation of peace, they will contact each other without delay in order to concert their positions with a view to removing the threat that has arisen or restoring peace." For "concert their positions," the Cairo version has the somewhat stronger "coordinate their stands." The two texts—the Russian *"soglasovanie svoikh pozitsii,"* and the Arabic *"tansīq mawqifayhima"*—overlap rather than coincide in meaning, and both translations, though divergent, are reasonably faithful to their respective originals. *Tansīq,* a late Ottoman term that has become common in modern bureaucratic Arabic, has a connotation of authority. It is often used in the sense of "coordinate"—e.g., of boards and committees, the task of which is to oversee and coordinate lower levels of administration. It is sometimes used in the sense of "to organize or systematize," or even in the context of a planned economy. The Russian word *soglasovanie,* in contrast, has a connotation of agreement and concurrence. Related words denote harmony and conciliation. This formula of "contact and consultation" is taken from the Soviet-French Protocol of 13 October 1970.

By the provisions of this article, both parties accept some limitation of their freedom of action in the event of war or threat of war in the Middle East. On the purely textual evidence of the Russian and Arabic versions, and the corresponding English translations, the Soviets are less limited than the Egyptians. This also corresponded with the power relationship between the two at the time. This limitation did not prevent the Egyptian offensive in October 1973.

In Article 9, each of the parties, in the Soviet version, "states that it will not take part in any groupings of states, or in actions or measures directed against the other high contracting party." This too constitutes an important limitation on the freedom of action of both parties, this time not only in regional, but also in international relations. The intended effect presumably was to preclude Egypt from joining any group or taking part in any "actions or measures" judged by the Soviet government to be anti-Soviet. That the Soviet Union was similarly precluded from joining an anti-Egyptian bloc could hardly at that time be considered a major diplomatic success.

In return for accepting these limitations on its domestic, regional, and international freedom of action, the government of Egypt received certain assurances of a military character from the Soviet Union. These fell short of a military alliance. The clause that appears, with minor variations, in all the East European treaties stating that the Soviet Union will "render immediate assistance" in case of aggression[8] is missing in the Egyptian treaty. The promise to Egypt of contact and consultation falls a long way short of these undertakings and instead uses the language of the "Protocol of Political Cooperation" with France—a Western power.

But that is not all. Article 8, which President Sadat described at the time as the most important in the treaty, provided for the development of "cooperation in the military field on the basis of appropriate agreements. . . ." The "appropriate agreements," in the UAR version "suitable agreements," were no doubt practical arrangements and were of course secret. The article, however, specified "assistance in the training of UAR military personnel and in mastering the armaments and equipment supplied to the United Arab Republic, with a view to strengthening its capacity to eliminate the consequences of the aggression, as well as increasing its ability to stand up to aggression in general." In a small but subtle divergence, in place of "mastery" (*osvoenie*), the UAR text has "assimilation" (*istīʿāb*).

Significantly, the definite article before the first use of "aggression" appears in both the Soviet and UAR English translations of Article 8, making it clear that both parties had a specific aggression in mind. In Russian there is no definite article; in Arabic the sentence requires the definite article. In English, the use of the article in this sentence is awkward and unidiomatic.[9] It would be interesting to know at what level the inclusion of the article in both English texts was decided. "The aggression" is not specified in the treaty, and both parties were thus free to define it as they chose—as the war of 1967, which left Israel in possession of Egyptian and other Arab territories, or as the earlier events involving the establishment of Israel in 1948. The former was the usual Soviet interpretation; both interpretations occur in Egyptian and other Arab writings.

In any case, the general purpose is clear, and "eliminating the consequences of the aggression" was obviously an Egyptian contribution to the text of the treaty. This formula, usually understood to refer to Egyptian territory, was basic in Egyptian diplomacy from its first use in the resolutions adopted at Khartoum on 1 September 1967 until the recovery of Sinai by the terms of the peace treaty with Israel signed on 26 March 1979.

The inclusion of this formula in the Soviet-UAR treaty was no doubt felt to establish an important principle for Egypt. On closer examination, however, its effect seems questionable. In the first place, there is nothing in the treaty that commits the Soviet Union to accepting the UAR interpretation of this formula. In the second place, on any interpretation of the formula, it is the armed forces of the UAR, duly strengthened for this purpose, that are to undertake the elimination. There is no provision in the article, or elsewhere in the treaty, for any participation by the Soviet Union in this action.

There are some additional discrepancies that may or may not be significant. Thus, for example, in Articles 1 and 5, in the enumeration of the areas of cooperation between the two parties, the Russian term *nauchno-tekhnicheskii* caused difficulties to the translators of both parties. In the Soviet English version it is rendered "scientific, technological," while in the UAR text, it appears as *al-'ilmī wa'l-fannī* in Arabic and as "scientific, technical" in English. A more substantial, but probably no more significant, discrepancy occurs later in Article 5, in reference to a specific field of cooperation, namely "the development of sources of energy." This phrase, which is used in the Cairo English version, corresponds exactly to the Arabic *tanmiyat maṣādir al-ṭāqa*. The Russian text has *razvitie energetiki*, which could convey the same meaning, while the Soviet English version reads "the development of power engineering," which conveys a somewhat different meaning. It seems likely that this phrase, more precisely expressed in the UAR versions and more specifically related to UAR needs, was an Egyptian contribution to the treaty. In that case, one might assume that the Russian draftsman followed the UAR text and that the Moscow English translator made a wrong choice among possible interpretations of his Russian original. An interesting variation occurs in Article 6, in which both parties agree to work for increased cooperation and contact between what the Moscow English text calls "political and public organisations of the working people." The Cairo English version reads "workers' political and social organisations." The UAR term, "social" in English and *ijtimā'ī* in Arabic, and the Soviet English term "public," both represent the Russian *obshchestvennyi*, which can be used in both senses. The choices made by the translators may perhaps shed some light on how these organizations were perceived in the two societies.

In Article 4, both contracting parties declare themselves to be guided by the ideals of liberty and equality for all peoples and condemn imperialism and colonialism in all their forms and manifestations (UAR version: "aspects"). The irony of the last European imperial and colonial power joining with the UAR in the condemnation of imperialism and colonialism "in all their forms and aspects" appears to have eluded both high contracting parties. Both were apparently in agreement on the general principle of this condemnation but differed on a specific application, set forth in the second part of the article. While in the Soviet version the parties undertake "to wage unswervingly the struggle against racialism [*sic*] and apartheid [*vesti neuklonnuiu bor'bu protiv rasizma i apartkheida*]," in the UAR version the struggle is only against "racial discrimination [*ḍidd al-tamyīz wa'l-tafriqa al-'unṣuriyya*]."

This difference, as one of the high contracting parties might have said at the time, was no accident. The UAR version follows the wording of the UN General Assembly Resolution of 1965, which calls for "the elimination of all forms of racial discrimination," but makes no reference to racism. In Arabic political discourse, the use of "racism" was at that time still recent and comparatively rare. "Racist" occurs in the Palestine National Covenant of 1964 (Article 19; it reappears in Article 22 of the amended version adopted in 1968) among the pejorative adjectives applied to Zionism, but is missing from the list of "enemies of the Arab masses" embodied in the Syrian Constitution of 1969 and from the amended version of 1971. These enemies are listed as "colonialism, Zionism, and exploitation." Racism did not become a common theme in Arabic writings until the mid-seventies, more especially after the adoption of the UN General Assembly Resolution of 10 November 1975, declaring that "Zionism is a form of racism and racial discrimination."

In the Soviet Union, the terms "racism" and "racist" had long been in common use for political purposes. Originally used to denounce the Nazis after they invaded Russia, the term was revived and applied to nationalist movements among the Soviet peoples, other than those that took the Soviet Union itself as the focus of identity and loyalty. An exception was made for Russian nationalism and, to a much lesser extent, those of the other Slavic peoples of the Union. Non-Slavic nationalisms were suspect, and particular hostility was directed against those movements—pan-Turkic, pan-Iranic, Zionist (i.e., pan-Jewish)—that aimed at some larger national unity and that had or could have a focus outside Soviet control. It was to these that the term "racist," in Soviet polemical and penal usage, was most commonly applied.

Perhaps the most remarkable term in the treaty for the historian of the modern Middle East is the very word that designates it—the word "treaty," in Russian, *dogovor*, in Arabic, *mu'āhada*. In Egypt, and in the countries of the Fertile Crescent, political life was dominated for half a century by the struggle against what were regarded as unequal treaties imposed on them by their former imperial rulers. The revolutionary eras in both Egypt and Iraq began with the rejection of treaties with Britain, and even the word for treaty, *mu'āhada*, was charged with evocative memories. The use of the same term can hardly have failed to revive such memories. The unequal language of the treaties and the visible presence of the Soviet armed forces in Arab cities must surely have given new life and new strength to old resentments.

In the event, the treaty was of brief duration. The following year, on 18 July 1972, President Sadat ordered the Soviet military experts to leave Egypt, and they went. The subsequent policies of the government of Egypt were not aligned with those of the Soviet Union in domestic, regional, or international matters.

Notes

1. My thanks are due to Professor Yuri Bregel, of Indiana University, and Ms. Jane Baun, of Princeton, for answering some questions that arose during the preparation of this version.

2. I have used the Russian version, as printed in *Izvestiia* (29 May 1971), and the Soviet-English translation, as printed in *Soviet News* (1 June 1971). The Arabic text, with official translations in English and French, was published by the Egyptian Ministry of Information, State Information Service, in a booklet entitled "Treaty of Friendship and Cooperation between the United Arab Republic and the Union of Soviet Socialist Republics, Cairo, May 27, 1971."

3. The Italian text of the treaty of Küçük Kaynarca is found in G. F. de Martens, *Recueil de Traités*, vol. IV [1761–1790 supplement] (Göttingen, 1798), no. 71, pp. 606–38; 2nd ed., vol. IV [1771–1779] (Göttingen, 1817), pp. 287–322.

4. In the Egyptian English version, "both texts have equal validity," while in the Soviet version, both texts are "equally authentic." This difference is, however, less serious than might at first appear, since the same formula appears in other Soviet treaties and represents the Russian phrase *"oba teksta imeiut odinakovuiu silu,"* literally, "have equal force."

5. The Soviet-Czechoslovak treaty was published in *Pravda* (7 May 1970); this and the other treaties may be found in the *United Nations Treaties* series.

6. The text of the Soviet-French Protocol appears in *International Legal Materials* for the year 1970, pp. 1165–66.

7. Max Jakobson, *Finnish Neutrality: a study of Finnish Foreign Policy since the Second World War* (London, 1968), p. 39.

8. See, for example, the treaties with East Germany (12 June 1964; Art. 5): "in the event of one of the high contracting parties being subjected to armed aggression in Europe by some state or group of states, the other high contracting party will render it immediate assistance . . ."; with Poland (10 April 1965; Art. 7): "shall immediately afford it every assistance including military aid, and also give it support with all the means at its disposal . . ."; with Hungary (7 Sept. 1967; Art. 6): "in the event of either high contracting party becoming the object of an armed attack . . . the other side . . . will immediately render it every assistance and will also support it by every means at its disposal"; with Czechoslovakia (6 May 1970; Art. 10): "regarding this as an attack against itself, shall immediately afford it every assistance, including armed assistance, and shall also support it by all means at its disposal . . ."; with Rumania (7 July 1970, Art. 8): "will immediately render it all-around assistance with all the means at its disposal, including military means, essential to repulse armed attack. . . ."

9. A similar problem arose over the interpretations of Article 1(i) of the Security Council Resolution 242 of 22 November 1967, requiring the "withdrawal of Israeli armed forces from territories occupied in the recent conflict." It has been argued, and generally conceded, that

the omission of the article before "territories" in the English text means that not necessarily all the territories are intended. The Russian text, which has no article since none exist in Russian, like the English text, leaves the question open. In the Arabic version—unofficial since at that time Arabic was not yet an official UN language—the article is present, as a stylistic if not a grammatical necessity.

20

A Taxonomy of Group Hatred

L et me begin with a disclaimer. I am neither a psychologist nor a sociologist and cannot therefore offer the insights, very appropriate to our topic of today, provided by these disciplines. I am by profession an historian, and it is only in historical prospective that I can look at our topic. In extenuation, however, I might plead that my area of specialization is the Middle East—a region rich in relevant examples.

Let me begin by distinguishing between individual and group hatred. Individual hatred usually has some minimum of rationality, even if not of justification. It starts with a sense of grievance, which in turn derives from some perceived slight or injury. This might be old or new, real or imagined, direct or vicarious; it is usually related, at least in the hater's mind if not in actual fact, to some specific action or—more especially in the Middle East—utterance. Normally, we hate those who we believe have wronged us, but it is not unusual to hate those whom we have wronged.

If hatred for someone is directed not only against him personally but also against others of a group to which he is seen to belong, then it is no longer individual; it is group hatred. In individual hatred, he is hated because of what he does or has done or is believed to have done. In group hatred, these may be present but are not required, since essentially he is hated not for what he does but for what he is. A single example may suffice. When the prime minister of Malaysia denounces Mr. George Soros as responsible for the economic troubles of his country, he is making an individual accusation, however implausible. When he levels the same charge against "the Jews," he is appealing to a group hatred, long familiar in Christian Europe, and in modern times transplanted to the world of Islam.

Let me begin with a proposition that may seem outrageous: to hate the other, the outsider, the one who is different, who looks different, sounds different, smells different; to hate, fear and mistrust the other is natural and normal— natural and normal, that is to say, among baboons and other gregarious animals, or in the more primitive forms of human existence, such as forest tribes, cave-dwellers and the like. Unfortunately, it survives into later forms of human development. It survives even in the most advanced and sophisticated civilized societies. It is, and we should not disguise this from ourselves, a very basic human instinct, not just human, but going back beyond our most primitive ancestors to their animal predecessors. The instinct is there, and it comes out in all sorts of unexpected situations. To pretend that it does not exist and that it is some sort of ideological aberration cannot lead anywhere useful.

At certain stages in the evolution of human societies, the approach to the problem, the eternal problem of the other, is transformed in a variety of ways. The way in which we perceive and define the other changes, as our perception of ourselves and the group to which we belongs changes.

In the earliest stage, definition is at once by blood, by place and by cult, the third being a natural concomitant of the first two. The three are usually indistinguishable. In more sophisticated stages of development other attributes assume greater importance. The two most articulate peoples of antiquity, those who have retained both their memories and their voices, that is to say, the Greeks and the Jews, devised special terms to define the outsider. Whoever was not Greek was a barbarian; whoever was not a Jew was a gentile. The one definition is cultural, the other, religious, and the two elements are closely inter-related. Both represent an important step forward in human evolution, in that the barriers they raise, though formidable, are permeable. One cannot change one's blood, one's race, one's kin. One can, however, adopt a culture and embrace a religion; and as we know from antiquity and medieval history, this has happened many times. Already in antiquity, there were Hellenised barbarians and Judaised gentiles, both directly and through Christianity. The Roman Empire added a new definition—citizenship, which was extended in stages until finally it included all the heterogeneous subjects of the Roman emperors.

Culture and religion can be changed by an act of will in the individual, or by assimilation in the group. Citizenship can be conferred or acquired by what in modern parlance is called naturalization. The examples that I have named show how some of the great religions and civilizations of humankind developed the capacity to assimilate, to absorb, to transform, and by so doing, to accept the other, who is then no longer perceived as other.

This raised a new problem, the problem of the outsider, the other, who wishes to retain his otherness; the one who dwells within the frontiers, but does not fully accept the identity, whether it be language, culture, religion, or citizenship, of the unity within which he lives—in other words, what we have got into the habit of calling minorities. Sometimes, of course, the minorities are majorities, but still have minority status—women, for example. This raises another kind of hatred, the kind known as misogyny—men's hatred of women as such. This, and its nameless equivalent, female hatred of men as such, require separate treatment, as does the newly-named homophobia, hatred of male and female homosexuals.

How does one deal with the recalcitrant other—the other who does not wish to be acculturated or converted—who persists, in spite of all the inducements offered to him, in retaining his otherness? Historically, three answers have been offered to this question. The first, and the most usual one, is to eliminate him in one or more of several ways—to absorb, extrude, or destroy him. These, forced conversion, expulsion, massacre, were the normal procedures in much of the world, particularly in central and western Europe during the Middle Ages and—in some regions—the modern period.

The second method is what we usually call tolerance or toleration; a word that has been used with a wide variety of meanings. What it normally meant was to allow the other, subject to certain conditions, to retain his otherness, his separate identity, and to grant him some, many, even most, but rarely all of the rights of citizenship. In Islamic law this is the system of the *dhimma*, whereby followers of certain approved religions, not all, were allowed to survive in that form, practising their own religions within their own communities, living by their own laws and institutions and enjoying many, though not all, of the privileges of full membership of the state. The degree of tolerance accorded in the different societies that practise it varies from minimal to maximal. Even at best, it remains a revocable concession, granted by a dominant group to a subordinate group.

The third is coexistence with mutual respect and equal rights. There are now many countries where such coexistence exists in theory, very few where it exists in fact; and even in those countries its history is short and checkered.

Religion may or may not be a source of hatred but it certainly provides an emotionally satisfying expression of hatred. Here it may be useful to distinguish between two kinds of religion, which may be described by the terms commonly used to denounce them—the one relativist, the other triumphalist. Relativist is a Catholic term, used to designate the theological error that all religions are valid and authentic—different ways by which human beings communicate with divinity and eternity, just as they use different inherited or acquired languages to communicate with each other. The obvious example of this approach is polytheism. For those who believe in many gods, one more or less makes little difference, and an additional god, brought by a newly-discovered people, can always be accommodated in the pantheon. A classical rejection of this view was given in a sermon of St. John of Capistrano, who accused the Jews—correctly on this occasion—of spreading the "deceitful" notion that "everyone can be saved in his own faith, which is impossible."

The alternative approach, condemned by its critics as "triumphalist," has been summed up in the formula: "I'm right, you're wrong, go to Hell." The most obvious examples of the triumphalist approach to religion are fundamentalist and some other Christians and Muslims, who share the conviction that they are the exclusive possessors of God's final revelation to mankind, which it is their duty to bring to those who do not yet possess it. The encounter of the two, with the same basic approach to religion in the same Mediterranean region, led inevitably to conflict, and to the long and bitter alternation of jihad and crusade, mission and counter-mission, conquest and reconquest.

In fighting an enemy, it is not absolutely necessary to hate him, but it is better for morale, and therefore for military effectiveness, if one does. Neither Christian nor Muslim teaching enjoins hatred of the infidel enemy. The desired emotion is rather compassion, giving rise to the desire to convert him to the true faith and share one's good fortune with him. This does not, however, fit well with launching and fighting a holy war.

For those who are spiritually less sensitive—that is, for the great majority of humankind—the most likely attitude of those who possess the truth to those who reject it is contempt. This is the normal response of the believer to the unbeliever, of the civilized to the uncivilized, of the insider to the outsider.

At what stage do these two responses, pity and contempt, give way to hatred? Why is it that even today, there are still places in the world where the cross is brandished as a substitute for the swastika, and what was conceived as a symbol of divine love is used to convey a message of human hate and rage?

The historical answer is clear—hatred takes over when love, compassion, even contempt are outweighed by envy and by fear. In the Middle Ages, European Christians knew that although theirs was the one true faith, they were overshadowed and threatened by the greater wealth, greater skill and greater armed power of the Muslims who were attacking Europe from every side—in Spain and Portugal, in Sicily, in the Balkans, in Russia. The result was a deep fear which readily turned to hatred of the invading infidel. Centuries later, the situation was reversed. Modern Muslims, like medieval Christians, knew beyond a doubt that theirs was the true faith, that those who did not share it were benighted infidels. At the same time, in the real world in which they lived, it was the infidels who triumphed over them both in the marketplace and on the battlefield. This imbalance, like the earlier one, gave rise to profound mistrust, fear, and ultimately hatred.

The same change in attitude may be seen, smaller in scale but no less pernicious in effects, in dealing with minorities, especially those defined by religion and culture. Minorities thus defined tend to give special importance to education, as a way to preserve their identity. But this may also give their children an advantage over majority children in the competition of life. Penalization, provided it is less than crippling, may even augment this competitive advantage. The most familiar example, in the Western world, is the position of the Jews in

Christendom. There are many others—South Asians in East Africa, Chinese in Malaysia and Indonesia, and Christians in some countries where they are a subordinate minority and not, as in the Western world, a dominant majority.

I spoke of the natural, basic, human and animal instinct to mistrust or fear the other. There is another element in these problems which we have to take into account. In a famous essay on toleration published in 1689, the English philosopher John Locke says: "Neither pagan nor Mahometan, nor Jew, ought to be excluded from the civil rights of the commonwealth because of his religion."[1] Locke does not include Catholics. That was no accident. "The pagan, the Mahometan, the Jew" were no threat to late 17th century England. The Catholic was. There was a struggle going on to decide whether England should be a Catholic or Protestant country, and tolerance, in the view of both sides, could give aid and comfort to a dangerous enemy.

This brings us to another aspect of our problem, when the source of hatred is not mere prejudice or xenophobia or bigotry, but a real conflict over real issues—to decide, for example, whether the Iberian peninsula should be an Arab Muslim country or a Spanish Catholic country; whether the six counties of Northern Ireland should be part of the United Kingdom or part of the Irish Republic; whether Basques or Kurds or Kosovars should have independent states. If Jews are persecuted in Spain or Poland or Germany, that may be ascribed to religious bigotry or racist Semitism or both. If Arabs and Turks are persecuted or discriminated against in Western Europe, that again may be ascribed to religious or racial prejudice. In the conflict between Jews and Arabs in Israel and Palestine, mutual hatred may be exacerbated by prejudice; it may give rise to prejudice, but it does not in itself arise from prejudice. This is a real fight over real issues. One could add many other examples.

These real issues come in a number of forms and they are, in themselves, a fertile source of hatred. Very often the hatred survives after the real issue has gone or been resolved or been forgotten. I mentioned the cases of Catholics in 17th century England and of Protestants and Catholics in present-day Northern Ireland. These are examples of a perceived threat from another group. The threat is most readily perceived and felt to be most dangerous when it is internal, coming not from some remote and unknown outsider but from someone present in the same place or nearby. For example, the wars between Protestants and Catholics in Christendom were far deadlier and evoked far more animosity than the encounters between Christendom and other religious communities.

One might argue that the wars between Christendom and Islam, waged over so many centuries in the Iberian peninsula, in the Levant, in Eastern and South Eastern Europe, were also an internal conflict. This made their mutual hostility both more intense and more intelligible. If we look at them in a wider global perspective, Judaism, Christianity and Islam are different branches of the same religion. Their resemblances are far greater than their differences. Compared with the religions of India, of China and of other places, they are as alike as peas in a pod. This of course is what gives particular virulence to the conflicts between them. When Christians and Muslims argued in the Middle Ages and continued into modern times and each said to the other: "You are an infidel and you will burn in hell," they understood each other perfectly. Such an argument would have been impossible between either a Christian or a Muslim on one side and a Buddhist or a Hindu on the other. They would not have known what they were talking about. Christians and Muslims understood each other because they both meant the same thing. Their heavens are significantly different but their hells are almost identical.

The question is sometimes asked: "How is it that racism and anti-Semitism flourished in Europe of all places—Europe of the enlightenment, of human rights and the rest?" My answer would be to say that it is precisely because of these that racism—that is to say, ideologically formulated hatred—flourished in Europe. In unenlightened times and places people are content to give way to their instincts; in some societies it is seen as normal, even as lawful, to enslave a defeated enemy and take his women as concubines. In enlightened times and places it is necessary to find rationalization and justification for such behavior. Individuals can do evil without compunction and without regret, but societies, civilizations, need to feel that what they are doing is right. If what they are doing is manifestly wrong they will find a justification for it. The modern world provides two perfect examples—racism, directed against Blacks and other non-Europeans; and a specific form of racism, anti-Semitism, directed against Jews. Expressions of dislike, disdain, even of hostility against other races are familiar from classical antiquity through both the Christian and Islamic Middle Ages, as well as in other civilisations. Theoretical, ideological racism began in Western Europe, and was a response to two specific problems.

One was the forced conversion of Jews and Muslims in Spain after the Reconquest. Forced conversion always arouses a suspicion of insincerity, particularly among the enforcers. That suspicion hardens into hatred when the so-called converts continue the professional and commercial successes of their unconverted forebears. The other arose from the expansion of European power into Africa, Asia and the Americas.

Modern racism, in its origins, is an attempt to justify the enslavement and exploitation of Black Africans by enlightened Europeans and Americans; anti-Semitism is the response of the secularized Christian, no longer able to use theological arguments, against the emancipated Jew. Both provide examples of the new and modern hatred—no longer primitive, not yet civilized, but rather an attempt to provide a civilized rationale for primitive instincts. Religious hostility against Jews, among Christians and to a lesser extent among Muslims, had of course existed since early times, but restating this in racist rather religious terms was a 19th century invention—an attempt to rationalize and to justify primitive bigotry. In enlightened, science-minded 19th century Germany, it was no longer acceptable to hate Jews because they had rejected Christ. One had to find a more modern and scientific reason. Anti-Semitism was the answer. Both the term and the ideology which it connotes date from 19th century middle Europe. They had the further advantage, from the point of view of their exponents, that they left the Jew with no way out. If you are persecuted because of your religion, you can change your religion. If you are persecuted because of your race, there is no escape. For the Jew as for the Black, his identity, thus defined, could not be changed.

In the same way, in the 18th and 19th centuries, Europe developed a pseudo-science and and a pseudo-philosophy, the purpose of which was to justify the enslavement of the Blacks in intellectually acceptable terms, according to the standards of the time. One could no longer say that it was the will of God, nor could one simply exercise the rights of the conqueror over the conquered, as would have been normal in earlier times, and was still normal in some parts of the world. Something that looked philosophical, better still scientific, was needed to justify and ideologise exploitation on the hand, and primitive hatred on the other.

In our own time, once again we see mounting tensions and hostilities, due in large measure to that early primitive human and animal instinct already mentioned—the mistrust of those who are different. In part of course it is also due to a genuine perception of threat from large new minorities, seen as unassimilable. The threat may or may not be genuine; the perception is certainly genuine, and has given rise to a new phenomenon, sometimes called Islamophobia, an equivalent of anti-Semitism, directed against the new Muslim residents in Christendom, as anti-Semitism was directed against the Jewish residents in Christendom.

Group hatred of this kind is transmitted in various ways. The oldest and most universal is through memory, stories told by parents or more often grandparents to the new generation, keeping alive and passing on the ancient grievances and hostilities. The Balkan Peninsula and the Middle East are particularly rich in these, going back for centuries, some of them for millennia.

Recorded memory, that is historical writing, may serve as a corrective to the distortions of primitive hatred. It may also, in certain circumstances and in certain hands, serve to deepen and intensify it. Here again the same regions provide tragic examples.

Sometimes old and waning hatreds may be deliberately revived to serve some purpose. During the Cold War, when NATO was extended to include Greece and Turkey, it became an important Soviet concern to destabilize this extension of the alliance by fomenting hostility within and between the new members, and, more especially, between them and the United States. This was done by rekindling and fanning old hatreds, religious and ethnic, and by adding to them new hatreds, nowadays often formulated in social and economic terms. The legacy of these revived and created hatreds remains with us to the present time. Another example is the Lebanese civil wars, which encapsulated all these different kinds of group hatred—religious, ethnic and regional, both spontaneous and induced.

I spoke of history. The perception that people have of their own history is of course the most effective single method of inducing, exacerbating, and—one hopes—reducing hatred. In the most primitive societies it comes in the form of tribal memory, developing into balladry and saga. In modern society these are replaced for most people by the primary school where we receive some grounding in the history at least of our own people, supplemented by the cinema and television screen from which most of us derive our knowledge of the earlier as well as of the more recent past. In dictatorships, all of these are strictly controlled, and they are frequently used to foment and maintain hatred of the currently designated enemy. In democratic societies, indoctrination is usually not government-directed. It is nonetheless present, being determined sometimes by interest, more often by fashion, especially in intellectual circles. Nowadays it seems that in democratic countries it is fashion more than anything else that determines how history—and with it the perception of other peoples—is taught in schools and colleges and conveyed through public entertainment. Even in democratic societies, the preaching of hatred still plays a significant part, but there it is usually hatred of one's self and one's own society rather than of the other.

We may now attempt a tabulation of the stages in the development of group hatred. The first and simplest is animal hatred—the hatred of the baboon family or the wolf pack for all who do not belong. The second might be called primitive hatred, when animal hatred is reinforced by two new potent forces—communication and memory. Loyalty to the tribe, however defined, and hatred of other tribes are at the very core of identity.

In the third stage identity has grown beyond its simple tribal origins, and the bond of blood is supplemented and ultimately supplanted by two new and interrelated factors—culture and religion. The hated outsider is still outside and is still hated, but there are procedures by which he may cross the barrier and be accepted as an insider provided he is willing to accept a certain level—differently defined in different societies—of assimilation. During this process hatred survives and may indeed acquire a new intensity, directed against the remaining outsider, seen as a rival and a threat, and against the new and still not fully assimilated insider, seen as his agent or ally. In certain societies the level of suspicion and hatred may actually increase with the progress of assimilation. Spain after the Reconquest and Germany under the Nazis are two examples. There are others.

Finally there is the modern form of hatred—the deliberate revival of old instinctive hatreds and even the creation of new ones, rationalized and disseminated in terms acceptable to what is believed to be the enlightened opinion of that time and place.

Mistrust, fear, hate of the other are part of the oldest, deepest layers of our being, going back to the beginnings of human life, and even beyond that. The rise of civilisation brought a wider and more inclusive definition of identity and therefore of otherness, through religion, culture, and citizenship. In the more enlightened societies, these forces have served to abate and control this primitive natural hostility, but even religion, culture, and civic loyalty have not been able to eradicate group hatred, and at times they themselves have been perverted to its use. The struggle continues.

Note

1. John Locke, *A Letter Concerning Toleration, With the Second Treatise of Civil Government*, ed. J. W. Gough, Oxford, 1946, p. 160.

21

Islam and the West

ᘓᕤᕤᕧᕤ

There was nothing unreasonable in believing that the Muslim world
would attain the power and prosperity of Europe by the same methods
Europe had used, and that this could be done without endangering
any of the essential values of Islam.

Elie Kedourie[1]

Until the nineteenth century, Muslims commonly spoke neither of the
West nor of Europe when they wished to designate the Western or
European world. The term West, when used in a cultural and political
sense, was applied inside and not outside the Islamic oecumene. In the form
maghrib—literally the land of the sunset—it designated North Africa west of
Egypt, that is the western part of the Islamic world, contrasted with *mashriq*,
the eastern half or land of the sunrise. The term Europe occurs in a few places
in early Arabic geographical literature, then disappears. It entered through translations from the Greek, as part of the Greek geographical system of continents,
which was adopted in a fragmentary form by Muslim geographical writers and
dropped at an early date. Even when it was used, the term Europe was purely
geographical, and was never injected with the cultural, historical, and latterly
even political content which the names of the continents acquired in European
and subsequently, under European influence, in universal usage.

For Muslims—as also for most medieval but few modern Christians—the
core of identity was religion, rather than nation, country, or continent, and the
basic divisions of mankind were religiously determined.

In discussions of the inhabitants of the outside world in general, the commonest designation until the nineteenth century, and in some regions later, was
kuffār, unbelievers. Where greater precision was needed in distinguishing

between different groups of unbelievers or different political entities among them, Muslim historians tended to use ethnic rather than territorial terms. The peoples of Christian Europe are variously referred to as Romans (*Rūm*), Slavs (*Saqāliba*), and, for the inhabitants of western Europe, Franks—a term which no doubt reached the Arabs via Byzantium, and was transmitted by the Arabs to the Persians, Turks, and other Muslim peoples. This practice of referring to the peoples of Christendom by ethnic names parallels the Western practice, until comparatively modern times, of denoting Muslims by such ethnic terms as Moors, Turks, and Tartars, in different parts of Europe.

The Muslim perception of these Western or European or Frankish lands passed through several phases. In the earliest Muslim accounts of Western Europe, mostly in geographical writings, these countries appear as remote and exotic, also as backward and unimportant. This perception was not greatly changed when the Westerners forced themselves on Muslim attention in Spain, Sicily, and Syria, and established direct contact in a number of ways.

In so far as there was a scholarly or scientific interest in the West, it was geographical. Muslim historians were not interested in the history of the outside world which, as they understood the value and purpose of history, lacked both value and purpose. Muslim theologians were little concerned with Christian doctrines—why after all should they be interested in an earlier and superseded form of God's revelation? And for the few that were interested, better information was more easily accessible among the many Christian communities living in the lands of Islam. There was no interest in the sciences and arts of Europe. They knew there was nothing of the one; they assumed there was nothing of the other. Only the geographers show some interest in the West, and even that a limited one. One geographical writer even apologizes for devoting some attention to these remote and uninteresting places. His excuse is the need for completeness.[2]

This indeed is the key to such interest as existed. Geography by definition should be universal, and a complete geographical survey must therefore include even the benighted and insignificant barbarians beyond the western limits. Some of these accounts include human as well as physical geography. Writers give some ethnological data, at times approaching almost an anthropology of the barbarian neighbours of Islam. Their sources of information were both written and oral. The written information came mainly from ancient Greek writings, from which Muslim scholars derived their first notions of the configuration of the European continent and islands. Oral information came from such few travellers as ventured from the Islamic world to Europe and back—captives, merchants, and an occasional diplomatic envoy.

The scientific, geographical interest was supplemented by another motive, a liking for the strange and wonderful (*al-'ajīb wa'l-gharīb*). There was a general taste for curious and wonderful stories that found its apotheosis in the *Thousand and One Nights*. Travellers from the East to Europe, like travellers from Europe to the East in another age, had no difficulty in finding wonders and marvels and curious tales with which to regale their readers. This element continues into comparatively modern times. Thus, an Ottoman janissary officer who visited Vienna in the early eighteenth century adorns his otherwise factual, prosaic account of his trip with strange and wonderful stories of miracles performed during the Turkish siege and retreat some years previous to his visit.[3]

Practical and material interest in western Europe was for long very limited. Until the discovery of America, the colonization of south and south-east Asia and the consequent enrichment of the maritime powers, western Europe had very little to offer by way of exports. English wool and a few other small items are occasionally mentioned in Muslim sources, but they do not seem to have been of great significance. For most of the Middle Ages the most important export to the lands of Islam from Europe was, as from tropical Africa, slaves. They were imported in great numbers across both the northern and southern frontiers of Islam. Both north and south of the Islamic lands slaves were sometimes taken in war, sometimes seized by raiders, sometimes—with increasing frequency—offered for sale by African or European slave merchants. The supply of slaves from western Europe was eventually reduced to a mere trickle, acquired through the efforts of the Barbary corsairs; the supply of east Europeans continued for much longer, as a result of the Ottoman wars in south-eastern Europe and the raids of the Crimean Tartars among the Russians, Poles, and Ukrainians. There is little evidence, however, that these white slaves from Europe had any great effect on Muslim perceptions or ways, any more than did the much greater numbers of black slaves imported from tropical Africa.

Another important element in the Muslim perception of western Europe, from the Middle Ages onwards, was the military. Muslim visitors to Europe looked around them, as men do in hostile or potentially hostile territory, and noted information of military value, such as the location of roads, bridges, passes, and the like. The early triumphs of the Crusaders in the east impressed upon Muslim war departments that in some areas at least Frankish arms were superior, and the inference was quickly drawn and applied. European prisoners of war were set to work building fortifications; European mercenaries and adventurers were employed in some numbers, and a traffic in arms and other war materials began which has grown steadily in the course of the centuries. As early as 1174, Saladin wrote a letter to the caliph in Baghdad justifying his action in encouraging Christian commerce in the territories which he had reconquered from the Crusaders and in buying arms from the Christian states. "Now," he says, "there is not one of them that does not bring to our lands his weapons of war and battle, giving us the choicest of what they make and inherit . . . ."[4] The result, he goes on to explain, was that these Christian merchants were supplying him with all kinds of armaments, to the advantage of Islam and the detriment of Christendom. The Christian church was of the same opinion, but all its efforts and denunciations failed to prevent the steady growth of this trade. Centuries later, when the Ottoman Turks were advancing into south-eastern Europe, they were always able to buy much needed equipment for their fleets and armies from the Protestant powers, and even obtain financial cover from Italian banks.

All this, however, had little or no influence on Muslim perceptions and attitudes, as long as Muslim armies continued to be victorious. The sultans bought war materiel and military expertise for cash, and saw in this no more than a business transaction. The Turks in particular adopted such European inventions as handguns and artillery and used them to great effect, without thereby modifying their view of the barbarians from whom they acquired these weapons.

The real change in attitude began when the Ottoman and later other Muslim governments found it necessary to adopt not just European weapons, but European ways of using them. In the early eighteenth century the great French soldier Maurice de Saxe, observing battles between the Austrians and Ottomans in south-eastern Europe, put his finger on the main reason for the Ottoman lack of success: "What they [the Turks] lack is not valor, not numbers, not riches; it is order, discipline, and the manner of fighting."[5] The important thing was "la manière de combattre," and it was this that gave the European enemies of the Ottomans their growing superiority in the battlefield. The Turkish commanders had certainly not read the *Rêveries* of Maurice de Saxe, but they had independently come to the same conclusion, and initiated a process of change which began as a limited military reform and culminated as a far-reaching social and cultural transformation.

Defeat in battle is the most perspicuous of arguments, and the lesson was driven home in a series of heavy blows. In the west, the Muslims were finally expelled from Spain and Portugal, and the triumphant Christians followed their former rulers into Africa and then into Asia. In the east, the Russians threw off the Tatar yoke and, like the Portuguese in the west but with far greater success, pursued their former masters into their homelands. With the conquest of Astrakhan in 1554, the Russians were on the shores of the Caspian; the following century they reached the northern shores of the Black Sea, thus beginning the long process of conquest and colonization which incorporated vast Muslim lands in the Russian Empire and brought the Russians as near neighbours to the heartlands of the Middle East. In central Europe the last great Ottoman attack failed before the walls of Vienna in 1683, and in the retreat that followed, the Ottomans lost Budapest, which they had held for a century and a half, and began their long rearguard action through the Balkan peninsula.

These changes gave a new importance to those elements in the Islamic world which were in one sense or another intermediaries between Islam and Christendom. They were of several kinds. The first group to achieve significance were the refugees who came from Spain and Portugal seeking asylum in North Africa and in the Ottoman lands of the eastern Mediterranean. These consisted of both Muslims and Jews, including some who had submitted under pain of death to enforced Christianization, and had then fled to more tolerant lands in order to declare their true religions. The Muslim Moriscos and the Jewish Marranos coming from Spain and Portugal to North Africa and the Ottoman lands brought skills, knowledge, and some wealth from what were then among the most advanced countries in Europe. Another group of newcomers from Europe, smaller but not unimportant, were those whom the Christians called renegades and whom the Muslims called *muhtedi*, one who has found the right path. Not all these adventurers found it necessary to adopt Islam. Some entered the Ottoman service while retaining their previous religions. These newcomers—converts, adventurers, mercenaries, and others—helped to initiate what one may now begin to call the Europeanization of Turkey.

By the seventeenth century the flow of newcomers from Europe, whether renegades or refugees, was drying up. But if Europeans were no longer coming to the Middle East, a new element was appearing to take their place: Middle Easterners going to Europe. These were from the Middle Eastern Christian communities who began to establish contacts with western Europe in various ways, notably by sending their sons to Italian and later other European colleges and universities for education. The Greeks were the leaders in this movement; other Christian communities followed. The Roman Catholic Church had always been interested in the eastern Christians. In the late sixteenth century the Vatican became increasingly active among these communities, sending missionaries to work among them in Lebanon and elsewhere, and founding colleges in Italy for the study of their languages and the education of their clergy. Their direct impact was in the main limited to the Uniate churches, breakaway groups of the eastern churches that had entered into communion with Rome and established close ecclesiastical and educational links with the Vatican. The indirect influence of these contacts spread to their orthodox co-religionists and even to their Muslim neighbours. The school and order founded by the Catholic Armenian Mekhitar became for a time the centre of Armenian intellectual life; the Uniate Maronites of Lebanon, the first Arabic-speaking community to communicate directly with the West, were later to play a crucial role in opening the Arab world to Western intellectual influence.

The Maronite impact on the Arab world did not become important until the nineteenth century. Long before that, Greek and Armenian Christians, for whom Turkish was a second or sometimes even a first language, were filtering Western knowledge and ideas to the dominant Ottoman Turks.

Apart from these various Westernized or Westernizing Middle Eastern Christians, there was, increasingly, a direct European presence which became more influential as the real power relationship between Europe and the Islamic world changed to the disadvantage of the latter. At first Westerners came mainly as traders or diplomats (the latter were for long seen by the Ottomans as also being concerned principally with trade). From the eighteenth century onwards, another group of Europeans begin to appear—military and naval officers assisting in the training of the new style Ottoman forces. At first, these were hired on individual contracts; later they were serving officers seconded by their home governments.

All these changes made for increased contacts between Muslims and Europeans. Educated Greeks, Armenians, and Maronites, able to speak and write a Western language as well as having a good command of Turkish or Arabic, created a possibility for genuine cultural exchanges, beyond the limited political, military, and commercial interpreting of earlier times. European instructors in Muslim military academies made it necessary, for the first time, for young Muslim cadets to view Europeans as dispensers of useful knowledge and not merely as infidels and barbarians. And the steady advance of European power—penetration, encroachment, domination, in some areas even annexation—was finally bringing increasing numbers of Muslim statesmen and soldiers to the view that a better understanding of this Western world was essential to their survival.

One noticeable change is in the literature of travel to Europe. Until the seventeenth century we have almost no information about Muslim travellers to Europe. While European travellers to the East—soldiers, pilgrims, merchants, captives—had already produced a considerable literature, there was nothing comparable on the Muslim side. Few Muslims travelled voluntarily to the lands of the infidels. Even the involuntary travellers, the many captives taken in the endless wars by land and sea, had nothing to say after their ransom and return, and perhaps no one to listen. In this they differed markedly from their European counterparts, whose reports of their adventures seem to have been in some demand. An Arab prisoner of war in Rome in the ninth century, an Andalusian diplomatic visitor to France and Germany in the tenth, a princely Ottoman exile in France and Italy in the fifteenth, these and one or two others have left a few notes and fragments which constitute almost the whole of the Muslim travel literature in Europe.

The first sign of a change came in the far west of Islam, in Morocco. This was the first Muslim country to perceive, and indeed to feel, the rise and expansion of European power. The Moroccans had seen the loss of Spain, for many centuries a part of the Arab Muslim world, and had received Spanish Muslim exiles in their own land. They had undergone invasion by both Spaniards and Portuguese and had had difficulty maintaining themselves. Already in the seventeenth century, the Moroccans were facing problems which Turks, Egyptians, and Persians did not have to confront until centuries later. This experience, and the resulting awareness of danger, is reflected in a series of Moroccan reports written by ambassadors to Europe and more particularly to Spain.

The earliest of these Moroccan ambassadors to leave a detailed record of his travels and impressions was the vizier al-Ghassani, who was sent to Spain by the sultan of Morocco in 1690–1. His book, the first description of Spain by a Muslim visitor since the end of the Reconquest, is of quite remarkable interest. His comments on Spanish life and affairs reveal him as a man of intelligence and discernment, keenly interested in what he saw, and with considerable powers of observation and analysis. His discussion is not limited to the moment and place of his mission but extends outwards to cover other countries in western

Europe, and backwards to embrace some centuries of European history. In addition to the political and military information which was presumably the primary concern of his government, he also devoted some attention to religious matters, including discussions of the confessional and the Inquisition; of social and economic matters, including some very revealing comments on Spanish customs and attitudes; and some perceptive remarks on the economic effects on Spain of the wealth of the Indies.[6] Al-Ghassani was followed by several other Moroccan ambassadors in the course of the eighteenth century. One of them, Muhammad ibn 'Uthman al-Miknasi, gives what is probably the first account in Arabic of the American revolution and the establishment of the United States.[7]

Ottoman travellers to Europe are, as one would expect, more numerous than Moroccans, but it was some time before their reports reached the level of interest and information that the Moroccan reports offer. Three examples may suffice, to illustrate successive phases in the Ottoman perception of the West and in the Ottoman manner of presenting their perceptions to their readers at home.

The first of the three was the famous traveller Evliya Çelebi, who went to Vienna in 1665 in the suite of a Turkish ambassador, Kara Mehmed Pasha. Evliya still represents an Islamic empire conscious of its unchallengeable superiority in religion and consequently also in wealth and power. In his comments he appears as amused, sometimes even playful, occasionally disdainful. But at the same time he offers something clearly different from the earlier tradition of unconcern and contempt. His description is very detailed and reveals to his Ottoman reader a society with many positive features—a well-disciplined army, a fair and efficient system of administration of justice, prosperous towns and countryside, and a thriving capital city. In general he avoids explicit comparisons between Ottoman and Austrian situations; the exceptions are for example his preference for European clocks and watches to those in use in Turkey, or his praise for the well-stocked and well-kept library of St. Stephen's Cathedral in Vienna, which he contrasts favourably with the mismanaged mosque libraries of Cairo and Istanbul.[8]

Evliya, even when he has something to praise, still reflects a society that is self-assured to the point of complacency. Yirmisekiz Mehmed Efendi, who went to Paris as ambassador in 1720–1, reflects a very different situation. Between Evliya's journey to Vienna and his own trip to Paris, much had happened. The Ottomans had withdrawn from Vienna and had lost Budapest, and their defeats at the hands of the Austrians had been sealed in the peace treaties of Carlowitz (1699) and Passarowitz (1718), in the second of which Mehmed Efendi himself had participated as Ottoman plenipotentiary. Even worse, the Ottomans were now acutely aware of a new and terrible danger, not yet perceived in Evliya's day—the threat of Russia from the north. Not surprisingly, therefore, Mehmed Efendi looked at France with a different eye, not that of a confident visitor from an unchallengeably superior power, but the anxious eye of an emissary from a state threatened on several sides. He came to Paris with a different purpose, seeking help and guidance and seeing for the first time in a west European country a possible model for reform, perhaps even, in a very limited sense, an ally against his sovereign's enemies.

Mehmed Efendi was interested in many things. He describes the observatory, the scientific instruments, the practice of medicine in France, industry and manufactures, the network of communications by road and canal, bridges and locks, and even says something about cultural activities, such as the theatre and the opera. In general, Mehmed Efendi does not make explicit comparisons, still less recommendations for change in a Westernizing direction. But these are implicit in some of his descriptions of French institutions, practices, and ways. His son, who accompanied him and later had a distinguished official career of his own, even learned French. This was a remarkable and for long a unique accomplishment.[9]

A document recently made known supplies an interesting addendum to Mehmed Efendi's account of his journey. On his return to Istanbul, he appears to have distributed a number of gifts to his colleagues, family, and friends. The new appetites which these aroused can be gathered from the list of items which the grand vizier shortly afterwards asked a French dragoman, going to Paris on leave, to bring with him on his return to Istanbul. They include optical instruments, eyeglasses, binoculars, microscopes, burning mirrors, Gobelin tapestries, small repeating watches, pictures of fortresses, towns, and gardens, as well as many other items. There was also, according to the dragoman in question, a verbal request for a thousand bottles of champagne and nine hundred bottles of burgundy. The Frenchman complied with most of these requests and in particular brought a thousand prints of fortresses and other scenes.[10]

The third example is 'Azmi Efendi, who went to Berlin as Ottoman ambassador in 1790. Between Mehmed Efendi's trip to Paris and his own journey to Prussia, the Ottoman position had again deteriorated, this time very sharply. A disastrous war with Russia had ended in the treaty of Küçük-Kaynarca of 1774, which gave the Russians immense territorial and other gains. This was followed by the Russian annexation of the Crimea and the rapid extension of Russian power in the Black Sea area. In 'Azmi's report, Europeans appear as powerful and advancing rivals, posing a major threat to the empire. In order to guard against them it was necessary to study them and perhaps even—so as to accomplish this purpose—to imitate some of their ways.

By this time the idea of imitation was no longer new or entirely strange in Ottoman circles, since several eighteenth-century writers had advanced it in various forms. 'Azmi's report, after the normal description of his travels and activities, contains a detailed account of the kingdom of Prussia under subject headings—the administration of the country, the inhabitants, the high government offices, the treasury, the population, the government food stores, the military, the arsenal, and the artillery magazines. 'Azmi speaks of the Prussian economic effort to foster trade and establish industry and to maintain a sound and healthy treasury. The most important passages are those in which he describes the structure of the Prussian army, with its system of training, and the efficiency of the Prussian state organization, with its hierarchy of established and competent officials. 'Azmi was not content, like some of his predecessors, to convey his recommendations by hints and suggestions. Instead, he ends his report with a series of specific recommendations for the improvement of the Ottoman governmental and military apparatus, by adopting some of the best features of the Prussian system. In time 'Azmi's report came to be an important text for Ottoman officers and officials pressing for urgently needed reforms. One of the interesting features of his report is his description of the Prussian system as what would now be called a meritocracy, and his recommendation that this be adopted in place of the traditional Ottoman system of patronage and clientage.[11]

From the late eighteenth century and during the nineteenth century—the date and pace differ from region to region—the Islamic world was subjected to the devastating impact of Western power, techniques, and ideas. Some regions were conquered and became part of the European empires of Great Britain, France, Holland, and Russia. Even the Ottoman Empire and Iran, though never formally conquered or occupied, found their independence in effect severely curtailed.

The first major change affecting Muslim perceptions of the West was in the channels and media of communication. Where previously Muslim visitors to Europe, even in the age of Ottoman retreat, had been few and far between, they now became frequent and numerous. From the end of the eighteenth century, the Ottomans and later other Muslim states established resident diplomatic missions in European capitals, thus bringing into being a whole group of government officials with direct knowledge of a European country and, increasingly, of a European language. This last was of special significance. Whereas previously Muslims had had to rely almost entirely on non-Muslims or new converts to Islam for interpretation and translation, there now emerged—at first slowly and reluctantly, then with rapidly gathering momentum—a new élite of native Muslims with a command of at least one European language. Such knowledge, previously despised, became tolerable, then useful, and finally indispensable. In the early years of the nineteenth century the first student missions were sent from Egypt, Turkey, and Iran to European schools—at first mainly military, then over the whole range of education. These few hundred students played an important role after their return to their own countries. They were the outriders of a vast army of eager young Muslims who lived for a while in a European city and, as is the way of students, learned more from their fellow-students than from their teachers. In the Europe of the 1830s and 1840s, there was much that was interesting to learn.

One result of the lessons learned was that after the mid-century, diplomats and students were followed by a third category of Muslim visitors to Europe—political exiles. Most important among these were the Young Ottomans, a group of liberal patriots who wished to bring their country the benefits of Western-style constitutional and parliamentary government, in which they saw the talisman of Western success and power. Before long groups of Muslim exiles, publishing manifestos, newspapers, pamphlets, and books, became a familiar feature of the European scene.

Perhaps the most important single development was education—not only of increasing numbers of Muslim students going to Europe but also, to an ever greater extent, by the establishment of Western schools and colleges in the Muslim lands and eventually even the partial Westernization of the schools established by the Muslim governments themselves. An important part of this process was the extension of military training through the modernization—which at that time meant the Westernization—of the armed forces. Western military advisers came from many quarters. Prussia, later Germany, maintained a series of military missions in Turkey from 1835 to 1919, with far-reaching effects on the Turkish army.[12] British and French military and naval officers also played a role, though a smaller one, in Turkey and a somewhat greater one in some of the Arab countries. The ending of a major war in the Western world often provided a supply of experienced military officers suddenly rendered supernumerary, and seeking an outlet for their talents. After the Napoleonic Wars, many French officers were available for service in Egypt. At the end of the American Civil War, retired American officers began to undertake the retraining and reorganization of the Egyptian army. Russian military lessons to the Muslim armies were for most of the eighteenth and nineteenth centuries administered on the battlefield rather than in the classroom. There were, however, some Russian officers training the Persian gendarmerie, and in more recent times Soviet military missions have begun to play a major role in several Muslim countries.

In this new phase the number of Muslim visitors to Europe increased greatly, and so too did the literature produced by them. For a long time the prevailing attitude towards Europe was one of respect, even of admiration. Muslim writers naturally enough did not regard the new masters of the world with any great affection, nor were they prepared to concede them any real merit in what was for them the most important aspect of all—the religious, a term which at that time, for them, included the cultural and intellectual. The old attitude of uninformed contempt, while still surviving no doubt among those who stayed at home, virtually disappeared among those who ventured abroad. The main stimulus was still the perception of their own weakness and poverty and the desire to emulate and if possible equal the wealth and power of the Western world. This desire became the more acute as events demonstrated with increasing urgency the dangers to which this inequality exposed the Muslim world—the dangers of domination, of exploitation, even of conquest.

There were, however, some differences of opinion as to the nature of the lessons to be learned; there were still some difficulties in making those lessons palatable among the largely unconvinced and unpersuaded public at home.

Among the earlier writers in this period of growing European domination, two themes predominate, both of them developments of themes already perceptible in earlier writings. They are respectively the military and the political. The one began as a concern with Western weapons, then with Western methods of warfare. This in turn developed into a concern with Western technology and eventually industry, as the realization spread that it was to no small extent on these that the superiority of Western armies depended. In the course of the nineteenth century, Muslim awareness of economic inferiority began to equal their awareness of the more dramatic and more obvious political and military weakness of the Islamic world, and some Muslim rulers began to be concerned with economic development along Western lines, not just as a support for better armies and navies, but for its own sake.

The second change was a growing interest in Western methods of government. At first Muslim visitors showed no interest whatever in this topic. Apart from a few passing references in medieval texts, a first brief account was given in the mid-seventeenth century by the well-known Ottoman scholar and polymath, Kâtib Çelebi. His information is scattered and fragmentary, on some points remarkably detailed, on others strikingly inaccurate. The book was never printed and is little known. Other Ottoman writers of the period show little or no interest in European affairs, even just across their border. Thus, the extremely voluminous Ottoman chronicles of the seventeenth century pay only the slightest attention to the events of the Thirty Years War, and even less to its causes and consequences. A brief reference to European laws and forms of government occurs in a Persian book written in 1732. The writer notes with regret that he had been unable to accept the suggestion of an English sea-captain whom he had met to visit Europe where, he implies, they order these things better. It is not until the mid-eighteenth century that we find the first factual account of European governments and armies, written and printed by a Hungarian convert to Islam who rose high in the Ottoman service.[13]

The last years of the century saw a major reform effort. A new printing press was installed in Istanbul, from which a number of books, both original and translated, were published; foreign officers in greater numbers were appointed as instructors in the military and naval schools; permanent Ottoman embassies were opened in London, Paris, Berlin, Vienna, and St. Petersburg, and the French—first through their embassy in Istanbul, then through their newly acquired bases in Greece and Egypt—began to disseminate information and ideas about the recent revolution in France. By the beginning of the nineteenth century, an Ottoman historian speaks approvingly of parliamentary institutions in the states of Europe, for which he uses the striking euphemism "certain well organized state,"[14] and suggests in a very tentative way that similar consultative institutions would have a place in the Ottoman governmental and administrative tradition. The idea of consultative and deliberative procedures is deep rooted in Islamic theory and Ottoman practice. What was new was the idea, imported from Europe, of freedom as a political and not merely a juridical concept—freedom in the sense of the rights of the subject against the state, rights to be enshrined in a code of laws and protected by the law and the judiciary. It was these notions that gave rise to the Muslim constitutional movement which grew steadily during the nineteenth century and reached its climax in the Persian and Ottoman constitutional revolutions of 1905 and 1908.

Since then there have been great disappointments. Western military methods did not win the hoped-for victories; Western economic and political panaceas brought neither the prosperity nor the freedom for which they had been prescribed. In a mood of outrage and revulsion, there has been a return to older perceptions and responses, and to many the West again appears as something alien, pagan, and noxious, still hostile, but no longer terrifying. For the time being Western values in general, and Western political ways in particular, enjoy little esteem or respect. But it would be rash to say that they are dead in the Islamic world.

Notes

1. Elie Kedourie, *Islam in the Modern World and Other Studies* (London, 1980), p. 7.

2. 'Umari, ed. M. Amari, "Al-'Umari, Condizioni degli stati Cristiani dell' Occidente secondo una relazione di Domenichino Doria da Genova," *Atti R. Acad Linc. Mem.*, xi (1883), text p. 15, trans. p. 87.

3. F. von Kraelitz-Greifenhorst, "Bericht über den Zug des Gross-Botschafters Ibrahim Pascha nach Wien im Jahre 1719," *Akademie der Wiss. Wien: Phil. Hist. Kl. Sitzungsberichte*, clviii (1909), 26–77.

4. Abu Shama, *Kitāb al-Rawḍatayn fi akhbār al-dawlatayn*, 2nd edition, ed. M. Ḥilmī Aḥmad (Cairo, 1962), i, pt. 2, 621–22.

5. Maurice de Saxe, *Mes Rêveries* (1757), i. 86–87, cited in *War, Technology and Society in the Middle East*, ed. V. J. Parry and M. E Yapp (London, 1975), p. 256.

6. Muhammad b. 'Abd al-Wahhab, al-Wazir al-Ghassani, *Rihlat al-wazir fi iftikak al-asir*, ed. and Spanish translation by Alfredo Bustani (Tangier, 1940). Bustani's edition is somewhat abridged. For a full French translation from a manuscript, see H. Sauvaire, *Voyage en Espagne d'un Ambassadeur Marocain* (Paris, 1884). On these Moroccan travellers in general, see Henri Pérès, *L'Espagne vue par les voyageurs musulmans* de 1610 [sic: recte 1690] *à 1930* (Paris, 1937).

7. Muhammad ibn 'Uthman al-Miknasi, *al-Iksīr fi fikāk al-asīr*, ed. Muh. al-Fasi (Rabat, 1965).

8. Evliya, *Seyahatname* (Istanbul, 1314 A.H.), vii; cf. German translation, R. F. Kreutel, *Im Reiche des Goldenen Apfels* (Graz, 1957).

9. There are several editions of the embassy report of Mehmed Said, in both the old and new Turkish scripts, with some variations in the text. The book was first published in Paris and Istanbul with a French translation as *Relation de l'embassade de Mehmet Effendi à la cour de France en 1721 écrite par lui même et traduit par Julien Galland* (Constantinople and Paris, 1757). A new edition of Galland's version, without the text but with many additional documents, was edited by Gilles Veinstein: Mehmet Efendi, *Le paradis des infidèles* (Paris, 1981). On these authors, see further B. Lewis, *The Muslim Discovery of Europe* (New York, 1982); and Faik Reşit Unat, *Osmanlı sefirleri ve sefaretnameleri* (Ankara, 1968).

10. Cited by Veinstein, pp. 48–49.

11. 'Azmi, *Sefaretname 1205 senesinde Prusya Kıralı Ikinci Fredrik Guillaum in nezdine memur olan Ahmed 'Azmi Efendinin'dir* (Istanbul, 1303 A.H.), p. 52. German translation by Otto Müller-Kohlshorn, *Azmi Efendis Gesandtschaftsreise an den preussischen Hof* (Berlin, 1918) (not seen).

12. On the German military missions to Turkey, see Jehuda L. Wallach, *Anatomie einer Militärhilfe: die preussisch-deutschen Militärmissionen in der Türkei 1835–1919* (Tel Aviv–Düsseldorf, 1976).

13. Ibrahim Müteferrika, *Usul al-hikem fi nizam al-umem* (Istanbul, 1144 A.H.); *idem*, French version, *Traité de la Tactique* (Vienna, 1769).

14. Şanizade, *Tarih* (Istanbul, 1290–1 A.H.), iv, 2–3.

PART TWO
CURRENT HISTORY

22

The Middle East, Westernized
Despite Itself

✐✐✐✐

1996

Recent decades have seen Western political influence reduced to a minimum in the Middle East, but, in every other respect, Western influence grew apace.

The most visible, the most pervasive, and the least recognized aspects of Western influence are in the realm of material things—the infrastructure, amenities, and services of the modern state and city, most of them initiated by past European rulers or concession holders. There was clearly no desire to reverse or even deflect the processes of modernization. Nor indeed were such things as aeroplanes and cars, telephones and televisions, tanks and artillery, seen as Western or as related to the Western philosophies that preceded and facilitated their invention.

Revolution in Iran

More remarkably, even some avowedly anti-Western states have retained the Western political apparatus of constitutions and legislative assemblies. The Islamic Republic of Iran claims to be restoring true Islamic government but it does so in the form of a written constitution and an elected parliament—neither with any precedent in Islamic doctrine or history.

Perhaps the most powerful and persistent of Western political ideas in the region has been that of revolution. The history of the Islamic Middle East, like that of other societies, offers many examples of the overthrow of governments by rebellion or conspiracy. There is also an old Islamic tradition of challenge to the social and political order by leaders who believed that it was their sacred duty to dethrone tyranny and install justice in its place. Islamic law and tradition lay down the limits of the obedience which is owed to the ruler and discuss—albeit with considerable caution—the circumstances in which a ruler forfeits his claim to the allegiance of his subjects and may or rather must lawfully be deposed and replaced.

But the notion of revolution, as developed in sixteenth-century Holland, seventeenth-century England, and eighteenth-century America and France, was alien and new. The first self-styled revolutions in the Middle East were those of the constitutionalists in Iran in 1905 and the Young Turks in the Ottoman Empire in 1908. Since then there have been many others, and by the last decade of the twentieth century, a clear majority of states in the region were governed by regimes installed by means of the violent removal of their predecessors. In early days, this was sometimes accomplished by a nationalist struggle against foreign overlords. Later it was usually achieved by military officers deposing the rulers in whose armies they served. All of these, with equal fervor, laid claim to the title "revolutionary," which in time became the most widely accepted claim to legitimacy in government in the Middle East. In a very few cases, the change of regime resulted from profounder movements in society, with deeper causes and greater consequences than a simple replacement of the men at the top. One such was surely the Islamic Revolution of 1979 in Iran, which invites comparison with the French and more especially Russian Revolutions in its origins, its modalities, and perhaps also its ultimate fate.

For better or for worse—and from the start there have been different views on this—what happened in Iran can be seen as a revolution in the classical sense: a mass movement with wide popular participation that resulted in a major shift in economic as well as political power and that inaugurated—or, perhaps more accurately, continued—a process of vast social transformation.

In Iran under the Pahlavis, as in France under the Bourbons and in Russia under the Romanovs, a major process of change was already under way, and had advanced to a point at which it required a shift in political power in order to continue. And in the Iranian revolution, as in the others, there was also the possibility that something might happen whereby the process of change was deflected, perverted, or even annulled. From an early stage, some Iranians, arguing from different and sometimes contrasting premises, claimed that this had already happened. As the revolutionary regime ensconced itself in power, more and more came to agree with them.

The revolution in Iran, unlike those earlier movements designated by that name, was called Islamic. Its leaders and inspirers cared nothing for the models of Paris or Petrograd, and saw European ideologies of the left no less than of the right as all part of the pervasive infidel enemy against whom they were waging their struggle. Theirs was a different society, educated in different scriptures and classics, shaped by different historical memories. The symbols and slogans of the revolution were Islamic because these alone had the power to mobilize the masses for struggle.

Islam provided more than symbols and slogans. As interpreted by the revolutionary leaders and spokesmen, it formulated the objectives to be attained and, no less important, it defined the enemies to be opposed. These were familiar from history, law, and tradition: the infidel abroad, the apostate at home. For the revolutionaries, of course, the apostate meant all those Muslims, and especially Muslim rulers, who did not share their interpretation of authentic Islam and who, in their perception, were importing alien and infidel ways and thus subverting the community of Islam, and the faith and law by which it lived. In principle, the aim of the Islamic revolution in Iran and eventually in other countries where such movements established themselves was to sweep away all the alien and infidel accretions that had been imposed on Muslim lands and peoples in the era of alien dominance and influence and to restore the true and divinely given Islamic order.

An examination of the record of these revolutionaries, however, in Iran and elsewhere, reveals that the rejection of the West and its offerings is by no means as comprehensive and as undiscriminating as propaganda might indicate, and that at least certain importations from the lands of unbelief are still very welcome.

Some of these are obvious. The Islamic revolution in Iran was the first truly modern revolution of the electronic age. Khomeini was the first charismatic orator who sent his oratory from abroad to millions of his compatriots at home on cassettes; he was the first revolutionary leader in exile who directed his followers at home by telephone, thanks to the direct dialing that the shah had introduced in Iran. Needless to say, in the wars in which they have been engaged, both formal and informal, the Iranian revolutionary leaders have made the fullest use of such weapons as the West and its imitators were willing to sell them.

There was, tragically, another respect in which the revolutionary regime in Iran borrowed from Europe. While its symbols and allusions were Islamic rather than European, its models of style and method were often more European than Islamic. The summary trial and execution of great numbers of ideologically defined enemies; the driving into exile of hundreds of thousands of men and women; the large-scale confiscation of private property; the mixture of repression and subversion, of violence and indoctrination that accompanied the consolidation of power—all this owes far more to the examples of Robespierre and Stalin than to those of Muhammad and 'Ali. These methods can hardly be called Islamic; they are, however, thoroughly revolutionary.

Like the French and the Russians in their time, the Iranian revolutionaries played to international as well as domestic audiences, and their revolution exercised a powerful fascination over other peoples outside Iran, in other countries within the same culture, the same universe of discourse. The appeal was naturally strongest amongst Shi'i populations, as in south Lebanon and some of the Gulf states, and weakest among their immediate Sunni neighbors. It was for a while very strong in much of the Muslim world where Shi'ism was virtually unknown. In these, the sectarian difference was unimportant. Khomeini could be seen, not as a Shi'i or an Iranian, but as an Islamic revolutionary leader. Like the young Western radicals who, in their day, responded with almost Messianic enthusiasm to events in Paris and Petrograd, so did millions of young and not-so-young men and women all over the world of Islam respond to the call of Islamic revolution—with the same upsurge of emotion, the same uplifting of hearts, the same boundless hopes, the same willingness to excuse and condone all kinds of horrors, and the same anxious questions about the future.

The years that followed the revolution were difficult years in Iran. The people suffered greatly from foreign wars, internal strife and repression, and a steadily worsening economic crisis. As in other revolutions, there was recurring conflict between rival factions, sometimes described as extremists and moderates, more accurately as ideologues and pragmatists. Because of these and other changes, the ideal of the Islamic revolution, Iranian-style, lost some of its appeal—but not all. Islamic revolutionary movements derived from, inspired by, or parallel to the revolution in Iran developed in other Muslim countries where they became serious and sometimes successful contenders for power.

All these various revolutionary regimes, as well as the surviving monarchies and traditional regimes, shared the desire to preserve and utilize both the political apparatus and the economic benefits which modernization placed at their disposal. What was resented was foreign control and exploitation of the economic machine, not the foreign origin of the machine itself.

Islam and Democracy

Like the British and the French before them, the Soviets and the United States in their rivalry in the Middle East tried to create societies and polities in their own image. Neither task was easy, one of them especially difficult. The sponsorship of authoritarian government presented no problem, but it was quite another matter to create a Marxist, socialist regime in an Islamic country. The task of creating a liberal democracy was no less difficult. But if democracies are more difficult to create, they are also more difficult to destroy. This in the long term worked to the advantage to the democracies, both inside and outside the region, and to the detriment of their authoritarian enemies.

In the debate about how the hard-won independence should be used, and the lot of the people bettered, there were two main ideological streams: Islam and democracy. Both came in many variant and competing forms. At a time when all the different imported methods that Muslims had used or copied or imitated had visibly failed, there was considerable force in the argument that these were the ways of foreigners and unbelievers, and that they had brought nothing but harm. The remedy was for Muslims to return to the faith and law of Islam, to be authentically themselves, to purge state and society of foreign and infidel accretions, and create a true Islamic order.

The alternative program was democracy—not the shoddy imitations of Western democracies practiced between the world wars, and operated only by small cliques of magnates at the top, but authentic, free institutions functioning at every level of public life, from the village to the presidency. Where the so-called fundamentalist Muslims and democrats are both in opposition, the former have an immense advantage. In the mosques and preachers, they dispose of a network for meeting and communication that no government, however tyrannical, can entirely control and no other group can rival. Sometimes a tyrannical regime has eased the path of the fundamentalists by eliminating competing oppositions. Only one other group in society has the cohesion, the structure, and the means to take independent action, and that is the army—the second major motor of political change in the region. At different times and in different places, the army has acted for democracy, as in Turkey, or for fundamentalism, as in the Sudan.

The proponents of both Islamic and democratic solutions differed considerably among themselves, and many variants of both have been propounded. For some, the two ideas were mutually exclusive. Fundamentalists—a minority, but an active and important one among Muslims—had no use for democracy, except as a one-way ticket to power; the militant secularists among the democrats made little effort to conceal their intention of ending, or at least reducing, the role traditionally played by Islam in the public life of state. The interaction between the Islamic tradition of a state based on faith and Western notions of separation between religion and government seems likely to continue.

For men and for women alike, the interlude of freedom was too long, and its effects too profound, for it to be forgotten. Despite many reverses, European-style democracy is not dead in the Islamic lands, and there are some signs of a revival. In some countries, parliamentary and constitutional systems are becoming increasingly effective. In several others there have been steps, still rather tentative, towards political as well as economic liberalization.

Culture and Society

In cultural and social life, the introduction and acceptance of European ways went very far and persisted in forms which even the most militant and radical either did not perceive or were willing to tolerate. The first to change were the traditional arts. Already by the end of the eighteenth century, the old traditions of miniature painting in books and of interior decoration in buildings were dying. In the course of the nineteenth century they were replaced in the more Westernized countries by a new art and architecture that were at first influenced and then dominated by European patterns. The old arts of miniature and calligraphy lingered on for a while but those who practiced them, with few exceptions, lacked originality and prestige. Their place in the artistic self-expression of society was taken by European-style painters, working in oils on canvas. Architecture too, even mosque architecture, conformed in the main to Western artistic notions as well as to the inevitable Western techniques. At times there were attempts to return to traditional Islamic patterns, but these often took the form of a conscious neoclassicism.

Only in one respect were Islamic artistic norms retained, and that was in the slow and reluctant acceptance of sculpture, seen as a violation of the Islamic ban on graven images. One of the main grievances against such secular modernizers as Kemal Atatürk in Turkey and the shah in Iran was their practice of installing statues of themselves in public places. This was seen as no better than pagan idolatry.

The Westernization of art was paralleled in literature, though at a slower pace and at a later date. From the mid-nineteenth century onwards, traditional literary forms were neglected, except among some diehard circles with limited impact. In their place came new forms and ideas from the West—the novel and the short story, replacing the traditional tale and apologue; the essay and the newspaper article, and new forms and themes that have transformed modern poetry among all the peoples of the region. Even the language in which modern literature is written has, in all the countries of the region, been extensively and irreversibly changed under the influence of Western discourse.

The change is least noticeable in music, where the impact of European music is still relatively small. In Turkey, where European influence has lasted longest and gone deepest, there are talented performers, some of them with international reputations, and composers working in the Western manner. Istanbul and Ankara are now on the international concert circuit, as are of course the chief cities of Israel, itself in effect a cultural component of the West. In these places, there are audiences large enough and faithful enough to make such visits worthwhile. Elsewhere in the Middle East, those who compose, perform or even listen to Western music are still relatively few. Music in the various traditional modes is still being composed and performed at high level and is accepted and appreciated by the vast majority of the population. Of late there has been some interest in the more popular types of Western music but even this is, in the main, limited to comparatively small groups in the larger cities. Music is perhaps the profoundest and most intimate expression of a culture, and it is natural that it should be the last to yield to alien influence.

Another highly visible sign of European influence is in clothing. That Muslim armies use modern equipment and weaponry may be ascribed to necessity, and there are ancient traditions declaring it lawful to imitate the infidel enemy in order to defeat him. But that the officers of these armies wear uniforms and, more remarkably, visored and peaked caps cannot be so justified, and has a significance at once cultural and symbolic. In the nineteenth century, the Ottomans, followed by other Muslim states, adopted European-style uniforms for both officers and men, and European harnesses for their horses. Only the headgear remained un-Westernized, and for good reason. After the Kemalist Revolution in Turkey, even this last bastion of Islamic conservatism fell. The Turkish army, along with the general population, adopted European hats and caps, and before long they were followed by the armies, and eventually even many civilians in almost all other Muslim states.

The situation was different for women. During the nineteenth and early twentieth centuries, the Europeanization of female attire was slower, later, and more limited. It was strongly resisted, and affected a much smaller portion of the population. At many levels of society, where the wearing of Western clothes by men became normal, women still kept—or were kept—to traditional dress. By the mid-twentieth century, however, more and more women were adopting a Western style of clothing—at first among the modernizing leisured classes, and then, increasingly, among working women and students. One of the most noticeable consequences of the Islamic revival has been a reversal of this trend and a return, by women far more than by men, to traditional attire.

Women

Of all the changes attributable to Western example or influence, the profoundest and most far-reaching is surely the change in the position of women. The abolition of chattel slavery, in the European dependencies in the nineteenth century and in the independent states in the twentieth, made concubinage illegal, and though it lingered on for some time in the remoter areas, it ceased to be either common or accepted. In a few countries, notably Turkey, Tunisia, and Iran until the fall of the shah but not after, even polygamous marriage was in effect outlawed, and in many of the Muslim states, while still lawful, it was subject to legal and other restrictions. Among the urban middle and upper classes, it became socially unacceptable; for the urban lower classes, it had always been economically impractical.

A major factor in the emancipation of women was economic need. Peasant women had from time immemorial been part of the work-force and had, in consequence, enjoyed certain social freedoms denied to their sisters in the cities. Economic modernization brought a need for female labor, which was augmented by mobilization for modern war. This became a significant factor in the Ottoman Empire during the First World War, when much of the male population was in the armed forces. The economic involvement of women and the social changes resulting from it continued in the interwar period and after, and even brought a few legislative changes in favor of women. These had some effect in social and family life. Education for women also made substantial progress, and by the 1970s and 1980s, considerable numbers of women were enrolled as students in the universities. They began in so-called "women's professions," such as nursing and teaching, traditional in Europe and gradually becoming so in the lands of Islam. Later, women began to appear in other faculties and professions.

Even in Iran there are women physicians for women patients and, more remarkably, women members of parliament. The enrollment of women even in the traditional professions was too much for some of the militants. Khomeini spoke with great anger of the immorality which he believed would inevitably result from the employment of women to teach boys.

The political emancipation of women has made significant progress in those countries where parliamentary regimes function. It matters little in the dictatorships, controlled by either the army or the party, both overwhelmingly male. Westerners tend to assume that the emancipation of women is part of liberalization, and that women will consequently fare better under liberal than under autocratic regimes. Such an assumption is dubious and often untrue. Among Arab countries, the legal emancipation of women went furthest in Iraq and South Yemen, both ruled by notoriously repressive regimes. It lagged behind in Egypt, in many ways the most tolerant and open of Arab societies. It is in such societies that public opinion, still mainly male and mainly conservative, resists change. Women's rights have suffered the most serious reverses in countries where fundamentalists have influence or where, as in Iran, they rule. The emancipation of women is one of the main grievances of the fundamentalists and its reversal is in the forefront of their program.

Nevertheless, it is clear that irreversible changes have taken place. Even those claiming to restore the Holy Law in its entirety are unlikely to reintroduce legal concubinage, nor is there much probability of a return to polygamy among the educated classes in Middle Eastern cities. Fundamentalist influences and rulers have in many ways changed the content and manner of education for women, but they have not returned them—nor are they likely to return them—to their previous condition of ignorance. And while, in Islamic lands as in Europe and America at an earlier age, there are women who speak and work against their own emancipation, the long-term trend is clearly for greater freedom. There are now significant numbers of educated, often Western-educated, women in Islamic lands. They are already having a significant impact, and Islamic public life will be enriched by the contributions of the previously excluded half of the population.

These changes, and the legal, social, and cultural transformations which preceded, accompanied, and followed them, have evoked sharply differing reactions among the population. For many women, they brought release and opportunity; for many men, they opened a way to a previously hidden world. In some places, the impact of the West brought wealth, often beyond any that could be imagined. Western technology and Western-style business introduced new ways of acquiring money; Western consumer culture offered a wide range of new ways of spending it. But for many, and not only those directly and adversely affected, the new ways were both an affront and a threat—an affront to their sense of decency and propriety, and a mortal threat to the most cherished of all their values, the religious basis of their society.

Economics

Modernization—or as many saw it, Westernization—widened the gap between rich and poor. It also made that gap more visible and more palpable. In most cities outside the Arabian peninsula, the rich now wore different clothes, ate different food, and lived by different social rules from the unmodernized mass of the population. And all the time, thanks to Western means of communication, especially the cinema and television, the deprived masses were more aware than ever before of the difference between them and the wealthy, and of what, specifically, they were missing.

In some countries, the pain and discomfort inevitable in a period of rapid change were palliated by wise and moderate governments. But in most they were aggravated by the economic mismanagement of autocratic regimes. There were real problems, notably the rapid growth of population unaccompanied by any corresponding increase in domestic food resources. But often even the considerable assets enjoyed by some countries were squandered. Part of the problem was the heavy cost of the security and military apparatus required to maintain order at home and to confront or deter potential enemies abroad. But these costs are not the whole explanation. The sad comment of an Algerian interviewed in a French news magazine is typical: "Algeria was once the granary of Rome, and now it has to import cereals to make bread. It is a land of flocks and gardens, and it imports meat and fruit. It is rich in oil and gas, and it has a foreign debt of $25 billion and two million unemployed." He goes on to say that this is the result of thirty years of mismanagement.

Algeria has a small oil income and a large population. Some other countries have large incomes and small populations, but have nevertheless managed to devastate their economies and impoverish their peoples. In the longer perspective, oil may prove to be a very mixed blessing for the countries endowed with it. Politically, oil revenues strengthened autocratic governments by freeing them from the financial pressures and constraints which, in other countries, induced governments to accept measures of democratization. Economically, oil wealth often produced a lopsided development, and left these countries dangerously exposed to such outside factors as the fluctuations in the world price of oil, and even, in the long run, to the uncertainties of oil itself. There are other sources of oil besides the Middle East; there are other sources of energy besides oil, and both are being actively pursued by a world that has grown weary of Middle Eastern pressures and uncertainties.

The Middle East, on Its Own

In the last decade of the twentieth century, the Middle East faces two major crises. One of them is economic and social: the difficulties arising from economic deprivation and, still more, economic dislocation, and their social consequences. The other is political and social—the breakdown of consensus, of that generally accepted set of rules and principles by which a polity works and without which a society cannot function, even under autocratic government. The breakup of the Soviet Union exemplifies the consequences of such a loss of consensus, and the difficulties and dangers of creating a new one.

In the last decade of the twentieth century, it became increasingly clear that in facing these problems, the governments and peoples of the Middle East were substantially on their own. Outside powers were no longer interested in directing, still less dominating, the affairs of the region. On the contrary, they displayed an extreme reluctance to become involved. The countries of the outside world—that is to say, of Europe, the Americas, and, increasingly, of East Asia— were basically concerned with three things in the Middle East: a rich and growing market for their goods and services, a major source of their energy needs, and, as a necessary means to safeguarding the first two, the maintenance of at least some semblance of international law and order.

The circumstances which would provoke outside military intervention were epitomized by Saddam Husayn's invasion and annexation of Kuwait, and the consequent immediate threat to Saudi Arabia and the Gulf states. This confronted the outside world with a double threat. The first was that the oil resources of the region, that is to say, a significant part of the oil resources of the world, would fall under the monopolistic control of an aggressive dictator. The second threat was to the whole international order established in the aftermath of the Second World War. Despite all the many conflicts in many continents, this was the first time that a member state of the United Nations in good standing was simply invaded and annexed by another member state.

Had Saddam Husayn been allowed to succeed in his venture, the United Nations, already devalued, would have followed the defunct League of Nations into well-deserved ignominy, and the world would have belonged to the violent and the ruthless.

He was not allowed to succeed, and an impressive range of forces, both from inside and from outside the region, was mobilized to evict him from Kuwait. But—this is the most telling indication of the new era—he was evicted from Kuwait, not from Iraq, and was allowed to resume his distinctive style of government and many of his policies in that country. The message was clear. If the Iraqis want a new and different form of government, they must do it for themselves; no one else will do it for them.

This broadly has been the message of the outside powers in the last decade of the twentieth century. These powers will, at most, act to defend their own interests, that is to say, markets and oil, and the interests of the international community, that is to say, a decent respect for the basic rules of the United Nations.

Otherwise, the peoples and governments of the Middle East, for the first time in two centuries, will determine their own fate. They may produce new regional powers, perhaps acting in concert, perhaps contending for regional hegemony. They may go the way of Yugoslavia and Somalia, to fragmentation and internecine chaos—and there are movements and individuals in the region who have made it clear that they would choose this rather than compromise on what they believe to be their religious duties or national rights. Events in Lebanon during the civil war could easily become a paradigm for the entire region. They may unite—perhaps, as some are urging, for a holy war, a new jihad which, again as in the past, might well evoke the response of a new Crusade. Or they may unite for peace—with themselves, their neighbors, and the outside world, using and sharing their spiritual as well as their material resources in the search for a fuller, richer, freer life.

For the moment, the outside world seems disposed to leave them in peace, and perhaps even to help them achieve it. They alone—the peoples and governments of the Middle East—can decide whether and how to use this window of opportunity while, in an interval of their troubled modern history, it remains open.

23

The Middle East in World Affairs

❦

1957

The Middle East today consists of a series of sovereign national states, almost none of which, in their present form, have any roots in the past. Some, like Turkey and Persia, are the metropolitan remnants of bygone empires, in which the former ruling peoples are feeling their way toward a national instead of an imperial identity and existence. Others are new creations, fashioned from the debris of empires, with frontiers drawn not by history and geography, but by statesmen on maps. These new political entities were for long irrelevant and unreal to the peoples who lived under them. The territorial and linguistic nation and the nation-state are both alien to the Muslim Middle East, where men's basic loyalties were determined not by language or fatherland, but by religion. Loyalty to a place was known, but it was to a village or a quarter, not a country; loyalty to one's kin was ancient and potent, but it was to the family or the tribe, not to the ethnic nation. The ultimate loyalty, the measure by which a man distinguished between brother and stranger, was religion, and political allegiance belonged to the dynastic sovereign of the Islamic state.

Today this has changed. The sense of Turkish, Persian, and Arab national identity is very strong, at least among those classes that have received a modern education or have been affected by modern ideas. Even the more specifically European sentiment of patriotism, love of country in the political sense, has made some headway. In Turkey the Kemalist government and its successors discouraged Pan-Turkish and Pan-Islamic tendencies, loyalty and politics by race or faith, and instead tried, with considerable success, to foster in the Turkish people a sense of communion with the country they inhabit. Egypt is a country well defined by both history and geography and has now been the center of a separate, modern state for a century and a half—long enough for a sense of separate territorial nationality to emerge. Iran, distinguished from its neighbors by both language and religion, has always had a strong sense of cultural identity and has, moreover, long been the seat of a sovereign and separate state. Israel, transplanted from overseas, has refashioned a unity of faith and destiny into a more or less European form of political loyalty and organization. Even in the Fertile Crescent the new states are beginning to take root in the loyalties and sentiments of their peoples and at times manifest a strong desire for separate survival. This is especially so where their politics coincide with ancient distinctions and rivalries, as for example between the eastern and western slopes of Lebanon or between the rulers of the Nile and of the Tigris-Euphrates valleys.

These forms and these allegiances are, however, new. Even where they are taking root they are still tender, immature, and precarious. They do not yet correspond to the feelings and loyalties of the great mass of the population; they cannot adequately express the instinctive and spontaneous responses even of the educated elite to the challenges of internal and international affairs. They cannot therefore provide us with a key to the understanding of those movements and policies in the Middle East that are due not to the calculations of groups or individuals, but to a real upsurge of popular sentiment and emotion.

To achieve some understanding of Middle Eastern attitudes in world affairs at the present time, we must view the Middle East not as countries, not even as nations, but as a civilization. It is unfortunate that we have formed the habit of calling the area the Near East or Middle East. The first of these names is diplomatic in origin; the second, strategic. Both are colorless geographical expressions that fail to express or even suggest a civilization, as real and distinctive an entity as Europe, India, or China, and very much more so than Africa or Asia.

We may define the area historically as that of the great Islamic empires of the caliphs and their successors, and of the classical Islamic civilization that grew up under their aegis. Its early, formative period ended before the Crusades. Its final flowering took place under the Turkish and Persian empires, which, from the sixteenth to the early twentieth centuries, divided what we call the Near and Middle East between them. Essentially, it was a civilization of three peoples and of three languages—Arabic, Persian, and Turkish. Its territorial core was Northeast Africa and Southwest Asia. In this sense the Middle East does not stop at the Soviet border, as in the rather artificial diplomatic and military usage, but includes extensive areas in Transcaucasia and Central Asia, which, from the Middle Ages until the Russian conquest, were under Arab, Persian, or Turkish rule and which are still inhabited by Persian- or Turkish-speaking Muslims.

Of those parts of the Middle East that are under Soviet rule there is little that can be said now. Our governments have for some reason followed the Soviet lead in excluding them from the consideration of Middle Eastern affairs, and in any case, despite a common background, their recent and present situation differs so much from that of the sovereign states of the Middle East that it is difficult to consider them together. I shall therefore confine my remarks to those parts of the Middle East that lie south of the Soviet border.

Now that the fog of battle and the mists of diplomacy are clearing from the Middle Eastern scene, it is becoming apparent that certain fundamental changes have taken place. One of these has been the decline of British power. The turning point came in July, 1954, when, a few weeks after the Eisenhower-Churchill conversations in Washington, Britain and Egypt reached agreement for the evacuation by the British of the Suez Canal zone. Great expectations were placed in that agreement. At the time, the hope was widely entertained and still more widely expressed that, with the removal of the final Egyptian grievance against the West, real friendship and co-operation would at last become possible.

For those who held them, those hopes have been disappointed. The general situation in the Middle East, far from improving, deteriorated rapidly. The Egypt-Israel border, after a period of comparative calm, became and remained the chief battlefield of Israeli-Arab conflict. The removal of the last specifically Egyptian grievance left the Egyptians free to take up the larger causes of those whom they call their Arab and African brothers. And finally, although the term power vacuum may be objectionable, the fact remains that the withdrawal of British influence has been preceded, accompanied, and followed by the growth of the influence of other powers.

It may be useful at this point to review, briefly and schematically, the chief phases in the development of great-power influence in the Middle East. After the victory of 1918, Great Britain and France were in exclusive control of the area, unchallenged except by one another. In the 1930s and 1940s Britain and France drew together to meet and, ultimately, defeat the attempt of the Axis powers to oust them from the area. Since then, first France and then—with a change in the casting, but not in the script—Great Britain have been eliminated from most of their positions of power and influence, leaving the center of the arena to a new set of contestants.

It would, however, be a misleading simplification to describe the present Middle Eastern situation only in terms of American-Russian rivalry. For one thing, Britain and France, though reduced in stature, can still call on certain reserves of good will and esteem in the Middle East. These, after reaching their lowest point at the time of the Suez incident, have begun to recover, and may be expected to grow still further as the Middle Eastern peoples come to realize that their protests against domination and tutelage, power politics, spheres of influence, and the rest must be delivered to new addresses.

Moreover, there are other heirs to Britain's Middle Eastern policy. Britain's direct interest in the Middle East dates from the late eighteenth century and was a consequence of the establishment of British paramountcy in India. It was after the end of that paramountcy that British interest in the Middle East began to dwindle, and it was not long before both the successor governments to the British raj in India began to pick up the pieces of its foreign policy on the

North-West Frontier, the Indian Ocean, the Persian Gulf, and the Red Sea—on the land and sea approaches to India, that is—and to fashion new Middle Eastern policies of their own. Their task is, of course, greatly complicated by the fact that there are now not one but two governments in the subcontinent and that neither of them possesses the military resources for an independent great-power policy. Both, however, possess in their dealings with the Middle East certain advantages that Britain and other Western powers could never have, and it would be a grave error to underestimate the role of either Pakistan or India in the Middle East—or to forget that their policies rest on genuine national and geo-political interests.

Another Asian contestant is China, which in recent years has for the first time begun to evolve a world-wide and not merely a Far Eastern foreign policy and has already shown many signs of an active and growing interest in the Middle East. It may be noted that Colonel Nasser's dalliance with Moscow was preceded and perhaps prepared by his meeting with Chou En-lai at Bandung.

But what of the Middle East itself—of this group of sovereign states and peoples who are no longer content, in a common phrase, to be the objects of history, but wish to become its subjects? Middle Eastern statesmen insist vehemently that there is no such thing as a power vacuum, that the Middle Eastern peoples must be masters of their own fate, and that they are not concerned with the rivalries of great-power blocs. There can be no doubting the sincerity of their wishes in this, but, as the great Arabic writer Hariri says: "You are in one valley and I am in another valley and what a difference there is between the wisher and the wish."[1] In fact no Middle Eastern state, nor any conceivable combination of Middle Eastern states, could in present circumstances play an active and wholly independent role in Middle East affairs—as can easily be seen in the maneuvers, in the last few years, of pro-Westerners, anti-Westerners (a more accurate description than pro-Communists), and the adherents of the a-plague-on-both-your-houses school.

A crucial question is: What are the relative strengths of the three schools? There are governments and politicians, groups and individuals, of all three tendencies, and some which seem to fluctuate between them. But of one thing there can be no doubt—it is the anti-Western policy that commands the widest, readiest, and strongest support in most of the countries of the Middle East. This was most strikingly demonstrated in September, 1955, when the Czech-Egyptian arms deal was announced. Far more significant than the arms deal itself was the wave of almost ecstatic joy with which the news of it was received all over the Arab world. The Syrian, Lebanese, and Jordanian chambers of deputies at once voted resolutions of congratulations to Colonel Nasser, and almost the entire Arab press greeted the news with exultation and delight.

This reaction was due, not to any special love for the Soviet bloc, nor to any desire to see its influence extended in the Arab world, but to a lively appreciation of the quality of Colonel Nasser's act as a slap in the face for the West. The

Colonel's slap, and the red-faced, agitated, and ineffectual Western response to it, gave dramatic expression to a mood and a wish that unite many people in the Middle East—the mood of revulsion from the West, and the wish to spite and humiliate it. There are many statesmen and even a few governments in the Arab world who believe that the long-term interests of their countries and peoples require co-operation with the West, help from the West. They can, however, only pursue such policies by disregarding or suppressing popular feeling. It is the policy of rejection and insult that arouses immediate and spontaneous enthusiasm among the mass of the people.

What is the reason for this anti-Western feeling?

There is no lack of answers to this question. First, there is the long list of specific political grievances, beginning with the Palestine question and including such other items as Algeria, Suez, and the rest. Then there are the economic and social dislocations resulting from the impact of Westernization in its various forms. These are, in the long run, far more important than the political grievances as a source of restlessness and resentment. By their nature, however, they are not easy to formulate and discuss on a political level, at any rate in countries that have no tradition of such discussion; nor can the blame for them readily be thrown on nameable and recognizable culprits. It is, therefore, the political grievances that are most to the fore, both as an outlet and as a focus for anti-Western feeling. Sometimes, indeed, it is difficult to tell whether a particular grievance is an irritant or a safety valve.

In discussing the relative importance of these various political grievances, Middle Easterners will naturally give primacy to those in which they themselves are directly concerned. Westerners, on the other hand, incline to the view that if those grievances that are directed against other Westerners could only be met, their own more reasonable requirements would find easy acceptance—and there is always someone ready to serve an interest or a prejudice by encouraging this belief. Variants of this view have been put before many different audiences in the past and have been argued, asserted, suggested, or hinted, according to the ductility of the evidence and the skill of the advocate. A current form of this interpretation, which enjoys a measure of popularity in some quarters today, is that were it not for the existence and persistence of the Israelis, the incompetence and greed of the French, and the duplicity and rapacity of the British, there could be an idyllic marriage of American interests and Arab nationalism, in which the latter would be firm and independent against all others, but gracefully acquiescent in American requirements. In that happy day there would be bases for the military, treaties for the diplomats, concessions for the businessmen, converts for the missionaries, and a general glow of mutual friendship and good will.

A pretty picture—but of an apocalyptic rather than a historical quality. The events of the last few years have shown that the removal of particular grievances produces no real alleviation, since the general upsurge of anti-Western feeling soon finds other outlets and expressions. They have shown, too, that though anti-Western feeling was directed chiefly against Britain and France, it was to no small extent in their capacity as leaders of the Western world. Today they are no longer the exclusive targets of hostility; soon they may no longer even be the chief targets.

Why should this be so? Why should the United States, which has never annexed or occupied an inch of territory in the Middle East, which on the contrary has shown a generosity without precedent in history towards the states of the Middle East, be included in this generalized hostility to the West?

We shall be better able to understand this situation if we view the present discontents of the Middle East not as a conflict between states or nations, but as a clash between civilizations. The "great debate," as Gibbon called it, between Islam and Christendom has been going on since the Arab Muslim conquerors first swept westward into Christian Syria, North Africa, and Spain. It continued with the Christian counter-offensive of the Crusades and its failure, the thrust of the Turks into Europe, and their hard-fought retreat and withdrawal. For the past century and a half Middle Eastern Islam has been subjected to the impact and domination of the West—political, economic, and cultural domination even where, as in most of the Middle East, there was no direct rule. This impact has shattered traditional patterns of thought and behavior, of political and social loyalty and organization, beyond repair, and has posed to the peoples of the Middle East an immense problem of readjustment, both in their dealings with the outside world and in their own internal affairs.

The change brought great benefits and will no doubt bring others in the course of time; but it would be a piece of myopic self-conceit on our part to deny that it has also done great damage and is the chief cause of the political and social formlessness, instability, and irresponsibility that bedevil the public life of the Middle East. In our own day the crisis has come to a head, and the anger that it engenders is directed outward, against the West—the millennial adversary and also the place in which these devastating changes had their origin.

In the twilight world of popular myths and images, the West is the source of all evil—and the West is a single whole, the parochial subdivisions of which are hardly more important than are those of the Middle East for the average Westerner. And in this mood of hostility, which we must concede has cause, if not justification, those who pander to anti-Western feeling will be able to count on a ready and fervent response, while those who seek to co-operate with the West will have to circumvent popular opposition by guile, stealth, or force. To many Americans it must have seemed incongruous, if not uncongenial, that their government should support a king against an elected parliament, but the outward forms of Middle Eastern political life should not mislead us into equating them with their Western originals. In the Middle Eastern poker game there is nothing inconsistent in a good republican's playing a hand of three kings—and hoping that no one else will play the aces.

The only people who have ever succeeded in ruling the Middle East for any
length of time, the Turks, had their own views on these matters. In a Turkish
manual of statecraft, written in the middle of the seventeenth century, the author,
Huseyn Hezarfenn, advises the sovereign to use fear as well as law to maintain
his authority:

> If the fear of punishment were to pass away from people's hearts, the
> evildoers would become more numerous and more arrogant. The right
> thing is that there should be fear among the bad and trust among the
> good people. Permanent fear and permanent trust are both harmful. While
> the people are between fear and hope, let the Sultanate be well-ordered
> and let the Sultan be generous.[2]

Between the Sixth Fleet and the Eisenhower Doctrine, as it were, let the
United States be both firm and munificent.

In what has gone before I have tried to raise the conflicts of the Middle East
from the level of a quarrel between states to that of a clash between civilizations.
But civilizations can have no foreign policies, and governments must. The question therefore remains: What action should the Western states take in the present
Middle Eastern situation? My own answer would be: As little as possible. The
peoples of the Middle East are going through a crisis of transition, which we
helped to precipitate, but which they alone can resolve. The United Nations has
the limited but overtaxing duty of keeping the peace or at least of curbing the
appetites of violence. We of the West can also do something to help, on non-
political levels, but should beware of proposing solutions that, however good,
are discredited by the very fact of our having suggested them. The West must,
of course, safeguard its minimum interests, which I leave to others to define; it
may also give some material help—though without hope of much political return. Apart from that, let us watch and wait, do little and say less, and hope
that in time the peoples of the Middle East may find their own way back to
stability and health.

But, of course, the great dilemma of such a policy of "masterly inactivity" is
how to leave the Middle East alone and at the same time insure that others also
will leave it alone. The point was well made by Walter Laqueur in his book on
Communism and Nationalism in the Middle East:

> It is quite true, as an Indonesian prime minister stated in Delhi re-
> cently to great applause, Asian affairs are no longer settled in London and
> Paris. What remains to be seen is whether the new rulers of the Middle
> East and South-east Asia will be able in the future to prevent Asian affairs
> from being decided in Moscow and Peking.[3]

Western rule in Asia has indeed gone, and a distinguished Indian scholar was
right in speaking of the end of "the Vasco da Gama era" in Asian history. It
would be both tragic and ironic if it were to be succeeded by a Khrushchev and

Bulganin era, which some future historian might also date from a voyage of exploration to the East.

Notes

1. *The Assemblies of Hariri* (Assembly XXXIV [al-Zabidiyya]), ed. F. Steingass (London, 1897), p. 282.

2. *Hezarfen Hüseyin Efendi'nin Osmanlı Devlet Teşkilatına dair Mulâhazalri,* ed. Robert Anhegger, *Türkiyat Mecmuasi* X (Istanbul, 1951–1953), p. 376.

3. W. Z. Laqueur, *Communism and Nationalism in the Middle East* (New York, 1956), p. 281.

24

Friends and Enemies

Reflections after a War

❧❧❧❧

1967

The measure of prudence and resolution is to know a friend from an
enemy; the height of stupidity and weakness is not to know an enemy
from a friend.

Do not surrender your enemy to oppression, nor oppress him yourself. In this respect treat enemy and friend alike. But be on your guard
against him, and beware lest you befriend and advance him, for this
is the act of a fool. He who befriends and advances friend and foe
alike will only arouse distaste for his friendship and contempt for his
enmity. He will earn the scorn of his enemy, and facilitate his hostile
designs; he will lose his friend, who will join the ranks of his enemies.

The height of goodness is that you should neither oppress your
enemy nor abandon him to oppression. To treat him as a friend is the
mark of a fool whose end is near.

The height of evil is that you should oppress your friend. Even
to estrange him is the act of a man who has no sense, for whom
misfortune is predestined.

Magnanimity is not to befriend the enemy, but to spare them,
and to remain on your guard against them.

From *The Book of Morals and Conduct,* Ibn Hazm of Cordova
(994–1064)

To begin with, the recent Arab-Israel dispute looked like what might be
called a normal crisis—a quarrel between states, with the usual wrangle
about the facts and rights of the situation. The crisis, it was agreed, was

due to aggression or the threat of aggression—by Israel against the Arabs, or by the Arabs against Israel, according to the contending parties and their sympathisers. As the crisis developed, however, it became clear that aggression meant different things to different people, and that more was involved than the mere facts of the case.

For the Arabs, the creation of Israel in an Arab country was an act of aggression; her survival is a continuing act of aggression. Consequently, any action taken by Arabs against Israel is defensive; any attempt by Israel to resist or oppose such action is aggressive.

For Israelis, the overriding fact is the Arab determination to destroy Israel and perhaps also its inhabitants. Israelis know from experience that there are men who can do such things, and others who can watch and acquiesce. In their eyes, therefore, Israeli action, being aimed at survival, is defensive; Arab action, aimed at destruction, is aggressive.

For the Soviet government, the only relevant fact was that Egypt and Syria were in their camp, while Israel was not. Any action by a pro-Soviet government is defensive; any action against a pro-Soviet government is aggressive. The Soviet government did not, in 1948, share the view that the creation of Israel was an act of aggression; on the contrary, they joined with the U.S.A. in bringing it about. They gave immediate recognition to the new state, and allowed Czechoslovakia to sell the arms which saved Israel from immediate destruction by her Arab attackers. Since then the Soviets, no doubt disappointed by the Israeli posture in world affairs and encouraged by Arab responses, have changed their attitude.

In the Western democracies, the term aggression denotes an act of war committed by one nation against another in violation of specific or general obligations under international law, and is defined in accordance with established rules and criteria. But even in the democracies, the Israel-Arab conflict was special; the usual rules and criteria were in effect substantially modified, and a cycle of raiding, sabotage and reprisal, accompanied by other war-like acts, was tacitly accepted as normal. The position seemed to be that routine harassment was tolerable, and became aggression only when it exceeded an ill-defined limit.

For the Russians and Arabs, the crisis began with an Israeli invasion threat against Syria—which the Israelis said was non-existent; for the Israelis, it began with Egyptian troop concentrations in Sinai and the blockade of the Straits of Tiran—which the Egyptians said was lawful. Politicians and historians will argue for a long time to come about what really happened, and about the guilt, complicity, stupidity or innocence of those involved. But as the tension mounted, in late May, the arguments about fact and law became increasingly irrelevant. Whatever the causes, whoever the authors of the crisis, it soon became clear to participants and observers alike that the question at issue was no longer a border or a blockade, but the whole problem of Arab-Israel relations. The Egyptian blockade and the Arab alliance, as President Nasser was at pains to make clear, were steps towards the destruction of Israel, and it was this—destruction or survival—that became the main issue in the confrontation. Some Arab spokesmen made a rather perfunctory distinction between the destruction of Israel and the extermination of the Israelis; others, like Ahmad Shuqayri, made it quite clear that they expected both. Whatever the intentions of the more responsible Arab leaders, even the most committed supporters of the Arabs can have few illusions about what would have happened if the Palestine Liberation Organisation and the Arab armies had entered Israel as conquerors.

Until the outbreak of war and the first news of Israeli victories, there was a real fear that this might happen, and it was this fear that largely determined the response to the crisis of public opinion. There were many people—not all of them Jews—who were resolved at all costs to prevent the destruction of Israel; there were others—not all of them anti-Semites—who were prepared, with greater or lesser regret, to accept it. In countries where opinion could be freely expressed, it was overwhelmingly in favour of Israel's survival; there is some evidence of such feeling even in countries where dictatorial governments, both Communist and Fascist, were pledged to the Arab cause. Especially in Europe, tormented by memories of the Nazis and their many accomplices, the threat of extermination brought a strong reaction in favour of the Jews.

As the magnitude of the Israeli military victory became known, opinion began to change. By demonstrating their proficiency in arms, the Israelis gained new friends in unexpected places. They also lost others. The Jew had defaulted on his stereotype as the frightened victim, to be despised and destroyed or pitied and succoured, according to the inclination of his superiors. Some found this profoundly disturbing. Many more were moved by the real change in the situation. Natural human sympathy for the underdog was transferred from the Jews to the Arabs, and was increased by reports of Arab suffering and humiliation. The Jews needed no compassion, and could be accused of making war to avert a danger which suddenly seemed absurd. As previously the threat of extermination, so now the plight of the refugees evoked pity and anger. The customary supporters of the Arab cause, freed from the taint of condoning genocide, recovered their strength and their voices, and were joined by many others. For a week or two after the end of hostilities, there was a strong reaction in the media against Israel and in favour of the Arabs. Thereafter the alignment of opinion in support of the two opposing parties began to return to its normal pattern.

This pattern shows interesting and curious features, with significant variations of motive and expression on both sides. There are sincere and honest believers in the justice of both the Arab and the Israeli causes, and others whose emotions are more complex.[1] There are some who believe that the creation of

Israel was just and necessary; others that it was a mistake or a crime. Similar disagreements exist concerning a number of the new states that have come into being since the war. In general, even those who opposed the creation of such new states would now concede to them the same legal rights of existence and self-defence as are enjoyed by older states, and would agree that the reversal of past errors would cause even greater suffering and injustice than their acceptance. Some however believe that in the special case of Israel the mistake should be rectified, and the Arabs allowed (and if necessary helped) to do the job—sometimes in the conviction that this is intrinsically desirable, sometimes in the rather messianic hope that with the disappearance of Israel all conflict between the Arabs and the West would cease and an era of idyllic friendship be inaugurated.

European and American attitudes to the dispute are greatly complicated by the fact that one party consists of Jews and the other of Arabs. Both peoples arouse powerful and irrational responses. This can be felt in the note of emotion, even of passion, that affects the public discussion of the problem—a passion that has few parallels in debates on other disputes between foreign nations.

Towards the Jews there are, on the one hand, feelings of pity and guilt, which sometimes find expression in emotional support for Israel; on the other there are feelings of hostility which can lead to equally emotional support for the Arabs. This is particularly true of those for whom anti-Semitism cannot openly be avowed in the circles in which they move or even, it may be, admitted to themselves.[2]

Towards the Arabs, too, there are feelings of guilt, arising from the memory of Suez and earlier imperial adventures, and also of sympathy among those who feel drawn by some personal affinity with Arab ways. These feelings are expressed in support for the Arab cause. Finally, just as anti-Semitism may be disguised as pro-Arab feeling, so too does anti-Arab prejudice find a more acceptable expression as support for Israel.

Powerful ideological, as well as psychological elements are involved. For many outsiders, the decisive factor is the type of régime existing on both sides. Israel is a liberal democracy, with a free press and parliament, an elected government of social democratic complexion, and a vigorous opposition. Egypt is an authoritarian state, with a controlled press, no legal opposition, and an official programme of radical nationalism and revolutionary socialism. Israel has a mixed economy; Egypt's is state-directed and largely nationalised. Both types of régime evoke automatic loyalties and antagonisms, in which political and economic considerations do not always coincide. Thus, Socialists are sharply divided. For some, Nasser's nationalisations atone for his repressions; for others, Israel's freedom atones for her partial capitalism. Support and hostility among the ideologists seem to be determined very largely by the choice of formulae, the outward aspect and external alignment of the régimes in question; they appear to be very little concerned with the real position or well-being of the people who live under these régimes.

More consistent in their responses are the obverse and reverse racialists, two groups who see the problem exclusively as a conflict between races. What matters, for them, is that the Arabs are an Afro-Asian people and Israel a state created by a population whose leadership is predominantly European in origin and attitude. For each of these two groups of racialists, one of the parties to such a dispute, irrespective of the circumstances, is necessarily right, the other necessarily wrong. The two groups are alike in their passion and their fury; they differ only in their choice. They include some grotesque and sometimes pathetic figures—the old-guard anti-Semite who becomes a champion of Israel, because he hates the Arabs even more than the Jews; the Anglo-American liberal, who claims a monopoly of sin for his country as fiercely and as absurdly as his parents claimed a monopoly of virtue; the tortured WASP radical, who sees the Arab-Israel conflict as, ultimately, one between Harlem and the Bronx, and makes a choice determined by his own personal mixture of prejudice and guilt.

Of all forms of partisanship, these are the most irrelevant, the least related to the realities of the Middle East. Both Arabs and Israelis show a very wide diversity of racial types, ranging from Nordic to African; none of the peoples of the Middle East have ever developed the acute consciousness of race and colour that afflicts their neighbours in Europe, Asia, and Africa. The conflict between Jews and Arabs may be seen as political and economic; as national, social, cultural, even religious; it is certainly not racial.

Finally, there are the simple souls for whom any cause licensed by Moscow must be progressive, even an alliance with religious fanatics and chauvinistic nationalists—and those others, equally simple, for whom the whole problem is merely the result of communist plots and subversion.

During the crisis and the war that followed it, there were many who responded predictably to the emotive words—Arab and Jew, imperialism and nationalism, socialism and democracy, Washington and Moscow. But the issues were not clear-cut, the responses were not consistent—and many fervent supporters of one side or the other were startled at the company in which they found themselves. On the continent especially, the Left was torn in two, with the larger group favouring Israel. Revered stalwarts of the leftist cause in Viet Nam, Algeria, and Cuba spoke up for Israel—and were joined by the survivors of *Algérie française*, still thirsty for vengeance against the Arabs. Sartre and Soustelle in a common cause made a strange sight. In England, liberal and socialist supporters of Israel were similarly embarrassed by the company of the friends of Rhodesia and the avengers of Suez. On the other side, left-wing defenders of Arab socialism and Afro-Asian rights were reinforced (to their alarm) by Nazis, Fascists, and professional anti-Semites—including those German veterans who had found a refuge and a new vocation in Cairo. Rumania broke ranks from the Communist bloc and showed sympathy with Israel, while Spain and Greece rallied to the Arab side. It was all very confusing. In Turkey, the two extremist student organisations, normally in conflict, both demonstrated in support of Nasser—the Right for Islam and the Holy War, the Left for socialism and the struggle against reaction.

One group, from whom some guidance might have been expected, in fact gave very little—the Arabists[3] and other scholarly specialists in the Middle East. The commitment of the Arabist to the Arabs is not based on the international or ideological alignment of Arab governments, to be abandoned or reversed when that alignment changes. He is not pro-Arab because the Arabs are pro-Russian or pro-Western or anti-Israel, and then anti-Arab when the Arabs change their minds. Such relationships rest ultimately on contempt or indifference; his rests on respect—the respect of a scholar for the people to whose language, history, and culture he devotes his life. For such a one, as for many Arabs who cannot speak out, the final test of Nasser or any other Arab ruler is not his attitude to Israel and the powers, but his treatment of the Arabs—those under his rule and those of other Arab countries. Arabists may hold various views on the rights and wrongs of the Arab-Israel conflict, and some of them have expressed these views. Many, however, confronted with a choice between condemning the Arabs and defending the régimes which represent them, have preferred to remain silent.

Some of course were silent because they did not have the opportunity to speak. Scholarly caution was of little use to the popular media, and singularly ineffective in debate with committed advocates. In general the editors of newspapers, programmes, and features seem to have preferred vigour to objectivity; the views and predilections of the regular commentators on Middle Eastern affairs were known, and an appropriate choice was easy to make. Some journalists and politicians managed to give a fair presentation and interpretation of the news; others were passionately partisan, and resorted (or submitted) to all the tricks—editorial, stylistic, dramatic, photographic—of propaganda, abandoning not only objectivity but even normal journalistic standards in their zeal to whitewash or blacken those whom they love or hate. At least one newspaper seemed to have become manic-depressive, with pro-Israel and pro-Arab phases on different days or even on different pages. A week after the end of hostilities it was clear to any reader or viewer that while, in certain circumstances, Jews and Arabs might sit down together and talk peace, with the pro-Jews and pro-Arabs there could only be war to the death. Meanwhile, such intemperate outbursts of support became in themselves a political factor, making peace more remote. Both sides, if they are influenced at all, become more obdurate; the one in the belief that help will be forthcoming, the other in the suspicion that counsels of moderation are inspired by ill-will.

Months have passed since the battle, and many of those concerned are having second thoughts. These are not easy, even for the outside observer. The manufacturers and distributors of lies continue their work, undeterred and unhampered by repeated exposure. The presentation even of the most basic facts is distorted by interest and prejudice, ideology and emotion. Yet the effort must be made to penetrate beyond the catchwords and slogans and to see the Middle East, not as a battlefield in an ideological, racial, or great power war, but as it is. Then perhaps men of good will may find it possible to be pro-Israel without being anti-Arab, and to be pro-Arab without endorsing the clowns and tyrants who have degraded and dishonoured a great and gifted people.

Notes

1. The possibility should not be overlooked that some who supported the Arabs or Israel did so because their livelihoods, directly or indirectly, depended on it.

2. The argument that Arabs and pro-Arabs cannot be anti-Semitic because the Arabs themselves are Semites is a mere quibble. Hebrew and Arabic are Semitic languages, but the peoples who speak them cannot be described as Semites in any scientifically meaningful sense.

In any case, the term anti-Semitism was an invention of the anti-Semites, to provide a pseudo-scientific cover for Jew-hating and Jew-baiting, and was never intended to apply to any "Semitic" people besides the Jews. A recent Arab writer on the "Jewish menace" has even argued that anti-Semitism, like Zionism, freemasonry, etc., was a Jewish invention, the purpose of which was to involve other Semitic peoples in the hatred that is rightly directed against the Jews.

It would be palpably unjust to assert that all critics or opponents of Israel are moved by anti-Semitism; it would be equally mistaken to deny that anti-Zionism can on occasion provide a cloak of respectability for a prejudice which, at the present time, is not normally admitted in public by anyone with political ambitions or cultural pretensions.

In Arab countries there is no such restriction, and publishers in Cairo and elsewhere have produced a rich and sometimes vividly illustrated anti-Jewish literature in Arabic. In the absence of indigenous source material, it is based mainly on the classics of European anti-Semitism. One of these, the so-called *Protocols of the Elders of Zion*, was commended by President Nasser himself. (*President Gamal Abdel Nasser's Speeches and Press-Interviews 1958*, Cairo, p. 402.)

3. The term *Arabist* is frequently misused in the popular press to denote an expert or participant in Arab politics, or an advocate of Arab causes. An Arabist may be any of these, but that is not what the word means. "Arabist" is a term of scholarship, and means a specialist in the field of Arabic studies—language, literature, history, civilisation. It is thus equivalent to Germanist, Slavist, Hispanist, and other similar terms. A Hispanist is not an adept at Spanish affairs, a former ambassador in Madrid or Costa Rica, or an admirer of bullfighters and of General Franco. He is a scholar in the field of Spanish language and culture. "Arabist" should be used in the same way.

25

Return to Cairo

&c/&c/&c

1969

The first impression that one gets returning to Egypt after an absence of some time is unmistakably one of greater freedom. In the past, criticism of the régime tended to be furtive, the speaker looking around carefully and making sure who was within earshot before he spoke. Now it is much more open. People tell jokes or make explicit criticisms even of the President at dinner parties and in public places without bothering to look around and see who is there. Only the presence of foreign correspondents seems on occasion to inhibit the expression of unorthodox views. Otherwise criticism is not only more outspoken but is much more violent. Whereas previously it tended to be directed against the régime as such rather than against Nasser in person, it is now both more vicious and more personal in tone. A line which was familiar at an earlier time, as also in other dictatorial régimes past and present—that the leader was good but the men around him evil—is no longer heard. Criticism of Nasser has become much more direct, and reflects even on his personal integrity. He is accused of favouring his family and allowing them to acquire positions of wealth, power, and above all comfort. During the first few weeks of my stay in Egypt I heard only one person speak well of Nasser and of the régime, and he was an Englishman. Egyptians were either silent or hostile.

In view of this overwhelming attitude of dissatisfaction and disapproval, I was puzzled by the dramatic events following Nasser's resignation in June 1967, and the apparently unanimous desire of the Egyptians or at least of the people of Cairo to have him back. I put this question to a number of friends, whose answers fell broadly into two groups. One school of thought was that the whole thing was a pre-arranged comedy, organised by the police or the Arab Socialist

Union—there were various nominees for the role of producer. Another view was expressed by a friend who put it this way: "When we heard the news of his resignation, our immediate reaction was that after having got the country into such a mess, he couldn't just walk out and leave it for someone else to clear up. What the crowds were in effect saying to him was 'You got us into this. Now you get us out of it.' . . ."

The greater degree of outspokenness is, however, misleading and does not really mean any greater freedom. On the contrary, the relaxation of pressure on the population in general is an excellent example of the skill of the régime in political manipulation—perhaps the only political skill which they possess to any degree. While, wisely, they are allowing people to talk more freely, they are allowing them far less scope to do anything about it. The means for the detection and suppression of *organised* opposition are much more effective. It is perhaps more striking and more significant that while there is more freedom in the country as a whole there is far less freedom within the ruling group. Whereas previously there was quite considerable scope for argument and criticism in Nasser's immediate circle, this has now ceased. The President now has his hands directly on the levers of power. Those who disagree with him or oppose his policies in any way, still more those who might conceivably form the nucleus of any kind of opposition group, have been systematically eliminated from positions of authority. They have not as yet been eliminated in any further sense but are still living peacefully in Cairo. They appear, however, to be under strict observation.

In the comparative gentleness with which opponents within the régime are treated, Egypt is still some distance from being a totalitarianism of the Central or East European type. The same kind of gap can be seen as between "Arab socialism" and the East European variety. Under Arab socialism as practised and applied in Egypt, the rich have been deprived of their riches, but apparently not of their ability to accumulate new riches. This has produced some curious results. Many former wealthy families whose wealth was in land or industry, finding themselves deprived of their former assets, have found new ways of using their talents. A number of them have invested what little remained of their money in such enterprises as night-clubs and restaurants, of which a surprising number have been established in Cairo in recent years. These are highly profitable institutions, and have the great merit of not figuring in the national development plans. They are patronised by wealthy Arabs from oil-rich countries such as Libya, Saudi Arabia, and Kuwait, who come with vast sums of money to spend. They are also patronised to some extent by what is left of the Egyptian middle and upper class. Wealth acquired by means of night-clubs and restaurants has several advantages from the point of view of defending oneself against taxation and sequestration—the two principal menaces of the Arab socialist programme.

In fact, those who make money in this and other ways seem to take good care not to accumulate any kind of visible capital, but to spend or remove their profits as quickly and as completely as possible. This means that a considerable amount of money is in very rapid circulation, inducing a rather febrile and specious prosperity in certain circles. It also means of course that nothing is being built up, and that the prospects of the economic future of the country are becoming steadily slimmer.

Many stories are told about the sequestration administration. Their general purport is to it as prejudiced and incompetent. Both charges are, alas, easy to prove. Sequestration orders were for long directed principally against foreign and minority-owned assets. The tripartite aggression in 1956 justified the sequestration of British, French, and Jewish (not Israeli—obviously there were none) assets. Belgian misdeeds in the Congo furnished the occasion for the seizure (as a matter of African solidarity) of Belgian property in Egypt. Land reform required the sequestration of land-holdings above the permitted maximum—and so towards a larger and more general programme of nationalization. Sequestered properties were not, however, simply confiscated. The previous owners retained a form of title, and in some cases received a monthly allowance from the sequestration authorities. Some of them qualified for other benefits. The large-scale dismissals of servants and other employees by suddenly impoverished plutocrats created distress and discontent. The authorities responded by arranging for these servants to stay at their posts, and draw their pay from the sequestration office. The former owners thus kept their servants, but with the uneasy knowledge that these were now paid by and answerable to another authority. In a few cases owners were able to obtain the annulment of the sequestration orders and the return of their property—except that usually there was nothing left to return. This was not due to corruption but to the apparently inevitable inefficiency of such arrangements.

The Crisis of National Identity

Nobody seems to have a good word to say for Arab socialism. Commercial, professional, and middle class elements bring against it the usual complaints which are brought against socialism in Western countries. Left-wingers dismiss Arab socialism with contempt as a half-hearted and inefficient compromise which has the merits neither of socialism nor of capitalism. According to them the only way to solve the economic problems of Egypt is to introduce "real" or "scientific" socialism—*i.e.*, the real thing as practised in Eastern Europe. According to this view Arab socialism is a mere sham—an ideological justification for the confiscation of Egyptian Muslim property when the supply of non-Egyptian and non-Muslim property for confiscation has run out. It has "nothing to do" with socialism in any real sense. The more pessimistic say that Arab socialism means socialism run by Arabs—and whatever kind of socialism they adopt in theory it will be "Arab socialism" when they put it into effect. In this respect Arab socialism will be the same as Arab democracy, Arab liberalism, and Arab capitalism.

I found this kind of rather neurotic self-criticism very frequent. It can be discerned for example in the political joke—that standard expression of dissent in autocracies. But whereas the political joke in Nazi Germany or Soviet Russia tended to be directed against the leader or against the régime, in Egypt it is as often as not directed against the Egyptian nation itself. It is not uncommon to find the expression of extreme nationalist views coupled with an almost nihilistic rejection of the Egyptian nation as incapable of anything at all.

The Egyptian nation? This raises another and interesting question. For a long time now the Egyptians have been suffering from what American psychologists and literary critics call "a crisis of identity." Are they Egyptians or are they Arabs? In the past they were quite happy to be simply Muslims or Copts, without worrying about a national designation. But in the modern world this is no longer adequate. There have been periods when they identified themselves—at least politically—as Egyptians, as inhabitants and citizens of a country called Egypt, which should find its political expression in an Egyptian state. During that period Egyptian intellectuals were inclined to argue that the fact that they spoke Arabic did not make them Arabs, any more than Mexicans were Spaniards or Americans were Englishmen. They expressed attitudes varying from sympathy to contempt for the Arabs of the East, but clearly differentiated themselves from them. They were Egyptians—the proud and legitimate heirs of the ancient glories of Pharaonic Egypt.

At other times they identified themselves as Arabs rather than Egyptians, and found their past heroes in the Arab caliphs rather than in the Egyptian Pharaohs. During the last fifteen years or more, the *Arab* rather than the *Egyptian* line has been dominant. It found its highest expression in the creation (in 1958) of the United Arab Republic after the union with Syria, and in the retention of that title by Egypt alone even after the Syrian secession. During this period even the very name of "Egypt" was wiped off the map. I was told that in elementary schools the history primers dealing with the ancient period spoke not of ancient Egypt but of "the ancient history of the southern region of the United Arab Republic". I do not know whether this is literally true, but it is not untypical of the attitudes that were current at that time. "Egyptianism" as distinct from "Arabism" was regarded as sectional and sectarian or, even worse, as an expression of Coptic influence. This was a damaging accusation.

During the last two years there has been a considerable revival of Egyptian as distinct from Arab identity. The war against Israel, the subsequent defeat, and the invasion by Israel of Egyptian territory helped to concentrate Egyptian feelings rather more powerfully on their own native land. With the enemy on the Canal and within gunshot of the Delta, it was Egypt herself that seemed to be threatened, and there were many Egyptians who began to ask how this came about. Many Egyptians still express loyalty to the Arab ideal and insist on the importance of the Arab world for Egypt—sometimes in political terms, sometimes more nakedly in economic terms (e.g., on the lines that the Arab world forms the natural economic hinterland of the rising Egyptian industry, or that Egypt requires the oil revenues which Arabia gets but does not know how to use). Others have adopted a rather more cynical view of Arab unity. Time and time again I heard people cursing the Syrians—"They got us into this and then they didn't fire a shot." This is perhaps not quite fair as a description of the Syrian role of the events of May and June 1967, but it is not altogether wrong.

One hears the same kind of opinions expressed regarding the Palestinians, who are believed to have got the Egyptians into a mess and done nothing to help themselves. It is curious that the Palestinian Arab guerrilla organisations, whose emergence as a new and powerful factor in Arab and Middle Eastern affairs occupies so much attention in the West, receive far less among Egyptians. During several weeks in Egypt and many conversations with many Egyptians, I only heard the Palestine guerrillas described once as a new and significant factor, and that was by a young man who was educated in England and returns to that country very frequently. I had the distinct impression that he derived his opinions from the B.B.C. and the *Observer* rather than from any local sources.

There had been earlier setbacks to the cause of Arabism in Egypt—such as the brief and ill-fated union with Syria, and the bloody and costly failure in the Yemen. These, however, worked both ways. The union with Syria, while it lasted, showed some of the advantages which such associations could bring to important groups of Egyptians, many of whom held positions of power and profit in the "northern region." Even the war in the Yemen was not without its rewards. Egyptian troops were rotated fairly rapidly, and many found the opportunity in Arabia, in the usual manner of armies abroad, to buy and sell their way to moderate and relative wealth. Many a Cairo taxi-driver acquired his vehicle with money brought back from the Yemen.

The defeat in 1967 was another matter. This time the defeat was immediate and overwhelming. It brought no gains to anyone—and it brought the enemy right into Egypt. In the inevitable search for scapegoats, "Our Arab Brothers," for whom Egypt had made such sacrifices and from whom Egypt had received so little help, were obvious candidates.

"Egyptianism" versus "Arabism"

This discussion of the nature and identity of the country—Egyptian or Arab—is one of the most hotly debated themes at the present time. The Copts, as one might expect, are almost solidly in favour of an Egyptian rather than an Arab identity, and indeed opponents of this point of view tend to dismiss it as a Coptic aberration, feeling that this is in itself sufficient to discredit it. It is, however, by no means limited to Copts. There are many Egyptians who begin to think once again in terms of an Egyptian patriotism rather than a Pan-Arab nationalism and to argue, not without some show of justification, that "Arabism" has brought many troubles and no gains to Egypt.

The Egyptian press remains of course strictly controlled and for the most part state-owned, but a careful reading reveals some of the problems and differences of opinion which agitate people. The question of Egyptian or Arab identity is a good example. The official line is still unremittingly "Arab," and any formal opposition to this would be impossible in the public media. The issue, however, finds expression in indirect form. During a recent conference held under the auspices of the Egyptian government to commemorate the thousandth anniversary of the foundation of the city of Cairo, a Soviet scholar—of all people!—submitted a paper in which he argued that the name "Cairo" is not, as everyone has hitherto thought, of Arab derivation, but goes back to an ancient Egyptian name. This paper was reported at some length in the official daily newspaper *Al-Ahrām*. This was followed by a lively controversy which ran for several weeks and attracted a great deal of attention. Quite obviously the contributors and readers of the newspaper were not working themselves into a passion over so obscure an issue as the etymology of the name "Cairo." What really interested them was the question whether they were Egyptians or Arabs, whether their Egyptian or Arab loyalty was supreme. The dispute on etymology was an argument on this question in disguise. The point was nicely summed up by an Egyptian-minded intellectual.

"I have heard of a woman pretending to be younger than she is," he said, "but not a civilization. Our civilization is 7,000 years old—and we invite the world to celebrate our 1,000th birthday! . . ."

There is one other field in which criticism—social and moral rather than political—appears in print, and that is in fiction. Egyptian novelists and short-story writers—and there are some very good ones working in Egypt today—present, for those who can appreciate it, a vivid picture of the quiet desperation of modern Egyptian life. It is perhaps fortunate that censors rarely understand literature.

Other questions of great public concern can be discerned dimly as through a glass in the arguments and discussions in the Cairo daily newspapers. The different factions do not put forward their views openly, but these can to some extent be detected through the accusations which groups make against one another. From this and other evidence one gathers the impression that there are within the ruling elite three main tendencies at the moment. In the centre there are the Nasserists *tout court*, those who support the President whatever he does, and have no political ideology of any kind other than such support. To the right of these there is the group of those who are alarmed at the too great influence which the Russians are acquiring in the country, and who feel that a more genuinely neutral policy would be desirable. To the extent that these desire to resume some sort of dialogue with the West, they might be described as "pro-Western"—but hardly more than that. On the other side, there are those who believe that Arab Socialism having failed, real or scientific Socialism must be tried. They would wish to collectivise or nationalise the economy of the country as a whole and apply the same sort of methods as have been applied in Eastern Europe. This would, of course, inevitably mean very much closer association with the Soviet Union—a consequence which is accepted with varying degrees of enthusiasm. Members of either one of these groups would have a good chance of seizing power if Nasser should fall.

Apart from these there are also the Muslim Brothers, who are of course not represented in the ruling group at any level, but who have very powerful and widespread support in the country as a whole. Their chances would come only if the régime is completely destroyed—a contingency which seems unlikely at the present time. A man high in the counsels of the Muslim Brothers was quoted to me as saying "I wish that the Israelis would really conquer Cairo—that would make our task much easier." I can see the logic of this rather strange pronouncement.

Attitudes to the nation and to the régime have of course a considerable bearing on the vexed problem of Israel. If the conflict is between a country called Israel and a country called Egypt, then the problem is much nearer to solution. Between Israel as Israel and Egypt as Egypt, there is no really fundamental problem at issue, and it should not be difficult to reach some sort of compromise. I found Egyptians who argued precisely along these lines. Another thing that struck me is that the passion against Israel and against the Jews which one has been led to expect from international press reports is usually lacking, or at least is no greater (and probably less) than before. There is of course a very strong feeling of anxiety at the danger which threatens the very heart of Egypt, and a great feeling of indignation. This indignation is not directed exclusively against the enemy. Often, it is directed against those, in Egypt and elsewhere, who got them into this trouble and who are now preventing them from getting out of it. One of the banners carried by student demonstrators last November read: "FORWARD, MOSHE DAYAN!" This was not of course an expression of pro-Israeli sentiments—though it was used by the prosecutors to support the absurd claim that the demonstrations were instigated by "Israeli agents." The rhetorical point that the student demonstrators were making is one often heard in conversation—that "any change," even an Israeli occupation, would be better than the present régime.

A picture that is often presented abroad is of Nasser as a moderate, holding back—with increasing difficulty—an infuriated Egyptian nation that is hell-bent for war. My own impression is the exact opposite—of a peaceable and weary people lashed and dragged by their leaders. The average Egyptian, young and old, is heartily sick of adventure and war. He asks nothing better than peace, even with Israel, on terms that are reasonable and honourable for Egypt. It is the régime which needs a state of war and a war-psychosis, with an endless series of incidents and crises, in order to maintain its rule over a reluctant country. Nasser himself is too heavily committed to pan-Arabism and the struggle against Israel to make peace even if he wants to—and the appearances are that he doesn't. There is in Egypt a great fear of the unknown, and even Nasser's bitterest critics sometimes express anxiety about what might happen after the fall. Even in France, incomparably more stable and less troubled than Egypt, there were similar misgivings before the departure of de Gaulle. How much more so the Egyptians, with their immense and manifold problems. A state of war increases their anxiety, and reinforces their unwillingness to risk a change. A state of peace would make the retention of Nasser less necessary, and make his rule less bearable.

Nasser himself would prefer a state of war, short of actual war. His problem is to restrain two groups who think otherwise—on the one hand, those who would like to make peace on "Egyptian terms," *i.e.* securing the evacuation of Egyptian territory and leaving the Arabs in the East to arrange their own affairs; on the other, the war party—the soldiers who are determined to wipe out the disgrace to Egyptian arms and honour, and the politicians who are irrevocably committed to "the Arab cause." It is by no means unlikely that a régime might emerge after him, or even a successor in the same régime, which is much more likely, who would be able to take a different point of view. One should not underrate the possibilities of rapid change of mood and direction in Egyptian politics.

The demand for the union of Egypt and the Sudan—the unity of the Nile valley—was one of the basic demands of Egyptian patriots for seventy years. King Farouk actually went so far as to proclaim himself King of Egypt and the Sudan, thus putting himself into a position from which he could not retreat on this subject. Yet the overthrow of the monarchy and the establishment of a new régime freed the Egyptian government from this embarrassing title and claim and made it possible to accept and recognise the independent nation which had meanwhile emerged in the Sudan. The long standing Egyptian demand for the union of Egypt and the Sudan was dropped—and the astonishing thing was that there was practically no objection in Egypt! The Egyptian interest in the Sudan is older and better grounded in reality than the Egyptian interest in Palestine. Although the Palestine issue has been embittered by three wars, it is by no means inconceivable that an Egyptian régime or ruler might emerge which would be prepared to cut its losses in Palestine in the same way as Neguib and Nasser did in the Sudan. In such a case there would no doubt be political opposition in Egypt, but I doubt if it would seriously incommode a determined Egyptian government. The problem of a settlement between Israel and her genuinely Arab neighbours in the East is of course quite another matter and would be very much more difficult—though on the other hand it is not easy to see what they could do once the great prop of the Egyptian support is removed.

Foreign newspapers can be obtained in Cairo—though occasional pages or even whole issues may be missing. They are however difficult and troublesome to get, and while I was there I relied on the local newspapers. These present a somewhat curious view of the world. One recognises the familiar outlines of places and people and events, but they appear in a strange and rather distorted form—with the perspective and realism of a medieval Islamic miniature. They are, so to speak, at some distance from reality and at a slant to it, and include a fair measure of pure fantasy. To begin with, I was able after my arrival to recognise the events and the situations to which newspaper articles and news items referred and to make the necessary adjustments. But after spending a little while in the country, I found my connection with reality slowly slipping. I began to feel myself much more influenced and affected by what I was reading, and unconsciously yielding to the Western-induced habit of believing that what one finds in print in a newspaper must have some sort of foundation of truth. One may doubt, one may feel that there is exaggeration, misrepresentation, or distortion, but one stops short of rejecting the entire story as a fabrication from start to finish. There were several items I accepted as truth because I had read them in the newspapers, and I did not discover until some time later that they were the purest invention.

One of the accusations commonly brought against the régime is that it had encouraged "immorality," or to put it in another way, that its activities have led to a breakdown of the old high Islamic moral standards. As usual, morality means primarily sexual morality, but not exclusively. Standards of honour among craftsmen, workmen, artisans, shopkeepers, etc. were once very high—in spite of the common Western belief to the contrary. They are now declining, to something more closely approximating a tourist or soldier's view of the Egyptians. This is a source of reproach. Even more sensitive is the sexual issue. In the new night-clubs and restaurants a visitor may see an astonishing sight. Young men and young girls sit together, publicly indulging in what the

Americans call "heavy necking." This is not entirely new—what is new is that the girls are no longer professionals of vaguely South East European extraction but young Egyptian Muslim girls of what I might perhaps be excused for calling good families. Such conduct would have been inconceivable up to a few years ago in what, despite all the social and political changes, remained a conservative society in its moral and religious aspects. It is now taking place on a wide scale, and is deeply shocking to those who still believe in the old standards and the old way of life. This may yet prove to be one of the most serious grievances against the régime.

The Minorities

One of the sadder changes that have happened in Egypt is the virtual destruction of the minority communities. It is often said that the Egyptian Jewish community has been a casualty of the Arab-Israel struggle. In a sense this is true—but it is not unlikely that the Egyptian Jewish community would have suffered the same fate even had there been no Arab-Israel struggle. The Jews in Egypt were by no means the only minority. There were also some 70,000 Greeks, 50,000 Italians, and smaller groups of Levantine Christians, Cypriots, Maltese, Armenians and others, many of them established in the country for generations. All these have suffered the same fate. Without actually being driven from the country, they have been induced to leave by the steadily increasing pressure of Egyptian Muslim nationalism, which made it very difficult for members of foreign communities or even minority religious communities to make a livelihood. The Greeks, the Italians and the rest have gone home, and the 65,000 Jews who once lived in Egypt are now reduced to barely 3,000. Theoretically, the Jews, who had been in the country for thousands of years, were an Egyptian religious minority like the Copts, not a foreign minority like the Greeks and Italians. But in fact this distinction was blurred. The poorer Jews were indeed genuinely Egyptian—poor, sick and down-trodden. The upper-class Jews, however, were mainly foreign by origin or adoption, and preserved their foreign language, culture, and citizenship. While the poor Jews spoke Arabic, the rich Jews usually spoke French or Italian, and were in consequence seen as part of the privileged alien domination. When the end came, they shared the fate of other foreigners in Egypt—but worse, because of the conflict with Israel.

Egyptians react rather angrily to any suggestion of "anti-Semitism." Sometimes they produce the rather illiterate argument that they cannot be anti-Semitic because they are themselves Semites. This is, of course, absurd. Egyptians and other Arabs are, however, justified in disclaiming the kind of hostility to the Jews which is to be found in Christendom. This is a Euro-American rather than an Afro-Asian phenomenon, and has no real equivalent in the lands of Islam.

Nevertheless, it is not surprising that the impression of Arab and Egyptian anti-Semitism should have got around. A visit to the bookshops of Cairo, even to the kerb-side kiosks, shows them to be full of the most virulent anti-Semitic literature, much if not most of it translated or adapted from European works. Arabic translations of the famous *"Protocols of the Elders of Zion"* are to be found everywhere, and are quoted and distributed by the government in its various propaganda and information agencies. Hitler's *Mein Kampf*, in Arabic, is another widely distributed classic. There is an enormous literature of books dealing with Zionism and Israel—natural and reasonable enough. Many of them, however, begin and conclude with statements about the wickedness of the Jews as such and the Jewish conspiracy against the human race, for which they rely very heavily on the *"Protocols"* and other European anti-Jewish literature. The choicer specimens include charges that the Jews use Christian and/or Muslim blood for religious ceremonies, were responsible for both World Wars as well as numerous earlier troubles, are trying to dominate the world by secret conspiratorial means, and—a recurring theme—thoroughly deserve the hatred and persecution which they have throughout their history attracted to themselves. This sometimes leads to the exoneration of Hitler and Eichmann, who are presented as martyrs in a worthy cause.

Even serious authors go in for this kind of theory. A well-known professor of political science, in a widely-read book on Zionism, quotes Hitler in support of the authenticity of the *"Protocols,"* which (he argues), is in any case demonstrated by the whole course of modern history; he goes on to argue that the study of what Hitler wrote about "World Zionism" is a vital necessity for the Arabs after what happened in 1948. Another, among many, is a distinguished diplomat, Ahmad Farrag Tayeh, who was Egyptian consul-general in Jerusalem during the final stages of the Palestine mandate, Minister to Jordan in 1951–52, and foreign minister after the revolution. This gentleman wrote an extremely important book describing what he saw in 1947 and 1948. His book begins with an introductory chapter based on the *"Protocols"* and French anti-Semitic tracts, on the Jewish plot to corrupt and rule mankind and their secret domination of the Anglo-Saxon countries. Most other books dealing with Israel, Zionism, or the Jews—and there are literally hundreds of them—bear to a greater or lesser extent in the same direction. Similar views are expressed in newspaper and magazine articles, and in radio and television programmes.

This general impression of "anti-Semitism" which one gathers from literature and journalism is reinforced if one considers some further factors, for example the presence of large numbers of Nazi refugees, many of them now disguised under Arab names. Most of them live in Meadi, once the favourite suburb of British administrators and officials in Egypt. The former English club at Meadi is now largely frequented by Germans of this and other kinds. It is a strange irony.

Yet in spite of this, in spite of the anti-Semitic literature, the Nazi advisers and the destruction of the Jewish community, the observer would be wrong in ascribing racial anti-Semitism to the Egyptians. Foreign visitors, accustomed to the anti-Semitism of Europe and North America, expect to find a physical and personal rejection of Jews. There is none, not even among the authors and translators of anti-Semitic propagandist works. The régime has no doubt tried very hard—but it has failed. From the Egyptians in general, and what is more important from those Jews themselves who still remain in Egypt, I was assured again and again that "there is no real hostility." Action taken against the Jews in Egypt is purely and entirely the work of the régime and does not rest on any real popular feeling. It is astonishing to what extent the flood of hostile propaganda in books, newspapers, magazines, radio and television has failed to penetrate the Egyptian and to affect his basically kindly and tolerant attitude. The Egyptian is capable of violence in moments of passion and anger, but he is at root a humane and easy-going sort of person. It is difficult, for example, to see Egyptians engaging in the kind of blood-bath that has characterised changes of régimes in Iraq in recent years, or enjoying the public hangings which appear to be the most favoured spectacle in that country.

There remains, however, the genuinely difficult situation of the few thousand Jews who are still in Egypt. There is a certain irony, too, in that situation. During the last twenty years or more most of the Jewish community of Egypt have left. Some have settled in Israel, most have gone to Europe and the Americas. Those who have remained are the most authentically Egyptian of all. These are the poor Jews from the old Cairo ghettos, who still wear the *galabiya*, who speak nothing but Arabic, and who cannot conceive of life in any other place. Their life has always been hard and poor—the discrimination now levelled against them by the régime makes only a marginal difference. There have been other troubles in the past, they say, "and God has helped and they have gone"; these, too, will no doubt go in time. During the last two years the authorities have arrested several hundred adult male Jews, for no apparent reason; at least, no charges were ever proffered and no trials ever held. The reason given in statements abroad was that these were defaulters from military service. This is palpably untrue, since Jews are never permitted to serve in the armed forces, let alone be required to do so.

Several hundred Jewish heads of families were detained at the Toura prison near Cairo. After a while arrangements were made to release them in small batches, but this ceased after the death of General Riyad and the wave of indignation that followed it. The remaining prisoners, between 300 and 400 of them, were transferred to another prison near the Barrage, where they are being kept in conditions of great hardship. Those Jews who remain at large do not appear to be subject to any kind of restraint or persecution. They are allowed to follow their professions, and to move freely around the country. They are not, however, allowed to leave.

At the present time it is fashionable in Arab countries—no doubt under Soviet influence—to use "Nazi" as a term of abuse. This has not always been so in the past, and even now many Nasserists make no secret of their wartime sympathies for Nazi Germany. Anwar el-Sadat in his autobiography has spoken of his role in organising a group in Cairo to help German spies. President Nasser himself, in his recent interview (2 March 1969) with the *New York Times*, when asked who was the man who had influenced him most, named General Aziz Ali el-Masri. General Aziz Ali el-Masri was the leader of the group of dissident officers to which Nasser and his friends belonged. He was also strongly pro-German, and in touch with Hitler's command. At one point arrangements were made to send a German plane to fetch him. Fortunately or unfortunately, depending on one's point of view, the plot was discovered in time and the General was arrested. Many others played a similar role and are not averse to talking about it. Generally speaking this pro-Nazism was pro-German and anti-British rather than connected with Jews or Zionism as such. At that time they were concerned with "the freedom of Egypt," and they naïvely believed that this was the way to obtain it. There were some, however, who seem to have gone a little further, and these are occasionally embarrassing to their present-day friends and associates.

Last year the Arab Socialist Union held a meeting in Cairo in order to mobilise international support from Left-wing elements in favour of the Arab cause. Quite a number of Leftists (both new and old) were present, including several Jews. At the final plenary session, to which resolutions were submitted from the various meetings, there was an untoward incident. One of the resolutions proclaimed the support of the meeting for all progressive movements wherever they might be, including Israel. The Syrian representative objected to the last two words "including Israel" on the grounds that since Israel was by definition aggressive, since its very existence constituted an aggression, to talk of progressive elements inside Israel was a contradiction in terms. The Chairman, a self-proclaimed wartime Nazi sympathiser now high in the councils of the Arab Socialist Union, appeared to agree, and summarily deleted the offending words. Among those who tried to raise their voices in protest was a European Jewish Marxist, who had come, so he explained, out of progressive solidarity with the Arab cause, and therefore deplored the spirit behind this change. The Chairman would not allow him to speak, and gave his reasons, with some vigour. He knew, he said, why "this Jew" had come; he knew what "this Jew's" real purpose was, and he would not let "this Jew" have his way. These remarks were of course made in Arabic and it is not known whether they were translated for the benefit of "this Jew" and other Marxist Jewish visitors.

Both Jews and Copts, during the period of Western cultural domination, began to give their sons European first names; Muslims did not. An Egyptian with a given name like "Louis" or "George" might be either a Jew or a Copt. If the latter, he may need from time to time to prove his Coptic identity—usually by producing a certificate from a Coptic priest. This has the advantage of proving that he is not a Jew; it has the corresponding disadvantage of proving that he is not a Muslim.

The position of the Copts continues to be curiously anomalous. The Copts are native and Arabic-speaking. They are undoubtedly the most authentically Egyptian of all the inhabitants of the country. They are Christians—but of an Egyptian national church which existed before the coming of the Arabs or Islam. Of all the inhabitants of Egypt they alone can claim to be the authentic descendants of ancient Egyptians, unmixed with Arab or Turkish or Circassian or Mamluk blood. While remaining Christian they did, however, adopt the Arabic language and to this extent became incorporated in the new identity which Islam imposed on the country. They have been rather luke-warm on the subject of "Arabism," still more so of pan-Arabism. In the old order which was officially based on Islam, the Copts had a recognised and accepted place as a tolerated minority. In the new order based on nationality, they should have been accepted as full equals—but they never really were. Their position was rather weakened during the period of the British occupation, when as Christians they enjoyed a certain favour from the occupying power to whom they were able in various ways to make themselves useful. That no doubt is the reason why anti-British attacks during the occupation and, more recently, during the struggle for the evacuation of the Suez Canal Zone, were not infrequently accompanied by campaigns against the Copts as well. At the present time the régime theoretically maintains the position that the Copts are fellow-citizens and complete equals, but it is not always so in practice. The Copts cannot really complain of any genuine persecution—though this does not stop some of them from doing so. There is, however, a very definite ceiling to their advancement in government service of any kind—and in the socialist society of the present time the term government service embraces an ever wider range of activities. Some Copts complain with equal vigour of what they regard as the neurotic tendency of their co-religionists to see anti-Coptic discrimination where there is none, and to attribute their own personal setbacks to prejudice against the group to which they belong. The real problem is one of insecurity. The Copts, particularly but not only the middle and upper classes and those with any kind of professional ambitions, do not feel at ease in modern Egypt.

This is one of the factors which has led to an entirely new phenomenon in Egyptian life—emigration. For hundreds and indeed thousands of years Egypt has been a country of *immigration* not of emigration. The hospitable land and people of Egypt, the wealth of the Nile valley, have in ancient, medieval and modern times attracted immigrants from many other countries who have come to Egypt, settled there, and contributed to its growth and development.

Egyptians themselves have never shown the slightest inclination to leave their country, even in times of real poverty and distress. Perhaps the most striking change the present régime has introduced in Egypt is in this respect—there is no immigration but, on the contrary, there is now considerable emigration. As a local wit put it, "Nasser began by wiping the name of Egypt off the map—now he is getting rid of the Egyptians too. . . ." Many thousands are already reported to be in Canada, where they have joined the Syrian, Lebanese, and other Christian émigrés from the Arab world. This represents a very significant development, for such a group constitutes a real bridgehead, a sufficient number of brothers, uncles, cousins, etc., to welcome a very much larger number. Egyptians are also going to other countries which are willing to receive them. Copts form a substantial proportion of the emigrants, but by no means the whole. Even Muslim Egyptians are now leaving Egypt and settling in countries overseas. The régime, after some initial reluctance, has apparently decided to allow this emigration. From its point of view it has the merit of siphoning off active and discontented elements who might otherwise cause trouble at home. Also it has, incidentally, the effect of draining away the most active and enterprising and often the best qualified elements in the country. This constitutes a permanent and perhaps irreparable loss. From the official point of view, however, the departure of dissident elements is a gain which far outweighs the loss of qualified elements.

Moscow to Cairo

The Communists are once again very much in evidence in Cairo. At one time they were rather severely repressed and a number of them were sent to a special concentration camp in the desert, where it is understood that they were very badly treated. Later they were released and a curious episode followed. According to the version that was put about, the Egyptian Communist Party had a meeting at which it agreed that in the present state of Egypt's development, a Communist Party was not required. It was accordingly decided that the party should be dissolved and that its members should join the Arab Socialist Union as individuals and work for the accomplishment of socialism in this way. It was noted after this that a number of Communists were appointed to positions of some influence and power, especially in the mass media. They can be heard and read almost daily on radio, TV, and in the main daily and weekly papers. The suspicion is general (and probably justified) that this was part of a deal imposed upon Nasser by his Russian friends—the release of the Communists and their appointment to certain positions, in return for the formal dissolution of the Party and support for the régime.

These Communists are a rather interesting lot. Generally speaking—though there are exceptions, especially in the universities—they are among the most intelligent, educated, and cultivated people that one meets in Egypt. They are also purposeful and determined. Often they are the sons and daughters of the great families in the past, a surprising proportion of them being the offspring of Turco-Circassian Pashas. Many of them were educated in French schools, often mission schools, and in French universities, where they acquired a characteristic French intellectualism and *gauchisme*. At the present time most of those who are still in Egypt seem to be fairly pro-Muscovite; the "Pekingese" have either gone into hiding or into exile. There are also quite a number who remain pro-Communist but with a certain detachment from Moscow (after the events in Czechoslovakia). Egyptian acceptance of the Russian action in Czechoslovakia is by no means as unanimous as one might gather from reading the press and listening to the radio.

Another place where Communist influence can be seen is in the bookshops. The selections of books on current affairs, politics, and history show a much wider range than in the past. A few years ago, one would have found books on Egypt, on Arab affairs, and of course on Israel and the Jews—but very little else. Now there are books on Asia and on Black Africa, on Europe and on Latin America, as well as on a wide variety of political, social, and economic topics. These present, overwhelmingly, the Muscovite line. It is, of course, anti-imperialist, and imperialism is another name for the West. Both the vocabulary and the ideology reveal the source. Books on earlier history show a much wider range of ideological commitments, but the modern world can, it would seem, be seen only from one viewpoint. Only on Israel is there some disagreement in the literature. For one school of thought, the enemy is "world Jewry," which cunningly manipulates American politicians; for another the enemy is "American imperialism," of which Israel is the dupe and puppet.

Another interesting feature of the bookshops is the output of literature on the Crusades—which are now a subject of considerable popular interest. They are also a common theme in journalism and even conversation. The attraction is obvious, and both writers and readers find comfort and encouragement in the story of how the Crusaders came from Europe, established themselves by force and aggression, maintained their states for a while, and were finally driven into the sea. The parallels are, so to speak, interchangeable. The Crusaders were early imperialists; the imperialists are modern Crusaders. The Muslim Holy War was yesterday's nationalist struggle; the nationalist struggle is today's Holy War. The Latin kingdom was a Zionist enclave, and Saladin was the Nasser of his time, who overcame the tripartite aggression of the Third Crusade. The end, it follows, must be the same. A European visitor who pointed out that the end was the Mongol invasions aroused some displeasure.

One of the really striking things that a traveller returning to Egypt after an absence notices is the immense unpopularity of the Russians. The kindest remark I heard about the Russians from anyone was: "We can't do without them—we need them in our present troubles." Even this rather unenthusiastic commendation was rare. Usually what people said about the Russians was very much harsher—though expressed with greater caution and more precaution than criticism of Nasser and his government. People appear to be more afraid of Russian reprisals than of those of their own rulers. Some, such as military officers who had dealings with them, complained of Russian crudity and bullying. Shop-keepers, guides and others complained of their parsimony. In shop after shop, particularly in the quarters dealing with tourist goods, I was told how sad it was that the Americans and British were no longer coming—just a few very rapid French tour parties. "But you have the Russians," I said. This was usually greeted with a storm of abuse. The Russians buy nothing and give nothing. They even get their cigarettes in their own clubs—and they won't, if they are asked, give anyone a cigarette either. The Russians apparently have not yet learnt that one of the ways in which a foreign presence can make itself tolerable is by spending money—preferably not too lavishly, but noticeably—among local shopkeepers. A more serious complaint about the Russians relates to their grow-ing domination. I was, for example, told again and again by various friends that any member of the Soviet Embassy, even the humblest third Secretary, can call President Nasser at any time of the day and night and see him immediately if he wishes. I do not for a moment believe the truth of this story, which is altogether too improbable; but the mere fact that it is related—frequently and by many people—is in itself a political fact. There is a widespread belief that the Russians need Nasser because he keeps them in Egypt, and Nasser needs the Russians because they keep him in power. This belief does not add to the pop-ularity of either Nasser or the Russians.

Of Milk and Beef

Egyptians in conversation tend to make frequent comparisons between the Rus-sians and the Americans, the two great super-powers. They compare the way they behave, their attitudes to Israel and to the Arabs, their cultural, commercial and political methods, their colleges and universities, their ways of dealing with their "clients." The comparisons are by no means always in favour of the Russians, and frequently quite to the contrary. There is a growing tendency, particularly among intellectuals on the one hand and among business people on the other, to recall sadly "the days when Egypt had free and open contact," and exchanges both of goods and ideas, with the West. Russian films are found to be heavy and didactic and quite incredibly boring. Cinemas which show American or West European films are usually crowded; those which show Russian films are almost invariably half-empty. This is a source of quiet satisfaction to many Egyptians and of baffled resentment to Russians. In the same way sophisticated Egyptians, accustomed to the "Western ways," are repelled by the Russian political and even intellectual style, and sigh wistfully for their lost association with the intellectual and cultural life of the Western world.

Another comparison which is frequently made is between the Russians and the British. This is in itself rather sinister, for it means a comparison between the two powers which at one time or another have dominated and occupied Egypt. Egyptians are painfully aware that the British occupation began in circumstances rather similar to those which prevail now. A hundred years ago the master of Egypt was the Khedive Ismail, an ambitious and extravagant ruler who squandered vast sums on useless display at home and fruitless adventures abroad. To pay the cost, he borrowed money in Europe, and tried to curry favour with his creditors. President Nasser is seen as "the Khedive Ismail of the present time."

Where Ismail aped West European liberal democracy, Nasser apes East European socialism—and the one resembles its original about as closely as the other. Where Ismail ran up debts with British and French bankers, Nasser runs up debts in Eastern Europe, and the result could well be the same. Already the Soviet Embassy in Cairo is conducting itself in much the same way as the British Residency in the old days, and the Russian Ambassador is behaving, so I was told, "like a High Commissioner." Egyptians are caustic on the subject of Nasser's speeches about the selfless generosity of the Russians and their unwillingness to ask for anything in return for their aid. "Why should they ask for anything," someone remarked, "when they get all they want without asking?" The Russians have not yet established a real military presence, but they are moving rapidly and dangerously in that direction. Egyptians feel that their independence is now in real danger, that they may be seeing the beginnings of a Russian occupation which will be harsher and, above all, longer than the British one. Several friends in conversation drew attention to the fact that the Russian tendency is not merely to exploit but to "eat" the countries into which their troops and experts move. "We shall share the fate of the Tartars and the Uzbeks" was a dreary comment which I heard more than once.

Egyptians like to quote the story of the Arab general Amr Ibn el-As, who conquered Egypt thirteen centuries ago. He expected the Caliph in Arabia to appoint him governor of the country, but the Caliph only offered him the command of the troops in Egypt, while another man became governor. Amr refused this command, in the memorable phrase: "Why should I hold the cow's horns while someone else milks her?" The British, too, came to Egypt for milk. The Russians, it is feared, may want beef.

26

Middle East at Prayer

ೞ⁄ভ ৩৲৩

1969

There is a well-known story, dating back to the early days of the Arab-Israel conflict, about an American representative at the United Nations who found himself involved in a more than usually acrimonious argument between the spokesmen of the two sides. Forgetting for a moment where he was and to whom he was speaking, he urged the Arabs and Israelis to settle their quarrels like Christians. A less frequently cited addendum explains that this is precisely what they have been doing ever since.

The reader of these two volumes (A. J. Arberry, ed., *Religion in the Middle East: Three Religions in Concord and Conflict*, C.U.P., 2 vols.) on religion in the contemporary Middle East—so rich in conflict, so poor in concord—may be excused for recalling both the anecdote and its sequel. The title is self-defining. Religion, in the Middle East, means Judaism, Christianity and Islam, in historical sequence. The earlier religions of the region have disappeared—though one contributor records that certain theologians feared lest a lecture on Osiris by a Dutch scholar "might conceal missionary tendencies."

The more difficult term "Middle East" is correspondingly defined as the area where the three religions meet. Besides the regions of North Africa and South West Asia to which the term is normally applied, it includes the Christians and Muslims of Ethiopia, India and Pakistan, the Muslims (but not Christians) of East and West Africa, the Jews (but not the Christians or Muslims) of the United States, and the Muslims (but not Christians or Jews) of the Soviet Union and the Balkans. The first volume is devoted to Judaism and Christianity, the second to Islam and a final general section on broad topics, such as doctrine, law, politics and culture, affecting all three religions. Among the chapters in this section, that of M Linant de Bellefonds on law stands out in particular.

There are many ways of writing about religion—the prayer-book, the guide-book or the blue book, the tract, the pamphlet or the homily, the scholarly monograph or the annual report. Most of them are cultivated by one or other of the contributors to these volumes, which in consequence display a striking variation in manner, content and worth. The editing of such co-operative works is always difficult; indeed, by a form of exegesis familiar to all three faiths, one might read a ban on such enterprises into the pentateuchal commandment not to yoke creatures of unequal size and strength.

There is inequality in the treatment accorded to the three religions. Of the four chapters on Judaism, all are by Jews, two of them Rabbis. Of the nine chapters on Christianity, eight are by clerics, one—the most clerical of all—by a Christian layman. Of the nineteen chapters on Islam, only two or three are by Muslims, none of whom are professional men of religion. The remainder are by Western scholars, for whom Islam is an object of study, rather than a source of guidance.

It is perhaps for this reason that, for the Western lay reader at least, the Islamic section is by far the most satisfying, the Jewish section a poor second, and the Christian third. The Islamic section begins with an historical introduction by Dr R. B. Serjeant, which offers new insights to the specialist as well as general guidance for the beginner. This is followed by two series of chapters, the first on the condition of Islam in various regions, the second on Islamic sects and schools. With one grotesque exception, all these chapters are good; several are outstanding.

The chapters on Judaism deal with modern trends in Jewish religious thought, chiefly in Europe and America; with Judaism in modern Israel; and with the Jewish communities in oriental countries. The chapter by Professor H. Z. Hirschberg on the Jews under Muslim rule runs to more than a hundred pages, and covers the whole period from the rise of Islam to the present day. Though perhaps disproportionate, it is one of the most valuable contributions in the book, offering a scholarly and detailed exposition of a subject that has suddenly acquired topical interest. Also valuable is Dr W.H.C. Frend's somewhat shorter introductory survey of Christianity in the Middle East, down to AD 1800.

The chances are that this will become a work of reference, which will be consulted, a few pages at a time, by those who seek information on the state of the Druze, the beliefs of the Ismailis, the hierarchy of the Armenians, and similar topics. The structure of the book encourages such treatment. If so, it will be a pity, for while the factual information is sometimes inaccurate and frequently transitory, there are several major themes—concerning beliefs, institutions and events—that are of more general and permanent interest.

The student of modern theology will probably be disappointed, for Muslims have not yet begun to discuss the death of Allah, and their Jewish and Christian neighbours are similarly unenlightened. In the Middle East religion is a matter of practice more than of belief, and its main demand is for loyalty rather than for orthodoxy. In Israel, it would appear, even the left-wing marxist labour party "accepts God *de facto* but not *de jure*." Law—which for Muslims is a central part of the faith—is of more practical importance than theology, which has limited appeal even for professional theologians.

It is interesting to learn that only three countries in the area have formally outlawed polygamy—Turkey, Tunisia, and Israel. The list is noteworthy. All the rest, including the revolutionary and "progressive" states, have retained legal polygamy, and for the most part have also retained the Islamic rule of law by which a Muslim man may marry a non-Muslim woman, but a non-Muslim man may not in any circumstances marry a Muslim woman. In Israel, we are told, the law forbidding polygamy was challenged in the supreme court by a Muslim citizen, who claimed that it violated freedom of religion. His plea was rejected, on the ground that Islam permits polygamy, but does not require it.

Another important general theme which, though not the subject of separate treatment, emerges from the work as a whole is that of tolerance and intolerance in the three religions. Here the almost unanimous testimony of the contributors leads to the chastening conclusion that modernisation—political, social, ideological—has led to a serious deterioration. In traditional society there were no doubt religious hatreds, especially between different branches of the same religion. It was a Greek monk, not a Muslim or Jew, who wrote after Richard Coeur de Lion's failure to capture Jerusalem in 1191: "It did not please Divine Providence to chase out the dogs from the Holy City in order to put wolves in their place."

The treatment accorded by the dominant religion to Christians and Jews certainly fell a long way short of the inter-faith utopia invented by modern political propagandists, but it was one which enabled them to survive and at times even flourish. To the modern ear, "second-class citizen" sounds like a condemnation—but second-class citizenship effectively maintained is better than first-class citizenship on paper only. During the nineteenth and early twentieth centuries, the new liberalism gave the minorities full legal equality as individuals, in place of their former inferior but protected status as tolerated communities; European economic and political influence sometimes gave Christians even more. In more recent times, the new intolerance has left them rather worse off than before. Constitutional rights, in countries where such concepts have little meaning, have proved a poor substitute for entrenched and recognised privileges.

The liquidation of the Jewish communities in Arab countries since the creation of Israel is well known. Less well known, since it raises no current political issues, is the emigration of Christians. From the chapter on the Orthodox Church, we learn that about 100,000 Orthodox Christians have migrated from Syria to Lebanon in recent years, and tens of thousands from Egypt, where the Orthodox community has been "virtually liquidated." One might add the growing emigration of Copts, especially to Canada and Australia. The chapter on the Roman

Catholic Church speaks of Christian, especially Catholic, emigrants from Egypt and other Muslim countries to Lebanon and North America, and quotes, without entirely approving, the reasons given by those who go: " 'Christians,' they say, 'have no future in a country which is becoming all the time more socialist and totalitarian. . . . To remain is to condemn oneself to death by suffocation. It is better to go in search of a milder climate.' " It is a sad change from the days when the Ottoman Empire was the only state in Europe that offered freedom and safety to Christians and Jews of all sects and churches.

Apart from these larger matters, *Religion in the Middle East* is full of fascinating details and side-lights. In the Yemen, women, not men, wear trousers, and of an effeminate man it is said: "He wears the trousers." A Coptic saint, St Moses the Robber, exemplifies asceticism resulting from a "deep sense of guilt." Arab Protestants are embarrassed by a hymn-book which sings the songs of Zion and blesses the Lord God of Zion. One point—perhaps the only one—which the book proves conclusively is the importance of the diacritical transcription signs used by Arabists and sometimes criticised by others as useless pedantry. A contributor quotes an Arabic book called *Kitâb al-Zîna*, but by an unfortunate misprint the macron in *Zîna* appears over the "a," thus making it a quite different word. In Arabic, written or spoken, the two words are distinct, and could not be confused. In transcription, the misplacement of the macron transforms adornment into fornication.

27

At the United Nations

❧❦❧

A Dangerous Place. By Daniel Patrick Moynihan with Suzanne Weaver. Atlantic-Little, Brown. 297 pp.

For a few months in 1975 and 1976, Daniel Patrick Moynihan was United States Ambassador to the United Nations. His brief tenure, which forms the theme of this book, attracted to the proceedings of the United Nations a degree of attention which they have not often received before or since. At that time, I had as temporary neighbor a distinguished social scientist from the West Indies, and, as a chorus of condemnation began to gather strength and volume, denouncing Ambassador Moyhnihan for what was described as his offensive and insulting demeanor toward Third World countries, my neighbor took a diametrically opposite point of view. Far from being offended by Ambassador Moynihan's remarks, he was delighted with them. "For the first time," he said, "an American politician is treating us as responsible adults." This, he said, made a welcome change from the normal tendency to treat Third World nations and their representatives as neurotic children or, at best, retarded adolescents to be humored and cared for but not taken seriously.

The prevailing attitude was well-illustrated in the affair of the Spanish terrorists to which Moynihan devotes a few pages in this account of his mission. In mid-September 1975, the Spanish government announced that five terrorists convicted of murdering policemen would be executed. This was routinely denounced by the Soviets and their clients, and received with genuine outrage by liberal opinion in Europe and America, which tried to influence the Spanish government with pleas and protests and appeals. An attempt to use this as a

❧ 269

means to maneuver the United States into defending Franco was adroitly foiled by Moynihan, who by joining Franco's accusers was able to score some telling points against them. This was a normal example of the double standard which had been institutionalized at the United Nations—the denunciation and condemnation of offenses against human rights by a right-wing government while offenses by left-wing dictatorships pass unnoticed.

But there is another aspect of the matter besides the double standard between Right and Left. There is also the double standard between black and white. While General Franco was being condemned for his executions, President Amin in Uganda was killing black Ugandans in numbers and by methods which made Francoist Spain look like a family Christmas party. Liberal opinion, however, though outraged by events in Spain, remained unmoved by what was happening in Uganda. There are two possible explanations of this silence. One is that white victims are so much more important than black victims that five Spaniards count for more than thousands of Ugandans. The other is that higher standards of behavior are expected from a European, even a Spanish fascist government, than from an African ruler. Either of these explanations would indicate a profoundly racist attitude.

But in the surrealist politics of the United Nations, none of this mattered. True or false, right or wrong, just or unjust—all such questions were irrelevant to the battle of the blocs. When the organization was founded there were two main groups—the West and the Soviet Union. Given the predominance of the West at that time, special arrangements were made to redress the balance in favor of the Soviet Union, which was allowed two additional votes for two of its component republics, Byelorussia and the Ukraine. These possessed far less independence than the states of, say, Delaware or Rhode Island, but probably not much less than Bulgaria or Czechoslovakia. Since the foundation of the organization, the balance of forces has changed greatly to the advantage of the Soviets. This is due not so much to the increase in the number of Communist states, though here too there has been some erosion, as to the emergence of two new blocs. One of these is the Arab bloc, which has increased its voting strength from the original five to the present twenty-one and, in addition, gained enormous financial resources. Another is the so-called nonaligned bloc consisting predominantly of Third World nations.

Of these four blocs, Western, Soviet, Arab, and nonaligned, only two, the Soviets and the Arabs, have enjoyed any unity of purpose and policy. The West has been deeply divided by rivalries among the states composing it and by irresolution and uncertainty within the leadership of its most important nation, the United States. The Soviet bloc, being centrally directed and commanded, operates like a well-drilled phalanx in all agencies of the United Nations. The Arab bloc, though split by serious conflicts within itself, was until recently completely unanimous in its policy on the struggle against Israel, which for most of the Arab states has constituted the be-all and end-all of their international relations. The nonaligned states have negative rather than positive features in common, and tend to gravitate toward one or another of the most important blocs. The Arab carrot and the Russian stick have proved a powerful combination.

There is in the Euphrates area where Syria and Iraq meet, near the Turkish frontier, a little-known Kurdish sect called the Yazidis, an aberrant offshoot separated from Islam at an early date. They are described by their neighbors as devil worshippers. This is a slander. The Yazidis are in fact dualists, surviving holders of a religious belief, once widespread in the Middle East, that there is not one but two eternal spirits, one of good, the other of evil, contending for the domination of the universe. Since the good spirit is by definition good and will remain so, the Yazidis devote most of their worship to propitiating the spirit of evil. Given their assumptions, this makes good sense. It is, thus, unfair to call their beliefs devil worship; they might more appropriately be described as theological nonalignment.

Similar considerations affect the policies of many countries at the United Nations. To attract or offend the Soviet Union can be dangerous; to differ from the Arabs, costly and perhaps also hazardous. To attack the United States and its policies, on the other hand, brings no penalties. On the contrary, in addition to gratifying the Soviet bloc and its allies, attacking the United States wins acclaim and respect from large segments of American opinion, including many policy-makers and, above all, the media. In these circumstances, the choice is not difficult, and it is not surprising that before very long the United States found itself in a permanent minority, where the best it could hope for was abstentions by its more devoted and loyal friends.

Many observers, and even participants, have come to take this as a normal state of affairs and, when challenged, dismiss what happens at the United Nations as being in any case unimportant and without effect. Many, but not all. In February 1974, Moynihan, at that time American Ambassador in India, delivered an address on the fiftieth anniversary of the death of Woodrow Wilson, an expanded version of which appeared in COMMENTARY in May of the same year ("Was Woodrow Wilson Right?"). In this article, Moyhihan set forth a strategy "for the United States deliberately and consistently to bring its influence to bear on behalf of those regimes which promise the largest degree of personal and national liberty." In the following year, these ideas were modified and developed in a further article, "The United States in Opposition," also published in COMMENTARY, arguing that the United States must recognize that it was now a minority and an opposition, and conduct itself accordingly. The move from apology to opposition, he said, "would be painful to American spokesmen but it could be liberating also. It is past time we cease to apologize for an imperfect democracy. Find its equal. It is time we grew out of our initial—not a little condescending—super-sensitivity about the feelings of new nations. It is time we commenced to treat them as equals, a respect to which they are entitled."

The article attracted considerable attention at the time, not least from Secretary of State Kissinger, who called Moynihan "to say that he had read it through at one sitting and had to tell me straight off that he found it 'staggeringly good.'" Not long after, Moynihan was offered the post of Ambassador to the United Nations and given an opportunity to put his ideas into practice. This book is an account of his mission, written with the wit and fire for which he has been both praised and blamed, and with a devastating frankness in exposing errors and failures, his own not excluded.

Almost from the start he was impeded by strong opposition, more effectively from his own side than from his opponents. Powerful arguments were adduced against the case which he presented—that he was flamboyant, discourteous, self-seeking, needlessly offensive. Even if these accusations were well founded, they would in no sense constitute a reply to the well-reasoned case which Moynihan made in his articles, his speeches, and now in this book. His real offense was that he did not share the fashionable feeling of guilt, with its arrogant assumption of ultimate responsibility for all that goes wrong as well as right, and its patronizing tendency to treat smaller and weaker nations as smaller and weaker beings. A second and almost equally important offense was that he refused to wrap his meaning in layers of verbiage, but insisted on making speeches which were frank, direct, and, greatest crime of all, easily understandable.

It could not last, and after a tenure of only eight months he was placed in a situation where there was nothing for him to do but offer his resignation. This, it would appear, was gratefully accepted.

Nevertheless, those eight months were rich in accomplishment. It is true that in the battlefield of the General Assembly there was a sequence of defeats, notable among them the passage of the famous anti-Zionist resolution and the ignominious withdrawal of the American proposal for a universal amnesty for political prisoners. It is significant, however, that the majorities cast against American proposals, or in favor of anti-American proposals, were during this period, on the whole, smaller, not greater, than had become and has since remained the norm. This would seem to dispose of the accusation that Moynihan by needless aggressiveness antagonized Third World nations which might otherwise have supported the American line. Their anti-colonial fervor against the American presence in Puerto Rico and Saint Thomas as contrasted with their extremely cautious responses to Russo-Cuban activities in Africa or Vietnamese expansion in Indochina would seem to suggest otherwise.

Moynihan's policy, carried through logically, might have injected some reality into the debates of the United Nations and given it a positive role in international politics. But this did not happen. Instead, the corruption of the United Nations has continued and has been greatly worsened by the normalization of falsehood and intimidation, now essential features of the procedures of the United Nations as of the majority of the regimes which constitute its membership.

There was a time when high hopes were placed in the United Nations, which was to succeed where its predecessor, the League of Nations, had failed, and truly become the parliament of mankind. This particular aspiration was impossible from the start and arose from a confusion between diplomatic and parliamentary relationships and processes. The United Nations may be a Reichstag or a Soviet; it can never be a parliament. It might well, however, have served some other useful functions, notably in the cause of peace and human decency. Instead, it has become, in the words of the late Tibor Szamuely, an organization for the conservation of conflict, so that when, after thirty years, a first attempt was made to negotiate an Arab-Israel peace, all parties agreed on one thing if nothing else—that to give their negotiation any chance of success, it must be kept away from the explosive and contaminating influence of the United Nations. It is indeed "a dangerous place," and Senator Moynihan's lively, detailed, and remarkably outspoken account of his own term of service may help to warn us against some of its dangers.

28

The Anti-Zionist Resolution

❦❦❦❦

1976

On November 10, 1975, the General Assembly of the United Nations adopted a Resolution declaring that "Zionism is a form of racism and racial discrimination." Seventy-two votes were recorded in favor of the Resolution, and 35 against. There were 32 abstentions, and three countries—Romania, South Africa and Spain—for different reasons, were recorded as absent.

The Resolution attracted a great deal of attention, and has been much used to attack both Zionism and the United Nations. In the Soviet and Arab camps the Resolution was regarded as constituting formal condemnation, before the tribunal of mankind, of Zionism and of the state which it established. In other quarters it was regarded as evidence of the decline and fall of the United Nations.

The Resolution was not an isolated phenomenon, but part of a continuing process. The campaign to secure a U.N. condemnation of Zionism[1] was launched at the World Conference of the International Women's Year held in Mexico City in late June and early July 1975; the "Declaration on the Equality of Women" issued on that occasion repeatedly stresses the share of women in the struggle against neocolonialism, foreign occupation, Zionism, racism, racial discrimination and apartheid.[2] On October 17 the Third Committee of the General Assembly—concerned with social, humanitarian and cultural affairs—agreed by a substantial majority that Zionism was a form of racism and called upon the General Assembly to do likewise. This was duly done, and the Resolution made the basis for a series of further condemnations in different agencies and at various meetings of the United Nations, most recently at the Habitat conference in Canada.

II

An inquiry into the Resolution, its genesis and its consequences, might begin with the double question: How much truth is there in the charge that Zionism is a form of racism? How much truth is there in the countercharge leveled by some Zionists and some of their friends that the Resolution is a thinly disguised form of anti-Semitism and is itself a return to the racial politics of Nazi Germany and its allies in the 1930s?

Zionism is basically not a racial movement but a form of nationalism or, to use the current nomenclature, a national liberation movement. Like other such movements, it combines various currents, some springing from tradition and necessity, others carried on the winds of international change and fashion. Most important among the former is the Jewish religion itself, with its recurring stress on Zion, Jerusalem and the Holy Land, and with the interwoven and recurring themes of bondage and liberation, of exile and return. The messianism and movements of religious revival which arose among Jews from the seventeenth century also made an important contribution to the genesis of this movement. The persecutions to which Jews were subject, especially in Central and Eastern Europe, gave an enormous impetus to its development.

In its political form, Zionism is quite clearly a nationalist movement of the type which was common in parts of Europe in the nineteenth century and which spread to much of Asia and Africa in the twentieth century. It is no more racial and no more discriminatory than other movements of this type—indeed less than most, since it is based on an entity defined primarily in religious rather than ethnic terms. The definition of a Jew according to rabbinical law is one who is born of a Jewish mother irrespective of the religious or racial origin of the father, or one who is duly converted to Judaism. This is not a racial definition; for the racist, fathers are at least as relevant as mothers, and identity cannot be changed at will. Zionism has always accepted this definition of the Jew, and the laws of the modern state of Israel recognize a convert to Judaism as a Jew and a convert from Judaism as a non-Jew. Zionism is certainly a form of nationalism, and the state of Israel may therefore practice some forms of discrimination, but these are not racial, insofar as this word retains any precise meaning at the present time.

The contrary accusation, that anti-Zionism is a form of anti-Judaism, is also false. Zionism is a political ideology, which Jews and others may accept or reject at will. There are good and faithful Jews who are non-Zionists or even anti-Zionists, and an anti-Zionist posture does not *necessarily* mean that its holder is an anti-Semite.

In any case, the Jews are not a race as that word is used at the present time. It was only in the pseudoscience of the Nazis and those who were duped by them that the Jews were regarded as such. Zionism is concerned with the claims of what it asserts to be a nation, and has both the merits and the defects common to nationalist movements. If Zionism is racist, then so too are the various nationalisms of Asia, Africa and elsewhere.

In examining any accusation, the question may be asked whether the accusers come with clean hands. Are they themselves racists? Do they themselves practice racial or other discrimination? And are they honest in their claim that their hostility is political, against Zionism, and not ethnic or religious, against Jews?

Some form of discrimination against groups other than the dominant group—whether defined by religion, race, culture, language, social origin or sex—exists in virtually every member-state of the United Nations, in some more actively and perniciously than in others. The inquiring reader may find it instructive to look through the lists of supporters, opponents, and abstainers with this in mind. The Arab countries of the Middle East are on the whole not racist, though other forms of discrimination flourish there no less than elsewhere. One may be less sure of the attitudes and policies of the Soviet Union and its satellites.

The claim put forward that the non-communist accusers attack Zionism but have reverence for Judaism as a divine religion is open to doubt. There is a vast literature of denigration and denunciation of the Jews published in Arabic, ranging over the whole of Jewish history from remote antiquity to the present day and including all kinds of accusations culled, in the main, from European anti-Semitic literature. Paradoxically, Arab authors appear to show more respect for Israel and Zionism than for Jewish religion and history. Discussions of the former are occasionally serious and factual; on the latter they rarely rise above the level of uninformed polemic and abuse, drawn partly from local stereotypes but relying very largely on such typical products of Christian anti-Semitism as the Protocols of the Elders of Zion. This well-known anti-Semitic fabrication now has more editions in Arabic than in any other language. It is universally cited in Arabic literature on Jewish matters, has been endorsed by heads of state and other prominent personages, and is taught as a basic Jewish text in some Arab university courses in comparative religion.[3] . . . More practical attitudes are illustrated by the fate of the Jewish communities in Arab countries, and by such noteworthy cases as the refusal by Saudi Arabia a few years ago to grant an *agrément* to a distinguished British diplomat, appointed as Ambassador, when it became known that he was of Jewish origin.

III

Who were the sponsors of the Resolution and what were their aims? In part, the Resolution was a stepping stone for the Arab states toward their next objective, Israel's expulsion from the United Nations. No doubt they will return to this goal; meanwhile the Resolution serves a useful propaganda purpose. In part it was probably intended as a maneuver against Egypt—to embarrass the Egyptian government by forcing it to join in this exercise and to sabotage independent Egyptian moves toward peace. In this, the sponsors of the Resolution achieved some initial success, notably when President Sadat was provoked into making remarks about Jewish predominance in the Egyptian economy which were reminiscent of banal street-corner anti-Semitism. The unwonted clumsiness with which President Sadat handled this matter suggests that, for the Egyptians at least, it came as something of a surprise.

In part again it was an attempt, by no means without effect, to win wider support for the Arab view of Zionism. It had little success with the liberal and open societies of Northern and Western Europe and North America which lined up with impressive unanimity (this time including even France) in rejecting it. It was more successful with the countries of the Third World, for whom the issue is abstract and remote, and who have little knowledge of Jews or of Zionism. They are, however, much concerned with racism and with the particular manifestation of it in Southern Africa, and the Resolution was, among other things, designed as a bid for their support.

The co-sponsors of the Resolution were the Arabs and the Russians, and their attitudes to the problems of both Zionism and racism are significantly different, not only from each other but also from the Afro-Asian and other countries whom they persuaded to join them.

For the Arabs, the conflict over the Palestine question long antedates any interest on their part in Zionism. Indeed, the quite extensive literature produced in Arabic from the late nineteenth century until the period following the Second World War shows a remarkable lack of concern with Zionist theory and doctrine. On the whole, the Arabs saw the conflict—rightly one may say—as one between two groups of people both desiring the same territory. Such abstract questions as the varying nationalist theories of the one side or the other were of limited interest, and the Arabic literature on Zionism until after the Second World War is meager and very largely derivative. In the main it seems to rely either on accounts written by Zionists themselves, some of which were translated or adapted from English into Arabic, or, increasingly from the mid-1930s, on accounts of Fascist or Nazi provenance, depicting Zionism as a dangerous form of left-wing radicalism. At that time, anti-Zionist propaganda described Zionism as a revolutionary and pro-Bolshevik or socialistic movement which was introducing radical social ideas and practices into the Middle East and should therefore be opposed. This was the main burden of propaganda for a long time, and was used even by Nasser in his early years, until his change of ideology and alignment made "radical" and "socialistic" compliments instead of insults, and therefore no longer appropriate labels for Zionism. The late King Faisal preferred the old line to the new one and went on using it until his death. Others were more sophisticated, and from the 1960s, Arab attacks on the Zionist enterprise and on Zionist theory began to make extensive use of such terms as *racist*, and to seek resemblances between Israel and South Africa, and, even more remarkably, between Zionists and Nazis.[4]

The German Nazis were of course the arch racists of our time, and it is instructive to review the evolution of Arab attitudes toward them. During the lifetime of the Third Reich and for some time after, the word *Nazi* in the Arab world was in general not an insult, and an association with Hitler and his regime was a matter of pride rather than of shame. Many of the leaders of Arab nationalism, including some in power at the present time, were closely associated with the Nazis, and speak proudly of their efforts in memoirs and elsewhere. In the early years of the Nasser regime, Egypt came to share with some Latin American countries the dubious honor of being a haven for Nazi and other Axis war criminals, and the influence of Nazi experts could be seen in the techniques of both repression and propaganda. Some Arab authors, even including leftists, found it hard to condemn the Nazi crimes against the Jews, and felt impelled to justify, extenuate, diminish, or even deny them.

Only with the rise of Soviet influence in the Arab countries from the mid-1950s onward did this begin to change. Nazi appears to have been used for the first time as a term of abuse in the Arabic political vocabulary by Qasim of Iraq criticizing Nasser of Egypt, and this use of the term, at the time, was a danger signal of the growth of Soviet influence in Baghdad. Times have changed, and the term *Nazi* is now generally used as a synonym for the commoner term *Fascist* to denote reactionary movements condemned by the current radical regimes. The racial aspect of Nazism was less important in Arab political discussion. In modern times, race has on the whole not been an issue in Arab politics, and even such major conflicts as those between Arabs and Kurds, Arabs and Persians, and above all Arabs and Jews have not been seen in racial terms. Thus, the preamble to the Syrian Constitution of 1969, amended in 1971, lists the enemies against which the Arab masses are struggling as "colonialism, Zionism and exploitation"—not racism. But the new theme has been slowly emerging. In Article 19 of the Palestine National Covenant of 1964,[5] *racist* is added to the list of pejorative adjectives applied to Zionism, while in 1965 a publication of the PLO, significantly in English, classifies Zionism as a form of racism.[6] Before long, Jewish racism was traced back to antiquity, and its sources found in the Bible and the Talmud. The reasons for this change are obvious enough. For one thing, racism can be identified with imperialism, with alien domination. For another, the fashionable enemy in the West in our day is the racist, just as a few years back he was the communist.

But what does the word *racist* actually mean? It is a fairly recent innovation in American English, and even more so in British English. Both this word, and the earlier British term *racialist*, were at first principally applied to the doctrines of the Nazis, including their precursors and their disciples; the Nazis used the words *racist* and *racism* of themselves and their beliefs, and thus brought them into general circulation.

But all that is past and, except among the surviving victims and some readers of history, forgotten. For a long time now the word has been used and understood mainly in its American adaptation—i.e., as referring to the relations between whites and non-whites. By choosing the racist as enemy and defining him in these terms, the international community, in this as in so many other respects, is taking its cue from the United States—the most important open society in existence, the forum where the issues in the world's debates are formulated and argued, the theater where the U.N. General Assembly enacts its dramas. If, as is not impossible, the racist is at some future time replaced by some other fashionable enemy, then no doubt the denunciation of Zionism will be adjusted accordingly. For the moment, however, the racist retains his primacy as enemy number one, and is commonly defined in terms of color; this accords well with the experience of many Asian and African countries—of white supremacy and imperial domination—and is so understood in most parts of the world.

In most, but not all. In Israel, color was never much of an issue, and the problem of race, as understood in America and Africa is irrelevant and meaningless. Among a people whose dominant memory is of the Holocaust, racism still connotes Nazism and anti-Semitism, and the accusation was thus received with a special kind of outrage.

IV

But it is not only for Israelis that the word *racist* still evokes the Nazi meaning, with all its appalling associations. The Russians, too, use it largely in that sense. In Eastern Europe, in general, the problem of color is of minor importance, the colonial experience is of an entirely different character, and the memory of the Nazis and their enormities is still vivid. This memory, and the fear and revulsion it arouses, has been much used in Russia, where the word *racist* has undergone another process of semantic development, related on the one hand to the Nazi past, and on the other to the internal problems of the Soviet Union. Specifically, in the technical vocabulary of Soviet vituperation, the term *racist* is applied to nationalist movements linking the non-Slavic peoples of the Union with their kin elsewhere.

In Soviet Russia only Soviet patriotism is approved and this, in fact, though not in theory, now embraces Great Russian nationalism. The nationalisms of other peoples within the Union are suspect and are variously described by such epithets as feudal, bourgeois, reactionary and clericalist. The term *racist* is used more particularly of those movements which have an actual or potential focus outside the Soviet Union. Many of the peoples in the Asian Republics of the U.S.S.R. speak a Turkish or an Iranian language, and pan-Turkism and pan-Iranism—linking divided peoples and, potentially, looking toward Ankara and Tehran—thus represent a danger to Soviet unity. Condemnation of these movements, and of pan-Islamism as well, is therefore fierce and unremitting, and is a feature of Soviet polemic literature, both political and academic. The charge of racism is often brought against such movements, and its extension to

Zionism—a kind of pan-Judaism, with a focus in Israel—is a development of its use against pan-Turkism and pan-Iranism. The offense is the same: a group or groups of Soviet subjects identify themselves with others of the same religion, culture or origin outside the Soviet Union, and therefore constitute a possibly disruptive element.[7]

A new major Soviet attack on pan-Turkism, pan-Iranism and pan-Islamism was launched in the years following World War II. Charges of racism figured prominently in the campaign and were given some color of plausibility by the collaboration of elements among the peoples concerned with the German invaders. (The collaboration of large numbers of Russians and other Slavs gave rise to no such inferences.) By labeling even cultural movements among the subject peoples as "racist," the Soviets sought to link them with the Nazis, and thus hold them up to universal execration.

The Jews, as so often, are a special case. Unlike the Uzbeks, Tajiks, and other "nationalities," they have no regional homeland within the U.S.S.R.; Soviet attempts to create a Jewish district in Birobidjan, in the Far East, have so far been desultory and ineffective. Neither have the Jews, to any extent, retained a separate and distinctive culture; Soviet restrictions on religious practice and on Jewish cultural activity have seen to that. Instead, Jews in Russia, as in the West, are increasingly becoming an assimilated minority, indistinguishable in language and culture from those among whom they live. There is however one significant difference from the West. We speak of American Jews, French Jews, Dutch Jews, and by extension of Russian Jews—but in the Soviet context this expression is a contradiction in terms. One is either a Russian or a Jew, but one cannot be both, since "Russian" and "Jew" in Soviet law are both "nationalities" (*natsionalnost*), within the common Soviet citizenship, and are, therefore mutually exclusive categories. The Soviets do not recognize religion as a form of identity, but maintain Jewish separateness through the principle of a Jewish *natsionalnost*. The word *Jew* is inscribed on every Soviet Jew's identity documents, and in many ways affects the treatment he receives. The Jew, like the Uzbek or the Armenian, belongs in Soviet law to a national minority; unlike them, he has no territorial base or political institutions, and little opportunity to develop and express a distinctive cultural identity. Soviet practice allows him neither to remain a Jew nor to become a Russian, and thus places him in an agonizing dilemma, which is worsened by widespread and deep-rooted hostility. Emigration, when permitted, is one answer. Zionism, which in a sense arose as a Jewish response to this kind of situation, has been outlawed in the U.S.S.R. almost from the beginning, and subjected to both repression and propaganda attacks. In recent years these have assumed a familiar demonological aspect, and the Zionist has become the root of all evil, both at home and abroad.

The charge of Nazi collaboration was not of course brought against the Jews or the Zionists in the years 1939–40, the period between the Soviet-German pact and the German invasion of Russia. Even during the war, the Soviets seem to have made considerable efforts to blur the fact that the Nazis persecuted Jews. To stress it could have had untoward effects—either by arousing sympathy for the Nazis, or by arousing sympathy for the Jews, both undesirable in Soviet eyes.

Until the Israeli victory of 1967, however, the problem of Zionism in the U.S.S.R. was manageable, and individual suppression sufficed. The Israeli victory in the Six-Day War generated enormous enthusiasm among Soviet Jews and a certain amount of sympathy even among Soviet non-Jews; for the first time, Zionism was seen as a serious problem, comparable with other nationalist movements which had plagued the colonial administrators of Tsarist Russia and their Soviet successors. The results were immediately visible in a vehement campaign of abuse, particularly in the attempt to equate the Israelis with the Nazis as aggressors, invaders, occupiers, racists, oppressors and murderers. Some of the literature produced at the time in the Soviet Union and its satellites was anti-Semitic and not merely anti-Zionist, sometimes even resorting to such classical themes as the world Jewish conspiracy and the use of Gentile blood for religious purposes.[8]

Some Jews, alarmed by such propaganda and its effects on Jews in communist countries, have seen in the Soviet Union a new danger to Jews and Judaism comparable with that of Nazi Germany. Certainly there are resemblances—in the totalitarian character of the two societies, and in the ruthless use of chauvinism and prejudice where appropriate and helpful to the purposes of the state. A further resemblance is that the Russian Communists have learned the value of anti-Jewish propaganda as a divisive force among their foreign clients or adversaries. The Nazis, by fostering anti-Semitic feeling in the West, tried to weaken and divide their opponents, sometimes achieving a measure of success that helped their conquests in Europe; the Russians are playing intensively on the anti-Zionist theme, and trying to persuade the non-Jewish majorities in both East European and Western countries that resistance to Soviet demands means pandering to Zionist (i.e., Jewish) interests, and that their Jewish compatriots are disaffected and dangerous. "Zionist" conspirators were blamed for dissident trends in Poland, Czechoslovakia, and other Soviet allies, and great stress was laid on the Jewish background, sometimes real and sometimes invented, of some of the protagonists. A favorite theme is the presumed disloyalty of Western Jews. Thus, even Mr. Kissinger has been called a "Zionist agent,"[9] and Jewish members of the U.S. Congress are alleged to place loyalty to Tel Aviv above loyalty to their country. (The loyalty of American citizens is of course a prime concern of the Soviet government.)

There is another respect in which the Anti-Zionist Resolution may be important, especially for the Soviets. In bygone days Jews were persecuted on religious grounds. In the twentieth century, religious oppression was no longer acceptable or even believable; when the Nazis sought to eliminate Jews from German life, they did not appeal to outdated religious doctrines and prejudices, but instead took their stand on the "scientific" grounds of race. Jews were different and had to be dealt with, not because they followed a false doctrine but because they belonged to an alien and inferior race. Today, a new rationale is needed, to replace race as race replaced religion—and Zionism provides the answer. In the Soviet Union, where religion and race are both equally taboo in official doctrine, only ideology provides a possible basis in law and public statement for separation, discrimination and repression. Zionism is therefore condemned as an ideological transgression, and those who support it or can be alleged to support it (this last is an important point) may be punished without any danger of a charge of religious or racial discrimination or prejudice. The case is strengthened if it can be shown that this transgression has been condemned by the "forum of mankind," the General Assembly of the United Nations. The speed with which the passage of the Resolution was announced by the Soviet information media, in contrast to their usual slowness, is instructive. Anti-Zionism thus serves a double purpose for the Soviet Union. At home it provides the necessary ideological instrument for the containment of what is seen as a danger to the political loyalties of an important group of Soviet subjects and a potentially disruptive force extending to other national liberation movements among the subject peoples of the Soviet Union and of the larger Soviet Empire. Abroad it helps to create suspicion and disunity and thus weaken resistance to Soviet purposes.

It has been said before that anti-Zionism is not the same as anti-Semitism and that many anti-Zionists hold such views with the best intentions unrelated to any form of prejudice. The disagreeable fact remains that anti-Zionism is very often a cloak for vulgar anti-Semitism, for which it provides possibilities of expression and action previously lacking. Particularly in the English-speaking world, anti-Semitism has never acquired the degree of intellectual or political respectability which, at various times, it achieved in Germany and, to a lesser extent, in France, and no one with political ambitions or intellectual pretensions can openly avow it. It is an ironic achievement of Zionism to have lent it a veil of respectability.

V

The coalition that passed the anti-Zionist Resolution was made up of disparate elements: the innocent majority, beguiled by semantic sleight of hand and irrelevant slogans and diverted from their own needs and interests; the trimmers, daunted by the power or tempted by the wealth of one or other of the sponsors, offering private apologies for their public actions; the Arabs and their associates, obsessed with one danger, oblivious of others; the Russians, as always carefully pursuing their special purposes, and convoking the grand alliance of all who oppose the West, its institutions, its way of life, its friends.

Between the Arab and Russian co-sponsors of the Resolution there is some convergence, but greater divergence of purpose. For the Arabs, the aim is to delegitimize the state of Israel. The condemnation of its ideological basis, for whatever reason, is an important step toward that end and, together with excluding Israel from UNESCO, the ILO, and other U.N. bodies, forms a kind of incantatory prefigurement of the expulsion of Israel from the United Nations and the ultimate dismantling of the "Zionist state." For the Russians, the purpose is to delegitimize, not just the state of Israel, but the Jewish people, or at least Jewish peoplehood, and to obtain for their actions toward this end a seal of international approval. It is a somber prospect.

All this has nothing whatever to do with the rights and wrongs of the Arab-Israel conflict which, despite its bitterness and complexity, is basically not a racial one. It is no service to the cause of peace or of either protagonist to inject the poison of race into the conflict now.

Notes

1. A General Assembly Resolution of December 14, 1973, condemning, *inter alia*, "the unholy alliance between South African racism and Zionism" had no immediate effect.

2. It is striking that while the Declaration condemns Zionism four times, it calls just once for the elimination of "rape, prostitution, physical assault . . . child marriage, forced marriage or marriage as a commercial transaction," and makes no reference to polygamy or concubinage.

3. A Marxist author (Jalāl Sādiq al-ʿAzm, *Al-Naqd al-Dhātī baʿd al-hazīma*, Beirut, 1972, pp. 53 ff.) pours ridicule on personal and conspiratorial explanations of history, such as those relying on the Protocols, but without in any way indicating they are a fabrication. On the Protocols and other anti-Semitic literature in Arabic, see Y. Harkabi, *Arab Attitudes to Israel*, trans. Misha Louvish, Jerusalem: Israel Universities Press, 1972, especially pp. 229 ff.; Norman A. Stillman, "New Attitudes toward the Jew in the Arab World," in *Jewish Social Studies, 37,* 3–4: 197–204 (1975); X, "The 'Protocols' among Arabs," in *Patterns of Prejudice, 9,* 4:17–19 (1975). In 1969 a UNESCO expert commission with American, French and Turkish members reported on its investigation of an Israeli complaint about anti-Semitic material in Arabic school textbooks used in UNRWA camps. Out of 127 books examined for this purpose, the commission recommended that 48 be retained, 65 modified before further use, and 14 withdrawn entirely.

4. A macabre example is the claim sometimes put forward by PLO spokesmen that while the Israelis are the heirs of Hitler, they themselves are the heirs of the heroes of the Warsaw ghetto. Who, one wonders, are the heirs of Hitler's faithful coadjutor, the former Mufti of Jerusalem, Hāj Amīn al-Husaynī?

5. Article 22 of the amended version adopted in 1968.

6. Hasan Saʿab, *Zionism and Racism*, Palestine Essays No. 2, Research Centre, PLO, Beirut, December 1965.

7. See Vincent Monteil, "Essai sur l'Islam en U.R.S.S." in *Revue des Études Islamiques*, pp. 107–25 (1952); Alexandre A. Bennigsen, "The Crisis of the Turkic National Epics 1951–1952: Local Nationalism or Internationalism?" in *Canadian Slavonic Papers, 17,* 2–3: 453–74 (1975).

8. See William Korey, *The Soviet Cage: Anti-Semitism in Russia*, New York: The Viking Press, 1973; Baruch A. Hazan, *Soviet Propaganda, a Case Study of the Middle East Conflict*, Jerusalem: Keter Publishing House, 1976.

9. Hazan, *op. cit.*, p. 186.

29

Right and Left in Lebanon

⚜

1977

I t is a fact well known to all students of the press that the recent civil war in Lebanon was basically a conflict between right and left and, furthermore, that in Lebanon as everywhere else in the world, the right represented the wealthy who wished to preserve the existing order while the left represented the poor who wished to change it. Some of the more intellectually ambitious newspapers sometimes spoke of "Christian rightists" and "Muslim leftists," indicating that there might be some connection between Christendom and the right on the one hand and Islam and the left on the other. But this was easily explained by the equally well-known fact that Christians were rich and Muslims were poor and that consequently Muslim hostility to Christians—like all authentic hostility— was socioeconomic in origin.

Occasionally, some small news item might appear to throw doubt on the validity of this picture—for example a report that at the height of the conflict muezzins called from the minarets of Beirut summoning the faithful to battle for the leftist cause; or, more recently, a report that followers of the leftist leader Kemal Jumblatt had avenged his death by murdering between 100 and 200 Christian villagers. If newspaper readers also had been able to follow the Arabic press, they might have found some other discrepant details, such as an interview granted by Jumblatt to the Lebanese newspaper *Al-Bayrak* in which he spoke warmly of Hitler ("At least he would have saved us from the Zionists") and of Nazism ("We must not take a strong stand against Nazism, just as we must not agree with everything the leftists say—Nazism should be revived somewhat").

But such information remains mostly unknown to the Western reader, while the few disturbing details that manage to seep through are easily cast aside. For some time now, Westerners, with few exceptions, have ceased to give religion a central place among their concerns, and therefore have been unwilling to concede that anyone else could do so. For the progressive modern mind, it is simply not admissible that people would fight and die over mere differences of religion. The very suggestion, particularly when speaking of Asians and Africans, is seen as an affront by liberal opinion. Even in their present mood of self-flagellation Westerners still tend to make themselves the model and pattern of mankind, and feel that it is an intolerable insult to suggest that other people, in other places, may have standards and loyalties different from their own.

These attitudes help to explain the common failure of journalism, scholarship, diplomacy, perhaps even intelligence, to perceive and describe the power of religious and communal loyalty in the affairs of the Middle East; instead, they resort to the language of right wing and left wing, progressive and reactionary, and the rest of our parochial Western vocabulary, the use of which in explaining Middle Eastern movements and events is about as enlightening as would be an account of an American presidential election in terms of tribes and sects.

"Render unto Caesar the things which are Caesar's; and unto God the things which are God's." This distinction, which forms a recurring theme throughout the history of Christendom, is foreign to Islam. Christianity, in its early formative years, was distant from and indeed persecuted by the state, with which it did not become involved until after it had created its own separate institution, the Church. Islam, from the lifetime of its founder, *was* the state, and moreover one favored with success and victory. The linkage of religion and power, community and polity, thus was established for its people by revelation and confirmed by history.

One result is that for Muslims religion is not, as for Christians, concerned with one part of life, leaving the rest to the State; it is concerned with the whole of life. And its ruling institution is Church and State in one. It was comparatively recently, under Christian influence, that the concept of a separation between lay and ecclesiastical, secular and religious, in other words between Church and State, began to appear, and terms were coined to express this dichotomy.

A second result is that religion—rather than country, language, descent or nationality—has been the primary basis and focus of identity and loyalty, that which distinguishes those who belong to the group and marks them off from others outside the group. The imported Western idea of ethnic and territorial nationhood has had an extraordinary impact; but it remains, like secularism, alien in origin and imperfectly assimilated.

During the early decades of this century [the twentieth], when the influence of the liberal democracies of Western Europe was paramount in the world, and when political life in Middle Eastern countries was dominated by a small, privileged, Western-educated elite, the idea of a multi-denominational nation-state with a secular, liberal democratic regime enjoyed wide support. The rise of new and more radical ideologies in recent years, together with the emergence of new and more authentically indigenous movements, has, paradoxically often brought a return to much more traditional forms of loyalty.

Lebanon is a classical example of Middle Eastern identity problems. Lebanon is more than just another Middle Eastern state. Among the numerous new states that were fashioned out of the debris of the Ottoman Empire in Asia at the end of the First World War, it was the only one with a real and deeply rooted historic identity. Most of the others were artificially constituted and arbitrarily defined; they were given new names, exhumed and reconditioned either from classical antiquity, like Syria and Palestine, or from medieval Islam, like Iraq. These names had not been used for centuries in the area and at that time had no real roots in the consciousness and loyalties of the inhabitants of the countries which they designated.

The Republic of Lebanon was quite different. It continued an established and living tradition of autonomy and separate identity, maintained, often under conditions of great difficulty, through the centuries of Ottoman rule. The Lebanese heartland consisted of the Mountain, with a very rough rectangle of territory extending from just south of Tripoli to just north of Sidon on the coast and slanting inland, northward and southward, to a line running from north to south through Zahle. It was inhabited primarily by Christians, most of them Maronites, and by Druze and Shi'ites, followers of what were seen as heterodox Muslim sects. With its difficult terrain and its nonconformist population, it had long been a refuge of social, intellectual and, in some measure, even of political independence within the Ottoman world.

Relations between the Lebanese Christians and the West go back many centuries, to a time when the Muslim peoples of the Middle East were sealed off from all contact with Western civilization. The Maronite Christians belong to a Uniate church. They have been in touch with Rome and Europe intermittently since the Crusades, and consistently since the 17th century. From the 1830s the port of Beirut grew rapidly in size and importance, and a new Christian commercial bourgeoisie played a major part in its growth. By the mid-1800s, the region boasted something which previously had been entirely lacking—a prosperous, educated, Arabic-speaking middle class. That they were almost exclusively Christian greatly limited their economic impact and almost entirely inhibited any social and political impact. But a change in the political circumstances of Lebanon and later of Egypt opened a new era for them.

In 1858, a development occurred of far-reaching significance. This was a rising among the Maronite peasantry of Kisrawan against their predominantly Druze landlords. The struggle was transformed into a more general conflict between Christians and Muslims, especially Druzes, culminating in what was, by the gentler standards of the mid-19th century, a major massacre. Some 11,000 Christians are said to have been killed in the Mountain and a few thousand more in Damascus. This led directly to French military intervention and, under Western diplomatic pressure, to the creation in 1861 of a special regime for Lebanon known as the *Règlement Organique.*

Under this regime, the Mountain and the immediately adjoining areas were to form an autonomous entity, governed by a Christian governor who would be an Ottoman subject but not a Lebanese, and whose appointment was to be approved by the Powers. He was to be assisted by an administrative council of 12 elected members, representing the different religious communities: four Maronites, three Druze, two Greek Orthodox Christians, one Greek Catholic Christian, one Sunni Muslim and one Shiʻite Muslim. The territory was to be divided into seven districts, each governed by a district officer of the locally dominant religious community. Similar administrative appointments were to be made in sub-districts and even in villages. Order was to be maintained by a locally recruited Lebanese gendarmerie; money to be raised by locally collected taxes and administered through a Lebanese budget. Only the surplus, if any remained after meeting local expenses, was to be remitted to the central Ottoman government in Istanbul. Justice, taxation, education, transport and other services all were locally administered. The *Règlement* provided for the abolition of feudal privileges and the establishment of full equality before the law of all Lebanese.

The autonomous Lebanese principality set up by the *Règlement Organique* of 1861 enjoyed an enormous success. The Christian Lebanon already possessed a thriving commercial middle class and now also had an active and enterprising smallholding class. The new political order provided a framework of peace, security and good government; it also allowed a rapid development of education and, consequently, of cultural and intellectual life. In a sense, it was in the Christian Lebanon that the Arab revival began. The Lebanese were Christians and rather Western in their outlook. But their language of expression was Arabic, and their energy and skills enabled them to make an immense contribution to Arab life. The relatively open society and stable regime in Egypt in the later 19th century created similar conditions and Lebanese migrants, attracted by the larger opportunities and greater security of that country, were among the founders of modern Egypt.

From the beginning, Christians played a leading role among the exponents and leaders of secular nationalism. As members of non-Muslim communities in a Muslim state, they had occupied a position of stable, privileged but nevertheless unmistakable inferiority; in an age of change even the rights which that status gave them were endangered. In a state in which the basis of identity was to be not religion, not community, but language and culture, they could hope to achieve the full membership and real equality that had been denied to them under the old dispensation. Christians figure very prominently among the outstanding poets, novelists, editors and ideologists in the earlier stages of modern Arab literature. Even in the nationalist movements, many of the leaders and spokesmen were members of Christian minorities. This prominence in cultural and political life was paralleled by a rapid advance of the Christian minorities in material wealth.

The Lebanon of the *Règlement Organique* came to an end in the First World War. After the war and the destruction of the Ottoman Empire, the French government as Mandatory Power for the Syrian lands created a new "Greater Lebanon" by adding a number of adjoining districts to the original Lebanese heartland. The purpose of this change was to create a larger and therefore presumably more viable Lebanese state. Its effect was to reduce the Christians to the role of one minority among others and ultimately to place their cherished ascendancy or even autonomy in peril.

In recent decades, this Christian prominence has ceased to be tolerable to Muslims. Partly through measures of nationalization adopted by Socialist governments, partly by other more direct means, the economic power of the Christians as of other minority communities has been reduced in one country after another and now has been challenged in its last stronghold, Lebanon. Christian predominance in Arab intellectual life has been ended long since and a new generation of writers and editors has arisen, the overwhelming majority of whom are Muslims. There still are Christian politicians and Christian ideologists, but their role is very much circumscribed in a society increasingly conscious of its Muslim identity, background and aspirations. It is noticeable that many of the more violent terrorist organizations tend to be Christian in membership, for in the radical extremism professed by these groups, Christians still hope to find the acceptance and equality which eluded them in mainstream nationalism. The aspirations—and disappointments—of Jewish radicals in Czarist Russia offer an instructive parallel.

As the nationalist movement has become more genuinely popular, it has become less national and more religious. In moments of crisis, and there have been many of these in recent decades, the instinctive communal loyalty outweighs others.

Against this background, the mystifying confrontation of right and left may be a little easier to understand. The Jumblatts are a family of emirs, apparently of Kurdish origin, Druze by religion. For centuries they have been leaders of what in the past was called the Jumblatti party. The Jumblatts are first heard of in Syria and appear to have settled finally in Lebanon during the early 17th century. By the early 18th century they were playing a major part in the interplay of Lebanese feudal politics. The Jumblatt party had its own armed forces and even its own flag—scarlet edged with green, bearing a hand and a dark green scimitar. They played an important part in all major developments in Lebanon. Said Jumblatt, for example, was one of the Druze leaders in the troubles of 1860. In the aftermath he was condemned to death by the Ottoman authorities and died in prison in 1861. Through the centuries the Jumblatt party—composed of peasants and retainers of the Jumblatt emirs—has gone through many forms, the most recent of which is the Progressive Socialist Party, founded by Kemal Jumblatt in 1949.

So much for the leftists. The term rightist is about equally appropriate in describing the Lebanese Phalanges. The name which this party gives itself is *Katā'ib*, the plural of a medieval Arabic term denoting a military formation which might be translated *phalanx*, but would be better translated *troop, squadron* or *regiment*, since it is usually applied to cavalry. The French translation *phalanges* was probably adopted in imitation of the Spanish party of that name and was abandoned years ago by the Kata'ib when this association became embarrassing. Their abandonment of the name has not prevented others from continuing to use it and from implying that this verbal similarity connotes an identity of political method and purpose.

The Kata'ib were founded in 1936 as a paramilitary youth movement. This was the age of political and militant "shirts," when blue, green, gray, white, khaki and tan shirts were used to clothe youth movements and proclaim their ideologies in Egypt, Syria, Iraq and Lebanon. Many of these paramilitary youth groups found their models in Nazi Germany, Fascist Italy and Francoist Spain, and some of their leaders were no doubt affected by the Fascist ideologies of those countries. In this they were by no means alone in the Arab world, and a large proportion of present-day Arab leaders and movements, including those of the left and extreme left, emerged from the same school.

The initial aim of the Kata'ib was not strictly political. The founders laid great stress on sport and spoke at the time of the Czechoslovak Sokol movement as their model—something very different from the Nazi storm troopers.

It was not until 1952, after the final departure of the French and the beginnings of independent political activity in a sovereign Lebanon, that the Kata'ib constituted themselves as a political party. They retained their paramilitary force but began to participate in elections. After that, they grew greatly in importance and came to occupy a leading position in the politics of the Christian, and more especially of the Maronite community.

Besides Kata'ib, the party has another name: the Social Democratic Party of Lebanon. This is by no means a meaningless label. The Lebanese Kata'ib stand for parliamentary, constitutional democracy and for a mixture of private enterprise and state assistance. These aims, coupled with Lebanese patriotism, might perhaps be described as rightist in the context of Middle Eastern politics, but it is or should be surprising to find this label used by the Western press.

The seating arrangements of the first French National Assembly after the Revolution do not express a law of nature, and the practice of classifying political ideas, interests and groups as right or left obscures more than it illuminates even in the Western world where it originated. As applied to other societies, shaped by different experiences, guided by different traditions, moved by different aspirations, such imported labels can only disguise and mislead.

30

The Shiʿa

❦

1985

T he anger of the Shiʿite Muslims, of which so much has been heard of late, has a long history, going back to the beginnings of Islam and rooted in the very nature of Muslim religion and government. When the Prophet Muhammad died in the year AD 632, he had founded a new religion. In doing this, he had also created a community, of which he was the leader and guide, and established a state, of which he was sovereign. He had begun his preaching in his birthplace, the oasis city of Mecca, and had won a number of disciples among its people. But the ruling oligarchy of Mecca rejected his message, and in 622 the Prophet and his disciples felt obliged, under growing pressure, to leave their homes and move to another oasis town, henceforth known as Medina.

T he migration—in Arabic, *hijra*—of the Prophet and his companions marks the beginning of the Muslim era. In Medina the Prophet was welcomed by the townspeople, who made him their judge and eventually ruler. By this, his position, and in some measure even his teaching, were radically transformed. In Mecca he had been a critic and an opponent of authority, seeking to replace both the ruling hierarchy and its pagan beliefs, the one by the Muslims, the other by Islam. In Medina he himself was authority, and Islam was the dominant creed.

During the last ten years of his life Muhammad was the accepted ruler of the oasis and, increasingly, of the surrounding tribes, and as such performed the political, military, judicial, and other tasks associated with government. He was even able to extend the authority of the Muslim state in Medina over the surrounding desert tribes, and, before his death, to conquer his birthplace, Mecca, and incorporate it in the new Muslim polity. By his migration from Mecca to Medina, the Prophet was transformed from a rebel to a statesman; at the time of his death the state that he had founded was in the process of becoming an empire. His revelation, the Qur'an, reflects these changes. The earlier chapters, revealed in Mecca, are concerned with moral and religious issues. The later chapters, revealed in Medina, deal with law, taxation, warfare, and other public matters.

As Prophet, Muhammad could have no successor. He was in Muslim parlance "the seal of the Prophets," and his book was the final and perfect form of God's revelation to mankind. But as head of the new Islamic state he needed a successor—and quickly, if the state was not to collapse in anarchy and its people revert to paganism. A group of his closest and ablest companions took immediate action, and agreed on one of their number, Abu Bakr, who assumed the headship of the community and state. Monarchical titles were odious to the early Muslims, and Abu Bakr preferred to be known by the modest term *khalīfa*, an Arabic word which, by an ultimately fortunate ambiguity, combines the meanings of deputy and successor. Thus was founded the great historic institution of the caliphate, which provided the political frame of the Islamic community for centuries to come. The first four caliphs, known in Sunni Muslim historiography as the Rightly Guided, were chosen from among the companions of the Prophet. Thereafter the caliphate became hereditary in two successive dynasties.

From the first, there were some who felt that Abu Bakr was not the best candidate, others who went further and condemned him as a usurper. Many of these saw in 'Ali ibn Abi Talib, the kinsman of the Prophet, husband of his daughter Fatima and the father of his grandchildren, the true and only rightful successor. As the polity and community of Islam grew rapidly through conquest and conversion, its people were subjected to increasing strains, and growing numbers of them began to feel that Islam had been deflected from its true path, and that the Muslims were being led back into the paganism and injustice from which the Prophet had been sent to save them. For those who held such views, the reigning caliphs appeared more and more as tyrants and usurpers, while for many, the claims of the kin of the Prophet, embodied first in 'Ali and then in his descendants, came to express their hopes and aspirations for the overthrow of the corrupt existing order and a return to pure, authentic, and original Islam.

These tensions reached a crisis in the year AD 656, when the murder of 'Uthman, the third caliph in succession to the Prophet, by a group of mutinous Muslim soldiers started the first of a series of civil wars that divided and devastated the Islamic state and community.

The issues in the first civil war were defined by the killing of the caliph. For one side, 'Uthman was the legitimate ruler of the Islamic state; those who killed him were murderers, and should be punished according to the law. For the other

side, 'Uthman was a usurper and a tyrant; those who killed him were executioners, carrying out a just and necessary task, and entitled to protection. By
granting them that protection, 'Ali, who succeeded 'Uthman as the fourth caliph, was in effect condoning an act for which he had in no way been responsible.
In the civil war that followed, 'Ali himself, after some initial victories, was
murdered in AD 661, and the caliphate became hereditary in the house of Uma-
yya, to which 'Uthman had belonged.

In time, those who accepted the legitimacy of the early caliphs came to be
known as Sunni, from *"sunna,"* an Arabic word meaning usage or custom, and
applied particularly to the body of precedent constituted by the actions and
utterances of the Prophet and his immediate successors. These, handed down by
tradition, were regarded as legally and religiously binding in Sunni Islam. Those
opponents who followed 'Ali and his descendants came to be known by another
Arabic word, Shi'a, meaning party or following—at first as the Shi'a of 'Ali,
and then simply as the Shi'a. The individual adherent to this cause was called
a Shi'i, or in common English usage, Shi'ite.

The Sunnis and the Shi'ites were by no means the only schools in early
Islamic history, but they are by far the most important, with Sunnism as the
dominant, mainstream form of Islam, and Shi'ism as the most powerful and
challenging of the alternatives. Sunnis and Shi'ites faced each other in all the
early civil wars and struggles, and for some time the outcome of the struggle
between them for leadership and domination of the Islamic world was far from
certain. It was not until the high Middle Ages that the Sunnis were able to
establish themselves at the prevailing form of Islam, while the Shi'ites, more
and more, came to be a minority associated with deviant doctrines and political
dissent.

In its origins the Shi'a of 'Ali was thus primarily political—the supporters
of a candidate for office, or of a family with claims to dynastic legitimacy. But
in a religion as political as Islam, in a polity as religious as the early caliphate,
a political party quickly and easily becomes a religious sect. In the course of this
transformation, certain events in their history were of decisive importance, and
gave rise to some of the characteristic and recurring features of the Shi'a.

In their own perception, the Shi'a were the opposition in Islam, the defenders
of the oppressed, the critics and opponents of privilege and power. The Sunni
Muslims, broadly speaking, stood for the status quo—the maintenance of the
existing political, social, and above all religious order. They even had a doctrinal
basis for this. After the death of the Prophet and the completion of the revelation
vouchsafed to him, God's guidance, in Sunni belief, passed from the Prophet to
the Muslim community as a whole. According to a much quoted saying of the
Prophet, "God will not allow my people to agree on an error." The notion of
consensus, embodied in this dictum, was the guiding principle of Sunni theology

and jurisprudence, including the political and constitutional provisions of the holy law. History therefore, for the Sunni, is of profound importance, since the experience of the Sunni community reveals the working out of God's purpose for mankind. In another much quoted saying, the Prophet urges the believer "not to separate himself from the community." This gives a special, even a theological value to precedent and tradition, and makes conformism and obedience basic commandments. Failure to observe these is a sin as well as a crime.

In principle, the Shi'ite philosophy is the exact opposite. After the death of the Prophet, and still more after the murder of 'Ali thirty years later, history in the Shi'ite view took a wrong turn, and the Muslim community has, so to speak, been living in sin ever since. For the Sunni, obedience to authority is a divine commandment. For the Shi'ite, obedience to the existing authority is a political necessity, to be given only as long as it cannot be avoided. The Shi'ite doctrine of *taqiya*, dissimulation, even permits, under duress, some measure of conformity in doctrine and practice against Shi'ite principles, but only if this is necessary in order to survive. For the Shi'ite, therefore, obedience is owed as long as it can be exacted, and no longer.

For Sunni and Shi'ite Muslims alike, the life of the Prophet is a model and example (Qur'an, 33, 21). But while Sunnis find their prophetic model in the Prophet in Medina, in the Prophet as ruler, commander, and judge, the Shi'a in contrast find their inspiration in the Prophet in Mecca—as leader and spokesman of the oppressed and downtrodden, against the pagan ruling oligarchy. It would be an oversimplification to classify the Sunnis as the quietists, the Shi'a as the activists of Islam. During most of their history, the Shi'a have practiced dissimulation and submission rather than open opposition, while the Sunnis have their own doctrine of limited obedience, expressed in the prophetic saying, "there is no obedience in sin." This was usually interpreted as meaning that when the ruler commands something which is contrary to God's law, the Muslim's duty of obedience lapses. Some even go on to argue that it is replaced by a duty of disobedience.

But the circumstances in which this principle might be invoked were never precisely defined, and in practice most Sunni jurists, even while recognizing the evils of the existing order, continued to preach conformism and submission, generally quoting yet another principle, that "tyranny is better than anarchy." The Shi'a, on the other hand, even while submitting, maintained their principled rejection of the Sunni order, and from time to time, more frequently in the early centuries than in the later, rose in revolt in an attempt to overthrow the existing order and replace it with another more in accord with God's purpose as revealed in Islam.

It was these revolts, and especially their almost invariable failure, that gave a distinctive quality to Shi'ite Islam. Certain recurring features may be seen especially in the participants, the tactics, the leadership, and the doctrines of these revolts. As challengers of the existing order, the Shiʿa very naturally found their main support among those who saw themselves as oppressed by it, and Shiʿite writings lay great stress on their appeal to the wronged, the downtrodden, the deprived. While the Shiʿa certainly had their own wealthy and learned families, their main following seems to have been among the artisans and workers in the cities and among peasants in the countryside. At certain periods, Shiʿite ideas had a considerable appeal for intellectuals. In most Muslim lands, the Shiʿa were a minority. Even where they became a majority, with the exception of Iran, they remained in a subordinate position. A striking case is that of Iraq, where a Shiʿite majority has remained subject to a Sunni ascendancy—to borrow a word from Anglo-Irish history—that can be traced back from the republic regime to the monarchy, the British Mandate, the Ottoman Empire, and beyond into the Middle Ages.

The one major political success gained by the Shiʿa since the Middle Ages was the accession to power of the Shiʿite Safavid dynasty in Iran at the beginning of the sixteenth century. Until then, Iran, like most other Muslim countries, was predominantly Sunni. The Safavids and their supporters were fervent Shiʿites, and succeeded not only in imposing Shiʿism as the state doctrine of Iran, but also in winning the adherence of the majority of the population. In its initial phase, the Safavid movement belonged to a radical, extremist branch of the Shiʿa, with millenarian overtones and far-reaching aspirations. These were contained by the surrounding Sunni powers in Turkey, central Asia, and India, and in due course were abandoned even in Iran. Before the sixteenth century, there were several other cases of Shiʿite leaders who succeeded in gaining power. But without exception, they failed to fulfill their promise. The great majority were ousted after a longer or shorter interval; the remainder, once established in power, forgot their earlier program, and conducted their affairs in ways not significantly different from those of the Sunnis whom they had overthrown.

The normal method of Shiʿite rebels was propaganda, followed by armed attack. In this too the career of the Prophet offered an example. Muhammad had begun by trying to win Mecca to his cause. Failing to do this, he had gone elsewhere, to Medina. There he had formed a new center of power, from which in time he was able to return as victor to Mecca and bring Islam to his native city. Many other rebel leaders tried to follow his example, a few of them with some success.

Most of the time, the Shiʿite preaching won only a limited response, while the armed insurrections that they launched were almost all suppressed by the vastly stronger armies of the Sunni state. From time to time there were some who found another way, which may be described either as tyrannicide or as terrorism; it was a method better suited to a movement whose numbers were few but whose followers were passionately devoted to their leaders. The killing of the caliph 'Uthman was the classical model of the removal of a ruler seen as unlawful and sinful. There were others after him.

The most famous of the terrorist groups was a small but important extremist Shi'ite sect, whose leaders were based in Iran and who established a branch in Syria during the twelfth century. Their method was to target and kill selected leaders, so as to terrorize others. They came to be known by the name of their Syrian branch, the Assassins (Arabic *ḥashīshiyya*). The Crusaders brought stories of these dreaded sectaries back to Europe, where the word assassin acquired the generalized meaning of murderer, more particularly the dramatic murderer of a public figure . . .

Contrary to a widespread but erroneous belief, the Assassins were not primarily concerned with war against the Crusaders, and comparatively few Crusaders fell to their daggers. Their enemy was the Sunni establishment, and their purpose was to frighten, weaken, and finally overthrow it. Their victims were the princes and officers of the Sunni state, and the qadis and other dignitaries of the Sunni religious hierarchy. Their emissaries, with negligible exceptions, made no attempt to escape, but died in the accomplishment of their mission. This was indeed part of the mission, and added greatly to the terror which they struck.

Like all their predecessors, the Assassins failed. After a long, hard struggle their strongholds were captured, their leaders killed, and their followers gradually transformed into peaceful and law-abiding peasants, artisans, and merchants. They are mainly found today in India and Pakistan, with smaller communities in central Asia, Iran, Syria, and East Africa. They are known as Isma'ilis, and their religious head is the Aga Khan.

The Isma'ilis, of whom there are several subsects, are a branch of the Shi'a. For some centuries in the Middle Ages, they were its most active and important branch, inspiring on the one hand the Fatimid caliphate which ruled in Egypt, on the other the dreaded Assassins of Iran and Syria, as well as a series of Muslim philosophers, theologians, and poets. But with the loss of their bases of power, they rapidly declined into one of the minor sects within the Shi'ite fold.

Their rise, efflorescence, and decline illustrate another characteristic aspect of Shi'ite history—the recurring tendency to split into rival and sometimes conflicting groups. In these conflicts among the Shi'a, as in the larger dispute between the Shi'a and the Sunni Muslims, the original issue was a political one—the question of leadership. All the Shi'a were at one in rejecting the Sunni caliph, but they often differed among themselves over his replacement. Virtually all agreed that the rightful ruler should be of the kin of the Prophet, through his daughter Fatima and his son-in-law 'Ali. But which? There were many claimants, each with his own following and disciples. The term which the Shi'a used for these claimants was "imam," from an Arabic word whose root meaning is "in front of" or "before." In Shiʿite usage it came to have an almost sacred significance. While the Sunni caliph was, theoretically at least, chosen by the faithful from among their own numbers, the Shiʿite imam was believed to be divinely appointed from among the descendants of the Prophet. The Sunni caliph held a religious office in the sense that it was established and regulated by holy law, but he was not a man of religion and had no legal power to modify or even interpret that law, which it was his primary duty to maintain and enforce.

While the Sunni caliph exercised religious but not spiritual authority, the Shiʿite imam was accorded a spiritual status by his followers, who saw in him the continuing embodiment of God's guidance to the believers. As one imam pretender after another followed the path of insurrection and defeat, they acquired, in the perception of their followers, an almost Christ-like quality, with the related themes of betrayal and suffering, passion and martyrdom, and even, ultimately, return.

From an early date two motifs become characteristic of insurrectionary Shi'ism—concealment and return. The imam is not really defeated and dead; he has been hidden away by God. And in God's good time he will return and establish the Kingdom of God on earth. In a much quoted dictum, also attributed to the Prophet, "one of my descendants will arise and fill the world with justice and equity as it is now filled with injustice and tyranny." This kind of messianism is not unknown in Sunni Islam, where similar conditions produced similar results, but it is characteristic of the Shiʿa, for whom it forms a central theme.

After many early disagreements about the imamate, most of the Shiʿa agreed on a sequence of twelve imams. These consist of ʿAli, his sons Hasan and Husayn, and the latter's descendants down to the twelfth imam, known as Muhammad al-Mahdi, who disappeared in about the year AD 873. Some branches of the Shiʿa have recognized other imams, notably some of the Ismaʿilis, whose line of imams has continued to the present day. But the great majority of the Shiʿa are known as Twelvers, because of their acceptance of the twelve imams. They believe that the twelfth imam went into concealment and it is he who will return, as *mahdī*, at the end of time.

While, therefore, there will be no more imams in this special sense for the Twelver Shiʿa, the word "imam" has continued to be used, rather loosely, by both Sunnis and Shiʿites, for other religious teachers and leaders, and even for the local officiant who leads prayers in the mosque. There may therefore at times be some uncertainty whether the term "imam" is being used in this lesser sense, or whether it implies a more far-reaching, indeed an eschatological claim. The imam Khomeini was asked about this, more than once, and gave no clear answer.

The great age of the Shiʿa, whether as an intellectual force challenging existing orthodoxies, or as an insurrectionary movement seeking to overthrow the existing order, had ended by the thirteenth century. Since then, its one great success was the takeover of Iran in the sixteenth century, and that was in time limited to one country and modified even there.

The Shi'a have remained a minority in the Islamic world as a whole, as well as in most Muslim countries. In the African continent, among Arab and black Muslims alike, Shi'ism is little known. It is represented only by Indian and Pakistani immigrants in East Africa. Shi'ites are equally scarce in Southeast Asia. As one might expect, the largest Shi'ite populations are in the countries around or near Iran—in the Indian subcontinent, in Afghanistan and central Asia, in Iraq and the Gulf. The Soviet Republic of Azerbaijan, which until its annexation by the Russian empire was an Iranian province, is overwhelmingly Shi'ite. In Syria there are no Twelver Shi'a, but three of the other branches of the Shi'a are represented—the Druze, the Isma'ilis, and the 'Alawis, also known as the Nusayris, to which President Asad and many of his closest associates belong. There are also Isma'ili and other non-Twelver Shi'a in Yemen. The Shi'a of Lebanon, for long known as the Matawila, are the only important group of Twelver Shi'a west of Iraq and the gulf province of Saudi Arabia. For a long time, the Lebanese Shi'a, consisting mostly of impoverished peasants, have been the forgotten men, both within the Lebanese political system and within the larger Shi'ite community. They are changing all that now.

Shi'ite and Sunni Muslims share the same basic beliefs in the unity of God, the apostolate of Muhammad, the finality and perfection of the Qur'anic revelation, and the principles and obligations of the holy law. Apart from the crucial issue of the imamate, there are no major theological differences between them, and only relatively minor differences of ritual and law—though the latter, in such social matters as marriage and inheritance, may at times acquire a disproportionate significance. There is thus no meaning to the parallels that are sometimes drawn between the Sunni-Shi'a cleavage in Islam and the schisms and heresies that have riven the world of Christendom. The original difference in Islam was political, concerning candidates for office. But in the course of the centuries, as the two main groups grew apart, other differences arose, the most important of which were psychological and emotional—the differences of mood and direction resulting from their greatly different experience. This is true not only of the differences between Sunni and Shi'ite Muslims, but also of the many disagreements that arose among the Shi'a themselves, dividing them into innumerable schools and sects. Here too the differences were in origin political—about which of several claimants was the rightful imam, the rightful head of Shi'ite and ultimately of all Islam. And here again, in the course of time, other differences—in belief and practice, in tactics and strategy—were added.

One of the most important of these is a recurring tension between what some have called the moderates and extremists, others, more accurately, the pragmatists and radicals. Differences of this kind underlie the original parting of the Twelver and other Shiʿites; they reappear within each of the two camps, and continue in a multiplicity of splits and sectarian groups. Broadly speaking, the pragmatists were those who recognized existing political facts and were willing to make what they saw as the necessary accommodations. When the Sunni order was too strong to be shaken, this meant resigning themselves to the role of a kind of loyal opposition. When they were able to seize power, it meant accepting the compromises that the continued exercise of power necessarily entailed. And at every stage, both in opposition and in government, the pragmatists were attacked by new groups of radical Islamic purists who saw them as betrayers of the true cause, and as imitators of the impious regimes which it was their primary task to destroy and replace. The same conflicts between pragmatists and radicals can be seen at the present day—in Iran, between those who are satisfied with Shiʿism in one country and with an Iranian foreign policy and those dedicated to the universal Islamic revolution; in Lebanon, between those committed to specific objectives within the Lebanese political system and those who share the Iranian radical dream.

31

Islamic Revolution

eulG euG

1988

1.

I n revolutions, even more than in other forms of political activity, there is an element of theater. This is evidenced by the almost universal use of such words as *drama, stage, scene, role,* even *actor,* in speaking of revolutionary events. Revolutionaries are, of course, conscious of this dramatic element. Some indeed, Karl Marx among them, have even used such unkind words as *farce* and *burlesque* to describe certain revolutionary activities. We do not hear these words applied to the revolution in Iran.

Playwrights and actors alike are especially aware of their audiences, both present and future. This awareness affects revolutionaries as they write, direct, interpret, and perform their roles in the revolutionary drama. The theater of revolution is essentially participatory, requiring more than the usual rapport between actors and audience. It depends on knowledge and empathy on the part of the public, who are not just spectators. As in Greek tragedy, the Japanese No, the Turkish or Egyptian shadow play, the English Punch and Judy, and the American western, the audience must know, preferably know intimately, the essentials of the plot, the characters and roles of the good and evil figures, and the desired, indeed the inevitable, outcome. The dramatist, the director, and the actors can appeal to a shared frame of reference, and, more important, of allusion, of memories: symbols that they can invoke to gain the interest, sympathy, and finally the enthusiastic participation of the audience.

During the last two hundred years, the dominant models of successful revolution in most of the world have been those of France and Russia, and the most dramatically effective roles those of the Jacobins and the Bolsheviks. In the nineteenth and early twentieth centuries, many revolutionary leaders attempted, in the differing conditions of their own countries, to reenact the magnificent climax of the storming of the Bastille and the proclamation of the Republic. After 1917, many tried to act out the Bolshevik script, sometimes with the aid of a prompter, sometimes without.

These models were most influential in societies that shared with France and Russia a common heritage of usable allusions and symbols, drawn from their European or Europe-derived culture, and from its ultimate sources in the Greco-Roman and Judeo-Christian traditions. At a time when Europe was paramount in the world, they were also adopted by aspiring non-European revolutionaries, at first against their own "old regimes," later against their European imperial masters. There have been several movements called revolutionary in the lands of Islam in this century, starting with the Persian and Turkish constitutional revolutions in 1905 and 1908, followed by many others after the withdrawal of Britain and France and the collapse of the regimes to which they had transferred power. In the early years of the century, it was the French model that prevailed among Westernizing Middle Eastern elites, to be supplemented, in the interwar and postwar decades, by other examples drawn first from Eastern and then from Southern and Central Europe. Public life in Muslim countries was enriched—if that is the right word—with a new system of values and symbols, drawn from European thought and from the European past.

The Islamic revolution which won power in Iran in 1979 and offers a major challenge to existing regimes in other Islamic lands uses none of these symbols. For the Ayatollahs and those who respond to them, neither the Bible nor the Latin and Greek classics, neither Jacobins nor Bolsheviks, neither Paris nor Petrograd provide usable models or evocative symbols. This of course does not mean that they have none. Islam has its own scriptures and classics. Islamic history provides its own models of revolution; its own prescriptions on the theory and practice of dissent, disobedience, resistance, and revolt; its own memories of past revolutions, some ending in success, others, in the historic memory the more significant ones, ending in failure and martyrdom. It is against this background of Islamic action and ideas, memories and symbols, that the Islamic revolution must be studied and may, just possibly, be understood.

Two preliminary questions must be asked and answered. Is the Islamic revolution in Iran a real revolution as that word has been used in the Western world, where it was first coined and applied, and if so, why is it called Islamic; why apply, to a major political, social, and economic transformation, a religious label? At one time the word *revolution* carried a connotation of profound and far-reaching change in the polity and perhaps also in the society, of some epoch-making upheaval in human affairs. It was in this sense that seventeenth-century Englishmen spoke of the first true national revolution, that eighteenth-century

Americans and Frenchmen and twentieth-century Russians and Chinese denoted the profound transformations that they brought to their countries.

Since then, the word *revolution*, like most other things in our world, in our time, has undergone a process of continuous devaluation, and is nowadays used for all kinds of trivial changes and innovations. In the West, the term *revolution* is now most commonly used to denote some above-average variation in style of life, production methods, or marketing; elsewhere it serves to designate violent seizures of power of the kind that used to be called *coup d'état*. All too often, the "revolution" is accomplished by a squadron of tanks, the officers of which seize the office of the president or prime minister, the central telephone exchange, the telegraph office, and one or two other strategic points, and proclaim a new regime administered by a *soi-disant* revolutionary command council, otherwise described as a military junta.

The Islamic revolution in Iran was, in its way, as authentic a revolution as the French or the Russian. For better or for worse—which remains to be seen— what happened in Iran was a revolution in the classical sense, a mass movement with wide popular participation that resulted in a major shift in economic as well as political power, and that inaugurated, or, perhaps more accurately, continued, a process of vast social transformation. As with other revolutions, it was preceded by a long period of preparation in which the transfer of power was merely a stage, introduced by what went before and facilitating what came after. It arose from deep discontents; it was inspired by passionate beliefs and driven by ardent hopes. And it still has some way to go before it works itself out, and before one can determine its nature and consequences.

As in France under the Bourbons and Russia under the Romanovs, so also in Iran under the Pahlavis, a major process of change was already underway, and it had advanced to a point at which it required a change in political power in order to continue. And in the Iranian as in other revolutions, there was always the possibility that something might happen whereby the process of change was deflected, perverted, or even annulled. Some Iranians, arguing from very different premises, would claim that this has already happened. But there is still some way to go before we, or for that matter the Iranians themselves, can say what kind of revolution this is or in which direction it is going.

So much for "revolution." What about "Islamic"? Why an Islamic revolution? We do not speak of the Tupamaros and Montaneros and other picturesquely named groups in Latin America as Christian revolutionaries, nor do we refer to the various upheavals that have taken place in Christendom in the last few centuries as Christian revolutions. Why then Islamic revolution? The first and obvious answer is: that is how they themselves describe it, how the revolutionaries, both the actors and the theorists, perceive and present their aims and their achievements. And in a very important sense, the Islamic revolutionaries are historically right in so doing, in seeing the Islamic revolution as a reassertion of certain basic loyalties, a return to the mainstream of their own history.

Revolutions move to different scripts, and their actors assume different roles. The French Revolution, with its ideological background in the eighteenth-century enlightenment, formulated its ideals as liberty, equality, fraternity. The Russian Revolution, with a background of nineteenth-century socialism, expressed its ideal as a classless state to be achieved through the dictatorship of the proletariat. The Iranian revolution expresses itself in the language of Islam, that is to say, as a religious movement with a religious leadership, a religiously formulated critique of the old order, and religiously expressed plans for the new. Muslim revolutionaries look to the birth of Islam as their model, and see themselves as engaged in a struggle against paganism, oppression, and empire.

When we in the Western world, nurtured in the Western tradition, use the words *Islam* and *Islamic*, we tend to assume that religion means the same for Muslims as it has meant in the Western world, even in medieval times: that is to say, a section or compartment of life reserved for certain matters, and separate, or at least separable, from other compartments of life designed to hold other matters. This is not so in the Islamic world. It was never so in the past, and the attempt in modern times to make it so may perhaps be seen in the longer perspective of history as an unnatural aberration that has come to an end in Iran and may also be ending in some other Islamic countries.

What then is the power, the attraction of Islam as a revolutionary appeal? This is a large and complex question, from which it may be useful to isolate a few points. The first is that in most Muslim countries Islam is still the basic criterion of group identity and loyalty. It is Islam that distinguishes between self and other, between in and out, between brother and stranger. We in the West have become accustomed to other criteria of classification: by nation, by country, and by various subdivisions of these. Both nation and country are of course old facts in the Islamic world, but as determinants of political loyalty they are modern and intrusive notions. Some countries—notably Turkey and Egypt—have become more or less accustomed to these notions. But there is a recurring tendency, in times of emergency, for Muslims to find their basic identity and loyalty in the religious community—that is to say, in an entity defined by Islam rather than by ethnic or territorial criteria.

A second, related, point is that Islam is still the most acceptable, indeed in times of crisis the only acceptable, basis for authority. Political authority, even in an authoritarian polity, requires some legitimacy. It can be maintained for a while by mere force, but not indefinitely, not over large areas for long periods. Power seeks legitimacy, and attains it more effectively, among Muslims, from Islam rather than from national or patriotic or even dynastic claims, still less from the Western notion of national or popular sovereignty. To Muslims Islam offers the most intelligible formulation of ideas, on the one hand of social norms and laws, on the other of new ideals and aspirations for the future.

And finally, a practical matter, but one of considerable significance; Islam, as recent events have demonstrated again and again, provides the most effective system of symbols—one might say of slogans, though no derogatory sense is meant—for mobilizing public opinion, for arousing the people in defense of a regime that is perceived as possessing the necessary legitimacy, or against a regime that is perceived as lacking that legitimacy, in other words, as not being Islamic. It was and is in Islamic terms that those who overthrew the Shah, murdered Anwar Sadat, seized the Great Mosque in Mecca, and now threaten the existing order in many Muslim countries justified their actions and appealed for popular support.

It is by now a truism that in Islam there is no distinction between church and state. In Christendom the existence of two authorities goes back to the founder of Christianity, who enjoined his followers to render to Caesar that which is Caesar's and to God that which is God's. There are two powers: God and Caesar. They may be associated, they may be separated; they may be in harmony, they may be in conflict; one or the other may dominate; one may interfere, the other may protest, as we have recently been reminded. But always there are two; God and Caesar, Church and state. In classical Islam, that is to say in pre-Westernized Islam, there is no such distinction. There were not two powers but one, and the question of separation did not therefore arise.

This difference between the religions goes back to the very beginnings of Islam and to the career of its founder. Unlike Moses, Muhammad lived to enter and conquer his promised land. Unlike Jesus, he triumphed in his lifetime over his worldly enemies and established an Islamic state in Medina of which he was sovereign. As the Ayatollah Khomeini has reminded us, Muhammad exercised the normal functions of a head of state—he dispensed justice, he raised taxes, he promulgated laws, he made war, he made peace. In other words, from the very beginning, in the sacred biography of its Prophet, in its earliest history enshrined in scripture and tradition, Islam as a religion has been associated with the exercise of power. Again to quote Khomeini: "Islam is politics or it is nothing." Its founder was judge, statesman, and general, as well as prophet. Church and state were not separable since they did not exist as different institutions or even as different concepts. These came, but much later and from elsewhere.

There are many different strands in the rich and varied traditional culture of Islam. There are in particular two political traditions, one of which might be called quietist, the other activist. The arguments in favor of both are based, as are most early Islamic arguments, on the Holy Book and on the actions and sayings of the Prophet.

The quietist tradition obviously rests on the Prophet as sovereign, as judge and statesman. But before the Prophet became a head of state, he was a rebel. Before he traveled from Mecca to Medina, where he became sovereign, he was an opponent of the existing order. He led an opposition against the pagan oligarchy of Mecca and at a certain point went into exile and formed what in modern language might be called a "government in exile," with which finally he was able to return in triumph to his birthplace and establish the Islamic state in Mecca. The Prophet's departure from Mecca—the *hijra*—marks the starting point of the Muslim era. The struggles in adversity that preceded his exile, like the ultimate triumph that ended his career, are all part of the Islamic tradition, of the holy life of the Prophet.

Of these two traditions, that of the Prophet as sovereign is obviously far better known and far better documented, but the tradition of the Prophet as rebel is also old and deep-rooted, and it recurs throughout the centuries of Islamic history. The activist tradition has been stronger and more explicit among the Shiʿa, but it is not exclusive to them, and there has been no lack of Shiʿi quietists and Sunni dissidents in Islamic history. The Prophet as rebel has provided a sort of paradigm of revolution—opposition and rejection, withdrawal and departure, exile and return. Time and time again movements of opposition in Islamic history tried to repeat this pattern, a few of them successfully. The rebels who carried out the first great Islamic revolution in the eighth century went to Eastern Iran and from there they came to Iraq and founded the great Abbasid Caliphate in Baghdad. Another group of religiously inspired rebels, in the tenth century, went to Yemen and then to North Africa, and from there they conquered Egypt and established the great Fatimid Caliphate in Cairo. Khomeini went to Iraq, and thence to Neauphle le Château, outside Paris, and from there he returned to rule in Tehran.

Does all this mean that Islam is a theocracy? Different observers have answered both yes and no. Some Western observers, particularly of late, have described Islam as a theocratic system. Most Muslim writers reject this with indignation. In the terms in which they argue, both sides are right, depending on what is meant by theocracy. From the point of view of Muslim scholars, historians, theologians, and others, who reject the idea of Islam's being a theocracy, the meaning of the word is very clear. There is, as they rightly point out, no church in traditional Islam. There is no priesthood in the sense of an ordination and a sacred office. There is no Vatican, no pope, no cardinals, no bishops, no church councils; there is no hierarchy such as exists in Christendom. Consequently, they argue, since theocracy means government by the church, rule by the priests, and since Islam has neither church nor priests, it follows that Islam is not, indeed cannot be, a theocracy.

The opposing argument takes theocracy in a rather different sense. Proponents of this view concede that there is no priesthood in Islam in the sense of an ordained intermediary performing some sacred office between God and man, but they claim that there is a very important priesthood in a sociological sense. It consists of a class of professional men of religion whose status is acquired by learning rather than by ordination and hierarchic rank, but who nevertheless function in most respects as a clergy. And these men of religion, the theologians and the jurists (the two in Islam are intimately associated), represent God and God's law for most practical purposes, and therefore in a very real sense exercise authority, though not the ultimate political authority, which until the present regime in Iran has never been exercised by the professional men of religion. In this respect, the Iranian Mullahs are not, as they claim, restoring the order that existed in antiquity; they are creating something entirely new in Islamic doctrine or history.

Islam is in principle, if not in practice, theocratic in another and deeper sense. Theocracy literally means the rule of God. And in this sense Islam has, in theory, always been a theocracy. In Rome, Caesar was God. In Christendom, God and Caesar coexist. In Islam, God is Caesar, in that he alone is the supreme head of state, the source of sovereignty and hence also of authority and of law. The state is God's state, the law is God's law. The army is God's army—and of course the enemy is God's enemy.

"The enemies of God" is an expression that is often heard nowadays in Iran, both in political polemics against enemies abroad and in criminal charges against enemies at home. The notion of God's enemies is a very old one; it becomes much more intelligible in its modern context if we bear in mind the Islamic perception of God as the head of state. Those who exercise authority do so on behalf of God, in the same way and perhaps to the same extent as the prime minister of England exercises authority on behalf of the Queen and the president of the United States on behalf of the people. And since the state undoubtedly can have enemies, it follows that the enemies of the state are the enemies of God.

2.

The larger question arises of the definition of the other, the outsider, the stranger. If the definition of self is by Islam, if the insider is the Muslim, it follows that the "other" is the non-Muslim, the unbeliever, the Kafir. And this for most purposes is seen as the basic division of mankind.

In classical usage, the difference between Muslim and unbeliever was one of creed and allegiance. The Iranian revolutionaries have given this ancient dichotomy a modern dimension, by linking it with another distinction drawn from the Qur'an, between the humbled and the haughty. In the religious and political language of present-day Iran, the humbled (one might also translate the Arabic word *mustaḍ'af* as deprived, downtrodden) include even the non-Muslim oppressed, who benefit from a kind of Islam of grace. Similarly the haughty (in Arabic *mustakbir*, which in the Qur'an means something like hubristic) include even those, both at home and abroad, who profess the Islamic religion but do not accept the teachings and discipline of the revolution. They too are counted among the enemies of God, and against them there is a perpetual obligation of struggle (in Arabic *jihād*, usually inaccurately translated as "holy war"), until all mankind adopts the faith and obeys the law of Islam.

These enemies are perceived as falling into two basic categories: the external and the internal. The external enemy means the non-Islamic world, relations with which, in war and in truce, are elaborately regulated by Islamic Holy Law. But for the revolutionaries, it is the enemy within Islam that is their first and main concern.

Since we are talking about religiously defined politics, a term that would most naturally occur to a Western observer is heresy. It would not be appropriate. Heresy is not an Islamic notion; there is not even an Islamic term corresponding to it. Heresy is a Christian term meaning a deviation, officially defined as such, from, an officially defined orthodoxy. And since Islam has no councils or churches or hierarchy, there is no officially defined orthodoxy and there cannot therefore be any officially defined and condemned deviation from orthodoxy. What can happen is something much more serious and much more dangerous. If a Muslim deviates from Islam to the point where he is no longer regarded as a Muslim with the minimum of correct belief, he is something much worse than a heretic. He is an apostate. The process by which one is declared to be an apostate is called *takfīr*, naming and denouncing a Kafir, an unbeliever. This term is much used in religious movements nowadays, notably by the group responsible for the murder of Sadat.

The penalty for apostasy, in Islamic law, is death. Islam is conceived as a polity, not just as a religious community. It follows therefore that apostasy is treason. It is a withdrawal, a denial of allegiance as well as of religious belief and loyalty. Any sustained and principled opposition to the existing regime or order almost inevitably involves such a withdrawal. In fourteen centuries of Islamic history there have been many opposition movements within Islam. Almost all of them and certainly all those of any significance were religiously expressed. Opposition to the prevailing order, criticism of an existing regime, found expression in religious terms, just as the prevailing regime defined its authority and its legitimacy in religious terms. To confront a religious regime, one needed a religious challenge.

In a sense, the advent of Islam was itself a revolution, which after long struggles only partially succeeded. After the Islamic conquests of the seventh century, there was a continuing tension between the new religion and its message and the very old societies of the countries that the Muslims conquered. Islam came, not into a new world, like Christendom in Europe, but to lands of ancient civilization and deep-rooted traditions. This tension between Islamic dynamism and the older forces of the river-valley societies continued through medieval into modern times. For example, Islamic doctrine is basically egalitarian. It is true that the equality of Islam is limited to free adult male Muslims, but even this represented a very considerable advance on the practice of both the Greco-Roman and the ancient Iranian world. Islam from the first denounced aristocratic privilege, rejected hierarchy, and adopted a formula of the career open to the talents.

Resistance to all this was, of course, very powerful. On the whole Islam triumphed only in certain limited spheres of social and family life. In most political and public matters it was overwhelmed by the more ancient traditions of the regions, which survived in an Islamic disguise, notably in the persistence of the autocratic, monarchical form of government. So we find through the centuries a recurring theme of revolt: a feeling that history had somehow taken a wrong turn; that Islam had been perverted; that the Islamic community was being ruled by non-Muslims, by bad Muslims, by renegade Muslims, by those who had betrayed the heritage of the Prophet and were leading the community as a whole into sin; and that therefore it was the duty of the Muslims to overthrow and replace such an evil regime. In time, this belief began to acquire a messianic character, and a whole cluster of traditions and practices developed, associated with the figure of the Mahdi, the divinely guided one who will come in God's good time, overthrow the kingdoms of evil, and establish the world of justice and divine law.

Normally this was to be accomplished by armed insurrection against the existing order. But armed insurrection was not always feasible and when it was not, according to the more extreme Shiʿites, it was permissible to have recourse to what we would nowadays call terrorist methods. At quite an early stage there were extremist and deviant Shiʿite groups who not only practiced terror but made a kind of sacrament of it. The most famous of course were the Assassins, the ones who took up the patent of the procedure that still bears their name . . . Theirs was a revolutionary struggle against the Lords of Islam at that time.

A familiar feature of revolutions, such as the French and the Russian, is the tension, often conflict, between moderates and extremists—Girondins and Jacobins in the French Revolution, Mensheviks and Bolsheviks in the Russian, as well as numerous smaller splinter groups. Some historians have found similar differences in Islamic revolutions of the past; some observers have discerned them in the course of events in Iran. Certainly there has been no lack of such tensions and conflicts between rival groups, factions, and tendencies within the revolutionary camp. The distinction between moderates and extremists is, however, one derived from Western history, and may be somewhat misleading when applied to the Islamic revolution in Iran.

A more accurate description, for this as for other previous Islamic revolutions, would present the conflict as one between pragmatists and ideologues. The latter are those who insist, against all difficulties and obstacles, on maintaining the pure doctrine of the revolution as taught by them. The former are those who, when they have gained power and become involved in the processes of

government at home and abroad, find it necessary to make compromises. Sometimes they go so far as to modify their revolutionary teachings; more often, they
tacitly disregard them. This conflict, between those who reject and those who
practice compromise, can be traced throughout Islamic history, from the vener-
ated Companions of the Prophet—those who embraced Islam and joined him
during his lifetime—to the henchmen of Khomeini. In times of revolution, it
becomes particularly bitter.

Each side has certain advantages. The ideologues have the better rhetoric, the
stronger appeal, the greater popular support. The pragmatists are better equipped
to deal with the practical problems of government, at home and abroad. Part of
their pragmatism is to try to avoid an open clash with the ideologues. When
they fail, and a clash occurs, they are usually defeated, since in a time of revolutionary change the ideologues are better placed to mobilize support. It is not
easy to rouse the masses for such tasks as compromising with Iraq, mending
fences with the United States, or slowing the pace of revolutionary change. When
pragmatists in office go too far, they are ruthlessly suppressed, and their careers
end in exile, imprisonment, or death. At best, they fade out of public life and
are rendered innocuous. Such have been the various fates of once prominent
figures like the former foreign minister Sadeq Qotbzadah, who was executed; the
former president Abolhasan Bani Sadr, who escaped to Paris; and the first prime
minister of the revolutionary regime, Mehdi Bazargan, who, though alive and
in Iran, has been excluded from power and reduced to insignificance. The ideologues rule, and since the practical problems remain, in time a new group of
pragmatists emerges among the victorious ideologues, and the conflict is renewed, usually with the same result. The process continues until the revolutionary passion is spent, and a group of pragmatists survives, succeeds, and remains
in power. Then the ways of government return to normal, and the ideologues
return to the world of theory and preaching from which the revolution had
enabled them, briefly, to emerge. It would seem that this stage has not yet been
reached in Iran.

In recent years it has become common practice to use the Western term *fundamentalist* to denote a wide range of militant Islamic movements, both radical
and conservative. The term has spread from English to other European languages,
and of late—the ultimate irony—it has even been translated into Arabic and is
used by secularized Muslims to describe their militant Islamic compatriots. Despite its common use, the term is inaccurate and misleading. *Fundamentalist* is a
term originating in the United States in the early twentieth century, and used
to refer to certain Protestant groups that asserted, against the growing influence
of liberal theology and critical Bible studies, their belief in the literal divine
origin and textual inerrancy of the Bible.

The so-called Muslim fundamentalists are something quite different. In principle, all Muslims believe in the literal divine origin and textual inerrancy of the Koran. No one within Islam has ever asserted otherwise, and there is no critical Qur'an study against which a protest or reaction might be necessary. Reformist theology has been an issue among Muslims in the past, and may again be one in the future. It is not the issue today. Where the so-called Muslim fundamentalists differ from other Muslims—and incidentally also from Christian fundamentalists—is in their scholasticism and their legalism. The gravamen of their case against existing regimes and prevailing ideologies is the abandonment of the Shari'a, the systematized law of Islam, and the adoption of what they see as infidel laws and customs. In his denunciation of the misdeeds of the Shah, Khomeini laid special emphasis on the Western-style emancipation of women, and the sharing of political power with non-Muslims. Other proponents of re-Islamization, in Egypt and elsewhere, have made similar complaints. Their critique is not, however, limited to these issues, but covers the whole range of social and cultural modernization. Their declared purpose is to undo all the political, legal, and consequent social changes that have been introduced during the period of Westernization, and to restore the full panoply of the Islamic state and the Islamic holy law. Only when the neopagan apostates who rule in Islamic lands have been deposed, and their laws and institutions abrogated and annulled, will the true Islamic life become possible, and the true mission of Islam be accomplished.

For the most consequent of these radicals, the fight against foreign enemies is at this point a distraction. The true enemy is at home, and only when he has been conquered will the fight against the alien intruder become necessary and victory against him desirable. In Iran, according to the exponents of the Iranian revolution, the first stage has already been accomplished, and the second is under way. In other Islamic countries, the first task still remains.

The external enemy Iran now confronts is, for the present rulers of that country, defined by Islamic law and identified by Islamic history. In the classical and sanctified texts that determine their view of the world, mankind is divided into two parts: the House of Islam and the House of Unbelief, more commonly called the House of War. Historically, in the Muslim perception, the House of War par excellence has been Christendom, later called Europe, in modern times redefined as the West. To the east and south of the classical Islamic world there were only pagans, some of them, as in India and China, with high levels of material culture, but both essentially regional, and neither offering a serious challenge to Islam. Only in the West was there a major adversary—an alternative dispensation, expressed in a rival world civilization and a competing world power. This perception was reinforced by centuries of conflict—jihad and crusade, conquest and reconquest, the Muslim invasions of Europe and the European invasion of Islam. If the main rival was the Christian and Western world, the archenemy was whoever was seen as the leading power of that world—at different times the Byzantine and Holy Roman Emperors, the imperial powers of Europe, and now the United States of America, described, in the theologically colored language favored by Khomeini, as "the great Satan."

This role came to the United States by inheritance and is retained by leadership, as the preeminent power of the West and the ultimate custodian of Western values. With that leadership comes the inevitable price of hatred. The United States might escape this hatred by changing its civilization—hardly a serious proposition—or by relinquishing its leadership and relapsing, like former leaders, into relative insignificance and perceived harmlessnesss. There may be another way—when the Muslim leaders are persuaded that it is no longer the West or Christendom that is the main enemy and the main danger, but another creed and another power that offer a far greater threat to all that they cherish.

Though recent events do not encourage such a perspective, some Muslim leaders have already begun to look in that direction. But most find it easier—and much safer—to direct their hostility against the West, the source of most of the changes that have come to the Islamic lands in modern times and, as they see it, have undermined and disrupted the Islamic way of life. In principle, the aim of the Islamic revolution, in Iran and eventually elsewhere, is to sweep away all the alien and infidel accretions that were imposed on Muslim lands and peoples in the era of alien dominance and influence, and to restore the true Islamic order as it existed in the days of the Prophet and his companions. An examination of the record however, in Iran and elsewhere, reveals that the rejection of Europe and its offerings is by no means as comprehensive and as undiscriminating as the propaganda might indicate, and that some of the importations from the lands of unbelief are still very welcome.

Some of these are obvious. The Islamic revolution in Iran was the first truly modern revolution of the electronic age. Khomeimi was the first charismatic orator who sent his oratory to millions of his compatriots at home on cassettes; he was the first revolutionary leader in exile who directed his followers at home by telephone, thanks to the direct dialing that the Shah had introduced in Iran and that was available to him in France (though not in Iraq). Needless to say, in the long war in which they have been engaged with Iraq, the Iranian revolutionary leaders have made the fullest use of such weapons as the West and its imitators are willing to supply—guns, rockets, tanks, and planes on the one hand, radio, television, and the printing press on the other.

There is another respect in which the Islamic revolutionaries in Iran have, alas, borrowed from Europe. While their symbols and allusions are Islamic rather than European, the leaders and practitioners of the revolution have found their models of style and method in European history. The summary trial and execution of great numbers of ideologically defined enemies; the driving into exile of hundreds of thousands of men and women; the large-scale confiscation of private property; the mixture of repression and subversion, of violence and indoctrination that accompanied the consolidation of power—all this owes far more to the examples of Robespierre and Stalin than to those of Muhammad and ʿAli. These methods are deeply un-Islamic; they are, however, thoroughly revolutionary.

But that is not all. In addition to the necessary technology of warfare and propaganda, there were other innovations that at first sight would appear to be neither Islamic nor necessary. The Islamic Republic of Iran has a written constitution and an elected parliament, in which lively debates take place. None of these things existed in the Islamic past, and there has been no serious attempt to argue that they did. While Western-inspired laws have been abrogated and replaced by the Shariʿa, Western-style legal procedures remain, and there are courts and lawyers to administer them. These too are not insignificant remnants of the age of European influence. There has been no loss of interest—if anything rather an increase—in the study of foreign languages, and the books to which a knowledge of foreign language gives access.

What then, in Islamic ideology, is the revolution about? What are the grievances that have aroused such passionate anger, and that call so urgently for remedy? A study of revolutionary writings and speeches reveals two main theses. One of these themes might be called religious in the narrower, Western sense of the word—that is to say, relating to belief, ritual, and observance. While no one, apart from a few Marxists and they at peril of their lives, has openly challenged Muslim beliefs, there has been a growing laxness among the educated classes, particularly those who have received some measure of Western or Westernized education. Even more offensive—since Muslims have always been more concerned with practice than with belief—is the laxness in Muslim observance, and in respect for the basic norms of the Muslim way of life. In many Muslim cities, forbidden food and drinks are freely available and openly consumed, to the scandal of the believers, while the cinema and the television screen bring indecency and immorality into both the public place and the private home.

Linked with this is the second theme, the polemic—itself a borrowing from the West—against consumerism and the cult of worldly goods, and the championing of the poor and oppressed against their rich and powerful oppressors. There had always been rich and poor in the Islamic world, and the difference between them was accepted and in a sense sanctified by Islamic law, which recognizes private wealth, regulates inheritance, and prescribes charity. But Westernization made the gap between rich and poor both greater and more visible. It also—through a rapidly rising rate of natural increase—made the poor much more numerous. Western commerce and industry created vast new opportunities for both enrichment and expenditure; the Western press and television have made the poor, as never before, conscious of their own poverty and of the wealth of their neighbors. In the past, rich and poor had basically worn the same kind of clothes, eaten the same kind of food, lived the same kind of life, and been held together by a complex web of loyalties and obligations. In the modern age, a Westernized elite and an un-Westernized populace live in different worlds, and the loyalties that once held them together have been broken or discredited. Such disparities did much to provoke and exacerbate the alienation and anger that destroyed the head of state in Egypt, and the entire regime in Iran.

L ike the French and the Russian in their time, the Iranian revolutionaries play to international as well as domestic audiences, and their revolution exercises a powerful fascination over other peoples outside Iran, in other countries within the same culture, within the same universe of discourse. The appeal was naturally strongest among Shi'i populations, as in South Lebanon and some of the Gulf states, and weakest among their immediate Sunni neighbors. It was and remains very strong in the greater part of the Muslim world, where Shi'ism is virtually unknown. In these, the sectarian difference is unimportant; Khomeini can be seen not as a Shi'ite or a Persian but as an Islamic revolutionary leader. Like the Western radicals who, in their day, responded with almost messianic enthusiasm to the events in Paris and Petrograd, events "that shook the world," so did millions of young and not so young men and women all over the world of Islam, from West Africa to Indonesia, from the Sudan to Sarajevo and Kosovo in Yugoslavia, and, more recently, among the millions of Muslim immigrants and guest workers in Western Europe. Sarajevo is a particularly striking case. Though its population is predominantly Muslim, Sarajevo is a European city in a country that had by then been under communist rule for thirty-five years. Nevertheless, the appeal of the Iranian revolution was so strong that the Yugoslav papers reported trials of young men in Sarajevo accused of plotting to overthrow the regime and establish an Islamic republic in Bosnia. If that could happen in Sarajevo, one wonders what might be happening among the sixty million Muslims in the Soviet Union, far closer to Iran, in both geography and culture, than those of Yugoslavia.

The parallel is again very close between what happened in the Islamic world in our day and what happened in Europe and beyond following the Russian and French Revolutions—the same upsurge of emotion, the same uplifting of hearts, the same boundless hopes, the same willingness to excuse and condone all kinds of horrors, and the same questions. Where next? Who could have predicted in 1795 or in 1925 the further development of the French or Russian revolutions and the careers of Napoleon or Stalin? I shall not attempt it for Iran. Only this much can be said: that what is in progress is producing vast, deep, and irreversible changes, that the forces that are causing these changes are not yet spent and that their destination is still unknown.

32

The Enemies of God

❧❦❧❦

1993

Recent events in parts of the Muslim world have revived memories of the Islamic revolution in Iran, and aroused fears that more such revolutions may be in preparation and new Islamic fundamentalist regimes about to emerge, with similar consequences both at home and abroad. Western observers in particular recall with alarm what they saw as the ferocity of the Iranian revolution, when large numbers of people were summarily arrested, tried in batches, and executed, sometimes within hours. Many were deeply shocked by this method of dealing with political opponents by execution, which in various parts of the Western world had been abandoned centuries, or at least decades, ago.

This kind of ferocity, this resort to ruthless, large-scale, summary trial and execution, however, is not characteristic either of Iran or of Islam. It is very characteristic of revolutions. Of the three components, Islam, revolution, and Iran, it is rather to the revolutionary than to the Islamic or Iranian aspects of what has been happening that we should look. This does not of course mean that such things are unknown in either Iranian or Islamic history. In the early days of the revolution, at the height of the anti-American campaign, one of the accusations that were frequently brought against the United States was that the CIA was responsible for instructing the Shah's men in torture and repression. This would be rather like accusing the Iranians or the Arabs of having introduced sharp business practices to the United States.

A certain level of repression, of violence, has been endemic in the Middle East, but mass killing has not. Similarly, although Islamic penal law and regional political usage can be very severe, there is nothing in either to justify mass political executions of the kind that we have seen. These events are, however, characteristic of revolutionary situations, such as those others, in Europe and elsewhere, with which the Iranian revolution may reasonably be compared. Successful revolutionaries generally seem to find it necessary to remove their domestic opponents in large numbers and at high speed—usually in larger numbers and at higher speeds than the tyrannical regimes which they overthrow and replace. This phenomenon is familiar from the histories of the French and Russian revolutions. Even within the Middle East, after the Young Turk revolution of 1908—the liberal constitutional revolution which overthrew the legendary tyranny of Sultan Abdulhamid II—the Young Turks managed to kill more Turks in three years than the old Turks had killed in the previous thirty years.

The Iranian revolution has kept up with this tradition, and has its own definition of the enemy it seeks to destroy. Earlier revolutions had defined their opponents in various ways. The French Revolution defined them socially as aristocrats, economically as feudal, ideologically as reactionary. The Russian Revolution defined them socially as bourgeois, economically as capitalist, ideologically as counterrevolutionary. The Islamic revolutionaries in Iran, and those who seek to follow their example in other Muslim countries, define their opponents with a term that covers both the social and ideological aspects, as "the enemies of God," and their crime as corruption or evil-doing (the Qur'anic Arabic word is *fasād*) on earth. And in case there should be any misunderstanding of the significance of this expression, the enemies of God are named more precisely as the followers of Satan, and Satan himself, qualified as "Great," is identified with the United States.

We all think we know what evil-doing means, and many of us nowadays have direct experience of it. For religious radicals, it can serve as a theological way of denoting what other revolutionaries call repression or exploitation, or—if we look at the vocabulary of "scientific" revolutionaries—incorrect policies. There is, as is well known, an extraordinary belief in some circles that politics is an exact science like mathematics; and that there is, so to speak, one correct answer to any problem, all the others being incorrect. It is a delusion, a false theory, and its forcible application has brought untold misery to untold millions of people, and has in particular deprived the Russian people, and those other peoples over whom they ruled, of almost a century of their history. The language of the Iranian revolutionaries in Iran and elsewhere indicates something of the same kind—a similar belief in a correct policy, which of course is God's policy, as opposed to all others which are incorrect, and therefore opposed to God.

Since the overthrow of the Shah in 1979 and the definition and denunciation of the "old regime" and its supporters, the course of events in Iran has followed familiar revolutionary patterns. These revolutionaries inflicted and suffered their reign of terror—worse than the French, though not as bad as the Russian. They faced and overcame the forces of foreign intervention, and themselves evoked a widespread international response, for which they created an appropriate international organization. They have their Jacobins and their Bolsheviks, with the fierce enthusiasm of the one, the rigid certitudes of the other, and the ruthless violence of both. Sooner or later, they will probably give way to some sort of restoration. Before that, they may yet—though this is unlikely—produce their Napoleon or their Stalin, to achieve new heights in the war against the enemies of God.

This term, the "enemies of God," which recurs so frequently in the statements of the Iranian revolution, both in its judicial proceedings and in its political pronouncements, must seem very strange to the secular-minded modern outsider. The idea that God has enemies, and needs human help in order to identify and dispose of these enemies, is a little difficult to understand. It is not, however, all that strange. The concept of the enemies of God is familiar in preclassical and classical antiquity, in both the Old and New Testaments as well as in the Qur'an, and occupies a central position in the ideology of the modern radical Islam.

The concept comes in various forms. The ancient Greeks recognized several kinds of enemies of the gods. One was the super-hero who actually defied the gods, and was presented in a favorable rather than an unfavorable light. Another was the enemy of the gods in that he was, so to speak, not their opponent but rather their victim, the object of the spite, the rancor, the envy of the gods. Yet another group consisted of those titans or heroes who were engaged in a sort of cosmic warfare against the gods, or who, unfortunately for themselves, inadvertently became involved in internecine warfare among the gods.

A particularly relevant version of the idea occurs in the dualist religions of ancient Iran. Most of the religions of Iran before the advent of Islam in the seventh century were to a greater or lesser degree dualist, believing not in one but in two cosmic powers. The Zoroastrian devil, unlike the Christian or Muslim or Jewish devil, is not one of God's creatures performing some of God's more mysterious tasks, but is an independent power, a supreme force of evil engaged in a cosmic struggle against God. This belief influenced a number of Christian, Muslim, and Jewish sects, through Manichaeism and other traditions. Although the Manichaean religion has almost disappeared, its name is still used—with some injustice to a complex theology—to designate a simplistic view that sees the world and all its problems as a stark struggle between good and evil.

The Bible also contains some indications about enemies, not of course of the gods, as in Greece, but of God. One is the distinction between those who love God and those who hate God, presumably meaning those who do not love God. In a key text in Exodus 23:22, God says: "If thou wilt indeed obey, then I will be an enemy unto thine enemies and an adversary unto thine adversaries." The same notion is expressed in a more passionate and personal form in many of the Psalms. In the Qur'an the enemies of God are specified as the unbelievers, and are doomed to Hell-fire (2:98; 41:19 and 28); the believers are commanded to "strike terror into God's enemy and your enemy." But the struggle need not be to the death. "If the enemy incline towards peace, do you also incline towards peace, and trust in God," who in His omniscience will give sufficient protection against any trickery that the enemy may intend (8:60–62). According to the historical record, those who fought against the prophet in his lifetime submitted to him. For some of the so-called Islamic fundamentalists of today, it would seem, this alone is what the sacred text means by peace.

In the teachings of the monotheistic religions, it is not God calling on mankind to help Him against His enemies; it is mankind, or rather some parts of it, calling on God to help them against their enemies, to adopt their enemies as His. They are, so to speak, recruiting God not—as in dualist religion—being recruited by God. The same approach is often adopted in modern times, as for example in the many hymns and anthems and special military prayers in which God is requested, or sometimes even instructed in somewhat peremptory terms, to save our King, Queen, Kaiser, Tsar, republic, or country, and of course to frustrate our enemies by adopting them as his own.

With the advent of Christianity, the Jewish concept expressed in the Old Testament was greatly developed. As the notion of God was broadened, and included Christ, the notion of enmity to God was correspondingly broadened and acquired a new significance. It was now possible for human beings not merely to be enemies of God, but also to wound or even, in a sense, to kill God. And so, in the early Christian patristic literature, there are many and frequent references to the enemies of God. This term, which had in the past been used by pagans about Christians, was now used by Christians about Jews and about heretics, who were seen as enemies of Christ and thus of God.

In Islam the notion of the enemies of God assumed a much greater role. The Qur'an is of course strictly monotheistic, and recognizes one God, one universal power only. There is, according to the Qur'an, a struggle in men's hearts between good and evil, between God's commandments and the tempter, but this is seen as a struggle ordained by God with its outcome preordained by God. It is a struggle that serves as a test of mankind, and not, as in some of the old Iranian dualist religions, one in which mankind has a crucial part to play in bringing about the victory of good over evil. Despite this monotheism, Islam, like Judaism and Christianity, was at various stages in its development influenced by Iranian dualist notions, by the idea of a cosmic clash of good and evil, light and darkness, order and chaos, truth and falsehood, God and the Adversary, variously known as devil, Iblis, Satan, and other names.

For Muslims, this cosmic struggle of good and evil could easily acquire political and even military dimensions. Muhammad, it will be recalled, was not only Prophet and teacher, like the founders of other religions; he was also the head of a state and of a community, a ruler and a soldier, and the founder of what became a vast empire. Hence the struggle became one involving states and their armed forces as well as individual believers. If the fighters in the war for Islam, the holy war "in the path of God," are fighting for God, it follows logically that their opponents are fighting against God. And since God is in principle the sovereign, the supreme head of the Islamic state, with the Prophet, and after the Prophet the caliphs, as His vice-regents, then God as sovereign commands the army. The army is God's army and the enemy is God's enemy. The duty of God's soldiers is to dispatch God's enemies as quickly as possible to the place where God will chastise them, that is to say in the afterlife. In the chronicles of the various holy wars that Muslims waged against infidels, the reported death of a Muslim is customarily followed by some such formula as "Peace be upon him" or "God have mercy on him"; the death of an infidel enemy is often accompanied by the phrase "God speed his soul to hell."

The holy war fought in the cause of God and against God's enemies is normally fought against infidels who must be induced, by force of arms if necessary, either to accept Islam or to submit to the rule of the Muslims. But there is another enemy, more insidious and more dangerous than the alien infidel beyond the frontiers of Islam, and that is the apostate—one who was brought up in Islam and bears a Muslim name and appearance but has abjured the faith and works in secret to destroy it from within. Already in medieval times, some jurists discussed the possibility of an internal jihad against a renegade regime. Among modern fundamentalists this has been developed into an ideology of revolution. The murderers of Sadat and the destroyers of the Iranian monarchy shared the belief that they were engaged in a sacred struggle against apostate rulers and regimes that had abandoned God's revelation and were seeking to abrogate God's law and replace it with new laws and new ways copied from the infidel West.

The archetype of the enemy of God is, of course, Satan, who appears frequently in the Qur'an and against whom the Believers are given many warnings. And in the demonology of the Islamic Republic, Satan has been given a local habitation and a name in the Western hemisphere. In Muslim scripture and tradition, Satan expresses his enmity to God by constantly trying to lead God's people astray. Since the First Temptation of Adam and Eve, he has never desisted from this evil endeavor. The final sura of the Qur'an, which ranks after the first sura as the best known and most widely repeated among Muslims, reads as follows: "I seek refuge with the Lord of men, the King of men, the God of men, from the mischief of the insidious whisperer who whispers in the hearts of men . . ."

From the writings of Khomeini and other ideologists of Islamic fundamentalism, it is clear that it is the seductive appeal of American culture, far more than any possible hostile acts by American governments, that they see as offering the greatest menace to the true faith and the right path as they define them. By denouncing America as the Great Satan, the late Ayatollah Khomeini was paying an unconscious tribute to that seductive appeal.

In modern as in medieval times, among Muslims as among Christians, Jews, and followers of other faiths, many, often most, have been willing to see their quarrels in less apocalyptic terms and to conduct themselves accordingly. Between human opponents fighting over human issues there can be dialogue and compromise and, as the Arab-Israeli peace talks have shown, even a prospect of peace. For God's self-appointed executioners, there can be no such prospect.

For those who wage war against the enemies of God, their struggle can end only in death or victory. For death in God's cause, so they believe, holy writ promises ineffable rewards in the hereafter. In victory, the same authority grants the victor rights over the persons and possessions of the vanquished greatly in excess of anything recognized in modern secular laws. In such a war, there can obviously be no peace, still less good will—only endless warfare until the final triumph of good over evil, of God over Satan. At most, the war may be interrupted by truces—tactical pauses until such time as it is convenient and expedient to resume the divinely ordained struggle. Peace, and with it good will, can only come when those who now perceive themselves as the warriors or the Party of God are ready to redefine the identity of the adversary and the purpose of the conflict.

Until they do—as most such movements have sooner or later done in the past—unfanatical believers of all faiths may agree that if indeed God is troubled with human enemies, then the most noxious are surely those who defame his name by portraying him as a patron of kidnappers and assassins, as a deity whose gospel is hatred and bloodshed, and whose greatness is proclaimed by the random slaughter of unoffending strangers—young and old, male and female—with bombs, guns, and kitchen knives.

33

The Roots of Muslim Rage

ꮯꭶꭹꭹ

1990

In one of his letters Thomas Jefferson remarked that in matters of religion "the maxim of civil government" should be reversed and we should rather say, "Divided we stand, united, we fall." In this remark Jefferson was setting forth with classic terseness an idea that has come to be regarded as essentially American: the separation of Church and State. This idea was not entirely new; it had some precedents in the writings of Spinoza, Locke, and the philosophers of the European Enlightenment. It was in the United States, however, that the principle was first given the force of law and gradually, in the course of two centuries, became a reality.

If the idea that religion and politics should be separated is relatively new, dating back a mere three hundred years, the idea that they are distinct dates back almost to the beginnings of Christianity. Christians are enjoined in their Scriptures to "render . . . unto Caesar the things which are Caesar's and unto God the things which are God's." While opinions have differed as to the real meaning of this phrase, it has generally been interpreted as legitimizing a situation in which two institutions exist side by side, each with its own laws and chain of authority—one concerned with religion, called the Church, the other concerned with politics, called the State. And since they are two, they may be joined or separated, subordinate or independent, and conflicts may arise between them over questions of demarcation and jurisdiction.

This formulation of the problems posed by the relations between religion and politics, and the possible solutions to those problems, arise from Christian, not universal, principles and experience. There are other religious traditions in which religion and politics are differently perceived, and in which, therefore, the problems and the possible solutions are radically different from those we know in the West. Most of these traditions, despite their often very high level of sophistication and achievement, remained or became local—limited to one region or one culture or one people. There is one, however, that in its worldwide distribution, its continuing vitality, its universalist aspirations, can be compared to Christianity, and that is Islam. . . .

Like every other civilization known to human history, the Muslim world in its heyday saw itself as the center of truth and enlightenment, surrounded by infidel barbarians whom it would in due course enlighten and civilize. But between the different groups of barbarians there was a crucial difference. The barbarians to the east and the south were polytheists and idolaters, offering no serious threat and no competition at all to Islam. In the north and west, in contrast, Muslims from an early date recognized a genuine rival—a competing world religion, a distinctive civilization inspired by that religion, and an empire that, though much smaller than theirs, was no less ambitious in its claims and aspirations. This was the entity known to itself and others as Christendom, a term that was long almost identical with Europe.

The struggle between these rival systems has now lasted for some fourteen centuries. It began with the advent of Islam, in the seventh century, and has continued virtually to the present day. It has consisted of a long series of attacks and counterattacks, jihads and crusades, conquests and reconquests. For the first thousand years Islam was advancing, Christendom in retreat and under threat. The new faith conquered the old Christian lands of the Levant and North Africa, and invaded Europe, ruling for a while in Sicily, Spain, Portugal, and even parts of France. The attempt by the Crusaders to recover the lost lands of Christendom in the east was held and thrown back, and even the Muslims' loss of southwestern Europe to the Reconquista was amply compensated by the Islamic advance into southeastern Europe, which twice reached as far as Vienna. For the past three hundred years, since the failure of the second Turkish siege of Vienna in 1683 and the rise of the European colonial empires in Asia and Africa, Islam has been on the defensive, and the Christian and post-Christian civilization of Europe and her daughters has brought the whole world, including Islam, within its orbit.

For a long time now there has been a rising tide of rebellion against this Western paramountcy, and a desire to reassert Muslim values and restore Muslim greatness. The Muslim has suffered successive stages of defeat. The first was his loss of domination in the world, to the advancing power of Russia and the West. The second was the undermining of his authority in his own country, through an invasion of foreign ideas and laws and ways of life and sometimes even foreign rulers or settlers, and the enfranchisement of native non-Muslim elements. The third—the last straw—was the challenge to his mastery in his own house, from emancipated women and rebellious children. It was too much to endure, and the outbreak of rage against these alien, infidel, and incomprehensible forces that had subverted his dominance, disrupted his society, and finally violated the sanctuary of his home was inevitable. It was also natural that this rage should be directed primarily against the millennial enemy and should draw its strength from ancient beliefs and loyalties.

Europe and her daughters? The phrase may seem odd to Americans, whose national myths, since the beginning of their nationhood and even earlier, have usually defined their very identity in opposition to Europe, as something new and radically different from the old European ways. This is not, however, the way that others have seen it; not often in Europe, and hardly ever elsewhere.

Though people of other races and cultures participated, for the most part involuntarily, in the discovery and creation of the Americas, this was, and in the eyes of the rest of the world long remained, a European enterprise, in which Europeans predominated and dominated and to which Europeans gave their languages, their religions, and much of their way of life.

For a very long time voluntary immigration to America was almost exclusively European. There were indeed some who came from the Muslim lands in the Middle East and North Africa, but few were Muslims; most were members of the Christian and to a lesser extent the Jewish minorities in those countries. Their departure for America, and their subsequent presence in America, must have strengthened rather than lessened the European image of America in Muslim eyes.

In the lands of Islam remarkably little was known about America. At first the voyages of discovery aroused some interest; the only surviving copy of Columbus's own map of America is a Turkish translation and adaptation, still preserved in the Topkapi Palace Museum, in Istanbul. A sixteenth-century Turkish geographer's account of the discovery of the New World, titled *The History of Western India*, was one of the first books printed in Turkey. But thereafter interest seems to have waned, and not much is said about America in Turkish, Arabic, or other Muslim languages until a relatively late date. A Moroccan ambassador who was in Spain at the time wrote what must surely be the first Arabic account of the American Revolution. The Sultan of Morocco signed a treaty of peace and friendship with the United States in 1787, and thereafter the new republic had a number of dealings, some friendly, some hostile, most commercial, with other Muslim states. These seem to have had little impact on either side. The American Revolution and the American republic to which it gave birth long remained unnoticed and unknown. Even the small but growing American presence in Muslim lands in the nineteenth century—merchants, consuls, missionaries, and teachers—aroused little or no curiosity, and is almost unmentioned in the Muslim literature and newspapers of the time.

The Second World War, the oil industry, and postwar developments brought many Americans to the Islamic lands; increasing numbers of Muslims also came to America, first as students, then as teachers or businessmen or other visitors, and eventually as immigrants. Cinema and later television brought the American way of life, or at any rate a certain version of it, before countless millions to whom the very name of America had previously been meaningless or unknown. A wide range of American products, particularly in the immediate postwar years, when European competition was virtually eliminated and Japanese competition had not yet arisen, reached into the remotest markets of the Muslim world, winning new customers and, perhaps more important, creating new tastes and ambitions. For some, America represented freedom and justice and opportunity. For many more, it represented wealth and power and success, at a time when these qualities were not regarded as sins or crimes.

And then came the great change, when the leaders of a widespread and widening religious revival sought out and identified their enemies as the enemies of God, and gave them "a local habitation and a name" in the Western Hemisphere. Suddenly, or so it seemed, America had become the archenemy, the incarnation of evil, the diabolic opponent of all that is good, and specifically, for Muslims, of Islam. Why?

Some Familiar Accusations

Among the components in the mood of anti-Westernism, and more especially of anti-Americanism, were certain intellectual influences coming from Europe. One of these was from Germany, where a negative view of America formed part of a school of thought by no means limited to the Nazis but including writers as diverse as Rainer Maria Rilke, Ernst Jünger, and Martin Heidegger. In this perception, America was the ultimate example of civilization without culture: rich and comfortable, materially advanced but soulless and artificial; assembled or at best constructed, not grown; mechanical, not organic; technologically complex but lacking the spirituality and vitality of the rooted, human, national cultures of the Germans and other "authentic" peoples. German philosophy, and particularly the philosophy of education, enjoyed a considerable vogue among Arab and some other Muslim intellectuals in the thirties and early forties, and this philosophic anti-Americanism was part of the message.

After the collapse of the Third Reich and the temporary ending of German influence, another philosophy, even more anti-American, took its place—the Soviet version of Marxism, with a denunciation of Western capitalism and of America as its most advanced and dangerous embodiment. And when Soviet influence began to fade, there was yet another to take its place, or at least to supplement its working—the new mystique of Third Worldism, emanating from Western Europe, particularly France, and later also from the United States, and drawing at times on both these earlier philosophies. This mystique was helped by the universal human tendency to invent a golden age in the past, and the specifically European propensity to locate it elsewhere. A new variant of the old golden-age myth placed it in the Third World, where the innocence of the non-Western

Adam and Eve was ruined by the Western serpent. This view took as axiomatic the goodness and purity of the East and the wickedness of the West, expanding in an exponential curve of evil from Western Europe to the United States. These ideas, too, fell on fertile ground, and won widespread support.

But though these imported philosophies helped to provide intellectual expression for anti-Westernism and anti-Americanism, they did not cause it, and certainly they do not explain the widespread anti-Westernism that made so many in the Middle East and elsewhere in the Islamic world receptive to such ideas.

It must surely be clear that what won support for such totally diverse doctrines was not Nazi race theory, which can have had little appeal for Arabs, or Soviet atheistic communism, which can have had little appeal for Muslims, but rather their common anti-Westernism. Nazism and communism were the main forces opposed to the West, both as a way of life and as a power in the world, and as such they could count on at least the sympathy if not the support of those who saw in the West their principal enemy.

But why the hostility in the first place? If we turn from the general to the specific, there is no lack of individual policies and actions, pursued and taken by individual Western governments, that have aroused the passionate anger of Middle Eastern and other Islamic peoples. Yet all too often, when these policies are abandoned and the problems resolved, there is only a local and temporary alleviation. The French have left Algeria, the British have left Egypt, the Western oil companies have left their oil wells, the westernizing Shah has left Iran—yet the generalized resentment of the fundamentalists and other extremists against the West and its friends remains and grows and is not appeased.

The cause most frequently adduced for anti-American feeling among Muslims today is American support for Israel. This support is certainly a factor of importance, increasing with nearness and involvement. But here again there are some oddities, difficult to explain in terms of a single, simple cause. In the early days of the foundation of Israel, while the United States maintained a certain distance, the Soviet Union granted immediate *de jure* recognition and support, and arms sent from a Soviet satellite, Czechoslovakia, saved the infant state of Israel from defeat and death in its first weeks of life. Yet there seems to have been no great ill will toward the Soviets for these policies, and no corresponding good will toward the United States. In 1956 it was the United States that intervened, forcefully and decisively, to secure the withdrawal of Israeli, British, and French forces from Egypt—yet in the late fifties and sixties it was to the Soviets, not America, that the rulers of Egypt, Syria, Iraq, and other states turned for arms; it was with the Soviet bloc that they formed bonds of solidarity at the United Nations and in the world generally. More recently, the rulers of the Islamic Republic of Iran have offered the most principled and uncompromising denunciation of Israel and Zionism. Yet even these leaders, before as well as after the death of Ayatollah Ruhollah Khomeini, when they decided for reasons of their own to enter into a dialogue of sorts, found it easier to talk to Jerusalem than to Washington. At the same time, Western hostages in Lebanon, many of them devoted to Arab causes and some of them converts to Islam, are seen and treated by their captors as limbs of the Great Satan.

Another explanation, more often heard from Muslim dissidents, attributes anti-American feeling to American support for hated regimes, seen as reactionary by radicals, as impious by conservatives, as corrupt and tyrannical by both. This accusation has some plausibility, and could help to explain why an essentially inner-directed, often anti-nationalist movement should turn against a foreign power. But it does not suffice, especially since support for such regimes has been limited both in extent and—as the Shah discovered—in effectiveness.

Clearly, something deeper is involved than these specific grievances, numerous and important as they may be—something deeper that turns every disagreement into a problem and makes every problem insoluble.

This revulsion against America, more generally against the West, is by no means limited to the Muslim world; nor have Muslims, with the exception of the Iranian mullahs and their disciples elsewhere, experienced and exhibited the more virulent forms of this feeling. The mood of disillusionment and hostility has affected many other parts of the world, and has even reached some elements in the United States. It is from these last, speaking for themselves and claiming to speak for the oppressed peoples of the Third World, that the most widely publicized explanations—and justifications—of this rejection of Western civilization and its values have of late been heard.

The accusations are familiar. We of the West are accused of sexism, racism, and imperialism, institutionalized in patriarchy and slavery, tyranny and exploitation. To these charges, and to others as heinous, we have no option but to plead guilty—not as Americans, nor yet as Westerners, but simply as human beings, as members of the human race. In none of these sins are we the only sinners, and in some of them we are very far from being the worst. The treatment of women in the Western world, and more generally in Christendom, has always been unequal and often oppressive, but even at its worst it was rather better than the rule of polygamy and concubinage that has otherwise been the almost universal lot of womankind on this planet.

Is racism, then, the main grievance? Certainly the word figures prominently in publicity addressed to Western, Eastern European, and some Third World audiences. It figures less prominently in what is written and published for home consumption, and has become a generalized and meaningless term of abuse—rather like "fascism," which is nowadays imputed to opponents even by spokesmen for one-party, nationalist dictatorships of various complexions and shirt colors.

Slavery is today universally denounced as an offense against humanity, but within living memory it has been practiced and even defended as a necessary institution, established and regulated by divine law. The peculiarity of the peculiar institution, as Americans once called it, lay not in its existence but in its abolition. Westerners were the first to break the consensus of acceptance and to outlaw slavery, first at home, then in the other territories they controlled, and finally wherever in the world they were able to exercise power or influence—in a word, by means of imperialism.

Is imperialism, then, the grievance? Some Western powers, and in a sense Western civilization as a whole, have certainly been guilty of imperialism, but are we really to believe that in the expansion of Western Europe there was a quality of moral delinquency lacking in such earlier, relatively innocent expansions as those of the Arabs or the Mongols or the Ottomans, or in more recent expansions such as that which brought the rulers of Muscovy to the Baltic, the Black Sea, the Caspian, the Hindu Kush, and the Pacific Ocean? In having practiced sexism, racism, and imperialism, the West was merely following the common practice of mankind through the millennia of recorded history. Where it is distinct from all other civilizations is in having recognized, named, and tried, not entirely without success, to remedy these historic diseases. And that is surely a matter for congratulation, not condemnation. We do not hold Western medical science in general, or Dr. Parkinson and Dr. Alzheimer in particular, responsible for the diseases they diagnosed and to which they gave their names.

Of all these offenses the one that is most widely, frequently, and vehemently denounced is undoubtedly imperialism—sometimes just Western, sometimes Eastern (that is, Soviet) and Western alike. But the way this term is used in the literature of Islamic fundamentalists often suggests that it may not carry quite the same meaning for them as for its Western critics. In many of these writings the term "imperialist" is given a distinctly religious significance, being used in association, and sometimes interchangeably, with "missionary," and denoting a form of attack that includes the Crusades as well as the modern colonial empires. One also sometimes gets the impression that the offense of imperialism is not— as for Western critics—the domination by one people over another but rather the allocation of roles in this relationship. What is truly evil and unacceptable is the domination of infidels over true believers. For true believers to rule misbelievers is proper and natural, since this provides for the maintenance of the holy law, and gives the misbelievers both the opportunity and the incentive to embrace the true faith. But for misbelievers to rule over true believers is blasphemous and unnatural, since it leads to the corruption of religion and morality in society, and to the flouting or even the abrogation of God's law. This may help us to understand the current troubles in such diverse places as Ethiopian Eritrea, Indian Kashmir, Chinese Sinkiang, and Yugoslav Kosovo, in all of which Muslim populations are ruled by non-Muslim governments. It may also explain why spokesmen for the new Muslim minorities in Western Europe demand for Islam a degree of legal protection which those countries no longer give to Christianity and have never given to Judaism. Nor, of course, did the governments of the countries of origin of these Muslim spokesmen ever accord such protection to religions other than their own. In their perception, there is no contradiction in these attitudes. The true faith, based on God's final revelation, must be protected from insult and abuse; other faiths, being either false or incomplete, have no right to any such protection.

There are other difficulties in the way of accepting imperialism as an explanation of Muslim hostility, even if we define imperialism narrowly and specifically, as the invasion and domination of Muslim countries by non-Muslims. If the hostility is directed against imperialism in that sense, why has it been so much stronger against Western Europe, which has relinquished all its Muslim possessions and dependencies, than against Russia, which still rules, with no light hand, over many millions of reluctant Muslim subjects and over ancient Muslim cities and countries? And why should it include the United States, which, apart from a brief interlude in the Muslim-minority area of the Philippines, has never ruled any Muslim population? The last surviving European empire with Muslim subjects, that of the Soviet Union, far from being the target of criticism and attack, has been almost exempt. Even the most recent repressions of Muslim revolts in the southern and central Asian republics of the USSR incurred no more than relatively mild words of expostulation, coupled with a disclaimer of any desire to interfere in what are quaintly called the "internal affairs" of the USSR and a request for the preservation of order and tranquillity on the frontier.

One reason for this somewhat surprising restraint is to be found in the nature of events in Soviet Azerbaijan. Islam is obviously an important and potentially a growing element in the Azerbaijani sense of identity, but it is not at present a dominant element, and the Azerbaijani movement has more in common with the liberal patriotism of Europe than with Islamic fundamentalism. Such a movement would not arouse the sympathy of the rulers of the Islamic Republic. It might even alarm them, since a genuinely democratic national state run by the people of Soviet Azerbaijan would exercise a powerful attraction on their kinsmen immediately to the south, in Iranian Azerbaijan.

Another reason for this relative lack of concern for the 50 million or more Muslims under Soviet rule may be a calculation of risk and advantage. The Soviet Union is near, along the northern frontiers of Turkey, Iran, and Afghanistan; America and even Western Europe are far away. More to the point, it has not hitherto been the practice of the Soviets to quell disturbances with water cannon and rubber bullets, with TV cameras in attendance, or to release arrested persons on bail and allow them access to domestic and foreign media. The Soviets do not interview their harshest critics on prime time, or tempt them with teaching, lecturing, and writing engagements. On the contrary, their ways of indicating displeasure with criticism can often be quite disagreeable.

But fear of reprisals, though no doubt important, is not the only or perhaps even the principal reason for the relatively minor place assigned to the Soviet Union, as compared with the West, in the demonology of fundamentalism. After all, the great social and intellectual and economic changes that have transformed most of the Islamic world, and given rise to such commonly denounced Western evils as consumerism and secularism, emerged from the West, not from the Soviet Union. No one could accuse the Soviets of consumerism; their materialism is philosophic—to be precise, dialectical—and has little or nothing to do in practice with providing the good things of life. Such provision represents another kind of materialism, often designated by its opponents as crass. It is associated with the capitalist West and not with the communist East, which has practiced, or at least imposed on its subjects, a degree of austerity that would impress a Sufi saint.

Nor were the Soviets, until very recently, vulnerable to charges of secularism, the other great fundamentalist accusation against the West. Though atheist, they were not godless, and had in fact created an elaborate state apparatus to impose the worship of their gods—an apparatus with its own orthodoxy, a hierarchy to define and enforce it, and an armed inquisition to detect and extirpate heresy. The separation of religion from the state does not mean the establishment of irreligion by the state, still less the forcible imposition of an anti-religious philosophy. Soviet secularism, like Soviet consumerism, holds no temptation for the Muslim masses, and is losing what appeal it had for Muslim intellectuals. More than ever before it is Western capitalism and democracy that provide an authentic and attractive alternative to traditional ways of thought and life. Fundamentalist leaders are not mistaken in seeing in Western civilization the greatest challenge to the way of life that they wish to retain or restore for their people.

A Clash of Civilizations

The origins of secularism in the West may be found in two circumstances—in early Christian teachings and, still more, experience, which created two institutions, Church and State; and in later Christian conflicts, which drove the two apart. Muslims, too, had their religious disagreements, but there was nothing remotely approaching the ferocity of the Christian struggles between Protestants and Catholics, which devastated Christian Europe in the sixteenth and seventeenth centuries and finally drove Christians in desperation to evolve a doctrine of the separation of religion from the state. Only by depriving religious institutions of coercive power, it seemed, could Christendom restrain the murderous intolerance and persecution that Christians had visited on followers of other religions and, most of all, on those who professed other forms of their own.

Muslims experienced no such need and evolved no such doctrine. There was no need for secularism in Islam, and even its pluralism was very different from that of the pagan Roman Empire, so vividly described by Edward Gibbon when he remarked that "the various modes of worship, which prevailed in the Roman world, were all considered by the people, as equally true; by the philosopher, as equally false; and by the magistrate, as equally useful." Islam was never prepared, either in theory or in practice, to accord full equality to those who held other beliefs and practiced other forms of worship. It did, however, accord to the holders of partial truth a degree of practical as well as theoretical tolerance rarely paralleled in the Christian world until the West adopted a measure of secularism in the late-seventeenth and eighteenth centuries.

At first the Muslim response to Western civilization was one of admiration and emulation—an immense respect for the achievements of the West, and a desire to imitate and adopt them. This desire arose from a keen and growing awareness of the weakness, poverty, and backwardness of the Islamic world as compared with the advancing West. The disparity first became apparent on the battlefield but soon spread to other areas of human activity. Muslim writers observed and described the wealth and power of the West, its science and technology, its manufactures, and its forms of government. For a time the secret of Western success was seen to lie in two achievements: economic advancement and especially industry; political institutions and especially freedom. Several generations of reformers and modernizers tried to adapt these and introduce them to their own countries, in the hope that they would thereby be able to achieve equality with the West and perhaps restore their lost superiority.

In our own time this mood of admiration and emulation has, among many Muslims, given way to one of hostility and rejection. In part this mood is surely due to a feeling of humiliation—a growing awareness, among the heirs of an old, proud, and long dominant civilization, of having been overtaken, overborne, and overwhelmed by those whom they regarded as their inferiors. In part this mood is due to events in the Western world itself. One factor of major importance was certainly the impact of two great suicidal wars, in which Western civilization tore itself apart, bringing untold destruction to its own and other peoples, and in which the belligerents conducted an immense propaganda effort, in the Islamic world and elsewhere, to discredit and undermine each other. The message they brought found many listeners, who were all the more ready to respond in that their own experience of Western ways was not happy. The introduction of Western commercial, financial, and industrial methods did indeed bring great wealth, but it accrued to transplanted Westerners and members of Westernized minorities, and to only a few among the mainstream Muslim population. In time these few became more numerous, but they remained isolated from the masses, differing from them even in their dress and style of life. Inevitably they were seen as agents of and collaborators with what was once again regarded as a hostile world. Even the political institutions that had come from the West were discredited, being judged not by their Western originals but by their local imitations, installed by enthusiastic Muslim reformers. These, operating in a situation beyond their control, using imported and inappropriate methods that they did not fully understand, were unable to cope with the rapidly developing crises and were one by one overthrown. For vast numbers of Middle Easterners, Western-style economic methods brought poverty, Western-style political institutions brought tyranny, even Western-style warfare brought defeat. It is hardly surprising that so many were willing to listen to voices telling them that the old Islamic ways were best and that their only salvation was to throw aside the pagan innovations of the reformers and return to the True Path that God had prescribed for his people.

Ultimately, the struggle of the fundamentalists is against two enemies, secularism and modernism. The war against secularism is conscious and explicit, and there is by now a whole literature denouncing secularism as an evil neo-pagan force in the modern world and attributing it variously to the Jews, the West, and the United States. The war against modernity is for the most part neither conscious nor explicit, and is directed against the whole process of change that has taken place in the Islamic world in the past century or more and has transformed the political, economic, social, and even cultural structures of Muslim countries. Islamic fundamentalism has given an aim and a form to the otherwise aimless and formless resentment and anger of the Muslim masses at the forces that have devalued their traditional values and loyalties and, in the final analysis, robbed them of their beliefs, their aspirations, their dignity, and to an increasing extent even their livelihood.

There is something in the religious culture of Islam which inspired, in even the humblest peasant or peddler, a dignity and a courtesy toward others never exceeded and rarely equalled in other civilizations. And yet, in moments of upheaval and disruption, when the deeper passions are stirred, this dignity and courtesy toward others can give way to an explosive mixture of rage and hatred which impels even the government of an ancient and civilized country—even the spokesman of a great spiritual and ethical religion—to espouse kidnapping and assassination, and try to find, in the life of their Prophet, approval and indeed precedent for such actions.

The instinct of the masses is not false in locating the ultimate source of these cataclysmic changes in the West and in attributing the disruption of their old way of life to the impact of Western domination, Western influence, or Western precept and example. And since the United States is the legitimate heir of European civilization and the recognized and unchallenged leader of the West, the United States has inherited the resulting grievances and become the focus for the pent-up hate and anger. Two examples may suffice. In November of 1979 an angry mob attacked and burned the U.S. Embassy in Islamabad, Pakistan. The stated cause of the crowd's anger was the seizure of the Great Mosque in Mecca by a group of Muslim dissidents—an event in which there was no American involvement whatsoever. Almost ten years later, in February of 1989, again in Islamabad, the USIS center was attacked by angry crowds, this time to protest the publication of Salman Rushdie's *Satanic Verses*. Rushdie is a British citizen of Indian birth, and his book had been published five months previously in England. But what provoked the mob's anger, and also the Ayatollah Khomeini's subsequent pronouncement of a death sentence on the author, was the publication of the book in the United States.

It should by now be clear that we are facing a mood and a movement far transcending the level of issues and policies and the governments that pursue them. This is no less than a clash of civilizations—the perhaps irrational but surely historic reaction of an ancient rival against our Judeo-Christian heritage, our secular present, and the worldwide expansion of both. It is crucially important that we on our side should not be provoked into an equally historic but also equally irrational reaction against that rival.

Not all the ideas imported from the West by Western intruders or native Westernizers have been rejected. Some have been accepted by even the most radical Islamic fundamentalists, usually without acknowledgment of source, and suffering a sea change into something rarely rich but often strange. One such was political freedom, with the associated notions and practices of representation, election, and constitutional government. Even the Islamic Republic of Iran has a written constitution and an elected assembly, as well as a kind of episcopate, for none of which is there any prescription in Islamic teaching or any precedent in the Islamic past. All these institutions are clearly adapted from Western models. Muslim states have also retained many of the cultural and social customs of the West and the symbols that express them, such as the form and style of male (and to a much lesser extent female) clothing, notably in the military. The use of Western-invented guns and tanks and planes is a military necessity, but the continued use of fitted tunics and peaked caps is a cultural choice. From constitutions to Coca-Cola, from tanks and television to T-shirts, the symbols and artifacts, and through them the ideas, of the West have retained—even strengthened—their appeal.

The movement nowadays called fundamentalism is not the only Islamic tradition. There are others, more tolerant, more open, that helped to inspire the great achievements of Islamic civilization in the past, and we may hope that these other traditions will in time prevail. But before this issue is decided there will be a hard struggle, in which we of the West can do little or nothing. Even the attempt might do harm, for these are issues that Muslims must decide among themselves. And in the meantime we must take great care on all sides to avoid the danger of a new era of religious wars, arising from the exacerbation of differences and the revival of ancient prejudices.

To this end we must strive to achieve a better appreciation of other religious and political cultures, through the study of their history, their literature, and their achievements. At the same time, we may hope that they will try to achieve a better understanding of ours, and especially that they will understand and respect, even if they do not choose to adopt for themselves, our Western perception of the proper relationship between religion and politics.

To describe this perception I shall end as I began, with a quotation from an American President, this time not the justly celebrated Thomas Jefferson but the somewhat unjustly neglected John Tyler, who, in a letter dated July 10, 1843, gave eloquent and indeed prophetic expression to the principle of religious freedom:

> The United States have adventured upon a great and noble experiment, which is believed to have been hazarded in the absence of all previous precedent—that of total separation of Church and State. No religious establishment *by law* exists among us. The conscience is left free from all restraint and each is permitted to worship his Maker after his own judgement. The offices of the Government are open alike to all. No tithes are levied to support an established Hierarchy, nor is the fallible judgement of man set up as the sure and infallible creed of faith. The Mahommedan, if he will to come among us would have the privilege guaranteed to him by the constitution to worship according to the Koran; and the East Indian might erect a shrine to Brahma if it so pleased him. Such is the spirit of toleration inculcated by our political Institutions. . . . The Hebrew persecuted and down trodden in other regions takes up his abode among us with none to make him afraid. . . . and the Aegis of the Government is over him to defend and protect him. Such is the great experiment which we have tried, and such are the happy fruits which have resulted from it; our system of free government would be imperfect without it.
>
> The body may be oppressed and manacled and yet survive; but if the mind of man be fettered, its energies and faculties perish, and what remains is of the earth, earthly. Mind should be free as the light or as the air.

34

The Other Middle East Problems

&(&@)

1995

Not long ago I was having lunch with a Saudi Arabian in Washington, and in the course of the conversation he rounded on me and said: "Why is it that when you Westerners want to talk about the Arab-Israeli conflict, you call it the Middle East problem?" "Do you think," he said "that it is the only problem we have? Do you think that is the worst problem we have? I wish it were; it would be a piece of cake."

"Piece of cake" was no doubt an exaggeration, but he had a valid point. Certainly the Arab-Israeli conflict is not the only problem of the Middle East, nor is it by a long chalk the bloodiest. The Iraq-Iran war produced more casualties than all the Arab-Israeli wars put together, including all the participants. The Gulf War of 1990–91, not to mention the civil wars in Lebanon and Iraq and elsewhere, would also score higher in sheer destructiveness. On a scale of bloodiness, the Arab-Israeli conflict would indeed rank rather low.

Nor is it the most dangerous. It appeared so at one time when rival superpowers were involved, but it was precisely that involvement that made it less dangerous, in that the superpowers were able to exercise some restraint and, thanks to them, the dangers were known, measured, assessed and managed. The limits were set; it was dangerous and destructive to the participants as are all such conflicts, but it had long ceased to be dangerous to anyone else.

It is certainly not the most complicated of the problems of the Middle East. Indeed basically, the Arab-Israeli conflict is a very simple problem; it consists of three simple questions which I put in sequence: Should Israel exist? If so, where should its frontiers be? And, what should there be on the other side of those frontiers?

Is it the conflict which has caused the most suffering? No, by no means. No one can fail to be deeply moved by the long drawn-out sufferings of the Palestinian refugees. But in the awful arithmetic of the twentieth century, they are among the privileged of refugees as compared to the countless unrepresented, unsponsored, unsupported millions of others who have fled or been driven from their homes in Europe, in Asia, in Africa, in Central America and elsewhere.

But assuredly it remains the most visible and the most audible of the problems of the region, the one which attracts and receives the most attention, to the extent that some have even claimed that this problem is the key to all the others, with the bizarre corollary that if this problem could be solved, all the others would miraculously disappear. It is possible, nowadays with very little effort of imagination, to conceive a situation in which there is peace between Israel and the Arab world. It is even possible, with somewhat more imagination, and evoking a more remote and complicated contingency, to imagine a situation in which there is peace between Israel and the pro-Arabs. But if even that could be attained, the fundamental problems of the region would surely still remain; they would be no nearer solution.

What are these other problems? It might be useful to begin by looking at the long war which was fought between Iraq and Iran, two regional powers; a war which went on for many years and caused untold destruction to both parties. What were they fighting about? One could give many different answers, all of them in some measure, in some sense, true. We can look at it as a simple, old-fashioned territorial war, a war over turf, over the specific issue of the Shatt al-'Arab waterway—that piece of coast at the southern end of the two rivers of Iraq, at the northern end of the Persian Gulf, control of which was vital to both parties. This was certainly an important element in the war, and exemplifies one of the major themes of Middle Eastern conflicts: territorial disputes.

It could also be seen as a national conflict. One of the contestants—Iraq—is Arab. The other—Iran—is Persian. Though both Muslim, these are different peoples, speaking different languages, with different cultures. There is a Persian minority in Iraq; there is a much larger Arab minority in southwestern Iran, and the war could be, and sometimes was, perceived or presented as a national, or even ethnic conflict between Arabs and Persians. It also had a religious dimension in that Iran is Shi'a and is indeed ruled by a militant Shiite hierocracy while Iraq, though inhabited by a Shi'a majority both in the country and in the capital, is ruled by a Sunni ascendancy. This was an important theme in the propaganda of the Iranians against Iraq during the war, and one naturally avoided by the Iraqis.

The war could be seen, and was interpreted, as an ideological clash between radical, fundamentalist Islam as represented by the Iranian regime and secular modernism, as represented, particularly in its own propaganda, by the Iraqi Ba'thist regime. Much of the Iraqi propaganda of the time presented Saddam

Hussein as the defender of secular modernism against obscurantist religious reaction. Later, it will be recalled, he changed his mind on this point.

The war could be explained in economic terms, as a dispute over oil interests; as a conflict between regional powers for regional hegemony—for control of the Gulf, of the eastern half of the Middle East, possibly with eventual subsequent ambitions even for the western half. Some have remarked, then and subsequently, that the Iranian revolution has been going through the classical phases established in both the French and the Russian revolutions. They inflicted and endured the Terror; they achieved their Valmy; they entered and have not yet emerged from their Thermidor; Napoleon—or Stalin—might come next.

The war can also be seen and has often been much presented as a clash of personalities. Khomeini himself seems very much to have seen it in that light, and is often quoted as having named as his principal adversaries the Shah, President Carter and Saddam Hussein. He swore that before his death he would get rid of all three of them. Two out of three was not a bad score.

All these elements were present; all of them appeared, not only in the discussions about the war but also in the self-projection and propaganda of the participants on both sides, sometimes using the same material in interestingly different ways. The Iraqis, for example, made great play with the Battle of Qadisiyya, fought in the early days of Islam when, in Iraqi terms, an Arab army defeated a Persian army, thus setting an example to be followed by their remote descendants at the present time. From the Iranian point of view, of course, this was an Islamic army defeating a pagan army, and thus a blessed event, preparing the way for the Islamization of pagan Iran. Both sides claimed the same victory; both sides did so justly. I was reminded of my school days in England when the Battle of Hastings was taught as having been won by the Normans over the Anglo-Saxons and we as Britons were taught to identify with both.

Let us start with the easiest of these different types of problem: the political, i.e., territorial, national and ethnic, disputes; and among those, let us start again with the clearest and simplest problem, that of frontiers. If we look at the map of Europe, we see a number of lines on the map, most very irregular lines, except for a few that follow geographical features; lines drawn by a thousand years of history and struggle. The frontiers on the map of the Middle East are to a remarkable extent straight lines. They were mostly drawn by statesmen with rulers on maps—statesmen who were not Arab, not Persian, not Turkish, but British or French or occasionally Italian. In this respect the map of the Middle East looks rather like the map of North America where similar reasons produced similar results, with the extraordinary difference that this was not an area of new settlement but of ancient civilizations.

The frontiers, and the entities which those frontiers enclose, are, with few exceptions, early modern or recent creations. The older ones are Ottoman, the more recent are European imperial artifacts. Not surprisingly, these artificial entities, with their artificial frontiers, were for long not fully well accepted or understood by the people who lived in them. The legacy of imperial partition consisted of a whole series of disputes—over frontiers, over minorities, and a variety of claims arising from these. I want to enumerate and classify the more important of these disputes and claims, those which have caused, or continue to cause, most trouble.

Let us start with inter-Arab problems, disputes between Arab states over frontiers. These are of two kinds. In the first, an Arab state claims territory from another, neighboring Arab state. In the second, an Arab state claims the whole of another Arab state, which it does not recognize as a legitimate sovereign entity. There are many examples of the first kind. They have included, in the past, the disputes between Algeria and Morocco over certain border areas between the two countries; between Egypt and the Sudan; between Egypt and Libya; and between Iraq and Kuwait when that conflict was over frontier adjustments. The importance of such disputes may vary according to who lives on top of the soil and what resources are hidden underneath it.

More troublesome are the cases where the claim is not to rectify but to remove the frontier and annex the entire country. This was the nature of the Iraqi claim to Kuwait, of which we have recently been reminded, but which was by no means new. According to this claim Kuwait was Iraq irredenta, part of Iraq unjustly separated by British imperialism. For a long time there was a similar Egyptian claim to the Sudan, but this now seems to have been abandoned. The Syrians maintain—though they do not always assert—their claim to Lebanon in its entirety, and not just to Lebanon but also to Greater Syria, including all the lands between Taurus and Sinai. The Moroccan claim to the former Spanish territories to the south is of the same nature.

All these are disputes between Arab states. There are also territorial disputes, some quiescent, some active, between Arab states and non-Arab states. One such is the Iranian claim to Bahrain; another is the Turkish claim, now in abeyance, to Mosul. In both cases, the claimants can justly point out that the existing frontiers were imperial arrangements made without reference to the needs or desires or rights of the inhabitants. The Turkish claim to Mosul is certainly no weaker, to say the least, than the Iraqi claim to Kuwait, and one may think that in legal terms it was unwise for Iraq to raise that particular issue.

There are also claims by Arab states on non-Arab states, such as the Syrian claim, never renounced, to the Sanjak of Alexandretta; the Libyan claim to territory in Chad; and the Moroccan claim to the Spanish Presidios. Some claims are not specifically about land or people but about resources, the most important being the Turkish control over the headwaters of the Tigris and Euphrates, an irritation to Syria and still more to Iraq. There are many more such claims which have been or may be asserted between the former Soviet republics in Central Asia and Transcaucasia. If the Soviets had devised the frontiers with a view to causing future trouble, they hardly could have done a better job.

On both sides of the frontiers, wherever drawn, there are minorities, giving rise to ethnic, religious, and sometimes even racial clashes. There are Persians in Iraq and in the Gulf States. There are Turks in Iraq—perhaps as many as a million or more. There are Blacks all along the southern edges of the Arab lands in North Africa, from the Sudan through Chad to Mauritania, in regions of ancient grievances and an endemic state of conflict going back for more than a millennium. There are significant ethnic minorities within these states: the non-Arab, non-Muslim Southerners in the Sudan; the Berbers all across North Africa; the Kurds in northern Iraq and the neighboring areas. There are religious minorities. The Jews have gone, the Christians are diminishing in numbers and influence, and in some areas are under threat. But Muslim religious minorities in Muslim lands remain: the Shi'a, not a minority but a subjugated majority in Iraq; important Shi'a populations in the eastern province of Saudi Arabia and in several of the Gulf States; and a religious mosaic in Lebanon.

Underlying all these national, territorial, ethnic and religious differences and disputes, there is the deeper problem affecting the whole area: the unresolved clash of identities, of loyalties, of allegiances. On the one hand, there is the imported, still not fully assimilated European notion of country and nation, and the idea of popular government deriving its legitimacy from the people over whom it rules and operating through some kind of legislative assembly elected by and responsible to the people. Against these, there is a very different tradition of identity defined not by country or nation, which are regarded as minor or insignificant, but by community, by religious belief and practice. In this tradition, the individual owes his primary loyalty to the community and to the polity that is based on it. Its government is regulated by immutable and eternal divine law, and its ruler is indeed responsible—not to the people, but to God.

A classic example of the clash of identities and allegiances can be seen in Egypt, a nation and a country sharply defined by both history and geography, but with three different over-lapping identities. At various times in their history, Egyptians have defined themselves in different ways. For some, they are Arabs because they use Arabic and share a common culture with other countries of Arabic speech. Others see themselves primarily as Egyptians, with a sense of identity and continuity going back to remote antiquity. Others again regard both the Egyptian and the Arabic identities as unimportant and outweighed by the common brotherhood of Islam. These three identities—Arab, Egyptian, Muslim—are expressed in different ideologies, and pursued with great vigor by different political groups, parties and alignments, often in conflict and of course expressed also in different notions of sovereignty.

Immediately after the murder of Anwar Sadat, the leader of the group of four assassins who murdered him exclaimed to the world "I have killed Pharaoh!"—a remarkable comment if one considers that this was an Egyptian speaking in a country where they have now been taught for several generations that Pharaoh was not the figure of evil depicted in the Qur'an but a great heroic figure of antiquity, a source of legitimate Egyptian national and patriotic pride. The murderer of Sadat obviously did not think of Pharaoh in those lines; he did not admire and claim Pharaoh as, for example, Saddam Hussein admires and claims Nebuchadnezzar, but rather was reverting to the Qur'anic Pharaoh who, far from being a hero, is the very paradigm of the unjust and tyrannical ruler.

Apart from Egypt, there are very few other countries where one can detect and trace back a continuing identity through a very long period of time. Yemen is one; Morocco is another; and the rest become more doubtful. Algeria and Tunisia are really Ottoman creations, owing their identity in their present forms to developments during the Ottoman period. Others are still more recent: the states of the Fertile Crescent fashioned in the Anglo-French carve-up; and Libya, invented by an official in the Italian Colonial Ministry and endowed with a name taken from Roman political geography.

It is hardly surprising, in these circumstances, that in such countries there should be a yearning, a striving for something nobler, vaster, higher, greater than the petty sovereignties into which they divided, and something better than the often rather squalid politics with which the affairs of these countries are conducted and their peoples governed. For a while it seemed that the response to this striving was pan-Arabism, the hope for a greater, vaster Arab state, but that seems to have failed and it has left a vacancy for the alternative program of pan-Islamism. That has not yet failed. It remains a very powerful and attractive cause in many of these countries.

We can better understand what is happening and see what the dangers for the future are likely to be in these countries, if we envisage their identities at three levels. There is the intermediate level, the one which is normally operative and at which most public affairs are conducted—that is, the level of the sovereign state. Above that level, there is some larger entity to which they feel that they belong, which may be Arab or, at the present time, is more likely to be Islamic. Such notions as Asianism or Africanism, though they may be powerful in other places east and south of the Middle East, have very little impact in the countries of the Arab and Muslim world. Asia and Africa are not Arab or Muslim notions. They are inventions of Greek geography with little or no impact on Muslim or Arab thought.

At the lower level, there is the older, deeper, more intense loyalty of the tribe, the ethnic group, the sect, the faction, the region and the like. There is a famous line in Browning's *The Grammarian's Funeral* describing the Grammarian "aiming at a million, missing a unit." It often happens that aiming at the higher level and missing, the State disintegrates into its component parts, to the lower level of the squabbling, feuding, fighting mini-states based on regional or ethnic or sectarian loyalties. This leads to the kind of situation for which the term "Lebanization" or "Lebanonization" has been devised, to indicate the fragmentation of the body politic into its component parts, through the loss of power on the part of the State and its inability either to evoke loyalty or to impose obedience.

These political differences also have important cultural counterparts. There is for example the question of language: what form of language should be the national language, the state language? Not an easy question; but it can be one of enormous importance. The Arab world, from the frontier of Iran to the Atlantic Ocean, has in principle one language; that is to say, one written language, an artificial language in the sense that it is not spoken naturally in any part of that vast region, but nevertheless a vibrant, evolving language and an important binding force. There are some who have argued in the past, though latterly one hasn't heard this so much, that the common literary language, far from being a progressive factor, has been the precise opposite; that by tying their education to what is in effect a dead language, they have prevented the natural development and evolution which occurred in Western Europe when bad Latin gave way in time to French, Spanish, Italian and Portuguese and produced a new literature of a liveliness and vigor quite impossible for medieval Latin. Arabic, according to this argument, is still at the stage of medieval Latin.

The Turks may soon confront a similar problem: spoken Turkish does not differ more from Istanbul to Tashkent than Arabic does from Baghdad to Marrakesh, but the Turks, unlike the Arabs, have no common written language. This raises profoundly important educational questions, such as the nature of cultural identity in these countries and the possibility of intellectual interaction.

By now it is hardly necessary to draw attention to the economic problems of the region, and more articularly to the problem of rising population unmatched by any corresponding increase in resources. There is difficulty in feeding that population, which in turn is linked with the lack of technical development. The recent war in the Gulf demonstrated graphically that you may buy technology and technologists if you have the money, but that does not make you a technologically advanced society. This technological backwardness of the region is not new. Some research recently conducted by my Princeton colleague Charles Issawi illustrates this in a very interesting way. The earliest technological device for producing energy is the mill—the water-mill or the wind-mill or the wind-mill, which are the first innovations that take us beyond the stage of human or animal strength. Mills are high visible and not easily movable and are therefore taxed, and since they are taxed they figure in documents and archives. We can thus pinpoint the number of mills with surprising accuracy in many places.

In the sixteenth century, at the height of Ottoman power and greatness, there were considerably fewer mills to the population in the Ottoman lands than there were in eleventh century England when the Domesday book was compiled after the Norman Conquest. One may find other reasons for that, but the fact in itself is significant and tallies well with other evidence pointing to a technological lack of development.

Another problem of the region has been mismanagement of the economy for a variety of reasons, among them ideology. . . .

Without great effort, one can list a number of other problems already acute and likely to become more so: overpopulation, leading to emigration and perhaps in time to a collision with Europe; and decline in the value of oil and eventually even the end of the oil era in human history. There was a time when mankind managed without oil, and the time will come when technological progress elsewhere in the world will make oil obsolete as a major source of energy. Even short of that, economic mismanagement has greatly diminished the benefits which might have been derived from oil. One is sometimes left with the conclusion that those countries which have no oil have, for this very reason, done rather better economically than those that have.

All these difficulties lead to something that we see happening around us all the time—to what we might call a breakdown of the consensus, of that generally accepted set of rules and principles by which a polity can survive, and without which the society cannot function even under autocratic government, as the Soviet Union demonstrated. This is a time when we see not a revaluation of values, as Nietzsche called it, but a devaluation of values, in which the old values are discredited and the new values offered in their place are neither understood nor accepted. The result is a social fragmentation, often a flight from reality, and a series of political changes culminating sooner rather than later in the characteristic combination of tyranny and terror that has marked so many of the governments of the region.

What does one do about it? The anger, the resentment, the frustration are clear all over the region and no one can dispute that they are well grounded. For the time being, two different solutions are being offered. One is Islam. If all the different imported methods that Muslims have used or copied or imitated have failed, there is obviously considerable persuasive force in the argument that these are the ways of foreigners and unbelievers. They have brought nothing but harm, so the only sensible thing for Muslims is to return to the tired and trusted ways of their ancestors, to be authentically themselves. It is a plausible, indeed a persuasive argument, except of course that one can never re-create the past; one can only imagine a past and try to create it, which is not at all the same thing.

There is the alternative, now much discussed, of democracy: not the rather shoddy imitations of western democracies, consisting of a set of rules and institutions at the very top of the state, with nothing to support them underneath, but something new—a democracy which, to use the old English phrase, would begin at the parish pump and ascend from there. One sees the argument between these different views in an acute form in the former Soviet republics with Muslim majority populations.

To return to my Saudi interlocutor: if there are so many problems, such difficult problems, such urgent and bloody and dangerous problems, why then does the world focus so much attention on the Arab-Israeli conflict, almost to the exclusion of anything else? There are a number of reasons which one can adduce for this.

One of them is curiosity. The attention of the world is increasingly determined by what the media put out. The people who sit in government offices have vast networks of services providing them with immense quantities of information day by day and hour by hour. But what really shapes their outlook and their policies is the 6:30 news on television. This is particularly true in democracies, perhaps less so in autocratic regimes. And the public in general is interested in Jews; it is not interested in Kurds or Berbers or other peoples whose names they don't even remember. Jews—as it used to be said—are news. For one thing, there are the Jews themselves who constitute a not insignificant proportion of both the consumers and producers of media news coverage. Then there are the people who dislike Jews to varying degrees, but usually for the same reasons. These again are not an insignificant proportion. Anything in which Jews are involved, either as parties or as opponents, arouses interest. Jews sometimes tend to assume that this interest is invariably and inevitably hostile; but this is not so at all. It is sometimes friendly, sometimes hostile, but is mostly neither the one nor the other, expressing an overwhelming curiosity to know about these peculiar, extraordinary people and to seek better or fuller information about what they are up to, what they are doing, and why.

There is no comparable interest outside the region in these other problems, no similar curiosity, not even in the Christian world about the fate of Christians. One of the more remarkable features is the extent to which the western Churches are far more concerned about what happens in Israel than they ever were about the fate of the Christian communities in Lebanon during the Civil War. (I remember a Lebanese Christian asking at the time in anguish "how much oil does the Pope need?", thinking no doubt of those divisions which Stalin enquired about in his famous question.)

Not only is there greater curiosity about Jews and their opponents; there is also far greater opportunity to satisfy that curiosity. The fact that Israel is a democracy and to a very considerable extent an open society makes it possible to produce the news to satisfy the curiosity, to give the customers what they want, which is after all an important principle of free enterprise business, whether dealing in news or other commodities.

Thanks to this open society, a large press corps is able to maintain a continuous supply of detailed and sometimes even accurate information about what is going on. It is possible to interview various parties and to hear complaints and grievances. After all, where else in the entire Middle East and North Africa is it possible to get an opponent of the government on television to denounce the government as conducting a police state? You might infer from this that Israel is the only police state in the region, or you may find another explanation. This other explanation might, however, raise other problems.

In promoting a cause, it is very important to select the right enemy. This may help of course to win a victory, but more important it will help to arouse curiosity. This curiosity, and the means of gratifying it, are probably the two most important reasons for the greater prominence of the Arab-Israeli conflict in the media. Apart from that, there are of course a variety of what one might call special interests. There are those who are moved by loyalty to one side or another or by ulterior motives of one kind or another; those who support Israel because it is Jewish and those who oppose Israel for the same reason. There are those who choose their side for professional or commercial reasons; many careers have been built up on the Arab-Israeli conflict and its solution may cause havoc and devastation, particularly in the academic world to which I belong. Think of all the lectures and research projects which may go down the drain. It has become a major industry in itself.

It is also of particular interest to religious people, and here I am thinking more specifically of Christians, the interests of a variety of ecclesiastical gentlemen and now, I should also add, ladies, who have developed a set of more or less standardized attitudes. For Christians, Israel and its people have a quite special importance, going back to the very roots of their religion and their civilization. The land of Israel, with its topography, its place-names, and a part of its history, are as familiar to them as their own, and sometimes more so. So, too, is the people of Israel. There is no comparable interest among Muslims. The Hebrew Bible was adopted by the Christians as a sacred book. Renaming it the Old Testament, they added a New Testament and the two constituted the Christian Scripture. There was no parallel development among Muslims, who simply declared both the Old and New Testaments to be obsolete and brought a new Scripture not to supplement but to supplant the existing ones. Elements from the Old Testament have some part in Islam, but it is insignificant compared with their place in Christian teaching, belief and experience.

The land, the people, do not matter to Muslims in the same way as to Christians; Islam did not come to complete Judaism or to fulfill prophesies to the Jews, as is the claim of Christianity. That makes for an entirely different relationship and of course a correspondingly greater, more intimate and more emotional attitude on the Christian side. There is a continuing awareness of the Jews: the Jews always figure prominently in the history of Europe, and in English, French, German and other literatures. Until very recently there was no comparable Jewish presence in Arabic or Persian or Turkish literature; there is no concern, such as one finds in Christendom, to persuade and convert the Jews. For Muslims, the more usual attitude is one of join if you want to, don't if you don't want to, that's your affair.

There is also the interesting element of guilt. This was extremely important in the early days of the history of the State of Israel and the conflicts in which it was involved, but is becoming less so. The feeling of guilt, particularly guilt for the Holocaust, can operate in more than one way. One can expiate it, by supporting Israel even when it's wrong; or one can escape from it, by denouncing Israel even when it's right. For the clergy in particular, the problem of guilt for the Holocaust has been an extraordinarily difficult one, and to deal with Jews as accused and not accusers brought welcome relief. It enabled them to abandon the uncomfortable and unfamiliar posture of contrition and penitence, and to return to the more familiar and comfortable posture of moral superiority and stern reproof. This again is an important element in attitudes to this problem, and may be among the reasons for the vastly greater interest that it arouses—the vastly greater emotional involvement, as compared with other, at least equally serious and probably greater and more dangerous problems.

Many who condemn Israel are surely moved by genuine compassion for Palestinian suffering, but there is a discrepancy between this vocal and active concern and the relative lack of interest in wrongs done by others to the Palestinians or, more generally, in violations of human rights by Middle Eastern governments other than that of Israel. At times, the attitude of the media to Israel appears to be that described in the book of Amos (III, 2): "You only have I known of all the families of the earth; therefore I will punish you for all your iniquities." In this spirit, it is often argued that the difference arises because Israel is held to a higher standard. This argument—at once a compliment to Israel and an insult to its neighbors—may be sincerely meant. It does not however explain the ethical relativism and selective indignation of those who make the judgments.

As I suggested before, even a solution of the Arab-Israeli conflict would not resolve or remove these other major problems. Indeed it might even aggravate them, by removing some distractions which have at times been useful. It would however accomplish one thing: it would release energy and attention now deflected from real problems. And here I am speaking of the peoples of the region rather than people outside. My impression is that if there is a solution of the Arab-Israeli conflict, so that it no longer arouses the interest of the outside world, the outside world will forget about the Middle East and will care no more about its problems and conflicts than it does about the problems and conflicts of Inner Africa, except of course to the extent that they affect vital interests like oil, as long as that remains a vital interest. But within the region, a solution would release interest and energy and attention, and make it possible to work for a better understanding of the other problems, and perhaps even ultimately for their solution.

35

Did You Say "American Imperialism"?

Power, Weakness, and Choices in the Middle East

❧❧❧❧

2001

In February 1991, as the defeated and shattered forces of Saddam Hussein were fleeing back into Iraq, the military commanders and political leaders of the victorious coalition faced a number of choices. One of these was to pursue and destroy Saddam's Republican Guard, the main prop of the regime. This, some argued at the time, could be done quickly and would enable the Iraqi people and perhaps even much of the Iraqi army to rise against Saddam and overthrow the regime. Others, more cautious, believed that to achieve any real change it would be necessary to advance on Baghdad, occupy the capital, and preside over the installing of a friendly regime. Opponents of this policy argued that such a regime would require continuing support—a military presence, at least for a while, and an ambassador with vice-regal authority. This, they said, would be the imperial method, as used by the British and French, and more recently, in a much harsher form, by the Russians and the Chinese. But the imperial way was not the way of the Americans, who lacked the desire—and some would add the skills—for such a policy.

President Bush decided to end hostilities after a hundred hours on the ground. Like the Israel-Arab Six-Day War of 1967, this war was concluded without the occupation of an enemy capital or the overthrow of an enemy regime. America's war aims had been accomplished. They included the liberation of Kuwait from foreign occupation and of Saudi Arabia from the threat of invasion. They did not include the liberation of Iraq from domestic tyranny.

In the Kurdish area adjoining the Turkish frontier, however, the United States joined in establishing a "safe haven" to protect the Kurds from Saddam Hussein's vengeance and the neighbors from an influx of refugees. A couple of years later, the Kurdish factions briefly joined forces and, under the leadership of the Iraqi National Congress, the democratic opposition, sought some American indication of sympathy for their proposal to establish a provisional government of Iraq in the zone.

They received neither encouragement nor support. The scheme had some merit, and there were many indications that the Iraqi National Congress could draw on broad national support—including much of the military—in establishing a free Iraq.

But it did not happen. The Kurdish factions, because of American indecision, resumed their quarreling, making the position of the Iraqi democratic opposition increasingly difficult and the government of the United States increasingly reluctant to become involved. Such an involvement, again, would have been the imperial way—and was therefore unacceptable, above all to the Americans themselves. Rather than risk the possibility of having to station a garrison in Iraq, the administration preferred what it seemed at the time a smaller and simpler option: to leave Iraq to Saddam Hussein, and to station troops in Saudi Arabia, at the invitation of the rulers of that country, to protect them from a renewed Iraqi attack.

"Infidels" on "Holy" Land

This simpler option brought unforeseen complications. For Christians and Jews, the term "Holy Land" refers to the country that has been known, at various stages in its history, as Canaan, Israel, Judea, and Palestine, in which the early formative events of Jewish and Christian history took place. For Muslims, some of these events have some importance, but the true "Holy Land" is Arabia, where the Prophet Muhammad was born, lived and died, and promulgated the Qur'an. During the great days of the British Empire, the British nibbled at the edges of Arabia—Kuwait, Bahrain, Oman, Aden—but took care not to land troops on the holy soil of the Prophet's homeland. The presence of American oilmen was accepted, however reluctantly, because they were necessary, for a while at least, to extract and market the oil. The presence of American troops—even by invitation, even to defend the Saudis against aggression—was more difficult to swallow, and was the first and main casus belli in Osama bin Laden's declaration of war against the United States. Osama bin Laden and his followers define the American enemy not as imperialists but as Crusaders (an earlier offender). They have no objection to imperial domination as such, provided that it is the true believers who rule the unbelievers, and not the reverse. This was what happened a thousand years ago, when the Abbasid caliphs in Baghdad ruled a vast and expanding empire, and five hundred years ago, when the Ottoman sultans in Constantinople took over the leadership of Islam and seemed ready to incorporate Europe in their imperial domains. Now the leadership of Christendom has passed from Europe to America, and for Osama bin Laden, as emerges clearly from his writings and utterances, the important point about American imperialism is that it is in decline, and due to share the fate of Rome and Byzantium.

Imperial rule, from the days of the Romans to that of the Soviets, may bring peace and order—the classical prototype is the Pax Romana—but at the price of foreign domination. At the present time, this is a deal in which neither side, American or Middle Eastern, has declared any interest. The foreign policy of the United States, like that of any other sovereign state, is—one presumes—primarily concerned with the defense and advancement of national interests, and for most Americans there are only two such in the Middle East: the supply of oil and the survival of Israel. The survival of Israel can be left to the Israelis, who request financial and some technological help, but not military support. The supply of oil is a more complex business. Some argue that whoever controls the oil will have to sell it and that we need not therefore concern ourselves with regional political squabbles. Some, while recognizing that such squabbles might endanger the supply, nevertheless maintain that since other countries—notably in Europe and the Far East—consume a far larger proportion of Middle Eastern oil than does the United States, it is their responsibility to maintain order. There is however some doubt whether they have the will or the power to discharge this responsibility. The prevailing view is that only the United States is able to maintain political stability in the oil-producing countries and, in particular, to prevent the monopolization of Middle Eastern oil by an aggressive dictator. This, it is argued, requires the protection of existing regimes, at least from external attack.

The message that U.S. actions and utterances in 1991 and after communicated to Saddam Hussein was very clear: Don't touch Kuwait or Saudi Arabia or in any other way interfere with the supply of oil. What you do in the north is not our concern—but don't be too obvious about it. A civil war between rival Iraqi factions would call for no involvement on our part unless our own vital interests were threatened.

This position—the reverse of the much-cited hegemonic approach—was well understood by the coalition allies and especially the Arab governments, and may help to explain their extremely cautious responses. Some, for example the Saudis, are alleged to have preferred it that way, though this has been denied. They and other Arab governments might have been willing to support a really determined effort to deal effectively with Saddam Hussein, such as they mistakenly expected in 1990. They would not risk the discontents of their own populations merely in order to support a severely limited action in defense of limited U.S. national interests—an action that would be sufficient to annoy but not to destroy Saddam Hussein, and would leave them, perhaps unaided, to face his anger and his vengeance. A military action carefully designed so as neither to suffer casualties nor to inflict them on the enemy may be seen as a noble example of civilized compassion. It does not, however, carry much conviction among regimes where such qualms are not shared or even understood. They would attribute such restraint to reasons other than compassion, and draw the appropriate inferences. These inferences—of fear and irresolution—would be reinforced by U.S. actions like the withdrawal of the Marines from Lebanon after the terrorist attack in October 1982, and of the troops from Somalia ten years later. In the view of most Americans, these were sent on missions of mercy, in countries where no real American interests were involved. They were withdrawn when the intended beneficiaries proved murderously ungrateful. The idea that any American government would wish to add Somalia to its responsibilities is mistaken to the point of absurdity. In the view of many Middle Easterners, however, these Americans were engaged in an imperialist adventure. When attacked, they flinched and fled.

To Destroy En Masse

Saddam Hussein's pursuit of weapons of mass destruction raises another issue. The possession of such weapons is clearly his first priority. For it, he is willing to sacrifice the health and lives of countless Iraqis, through the effect of sanctions that he could end at any time simply by complying with U.N. resolutions and with the terms of the 1991 cease-fire. Even without ending his defiance, he could still have spared his people suffering by using his not inconsiderable income to fund life rather than death. No less significant, though rarely mentioned, is his willingness to sacrifice his conventional weaponry to the same purpose. In tanks, guns, and the like, the Iraqi armed forces are in a parlous state. They are probably good enough to deal with ill-equipped and unaided rebels or neighbors, but not good enough to confront a serious military adversary.

The ruthless quest for non-conventional weapons, by Saddam and also, one may add, by the rulers of Iran, reflects their assessment of what happened in 1991, and the conclusions they drew from it. The swift and overwhelming American victory confirmed the lessons of earlier wars—that a pre-modern army, however richly provided with modern weaponry, cannot equal the army of a modern state, and, therefore, that a head-on military confrontation with such a state or states would inevitably end in defeat.

But there was a political as well as a military lesson drawn from the events of 1990–91. Already at the time, it was clear that American opinion was far from unanimous on the need to force Saddam out of Kuwait, and that it was only by a narrow margin that the U.S. decided to intervene in this inter-Arab conflict. In Iraq and also in Iran, it was deduced at the time that had Saddam already possessed a nuclear or comparable deterrent, the U.S. would have decided that intervention in an ultimately marginal affair was not worth the risk, and would therefore have left Kuwait—and the Middle East—to their fate. Such a deduction, certainly plausible and possibly correct, underlies the frantic search in both countries for weapons of mass destruction. With America on the sidelines and no other outside power capable—as yet—of intervening, the way would be open for an unimpeded Middle Eastern showdown. The real threat to the peace of the region is not the American presence, but the possibility of an American loss of interest and withdrawal. It may be recalled that the only confirmed use of chemical weapons since World War II has been in the Middle East—by Nasser in Yemen in the Sixties, by Qaddafi in Chad in 1987, and by Saddam against Iran and against his own countrymen in 1988. At least 5,000 of the latter were killed. All these attacks were against local adversaries, incapable of retaliation.

All this does not of course prevent the usual Middle Eastern accusations of "American imperialism"—a charge that reveals an imperfect understanding, not only of American policy, but also of the nature of imperialism. Perhaps because of some similarities of language and institutions, there is a widespread illusion in the Middle East that the United States is the old British Empire back in business, with new top management and a new head office. Some, in the radical Islamist camp, look back to more remote antecedents, and see the Americans as the leaders of Christendom, the successors of the Christian emperors and the Crusaders in the millennial struggle of the two world religions for world supremacy. This view emerges very clearly in the various writings of Osama bin Laden. For those who see the world in those terms, neither the American defense of Muslim Kosovo nor the Russian attack on Muslim Chechnya affects the basic reality of America's primacy. Even for those who may not believe this explicitly, both their accusations and their expectations seem to indicate some such assumption—often coupled, without concern for consistency, with the denunciation of a satanic America as the fountainhead of immorality and depravity in the world.

Such assumptions are of course profoundly, indeed absurdly, false. But they are natural enough—perhaps indeed inevitable. In the Middle East, as elsewhere in the world, it is always much easier to blame others for what goes wrong than to accept responsibility oneself. So much has gone wrong—and who else is there to blame? The British and French empires have long since departed. The Russians, who once shared and contested responsibility with the United States, have, at least for the time being, been reduced to a lesser and sometimes even supportive role, and no one remains but the United States, the only surviving candidate for the heavy role of imperialist arch-villain. Resentment of America as the sole surviving superpower, capable of unilateral political or military action when and where it chooses, is normal enough, and is not limited to the Middle East. There as elsewhere, the fear and envy of America are based less on American actions than on a kind of projection—the expectation that America will act as they themselves would act if they possessed America's power. But in the Middle East, anti-Americanism is nourished not so much by America's power as by the sources of that power—America's freedom and plenty. These are seen as a constant threat to the shabby dictatorships that rule much of the region, and—more accurately—as a constant temptation to their oppressed and deprived peoples.

This is true even of regimes that profess friendship and receive military or financial support from the United States, but allow vicious anti-American propaganda in their controlled media. The threat is more acutely felt by regimes like that of Iran, whose policies are resolutely anti-American and whose people therefore look to America with sympathy and hope.

The Feeling in "The Street"

For America to seek friendship or even good relations with such regimes is a forlorn hope. But to win respect is both possible and necessary. Generally speaking, popular good will towards the United States is in inverse proportion to the policies of their governments. In countries like Saudi Arabia and Egypt, with governments seen as American allies, the popular mood is violently anti-American, and it is surely significant that the majority of known hijackers and terrorists come from these countries. In Iran and Iraq, with governments seen as anti-American, public opinion is pro-American. The joy displayed by the Afghan people at the ending of Taliban rule could be repeated, on a larger scale, in both these countries. It is no doubt for this reason that the Afghan festival of liberation—unveiled women, beardless men, and the rest—has not been found newsworthy in most of the Middle East.

Some, especially among the more sophisticated politicians, are aware of American reluctance and perhaps even unconcern. But not all. One is constantly astonished at the conviction of even educated and otherwise rational Middle Easterners that everything that happens in their region—including the Khomeini revolution, the Lebanese kidnappings, and the Iraqi attack on Kuwait—is part of a deep-laid, long-term American strategy pursued relentlessly over decades. For anyone with even a minimal acquaintance with how Washington works and how Washington officials deal with problems, such a view is not only absurd; it is grotesque. But for many it remains an article of faith, and a refusal to accept it is seen as evidence of either naïveté or duplicity.

These charges persist, and there are others, less explicit, that reveal a similar misreading. Thus, for example, the accusation is often made, not only against the United States but against the West in general, that they have a "double standard." This is a most unfair accusation—why should we be limited to only two standards? Obviously, the U.S. government, like every other, has not a double but multiple standards to deal with differing and changing situations.

A comparable charge is the lack of "evenhandedness." This again rests on a total misunderstanding of the situation. Evenhandedness is a desirable quality in judges, juries, police forces, and other agencies of law enforcement. It is also appropriate to an imperial suzerain, trying to maintain some balance between contending protégés and native princes. But it is irrelevant to the policies of a power protecting its interests as best it can in a dangerous and troubled region. The real thrust of these complaints is not that America is pursuing imperialist policies, but that America is failing to live up to its imperial responsibilities.

A similar misunderstanding affects the perception of and the desire for an American role as "honest broker" in Middle Eastern disputes, notably the Arab-Israel conflict. Here there is an important distinction to be made between the roles of facilitator and mediator. In the secret bilateral negotiations and agreements between President Sadat of Egypt and Prime Minister Begin of Israel that preceded Sadat's public declaration, the King of Morocco and President Ceausescu of Romania rendered valuable services in arranging meetings and ensuring the necessary secrecy, but played no part in the actual peace process. Mediation is another matter. The role of mediator can be both honorable and useful, and the United States has, on occasion, rendered signal service to the warring parties. But on the whole they are likely to do better when they meet face to face, preferably in secret. With a superpower mediator, the parties will tend to negotiate with the mediator rather than with each other. This is specially relevant to the Israel-Palestine conflict, where the ultimate issue is the survival or destruction of a nation. Any arrangement short of this is seen as temporary and provisional. On the basic issue, clearly, there is no possibility of compromise or even of meaningful negotiation. In this context, the call for an American role can only mean a call for decision and enforcement—for a truly imperial role. And this in turn leads, inevitably, to renewed charges of double standards and lack of evenhandedness.

It is not difficult to document both charges—for example, in the different policies pursued towards Israel and most of the Arab states; more dramatically, in the West's inconsistencies, as between the different Arab states, in accepting, tolerating, or condemning human-rights abuses perpetrated by friendly, neutral, or hostile governments.

But such charges are, in a profound sense, irrelevant. If "evenhandedness" means treating all alike, it would be a manifestly suicidal policy for any kind of government, American or other, to pursue. In the Middle East as in most other places, one is expected to help one's friends and to harm one's enemies. This is well understood, and was classically formulated, a thousand years ago, by the Arab moralist Ibn Hazm: "He who treats friends and enemies alike will arouse distaste for his friendship and contempt for his enmity." The occasional American tendency to harry friends and court enemies causes understandable bewilderment, and, for lack of a more rational explanation, arouses fear of deep-laid, far-reaching plots.

To Be Rid of Oil

In time, the advance of science and technology, which first made oil necessary, will make it obsolete, and replace it with cleaner, cheaper, and more accessible sources of energy. When that happens, oil wealth will no longer be available to sustain tyranny at home and finance terror abroad, and the outside world will no doubt view the struggles and upheavals of the Middle East with the same calm detachment—or as some might put it, callous indifference—as it now views the civil wars in Somalia and Sierra Leone. Until then, the consumer countries— Europe and the Far East much more than the U.S.—will be anxiously dependent on whoever rules the oil wells and the oil routes, and will have to devise and apply their policies accordingly. It will be neither a safe nor an easy task.

Meanwhile it is not sufficiently realized that a major change is taking place in American government policy and more profoundly in American national attitudes towards the Middle East. During the Cold War, the overriding American interest in the Middle East as elsewhere in the world was to prevent Soviet penetration and domination. American concern about Soviet intentions towards the Middle East began in 1945, when the Soviets, as part of the victorious alliance, presented territorial demands against Turkey and tried to establish a Soviet puppet state in northwestern Iran. The CENTO pact was created to answer this threat; so too the expansion of NATO to Greece and Turkey. The problem became acute in the 1950s with the rapid spread and entrenchment of Soviet power in Egypt and then in some other Arab countries. It is sometimes forgotten nowadays that the closer American strategic relationship with Israel was a consequence, not a cause, of Soviet successes in the Arab world. Before that, American policy towards Israel had been cautious, and American support limited— far less, for example, than that of the Soviet Union in the early years and later of France, whose planes and weaponry made possible the Israeli victory in the Six Day War. The Soviet threat remained a constant preoccupation, and American policy in the region was primarily concerned with meeting it.

This aim was successfully accomplished, and there can be little doubt that without American involvement the Middle East would have fallen under Soviet domination and shared the fate, at best of Eastern Europe, more probably of the Central Asian and Transcaucasian republics.

But that is over and finished, and there is no present external threat. At some future time the Middle East may again be threatened by a new domination from outside; perhaps by a resurgent Russia, perhaps by a superpower China. Indeed, if the various governments and peoples of the Middle East continue in their present self-destructive way, the neighboring greater powers may be drawn, even without deliberate purpose, into the politics of the region.

But this is not likely in the immediate future, and for the time being the peoples of the Middle East, or more precisely, the governments that rule them, are free to determine their own fates. This means also to make their own mistakes and suffer the consequences.

In the theater of Middle Eastern politics, the United States is cast in several roles—sometimes as arbiter and enforcer, i.e., as suzerain; more often, and more popularly, as villain and scapegoat—and is variously denounced, sometimes by the same people, for claiming and shirking an imperial mission. The range of American policy options in the region is being reduced to two alternatives, both disagreeable: Get tough or get out.

36

The Law of Islam

⚱⚱⚱⚱

1989

I have not read *The Satanic Verses* and can therefore express no opinion on its literary merits or on whether it is likely to be insulting to Muslims. My opinion on both questions would in any case be irrelevant. The issue of freedom of speech applies equally to good and to bad books (otherwise, who is to decide?), while only Muslims can determine what is offensive to them.

What might properly concern us is three questions: 1) Is Khomeini's response justifiable within Islam, and in Islamic terms, 2) why now, and 3) how does this affect us?

On the first question: certainly, insulting the Prophet is an offense in Muslim law, and the jurists devote some attention to discussing its definition and appropriate punishment. Almost all these discussions turn on the question of a non-Muslim subject of the Muslim state who insults the Prophet. The jurists devote considerable attention to the definition of the offense, the rules of evidence and the punishment. They are concerned that accusations of this offense should not be used to achieve some private vengeance, and insist on careful scrutiny of evidence before any sentence is pronounced. The majority opinion is that a flogging and a term of imprisonment are sufficient punishment—the severity of the flogging and the length of the term to depend on the gravity of the offense.

The case of a Muslim who insults the Prophet is hardly considered, and must have been very rare. Where it is discussed, the usual view is that this is tantamount to apostasy. Apostasy for all schools of classical Islamic jurisprudence is a capital offense. The apostate, even if he recants and repents, cannot be pardoned, and must be put to death. It is presumably to this rule that the ayatollah was referring in his second statement.

At one time the law on apostasy was indeed enforced, and Muslims who were converted to some other religion were put to death, as were backsliders in parts of Christian Europe. This has not been done for a considerable time, and I doubt if anyone today would demand that Muslims who have embraced Christianity or Marxism should be killed for that offense. Should anyone, however, choose to raise this issue, the arguments would be the same as in the present case.

In saying that insulting the Prophet, or for that matter apostasy, is an offense in Muslim law, I would stress the word law. Islamic jurisprudence is a system of law and justice, not of lynching and terror. It lays down a procedure according to which a person accused of an offense is to be brought to trial, confronted with his accuser and given the opportunity to defend himself. A judge will then give a verdict and, if the accused is found guilty, pronounce sentence. I am not aware that this procedure has been followed in the present case.

A second question is why the ayatollah and some other Muslim leaders have waited until now to condemn the book and sentence its author to death by assassination. *The Satanic Verses* was published in England in September [1986] and was reviewed in an Iranian magazine a couple of months later. It is difficult to see a religious reason for the long delay, though the timing of the present response to coincide with the American publication of the book might suggest a political reason. There is an obvious and striking parallel with the seizure ten years ago of the American Embassy and diplomats, which stopped and reversed a movement in Iran to mend fences and restore relations with the United States, and which left the radicals in full control. The Rushdie affair has stopped a similar move to restore relations with Europe and will probably have a similar effect on the internal balance of forces in Iran.

What Muslims decide and do in their countries is their business and not ours. We have no legal right of interference, though we may have a legitimate concern with what goes on, and a natural sympathy with those whose human and civil rights are affected by it. We can only commiserate with our browbeaten Muslim friends and colleagues, and lament the growing tendency in the non-Muslim world to perceive and portray the Muslim as a tyrant at home, a terrorist abroad and a bigot in both.

This false and libelous picture of one of the great religions of the world and of the rich and original civilization that grew up under its aegis is a major tragedy of our time. The wide dissemination of this picture is due not to anti-Muslim polemicists or dissident Muslims, whose impact on world opinion would have been minimal, but to the self-appointed spokesman of Islamic purity.

The third question is how this concerns us in the Western world. Muslim jurists claim no jurisdiction over infidels in their own countries, and are not agreed on whether, and if so how far, Muslim jurisdiction extends over Muslims in lands not under Muslim government. That, however, is surely not the question as far as we are concerned. Our question is whether we still value the freedoms which our forebears won and bequeathed to us, and whether we are prepared to defend them. If we are not—and the silence or mumbling of large parts of the political, commercial, literary, academic and ecclesiastical establishments in various Western countries is not encouraging—then the further erosion of our freedom at home will certainly be rapid and probably irreversible. And that would also be a terrible loss for the world of Islam.

37

Not Everybody Hates Saddam

ɔ/ʕ ʕ\ɔ

1990

In the Middle East nothing is quite what it seems to be, and there are always
differing, sometimes conflicting, explanations of whatever happens. The recent war between Iraq and Iran was variously explained as a struggle for
hegemony between two regional powers, as an ethnic conflict between Arabs and
Persians, as an ideological clash between Ba'thist secularism and Islamic fundamentalism and even as a sectarian squabble between Sunni and Shi'a Muslims.

Similar variety may be seen in reactions to the current Middle Eastern crisis,
launched by Saddam Hussein's invasion and annexation of Kuwait. In the broader
world outside the Middle East, the perception of what has happened and of what
needs to be done shows a unanimity unknown since the defeat of Adolf Hitler.

Kuwait is after all a classical example of a small, unoffending, peaceful country, invaded and swallowed by a ruthless and aggressive neighbor. It is indeed
difficult to find, even in the checkered history of this century, so clear a case of
unprovoked aggression. The Kuwaitis never attacked Iraq in word or deed, oppressed no Iraqi minority and gave no shelter or encouragement to terrorist or
guerrilla opponents of Iraq—on the contrary, they provided vital help to the
Iraqis during the long war against Iran, and ran one of the least repressive
regimes in the region.

But not everyone shares the Western, and especially the European, perception
of Saddam Hussein as another Hitler without Hitler's charm, nor would such a
comparison be seen by all as wholly negative. In the Middle East, some other
perceptions have been expressed, notably in the English-speaking samples of
public opinion provided to Western media correspondents by local support services. According to one view, energetically promoted by the government of Iraq

and its supporters, the rulers of Kuwait—and by implication others like them—were Western lackeys, agents of foreign imperialism in the Arab lands, and Saddam Hussein is an Arab hero, who, by annexing Kuwait, took the first step toward the liberation and unification of the Arab world.

In this perception, he is the heir of Nasser, of Saladin, and—in his own rhetoric—of Nebuchadnezzar. He will resume and complete the unfinished work of Nasser, and deal with the enemies of the Arabs as Saladin dealt with the Crusaders and Nebuchadnezzar with the Jews. Neither was an Arab, but both were natives of Iraq.

In another perception, often linked with the first, his role model—not named of course—is not so much Nasser or Saladin, as Robin Hood. This involved an abrupt switch. During the war with Iran, Saddam Hussein was the defender of the sheikhly order in the Gulf against Iranian revolutionary subversion. In his new role, he is himself the subverter of rich and tyrannical old regimes, in the name of social justice and pan-Arab egalitarianism.

In a speech Friday, Saddam Hussein attempted yet another, even more startling switch—from secularist bulwark against Islamic fundamentalism at home and abroad to defender of the faith and claimant to the custody of the holy places, until now a duty and privilege of the House of Saud. The call to jihad will always have some appeal, though Saddam Hussein's guise as holy warrior may lack plausibility. There is surely a note of desperation in this appeal to religious passions.

In the first two of these roles, perhaps even in the third, he may win some support among the many discontented—though more outside than inside Iraq. There is still a deep yearning for a great Arab Muslim leader who will end foreign and infidel ascendancy and restore Arab glory; there is also a profound social resentment against the oil-rich rulers who are condemned equally whether they squander or invest their wealth. In all these roles—as champion of the Arabs, as sword of Islam and as avenger of the poor—support for Saddam Hussein will be reinforced by the respect that is owed to power and the will to use it—to ruthlessness and of course, to success.

But even among those who respond emotionally to such appeals, there are doubts. Is he really working for the greater Arab or Muslim cause or just for his own personal aggrandizement? Will he really bring about a redistribution of the wealth of the old regimes, or merely transfer it to his own control, and in the meantime deprive great numbers of young men from Jordan and Egypt and elsewhere of the employment opportunities that the Gulf states and Saudi Arabia offered? The past record of Iraq is not encouraging.

As well as those who accept Saddam Hussein's claims, there must be significant numbers of Arabs and other Middle Easterners who share the perception of the rest of the world—that the invasion of Kuwait was an act of blatant aggression, which must not be allowed to succeed. In the Middle East as elsewhere, those old enough to remember or wise enough to learn from history will recall an earlier sequence of events—the Japanese invasion of Manchuria, the Italian invasion of Ethiopia, the German seizure of Austria and then Czechoslovakia. These events led directly to the collapse of the international order and the outbreak of World War II. If Saddam Hussein succeeds in his gamble, the United Nations, already devalued, will follow the defunct League of Nations into ignominy. The world will belong to the violent and the ruthless, and we shall all be on the way to a Third World War.

38

Mideast States

Pawns No Longer in Imperial Games

❧❦❧

1991

For as far back as living memory can reach, and a while further, the countries of the Middle East were disputed between rival, more developed outside powers. There were times—before the rise of Rome, and again after the fall of Rome—when Middle Eastern powers competed for the domination of the known world. But those times are long past, and for many centuries the countries of the Mideast have, variously, enjoyed and endured the attention of outside powers—first the commercial and diplomatic rivalries of mercantilist European states, then the successive clashes of the British, French and Russian empires, of the Allies and the Axis, and most recently, of the U.S. and the U.S.S.R. In both peace and war the governments and sometimes the peoples of the Mideast were the object of intensive efforts by outside powers to win their hearts and minds so as to gain access to their communications and resources.

And now the picture has changed completely.

For the first time ever, there is only one power, with overwhelming wealth and strength, and no real rival to challenge it. Russia, because of its internal problems, is, at least for a while, out of the game. The powers of Europe are out, probably for good. As yet there is no sign that their role will be taken up by the European Economic Community—which, in the words of the Belgian foreign minister, has shown itself to be "an economic giant, a political dwarf and a military worm." Russia, because of its vast numbers, extent and resources, will probably be back, and may again develop that characteristic combination of greed, smugness and sense of mission that constitutes the imperial mood. This is not likely, however, to happen for some time, probably not before the next century. And in the meantime, the U.S. remains alone.

But the U.S. is not an empire, and has no taste or desire for imperial expansion or domination, which are in fact precluded by the American kind of mass democracy. Americans have no wish to fight and die in foreign lands for imperial interests. (Neither of course did Englishmen, Frenchmen and Dutchmen. Their empires ended when modern democracy prevailed and when new democratic ideas affected both rulers and subjects, making the one unwilling to subdue, the other to submit. The same could conceivably be happening in Russia.) It is already clear that American democracy will not permit the retention of American forces in the Middle East for a day longer than is manifestly necessary, and perhaps not even for as long as that.

All this has brought a profound change, which is not yet fully understood. Generations of statesmen in Arab countries have been accustomed to a situation in which they were able—were indeed required—to perform a balancing act between rival great powers, and could sometimes turn it to advantage. In most of these countries, such conditions have prevailed since the beginning of modern independence, and no other is known. It is this relationship that has shaped the outlook of their statesmen; it has also shaped that of the specialists in the developed countries, whose professional task it is to deal with these statesmen, and who interpreted their task as doing whatever was necessary to gain and to retain their good will.

Neither the statesmen of Middle Eastern countries, nor the Middle East specialists of the powers, appear to have yet grasped the change that has taken place.

The Middle East still retains considerable importance, notably through its possession of vast reserves of oil. But recent events have made it clear that the West will more easily find other sources of energy than the oil-producing states can find other cash customers. And the main reason for foreign involvement in the past—to deny the region to a rival—no longer arouses much interest.

Today the only serious restraint on American power is American public opinion. Perhaps the greatest of Saddam Hussein's many blunders was to antagonize both at the same time, while forgetting that there was no countervailing power in the world that he could call to his aid against the U.S.

It may be some time before American and European Middle East specialists fully realize that it is no longer necessary for them to ingratiate themselves with whatever tyrants happen to rule in Middle Eastern countries. It probably will take less time for Middle Eastern rulers to realize that they can no longer compel the aid of foreign powers, or plausibly blame them when things go wrong. This change, when it comes, can only be beneficial to both sides, opening the way to a more natural and more healthy relationship. And when that happens, Middle Eastern peoples, freed from foreign bullies and toadies and derived of foreign scapegoats, may at last confront the real problems of their societies.

They will have several choices before them:

It may turn out that the civil war that destroyed Lebanon was a pilot project for the whole region, and that with very few exceptions states will disintegrate into a chaos of squabbling, feuding, fighting sects, tribes and regions.

It may be that, to avoid such a fate, the peoples of the Middle East will submit to the direction of those whose idea of a security plan for the region is one in which each country's tyrant confines his tyranny to his own subjects and does not trouble his neighbors—until one or another of these tyrants breaks the rules and launches a regional war from which the outside world will keep its distance.

Or it may be that the peoples of the region will free themselves at last from the politics of bribery, cajolery, blackmail and force, and find their way to the freer and better life to which they have so long aspired.

The important change is that the choice is now their own.

39

What Saddam Wrought

❧❦❧

1991

After Saddam Hussein's invasion of Kuwait a year ago today, again after the launching of the coalition offensive, and again after the ceasefire, it was said by many that as a result of these events the Middle East had changed beyond recognition, and that nothing would ever be the same again. And then, when a new and different Middle East failed to materialize, the same or other voices were raised to assert that nothing had changed at all.

There is not as yet sufficient evidence to test the validity of the first proposition. When a new political configuration emerges, it may take years before the shape or even the fact of the new order becomes clear. The ignominious failure of the Arab states to strangle Israel at birth in 1948 was followed by the assassination or removal of every Arab ruler that had participated in the fiasco, and the emergence of a new political order in the Arab world. But it was not until 1958 that the last of the participants, the Iraqi monarchy, was overthrown.

The second proposition, that nothing has changed, can already be rejected as demonstrably false. Many things have changed, both in the understanding of old realities, and in the emergence of new ones. Perhaps the most striking and obvious is the final discrediting of sanctions. Many no doubt argued for them in good faith, but some of those who pleaded, "give sanctions time to work," had an unspoken second line, "and if they don't work, let's forget about it." At the present time, after a military debacle and a major rebellion, Saddam Hussein remains in power and in control of his political and military apparatus, and it seems clear that he and his ruling elite are in no way discommoded by the continuing sanctions, either in their personal comfort, or in their pursuit of weapons of mass destruction. The idea that sanctions could ever have succeeded in dislodging him from Kuwait is now seen as a grotesque absurdity.

Supply and Price of Oil Unaffected

Another widely held belief now proved to be false is that war in the Gulf would disrupt the flow of oil, and cause major upheavals in the world. Nothing of the kind happened. Two major suppliers of oil have virtually ceased to function—Kuwait, because of Iraqi sabotage, and Iraq, because of U.N. sanctions. All this appears to have had no discernible effect on the supply of oil, or even on prices, which if anything have fallen slightly. It is always possible that the manipulation of Middle Eastern oil might once again pose a major threat to the industrial world. To reach this point would however require a degree of negligence and incompetence on the part of both Western governments and businesses which, though unfortunately not impossible, is increasingly unlikely.

Another myth that is being reluctantly relinquished concerns the strength and effectiveness of pan-Arabism or, as it is sometimes expressed, of the Arab world. No one could dispute the passionate belief of the Arabs in their common cultural identity; few would question the hatred for the West that still dominates much of their public life. Yet neither the passion nor the hatred has provided a usable political force. Time and time again the pundits have warned that this or that action or policy would raise the whole Arab world in arms against us— but it did not happen. Even such events as the American bombing of Tripoli in 1986 and the Israeli invasion of Lebanon to expel the PLO in 1982 raised barely a ripple in Arab countries, where for the most part they were received with almost total indifference. The Gulf crisis, which was essentially an inter-Arab conflict into which outsiders were drawn, finally demonstrated the falsity of this belief, except perhaps for the most obdurate of pundits and the most amnesiac of audiences. The Arab world as a cultural, intellectual and social entity remains of the greatest importance. But the Arab world as a political bloc has no more reality than Latin America and much less than southeast Asia.

Some other myths have been, if not destroyed, badly damaged. One example is the belief among some Middle Eastern powers that the purchase of costly and sophisticated weaponry would enable them to defend themselves against aggression and obviate the need for outside help. Another is the remarkably persistent belief, among outside powers, that it is possible to solve problems and attain policy goals in the Middle East, by "friendship" or other arrangement with some regional dictator.

All these changes are not in themselves new, but arise from a clearer perception of old realities. There are also new realities, but it will take somewhat longer for these to be fully observed and understood.

One change however is already becoming clear, though it may be some time before its implications and consequences take shape and are recognized. This change is in many ways the most momentous to affect the Middle East in centuries, and its effects—if the new situation continues—may require centuries for their fulfillment. For the first time since the decline of the Ottoman and Persian monarchies and the rise of Europe, the Middle East is no longer contested between rival outside powers, and no longer in danger of domination by them.

Many contestants have come and gone in the struggle for the domination of the Middle East. In recent years, only two remained—the Soviet Union and the United States. The crisis, the war, and their aftermath have made it clear that of these two superpower rivals, the one is unable, the other unwilling, to play any kind of imperial role. For the first time in centuries, the governments and perhaps even the peoples of the Middle East will be able to make their own decisions, and devise and apply their own policies. They will also have to accept responsibility for those decisions—a salutary change. It is to be hoped that the governments, or if not the governments, the peoples of the region will rise to the challenge.

There are some who would add to the list of shattered illusions the hope for Arab democracy. The record, they say, shows that only a strong autocratic government can maintain itself and survive in this political culture. In Kuwait, the horrors of occupation were followed by the horrors of liberation, and wherever a regime is foolish enough to allow the people to vote, they will, it is said, inevitably choose some group of religious or nationalist fanatics, who, once ensconced, will take good care not to repeat the foolishness of their predecessors and allow themselves to be voted out of power.

It is, to say the least, a plausible hypothesis. It has been true in the past, and it may prove true in the future. But it is too soon to dismiss the Arab democratic movement as a sham or a failure, and there are many signs of a new interest in freedom, and a new understanding of what it means. Perhaps most important of all, there is a growing readiness among Arabs, in discussing the ills of their society, to seek the fault not in their stars—or in their enemies—but in themselves. Such readiness is a necessary, though not a sufficient, condition for progress.

Age-Old Autocratic Traditions

It is not easy to establish democratic institutions in a region of age-old autocratic traditions, where loyalties and responses have been determined by a kind of communal or ethnic collectivism. It is difficult—but, as the Turks have shown, it is not impossible, if significant numbers of men and women are willing to make the effort and face the risk. There is no guarantee that they will succeed, and even if they do, after how long and at what price.

But they have not yet failed, and in the meantime, we in the West face an agonizing choice. Even the choice can be variously formulated. Some might ask:

"Should we give at least moral support to those who share our ideals and aspirations, and seek a better, freer life for their peoples, or should we become known as the cynical accomplices of whatever tyrant, however odious, is willing for a time to serve our purposes while we serve his?" Either way, it is a difficult and also a dangerous choice that we must make.

40

The "Sick Man" of Today Coughs Closer to Home

♄♄♄

1991

In January 1853, in a conversation between Czar Nicholas I of Russia and the British ambassador, Sir Hamilton Seymour, the czar suggested that it was time for Britain and Russia to agree on the partition of the collapsing Ottoman Empire. "We have a sick man on our hands," said the czar, "a man gravely ill. It will be a great misfortune if one of these days he slips through our hands, especially before the necessary arrangements are made." Seymour, while not disputing the diagnosis, suggested that with proper treatment the "sick man" might recover, and thought that what was needed was a physician, not a surgeon. This disagreement between the British and Russian views led shortly afterward to the Crimean War, and to a long and sustained political conflict.

The phrase "the sick man" became famous and, despite differences of policy, reflected the common European view of the state of the Ottoman Empire. With the demise of the Ottoman Empire after the First World War, the sick man may be said to have died, and been succeeded by his sole legitimate heir, the Turkish Republic. The image, however, remained.

More recently, the Ottoman decline has often been cited as a paradigm for the decline and fall of the Soviet empire in Eastern Europe. The parallels are indeed striking—both in the challenge and in the collapse. For a while it seemed that the Ottoman power—centralized, disciplined and inspired by a militant and expansionist ideology—would inevitably triumph over a weak, irresolute and divided Europe. But it did not, and in time the Europeans came to realize that the sick man was losing both his strength and his will.

By the 19th century, the problem that the Ottoman Empire presented to

Europe arose not from its strength but its weakness, and from the scope that this weakness gave to hostile forces, both inside and outside the failing empire. It was in this latter phase that it came to be known as "the Eastern Question."

The decline of the Ottomans was due not so much to internal changes as to their inability to keep pace with the rapid advance of the West in science and technology, in the arts of both war and peace, and in government and commerce. The Turkish leaders were well aware of this problem, and had some good ideas for its solution, but they could not overcome the immense institutional and ideological barriers to the acceptance of new ways and new ideas. As a distinguished Turkish historian put it: "The scientific wave broke against the dykes of literature and jurisprudence." Unable to adapt to the new conditions, the Ottoman Empire was destroyed by them, as was the Soviet empire in our own day.

In comparing the fate of the Ottomans with present-day conditions, attention has focused mainly on the political and ideological elements—the explosive forces of nationalism and liberalism, the bankruptcy of old ideologies, the collapse of old political structures. In all these, the Russians have indeed been following the path once trodden by the Turks, and if they are fortunate, they will find a Kemal Atatürk to open a new chapter in their national history.

But there is another aspect of the Ottoman decline that suggests a different present-day parallel. The economic weakness of the Middle East, unlike that of the Soviet Union, was not due to an excess of central control, which on the contrary was almost entirely lacking. There was some economic regulation, mainly at the level of the craft guild and the country market, but in the mobilization and deployment of economic power, the Ottoman world was falling far behind Western Europe. It had also become a predominantly consumer-oriented society.

A rise of mercantilism in the producer-oriented West helped European trading companies, and the states that protected and encouraged them, to achieve a level of commercial organization and a concentration of economic energies unknown and unparalleled in the East, where—as a matter of fact more than of theory—"market forces" operated without serious restrictions.

The Western trading corporation, with the help of its business-minded government, represented an entirely new force. Thanks to this growing disparity of economic strength and purpose, Western merchants, later manufacturers, and eventually governments, were able to establish an almost total control of Middle Eastern markets, and ultimately even of major Middle Eastern manufacturers.

Middle Eastern textiles, once highly regarded in the West, were driven first from external, and then even from domestic, markets by more efficiently produced and aggressively marketed Western goods. Even coffee and sugar, two items that once figured prominently among Middle Eastern exports to the West, were in time produced by Western powers in their tropical colonies, and by the

18th century, thanks again to cheaper production and better marketing, were transferred from the export to the import side of Ottoman trade with Western Europe.

By the late 18th century, when a Turk or an Arab indulged in a cup of sweetened coffee, in all probability the coffee was brought by Dutch merchants from Java, and the sugar by French or British merchants from the West Indies. Only the hot water was of local provenance. In the course of the 19th century, even that was doubtful, as Western companies dominated the rapidly expanding utilities in Middle Eastern cities.

In our own day, it is not the former Soviet bloc that suffers from this particular economic problem. It is rather the consumer-oriented societies of Western Europe and, even more, North America, where manufacturers and merchants are faltering or failing in the struggle in the open market against the new mercantilism of competitors who have found new ways of mobilizing and deploying the economic power of their societies.

41

Revisiting the Paradox of
Modern Turkey

෫෮෯෮

1996

We live in an age of historical revisionism. In England, young historians are busy chipping away at Winston Churchill, trying to topple him from his pedestal and expose him as a man of many weaknesses and errors. Surely there must be some part of truth in this—Churchill was a man and not a god, and like other men he had his weaknesses and made his mistakes. But for the men and women of my generation, who fought and won a great war under Churchill's leadership, saving their country and, incidentally, the world from the most odious tyranny known to human history, nothing can belie his achievement or diminish the respect—or should I say reverence—in which we held him and still hold him.

Similar re-examinations of past assumptions and past heroes are in progress in many other countries. But not in all. Such a re-examination presupposes both the development of a critical faculty and the freedom to exercise it. For better or worse—and I am convinced that it is for better—Turkey is such a country, and Turks must confront the dangers and responsibilities as well as the pleasures and opportunities of freedom.

The re-examination of the past—including the achievement of the heroes of the past—is a right, indeed a duty of the historian, as the discovery of new evidence and documents and the development of new techniques of inquiry make such a re-examination necessary and possible. And if sometimes the re-examination takes the form of politically or ideologically motivated denigration, this too must be accepted as part of the functioning of a free society.

But after all the re-examinations and all the reassessments, even the most hostile, the achievement of Atatürk remains—perhaps reinterpreted, but surely

367

not diminished. What is that achievement? Obviously the answer to this question must come primarily, though not exclusively, from Turks. But sometimes the perspective of an outsider may be helpful.

Atatürk's first achievement, which made all the others possible, was military and political. Of the three major powers defeated in 1918, Turkey alone was able to reject the peace imposed by the conquering allies and to negotiate freely and on equal terms a peace securing its basic national objectives. At a time when almost all of the Islamic world was falling under the dominance of the imperial powers of Europe, Turkey was one of the very few that managed not just to preserve, but to reinforce its sovereign independence. By these two successes alone, the new republican regime was able to infuse in a defeated and dispirited people a new sense of pride—of self-respect concerning the past and self-confidence for the future.

On Sunday Turks observed the 58th anniversary of Atatürk's death. His true greatness, his lasting achievement, may be found not in his political and military victories, but in the use that he made of them. It was not easy to create a free nation-state from the ruins of an empire, and to do so surrounded by suspicious former enemies and resentful former subjects. It was no mean diplomatic achievement to establish peaceful and even friendly relations with both.

It would take too long to enumerate the many significant changes inaugurated by Atatürk and his generation. Let me just mention one of the most important—the revitalization of Turkish society by the fostering and encouragement of new elements. One of these was women. Already in the 1920s Atatürk spoke on more than one occasion of the impossibility of keeping up with the modern world if a country deprives itself of the talents and services of half its people. The emancipation of women—central to the whole process of modernization—made immense advances in his time and under his successors. Another was the emergence of new social groups—professional, technical and commercial—that were creative, independent and self-reliant. These were indispensable components of the new civil society, the ultimate basis on which Turkish democracy must rest.

Probably the most debated of his policies at the present day is that which is sometimes called Westernization, not easily distinguished from modernization. In a sense, his victories and those of his successors were a paradox—the first decisive victory in defiance of Western power, the first decisive steps in the acceptance of Western civilization. There is an old American saying: "If you can't beat them, join them." Atatürk did both.

42

We Must Be Clear

ℰ⁄ℰ ℰ⁄ℰ

September 16, 2001

T he attack on the World Trade Center and the Pentagon has been likened many times this week to Pearl Harbor. The resemblance goes further than the simple suddenness and cruelty of the assault. This too, like Pearl Harbor, is not an isolated act; it is the opening salvo of what is intended to be a war leading to victory. The Japanese assumption at the time was that the United States, despite its wealth and strength, was unmilitary and indeed cowardly, and would easily be frightened out of Asia. A similar calculation underlay the action on Tuesday: that the Americans have gone soft, cannot take casualties and will run if attacked. A similar purpose inspired the action—to expel the Americans, their economic tentacles, their corrupting culture and their local accomplices from all the world of Islam, wherever the frontiers of that world may ultimately lie.

The calculation is not at first sight unreasonable. The abandonment of Vietnam, the flight under attack from Lebanon and Somalia, the recent preemptive withdrawal and evacuation because of a (probably planted) intercept indicating a threat of terrorist action, all seem to point in that direction. So too does the anxious, propitiatory posture adopted by spokesmen in addressing the rulers of other countries, including those regarded as friends.

The words "friend" and "friendship," between states as between individuals, are used to denote two very different things: (1) a deep mutual commitment, based on shared principles and aspirations, or (2) a temporary arrangement, based on a perception of shared interests. The first is likely to be permanent, unaffected by changing circumstances. The second will last only as long as the interests and the perception last.

In political terms, the one means a relationship with a fellow democracy, perhaps differing in some details, but sharing the same basic way of life—free institutions, liberty under law, elected and responsible government. The second means an understanding with an autocratic ruler, valid only as long as he stays in power and does not change his mind.

Why would he change his mind? Discussions of these matters often make use of such terms as "public opinion," "climate of opinion," "constituency" and the like, all terms and concepts derived from the political life of democratic societies but having little relevance to the politics of an autocratic regime unhampered by such alien concepts as "civil liberties" and "freedom of expression." In a dictatorship the law of political survival is very simple: Jump on the bandwagon. The problem that sometimes arises in the more complex conditions of today is to identify the bandwagon in the traffic jam. A wrong choice may in the most literal sense be fatal.

Attitudes toward the terrorists and the governments that harbor and help them are not too difficult to understand. Saddam Hussein has made war against three of his neighbors and invaded two of them, doing great damage. Clearly, they are neither forgetful of the past nor confident of the future. Their dearest wish is certainly to see him removed and replaced by a less menacing regime. But they are not willing to take the risk of participating in yet another action that would go far enough to annoy him but not far enough to remove him, and would leave them to face his inevitable revenge.

Their primary need is not to evaluate the policies and purposes of dictators and terrorists, which they know well and understand accurately; it is to understand the policies and purposes of the United States—a much more difficult task. In this task, they have two guides: The first is history, which Middle Easterners read. In this the record is not encouraging. The second is their current dealings with U.S. statesmen, soldiers and diplomats, and the interpretations they put on what is said to them and what is asked of them.

Middle Eastern responses to American appeals for support will be determined by their assessment of America's position. What is needed is clarity in recognizing issues and alignments, firmness and determination in defining and applying policy. Even with these, there is no certainty of success in getting the necessary support from frightened neighbors—only a possibility. Without them there is a certainty of failure.

43

Deconstructing Osama and
His Evil Appeal

ぴそそ

2002

For most Westerners, Osama bin Laden presents an ogreish figure, equally indifferent to the suffering and death of his enemies, of his devotees, and of uninvolved bystanders. Some recent accounts have also suggested unpleasant personal traits—an arrogant and domineering personality, an inability to work with others. Yet he remains an enormously popular figure not only with the extremists and radicals who form his main support group, but in much wider circles in the Muslim and more particularly in the Arab world.

In a sense, the reason for his appeal is self-evident—that he responds, with words and with actions, to the seething resentment that has been growing for many years in the Muslim world, and offers some hope of vengeance and even of ultimate triumph. But others in the not-too-distant past have appealed to similar sentiments, and offered similar inducements, without evoking similar support. Something else is involved, which marks him off from earlier exponents of pan-Arab, pan-Islamic, and other revolutionary movements against Western domination.

The first and most obvious reason for his popularity is his eloquence, a skill much admired and appreciated in the Arab world since ancient times. Many tales are told of the great orators of the past. But in the modern Arab world there is little sign of eloquence, and indeed little need for it, since most rulers rely on repression rather than persuasion to secure the obedience of their subjects. Bin Laden is not a ruler, and therefore not tainted with tyranny and corruption. Most of the rulers are guilty of both, and not one of them has dared to submit either his accession to power or his retention of power to a genuinely free vote of his people.

Rule is personal; it is obtained and maintained by force; it is usually for life, and increasingly, it is hereditary even in states that call themselves republics. Older dynasties, especially those with claims to descent from the Prophet, like the Hashímites of Jordan and the ruling dynasty of Morocco, enjoy some legitimacy and can afford some relaxation. This is not enjoyed by more recent dynasties, still less by hereditary revolutionary presidents.

None of these has any need for persuasion and therefore for oratory, and some indeed have shown a quite remarkable lack of skill in handling the beautiful and supple Arabic language. At one time, during the political conflict between Egypt and Israel, the Arabic experts employed by Israeli radio made a point of recording some of President Nasser's speeches and then playing them back to the Egyptian public with a commentary drawing attention to his grammatical errors and stylistic infelicities. Thereafter, his speeches were marked by punctilious grammatical accuracy more than by eloquence. In his use of language, bin Laden brings a return to traditional virtues. Modern devices, notably satellite television, can bring his eloquence all over the Arab world.

Even more striking is the contrast demonstrated in his personal life, between himself and the present-day rulers of most of the Arab lands. The usual pattern—more so in republics than in monarchies—is rags to riches, a process by which people of humble, usually impoverished, origin contrive, through the exercise of military and hence of political power, to attain often great wealth, which they pass on to their children and extend to their kinsfolk. Osama bin Laden presents the inspiring spectacle of one who, by his own free choice, has forsaken a life of riches and comfort for one of hardship and danger.

But why would Arab governments, themselves threatened by his appeal to their subjects, show him such a remarkable degree of tolerance? Here there is a more practical consideration, involving rulers rather than subjects, and inducing them, at the very least, to take a more lenient line towards bin Laden and towards propaganda in his favor. More often than not, they confront a situation in which they have to choose between offending bin Laden and offending the U.S. In such a dilemma, the choice is not difficult.

If they offend Osama, the consequences can be very dire indeed. If they offend the U.S., they will suffer no penalties and may even—if the right people in Washington have their way—receive some reward. It therefore makes obvious good sense to do nothing against bin Laden, and even to pay him some hush money, a practice widely followed in some of the wealthier Arab countries.

All these helped to burnish his image as a latter-day Islamic Robin Hood, defending the poor and the downtrodden against a distant tyrant and his nearby henchmen. In the Middle East as in Europe, there is a strong tradition of bandit heroes, challenging authority and eluding capture. The tradition is indeed longer and stronger than in Europe, since it has continued from the Middle Ages into modern times.

The role of the Middle Eastern Robin Hood, unlike his Western prototype, is not to rob the rich and give to the poor, though some such expectation may lurk in the background; it is rather to defy the strong and to protect—and ultimately avenge—the weak. For Osama bin Laden and his merry men, the Sheriff of Nottingham is their local potentate, whichever that may be. The ultimate enemy, King John, lives far away, as he has always done—in Constantinople and Vienna, London and Paris, and now in Washington and New York.

This vision, comforting though it may be to those who hold it, is flawed at both ends. King John was not a democrat, and Robin Hood was not a terrorist. We live in a different world, and at a different level of reality. Those who cherish such delusions will sooner or later suffer a painful but salutary awakening.

44

Targeted by a History of Hatred

❧❧❧❧

2002

The immediate, general reaction as the facts of what happened on Sept. 11 became known was one of utter astonishment. Most people in the United States and more generally in the Western world find it impossible to understand the motives and purposes that drove the perpetrators of these crimes, those who sent them and those who applauded them with song and dance in the streets. We understand people who are willing to die—even to face certain death—for a cause in which they believe. The kamikaze pilots of Japan are an obvious example. But that was in wartime, and directed against military objectives. Many of our own people, in wartime, willingly sacrifice their lives for their country. Even in peacetime, on that same Sept. 11, firefighters and rescue teams risked, and many gave, their lives. But that was to save other people, not to kill them. That we understand. Why would anyone be willing to sacrifice his own life to accomplish the random slaughter of other people selected merely by the place where they happen to be, irrespective of age, sex, nationality and religion? An earlier example of the same indiscriminate slaughter was the attack by suicide truck-bombers on two American embassies in East Africa in August 1998, where, to make a point and to kill 12 American diplomats, the terrorists were willing to sacrifice 19 suicide "martyrs" and slaughter more than 200 Africans, many of them Muslims, who merely happened to be in the neighborhood at the wrong moment. This callous indifference to the suffering of others, even of their own people, is a common feature not of Islam as a religion but of these terrorist movements and of the regimes that use them.

The motive, clearly, is hatred, and from then until now the question is being asked, with growing urgency and bewilderment: "Why do they hate us so?" Some go further and ask the very American question: "What have we done to offend them?"

At one level the answer is obvious. It is difficult if not impossible to be strong and successful and to be loved by those who are neither the one nor the other. The same kind of envious rancor can sometimes be seen in Europe, where attitudes to the United States are often distorted by the feeling of having been overtaken, surpassed and in a sense superseded by the upstart society in the West. This feeling, with far deeper roots and greater intensity, affects attitudes in the Muslim world toward the Western world or as they would put it, the infidel countries and societies that now dominate the world. Most Muslims, unlike most Americans, have an intense historical awareness and see current events in a much deeper and broader perspective than we normally do. And what they see is, for them, profoundly tragic. For many centuries Islam was the greatest civilization on Earth—the richest, the most powerful, the most creative in every significant field of human endeavor. Its armies, its teachers and its traders were advancing on every front in Asia in Africa, in Europe, bringing, as they saw it, civilization and religion to the infidel barbarians who lived beyond the Muslim frontier.

And then everything changed, and Muslims, instead of invading and dominating Christendom, were invaded and dominated by Christian powers. The resulting frustration and anger at what seemed to them a reversal of both natural and divine law have been growing for centuries, and have reached a climax in our own time. These feelings find expression in many places where Muslims and non-Muslims meet and clash—in Bosnia and Kosovo, Chechnya, Israel and Palestine, Sudan, Kashmir, and the Philippines, among others. The prime target of the resulting anger is, inevitably, the United States, now the unchallenged, if not unquestioned, leader of what we like to call the free world and what others variously define as the West, Christendom and the world of the unbelievers.

For a long time politicians in Arab and some other Third World countries were able to achieve at least some of their purposes by playing the rival outside powers against one another—France against Britain, the Axis against the Allies, the Soviet Union against the United States. The actors changed, but the scenario remained much the same. And then, with the collapse of the Soviet Union, came a truly radical change. Now, for the first time, there is only one superpower, dominant, however unwillingly, in the world: the United States.

Some Arab leaders try frantically to find a substitute for the Soviet Union as patron and protector of anti-American causes and have evoked a limited and for the most part ineffectual response in some quarters in Europe. Others, notably Osama bin Laden, took a different view. As they saw it—and their view does not lack plausibility—it was they who, by the holy war they waged in Afghanistan, brought about the defeat and collapse of the Soviet Union. In their perspective, they had dealt with one of the infidel superpowers—the more determined, the more ruthless, the more dangerous of the two. Dealing with the soft and pampered United States would, so it seemed, be a much easier task.

The reasons for hatred are known and historically attested; the hatred has been growing steadily for many years and has been intensified by the conduct of some of the rulers whom we call friends and allies and whom their own people see and resent as American puppets. A more important question, less frequently asked, is the reason for the contempt with which they regard us. The basic reason for this contempt is what they perceive as the rampant immorality and degeneracy of the American way—contemptible but also dangerous, because of its corrupting influence on Muslim societies. What did the Ayatollah Khomeini mean when he repeatedly called America the "Great Satan"? The answer is clear. Satan is not an invader, an imperialist, an exploiter. He is a tempter, a seducer, who, in the words of the Qur'an, "whispers in the hearts of men." An example of this perception and the resulting attitude may be seen in a recent Arabic newspaper article in defense of polygamy. The writer argues as follows: In Christianity and more generally in the Western world, polygamy is outlawed. But this is contrary to human nature and needs. For 10 days a month during menstruation and for longer periods during pregnancy, a woman is not available. In the monogamous West, the deficiency is made up by promiscuity, prostitution and adultery; in Islam, by polygamy. Surely this, the writer argues, providing respectability for the woman and legitimacy for her children, is the better of the two. This makes good sense, if one accepts the writer's view of the relations between men and women.

Another aspect of this contempt is expressed again and again in the statements of bin Laden and others like him. The refrain is always the same. Because of their depraved and self-indulgent way of life, Americans have become soft and cannot take casualties. And then they repeat the same litany—Vietnam, the Marines in Beirut, Somalia. Hit them and they will run. More recent attacks confirmed this judgment in their eyes—the attack on the World Trade Center in New York in February 1993, with six killed and more than a thousand injured; the attack on the American liaison mission in Riyadh in November 1995, with seven Americans killed; the attack on the military living quarters in Khobar in Saudi Arabia in June 1996, with 19 American soldiers killed and many more wounded; the embassies in East Africa in 1998; the attack on the USS Cole in Yemen in October 2000, with 17 sailors killed—all those brought only angry but empty words and at most, a few misdirected missiles. The conclusion bin Laden and others drew was that the United States had become feeble and frightened and incapable of responding. The crimes of Sept. 11 were the result of this perception and were intended to be the opening salvo of a large-scale campaign to force Americans and their allies out of Arabia and the rest of the Muslim world, to overthrow the corrupt tyrants America supports, and to prepare the ground for the final world struggle.

The immediate and effective response against their bases in Afghanistan must have come as a serious shock to the terrorist organizations and compelled some revision of their earlier assessment of American weakness and demoralization. We must make sure that they are not misled by the unfamiliar processes of a democratic society to return to that earlier misjudgment.

45

A Time for Toppling

❧❧❧❧

2002

Among the many arguments that have been adduced for not taking action against the present regime in Iraq, two have received special emphasis. The first is that the governments and peoples of the Middle East attach far greater importance to the Arab-Israeli conflict than to Iraq or any other problem in the region, and that therefore one should begin by solving that. The second is that even a successful attempt at regime change in Iraq would have a dangerous destabilizing effect on the rest of the region, and could lead to general conflict and chaos.

Undeflected Anger

The conflict with Israel certainly receives overwhelmingly major attention in the Arabic media, but since this is the only specific grievance that may be publicly expressed in a region of numerous and painful problems, that is hardly surprising. One may therefore wonder whether Middle Eastern governments would indeed wish for a peace settlement, which would deprive them of this valuable safety valve, leaving them to face the undeflected anger of their subjects, including those who live under the rule of the Palestine authority. From the almost monotonous regularity with which a series of promising peace processes have failed at the moment when they seemed most likely to succeed, one may be driven to the conclusion that they prefer to keep the conflict unresolved, but at a low level—simmering not boiling, and usefully controllable.

In any case, requiring a settlement of the Palestine question as a prerequisite to dealing with Saddam Hussein sends him a clear signal that he must at all costs prevent such a solution. Saddam Hussein has indeed already responded to that signal in various ways, both secret and open. The most notable of his open responses is the increase of the bounty he pays to the families of suicide bombers from $10,000 to $25,000. This is the most public but probably not the most important of his contributions to the conflict. To make the settlement of that conflict—which even in its present form is more than half a century old—a prerequisite for any action concerning Iraq is a sure formula for indefinite inaction.

The fear of destabilization is both genuine and serious, and it is easy to understand the anxiety provoked in the regimes of the Middle East by the prospect of a regime change in Iraq. The crucial question here is not how or by whom Saddam is removed, but what comes in his place. The clear preference of some influential groups in this country and elsewhere is for his replacement to be a kinder and gentler tyrant, who would be amenable to our interests and requirements, while avoiding the hazards of regime change. This would certainly be the preference of our so-called allies in the region, most of whom would feel mortally threatened by the emergence of anything like a democratic regime in Iraq.

But why should we feel threatened by such a change? The overwhelming evidence is that the majority of our terrorist enemies come from purportedly friendly countries, and their main grievance against us is that, in their eyes, we are responsible for maintaining the tyrannical regimes that rule over them—an accusation that has, to say the very least, some plausibility. Apart from Turkey and Israel, the two countries in the region where the governments are elected and can be dismissed by the people, most of the countries of the Middle East can be divided into two groups: those with what we are pleased to call friendly governments, and therefore increasingly hostile people who hold us responsible for the oppression and depredations of those governments, and, on the other hand, those with bitterly hostile governments, whose people consequently look to us for help and liberation.

The most notable of these are Iraq and Iran. In countries under dictatorship, the political joke is often the only authentic and uncensored expression of political opinion. An Iranian joke, current during the campaign in Afghanistan, related that many Iranians put signs on top of their houses, in English, with the text:

"This way please!"

It is noteworthy that after the events of Sept. 11, great numbers of people came out into the streets in Iranian cities, where, in defiance of the authorities, they lit candles and held vigils in sympathy and solidarity with the victims in New York and Washington. This contrasted markedly with the scenes of rejoicing elsewhere. One is often told that if we succeed in overthrowing the regimes of what President Bush has rightly called the "Axis of Evil," the scenes of rejoicing in their cities would even exceed those that followed the liberation of Kabul.

The overthrow of a regime must inevitably raise questions, concerning first what will follow, and then what impact this will have in neighboring countries. A regime change may well be dangerous, but sometimes the dangers of inaction are greater than those of action.

There may indeed be, as is so often said, a link between a settlement of the Palestine conflict and a regime change in the region—but in the reverse order to that usually adduced. It is generally agreed that democracies do not start wars. Democratic governments are elected by the people and are answerable to the people, and with exceedingly rare exceptions, the people prefer peace. Even the great Winston Churchill—certainly no warmonger, but seen by his people as a war leader—was thrown out of power by the British people in the general election of 1945. It is equally true, but less recognized, that dictatorships do not make peace. The world war started by the Axis ended with its defeat. The Cold War started by the Soviet Union ended with its collapse.

The Tyranny of Conflict

In the same way, the dictatorships that rule much of the Middle East today will not, indeed cannot, make peace, because they need conflict to justify their tyrannical oppression of their own people, and to deflect their peoples' anger against an external enemy. As with the Axis and the Soviet Union, real peace will come only with their defeat or, preferably, collapse, and their replacement by governments that have been chosen and can be dismissed by their people and will therefore seek to resolve, not provoke, conflicts.

PART THREE
ABOUT HISTORY

46

In Defense of History

↬↬↬

L et me begin my defense with a word or two of explanation. To start with, let's look at this word history. Of late there has been a certain semantic change, a new, idiomatic, increasingly common use of the word history, which I can perhaps best exemplify by a familiar scene from a movie in which the heavy, the tycoon or the gangster chief, contemptuously dismisses his cast-off mistress with the words "you're history." The common phrase "that's history" now conveys the general meaning that it is, whatever it may be, of no relevance to present events, concerns, or purposes. History may have some antiquarian interest, or may provide entertainment, but no more.

This lack of concern with the past, this dismissal of the past as something unimportant, at most entertaining, and in the hands of most professional historians not even that, has precedents. Ancient India offers the example of an advanced, sophisticated society that did not think that history mattered, and took no trouble to record it. As serious Indian history-writing began with the coming of Islam, most of what we know about pre-Islamic India is either from fragmentary evidence or outside visitors, not from narrative historiography.

We find the same a-historical approach in rabbinic and diaspora Judaism. From the end of the ancient Jewish state until the impact of the Renaissance on Italian and French Jews, there is an almost total lack of historical writing, even a rejection of history. Thus Maimonides, a man of wide-ranging intellectual pursuits, condemns the preoccupation with the events of the past as of no value and of no interest. "[These books] neither possess wisdom nor yield profit for the body, but are merely a waste of time."[1] This lack of interest in history among Jews of that period and of that background is the more remarkable if we reflect that some of them were living among peoples with a very strong interest in history, like the Romans or the Arabs, and were in other respects profoundly influenced by the cultures in which they lived. Historians, in those days, were employed by the state or the church. Since the Jews had neither, they had no history.

I used the word relevance, and spoke of the dismissal of history as "not relevant." But there is another danger even greater than that of irrelevance, and that is the danger of relevance. The word relevant has acquired new and menacing overtones and undertones of meaning in our time. History, according to this view, is admissible, even useful, provided it is limited to "relevant history." Here we confront something worse than neglect. I shall try to make my point clear with two quotations. One will certainly be familiar, the other probably not. The first comes from Mr. Henry Ford, who once observed, with that brevity that is conventionally the soul of wit and sometimes also of its converse, that "history is bunk." Most historians would agree with that proposition as applied to some of the work of some of their colleagues. But, as a judgment of the profession as a whole and of the subject matter with which it deals, most of us would find it excessive.

My second quotation, probably less familiar, comes from a government department of education, laying down the purpose of the study and teaching of history in schools. "Its purpose is to strengthen the nationalist and patriotic sentiments in the hearts of the people, because knowledge of the nation's past is one of the most important incentives to patriotic behavior."

The passage in question comes from a circular of the Syrian government department of education.[2] But that is purely coincidental. I deal with the Middle East, so I come across Middle Eastern documents. I have no doubt that the sentiments expressed in this Syrian ministerial circular would be echoed in many other countries, and were indeed echoed in this country in the debate on national standards for the teaching of history.

These two quotations, from Henry Ford and some unknown Syrian ministry of education official, exemplify the twin dangers against which, I suggest, history is in need of defense: disuse and misuse—or, putting it differently, neglect and perversion. The two global superpowers that confronted each other during the cold war in a sense exemplified these two dangers. In the United States we have perhaps the greatest example of the neglect of history. Here, despite an enormous historical establishment comprising vast numbers of tenured historians organized in departments and societies and producing libraries of books, one cannot but be struck by the lack of a sense of history in the society, in the public discourse, and even, more specifically, in the conduct of government.

One sees this for example in the schools, even in primary and secondary education, where we read in one report after another that high school seniors cannot place Abraham Lincoln within a century, and have the vaguest ideas about major events in the history of their own country, not to speak of others. A recent quiz in an undergraduate class in a respected university revealed that fewer than half the students could say when World War II began and when it ended.

This happens partly through simple neglect and partly because history has been, so to speak, colonized, taken up and subsumed in the social sciences, the practitioners of which (let me be cautious in putting this), often have a somewhat different attitude to evidence from that of historians. One notices it also in the media and more generally in the public debate, where references to history are few and far between and, as often as not, inaccurate.

I would point here to the contrast with the Middle East. During the war between Iraq and Iran (1980–88), propagandists on both sides made frequent allusion—rapid, incomplete, passing allusion—to such matters as the reign of the Caliph Yazid (680–83) and the massacre of Kerbela (680). These and other events of the seventh and eighth centuries were immediately familiar to the mass audiences to whom those propaganda broadcasts and statements were addressed. Their knowledge of history may not have been very accurate, but it was certainly very detailed. One doesn't quite see modern Western politicians or propagandists making a point by allusion to the Lombard League or the Anglo-Saxon Heptarchy, approximately contemporary to those events.

One sees also the lack of a sense of history in government. Time and time again I have chatted with government officials concerned with the problems of the Middle East. They are always highly educated and often remarkably competent, with a detailed and intimate knowledge of the problem with which they are involved from the moment of their own involvement. But they sometimes display surprising gaps in their knowledge of what went before.

The opposite extreme, of misuse rather than disuse, is exemplified by the other party to the cold war, the Soviet Union and its satellites, which regulated or even dictated what might or might not be written and taught. In accordance with the general doctrines of that society, the state and the party maintained control of the means of production, distribution and exchange, of historical information and ideas, as well as of other things. It has been remarked that a new present and still more a new future require a new past, and constant readjustment was therefore necessary. This applied not only to the recent past but even to the remoter past. A Soviet historian tells us that the "working masses" of the Byzantine Empire saw the roving Slavic tribes as "their allies and deliverers."[3] This somewhat implausible assertion was clearly not based on any kind of evidence, but it served an obvious political purpose and conformed very well to Soviet-style political correctness.

The collapse of communism in the Soviet Union and elsewhere brought another historiographic problem. It soon became clear that Communist rule had acted as a kind of deep-freeze, in which historical notions and ideas and attitudes were frozen stiff and then, with the ending of the Communist controls, thawed out. In Russia they thawed out in 1917, with many of the attitudes and anxieties of that era. The Yugoslav peoples thawed out, roughly, into 1945, with the attitudes, the memories, the prejudices, and the hostilities of that year fresh as they were at the moment when they were frozen. And sometimes the freeze can last a very long time. It has been well said that the Serbs are still fighting their traditional enemies, the sultan and the pope.

There is of course a wide range of what one might call self-serving history, not only Communist and nationalist but many other kinds. There is also the less common but perhaps more interesting phenomenon of self-flagellating history, which raises psychological as well as other problems. In its noblest form, I suppose, self-flagellating history may be found in the historical and prophetic books of the Old Testament, in expressions of moral indignation at all the wicked things we—not they, not you, but we—have done. More recently this self-flagellating type of history is taking other forms. In part one might describe it as healthy self-criticism, in part as a kind of neurotic self-hate, but perhaps more than either of these, a continuation in another form of the rather arrogant, self-centered historiographic approach of earlier times.

Again I take the American example, though one could readily name others. It is no longer fashionable or acceptable for American historians to insist that the United States is the center of the world and the source of all that is good, from freedom to motherhood to apple pie. It is, however, perfectly acceptable to insist with the same self-centered arrogance that the United States is the source of all evil. Only we make mistakes or commit crimes, because—by unstated implication—only we make decisions or cause events. The rest of the world is passive and inert, and its fate is determined by what we do. In this sense, the currently fashionable self-flagellatory school of history is, at the very least, as arrogant and self-centered as the more traditional kind of self-serving history.

What, then, is there to defend, against what attack, and how? Let me begin with a defense against neglect, against disuse. Here I can do no more than offer the usual apologia for my craft and that of my colleagues: the need for memory, the dangers of deprivation of memory—in the individual with no memory, amnesia, with distorted memories, neurosis. The group, no less than the individual, needs some form of collective memory and record. Even running a business or selling a commodity requires the keeping of records, preferably accurate. A balance-sheet, for example, is a historical narrative. If it is missing or inaccurate, the enterprise faces grave dangers; if it is fraudulent, those dangers include indictment.

But even a balance-sheet, while remaining within the law, can be cooked and served in various ways, as any businessman knows. Let us look at the way in which historical records or narratives are cooked and served.

Here I turn from the dangers of disuse to the dangers of the misuse of history, by those who believe that history must serve a purpose. They agree that history has an important place in any system of education, but have their own ideas on why, and more especially how, history should be studied and taught.

The discussion of misuse raises further questions—by whom? For whom? Under what auspices? For what purpose and interest? A historian has a natural preference for answering this question historically, and tracing the stages. He might begin with the tribe and the tribal cult, reflected in ancient narratives, both tribal and religious. Such narratives are of several kinds, the most ancient and traditional being what one might call the bardic or mythological. From remote antiquity, feuding tribes had rival sagas sung by competing bards. Something of the sort continues to the present day. There is a parallel religious, or more precisely sectarian, historiography. The more old-fashioned approach to religion has been admirably summed up in three short phrases, "I'm right, you're wrong, go to hell." A good deal of religious, communal, and national historiography is of this kind.

In more modern times, there are new threats to history from what I am tempted to call the fashion tsars of the ideological hem-line—those who determine what ideas shall be worn this season—what length, what style, and what cut. The set of rules known as "political correctness" provides one version of this. There are others. According to some currently fashionable epistemological notions, good evidence and bad evidence are meaningless terms. All evidence is, so to speak, born free and equal. And since there is no such thing as truth, there is no such thing as authenticity; these are irrelevant and meaningless, even misleading, concepts. This approach serves a double purpose; it makes it possible both to discredit good evidence and to validate bad evidence, and this helps enormously in the process of falsification. We might call these "catahistorians," in contrast to the so-called metahistorians, who reflected on the nature of historical reasoning, and sometimes—the more rash among them—tried to formulate rules governing the historical process itself. I use the Greek prefix "cata" as in cataclysm, catastrophe and catalepsy.

What are the media by means of which historical narrative is reshaped and redirected?

The oldest, the most traditional, is of course mythology. The term mythology as used at the present day covers a number of different things—primitive science, to explain such natural phenomena as birth and death and the rotation of the seasons; primitive religion, to answer questions about man, God, time and eternity; and—our present concern—primitive history, to confirm identity, encourage loyalty, and, through legitimacy, to justify authority. The primary and most basic focus of history and religion is thus the tribe and the tribal cult. There are many surviving examples of these, expressing the historical self-image of the tribe and the religious projection of that self-image. In time the tribe develops into a people, then a state, the cult into a church or equivalent, and these in turn may subdivide into parties and factions and sects, each with its own version of history, designed to prove the rightness of its actions and the correctness of its beliefs, in contrast with other groups and cults with which it may come into contact and, usually, into conflict.

Historical narrative in the form of mythology—to which we must now add counter-mythology—still flourishes. In free societies, it survives primarily in elementary education and popular entertainment. In such societies, serious historians have long since learned to look with suspicion on any version of history in which their side is always right and its opponents are always wrong, and, since it is not in the nature of human entities to be invariably right, to question the hypotheses on which such narratives are based. In unfree societies such questioning is rarely permitted, and a more or less mythological version prevails unchallenged.

There are many such mythologies at the present time. One particular brand is what is sometimes called salvation-history, history presented as the coming of the truth that saves mankind, or at least part of it. The best known are of course the religious versions of history, each presenting the essential truth of its own brand of salvation, which washes whiter than the others. To these we may add the modern secular versions, liberal, Communist, nationalist, patriotic, and the rest. This kind of history may also be disseminated through preaching and teaching, song and balladry, and through religious and national commemorative ceremonies. The massacre of the Prophet's kin at Kerbela, mourned every year by the Shi'a, has enormously powerful evocative impact. The great battle of Kosovo in 1389, in which the Serbs were defeated by the conquering Ottomans, is another example of remembered suffering.

Sometimes a mythology becomes an orthodoxy. This term, from two Greek words meaning the right idea, was first used by Plato, and has come to mean a systematized statement of officially sponsored truth. There is of course historical orthodoxy in many societies, deviation from which can be dangerous and in certain circumstances even fatal—professionally in democracies, physically in dictatorships. For the dissemination and, where appropriate, enforcement of orthodoxies, modern technology has greatly strengthened traditional methods; propaganda, indoctrination, and an extreme form known at one time as brainwashing.

Historical mythologies are extraordinarily persistent. The French retreat from Moscow in 1812 was presented in traditional French schoolbooks as due entirely to the bad weather. It wasn't the Russians who defeated the Grande Armée; it was the Russian winter. Serious scholarship, even in France, eventually came to the conclusion that this was an oversimplification and that the Russian armed forces may also have had something to do with the retreat and defeat of the Grande Armée. This has even appeared in French school textbooks. Nevertheless, among Frenchmen other than trained historians, the myth that Napoleon's defeat in Russia was due to the weather and only the weather remains extraordinarily vigorous.

How does one actually set about distorting history? The best and most effective method of course is invention, supported by fabrication. One invents events, and if convenient or necessary one fabricates the evidence to support one's inventions. A fabrication may be personal and deliberate; it may be collective and unconscious. Both kinds can usually be detected by critical historical scholarship.

There are some celebrated historical fabrications. The Donations of Constantine for example, a document said to have been issued by the emperor Constantine to Sylvester, bishop of Rome, was used as the basis for the temporal power of the popes in the city of Rome. Purporting to be of the fourth century, first appearing in the eighth century, it was finally demonstrated to be a forgery in the fifteenth century. It probably had the longest run so far of any historical fabrication.

There are others. Under the auspices of the American Philosophical Society I may mention the statements attributed to Benjamin Franklin denouncing Jews and Catholics. These first appeared in the 1930s, when the international atmosphere was propitious to such fabrications. There are the so-called Protocols of the Elders of Zion, the Talât Pasha telegrams, and others of the same kind. The Protocols are by now pretty much discarded in the Western world, but they still flourish in other parts. My own copy, entitled *Jewish Conspiracy*, was printed in Tehran in 1985, and came to me by courtesy of the "Islamic Propagation Organization" in that city.

The misuser of history can to a considerable extent serve his purpose simply by defining the topic, that is to say, of what, of where, of whom, of when, he is writing the history. Take even a simple matter like the starting point. One has to start somewhere if one is going to write a book or an article or give a lecture on an historical topic, and the choice may in some measure predetermine the result. Any starting point is necessarily in some degree artificial. History is a seamless garment; periodization is a convenience of the historian, not a fact of the historical process. By choosing carefully, one can slant history without any resort to actual falsehood. For example, a writer on relations between the United States and Japan can start with Hiroshima, or he can start with Pearl Harbor. Even precisely identical narratives of events would look very different, if they start with the one or the other.

Another example is the Crusades. Nowadays it has become fashionable to present the Crusades as an early example of aggressive, predatory Western imperialism against the Muslim East. But how did the previously Christian East become Muslim? If we go back a few centuries we might notice that the Crusade was preceded by the Jihad—that is, a similar invasion moving in the opposite direction—and one might not unreasonably describe the Crusade as a long-delayed, limited Christian response to the Muslim Jihad. Again, it depends when we start.

And where. In choosing a topic, the historian must define the area as well of the period with which he is concerned, and this too will affect his perspective and may slant his result. Will he write the history of England, or of Britain? Of Denmark, or of Scandinavia? Of the Turks, or of the Ottoman Empire? These very different examples are but three among many.

Much may be determined—or at least suggested—by the simple choice and definition of the topic. Latterly, there have been many histories of resistance in Nazi-occupied Europe; there are few histories of submission and collaboration.

To some extent the result is predetermined by the accessibility of evidence—a fact of course known to the historian. Take for example the history of a conflict between two countries, one a closed society with sealed archives, the other an open society with open debate and open archives. Inevitably the historian will study the subject on the basis of what is available and accessible, and even without any intention to distort, he may well arrive at a rather slanted, one-sided picture, usually to the advantage of those whose archives are closed and who permit no adverse point of view to be expressed. The Cold War furnishes examples of that. So does the modern Middle East.

I spoke of invention sustained by fabrication as one major form of falsification. The counterpart of that, equally effective, is amnesia sustained by concealment— the unconscious forgetting of disagreeable episodes, or the deliberate suppression of shameful memories, sustained by the destruction of evidence. One thinks for example of the massive shredding of documents in the Paris prefecture of police at the moment of liberation, or the more recent example of the attempted destruction of Nazi era deposit records by a Swiss bank. These exemplify what one might call planned amnesia.

There are other less obvious examples. One such is slavery. Slavery is a very disagreeable fact in human history, not just American history. American historians faced this honorably, recognizing the fact, discussing it, documenting it, analyzing it without any attempt to offer excuses. It was not embellished, as it was not long ago at an African History Conference, where one of the most famous African slave traders was described as running "an intercontinental employment agency." There are societies in which slavery has been a fact of life, in some of them very recently, in some even to the present day. But the subject is taboo. Not long ago a graduate student who wanted to work on slavery in the medieval Middle East was strongly advised, not by any Middle Eastern authority but by a grant-giving body in this country, to choose some "less provocative" subject. To study the history of the Middle East without slavery would be as meaningful as to study the history of the American South or the Roman Empire without slavery. Nevertheless, it is widely done. Many books, indeed I suppose most general books on Middle Eastern history, either don't mention it or gloss over it, and research in that field is discouraged in a number of ways. The amnesia of the Nazi era is an obvious modern example, and here I must say that the Germans have been more honest in confronting the past than some of their former allies and collaborators in other countries.

Having fabricated your history, how do you put it across? This varies from country to country and from regime to regime. The most effective method of promulgating falsified history is of course coercion. This was universal in the Soviet Bloc, and although it is no longer applied there, it still persists in other parts of the world, where only one version of historical events is permitted, other versions being forbidden and punishable. Even in a democratic state the use of coercion is still a possibility, by selective legislation. For example the Loi Gayssot in France makes it a criminal offense to deny that the Holocaust took place. There is no such law either in the United States or in the United Kingdom, any more than there are laws making it criminal to claim that the earth is flat. Anyone who wishes to argue that the earth is flat is free to do so both in Britain and in America. In France, and also in Germany, which has a similar law for a similar reason, there is a somewhat different history. One can easily explain and one may try to justify the Loi Gayssot, but one cannot dispute that it constitutes a limitation on freedom of expression, and may be a dangerous precedent. I note in passing that legislation has been proposed in the French parliament that would extend the same limitation to other events in earlier history.

Coercion is the best method of falsifying history, but it is not always possible. The second best is intimidation. This can be quite effective. A number of years ago a history professor at the University of California at Los Angeles published a book that displeased some elements in the community. They picketed his lectures and his publishers and blew up his house. He and his family were in the house at the time. Miraculously they escaped. This seems to be an extreme and for most people unacceptable form of historical argumentation.

One step further down after coercion and intimidation come a number of methods that may be grouped under the heading of pressure. There is social pressure, through colleagues and neighbors and friends, which makes it difficult or even painful to express opinions that go against what is currently acceptable or fashionable. And of course there is material pressure, by the manipulation of the granting or withholding of visas to visit one or another country and research permits to work in them, as well as more professional matters such as grants, fellowships, appointments and promotions. All of these are frequently used as weapons to secure preferential treatment for one or other school of historical thinking or, to be precise, historical teaching and writing.

More generally, there is education, used in various ways. Education can be a very effective method to obtain some measure of control of historiography. This is illustrated in the argument in the United States over the so-called national standards, drawn up by a committee appointed under the auspices of the Department of Education and the National Endowment for the Humanities, to set standards in both United States history and world history. This gave rise to a passionate and ongoing debate as to the nature of these standards and what they are trying to teach our children.

Beyond education, perhaps even more important than education, there is entertainment. What after all do most people know about history, people—a growing majority—who have not studied history and who are not concerned with historical accuracy? Some years ago, the French historian Marc Ferro[4] observed that the idea that most of these people have of history is derived from two major sources: from the moldering relics of their primary school instruction in the subject, and from the cinema. These are the two major sources, I will not say of historical information, but of historical perceptions and attitudes.

The misrepresentation of the past in the cinema is probably the most fertile and effective source of such misinformation at the present time—certainly since the disappearance of the Soviet educational system, and I am not at all sure that it couldn't compare favorably even with that, in terms of skill and effectiveness in historical distortion and perversion. I have not seen the films about the Kennedy assassination and about Nixon and will therefore not discuss them. But I have seen some others. There was for example a film about Robin Hood that contained some very remarkable pieces of historical data. There was a Saracen who visited England in the twelfth century, in itself highly improbable, and was able to speak English. I set aside that it was—inevitably—American English, but the mere fact of a Saracen speaking English was a little odd. Even odder was that the Saracen was black and finally, being from a much more advanced civilization than that of the native English, he was able to dazzle them with a number of devices, one of which was a magnifying glass—one of the very few things in which Europe was more advanced than the Islamic world at that time.

With all these dangers one might indeed ask "Why bother?" Aren't we better off without history, since it is so subject to perversion, distortion, misrepresentation, and the rest? Let the Serbs forget about Kosovo. Let the rest of us forget about our past grievances.

If that were the real choice, I might even be tempted to agree, although I think I could resist the temptation. But it isn't the real choice, for two reasons. In the first place, it would mean leaving history to the falsifiers, unchallenged and unchecked, because they will not desist even if we do. And in the second place, more serious, we cannot abandon history, because whatever we may say about it, the historical process continues—not just versions or narratives or whatever may be the fashionable term, but historical processes which continue to shape the present and affect the future. We stand a better chance of being able to understand what is happening now and influence what will happen next if we have some knowledge of what happened in the past.

It is by now generally accepted that the sciences and the social sciences, in addition to their intrinsic intellectual merits, serve useful and practical purposes. The one may provide us with new tools and weapons; the other may, with luck, help us to live with their consequences. It was believed in the past, there may still be some remote and isolated places where it is believed in the present, that for the humanities their own intrinsic intellectual merit is sufficient, and their study is its own more than adequate reward. By now this is very much a minority point of view, but it deserves to be reiterated. Through philosophy and history we may hope to achieve some understanding of our place in the universe and of our experience in the past. Through the study of language and literature, in themselves historical records, we may be able to receive and be enriched by some understanding of what the great minds of the past have achieved, the experiences our predecessors recorded and transmitted for our guidance. In this way, the study of the humanities has at all times made an essential contribution to the refinement of the mind, the ennoblement of the soul, and, by these means, the education of the young to take their place fittingly in a civilized society. These purposes, and the values that underlie them, are now under heavy attack, and greatly in need of defense.

It must be admitted that history, for the educator, is in many ways an unsatisfactory subject. It is unreliable, changeable, inconsistent, fragmentary, often contradictory. Yet it is precisely for those reasons that it is valuable, in that it accurately reflects the human predicament, and is therefore an essential ingredient of our education, of our perception of ourselves, of our understanding not only of our past but of our present and whatever future may await us.

The past does not change, but our perception of the past is constantly changing, and every generation re-examines the past in the light of its own concerns, and to the extent of its own capabilities.

The rewriting of the past derives from several sources, some relatively straightforward, others complex and difficult. The former include the discovery of new evidence and the development of new techniques of enquiry. In our own day, the advance of archeological, epigraphical, archival, and documentary studies has vastly increased the amount of evidence at our disposal, while the progress of both the linguistic and social sciences has given us new methodologies for the exploitation of this new evidence. A very large part of current research is concerned with these tasks.

There is however another kind of revision of history, arising from changing conceptions of the very nature of the historical process, and the consequent enrichment of the content of historical research and writing. In its earliest and simplest form, history was just a chronicle of political and military events—the so-called "drum and trumpet" school of historiography. In the course of time, historians extended their studies to include cultural and intellectual, religious and scientific, economic and social history, all of which enormously increased the range, complexity, and value of historical study and exposition.

In our own day another new dimension of comparable importance has been added—gender history. This is sometimes dismissed as a fad or fashion of the politically correct, and in some hands it is indeed no more than that. But there is a lot more to gender history, and for the politically correct it can pose agonizing dilemmas. It is of course incorrect to say anything positive about Western civilization, or anything negative about non-Western civilizations—so how does one deal with the inescapable fact that the position of women in Christendom, though far from equality, was vastly better than in most other societies where polygamy and concubinage were legally and socially acceptable? The resulting contortions can sometimes be quite entertaining.

More seriously, there is a kind of revision of history, widely practiced today, that arises not from the opportunities but from the needs—or the passions—of our time. Basically, all research means putting questions, and historical research means putting questions to the past, preferably without torture, and trying to find answers there. The questions we put are necessarily those suggested to us by our own times and preoccupations, and these differ from generation to generation and from group to group.

It is inevitable and legitimate that this should be so. What is neither legitimate nor inevitable is that not only the questions we put to the past but also the answers we find there should be determined by our present concerns and needs. This can lead, particularly under authoritarian regimes, but also in free societies under pressures of various kinds, to the falsification of the past, in order to serve some present purpose.

Much of what purports to be history at the present time, in much of the world, is of this kind. We live in an age when immense energies and resources are devoted to the falsification of the past, and it is therefore all the more important, in those places where the past can be researched and discussed freely and objectively, to pursue this work to the limit of our abilities. It has been argued that complete objectivity is impossible, since scholars are human beings, with their own loyalties and biases. This is no doubt true, but does not affect the issue. To borrow an analogy, any surgeon will admit that complete asepsis is also impossible, but one does not, for that reason, perform surgery in a sewer. There is no need to write or teach history in an intellectual sewer either.

We should have no illusions about this. While some of us may prefer to forget history or to rewrite history to serve some present purpose, the facts of the past, as distinct from the record or perception of the past, cannot be changed. And the consequences of those facts cannot be averted by ignorance or misrepresentation, whether self-serving, or, as sometimes happens nowadays, compassionate.

In our own time there has been a considerable change in our perception of the scope and scale and content of history. In bygone times, it was considered sufficient if a country, a society, or a community concerned itself with its own history. In these days, when almost every action or policy has a global dimension, we know better. We also have a broader and deeper idea of what constitutes our own history.

The rapid changes of recent years have forced us—sometimes painfully—to realize that the world is a much more diverse place than we had previously thought. As well as other countries and nations, there are also other cultures and civilizations, separated from us by differences far greater than those of nationality or even of language. In the modern world, we may find ourselves obliged to deal with societies professing different religions, nurtured on different scriptures and classics, formed by different experiences, and cherishing different aspirations. Not a few of our troubles at the present time spring from a failure to recognize or even see these differences, an inability to achieve some understanding of the ways of what were once remote and alien societies. They are now no longer remote, and they should not be alien.

Nor, for that matter, should we be alien to them. Between the various countries and cultures that make up this world, the forces of modernization are creating, however much we may resist it, a global community in which we are all in touch with, and dependent on, one another. Even within each country, modernization is destroying the barriers that previously divided us into neatly segregated communities, each living its own life in its own way, suffering minimal contacts with the outsider. All that is ending, and we must learn to live together. Unfortunately, intercommunication has not kept pace with interaction, and we are still deplorably ignorant of each other's ways and values and aspirations.

Ignorance is of course not the only problem. There are real differences, which must be recognized and accepted; real issues, which must be confronted and resolved. But even real differences are exacerbated, real problems are aggravated, by ignorance, and a host of difficulties may reasonably be ascribed to ignorance alone.

Our education today should be concerned with the development of many cultures, in all their diversity; with the great ideas that inspire them and the texts in which those ideas are enshrined, with the achievements they made possible, and with the common heritage their followers and successors share.

History is the collective memory, the guiding experience of human society, and we still badly need that guidance.

Notes

1. As cited in S. W. Baron, "The Historical Outlook of Maimonides," *Proceedings of the American Academy of Jewish Research* 6 (1934–35), 7–8.

2. Decree of 30 May 1947. As cited in Anwar G. Chejne, "The Use of History by Modern Arab Writers," *Middle East Journal* (1960), 392–93.

3. E. A. Belyaev, *Arabs, Islam and the Arab Caliphate in the Early Middle Ages* (New York: Praeger, 1969), 9.

4. Marc Ferro, *Comment on raconte l'Histoire aux enfants à travers le monde entier* (Paris: Payot, 1981).

47

First-Person Narrative in the
Middle East

❧❦❧

After the Young Turk Revolution of 1908, there was a sudden outpouring of something that had long been rare: the writing and publication of memoirs. Two new circumstances combined to produce this flowering of the memoir. The first was an interval of freedom of expression and publication in Turkey that had no precedent in the past and very few parallels in the future. The second was the urgent need felt by a number of rather senior and important figures to provide some explanation of what they had been doing during the previous thirty years. And so we find Said Pasha, grand vezir and holder of various other offices under Abdülhamid, producing three volumes of self-exculpatory memoirs; Kâmil Pasha, colleague and rival, doing the same; Said Pasha then producing comments on Kâmil Pasha's memoirs; Kâmil Pasha producing comments on Said Pasha's memoirs; and each producing a reply to the other's comments as well as to comments by a number of lesser mortals. Memoir writing engaged not only pashas but even some of the revolutionary leaders. Some of these works were translated from Turkish into Arabic and helped to set afoot a similar trend in the Arabic-speaking world.

It has been claimed that this was the beginning of memoir writing in the Near Eastern Muslim world and that until that time it was not the practice for people to write about themselves. It has been remarked that, generally speaking, the tendency among writers of history in Arabic was to conceal their own personalities, and it is noteworthy that when inserting a personal testimony, they often do so in the third person. Tabari, for example, the great medieval historian, when wishing to make a comment or observation of his own, says *qultu*, "I said," instead of his usual narrative introduction *qāla*, "he said." But when he is producing a piece of evidence of his own, he says "*qāla* Abu Jarir," this being his own sobriquet, thus distinguishing between information provided by him and comment made by him.

The idea that autobiographical writing, first-person writing, memoir writing, whatever we may choose to call it, begins with the Young Turk Revolution is quite mistaken. Such writing goes back a very long time, and I shall try to demonstrate this by putting before you a sort of prospectus of the different types of first-person narrative that have at one time or another flourished in the region and that have contributed directly or indirectly to the growth of memoir and autobiography in modern times.

First-person narrative figures among the most ancient writings of the Middle East and therefore in the world. Amenemhet of Egypt, of the twelfth dynasty that flourished between 1991 and 1962 B.C., wrote some rather interesting autobiographical texts. In a description of a journey to the south and some campaigns, each paragraph begins with "I did this" or "I did that," the classical approach of the autobiographer. Even more remarkable is an autobiographical inscription from a Hittite king, Hatusilis, who felt called on in about 1275 B.C. to provide a justification for his accession to the throne. He felt, almost uniquely among ancient and indeed more recent rulers, that having obtained power to the disadvantage of other members of his own family, he had to provide a moral and legal justification for what he had done. So we have this rather strange spectacle of an ancient Hittite king saying in effect, "Well, I had to do this. It's true he was my brother . . ."

Another example is Tiglat Pileser, the Assyrian king who, writing about 1115 B.C., produced another of the classical types of first-person narrative; describing the innumerable countries he had conquered, cities he had devastated, and peoples he had killed or enslaved, thereby building up great glory for himself. Darius, the king of Persia, gives us another type in his Behistun inscription of about 520 B.C. that begins with his pedigree: his father, his grandfather, his ancestors.

When we pass from these and other for the most part now extinct Middle Eastern societies to that of the Jews, we have a somewhat different situation. In the Hebrew Bible, normally only God speaks in the first person. Normally, but not exclusively; there are exceptions. The Book of Deuteronomy, for example, is for the most part first-person narrative by Moses, or at least is presented as such, although it is hardly autobiographical. There are first-person passages in some of the Prophets and a genuine autobiography in the Book of Nehemiah, a personal statement of personal history probably unique in the ancient world. Another Jewish example is the autobiography of Josephus, written or at least surviving in Greek, in which he justifies his own rather questionable activities. M. Vidal Nacquet, the French classicist, described this as a manual of correct behavior in treason. Josephus gives us a perhaps classical example (classical because it was in Greek) of the self-justificatory memoir, explaining his life because it was necessary to answer a whole series of charges and accusations brought against him.

One interesting feature of Josephus's autobiography is that he begins with his pedigree. Apart from Darius, this is almost unique in antiquity. As far as I know, no other Greek or Latin author does so, and there are quite a number of autobiographical writings in Latin and Greek. Josephus begins with his ancestry, explaining that among the Jews, unlike other people, nobility is measured by priesthood, and he goes on to develop this theme at length. This practice of beginning with a pedigree became standard in Islamic times.

Of all the pre-Islamic societies that flourished in the Middle East, the one with the most recent and direct influence on early Islam was of course that of Iran. Unfortunately, we do not know a great deal about the literature of Iran in the period immediately preceding the advent of Islam, that is, in the Sasanid period, but we do have some information, including three documents that purport to be autobiographical and that survive in Arabic. One of them, ascribed to the Sasanid emperor Khusraw Anushirvan and preserved by Ibn Miskawayh, sets forth certain guiding principles that Khusraw as a king found it expedient to follow. This text is a mirror for princes, of a type common in Islamic literature, but is projected back into a pre-Islamic past and presented in the first person in the name of Khusraw; it is obviously not to be taken seriously as autobiography. Somewhat more autobiographical is a letter of advice from another Sasanid, Khusru Parviz, to his son Shiroye. This does make some personal statements and may in part be authentic.

Much more important than either of these is the brief autobiography of Burzoye, a Persian physician who was sent to India, knew Indian languages, and translated from Sanskrit the collection of animal fables that later came to be known as *Kalila wa-Dimna*. The introduction to his autobiography states that the king gave orders to set down the history of this man from the day of his birth, including his education, his studies, his travels, "until his heart was filled with all kinds of wisdom and knowledge." As we shall see, this short autobiography became the model for a vast number of autobiographical writings— fragments rather than autobiographies—by men of learning.

Having set the scene, I come to the heart of my presentation, namely, the Islamic period. For convenience of rapid treatment and at the cost of some inevitable oversimplification, we may divide first-person writings into certain major classes, the first of which I would designate by the Arabic term *fakhr*, the boast. Perhaps the earliest Arabic autobiography is the *Mu'allaqa* of Imr al-Qays, and to a lesser extent some of the other "hanging odes" of ancient Arabia. These are often lengthy first-person statements describing deeds done. Quite a number of other fragments survive from ancient Arabia; the stories of the *Ayyam al-'Arab*, and other ancient poems are often markedly autobiographical.

This kind of personal statement of deeds done finds expression in an impressive number of royal memoirs, written personally by rulers or under their immediate direction. A fascinating example comes from the far west of Islam. ʿAbdallah Ibn Buluggin, of the Zirid dynasty of Arabized Berbers who lived in the eleventh century, wrote a book-length account of life at court during his father's and his own lifetimes. A still better known autobiography is that of Usama ibn Munqidh, a local ruler in northern Syria in the twelfth century, who wrote what is probably the most informative single book in Arabic about what life was like in Syria at the time of the Crusades and what kind of human relationships existed between Muslims and Crusaders.

Such writings appear more frequently in the Persian than in the Arab or Turkish world. There are the pseudomemoirs of Timur, the genuine memoirs of Babar and of Tahmasp, and the still later first-person narratives of Nasir al-Din Shah. In contrast, the Ottoman sultans do not seem to have gone in for this kind of writing. They preferred to express themselves artistically by writing verse rather than memoirs. All the Ottoman sultans without exception composed poetry, and some of them were even poets.

Associated with the royal memoir is a rather special genre: the autobiographical biography, a book written by someone who is primarily a literary figure, who is closely associated with the ruler, and who writes a book that is at the same time a biography of the ruler and an autobiography of the writer, the two stories being commingled in order to show, among other things, the intimate position of the writer with the ruler. The best example of this genre is ʿImad al-Din's book about his life with Saladin. If he had been modern, he might have called it "My Life with Saladin" or "Saladin and I"; he actually called it *al-Barq al-Shāmī*. Displaying at times an almost epic quality, it is a remarkably informative document about Saladin and also about ʿImad al-Din. About the same time, ʿUmara al-Yamani, a courtier of the last Fatimid rulers of Egypt, a minor poet and a man of letters, wrote an autobiographical work that is also of considerable interest.

The first category of first-person narrative consists, then, of "things that I did." The second category might be defined as "places I went to and things I saw." In the Middle East, there is an extensive travel literature, arising from many different kinds of travel. Medieval Islamic society enjoyed a far greater degree of voluntary, personal mobility than did any other known premodern society. Men, and sometimes women, traveled; they planned, organized, and conducted long journeys.

The main impetus, of course, was the Muslim pilgrimage, which requires every Muslim once in a lifetime, whether living in Morocco, in Java, in Central Asia, in Central Africa, to go to the Hijaz, visit the holy places, and join with other Muslims in certain rites. An elaborate system of arrangements all over the Muslim world facilitated the pilgrimage. There were roads, relay stations, and other services, and we know of a large number of individual travelers. The pilgrimage became associated with other forms of travel, notably travel for trade and travel for study. Scholars went to study under different teachers: "Seek for learning even in China," says a *ḥadīth*. This is not meant in any sense to be derogatory to China; it simply means that even if you have to go that far, still go. This whole category of writings is devoted to "journeys I made, places I visited, teachers at whose feet I sat, whose courses I attended, whose lectures I noted down," and the like. People collected shaykhs, and books that are "shaykhs under whom I studied" form a recognized genre.

There were also diplomatic envoys who, exceptionally, had interesting things to say. There were captives who managed to get themselves ransomed and returned home. And, in more modern times, there were students who went abroad and came back with often very strange stories.

One of the earliest of these travelers was an Arab called Harun ibn Yahya, who was taken prisoner and sent first to Constantinople and then to Rome in about 886. He wrote a brief description of Rome and Western Europe that was preserved by a later geographer. Others, including such famous figures as Ibn Battuta (whose descriptions of the world are at least in part written in the first person), recounted personal adventures and experiences, personal contacts and relationships, conversations with other people, and personal reactions to the strange and wonderful things that they found.

In the Ottoman period we have accounts of India, such as that of the admiral Sidi Ali Reis, who went to India in the late sixteenth century. We have a number of Ottoman ambassadors to Europe, to Iran, to Central Asia, to India, and we have the unique and incomparable Evliya Chelebi, who died in 1684 and wrote of a whole series of adventures. Unfortunately one of the problems with Evliya Chelebi is his credibility. To call him a liar, as some have done, is an injustice; he makes it quite clear in the introduction to his book that his purpose is to entertain rather than to instruct. He is indeed one of the few authors who tells us why he is writing the book and what he is trying to accomplish. There is undoubtedly a great deal of personal information in his work. His account of Vienna, where he went as a member of the entourage of an Ottoman ambassador, is particularly interesting. He seems to have spent some time in the city, and the responses of an Ottoman gentleman to imperial Vienna in the seventeenth century make a remarkable document.

In the nineteenth century, the literature of travel acquired a new dimension with the process of European discovery and the growing number of students, then diplomatic envoys, and then political exiles who visited the lands beyond Islam. To these three major groups, we may add royal visitors.

If the first two categories are "what I did" and "what I saw," the third, more interesting in many ways, is concerned with "what I thought." These latter works are rarely book length. Most are short statements by scientists and philosophers, apparently written for inclusion in some larger biographical work. Reference has already been made to the existence in Arabic and later, to a much lesser extent, in Persian and Turkish of vast biographical dictionaries. Scholars were obviously concerned to have a proper and correct entry in these medieval versions of *Who's Who*, and some of them took care to provide an outline. Thus when Ibn Abi Usaybi'a compiled his famous biographical dictionary of physicians, many of the physicians in his book provided their own biographies directly. Quite a number of remarkable personal statements by medieval physicians are included in this and other biographical dictionaries, and some entries are preserved from earlier periods. From as early as 873, we have a kind of memoir by Hunayn ibn Ishaq, a translator, who talks about his work, his rivals, and his critics; a memoir by the great physician Muhammad ibn Zakariya al-Razi, who died in 925; and another by an Egyptian physician called Ibn Ridwan, who tells the heartbreaking story of his impoverished childhood and hard times, his inability to study properly because he had no money, and his success in completing his studies all the same: an intensely personal statement also offered as a moral lesson for others.

Not only the scientists and philosophers wrote in this manner, but also others with a more specifically religious purpose, and notably the Sufis. Muhasibi (d. 857) is an example. Hallaj left some autobiographical fragments. These writers want to tell us of their mystical experiences, for our enlightenment and for our guidance. Surely the outstanding and classical example of the religious autobiography in Islamic literature is Ghazali's (d. 1111) *Saviour from Error*. In it he tells of his struggle to achieve a true understanding of the world, the universe, and the predicament of humankind. He speaks of trying the way of the philosopher, the way of the theologian, and finding that each one was unsatisfactory. He finally found the true way, that of the mystic, and through that, with some changes, he managed to achieve the understanding that he sought. Among scholars, this introspection takes the different forms of autobibliography and what might be called autohagiography; an outstanding example of the latter is Sha'rani (d. 1565).

One religious autobiography is of particular interest, that by an Ismaili *da'i*, or propagandist, who worked in Iraq in the interest of the Fatimid caliph. He was a propaganda agent of subversion and influence in the territories ruled by the Buyids and eventually was recalled to headquarters in Cairo where, if I may translate it into modern language, he became first a high official in the ministry of propaganda and then minister of propaganda—the head of the *Da'wa*, or *dā'ī al-du'āt*. His narrative, one of the very rare book-length autobiographies, is a curious mixture of personal statement, religious testimony, and career intrigue. It consists of debates that he had with other people, speeches that he made, sermons that he delivered, letters that he wrote, and actions that he took—demonstrating how clever he was in various tricky diplomatic situations. In the last part, when he is in Cairo and working in the Fatimid government, he tells of his disagreements with other people and describes how this one and that one were treacherous and dishonest, or stupid and vicious, and how he got things right and was therefore deserving of credit and attention. This is the most modern of these books, an early prototype of the present-day memoir that consists of speeches, letters, debates and experiences, accusations against one's rivals, and above all self-justification.

I spoke a moment ago of the autobibliography. These became more and more common as the biographical dictionaries became larger, more capacious, more copious, and more numerous. Roughly from the thirteenth century onward, there were great numbers of short autobiographies and short memoirs—half a page, a page, rarely much more—that were someone's draft for his own *Who's Who* entry. More often than not, such entries were provided to disciples who then included them in their books. These disciples and compilers also offered self-portraits. The biographical dictionaries were normally arranged chronologically by years of death, and the individual entries were therefore not, so to speak, published until after the subject's death. But some compilers arranged their entries by the centuries in which they flourished and therefore felt able to include themselves in their own biographical dictionaries. Sometimes they spoke of themselves in the third person, a practice shared with such distinguished figures as Julius Caesar and Charles de Gaulle; at other times, they wrote in the first person. Some of these accounts are mixed, as for example that of the famous Ibn Tulun of Syria; he begins his autobiography in the third person and halfway through switches to the first person.

An outstanding book that combines many of these different features is the autobiography of the great Ibn Khaldun. This is not strictly speaking a book but part of a book, a book-length component in his vast universal history. In this he talks of his ancestry, his education, the shaykhs under whom he studied, his travels, his writings, his career, and his scholarship. It is certainly the most comprehensive and, as one would expect from Ibn Khaldun, intellectually the most interesting and the most satisfying.

A distinct group consists of autobiographies by those who lived in some sense on the margins of Islamic society, for example, the *dhimmīs*, non-Muslims living within the Muslim community who, for one reason or another, wrote memoirs or statements about themselves. Two Jewish figures are credited with probably apocryphal autobiographies, Eldad Hadani and David Reubeni; an interesting eighteenth-century figure from Jerusalem, Azulay, produced a real autobiography. Among Christians, there were several memoir writers in the nineteenth century, including Mikha'il Mishaqqa, Rustum Baz, and Arutin.

Some of these non-Muslims were converts to Islam. The Jew known as Samuel al-Maghribi was converted in 1163 and wrote a refutation of Judaism called *Ifḥām al-Yahūd*, to which he appended a brief statement about himself and his family, explaining that he had postponed his conversion because he did not want to distress his father. Ahmad Faris al-Shidyaq wrote extensive memoirs; an experienced convert, he became a Protestant first and then a Muslim.

A special genre consists of solicited memoirs, those written on request, usually of someone European, someone from outside the Islamic world. Some of these documents are interesting personal statements, in part because of the circumstances that brought them into existence. The Yemeni Jew Hayyim Habshush, for example, who escorted Halévy in his travels in the Yemen, was asked twenty years later by Edward Glaser to write memoirs of himself and Halévy. Habshush wrote an autobiographical cum biographical travel book, a kind of *al-Barq al-Shami* on a small scale. An Egyptian shaykh called Tantawi somehow found his way to Russia where he died in 1861, but not before becoming one of the founders of the Russian school of Arabic studies. Tantawi was asked by a Russian Orientalist of the time to write an autobiography, which he obligingly did. There was the Ottoman interpreter known as Mütercim Osman, a native of Temesvár, at that time an Ottoman city, who was in the service of the Pasha of Temesvár. Osman knew several languages, as apparently did everybody in Temesvár. He spoke Serbian and Hungarian as well as Turkish; after his capture by the Austrians in war, he spent eleven years in captivity during which he mastered German. He was then ransomed or exchanged and went home and got an excellent job as chief interpreter to the Pasha of Temesvár. He wrote two volumes of memoirs, fascinating books about the Turko-Austrian wars in and around Hungary. What is still more interesting is that each of these volumes survives only in a single manuscript, one in Vienna, the other at the British Museum, and that the work is totally unknown to Ottoman historiography or literature.

In the nineteenth century, again, a number of people wrote memoirs to order: Khayr al-Din al-Tunisi, for example, who was asked to write in French; As‘ad Khayat, who wrote in English; and a rather curious person known as Mme. Veuve Kibrisli Mehmet Pasha, the widow of Kibrisli Mehmet Pasha, whose book, written or at least published in English in 1872, contains the remarkable memoirs of an Ottoman lady.

What sort of pattern, if any, emerges from this kind of first-person writing, memoirs, autobiographical fragments, and the like, of which I have selected merely the high points? Certain things are almost standard. These writers begin with ancestry, although in Greco-Roman antiquity only Josephus does so. In Islamic autobiographical writing, this opening is practically universal and includes as many generations as possible. In extreme cases people will go back to Adam, but certainly as far back as ancient Arabia. They say where they were born, though not necessarily when they were born. (There seems to be a certain vanity that inhibits some of our memoirists from giving the date of their birth.) The place of birth is important, and some words of praise for the beauties of the place are often included, perhaps the citation of a well-known *ḥadīth*, *Ḥubb al-waṭan min al-īmān*, love of one's birthplace is part of the faith, and the like. Then, particularly among the scholarly autobiographies, education and travels follow, forming a kind of curriculum vitae. This section may include "the books I have read and the books I have written," and if the autobiography or fragment is a religious one, then of course the religious experience. The length varies enormously. Relatively few are separate books or even long enough to form separate books. The great majority are brief, running from a few lines to a few pages, and obviously written for inclusion in some larger book, either one's own or someone else's.

Finally, why? What are the purposes of these writings? Here again, at the risk of oversimplifying, I would put them in three main categories: to serve oneself, to serve others, and to serve posterity. To serve oneself covers, of course, the numerous apologia written to justify what one has already done or to facilitate what one hopes to do next. The two purposes are often linked. To serve others refers in particular to the religious works. There is no doubt about the religious sincerity of Ghazali or of Avicenna in writing for the intellectual guidance of their readers. And posterity is the intended audience of those who are concerned about their place in history, an important concern in Sunni Islam where, by the very nature of Sunni beliefs, the sense of history is strongly developed.

In the course of the nineteenth century, under the influence of European models, many memoirs of one kind or another were added. In the twentieth century, they became an unstoppable torrent.

48

Reflections on Islamic Historiography

♋♋⟐⟐

Consider the word *history*. It comes from a Greek verb meaning to learn by asking questions—a good way to learn, I think we would all agree. It has the further meaning of inquiring into a subject, and then the derived meaning of narrating what one has learnt by asking questions and inquiring.

Historia developed to mean the relating of a narrative. This may be of events which actually happened or are purported to have happened, or of which the narrator frankly admits himself to be the inventor. In English, we have a bifurcation of this idea of narrative into two kinds: history and story. French uses *histoire* in both senses, while German uses *Geschichte*—a different word from a different root, but still combining these two meanings from the Greek.

The same word, the same root, has found its way into Arabic too, but with a dramatic shift of meaning. The Arabic term is *usṭūra*. It too derives from the Greek *historia*, but in Arabic, it has the meaning of a tall story. *Usṭūra* is a fable, a myth, a patently invented tale, and it is interesting that this same term, by what route or channel I do not know, should have suffered so complete a change of meaning in Arabic. It is not that the Arabs, from the earliest times, were not interested in history, but they use a different term to designate it. This is the term *ta'rīkh*, which is used not only in Arabic but, as far as I know, in virtually every other Muslim language.

Now *historia*, as I mentioned earlier, means to learn by inquiry; *ta'rīkh* comes from an old Semitic word meaning the moon. It means, in other words, dating: a system of dating by natural phenomena, and it reflects the concern to establish a precise and accurate chronology. *Ta'rīkh* means, in the modern American idiom, to tell it like it was, or, in the more elegant phrase of von Ranke, "wie es eigentlich gewesen ist." This reflects a profound concern, from the very beginnings of Islamic historiography, to establish a sequence of events, to find out and relate what happened, precisely and accurately. I propose to consider how this was done, in what ways, for what purposes and to what effect.

Attitudes towards the Past

It may be useful to begin by underlining the difference between what one might call historical and ahistorical societies. There are some civilizations that have reached a high level of material, moral and intellectual culture without being interested in the past. The outstanding example is Hindu India, that is, India before the advent of Islam. . . . Another example of an ahistorical culture is that of post-exilic Judaism. There is a marked change from the pre-exilic concern with history to the post-exilic neglect of history. The Greeks were very interested in what we would call contemporary history, the chronicling of the here and now. But there is very little Greek writing about times that, for them, were ancient. The Romans were rather more interested in ancient history, principally their own.

All this is by way of background, to set the scene for a study of Islamic historiography. The first thing that strikes us, looking at the historical literature of the Islamic world, is its immense richness and variety, as contrasted even with other history-writing civilizations. It has been calculated that the historical literature of medieval Islam is far greater in bulk, just in Arabic, than the literatures of medieval eastern and western Christendom in Latin, Greek and all the vernaculars combined. Islam, from the very beginning, has attached enormous importance to history. Indeed, in many parts of the world, reliable history begins with the advent of Islam.

The first kind of historical writing to appear in Islam is that which we might call heroic: saga, epic, narratives of battles, stories of heroes, the old Arabian stories known as the *Ayyām al-'Arab* (Days of the Arabs) which tell of the great battles of pre-Islamic Arabia. (Reading the *Ayyām al-'Arab*, I am irresistibly reminded of American football: there is the same element of sport, and one has the impression that the battles recorded in the *Ayyām al-'Arab* were only slightly more dangerous to life and limb than American football.) This type of saga literature develops into the *maghāzī*, the tales of raids which become tales of conquests, the *futūḥ*, and form an important component of the traditional biography of the Prophet who, in addition to being the Prophet, was also an Arab hero in the traditional style.

This type of saga historiography is most important in the early period. It includes the saga of the Prophet himself, of his Companions, of those immensely successful wars which brought vast territories into the realm of Islam and subject to the rule of the Islamic state. But saga historiography doesn't end there; it continues into much later times, in the form of historical narrative that is halfway between chronicle and epic. Usually it centers around the career and achievements of some heroic figure, particularly in the jihad, the holy war for Islam. Thus, we have several Arabic biographies of Saladin, most notably the work by 'Imad al-Din, who combines Saladin's biography with his own autobiography, and whose frequent use of rhymed prose and heroic narrative qualifies his work as semi-epic literature. As a later example, I would mention the Ottoman accounts of the Hungarian wars of Suleyman the Magnificent, where the Ottoman historian Kemalpashazade again uses the same kind of literary style—part chronicle, part heroic poetry—to describe the achievements of his hero.

What is the purpose of this heroic literature? It is meant to stimulate, arouse, encourage, stiffen the sinews and summon up the blood, in Shakespeare's phrase. It also has some other purposes which become more important in later times. For want of a better term, I would call this purpose PR, public relations. This becomes almost formalized and certainly becomes a profession. Historical PR comes in a number of forms. The most universal is the poem. Nowadays, rulers employ public relations advisers or consultants. In classical Islamic times, they employed poets. The old histories of literature tell many stories of vast sums being paid by rulers to poets. Normally these were not expressions of literary appreciation, but were payments for services rendered. In a society where there are no mass media, radio, television, or newspapers, there are two ways by which the ruler can address the mass of his subjects: poetry and inscriptions. Inscriptions are there for whoever can read them, or have them read to him, and they proclaim the ruler's greatness, his achievements, and other things he would have his subjects believe about him. But the poet serves the same purpose rather more effectively, producing memorable and easily memorized verses lauding the greatness of his master. A good deal of classical poetry is PR: poems written in praise or eulogy, usually for a political or military chief. There is also negative PR, known as satire.

Rather more formal is the victory letter, a custom going back to remote antiquity, and very much developed in Ottoman times in the *fathname*. When an Ottoman sultan won a battle, the practice was to hire a historian who would then write it up in suitably grandiloquent language. This *fathname* would then be sent to other Muslim rulers, to say "Look what I've done."

Another major type of historical writing is that which is devoted to the collection, establishment and recording of precedents. The historian in these instances functions as the compiler of a casebook. This is needed for a variety of reasons, and there are several different kinds of historical writing that are collections of precedents. One type, predominant in the earlier period, is what one might call the Sunna approach, the *ḥadīth* narratives concerning the actions and utterances of the Prophet, followed by narratives of the doings and sayings of the Companions of the Prophet and the early rulers of Islam. The purpose of these was to establish rules of procedure: the Prophet said or did this, therefore this is right and is an example which should be followed. These are what modern lawyers call casebooks, and they pose two problems: how to treat history as law, and how to treat law as history.

One consequence of this desire to collect precedents and examples from the sanctified figures of the past is an almost obsessive concern with accuracy. If your purpose in history is to find out the manifestation of God's will—and from a Muslim point of view, Sunna is no less than that—it is obviously extremely important to get it right. From an early time, there are not only variant versions but even contradictory versions of the same event; hence the development, by early Muslim historians, of a very sophisticated science of source criticism, a comparative method far in advance of anything known in the world until that time. Modern scholarship has not always agreed with the methods used, but the information provided, sometimes perhaps half a dozen different versions of the same event, all laboriously tabulated, each supported by a chain of narrators attesting to its origins and its authenticity—all this provides a great wealth of material for the modern scholar.

The Sunna approach to history is not the only one concerned with precedent; there is another which we might call *adab*, using a different word that has a meaning similar to Sunna. *Adab* literature develops more in the Abbasid period and after, and its producers and consumers are not primarily men of religion but are rather "men of the pen," civil servants. A great deal of classical Arabic prose literature is written by civil servants for civil servants, to meet the needs of the civil service. These too are collections of precedents set by wise rulers and competent officials. There are also stories about unwise rulers and incompetent officials: one needs negative as well as positive examples. In this school of historical writing, accuracy—getting it right, what actually happened, the actual deeds done and words spoken—matters less than persuasive, convincing and elegant expression, raising all the problems of history as literature and literature as history.

These are the main types of history as precedent in Islamic historical literature. There is another type, relatively less important: biographical literature. Some of the biographical literature is an offshoot of the earlier *ḥadīth-khabar* type: it becomes necessary to establish biographies in order to verify the reliability of narrators and thus the authenticity of the texts which they narrate. Apart from that, biography takes two principal forms: martyrology and hagiography. Both of these are outside the Sunni mainstream of historical writing. Martyrology is Shiite, hagiography is primarily Sufi. From the point of view of the Shi'a, history does not have that central religious importance that it has for Sunnis, because from the Shi'ite point of view, after the murder of the Caliph 'Ali and the withdrawal of his son and successor, history can teach us nothing; it is a long saga of crimes, misdeeds and oppressions. This gives an entirely different quality to Shi'ite historiography from that of the Sunnis. It also produces that distinctively Shi'ite brand of historical writing: martyrologies, the record of those who were killed among the descendants of Abu Talib. As for the Sufis, they collect saints, and we have quite a number of collections of Sufi holy men.

Apart from these specialized varieties, biography—which is so important in some other historiographic traditions—is rather limited in the Islamic world. We have great numbers of biographical dictionaries, and I suspect that it was in the Islamic world that the biographical dictionary was invented. But the full-length individual biography is extraordinarily rare, and even the biographical dictionaries are mostly limited. Most were written by scholars and literati, collecting the biographies of scholars and literati, for a readership consisting largely of scholars and literati.

We do not find, as we find in some other societies, notably in Europe, biographies of monarchs. It is extraordinary that, with very few exceptions, even the most famous and active rulers of the Islamic world are not the subjects of individual full-length biographies. I mentioned Saladin before as one of the very few examples. It would be difficult to add many more. There is no real biography of any Abbasid caliph; there are only relevant sections of general histories. One possible explanation that comes to mind is the structure of the Muslim family, which makes it more difficult to achieve the kind of personal knowledge that biographers need. The biographer of an English or French monarch would know things about the monarch's mother, his upbringing, his early life, which for most Muslim rulers are simply unknowable. This information is unavailable even for Ottoman sultans, almost to the end of their dynasty, and that does make biography difficult.

What then is the subject matter of Muslim historiography? Here again we find striking contrasts between the Islamic and the medieval and later European approach. In the Islamic world, we do not find histories of nations. There is no history of the Arabs and no history of the Turks, very remarkable omissions. We do not find many histories of countries, and when we do, it is really city history. A history of Egypt usually means a history of Cairo; a history of Syria, *Shām*, usually means a history of Damascus. One will find local histories of a city and a province, mostly biographical, but no histories of countries in the sense that, further west, people were writing the history of England and the history of France. What we have is universal history, which of course for Muslims means Islamic history, sub-divided into dynastic histories, and to some extent regional histories, but only of the very large regions. (There are for example histories of Muslim Spain and Central Asia.)

Muslim Historiography and the "Other"

How does Muslim historiography look at the history of other peoples, countries, nations, religions? In the civilizations that preceded Islam, there was an almost total lack of interest in the "Other." The Greeks were not particularly interested in other people's history. There were books written about other civilizations, but they were compiled mainly by writers coming from those civilizations, such as the Babylonian Berossos on Babylon and the Egyptian Manetho on Egypt. It is surely significant that these books have not survived, but are known only from quotations. The Romans show a similar lack of concern with outsiders. The Byzantines do devote some attention to the history of other cultures, and particularly to that of their Islamic neighbor. But much of what the Byzantines write about Islam is in the nature of intelligence reports submitted to the Byzantine administration.

Muslim historiographical horizons did not extend much further. Some foreign history did find its way into the Islamic historiographic tradition, as it was needed by way of background. The Qur'an itself contains elements of earlier history. It deals with the prophets before Muhammad, and with various places and peoples of earlier times. Within the Islamic historiographic tradition it was permissible, indeed necessary, to include pre-Islamic material insofar as this was needed to interpret the Qur'an. For this purpose, we find elements of biblical, Greek and Roman history which became part of the Muslim historiographic tradition. But these amount to very little, and one is astonished by the extent to which the pre-Islamic past was forgotten and obliterated after the conversion of the central lands to the Islamic faith. Indeed, when the Persians began a kind of Persian national renascence in the ninth and still more in the tenth centuries, and tried to recover the history of the fairly recent glories of ancient Iran, they were not really able to do so. Much of the Iranian history that appears at that time is old Persian myth and saga rather than history. Firdawsi's famous *Shāh-nāme*, the Book of Kings, is not the real history of ancient Iran, but an entirely mythical saga.

Most astonishing is that the name of Cyrus was unknown in Muslim Iran until the last years of the nineteenth century, when it first became known through Persian translations of a French novel dealing with Cyrus, and some other writings dealing with ancient history. It was recovered through France, where it had been retrieved from the two surviving participants in the history of the ancient Middle East, the Greeks and the Jews.

Of course, one needed to know something about the enemy; it is always useful to have information about the current or prospective adversary whom one is likely to encounter on the battlefield or in the marketplace. But even here we find surprisingly little concern or interest. Crusade versus jihad—the great debate, as Gibbon called it, between Christendom and Islam—exemplifies this lack of interest in the "Other." Jihad was a holy war; the Crusade was a limited and belated Christian response to the jihad, but it extended over a vast area from Spain through southern Italy and Sicily to the Levant. Crusaders and Muslims confronted each other for several centuries in almost total ignorance of each other. The Crusaders show a remarkable lack of curiosity concerning their adversaries, and the Muslims show an even greater lack of curiosity concerning the Crusaders.

They knew little, they cared less. There are a few historians who give the Crusades a passing mention. A man of genius like the early thirteenth-century historian Ibn al-Athir was even able to detect a connection between the reconquest in Spain and Sicily and the arrival of the Crusaders in the Levant. For a man of his time, writing in Iraq, that was a quite remarkable piece of historical vision. But this was an exception.

We should therefore not be surprised to find a lack of any kind of empathy with the outsider. Now empathy is not a strictly modern phenomenon. The prophet Jonah was reminded that the people of Nineveh were also people, that one should not delight in their defeat. The Greek dramatist Aeschylus shows compassion for the defeated Persians in a war in which he himself had been a combatant. In contrast, I have not come across anything of that kind in Muslim sources.

This lack of interest and empathy continues right into the Ottoman centuries. One is struck by the fact, for example, that the Thirty-Years War—an event that should have interested the Ottomans, raging as it did just beyond their frontiers—is mentioned in the contemporary Ottoman chronicle only in a very brief and error-ridden entry of a couple of pages. But interest in outside history finally begins, as one would expect, with the Ottomans, and it begins when the Ottomans were becoming aware that things were going wrong, that these picturesque barbarians beyond the frontier could actually be dangerous.

We then find attempts to write historical accounts of Europe, one from the seventeenth century, two or three from the eighteenth century. Efforts begin in earnest in the early nineteenth century, when the Ottomans could no longer be unaware of the looming danger that Europe represented to the very survival of Muslim independence in the central lands. We then see the first translations from Western languages into Arabic, Persian and Turkish. The choice of books for translation is telling. A very large proportion are biographies: Napoleon, Catherine the Great of Russia, Charles XII of Sweden, and one wonders why a historiographic tradition which never took to royal biography becomes so concerned with the royal biography of others.

The Ends of History-Writing

What then has been the function and the purpose of history in the Islamic world? Why did people pay historians to write the stuff, and to teach it? Three major purposes emerge.

The first is what one might call the didactic: one needs to study the past and to relate and explain what happened in the past so that we may learn from the past and teach others. This is, I think, the most basic and important purpose, and it is for this that Islam especially assigns a central religious importance to history and accuracy. Here one might mention the example of the Ottoman *vakqanüvis*—the imperial historiographer, a court official appointed by the sultan whose job it was to chronicle current events. What is striking about the Ottoman court chroniclers is their extraordinary frankness. Major defeats, like the battle of Lepanto and the failures to take Vienna, are described with devastating candor. I remember a phrase of Silihdar, a contemporary Ottoman historian of the second defeat of Vienna. He tells the story in picturesque detail and ends by saying: "This is the most crushing defeat suffered by the house of Osman since the foundation of our state." It is difficult to imagine a modern historian in most countries of the Middle East using that kind of language about a contemporary defeat.

A second purpose is what one might call the practical: one learns about what people did in the past in order to repeat their successes and avoid their errors. Hence, a number of Muslim historical writings have the word *'ibar* in the title or something to the same effect—examples to be followed.

A third purpose of the writing of history is to legitimize, justify, advertise, promote, persuade, and indoctrinate. In pre-modern times, this is surprisingly rare. Historians on the whole tell it like it was. Occasionally, when they don't, they confess. There are some striking passages in Tabari, for example, where he confesses in so many words to suppressing some information as not being in the public interest. For the most part, however, such suppression is a modern practice that arrives only with nationalism and nationalist historiography. . . .

Whose History?

The question of the study of Islamic history is the last topic to which I shall refer. May we non-Muslims study it? Should we? And if the answer to both is yes, then how?

May we? Until a few years ago, it would not have occurred to anyone to ask the question. Now it is asked all the time, and it must be answered. There is a prevailing view, particularly in politically correct circles, that history is a national possession which belongs to the people who made it, and that others have no right to deal with it. We must let "them"—whatever that means—study "their" history, and be content with what they give to us for our edification. This is a point of view I find totally unacceptable. All that is human belongs to all of us, and I cannot see any justification, intellectual or other, for this kind of nationalized history. I derive great satisfaction from the fact that in my own university, Princeton, Talmud is taught by a Christian woman (which would seem to constitute not one but two strikes against her).

Should we? There are many people who ask why we should bother with these strange and exotic peoples. We have enough to do to learn our own history, which is all that really matters to us. Why go to the trouble? Again I think that we should bother; perhaps not all of us but certainly a lot of us. The history of Islam is a vital and essential part of human history without which even "our" own history is not fully intelligible.

And how? In a scholarly, meticulous, careful, precise way. No one can achieve complete freedom from bias. But . . . we do the best we can. This means using the new sciences that have been created for the study of documents, inscriptions, coins, and the like, and trying to achieve a better understanding of the past through methods and sources not previously available.

The study of Islamic history in the Western world has gone through three phases. In the first, historians believed everything they were told. They read chronicles, were impressed by their detail, quantity, and manifest concern for accuracy, and so assumed that whatever they said was true. Then came a second phase, when the great nineteenth-century scholars began to apply critical method, treating Muslim historians in the same way they had treated Greek, Latin, and their own historians, trying to detect biases, distortions, variant versions and so on. Here I am thinking particularly of the work of such founding fathers of our discipline as de Goeje, Wellhausen, Caetani and others. Then more recently comes a third phase, of almost total rejection. It is all false, it is all invented; we know absolutely nothing.

From my presentation, you will have gathered that I do not hold that opinion. What we have to do now is to find a more balanced approach, critical but not destructive, which will enable us to achieve a better understanding of the human history we all share.

49

The Ottoman Archives

A Source for European History

ಞೊಞಞ

The Ottoman archives of Istanbul have for long been one of the great unknowns of historical scholarship. For many years the general reluctance of Turkish officialdom to allow any questing foreigner to sail the uncharted backwaters of Turkish administration—a reluctance based on well-founded suspicions of Western intentions towards Turkey—was sufficient to exclude Western scholarship from all but the most cursory examination of the Turkish records. Historians were compelled—or rather permitted—to write the history of Europe without any reference to the documents of what was for long one of the greatest of European Great Powers, and even to write the history of Turkey and the Turkish provinces without reference to Turkish documents of any kind.

The first question we may fairly ask is how the Turkish archives come to be in existence when those of every other Middle Eastern state have perished. The simple answer is that Turkey herself still exists—almost the sole survivor of the Islamic political entities of earlier times. Archives are assembled for administrative use and not for the convenience of historians. When the institutions which produce them cease to exist, the archives, ceasing to serve any practical purpose, are scattered and lost. Of the older states of the Middle East, only the Ottoman Empire survived into a period when the value of archives to historians was recognized and respected. The Turkish archives were cared for and survived, albeit narrowly, the fall of the Empire.

The formation of the Ottoman archives begins with the rise of the Ottoman state, but the present collection dates only from the Turkish conquest of Constantinople in 1453. Earlier collections of documents were presumably left in the previous capitals in Bursa and Edirne. A number of documents is still to be found in Bursa. As far as I am aware nothing remains in Edirne, but I have been told that an important collection was in existence until the Balkan war of 1912 when it was destroyed by Bulgarian artillery fire. Even in the Istanbul collection there are a number of individual documents dating from before the conquest, including an autograph letter in Greek from the Byzantine Emperor John VIII of the year 1432, which has recently been published three times. The archives become really full in the sixteenth century, and continue to the end of the Empire.

There are many collections, in Istanbul as well as in Ankara and a number of provincial towns, pertaining to various branches of the Ottoman government. I shall deal only with those known at the present time as the Archives of the Office of the Prime Minister (*Başvekalet Arşivi*), and housed near the Vilayet offices in Istanbul. This is the biggest and most important collection. It consisted originally of the records of the Imperial Council (*Divan-i Hümâyun*) and of the office of the Grand Vezir (*Bab-i Asafı*), which in the seventeenth century grew into a separate bureaucratic organization and eventually took over most of the functions of the office of the Imperial Council.

In 1845 the reforming Grand Vezir Reshid Pasha erected a new building for the archives in the grounds of the office of the Grand Vezir and housed these two groups of records in it. The finance records of earlier periods, previously kept in the Mehterhâne (the barracks of the Grand Vezir's military band), were brought there, and later also other groups of documents, notably the cadastral survey registers (*tapu defterleri*), which were brought from the Defterhâne (House of Registers) in the neighbourhood of the Sultan Ahmed Mosque. These records were to some extent made available to the imperial historiographers, but seldom to other Turkish historians, still less to foreigners.

What we may call the discovery of the Ottoman archives begins after the Young Turk revolution of 1908. In 1911 the Ottoman Historical Society was formed; its first president was Abdürrahman Sheref, who was also the last imperial historiographer. The first issue of the journal published by the Society contains a statement of its aims, the first of which was the classification, study, and publication of archive documents.[1] In the years that followed, Turkish scholars in the archives began to sort and classify the documents, and also published many individual documents of the highest importance. A Hungarian scholar, Imre Karácson, was brought in to advise but unfortunately died of blood poisoning contracted from a document. After his death no foreigner was admitted for a long time.

The years 1918–1921—dark years of defeat, occupation, and struggle in the history of Turkey—were nevertheless good ones for the archives, for in this period the first serious attempts were made at a systematic cataloguing of the papers. The work was interrupted by the Turkish Revolution and War of Independence. The transfer of the capital from Istanbul to Ankara and the general mood of revulsion from the Ottoman past led to a period of neglect, culminating in the sale of nearly 200 bales of records to a Bulgarian paper-mill as waste paper. The deal was fortunately discovered in time to save some though not all of the material; the ensuing scandal had the good effect of making the Turkish government and public archive-conscious. A new start was made in 1932, and since then excellent work has been done in housing, cleaning and cataloguing the records. In 1936–1937 another Hungarian scholar, Professor Lajos Fekete, was invited to advise on the methods to be adopted in preparing the catalogue.[2] The task is an enormous one, and only a beginning has been made, but already work of great value has been done by the archives staff and also by Turkish scholars who have published and are publishing a growing number of documents.

In 1949 I was given permission by the office of the Prime Minister to work in the Istanbul archives. In that and the following year I was able to spend about nine months working on the records, and I have made a number of briefer subsequent visits.

I would like now to give a brief description of the contents of the archives. We may divide them very roughly into:

Evrâk—pieces of paper with writing on them, ranging from imperial decrees drawn up in due form to odd notes and minutes by minor clerks. Their number is estimated at several millions, of which only a small proportion has been catalogued or even examined.

Defters—bound registers, estimated at about 50,000. These may be divided into two main groups: statistical, containing figures and other information required and collected for administrative purposes; and diplomatic, containing the texts of outgoing orders, letters, and other communications addressed to authorities within the empire and to foreign states.

A first classification of papers was made in 1918–1921 by a committee under the direction of Ali Emiri, which sorted about 180,000 documents in chronological order. In 1921 a second committee, under Ibnülemin Mahmud Kemal, sorted about 45,000 documents, from the fifteenth to the nineteenth centuries, into 23 subject groups with a rough chronological sequence in each group. A third team, under Muallim Cevdet, worked from 1932 to 1937 on much the same lines as Ibnülemin, and sorted some 185,000 documents into 16 subject categories.[3]

In 1935, following the advice given by Fekete, a systematic chronological classification was inaugurated, divided into three main sections corresponding to the Imperial Council, the Grand Vezir's Office, and miscellaneous others. This has now been carried as far as the late-seventeenth century, and is being accompanied by an index of personal and geographical names. A working classification of registers, especially those of the finance departments, was introduced by the late Kamil Kepeci, of the archives staff. In addition, a whole series of other catalogues, both of registers and of documents, has been prepared or started by the staff. These include catalogues of imperial writings (*hatt-i hümâyun*), of decrees (*irâde*), of waqf documents, and, most interesting to the modern historian, of the personal papers and records of Sultan Abdülhamid II, which were transferred to the archives from the Yıldız Palace. These papers are of considerable interest for every aspect of the internal and external policies of the Sultan, and cover the whole period of his reign. More than half of them have so far been examined and catalogued under 40 subject headings, the last of which is Egyptian affairs.

In what follows I shall try to indicate briefly the value of the Ottoman archives for European history, under three headings:

Diplomatic history, that is to say, the relations between the Ottoman Empire and other states. There is not much that need be said of this, since the material we may expect to find is of much the same kind as in the record office of any other power. The texts of outgoing communications to foreign sovereigns and diplomats are recorded in the usual form and in full. The great dividing line in the Turkish foreign affairs records is the reign of Selim III (1789–1807). Until his time the Ottoman sultans had not maintained any regular diplomatic missions abroad but had dealt with foreign governments through their representatives in Constantinople. Only on few and rare occasions were special Ottoman missions sent to one or another foreign capital. Selim established resident embassies in Vienna, Berlin, London and Paris. Others followed. These embassies were suppressed for a while, but were restored and extended by Mahmud II and his successors.[4]

In the earlier period there was apparently no systematic preservation of incoming documents or even of the Turkish translations that were made for departmental use. The contents of incoming documents were, however, summarized in the preambles to the outgoing documents containing the replies, and one is able to follow a correspondence fairly well. Numbers of individual documents have survived, such as royal letters from various European sovereigns, as well as some others, including an autograph letter from Lord Nelson to the Grand Vezir.

Until 1836 foreign affairs were handled by the office of the Reis Efendi, which was a part of the Bab-i Asafi. In that year it became a Ministry of Foreign Affairs. At first a mere change of title, this new ministry in time became a reality, and its records are kept in a separate collection. For a period after the Crimean War, Ottoman diplomatic communications were in French.

Foreign activities in the Ottoman Empire. The most important source of information of this subject is the series of registers called *Düvel-i ecnebiye defterleri*— registers of foreign states. There are 106 volumes classified by states and running from 1567 to 1914. This series deals not with diplomatic but with consular and commercial affairs. I take the English series as an example. There are nine volumes from 1675 to 1914. The first four contain Ottoman orders and exequaturs granted to British consuls, consular agents, dragomans, and the like, giving them official recognition and confirming their privileges. Volumes 5 and 6 contain copies of the fermans issued to the civil, military, naval, and other authorities, including customs, on matters relating to British trade. Volume 7 deals with ships and includes information about British vessels calling at Turkish ports and customs reports on the goods brought or carried away on these ships. Volume 8 contains the texts of capitulations and commercial treaties and agreements entered into with England, together with correspondence, reports and orders arising from them. Volume 9, labelled miscellaneous, contains reports, decrees, and rulings on specific cases involving British subjects.

Similar series exist for most of the countries of Europe and for Brazil (1857–1906), Mexico (1865), and the United States (1829–1905). I should perhaps add that matters of this kind are also dealt with in other series of registers and papers.[5]

Internal history of the European territories under Ottoman rule. It is of course for this subject that the Ottoman archives offer the richest resources. I have dealt elsewhere at some length with the value of the archives as a source for the history of the Asian provinces of the Empire, and will not repeat what I said there.[6] Most of it applies with even greater force to the European provinces, in which Ottoman administration was more direct and effective, and the records therefore more detailed and extensive. I refer only in passing to the great series of registers on land, fiefs, waqfs; taxes, customs and tolls; tax-farms and leases; population, non-Muslims, tribes; supplies, ports, roads, services; army, navy, police, arsenals; laws, decrees, regulations; and the vast mass of correspondence between the central and provincial authorities.

The treasures of the Turkish archives are now fairly easily accessible in the physical sense. All that is necessary is to obtain permission from the Prime Minister's Office in Ankara, and it is now usually given to *bona fide* scholars. Though the catalogue is far from complete, sufficient material is already listed and accessible to occupy generations of researchers and to impose a rewriting of most of what has been written on Ottoman history. The archives are in the care of a competent and devoted staff who are always willing to place their time and knowledge at the disposal of the visiting scholar, with a personal helpfulness and courtesy that will surprise those with purely Western experience.

There remains, however, the difficulty of reading and understanding the documents—and it is not a small one. The first problem is that of the script. With relatively few exceptions,[7] the documents are written in the Arabic alphabet, of which a number of different forms are used. These present considerable palaeographic problems, and for the earlier periods especially the decipherment of a single document is often a long and exacting task. At opposite extremes are the *divani*, the ornate and convoluted script used in imperial letters, and *siyaqat*, the special script, half cipher half shorthand, used in keeping finance records. It served the double purpose of speed and secrecy, and still maintains some success in preserving the second. The reading of proper names, in particular, is often almost or quite impossible.[8]

The language is Ottoman Turkish,[9] the already not inconsiderable difficulties of which are increased, in the diplomatic documents, by the use of a complex and intricate chancery style, full of allusion and artifice. At its best, as in some of the imperial letters, it can produce magnificent and resounding prose; but all too often, in the hands of inferior manipulators, it degenerates into mere bombast—vast expanses of contorted syntax and swollen verbiage where the thin rivulet of meaning is lost in the endless wilderness of words.

Documents of an administrative rather than a diplomatic character—such as orders to provincial governors, qadis, etc.—are usually free from the worst excesses of the chancery scribes and deal briefly and clearly with the topics to which they refer. They present, however, a major difficulty of another sort—their technical vocabulary. The Ottoman sultans ruled over a vast empire, with an elaborately organized system of civil, military, and religious government. The recent rapid development of Ottoman historical studies in Turkey and elsewhere has shown us how little we have really known of this system. The effective use, for historical research, of Ottoman documents presupposes a knowledge of the administrative background to which they relate, and of the significance, at different times and in different places and contexts, of the technical terms they contain.

The treasures of the Turkish archives have for a long time been well guarded: the outer approaches by a suspicious and obstructive officialdom, the second line by a difficult language and an obscure script, the inner citadel by an involved chancery style and a highly technical official vocabulary. Today the outer barrier is down. The archives are in the care of a skilled and enlightened staff, and are open to all who can read them. Only the inner barriers await the assault of those with sufficient courage and curiosity.

Notes

1. See Paul Wittek, "Les Archives de Turquie," *Byzantion*, xiii (1938), 691–99.
2. See L. Fekete, "Uber Archivalien und Archivwesen in der Türkei," *Acta orientalia* (Budapest), iii (1953), 179–206.
3. The classifications are: Ali Emiri—by reigns from Osman to Abdül-Mejid. Ibnülemin—justice, military, naval, internal, mint and coins, old registers, petitions, legacies, special correspondence, exemptions and privileges, palace, genealogies, foreign affairs, imperial rescripts, robes of honour, mines, finance, health, complaints, appointments, fiefs, pious foundations, public works. Cevdet—justice, military, naval, municipal, internal, mint, pious foundations, economics, foreign affairs, health, public works, palace, fiefs, police, education, privileged provinces (those under foreign or autonomous administration, as Egypt, Lebanon, and Cyprus). For a general description and classification of the documents and registers, in Turkish, see Midhat Sertoglu, *Muhteva Bakımından Başvekalet Arşivi* (Ankara: University of Ankara, 1955).
4. Documents already published by Turkish scholars include the letters and reports of the Turkish ambassadors in Paris under the Directorate and Napoleon, the reports on the missions of Namik Pasha to London in 1832 and of Reshid Pasha to Paris in 1834–36, as well as many others.

5. For a description of the Danish series see Bernard Lewis, "A note on some Danish material in the Turkish Archives in Istanbul," *Acta orientalia* (Copenhagen), xxii (1955), 75–76.

6. See my "The Ottoman Archives as a source for the history of the Arab lands," *Journal of the Royal Asiatic Society*, October 1951, p. 144, n.1; "Studies in the Ottoman Archives—I," *Bulletin of the School of Oriental and African Studies*, xvi (1954), 469–501; and *Notes and documents from the Turkish Archives* (Jerusalem, 1952).

7. From the earlier periods there are some Turkish documents written in Uighur script.

8. For an introduction to Ottoman palaeography and diplomatic see L. Fekete, *Einführung in die Osmanisch-türkische Diplomatik der türkischen Botmässigkeit in Ungarn* (Budapest, 1926). A manual of Ottoman diplomatic was published in Polish in 1955 by A. Zajaczkowski and J. Reychman.

9. There are numbers of documents in Latin, Greek, and European languages, as well as in Persian and Arabic. The last named is used for waqf documents and some others dealing with religious matters. The great mass of documents, however, is in Turkish.

50

History Writing and National Revival in Turkey

❦❦❦❦

T he national revival of the Turks in the 19th and 20th centuries has long been recognized as one of the most significant developments in the modern history of Islam, with effects reaching far beyond the frontiers of Turkey. While the political aspects of this movement have received some attention from Western writers, the no less important cultural aspects have hitherto been little studied outside Turkey, with the result that the picture given of modern Turkish history has sometimes been one-sided and distorted. The sources for a history of intellectual movements in modern Turkey are vast and only imperfectly explored, and this article must therefore be taken as no more than a preliminary and tentative survey of a subject that still requires detailed investigation.

Nationalism, as we use the word today, is a 19th century importation to the Middle East. The idea and its content have been transformed in gradual stages as the concept of the linguistic and territorial nation percolated from Europe to the Islamic world, and in the process acquired a new shape and meaning. The subject at issue is the very nature of group identity, the basis of social and political cohesion. Historiography provides us with one possibility, among others—of following the changes in the concept of the community or social entity to which the individual feels himself primarily to belong. It is therefore principally as an expression of collective self-consciousness that I propose to look at Turkish historiography in the last century or so, and endeavor to ascertain, first, how historiography is affected by changing concepts of group identity, and second, how historiography in turn affects those concepts.

At the beginning of the 19th century the Ottoman Turk regarded the society in which he lived as the culmination of two lines of historical development—or rather, since it is questionable how far the notion of development is present in traditional Islamic patterns of thought, of two series of historical events. The first of these began with the mission of Muhammad, the rise of Islam, and the establishment of the Caliphate; the second with the rise of the House of Osman and the Ottoman Empire. The link between the two was provided by the invasion of the Seljuk Turks and the creation of the Seljuk Sultanates first of Persia and then of Anatolia. These events form the main theme of Ottoman historiography. The Ottomans, like most other Muslim peoples, produced a rich historical literature, and their historiography must rank among their greatest achievements. Soon rising above the level of formal chronicles and annals, Ottoman historians in the best period reached a high level of historical insight and often attained an epic quality. By the end of the 18th century the general decline in Ottoman civilization was reflected in its historiography, and the resonant periods of the great historians sometimes degenerated into mere verbiage and bombast.

The liberal and westernizing reforms of the 19th century brought important changes in the writing of history, which was necessarily affected by such things as the spread of the knowledge of Western languages, and with it the ability to read Western books and thus make the acquaintance of new facts and new methods. The new school of Ottoman history reached its climax in the work of Jevdet Pasha (1822–1895), whose twelve-volume history of the Empire from 1774 to 1825 is a masterpiece by both historical and literary standards.

The spread of printing in Turkey during the 19th century, and the increase in literacy resulting from the educational reforms, created a new public demand for historical works of a somewhat different type. From about the middle of the century we find a number of new books on Ottoman history, addressed to a general intelligent reading public and attempting to record and explain a past that was already beginning to fade. To meet the new and growing interest in Europe, translations from Western history books appeared,[1] followed before long by original works on Western history. As one would expect, several of these were works of Islamic interest, and such books as Sédillot's history of the Arabs and Conde's history of the Moors in Spain were adapted into Turkish. But these were not the only ones. In 1866 a work appeared called *Universal History*, in six volumes, translated and adapted by Ahmed Hilmi from Chambers' *Universal History*, published in Edinburgh. This, as far as I know, was the first world history in modern Turkish literature. A little later, in 1872, Victor Duruy's history of the Middle Ages was published in Turkish translation, and thereafter a series of other translations, adaptations, and original works. Particularly popular was a series of books on the histories of individual countries[2] by Ahmed Midhat (1841–1912), one of the most widely read Turkish writers of his time.

Despite the growth of European influences, the dominant outlook of the period was still Islamic and Ottoman, and the sentiment of loyalty primarily religious and dynastic. Thus, even a pioneer of patriotism like Namık Kemal (1840–1888), in an eloquent appeal to the patriotic pride of his readers, reminds them that they had produced such great sovereigns as Sultan Suleyman the Magnificent and the Caliph Omar, such men of learning as Farabi, Ibn Sina, Ghazali and Zamakhshari; and he saw nothing incongruous in including Arab and Persian Muslims in an appeal to Turkish pride. In his most important historical work, the *Evrak-i Perişhan* (published in 1884), he gives biographies of Sultan Mehmed II, Sultan Selim I, Emir Nevruz Bey, and of Saladin. Most of the other historical works of the period take the Ottoman Empire as the unit of study and seek its origins, not in the history of the ancient Turks, but in that of the Islamic Caliphate.

In this same period, however, we can see the first stages in the development of two new notions: the notion of Turkey, and the notion of Turks. It may seem strange that these two notions should be described as new among the Turks in Turkey, yet so they were in the Ottoman Empire in the 19th century. While traces of a Turkish awareness of identity can be found in the early Ottoman period, they were overlaid and effaced by the double weight of the Imperial and religious traditions. In Ottoman writings up to the middle of the 19th century, and in many of them much later, the word "Turkey" is not used. It was a Western term, used by Westerners to describe a country which the Turks themselves usually called "the lands of Islam," "the imperial realm," "the divinely guarded realm," "the Ottoman dominions," and similar expressions—and these were of course understood to include the whole of the Empire and not simply the area inhabited by the Turkish nation, the very existence of which was concealed. The word "Turk" was indeed used, but in much the same way as "fellah" is used in modern Arabic—to denote the ignorant peasant—and its application to the Ottoman gentleman of Istanbul would have been an insult. It is in the course of the 19th century, and under Western influence, that these two ideas appear and make headway: the idea of Turkey as a country inhabited by a certain people and constituting a natural entity, and the idea of the Turks as a nation, distinct from the Ottoman dynasty and Empire.

One of the most important sources of these ideas was the new European science of Turcology. From the 18th century onwards a series of scholars, working from Chinese, Islamic, and later Turkish sources, had studied the history and languages of the eastern and pre-Islamic Turks. From the work of scholars like Joseph de Guignes (1721–1800), Abel-Remusat (1788–1832), Stanislas Julien (1799–1873), Heinrich Julius Klaproth (1783–1835), Edouard Chavannes (1865–1918), Vilhelm Thomsen (1842–1927), Wilhelm Radloff (1837–1918) and others, a new picture emerged of the role of the Turkish peoples in the history of Asia and Europe, and new light was thrown on the hitherto obscure history of the Turks before they entered Islam. This new science was especially cultivated in Hungary, where the belief was held by some authorities in the common origin of the Turks and Magyars.[3] National and racial ideas were introduced to the Turks by Hungarian and other European exiles who settled in Turkey after the unsuccessful revolutions of 1848, and were also communicated to the Turkish students who began to go to Europe. One of the leading Hungarian scholars of the time was Arminius Vambery (1832–1913). During his long residence in Istanbul he came into contact with many Turkish intellectuals, whose friendship and attention he retained after his appointment to a chair of oriental languages in Budapest. His work was continued by his pupils Kunos, Thury, and others.

Of Western books two in particular seem to have had a considerable influence. One was the *Grammar of the Turkish language*, with a long historical introduction on the Turkish peoples, published in London in 1832 by Arthur Lumley Davids. A French translation appeared in 1836 and attracted Turkish attention. Its grammatical portions helped to inspire the *Kava'id-i Osmaniyye* of Fuad and Jevdet Pashas, published in 1851, the first modern Turkish grammar to appear in Turkey. More important for our present purpose, its introduction served as the basis of a defense of the *Turks* (not Muslims or Ottomans) by the journalist and essayist Ali Suavi (1838–1878) in the first issue of his journal *Ulum*, a fortnightly published in Paris in 1869 on behalf of the Young Ottoman group of liberal patriots. Another work that influenced Turkish thought was the *Introduction à l'Histoire de l'Asie*, published in France in 1896 by Léon Cahun, containing a semi-scientific, semi-romantic account of the history of Asia in which attention is called to the significant role of the Turkish nomads of the Central Asian steppe. Cahun's book was published in Turkish translation in 1899, and many Turkish writers testify to its formative influence.

Among the first pioneers of Turkism in Turkey, a few representative examples may be considered. Ahmed Vefik Pasha (1828–1891) is credited with being the first to stress that the Turks and their language were not merely Ottoman, but were the western most branch of a great and ancient family stretching across Asia to the Pacific. Suleyman Pasha (d. 1892) was the author of a universal history, published in 1876, which includes a section on the pre-Islamic Turks— the first in modern Turkish historiography—based chiefly on Davids and other European writers. Shemseddin Sami Frasheri (1850–1904) was an Albanian whose career illustrates the way in which the Balkan peoples, more accessible to Western influences, served as carriers for new ideas. Though a philologist rather than a historian, Sami Frasheri, by his lexicographic and encyclopaedic work, did much to help the growth of the new feeling of Turkish self-awareness. Perhaps the most important was Nejib Asim (1861–1935), the first real Turcologist in Turkey. He was much influenced by Cahun, whose works he translated into Turkish, and also by the Turcological discoveries and publications in Europe, especially in Hungary, with which he had close personal connections. Nejib Asim did much to make the findings of Western Turcology known in Turkey, and himself made independent contributions to the subject.

Towards the end of the 19th and the beginning of the 20th century, the movement towards Turkism received a political impetus from another source, the Russian Turks—Muslim Tatars and Turks from the Volga, Central Asia,

Azerbayjan and Crimea, numbers of whom came to live in the Ottoman Empire. These exiles from Russia were usually people of a high standard of education; some of them had been through Russian high schools and universities. They were acquainted with the very considerable achievements of Russian Turcology; they had encountered and reacted against the pan-Slav movement and mystique. At the same time they were familiar with the new national ideas current among some circles in the Ottoman Empire. Tatar intellectuals, led by the Crimean Ismail Gasprinski or Gaspiralı (1841–1914) began a new political pan-Turkish movement, the ideas of which were disseminated in Turkey by men like Akchuraoghlu Yusuf (1876–1933) and Agaoghlu Ahmed (1869–1939). Foremost among the pioneers of this new nationalism was Ziya Gökalp (1875–1924) who, in a series of important historical and sociological works, laid the intellectual foundations of the Turkist movement.[4]

After the Young Turk revolution of 1908 a new phase began in historiography, as in all else. In 1910 the Ottoman Historical Society was founded; its first president was the last imperial historiographer, Abdurrahman Sheref, who thus served as a personal link between the old and the new. This society published a journal which appeared regularly for nearly twenty years. The professed aims of the society were to fill the gaps in the existing histories of the Ottoman Empire, to report on and publish documents, and to prepare a new Ottoman history on the grand scale. A great deal was accomplished towards the fulfilment of the first two objectives. In the third project the society failed: only the first volume appeared, and that—an interesting detail—was on the pre-Ottoman period, written by Nejib Asim in collaboration with Mehmed Arif.

The journal of the Ottoman Historical Society maintained a high scholarly standard, and its many volumes are still indispensable to every serious student of Turkish history. Perhaps the most distinguished among its many contributors was Ahmed Refik (1881–1937), author of both scholarly and popular works of great merit, and an indefatigable editor of documents. The journal was devoted almost entirely to Ottoman history, with occasional articles on pre-Ottoman Turkish Anatolia. In a society under Imperial patronage, under a government devoted to the principle of Ottomanism—of a common Ottoman citizenship and allegiance as the basis of political identity—it is hardly surprising that the field of study is in the main limited to the Ottoman Empire.

But the non-Turkish peoples of the Empire, increasingly conscious of their own separate national identities, did not respond to pan-Ottomanism, and it is not surprising that their example impelled even the masters of the Empire to seek nationalist self-expression. Turkism, the beginnings of which were already discernible in the preceding era, developed and found expression in other journals, books and pamphlets. Foremost among these were Turkist political journals like *Türk Yurdu*, in which Akchuraoghlu Yusuf, Ziya Gökalp and others elaborated the Turkist political thesis and continued the separation of Turkish from Ottoman loyalty. More specifically devoted to learning was *Milli Tetebbüler*, edited by Köprülüzade Mehmed Fuad, later known as Fuad Köprülü.[5] Unfortunately only five issues of this journal appeared, between April and December 1915, but they are enough to make it a landmark in Turkish historical studies. The studies and articles published in this journal and elsewhere by Ziya Gökalp, Köprülü, and their collaborators present a new conception of the scope of Turkish history. For them it is primarily the history of the Turks and of Turkey—that is, of a people and a country, rather than of a dynasty or a religion, though these are still accorded some respect. Their field of study included not only pre-Ottoman Turkish Anatolia, but also the history of Turkish states and peoples far from Turkey, in Central Asia and India. In another respect, too, the scholars of that generation broadened the scope of Turkish historical studies. Ziya Gökalp was a disciple of the French sociologist Emile Durkheim, and he and Köprülü were primarily responsible for the introduction of the sociological method to Turkish history. Their articles and books deal with institutions, law, folklore and culture as well as with political history.

With the fall of the Empire and the establishment of the Republic, the Ottoman Historical Society became the Turkish Historical Society, a change of name that expresses the new basis of political identity of the Turkish state. The publications of the society and its members show no great change, however, until the late twenties and early thirties, when the old society in Istanbul was wound up, and a new Turkish Historical Society formed in Ankara, the capital of the Republic. It was at this time that Kemal Atatürk took the history of Turkey in hand. His aim was to destroy what remained of the Ottoman and Islamic feeling of identity, and to replace it by one that was purely Turkish. The Turkish Historical Society became the instrument of state policy for the imposition of certain historical theories. Its tasks included the drafting of programs and text-books on national lines, for use in schools and universities. In 1932 a Turkish Historical Congress was convened in Ankara, which was inspired by Atatürk and attended by professors and teachers of history from all over Turkey, as well as by scholars and delegates from abroad.

The theory propounded by Atatürk and his disciples was, briefly, that the Turks were a white, Aryan people, originating in Central Asia, the cradle of all human civilization. Owing to the progressive dessication of this area, the Turks had migrated in waves to various parts of Asia and Africa, carrying the arts of civilization with them. Chinese, Indian, and Middle Eastern civilizations had all been founded in this way, the pioneers in the last-named being the Sumerians and Hittites, who were both Turkish peoples. Anatolia had thus been a Turkish land since antiquity. This mixture of truth, half-truth, and error was proclaimed as official doctrine, and teams of researchers set to work to "prove" its various propositions.

It would be a grave error to deride all this as the whim of an autocrat. Atatürk was too great a man to organize an elaborate campaign of this sort out of mere caprice, or out of a simple desire for national self-glorification. One of the reasons for the campaign was the need to provide some comfort for Turkish national self-respect, which had been sadly undermined during the last century or two. First, there was the demoralizing effect of a long period of almost uninterrupted defeat and withdrawal by the Imperial Ottoman forces. Then there was the inevitable reaction to Western prejudice. It is difficult not to sympathize with the frustration and discouragement of the young Turk, eager for enlightenment; who applied himself to the study of Western languages, to find that in most of them his name is an insult. In the English dictionary the Turk shares with the Jew[6] and the Welshman the distinction of having given his name to a term of abuse. The mixture of prejudice, ignorance, and cynicism that disfigures most European writings about the Turks can have given him no very high opinion of the European ideal of disinterested historical enquiry and the search for truth. His opinion will not have been raised by the readiness with which some European institutions and scholars, for political reasons, lent their encouragement to the Turkish official thesis. Once upon a time the Turk had been accustomed to despise his neighbors and his enemies from the comfortable altitude of superior religion and imperial authority. Empire was gone, and the growth of secularism was depriving him even of the consolations of religion.

In addition to the encouragement of Turkish pride and self-respect, Atatürk had a further political purpose. The loss of the Empire was recent, and still rankled with many. In Turkist circles and especially among the Tatar exiles, the idea was current that a new Imperial destiny awaited the Turks, whose task it was, not to revive the polyglot Ottoman Empire, but to create a new pan-Turkish Empire of the Turkish and Tatar peoples from the Aegean to the Far East. It was with the idea of discouraging such dangerous adventures that Atatürk taught the Turks that Anatolia was their true homeland, and had been the center of their civilization since ancient times.

The bad effects of the historical campaign are obvious. The good effects include the extension of the range and scope of historical studies and the provision of resources which were put to better use at a later date. By no means all Turkish historians were ready to accept these doctrines. Since Atatürk's death they have been gradually modified and abandoned. Some degree of national bias remains, and is probably inevitable. As in most countries, it is most evident in popular works and school textbooks, less so in university textbooks, and least noticeable in serious research. The encouraging thing is that it appears to be decreasing.

Turkish historical writing during the last twelve years has grown vastly both in quantity and in quality.[7] From the universities, the Turkish Historical Society, the Ministry of Education Press, and other bodies, a steady flow of books and periodicals shows an increasing mastery of modern scientific and historical methods. The rich treasures preserved in Turkish libraries and archives are now being cared for, catalogued and studied, and the volume of published documents is already sufficient to demand the attention of students not only of Turkish but also of European history.

Only some general observations can be made here. The first point to note is that the field of study chosen for research by the overwhelming majority of Turkish scholars is the history of Turkey, that is to say, of a definite country, a territorial and national unit in the Western sense. Ottoman history, which for a while was despised and neglected because of its connection with the previous régime and with anti-national ideologies, is again a major subject of study and research, but it is treated as a phase in the history of Turkey, preceding the Republic and following the Seljuks. Many scholars work on pre-Ottoman Turkish Anatolia; others go back still further, to the Byzantine, Roman, Greek and Hittite periods of Anatolian history. Some work was done on Hittite archaeology in Turkey even before Atatürk. Since his day Hittite and Asianic studies have become an essential part of the national history.

After the history of Turkey in all its eras, the two chief subjects are Turkish history and Islamic history. The first includes the history of the Turks outside Turkey. A fair amount of research has been carried out on the ancient Turkish peoples of Central Asia, the understanding of whose history and languages is of great importance even for the history of Turkey. Surprisingly little on the other hand is published about the other Turkish peoples in more recent times—in Central Asia, Turkestan, Azerbayjan and Russia—and most of that is the work of émigrés from those countries. Islamic history as an academic discipline in Turkey nowadays is usually taken to mean the Islamic period of Turkish history before the Ottomans. A certain amount of work is done on the great Seljuks, who are the direct antecedents of the Anatolian Seljuks and therefore relevant to Turkey. Very little attention is given to the earlier history of Islam, or even to the Turkish dynasties of mediaeval Egypt, Persia, and India. This restriction of range applies of course only to original research. Compilations and general works for the student or general reader are available on almost every branch of world history, including China, Japan and India, as well as most of the countries of Europe.

In the evolution of Turkish historiography in the period under review, three main developments may be seen, which are in some measure characteristic of the change in Turkish life and letters generally. The first is the gradual transformation of the main field of study from Ottoman and Islamic to Turkish and Anatolian history, reflecting—and at the same time influencing—the changing basis of corporate identity. The second is the progressive westernization of historical studies, involving the adoption and acclimatization of European methods and techniques, and the extension of the scope of historical enquiry to new fields, especially social, economic, and institutional history. The third is the rise, transformation, and, in our own day, decline of the romantic view of history. In the 19th century, Ottoman historians, like those of other Muslim countries, reacted to European hostility and prejudice with a romantic conception of classical Islamic civilization, idealizing its very real achievements until it became for them the fountainhead of all virtue and progress. This apologetic, still to be found in other parts of the Islamic world, gave way in Turkey to another kind of romanticism, in which the ancient Turks replaced the mediaeval Muslims as the heroes of a sort of national historical idyll. This trend in historiography reached its peak in the early nineteen-thirties. Since then the best Turkish historical writing has shown a growing regard for the standards and an increasing familiarity with the methods of objective scholarship, and in so doing is acquiring an importance that goes beyond the frontiers of purely Turkish history.

Notes

1. The first Turkish translations of European history books were published in Cairo in the eighteen-thirties, under the auspices of Muhammad Ali Pasha. Some of them were later reprinted in Turkey.

2. The fourteen volumes of the series appeared as follows:

1871–72	1) England, 2) Denmark, 3) Sweden and Norway, 4) Russia
1875	5) France, 6) Belgium and Holland
1876	7) Germany
1880	8) Germanic states, 9) Austria
1881	10) Switzerland, 11) Portugal, 12) Spain, 13) Italy, 14) Greece

3. At a later date the Hungarian desire for Turkish support against the common danger of pan-Slavism gave rise to the political movement known as pan-Turanianism.

4. On Ziya Gökalp, see Uriel Heyd, *Foundations of Turkish Nationalism*, London, 1950.

5. For an appreciation of Köprülü work as a historian see Ettore Rossi, "Lo Storico Fuad Köprülü, Ministro degli Esteri di Turchia," *Oriente Moderno*, XXXI, 98–103, Apr.–June, 1951.

6. This may in part account for the prominence of Jews among European Turcologists and Turcophiles, such as Davids, Cahun, Vambery, and, of a different kind, Disraeli.

7. A classified bibliography of historical books printed in Turkey in the period 1729–1950 was recently published in Ankara by Enver Koray, of the Turkish National Library. It contains 4,128 items, of which 2,518 are subsequent to the introduction of the new alphabet in 1928. For an annotated bibliography of the years 1940–45 see Robert Mantran, "Les Etudes historiques en Turquie de 1940 à 1945," *Journal Asiatique*, 1946–47, 89 ff.

51

On Occidentalism and Orientalism

CR̃Ȣ̃

There is a little book, written by the Turkish polymath Hajji Khalifa in 1655, called *The Guide to the Perplexed concerning the History of the Greeks, the Romans and the Christians*,[1] in which he says that although these wretched people are bound in due course to roast in hell, they are in the meantime becoming obnoxious; they are approaching the divinely guarded (i.e. the Ottoman) realms from both sides and becoming a serious danger. They have already caused certain lands which were previously part of the house of Islam to become part of the house of war, and it is becoming urgently necessary to know something about them.

Unfortunately, says Hajji Khalifa, what we find in our histories consists "of ridiculous lies and grotesque fables"—a judgment with which few would quarrel. It is necessary, he says, that the Muslim peoples should awake from the long sleep of negligence which has allowed the Christians to advance against them, should learn something about them and thus be enabled to take appropriate action.

He then goes on to give what purports to be information about the world of the Greeks, Romans, and other Christians. He begins, as one would expect, with a discussion of religion, since that is, after all, the beginning of all knowledge and therefore of any research into problems, and he offers his readers a brief outline of the Christian religion. This is based in the main on earlier Arabic accounts, including some polemical texts written by converts from Christianity. Following his sources, Hajji Khalifa provides his reader with information about the disputes in the Church in the early Christian centuries, but surprisingly, offers virtually no information about such things as the schism between the eastern and western churches or the Protestant Reformation, which one might have expected to interest an Ottoman reader in 1655 rather more than the fifth-century disputes between the Nestorians and the Orthodox. Hajji Khalifa knew little or nothing about either the Schism or the Reformation. He speaks of the eastern patriarchs, whom he lists, as "lieutenants" (*qā'immaqām*) of the Pope, and notes that the English, the Danes and the Swedes reject the authority of the Pope. The viziers of the Pope, he explains, are called Cardinal. They number 72, and the Pope is chosen (*intikhāb*) from among them.

He then goes on to discuss the political order of Europe, which, he says, is divided into *madhhabs*, the term commonly used to designate the different schools of Muslim law. In Europe, he says, there are three *madhhabs*: monarchy, aristocracy and democracy, monarchy being the *madhhab* of Plato, aristocracy the *madhhab* of Aristotle and democracy the *madhhab* of Democritus.

There is a great deal more of the same sort, as well as some quite reasonable observations. He classifies the Republic of Venice as an aristocracy, and describes the voting procedures of the Grand Council by means of what he calls *ballotta*. He notes that the only democracies in Europe are in the Netherlands and in England, and has a brief description of electoral procedures in both. There are two long chapters on the Papacy and the Empire, consisting mainly of numbered and dated lists of popes, kings, and emperors. The first, 232 names, runs from Peter to Paul III, who died in 1549. The second names seven kings of ancient Rome, from Romulus to Tarquinius Superbus. The third list gives the names and dates of 117 emperors—of Rome from Gaius Julius Caesar to Honorius (no. 47); of Constantinople to Nicephoras (no. 73); and then of the Holy Roman Empire from "Carolus Magnus" to Ferdinand III, who was still reigning when Hajji Khalifa wrote this booklet. Of Charlemagne, Hajji Khalifa notes that "He was king (*pādishāh*) of France. He conquered Rome and Austria (*Nemçe*) and became emperor." He then goes on to survey briefly the major countries in Europe which, for this purpose, do not include England.

The impression with which one is left is of breathtaking triviality. Hajji Khalifa was no fool. He was a man of great learning and great intelligence. He was moreover rather exceptional among Muslims of his time in being interested in Europe. He even went to the trouble to procure copies of geographical and historical works by European writers and get them translated into Turkish for his use; the very triviality and inaccuracy of this little tract, which, not surprisingly, has never been printed, is an index of the lack of interest that prevailed in his time.

Hajji Khalifa wrote in 1655, that is to say, more than one hundred years after Hieronymus Beck von Leopoldsdorf (1525–1596) had brought a manuscript of the early Ottoman anonymous chronicles to Vienna in 1551, as a gift for the Emperor Ferdinand I. This book was translated into German and published in 1567; a fuller version also appeared in a Latin translation with analytical commentary by Johannes Löwenklau (known to scholars by the Latinized form of his name, Leonclavius). This book, published in 1588, was a contribution to the textual problems of early Ottoman historiography and the elucidation of early

Ottoman history, which is still respectable. 1655 was also a couple of decades after the establishment of the first chairs of Arabic at Cambridge in 1633 and at Oxford in 1636, much longer after the establishment of chairs in Paris and at the University of Leiden. This was the same century in which Bartholomé d'Herbelot (1625–1695) produced the *Biblothèque Orientale* and in which Golius (1596–1667), Erpenius (1584–1624), Edward Pococke (1604–1691), William Bedwell (1562–1632) and so many other major scholars were at work.

These illustrate a striking contrast in the way in which two major civilizations, facing one another, looked at one another. They are not the only example. During the long wars between Islam and Christendom, fought in Hungary and adjoining areas between the Holy Roman Empire and the Ottomans, in the Mediterranean between the Barbary Corsairs and their Christian opposite numbers, the piratical Knights of St. John and others, many from both sides were taken captive, stayed for a while on the other side and were duly ransomed or escaped. Christian captives returning from Barbary or from the East produced, in the 15th, 16th and 17th centuries, a considerable literature about the countries in which they had for shorter or longer periods been incarcerated. Of the many Muslim captives—North African, Turkish and other—who were in Europe, so far as I know, only two accounts have come to light. One is by a Turkish Kadi captured on his way to take up an appointment in Cyprus. He was carried off to Malta, spent a little while there, and wrote a brief memoir.[2] The other is by a certain Osman Aga from Temesvar in Ottoman-ruled Hungary, who was captured by the Germans, learnt German and wrote an autobiography. It exists in a unique manuscript in two parts, one in Vienna and the other in London, suggesting that the work did not arouse much interest among Turkish readers.[3]

One last example may illustrate this difference. By the end of the 18th century, that is to say the beginning of the Anglo-French penetration into the Arab East to which such importance has been attributed in the development of Orientalism, there were available in print in the languages of western Europe, of grammars: 70 for Arabic, 10 for Persian, 15 for Turkish; of dictionaries: 10 for Arabic, 4 for Persian, 7 for Turkish, not to speak of great numbers of texts, both editions and translations, chrestomathies, and the like. One may wonder why so much more attention was given to Arabic than to Turkish, at that time the language of government and commerce in the Middle East and even to some extent in North Africa—letters from the rulers of Algiers and Tunis preserved in Western archives are mostly in Turkish, the language of rulers, not Arabic, the language of their subjects.

The answer is clear. There were no chairs of Turkish in European universities for the same reason there were no chairs of English or French or German— modern languages were not a fit subject for scholarly teaching and research. Arabic, in contrast, was a classical and scriptural language, worthy to take its place with Latin, Greek, and Biblical Hebrew.

Christian Europe had compelling reasons to interest itself in the languages and culture of the Middle East. In addition to the obvious appeal of an older and richer civilization and the even more obvious threat of a powerful and invading enemy, there was the call of religion. For the Christian, even in the far north, the very heart of his religion was in the Holy Land, since the 7th century under Muslim rule. His Bible and the faith that it enshrined had come to him from the Middle East, much of it written in Middle Eastern languages, and recording events in Middle Eastern lands. His places of pilgrimage—Jerusalem, Bethlehem, Nazareth—were all under Muslim rule, and except for the brief interval of the Crusades, it was only by Muslim permission that he could visit them as a pilgrim.

The Muslim had no comparable concern with Christian Europe. His religion was born in Arabia; his prophet was an Arab; his scriptures were in Arabic, and his places of pilgrimage, Mecca and Medina, were safely in Muslim hands. Nor was there much else to attract Muslims to medieval Europe. Its primary export to the Islamic world was its own people, as slaves; indeed, until the beginning of the modern age, there was little else in Europe to arouse their interest or curiosity. True, they were very interested in certain parts of the heritage of ancient Greece, but their concern was limited to what was useful—medicine, chemistry, mathematics, geography, astronomy, and also philosophy, in those days still numbered among the useful sciences. The medieval Muslims translated—or to be precise, procured translations of—a large part of the philosophical and scientific literature of Greek antiquity; they did not however show any interest in the Greek poets, dramatists, or historians.

Nor did they find anything of intellectual value in the Europe of their own day. During the centuries of the Arab presence in Spain and Sicily, the Tatar presence in Russia, and, a little later, the Turkish presence in the Balkans, there is virtually no sign of any interest in either the classical languages of Europe or the vernaculars. Where translators were needed for practical purposes, Muslim rulers could always find them among their Christian or Jewish subjects, or among converts from those religions. One might put it this way: they were aware of belonging to the most advanced and enlightened civilization in the world, and of being the fortunate possessors of the richest and most advanced of languages. Everything worth reading or knowing was available in their language, or could be made available by immigrants or foreigners. It is an attitude which many of us today will easily recognize.

By the beginning of the 19th century, Muslims, first in Turkey and then elsewhere, were becoming aware of the changed balance, not only of power but also of knowledge, between Christendom and Islam, and, for the first time, thought it worth the effort to learn European languages. The Ottoman historian Asim, writing in about 1808, observes: "Certain sensualists, naked of the garment of loyalty, from time to time learned politics from them; some, desirous of learning their language, took French teachers, acquired their idiom, and prided themselves . . . on their uncouth talk."[4] It is not until well into the 19th century that we find any attempt in any of the languages of the Middle East to produce grammars or dictionaries which would enable speakers of those languages to learn a Western language. And when it did happen, it was due largely to the initiative of those two detested intruders, the imperialist and the missionary. This is surely a striking contrast and it has prompted many to ask the question: why were the Muslims so uninterested?

This, I would suggest, is the wrong question. It was the Muslims who were being normal, the Europeans who were not being normal. Not being interested in other cultures or even despising them is the normal state of mankind. It was a peculiarity of the European and one can, indeed, be more specific, of the Western European during a certain period in his history to exhibit this kind of interest in alien cultures to which he has no visible or ascertainable relationship. It was a peculiarity which requires explanation and which for many baffles understanding: of Western Europe, and later, under western influence, of Eastern Europe, but not of Asia (except for a Westernized Japan), not of Africa and, given the limited interest in American education in any subject the utility of which is not immediately demonstrable, one might say that it is probably not a characteristic of present-day America either.

The researches conducted by West European scholars in eastern lands gave rise to some puzzlement and to some suspicion. Why on earth would people travel great distances, endure hardships, discomfort, and often danger and disease, in order to dig up ancient monuments, try to decipher inscriptions in the long dead languages of long dead heathens? Why? Obviously, there had to be some rational explanation. At the simpler level, this was attributed to searches for buried treasures. At the more sophisticated level, it was assumed that archaeologists were spies or agents of their imperial governments. Some of them of course were, either full time or part time, but that is hardly a satisfactory explanation of so major a scholarly endeavor, beginning centuries before the imperialist expansion of Europe in the Middle East and including many countries which never took part in it. Even if one grants that English or French Arabists were motivated by the current or future activities of their countrymen in the Arab world, what were the motives that inspired Danes and Finns to take up these studies?

The same difficulty of understanding the purposes, the motivations, persists. One thinks of such figures as the Englishman Simon Ockley (1678–1720), a poor scholar with a large family, who went into a debtors' prison rather than earn a proper livelihood, and left his family to starve because of his obsession with the history of the early medieval Caliphate. One thinks of the German Johann Jakob Reiske (1716–1774), pinching pennies to publish the Arabic texts that he was editing at his own expense because no one else would print them.[5]

Why? What drove them? Let us consider some of the explanations that have been offered, some of the comments, the criticisms, or the attacks that have been made.

We may first look at this curious word, "orientalist." The word was created, as are so many, by analogy, after the model of such earlier terms as Latinist, Hellenist or Hebraist. A Latinist was one who studied Latin texts, a Hellenist one who studies Greek texts and so on. I am not aware that there has been any objection on the part of the Latins or the Hellenes to being studied in this way nor to having the studies so designated. The term orientalist, to us at the present time, seems remarkably vague, but when it first came into use it was not by any means as vague. The Orient meant what we now call the Middle East. Even as late at the 19th century, when diplomats talked of the eastern question (or *la question d'orient*) they knew perfectly well that they were talking about the Ottoman Empire and not about China or Japan or India. The Orient, literally the sunrise, meant above all that which lay immediately to the east of Europe, and for a very long time the terms orient and oriental, in West European usage, in fact meant the Islamic world. Levant, another word for sunrise, was even more restricted.

But then there was a reaction against the use of this term and a series of objections to it. The first is that which one might describe as professional, the objection which arose among those who were themselves orientalists or were so designated by others. They found, I think with some justification, that the term was no longer adequate; that it had become obsolete and obscure. It was too vague in regard to both the area and the period. The Orient was no longer the Middle East in the Islamic period; it was a much larger area in a much longer period, and the term orient, and therefore also oriental and orientalist, was too vague both geographically and chronologically. To complicate matters further, Orient and oriental in American, but not in European, usage, are usually applied to the Far East only.

"Orientalist" was also felt to be too vague in another respect, in that it did not designate any discipline. This did not matter in earlier times, when the discipline of scholarship was theological and philological and there was virtually no other. Even history is a comparatively latecomer. One cannot really speak of the professionalization of history until the 19th century and then not everywhere at the same time. Before that history was a pursuit for hired chroniclers or independent gentlemen. The extension and the range of disciplines, the expansion of the territories and periods studied, made this term seem inadequate, vague, confused.

This was an objection which arose from among the scholars themselves. There was also, not immediately, but at a somewhat later stage, an objection from those who, so to speak, represented the object of these studies, that is to say, those who came from the countries of Asia and Africa.

The debate among the orientalists was carried on for some time and came to a head on the hundredth anniversary of the 1st Congress of Orientalists. The first was held in Paris in 1873, another was held in Paris on the hundredth anniversary in 1973; and celebrated the centenary by officially abolishing the term orientalist. Henceforth, the Congress of Orientalists is not a Congress of

Orientalists. The International Association of Orientalists is not an international association of orientalists. The term "orientalism" or oriental studies has been replaced by "the human sciences with special reference to Asia and Northern Africa." I recall at the steering committee of the Paris meeting in '73, when this proposal was put forward, the strongest objection came from the late Professor Gafurov, leader of the Soviet delegation. He put in an impassioned plea for the retention of this term which "had served us well for more than a century" and which he saw no reason to change. At the time, I congratulated the Soviet delegate for his able statement of the conservative point of view, a compliment which didn't entirely seem to please him.[6]

There were objections too, increasingly, from the objects of study—not just to the name but to a great deal more. These objections did not come until a comparatively late stage. The attitude of the orientals (if I may be excused for using the this term for the moment) to the orientalist was at first either respectful or indifferent: indifferent where they either didn't know about them or didn't care about them or regarded them as engaged in pursuits totally irrelevant to their own interests. In time, scholars in the "Orient" became increasing respectful and sometimes even appreciative. Scholars from Islamic countries and possibly also from others began to attend some of the congresses of orientalists. At the congress held in Stockholm, for example, in 1889 there were a number from Middle Eastern countries and two of them, one Turk and one Egyptian, wrote long accounts of their attendance at these gatherings which are still worth reading.[7] Appreciation was shown by their willingness to utilize orientalist scholarship—books, dictionaries, editions of texts and the like, which they found of great value, and more tangibly through exchanges of visits, through the sending of students and even, increasingly, through the translation of the writings of orientalists into Arabic and other Middle Eastern languages.

Then, particularly in the post-war period, there came a considerable change which may be attributed, I think, to several factors. I shall enumerate some though I cannot claim pretend that this is a comprehensive list.

One is undoubtedly the intensifying conflicts between the Islamic world and the Western world, conflicts which do not arise from scholarship, at least not usually, but which obviously affect attitudes towards scholars, the things they write and the way they write them. It arises also from a resurgence, sometimes national, sometimes religious, sometimes both at the same time, an increasing self-awareness, including cultural self-awareness, and an increasing self-confidence. And, of course, the self-confidence in its turn was greatly encouraged and reinforced by the new wealth and power which some, though not all, of the countries of the Islamic world possess.

What are the accusations brought against orientalists at this period? These vary quite considerably from accuser to accuser, but there are some which tend to recur. One which does appear occasionally but on the whole with surprising rarity is the accusation of ignorance or incompetence. This would be easy enough to document merely by reading the self-criticism or, rather, the mutual criticism of orientalists, particularly if one looks at book reviews from periods and areas when book reviewing was still a contribution to scholarship and had not yet become a weapon in the armory of ideological and political warfare or of personal and professional self-advancement.

There are some accusations of ignorance and incompetence, but they are rare. One difficulty, I suppose, was that in order to make such accusations it was necessary to read a great deal of rather technical and difficult literature. The other was that, perhaps, raising this point might have been seen as hazardous to the accuser. No, defects were not normally attributed to ignorance or incompetence but to ill-will, to evil purposes, to ulterior motives sometimes verging on a sort of incarnation of evil in which orientalists are given a continuing corporate character through the centuries, engaged in a kind of conspiracy dedicated to certain dark purposes, pursuing its devious way.

One specific accusation, for example, is concealing or belittling Islamic achievements. The orientalists are accused of writing history in such a way as to obscure the great Islamic contribution to Western civilization. This, I suppose, is the unkindest cut of all. For one thing, the orientalists do not write Western history. More important, the glorious achievements of Muslim Spain and the major role of Muslims in the transition from antiquity to the modern world in the sciences and in philosophy is known very largely thanks to the efforts of orientalists.

They are accused of distortion, not just distortion of this or that individual theme, but a systematic, deliberate distortion conducted by orientalists as a profession or, more precisely, as a conspiracy. This is, of course, an old story and the accusation of *Taḥrīf*[8]—the charge that the Jews and Christians falsified their scriptures—goes back to classical times. According to this doctrine, the Jews and Christians had falsified the Torah and the Gospels, thus necessitating a new and final revelation. This is a new version of the same charge, and will presumably require a new, sacrosanct and final scholarship.

The Orientalists have sometimes also been accused of stealing the property of the people whose history and literature they study. This came out very vividly at the time of a conference held at the University of London in 1958 on the historiography of the Middle East—a gathering of historians, some from Western countries, quite a few from the Middle East, which eventually produced a large volume of studies on Middle Eastern historiography and on Western historiography relating to the Middle East. When it became known that this conference was to be held in London, before any part of it was actually published or even submitted, a press campaign was launched, the general purport of which was: this is my history. You have no right to study it. You are stealing something that belongs to me. This approach to scholarship and its problems has become sadly familiar, and has had some impact on these studies in the universities.

To sum up. There is a term which has become popular of late—the decolonization of history. The assumption is that the past is another territory which has been conquered, subjugated, settled and exploited by imperialist foreigners and the time has come to liberate the past by assault, by an intellectual liberation struggle. The struggle is on at the moment. It is in the guerrilla or, as some people would put it, the terrorist phase.

Notes

1. *Irshād al-Ḥayārā ilā ta'rīkh al-Yunān wa'l-Rūm wa'l-Naṣārā*. There are three known manuscripts of this treatise. For a description see V. L. Menage, "Three Ottoman Treatises on Europe," in *Iran and Islam*, ed. C. E. Bosworth, Edinburgh, 1971, pp. 421–23. I have used the manuscript in the library of the Turkish Historical Society (*Türk Tarih Kurumu*) in Ankara, no. 15.

2. The Kadi's memoirs were published by I. Parmaksizoğlu, "Bir Türk kadısının esaret hatıraları,"*Tarih Dergisi* 5 (1953):77–84.

3. Both volumes of Osman Ağa's memoirs were first published in German translation: see R. F. Kreutel and O. Spies, *Leben und Abenteuer des Dolmetschers 'Osman Ağa* (Bonn, 1954), and R. F. Kreutel, *Zwischen Pashas und Generalen* (Graz, 1966). The Turkish text of one part has been edited by R. R. Kreutel, *Die Autobiographie des Dolmetschers 'Osman Ağa aus Temeschwar* (Cambridge, 1980).

4. Ahmed Asim, *Tarih*, Istanbul, n.d., vol. 1 pp. 274–76.

5. On this and other Arabists of the time, see Johann Fück, *Die arabischen Studien in Europa bis in der Anfang des 20 Jahrhunderts*, Leipzig, 1955; P. M. Holt, *Studies in the History of the Near East*, London, 1973, *Part I. Early Students of Arab History in England*.

6. For a somewhat informal account of the proceedings, see Vamadeo Shastri, "Orientalists at Odds," in *Encounter*, December, 1973, pp. 56–60.

7. Muhammad Amīn Fikri Bey, *Irshād al-Alibbā ilā Mahāsin Ūrūbā*, Cairo, 1892, pp. 617ff; Ahmed Midhat, *Avrupada bir Jevel_n*, Istanbul, 1307 [1889–90], p. 130ff. See also Carter Vaughn Findley, "An Ottoman Occidentalist in Europe: Ahmed Midhat meets Madame Gülnar, 1889," in *American Historical Review* (103), 1998, pp. 15–49.

8. See *Encyclopaedia of Islam*, 2nd ed. s.v. *Taḥrīf* (by Hava Lazarus Yafeh).